CONTEMPORARY BUSINESS

*

D1713093

CONTEMPORARY BUSINESS

CHALLENGES AND OPPORTUNITIES

EDDIE V. EASLEY

College of Business Administration
Drake University

EARL F. LUNDGREN

School of Business
University of Missouri–Columbia

HARRY I. WOLK

College of Business Administration
Drake University

WEST PUBLISHING CO. ST. PAUL · NEW YORK · LOS ANGELES · SAN FRANCISCO

The authors are indebted to the following for permission to reproduce copyrighted materials.

Text

p. 405 From *The Closing Circle: Nature, Man and Technology* by Barry Commoner. Copyright © 1971 Alfred A. Knopf, Inc. Reprinted by permission.

p. 409 From "Tomorrow's Disaster: 'Gigantic'" in *Time*, The Weekly Newsmagazine. Reprinted by permission from *Time*, The Weekly Newsmagazine; copyright © Time Inc. 1977.

Illustrations and Tables

Fig. 4-14 From *Managerial Process and Organizational Behavior* by Alan C. Filley and Robert J. House. Copyright © 1969 by Scott, Foresman and Company. Reprinted by permission.

Table 8-1 From "Discretionary Spending for Three Years: 1950, 1960, and 1972." In *Conference Board: Statistical Bulletin*, Vol. 8, No. 11 (November 1975). Copyright © 1975. Reprinted by permission.

Table 9-5 From the August 12, 1974 and December 27, 1976 issues of *Advertising Age*. Copyright © 1974 and 1976. Reprinted by permission.

Table 11-4 Reprinted from the 1977 Fortune Directory. Copyright © 1977 by Time, Inc. Reprinted by permission.

Table 12-6 Reprinted from the September 20, 1976 issue of *Business Week* by special permission. Copyright © by McGraw-Hill, Inc.

Fig. 12-9 From *Macroeconomics* by J. Carl Poindexter. Copyright © 1976 by The Dryden Press, A Division of Holt, Rinehart and Winston. Reprinted by permission of Holt, Rinehart and Winston.

p. 417 Cartoon. From *Consumer Reports* (May 1974). Reprinted by permission of Roy Doty. Copyright © *Consumer Reports*.

Table 18-1 From "Nondiscrimination Policies: Are They Effective?" by Larry E. Short. In *Personnel Journal*, Vol. 52 (September 1973): 790. Copyright © September 1973 by *Personnel Journal*. Reprinted with permission.

Photographs

p. 39 McDonald's restaurant. Printed with permission of McDonald's Corporation.

p. 193 Buick price sticker. Printed with permission of Buick Motor Division, General Motors Corporation and Roy Eliot Buick.

p. 200 L'eggs panty hose carousel. Printed with permission of Hanes Corporation.

p. 214 Super Valu Store. Printed with permission of Super Valu Stores, Inc.

p. 239 Three film packages. Printed with permission of Agfa-Gevaert, Inc., Eastman Kodak Company, and Fuji Photo Film U.S.A., Inc.

p. 303 Optical scanning gun. Printed with permission of Sears, Roebuck and Company.

p. 303 Uniform Pricing Code. Printed with permission of General Mills, Inc.

p. 371 Cereal boxes. Printed with permission of General Mills, Inc., Kellogg Company, and Red Owl.

p. 386 Consumer communications office. Printed with permission of the Pillsbury Company.

Library of Congress Cataloging in Publication Data

Easley, Eddie V.
 Contemporary business.

 Bibliography: p. i–xvi, 1–495.
 Includes index.
 1. Business. 2. Small business.
I. Lundgren, Earl F., joint author.
II. Wolk, Harry I., joint author.
III. Title.
HF5351.E17   658.4   78–764
ISBN 0-8299-0166-3

To our wives and mothers

Ruth and Berta
Georgianna and Esther
Barbara and Rose

and our children

*

PREFACE

Writing a textbook is an exercise requiring both planning and patience. Indeed, it often parallels running a business because goals must be set, deadlines met, and coordination maintained.

Among the goals originally set and kept was a desire to emphasize the role of American business in its larger environmental setting during the last quarter of the twentieth century. The last section of this book, Responsibilities and Opportunities, attempts to hit this theme particularly hard without trying to pull any punches, though it attempts to be fair and unbiased throughout. While we are critical of business in this section, we are also attempting to show that there are tremendous opportunities for business to help in improving our economic, natural, and social environments.

Let there be no mistake, however. Immediately in Chapter 1, the strength, vitality, and importance of the capitalistic system in terms of satisfying economic needs and allocating resources in conjunction with a high degree of personal freedom are strongly emphasized.

Another feature of this book is the use of an illustrative case throughout the chapters in the functional areas of management, marketing, and finance as well as in several other chapters. The case itself is based upon a small business involving one of the authors. While we did use many actual examples and illustrations from business throughout the text, we decided that an extensive analysis of a small business situation would add significantly to the depth of the book and the interest of the student. For example, no other introductory business text that we are aware of deals at all extensively with the problems associated with organizing and starting a new business.

As teachers of business administration, we attempted to write particularly strong chapters in the functional areas. However, we found our wings constantly being clipped by our editors who urged us to scale down the material to the basic elements. Thanks to their prodding, we think the chapters provide a good, solid introduction to the concepts underlying these important areas rather than simply an encyclopedic list of definitions and terms.

We have tried to make the writing style simple, concise, and up-to-date. No matter how good the ideas in the book, if they are not written in a contemporary and easily comprehensible style, the book will not communicate. Both writers and readers will undoubtedly agree on this last point.

Finally, we wish to call your attention to what we believe is an unusually strong students' manual, instructor's guide, and set of transparencies. The student manual was carefully designed to maintain student interest with creative problems and puzzles. We believe that a student manual must involve the student if it is to be a useful learning tool. The instructor's guide provides additional teaching materials, if they are desired, as well as many other useful tools and materials. An extensive group of transparencies is provided, including many that are keyed into the additional teaching materials in the instructor's manual.

An important input to this book has been the many excellent comments from individuals who have received parts or all of this text. These persons have brought their extensive experience and considerable expertise to bear upon our work. Their efforts have added an important part to the shaping and thrust of this book. We particularly single out and thank James Agresta of Prince George's Community College, Michael Broida of Miami University of Ohio, Mel Choate of North Seattle Community College, Jack Duncan of the University of Alabama at Birmingham, William D. Evans of Wright State University, Marjorie Gilmore of the Community College of Denver, Donald Gordon of Illinois Central College, Gary Holt of Tarrant County Junior College, Ray Y. Jones of East Carolina University, Jagdish R. Kapoor of the College of DuPage, George Katz of San Antonio College, Ron Lee of Erie Community College City Campus, John Martindale of Tompkins–Cortland Community College, Curtis Mason of Tidewater Community College, Robert Masters of the University of Southern Colorado, John Myers of the University of Southern Colorado, Michael Pauritsch of Moraine Valley Community College, Joseph T. Straub of Valencia Community College, Ray Tewell of American River College, Percy O. Vera of Sinclair Community College, and James Webb of Lousiana Tech.

To our editors at West Publishing Company, we are deeply grateful for their high degree of professionalism, their numerous, excellent suggestions, their unflagging cooperation and, not least of all, the pleasure of working with them.

Special thanks also go to Professors Don Gordon of Illinois Central College and Ben Shlaess and Jack Zeller of Des Moines Area Community College for their excellent work in developing and preparing the Student Manual accompanying this text.

Finally, we wish to thank our typist, Sandy Huckstadt, who cheerfully and efficiently turned our often illegible script into finished manuscript form.

CONTENTS

CONTEMPORARY BUSINESS

†

PART ONE

HOW BUSINESS SERVES SOCIETY: INTRODUCTION AND BACKGROUND

☐ Business. It is all around us. But why study it?

☐ Profits. A necessary evil or a valuable part of our economic system?

☐ Even though business is all around us, it is doubtful if many people understand its role and function in American society. Part I attempts to answer some of the questions that may be puzzling you about business.

☐ Chapter 1 explains the basic nature of business and why there is a business system. It also describes the relationship between business and capitalism, shows how the making of profits performs a socially useful role, and discusses how socialism and communism differ from capitalism.

☐ But how did business get to where it is today? To understand this, you should have an appreciation of how business has developed. Chapter 2 provides a brief historical sketch of business development.

☐ How does one form a business and how does it work? Chapter 3 answers questions about the legal forms of business, different types of business, and the different cost structures of business. This chapter also discusses the relationship between supply and demand and how that relationship affects business operation.

*

WHY BUSINESS

LEARNING OBJECTIVES

When you finish this chapter you should:
- [ ] have a basic understanding of what business is and why it is necessary.
- [ ] realize the importance of profit and the profit and loss system.
- [ ] know how private property, the profit and loss system, the price system, and competition work together in a capitalistic system.
- [ ] understand the benefits and problems of capitalism.
- [ ] be familiar with the traditional, philosophical basis of business.
- [ ] understand the basics of other economic systems: specifically, socialism and communism.

KEY TERMS TO LEARN FROM THIS CHAPTER

business	depression	management	profit and loss system
business cycle	free enterprise	monopoly	protestant ethic
capital	gross profit	nationalization	recession
capitalism	inflation	net profit	robber barons
communism	labor	price system	social Darwinism
competition	laissez-faire	private enterprise	socialism
deflation	land	profit	welfare state

A group of college students decided to make some money as a part of their Homecoming football activities. On Saturday morning before the game, the campus was always alive with alumni renewing old friendships and viewing the Homecoming decorations. The group of students felt sure they could make money by selling peanuts and candy in the crowds. They obtained a temporary city permit for one day of selling and were able to obtain $300 worth of candy and peanuts from a local candy company. By buying a large quantity for the purpose of reselling, the students were able to buy at a reduced price.

Their effort was successful. By selling the peanuts and candy at a higher price than they had paid to buy them, the students ended their day with more than $400. Through their hard work and ingenuity, they had earned more than $100. In other words, the students had for one day successfully operated a business enterprise.

Many readers might say: "Why, I've done something like that, but I never thought of it as running a business." It is running a business, however, because the same basic ideas and activities apply as much to students selling candy and peanuts as to the largest business organizations in the world. A business can be anything from a newspaper route to the worldwide operations of General Motors.

The purpose of this opening chapter is to introduce you to what business is and why it is necessary. Business produces the goods and services that people need or want. The clothing manufacturer produces clothing that people need for protection as well as clothing that people want to be in style or to satisfy a personal whim. The retail clothing store produces or provides a service by stocking a variety of clothing that is conveniently accessible to the consumer in terms of location and shopping hours. In addition, every business organization hopes to make money through the production of its goods or services.

MAKING MONEY

As we saw in the opening illustration, the students who sold candy and peanuts earned over $100 as a result of their one-day selling effort. The $100 represented the difference between the $300 they paid for the candy and peanuts and the $400 plus they got for selling their goods. The $100 they earned was their *profit* or the difference between their dollar costs ($300) and their dollar sales ($400+). Of course, they did not charge themselves for their own labor, and they did not have any other costs. Their $100 was clear profit although subject to income tax.

A business usually requires labor costs and other costs such as rent, transportation, and utilities (gas and electricity, for example). Suppose the students had hired some salespeople at a cost of $50 and had bought some advertising signs for $20. Then their *net profit* would be around $30 because they would have to deduct their labor and other costs—a total of $70—from their *gross profit* of $100. Profit is very important to a business organization. For one thing, profit is essential to survival, for without profit a business will decline and eventually must fail. Profit is also one way to measure the success of a business. Good profits suggest a business is successful, while poor profits or no profits suggest a business is doing poorly. Finally, when profit is thought of as a goal, it motivates the business person to work hard in order to show a profit and have a successful business.

Being successful in business requires a lot of hard work, but there are many opportunities in business in both large and small organizations. There are also opportunities for the individual to start and run his or her own business.

OPPORTUNITIES IN BUSINESS

In recent years, there has been a resurgence of small-business entrepreneurs or business persons. From Seattle to Miami and from Los Angeles to Boston, small businesses are starting and succeeding. There are failures, too, since there is rarely a guarantee of success in the business world. Approximately 60 percent of all businesses that are started fail during the first five years of their existences. In numbers, about 100,000 small businesses fail during their first year, and 400,000 small firms go out of business each year in the United States.[1]

Nonetheless, changing consumer tastes and interests constantly create opportunities for the alert business person. The nostalgia craze is an example. Individuals have started businesses as brokers for baseball cards, comic books, and 78 r.p.m. phonograph records, to name just a few examples. There is a growing demand for the handicraft work of local artisans, stimulating the opening of retail outlets as well as manufacturing facilities. Recognizing this interest, several universities and colleges have begun offering courses in venture management, entrepreneurship, or how to start a business. In these courses, students learn the basic elements of accounting, finance, marketing, and management—the same areas of business operation that we will be discussing in this book.

Opportunities abound in the large business organization as well. Most individuals with an interest in a business career start out with a larger corporation. There are many attractions in this career track. It offers the continuing opportunity to specialize in a given area such as accounting or marketing. There is a challenge and a satisfaction to be found in association with a large operation that affects the lives of millions of people through the impact of its actions in both economic and social areas. And then there is the exciting challenge of reaching the top management levels—perhaps the presidency itself—in a major corporation.

Whatever one's interest, there is an opportunity in the business world. Interest in business can be combined with an interest in the arts, in agriculture, in sports, or in anything that is legitimate and needed or wanted. Hence we find that business serves the individual by providing goods and services for consumption and jobs and opportunities for people to earn a living and forge a career. But we may still ask a broad and important question. What is the justification for our society allowing business to function as it does—largely privately owned and relatively free from government regulation?

WHY BUSINESS

As we have become acutely aware in recent years, many of the world's resources are in short supply. In reality, however, resources have always been relatively scarce. Economists are people who study the utilization of our resources, and as a

[1]*Wall Street Journal*, October 26, 1976, p. 1.

result of their studies, they recommend various systems to develop resources effectively and efficiently and allocate them among the many segments of society. Further, many economists classify resources into four major kinds: *land, labor, capital,* and *management.* They call these four resources the factors of production.

Land includes natural resources such as oil and mineral deposits, water, forests, and land itself. Labor is the human resource which expends physical and mental energy in the production of goods and services. Capital is the means by which the human resource can more efficiently utilize land in the production of goods and services. Capital includes all types of equipment, tools, machinery, buildings, and transportation. The fourth kind of resource, management, is the people who have the skill and knowledge required to guide and direct successfully the operations of a business organization. Hence a business requires all of these resources in order to make a profit and to continue to exist, although the amount of each resource used will vary.

Because resources are scarce, they carry a value. In certain cases, a resource is abundant and its value goes down. India has a large population, and the price of labor in India is low. Where a resource is very limited, its value goes up. The value of real estate in mid-Manhattan is very high since the amount of land in that location is absolutely limited. What, then, is the best way to develop and allocate a nation's scarce resources? The United States has long favored a capitalistic system.

CAPITALISM

When we speak of *free enterprise, private enterprise,* or *business,* we usually mean *capitalism.* We can think of capitalism as a descriptive term for an economic system, while business is the chief instrument through which individuals and organizations practice the capitalistic system. The most important characteristic of capitalism is the *right to own and use property.* The Constitution of the United States, for example, guarantees that owners of private property are not subject to unlawful search, seizure, or trespass.

The Right to Private Property   A person who owns a parcel of land has the right to determine whether to graze cattle, to grow crops, or not to use it at all. As individuals, we control our own labor. We pursue the type of work which interests us and apply for employment with an organization that attracts us. We may, of course, decide not to sell our labor at all. Similarly, an individual or a business acquires equipment or builds facilities which are privately owned and controlled.

The right to own property is a great incentive. Through the wise use of the factors of production, there can be an increasing accumulation of land and capital as well as a capability for employing greater amounts of labor. Such accumulation comes about as a result of earning a profit, and the *potential of profit* is a second important characteristic of capitalism.

A Profit and Loss System   Business operates under a *profit and loss system.* As was illustrated in the example of the students selling candy and peanuts, being in business means that one has the opportunity to make a profit but also that one runs the risk of incurring a loss. This duality helps to define free enterprise in the United States and other countries. There is risk in business and the possibility of loss, but the *potential for profit is the driving incentive behind business effort.* Profit performs another function in capitalism. It serves as a measure of how efficiently and effectively a business or a total economy is allocating its productive resources. In addition to serving as a yardstick in this manner, profits also serve as a guide to action.

If a company finds that a particular good or service is earning very slim profits or operating at a loss, the company is likely to remove productive resources from that line if the problem cannot be corrected. If, on the other hand, a good or service is doing extremely well and earning handsome profits, the company will assign more resources to that good or service.

Similarly, if an entire industry operates at a loss, perhaps it is consuming a disproportionate share of the nation's resources. If an industry has high profits, there is a good chance more resources could and perhaps should be thrown into the high-profit industry. Another factor that helps to allocate resources efficiently is the price of a good or service, and the *price system* is another characteristic of capitalism.

The Price System The price system is a third important component of capitalism. It also aids in efficiently allocating productive resources. When the supply of a product or service is limited and demand is high, the price will usually rise. Under this condition, additional companies may enter the market and drive down the price. This activity has been apparent in recent years in the limited supplies and/or high prices of the hand-calculator and houseplant industries.

In certain instances, additional companies may not enter the market, and existing companies may not expand production. This inaction occurs when there is simply no more of the good or service to be had, when additional production requires a tremendous investment in capital, or when there is artificial restriction due to government regulation or control of the market by a few large companies. For example, we apparently do not have sufficient oil reserves to expand production greatly and reduce the price of oil and gas. In addition, drilling oil wells and building refineries costs a tremendous amount of money. Finally, some observers have suggested that a few large oil companies do exercise a substantial degree of control over the distribution and sale of oil products.

When supply is ample and demand low, prices tend to drop and companies tend to contract their operations or leave the market. Perhaps the reader has observed businesses such as small bakeries or drive-in restaurants closing operations when the number of outlets selling similar products increases. When the number of retail outlets increases, the individual shops often lower prices to attract customers and increase the volume of business. In so doing, however, the shops may discover they are losing money, and eventually they may have to close down.

Few people would suggest that the price system works perfectly, and most would admit that the price system has many inconsistencies and surprises. Nonetheless, there is a constant tendency for the price system to work as described above in the allocation of productive resources. Land, labor, capital, and management naturally flow to those areas commanding the highest prices and the greatest potential for profit.

Competition The fourth and last component of capitalism is *competition*. The price system and the potential for profit stimulate competition. Competition takes many forms, and we need only look at a business such as retail clothing to see a variety of competitive strategies. Some stores emphasize service and quality. Their store interiors are beautiful, they may employ models to show the clothes, their quality in clothing tends to be high, and so do their prices. Saks Fifth Avenue in New York City and other high-fashion clothing stores around the country are examples of this kind of store. These stores compete on the basis of prestige, status, and quality. On the other hand, there are rack shops where the customer can sort through clothes, try on outfits, and haul merchandise up to the cash register to make a purchase. K-Mart and Woolco are examples. This type of store is competing primarily on the basis of price.

The fact that competition exists is obvious to every consumer. TV, radio, newspaper, magazine, and billboard advertising stress the value and attractiveness of every conceivable good and service. Salespeople perform the same function on a more personal basis. Business has wide latitude in choosing the best means to compete, although there are guidelines for business competition. Over time, a set of laws and practices has developed that constrains competition in certain cases and encourages it in others. By and large, the purpose of these laws and practices is to protect the consumer, although in certain cases such as agriculture the target of protection also includes the producer or the farmer.

Limits on Competition The most apparent constraints reside in laws and regulations at the local, state, and federal levels. Local laws cover everything from sidewalk displays in front of retail stores to the size and location of advertising signs. State laws cover such things as standards of cleanliness, fraud, and interest rates that banks may charge on loans. The principal enforcer of federal laws and regulations governing competition is the Federal Trade Commission. It is generally charged under the Federal Trade Commission Act of 1914 with maintaining fair competition for the protection of both the business organization and the consumer. Under its charge, the FTC will investigate activities such as possible deceptive advertising or agreements among competitors that may restrain competition or result in unfair competition.

The actions of consumers as individuals and as groups also have an impact on the way in which businesses compete. The individual is perhaps most effective when dealing with a retail outlet in a small town or in a given neighborhood in a city. News of unfair competitive activities may quickly pass from person to person by word of mouth. Retaliation hits the retailer where it hurts most—in the pocketbook. In larger businesses, accumulated individual complaints, particularly when directed to the higher executive levels, often stimulate action to correct abuses.

Many newspapers now offer a service to their readers that helps to correct questionable business activities. Upon an inquiry or complaint from a reader, the newspaper will contact the company involved and will publish the results for all to see. A business that has any interest in good public relations will strive to avoid practices that will receive bad press notices in the news media.

Other avenues of appeal for the consumer include the Better Business Bureau, a private organization that tries to help consumers with specific complaints against companies; departments of city governments such as New York City which have responsibility for consumer protection; and consumer advocates such as Ralph Nader, who try to serve the consumer interest on many issues. For example, Nader was very effective several years ago in pointing out possible deficiencies in the Corvair automobile, produced by the Chevrolet Division of General Motors. Nader claimed among other charges that the Corvair could be blown off the road in high crosswinds.

Of the four components of capitalism that we have discussed, competition appears to be the one most subject to possible manipulation and abuse. The limits on competition such as laws and consumer actions serve as safeguards to help assure that the competitive system and capitalism can operate in a free and fair manner for the benefit of society. The importance of free and fair competition and capitalism will become increasingly apparent as we examine the benefits of capitalism for us.

THE BENEFITS OF CAPITALISM

Capitalism has been the economic system used in the United States for over 200 years. Although our environment has changed and the nature of business operations has changed, the basic ideas of capitalism are as much in use today as they were 200 years ago. And while today the government does regulate business activity to help assure fair competition and to protect the consumer from harmful practices, the government does little planning for the detailed allocation of resources. Hence there is decentralized decision making on most business matters. Each company decides for itself how many people it will employ, how much

The emphasis of the free enterprise system on profitably satisfying the needs of consumers.

and what kinds of equipment to buy and use, and how best to utilize land which it owns and occupies. Each individual has the right, within the confines of the law, to start and operate a business enterprise and, therefore, the right to own, rent, and hire productive resources; to earn a profit or take a loss; to set prices; and to compete on a fair basis.

The system incorporates almost complete freedom of action and has been successful for many years in developing and utilizing the nation's resources. This is the most important reason why our society encourages business development and success. All of us depend upon business to be efficient and effective in using resources to satisfy our needs and wants.

The consumer also has freedom of choice, of course, and it is the consumer who starts the chain of reaction that goes all the way back to resource allocation and utilization. The consumer chooses one car in preference to another or may choose to buy no car at all. The consumer chooses to eat steak, pork, ham, or no meat at all and affects the type of meat production that subsequently will occur. Business has the job of trying to figure out what the consumer wants and then competitively meeting that want. This is the essence of competition as well as of the entire private enterprise system.

SOME PROBLEMS OF CAPITALISM

No economic system has ever demonstrated perfection in operation, and capitalism is no exception. Among the imperfections of any system is an inability to maintain stable economic conditions over an extended period of time. Economies suffer from *depressions, recessions, inflation,* and *deflation.* A depression occurs when the economy slows to a crawl. Unemployment is high, production and sales are very low, and there is a general atmosphere of pessimism. A recession has the same characteristics as a depression, only in milder form. Inflation occurs when prices and wages are rising. An inflation may be very mild, with prices and wages rising only 2 or 3 percent per year, or it may be severe, when prices and wages rise at a 10 or 15 percent rate per year. An inflationary period can be particularly difficult for individuals when prices are rising faster than wages. When this happens, it means that any given paycheck will buy less food, clothing, and other items than the last paycheck. Even worse is the combination of a recession and inflation, called "stagflation," such as occurred in 1974–75. Then we have unemployment and rising prices both happening at the same time. Finally a deflation is the opposite of inflation. In a deflation prices and wages are generally falling. Deflations have been rare in the United States, especially in the past forty years, which have been marked for the most part by steadily increasing prices.

Alternating periods of recession or depression and prosperity result in *business cycles.* These cycles are the ups and downs in our economy which correspond to periods of prosperity and recession. Business cycles are often accompanied by periods of rapid inflation and sometimes by deflation. The latter is most likely to occur during a severe depression. Since World War II ended in 1945, the United States has experienced several recessions and two relatively severe inflations, including the most recent, which exceeded a 10 percent rate of increase in 1974. Figure 1–1 illustrates several business cycles.

The causes of recessions, depressions, inflations, and deflations are complex, and the capitalistic system has never developed the means to eliminate the severe fluctuations or ups and downs in economic conditions. In many instances,

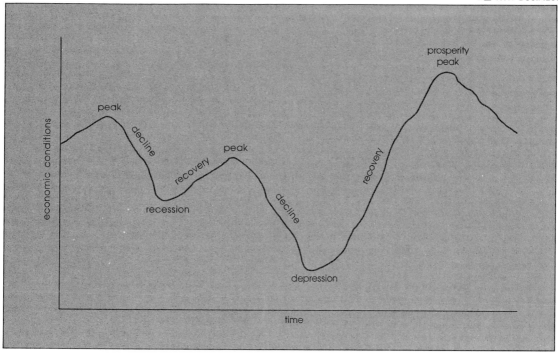

Figure 1-1   Business cycles.

the very characteristics of business capitalism worsen the fluctuations. For example, thousands of individual companies make competitive decisions every day. In a period of rapidly rising prices, a business person may perceive a competitive advantage in stocking up on certain supply items. The business person may do this because today's cost will be very low compared to future higher prices, and his or her profit will be correspondingly higher. As a result, however, the supply of those items may become scarce, thus adding even more pressure to push prices up. In 1974, sugar companies apparently accumulated vast inventories of sugar in anticipation of continuing price increases. Sugar prices reached all-time highs, and there were shortages for some consumers. Eventually prices dropped as companies ran out of space to store sugar and had to release it to the market. Multiply one such decision by thousands and you gain an idea of the immensity of forces that may affect prices.

Business Cycles in Other Nations   Do countries with different systems fare any better? In countries with a higher degree of centralized government control over economic decisions—such as Russia and Mainland China—there are also economic fluctuations. No system appears to be immune. Also, no economic system works in isolation. The United States depends on other nations for a substantial portion of its mineral resources. Other nations import machinery, equipment, and technical know-how from the United States. What happens economically in one country inevitably affects one or more other countries because of variations in trade between countries and the resulting effects on levels of production, employment, and prices. A recession in country A may reduce trade between A and country B and thus help depress economic conditions in B.

Of course, many uncontrollable factors contribute to economic problems. Weather is an important one. Partly because of poor weather for growing crops, there has been mass starvation in parts of Africa and India. Flooding, droughts, and cold weather have caused food shortages in the United States. Many people agree that capitalism has worked well, but it cannot control the weather and other factors that contribute to economic instability.

Inadequate Long-Range Planning   With millions of individuals making business decisions that often have some impact on resource allocation, there tends to be an overemphasis on short-range planning—especially in broad areas of concern to all of us. The energy shortage is an example. When the energy crunch first hit, people would ask, "Why didn't someone realize there was going to be an energy shortage twenty years ago and do something about it?" Back in 1953, a few individuals warned of impending shortages. But most companies and consumers were busily shifting from coal to fuel oil and natural gas in order to cut costs, while the energy producers were trying to keep up with the demand.

Even if there had been a widespread realization in 1953 of a shortage twenty years later, it still would have been very difficult to gain the cooperation of millions of consumers and producers to take effective action. The capitalistic system, with its decentralized decision making and built-in competition, usually does not yield to mass cooperation until a time of crisis.

Artificial Restraints on Competition   We saw earlier that possible excesses in competition such as false advertising and deceptive selling practices are limited by such factors as laws and consumer actions. It is also possible for a business to attempt to restrain competition to the point where only one company may control an entire market for a good or service. The capitalistic system encourages free and open competition, but occasionally a business organization has achieved a *monopoly* position in its market. In a monopoly, one company dominates a market to such an extent that there is no effective competition, enabling the monopoly company to control distribution, sales, and prices in the entire market for its goods or services. In a total monopoly, there are no competitors, or if there are, they exist only at the pleasure of the monopoly company.

If one automobile company, such as General Motors or Ford, controlled 90 percent of the automobile market, this would no doubt be a monopoly position. In most kinds of business, however, a monopoly is forbidden under federal law. When the government believes a company has a monopoly, the Justice Department will file suit in federal court to break up the monopoly. If the government wins, the court usually requires the monopolistic company to be split into two or more competing organizations. Certain companies such as public utilities, however, are granted a monopoly market position in a given area to avoid cumbersome and costly duplication. You can imagine the problems if three electric companies, for example, ran their own separate power lines all over a city. Public utilities pay a price for this market position, however, because they are highly regulated by the government.

Social Problems   Poverty, discrimination against minority groups, discrimination against women, discrimination against older persons, urban decay, and consumer exploitation have not been completely eliminated through capitalism. Many persons argue that business bears little or no responsibility for corrective action in these problems. Others claim that business should carry a major portion of the responsibility. Controversy continues over the role of business with respect to social problems even though most social problems have severe economic outcomes—that is, expansion of the welfare rolls, unemployment, declining real estate values, and others. These economic outcomes would seem to support the position of those who maintain that business should assume a major role in helping to solve social problems. The capitalistic system in a democratic setting does offer the potential for solving social problems, but it is up to business to take the initiative and realize the potential available through capitalism.

Up to the present time, the business community as a whole has not fully accepted the challenge of social problems, and it has been primarily through pressure groups forcing government legislation that measurable progress can be observed today. For many years, some individual business persons and companies have worked to reduce discrimination and environmental pollution, and most businesses do not deliberately seek to exploit the consumer. But the cooperative and directed action required to deal effectively with social problems has not developed to date within the private enterprise system.

We find, then, that even though capitalism has some limitations, societies in the United States and other countries accept an economic justification for its continuing existence. Capitalism's ability to allocate resources to meet society's needs and wants has been largely satisfactory. The very fact of continuing social problems has led, however, to greater expectations regarding the role of business. Consumer advocates such as Ralph Nader and organized groups representing minority interests exert great pressure on business to have more concern for and to be more active in social problems.

The public, through its elected representatives in Congress, reflects the pressure on business by supporting legislation such as Truth-in-Lending, which requires lenders to specify exactly the true rate of interest on loans, and the Occupational Safety and Health Act, which sets standards and enforces them for safe and healthy working conditions. Business has been forced to respond to some of these expectations by conforming to the law.

Business has also responded, in part, by voluntary action to reduce the severity of social problems. The National Alliance of Business, for example, is a voluntary organization that encourages industry to improve the skills of minority-group members and expand their employment opportunities. The Dow Chemical Company operates "zero discharge" plants that completely recycle wastes, an accomplishment requiring the investment of millions of dollars. International Business Machines Corporation (IBM) and other companies have successfully established manufacturing operations in ghetto areas. Hence there have been increasing demands on business in social problems and there has been a response. It appears that many businesses now accept some degree of social responsibility as one of their goals.

THE PHILOSOPHICAL BASIS OF BUSINESS

Why does business operate as it does in the United States today? Why did the private enterprise system develop? The answers to these questions go back to the founding of our country and the economic philosophy prevalent at that time. Two hundred years ago, Adam Smith, a Scottish political economist and philosopher, spoke of the "invisible hand" that could guide business activity for the benefit of all. According to Smith, if government would maintain a *laissez-faire* or hands-off policy, the "invisible hand" would be free to function. To put this philosophy into practice would require the government not to interfere at all with business activities. There would be no control over competition, no interference with the use of resources, and no attempt to influence economic factors such as the interest rate on loans or the amount of money in circulation. In other words, business would be completely free to operate in an economy free of governmental interference. The results, according to Smith, would be the lowest possible prices for the consumer, the development of all valuable resources, and the greatest wealth for the nation and its people.

While immigrants to the United States did not arrive carrying a copy of Smith's book, *The Wealth of Nations,* they lived and worked in their new country accepting Smith's basic ideas. Lack of opportunity in Europe combined with the immense, unknown frontier nourished the concept of rugged individualism and independent action. The vastness of the land itself made any sort of continuing, centralized control from the government impractical.

The lone sodbuster, rancher, and business entrepreneur struggled and sometimes succeeded, sometimes failed. In many cases, particularly on the frontier, those with the greatest strength, endurance, and/or the best brains survived and succeeded. It was survival of the fittest, and this idea became a popular philosophy in the late 1800s and early 1900s. It was called *social Darwinism* and was applied to all types of business organizations. The social application of survival of the fittest was an extension of the ideas of Charles Darwin in his book on biological evolution, *Origin of Species.*

The philosophy of survival of the fittest suggested that only the most fit succeeded and prospered. Those who were poor and had no job or held only the lesser jobs in an organization were obviously incompetent and unworthy. In short, they were unfit. Proponents of this philosophy claimed that each individual was master of his or her own destiny and was alone responsible for personal success or failure. Hence those who were successful obviously were fit. Since each individual was on his or her own and was personally responsible for success or failure, nothing should be allowed to interfere with this natural struggle. There should be no governmental programs to aid the poor, for example, nor any special privileges granted to the rich.

While traces of the philosophy of survival of the fittest may survive in some organizations today, as a society we have changed our outlook considerably. We recognize that conditions beyond individual control, such as the state of the economy, force people into unemployment and sometimes into poverty. Under certain conditions, such as in pioneer days, survival of the fittest may be applicable. Gaining control of the nation's vast resources—profitably working the land, developing the mineral deposits, and ultimately setting up manufacturing plants and distribution systems—required immense labor and the endurance of almost unbelievable hardship. Disease, injuries, lawlessness, and bad weather were unwelcome but frequent visitors. Fortunately, many of these conditions have been overcome, and the idea of survival of the fittest, at least as a philosophy of success or failure, does not seem to be directly applicable.

THE PREEMINENCE OF WORK

Another idea that was popular at about the same time as the philosophy of the survival of the fittest has been termed the *Protestant ethic.* It found its basis in the religious writings of John Calvin, a French theologian of the sixteenth century. Calvin instructed his followers that God looked with favor upon those who worked hard and saved their money. In the late 1800s, these thoughts of Calvin were interpreted to mean that businessmen, for example, were working in accordance with God's wishes when they worked hard to earn a profit and save it. More important, however, was the notion that the more successful and wealthy a person became, the more favorable was God's view of that person.

Since individuals were supposed to save money even though their incomes were huge, many wealthy businessmen lived quite modestly, including Andrew Carnegie, who accumulated hundreds of millions of dollars in the steel industry. Large savings also enabled business people to pour enormous amounts of money back into their businesses. This reinvestment of profit resulted in large-scale growth of industry over many years. Investing a portion of profit back into the business remains a basic idea of capitalism today.

Similar to the concept of survival of the fittest, the Protestant ethic tended to debase people who were poor and relatively unsuccessful. Poverty could only mean that a person was lazy and regarded by God with less esteem than those who were successful. This part of the Protestant ethic faded considerably by 1900, following the publication of newspaper articles that revealed corrupt practices and exploitation of the public by *"robber barons"* such as Jay Gould and Jim Fisk. It was certainly questionable that God would look with favor upon men who accumulated their fortunes through deception, dishonesty, and cheating.

What remained of the Protestant ethic was an emphasis on a close relationship between hard work and success. At the same time that newspaper writers and others were attacking the practices of big business, authors such as Horatio Alger were glorifying hard work and its potential for success and achievement. An Alger hero was usually a young and very poor boy who started at the bottom of the ladder in business. Through hard work (and sometimes with a bit of luck), the young boy grew into manhood and ever-increasing success. There is still no doubt a strong work ethic in the United States.

Overall, despite many governmental regulations and requirements, the traditional ideas of free competition, individual effort, and rewards for business entrepreneurship remain very much alive in the United States. Often when we think of business, we tend to think of the large, complex corporations. It is true that the 500 largest companies in the United States generate about 80 percent of gross sales in the private sector of the economy—that is, the business sector. But thousands of small companies thrive as well, many of them supplying goods and services to the large companies.

We have sketched a broad outline of what business is and how it functions in a society such as the United States. With this as background, let us now look at some economic systems in other countries.

OTHER ECONOMIC SYSTEMS

Two other major economic systems are in use by other nations in the world: socialism and communism. These systems have their disciples in the United States as well. They are active politically and spend a large amount of time trying to convince others that socialism or communism would be the best system for the

United States. The best-known socialist of this century, Norman Thomas, was on the ballot for president several times. The Socialist and Communist parties are legitimate political parties, and their members are entitled to run for elective office under their party labels. Given the importance, then, of *communism* and *socialism* as economic systems and political forces, it is helpful to have a basic understanding of how they operate in order to compare them to capitalism.

SOCIALISM

In a socialistic system, the government usually owns and operates major industries such as coal mines, steel mills, railroads, and communication networks. When a government takes over the ownership and operation of a company, the term applied to that action is *nationalization*. Britain, for example, has nationalized the radio and television networks, the railroads, and other industries. Outside of the nationalized portion of the economy, however, businesses are owned and operated as in a free enterprise system.

By owning basic industries, the government is often attempting to eliminate practices that can occur where competition among companies is limited. Railroads, for example, may charge high prices and restrict service to make a profit or reduce a loss. Yet railroads may be vital to the economy and national defense of a country. The government, therefore, may nationalize the railroads to assure their continued existence at the same time it attempts to offer a broader service at lower prices. In effect, the government often assumes a good chunk of the loss in continuing to run certain kinds of necessary industries. In contrast, a capitalist nation such as the United States would try to regulate these industries through legislation rather than through ownership and operation.

Socialist economies usually provide free social and health service for all of their citizens. Free medical and dental care, full retirement benefits, and food, shelter, and clothing when needed is an aspect of socialism that often identifies it as a *welfare state*. These free goods and services cost the government money, of course, which it must obtain through taxation. As a result, a socialist nation typically imposes heavy taxes on its people and companies.

High taxation accomplishes another purpose in socialism. It helps to even out the amount of money that people have left to spend after paying their taxes. Very heavy taxation of the higher incomes and of inheritances transfers money from the more wealthy people to the government. The government, in turn, transfers this money to the average citizen in the form of free or less costly goods and services. In theory, at least, people in a socialistic state need less money because they do not personally have to pay for such things as medical service. They have to pay, of course, in the form of taxation, but the tax burden does tend to fall more heavily on the rich.

Government spending at very high levels, as in Britain, does tend to strain a nation's resources and capability to tax and spend. Britain has had serious economic problems in the last few years, although one must be cautious in placing all the blame on its form of socialism. The volume of foreign trade, the increasing price of oil, and other world conditions have undoubtedly played a role in Britain's problems as well.

It should be stressed that socialism can exist side by side with a democratic political system in which free elections are held and numerous political parties are free to operate. Britain and Sweden are two excellent examples of this form of coexistence. It does appear that once a country nationalizes its major industries, it becomes difficult if not impossible to reverse its tracks and denationalize even in the presence of a democratic political process.

COMMUNISM

Communism is state ownership of virtually all the productive resources of a nation's economy. Minor exceptions might be made, such as allowing collective agricultural workers to farm their own small plots and profit from the sale of their produce at local markets. In a communistic system, market decisions are made on a central planning basis by the government bureaucracy. For example, central planners tell factories how much of what goods to produce. As a result there may be a de-emphasis of consumer goods while industrial goods and defense hardware receive top priorities. The communist consumer is then likely to find shortages and high prices for items such as shoes and cars.

Distribution of income—how much one gets paid for working—is set by government order. The government also controls the job market by controlling the number of young people allowed into training and education for different kinds of work and careers. This control is particularly apparent at the university level. Membership in the Communist Party is also frequently important in terms of opportunities for individuals.

There has been at least some minor amount of modification in the production-distribution system in Russia as it affects the consumer sector. In the past, central planners would tell factories how much of each product to manufacture. They would also determine how the goods would be distributed to the various retailing firms in the economy (such as the famous G.U.M. department store in Moscow). However, the goods were often shoddy and would simply pile up on store shelves because consumers refused to buy them. As a result, some decentralization of decision making occurred. Retailing outlets were given the freedom to buy from whatever factories they desired. In order to sell their products, factories were thus forced to emphasize the quality of their work as well as the quantity. This system is often called *Libermanism* after the Russian economist whose ideas were responsible for its adoption. It was seen as a slight movement by Russia toward a capitalistic approach, though its importance in that respect may have been over-emphasized.

A communistic system can hardly function with anything short of a very highly centralized and despotic national government. Furthermore, there must be rigid control over communications media such as press and television to prevent criticism of the government. Changes in the government usually come about as a result of plots within the party hierarchy if problems such as foreign policy or domestic strife arise that the present leadership is judged to have mishandled.

This is exactly what happened to Nikita Khrushchev in 1964, when he took what he thought was going to be a short vacation on the Black Sea. Dissident members of the inner circle acted quickly during his absence to get other members of the highest government ruling body (Politburo) to turn him out and bring in Leonid Brezhnev, until then a close lieutenant of Khrushchev's, into the chairman's office. Khrushchev's great failing was an unsuccessful agricultural policy.

The three major economic systems in the world today, then, are capitalism, socialism, and communism. In practice, each economic system is closely related to a political system. Capitalism operates under the democratic process, as does socialism in Britain and Sweden. At times a socialistic system may operate within a highly centralized political system, with the government exercising tight control over its citizens and restricting such basic freedoms as due process of law and free speech. Nondemocratic regimes of this nature have existed from time to time in Latin America. Communism tends much more to be associated with a highly centralized and dictatorial form of political system—as typified by Russia and Mainland China.

The so-called Third World nations or developing nations would very much like to progress from a condition of relative poverty to a standard of living approximating that of the more developed nations such as the United States or countries in Western Europe. To attempt this progress, the developing nations generally either choose to use a particular economic system or gravitate toward one as a result of influence from other nations.

The United States and some countries from Western Europe encourage developing nations to adopt a democratic and capitalistic system. Russia and Mainland China, usually going their separate ways, encourage others to adopt a communistic system. Such attempts at influence have taken the form of persuasion, economic help, and sometimes undercover activities. Unfortunately, these attempts to influence developing nations have also contributed to the tensions between the major powers of the world as they seek to extend their political systems and the amount of influence they have in world affairs.

Hence we find economic systems and political systems are closely related. And we cannot fully understand and appreciate one without being aware of the relationship to the other. We cannot fully understand and appreciate capitalism until we recognize its dependence upon the democratic process. In the next section, the authors will offer their philosophy on capitalism and business and will present a conceptual framework for the book.

THE PHILOSOPHICAL AND CONCEPTUAL FRAMEWORK

The authors fully support capitalism and the democratic process as economic and political systems that provide a supportive base and environment for the operation of business enterprise. Democracy provides the freedom to operate, while capitalism offers the incentive and potential reward.

At the same time, we must recognize that capitalism and business enterprise have not solved many of our social and environmental problems. The authors, therefore, also feel that the business community has a responsibility and obligation to work toward solutions of these problems—to reduce unemployment, to eliminate discrimination, to eliminate pollution, to assure fairness for the consumer, and to aid in areas of urban trouble. Business cannot solve these problems by itself but can work cooperatively with government and other institutions.

While the authors' philosophy is supportive of capitalism and the social responsibilities of business, the main purpose of their book is to introduce the student to the fundamentals of business. The introductory section of the book, Part One, demonstrates why we have our present business system and offers a broad description of business organization. Parts Two, Three, and Four analyze the several different kinds of activities required to run a business successfully. Some of the important skills and tools that can help a business to be successful are discussed in Part Five. The last part of the book, Part Six, identifies the major challenges and opportunities that confront the business community today. The conceptual framework of the book is portrayed graphically in Figure 1–2.

As an aid to understanding some of the concepts of business operation, a continuing example will be used in Parts Two, Three, and Four of the book. These parts deal with the important business functions of management, marketing, and financial management. In addition, Chapter 3, "The Framework of American Business," and Chapter 14, "Accounting," will use the example.

This example or case will become familiar to the reader, and, as a result, time can be more productively spent on explanation of concepts rather than on introducing a new case every time an illustration is desired. Of course, where it is necessary to use some particular type of example, such as a bank or railroad, the authors will do so.

The continuing case to be used casts Geri Rogers and Art Lindstrom in the lead roles. They will organize and operate a business called The Candy Emporium. The Candy Emporium is based on a real case. Some of the facts have been changed slightly for illustration. Geri Rogers worked on a newspaper and

Figure 1-2 Conceptual framework of the book.

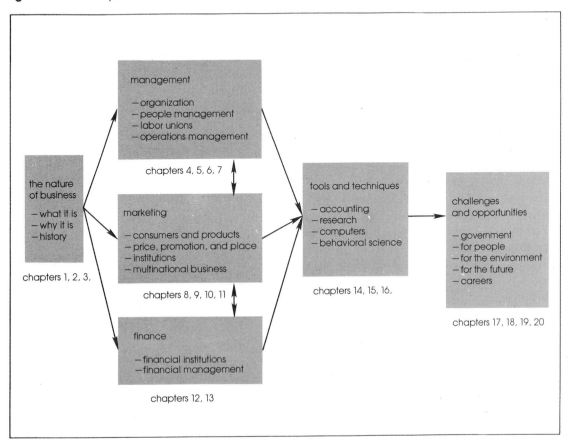

as a department store buyer in Omaha. She returned to her hometown, Warrenstown, due to the illness of her widowed mother. Geri was an excellent cook, and friends frequently complimented her and told her she should use her talents professionally.

While there were restaurant opportunities available, the hours involved were long. However, Geri and her friend Art Lindstrom, a geology professor at State College in Warrenstown, perceived a need for a candy store and associated services. The story of the formation of The Candy Emporium begins in Chapter 3.

SUMMARY

Business produces the goods or services that consumers need or want. It operates on a competitive, private enterprise basis that is encouraged by our national culture and legal structure. Our society has a basic belief that business provides the best means to develop and allocate scarce resources. Business operates within a capitalistic system that is characterized by the right to own and use property and make a profit, by a price system that aids in allocating resources, and by competition. Capitalism has problems, and these include economic cycles of prosperity, recession, depression, and recovery; inadequate long-range planning; and, to date, an inability to solve various social problems.

People in the United States have long believed in individualism and rewards for hard work. These beliefs find much of their basis in the religious philosophy of John Calvin and in the Protestant ethic. As a partial result, small business has existed continually along with big business in our history. Today there appears to be a resurgence of small business and greater emphasis on individual craft work.

Besides capitalism, the two other major economic systems in the world are socialism and communism. In socialism, the government usually owns and operates major industries such as the railroads, while in communism, the government usually owns and controls all economic resources. Capitalism and some forms of socialism are closely linked with the democratic process, while communism is usually associated with highly centralized government control and dictatorial power.

DISCUSSION QUESTIONS

1. What is the meaning of profit? Why is profit important to a business? What are some of the things that the amount of profit might tell about a business?

2. What do you think would be the differences in terms of challenges and opportunities between working for a very small business and working for a very large business such as General Motors?

3. Several years ago, a hand calculator cost $100 or more. Now some models of hand calculators can be bought for less than $10. Can you think of some reasons why the price has gone down so much?

4. Sometimes politicians and others speak of "free competition" in the United States. Is competition in the United States truly free? If not, in what ways is competition limited, and do these limits hinder a business in competing with other businesses?

5. Do you have any personal experiences that would suggest the country has been in a recession or an inflationary period? Do you think recessions and inflations can be prevented?

6. A company such as IBM is very successful. If IBM were to achieve a strong monopoly position in the computer market, why should the government try to break that monopoly?

Why should not IBM be allowed to enjoy the rewards of its efforts and success?

7. Can you think of some activities today where the philosophy of survival of the fittest still applies?

8. Some persons suggest that socialism is just a step on the road to communism. Do you think this is true? Are Sweden and Britain on the road to communism?

SHORT CASES

Hot Competition

Dan James owns an appliance store in a city of 100,000 people. There are three other appliance stores in town, and competition among the stores is very intense. Lately James's sales have been falling off, and he blames his relatively poor location for the decline in sales. He also notes, however, that his competitors have been doing a lot of advertising, emphasizing sale prices and special deals on certain items. James has done limited advertising and has run very few sales because he feels he needs to get the full price for an appliance in order to make a profit.

With sales going down, however, James feels it is time for drastic action. One weekend he carefully reads all the ads of his competitors and the sales prices on several specific appliances. The next weekend James splurges and runs a half-page ad in the local newspaper. In the ad he lists each of his competitors and the prices they are charging on certain appliances. Then he lists his own comparable appliances and their prices—in each case lower than his competitors'. The following week, James does more business than he has for the previous three years.

Do you feel it is proper for Dan James to advertise a comparison of his competitors' prices with his own in order to show that his prices are lower?

If you were one of Dan James's competitors, how would you feel about his advertising? What would you do?

Have you ever seen an ad that compared competitors' prices? What was your reaction?

The Case of the Disappearing Profit[2]

In 1975 Sharon Steel Corporation of Pennsylvania was trying to buy a controlling interest in a company called Foremost-McKesson, Inc., in order to take over the management of the latter company. It was a David versus Goliath struggle since Sharon had $360 million in annual sales, while Foremost-McKesson had $2.6 billion in sales. Apparently in order to increase its chances for the takeover and to make itself look attractive to the stockholders of Foremost-McKesson, Sharon Steel reported earnings in 1975 of $25.6 million.

Not wanting to lose its independence, Foremost-McKesson sued Sharon to block the takeover attempt. As a result of information brought out in the trial, the judge in the case said that Sharon's earnings for 1975 were much closer to $6.3 million rather than $25.6 million, a difference of $19.3 million. The judge said that almost $8 million of the reported earnings should not have been recorded at all, and almost $12 million were the result of unjustified changes in the value of the inventory and were, therefore, not real earnings.

According to the court, the effect of Sharon's overstatement of its earnings for 1975 was to distort its financial strength and capacity. As a result of the findings, Sharon withdrew its offer to buy stock in Foremost-McKesson.

As the case illustrates, it is possible for profits to vary considerably, depending on the accounting procedures that are used. Was Sharon Steel acting in an unethical and/or immoral manner when it reported 1975 earnings far greater than what Sharon Steel really earned?

Would you like to see the government require all companies to use exactly the same methods in figuring their profits? Would this requirement prevent problems such as occurred in this case?

---

[2] "A Court Untangles Sharon Steel's Books," *Business Week*, May 9, 1977, pp. 34–35.

SUGGESTED READINGS

Bach, George Leland. *Economics: An Introduction to Analysis and Policy.* 9th ed. Englewood Cliffs, N.J.: Prentice-Hall, 1977.

Clough, Shepard B. *The Economic Development of Western Civilization.* New York: McGraw-Hill Book Co., 1959.

Monsen, R. Joseph, Jr. *Modern American Capitalism.* Boston: Houghton Mifflin, 1963.

Nove, Alec. *The Soviet Economy.* New York: Praeger, 1961.

HISTORICAL PERSPECTIVES

LEARNING OBJECTIVES

When you finish this chapter you should:

☐ know the important periods of development in business history.

☐ understand the role of the industrial revolution and its many inventions in business development.

☐ understand how monopoly positions played a role in the development of some of our largest corporations.

☐ be familiar with the succession of periods — the prosperous twenties, the depression of the thirties, and World War II — leading to the present, modern era.

KEY TERMS TO LEARN FROM THIS CHAPTER

cottage system
holding company
industrial revolution
interchangeability of parts

mass production
share of stock
watered stock

Business development in the United States over the past 200 years has been rapid and has occurred in several well-defined stages. Wars, depressions, and periods of great prosperity have often marked the beginnings and endings of these historical stages. The purpose of this chapter is to give the reader a perspective on how the United States arrived at its present stage of business development. Chapter 1 provided a philosophical basis and justification for American business, and this chapter will help the reader understand business by offering historical illustrations of business in practice.

In 1606, the British government chartered the London Company and the Plymouth Company to travel to the New World to establish trade in furs, precious metals, and whatever else might prove profitable. Unfortunately, both companies established a long-term habit of losing money. Their precedent did not create an irreversible trend, however, and subsequent commercial ventures fared well enough to establish continuing operations in the colonies and the United States.

Business in the New World throughout the seventeenth century was predominantly agricultural. Cattle and particularly sheep were introduced, and trade slowly began in furs, meat, wool, cotton, tobacco, and leather. At that time, most raw materials were shipped to other countries in trade for finished products such as furniture, machinery, wines, and fine clothing. The traders or merchants in these items began to accumulate tidy amounts of money over the years.

The surplus funds of the merchants were invested in land and gradually in manufacturing operations. In the eighteenth century, most manufacturing was done by skilled craftsmen in their own shops or by means of the *cottage system*. Under the latter system, manufacturers delivered raw materials to homes where entire families might work to convert the raw materials to finished products. These products were then picked up at the workers' homes and sold to merchants or the final consumers. Clothing often was produced in this manner.

THE FACTORY

By 1800, manufacturers had established many factories—that is, they had physically placed under one roof all the production processes required to complete a product. Instead of having materials brought to their homes, workers went to the factories every day. The first factories included such operations as flour and saw mills, textile mills, and shoemaking. These early manufacturing and processing plants were small and simple, of course, and primarily utilized water power and, to a much lesser extent, steam power.

Then, in 1793, Eli Whitney invented the cotton gin—a mechanical method of removing seeds from cotton. The productivity increase over hand methods of cleaning cotton was fantastic, and cotton boomed. Planters put every possible acre into growing cotton. Slavery, which had been gradually phasing out, suddenly became the principal means for exploitation of the land. Cotton mills, textile manufacturers, and banks in the northeastern part of the country prospered from cotton. For seven decades after 1793, cotton was king and slaves suffered as victims of the southern cotton economy.

Other industry developed as well. After being exploited himself in the financial and legal maneuvering over his patent on the cotton gin, Eli Whitney turned to a new challenge—the manufacture of muskets in quantity. At that time, musket makers would contract to produce several hundred muskets at most. Each gun had to be individually tooled and assembled. On the basis of an idea, however, Whitney contracted for 10,000 muskets with the United States government.

His idea was *interchangeability of parts.* The importance of interchangeability in manufacturing practice was that any musket barrel, for example, could be used in combination with any trigger and all the other necessary component parts to produce a complete musket. Whitney could see tremendous savings in comparison with the laborious handwork required to individually make and fit together all the parts for one musket.

To realize the potential of his idea, Whitney had to develop the specialized machinery and tools that would make possible the manufacture of standardized parts. Fortunately, he had the creativity and practical know-how to accomplish his goal. In so doing, Whitney achieved the first *mass production* of a complex product. He also achieved his projected cost savings, principally by being able to employ semiskilled workers to run the machines rather than highly skilled and specialized gunsmiths.

After initial difficulties, Whitney fulfilled his contract with the government for muskets. More important, standardized, interchangeable parts opened up whole new vistas in manufacturing—leading ultimately to the mass production of automobiles and other products.

THE INDUSTRIAL REVOLUTION

Invention followed upon invention in England during the eighteenth century. Richard Arkwright, James Hargreaves, Samuel Crompton, and Edmund Cartwright successively invented improvements for textile machinery. James Watt invented the steam engine in 1765. There were others, but inventiveness was not confined to the British Isles, as Eli Whitney convincingly demonstrated. Events began to move ahead quickly in the United States after 1800. Robert Fulton bolted down a steam engine in his boat, the *Clermont,* in 1807 and successfully chugged up and down the Hudson River. Steamboats flourished, culminating in steam power for ocean-going vessels, coastal ships, and the side-wheelers and stern-wheelers that plied the Mississippi in great numbers.

Railroads were starting up in the early nineteenth century. By the 1830s, the government had chartered the Baltimore and Ohio, the New York and Erie, the Charleston and Hamburg, and the Mohawk and Hudson. Horses pulled the first trains. To demonstrate superior efficiency and economy, Peter Cooper, a highly successful Baltimore businessman, built "Tom Thumb," a steam locomotive. In a thirteen-mile race with a horse, the "Tom Thumb" almost won. The results were sufficiently convincing to railroad managements, however, and orders poured in for locomotives in the following years. Tremendous expansion of the railroads followed, achieving a grand climax on May 10, 1869, when Leland Stanford drove the last spike at Promontory, Utah, to complete a transcontinental railroad.

Famous and infamous names were associated with the railroads: Commodore Cornelius Vanderbilt and the New York Central; Daniel Drew, Jim Fisk, and Jay Gould with the Erie; Leland Stanford and the Central Pacific; and Edward Harriman and the Union Pacific. Drew, Fisk, and Gould in particular earned reputations as financial pirates for their dealings in *watered stock* (shares of stock issued beyond the value of a company) and other questionable practices. At times, the railroad tycoons waged monumental battles over rate cutting and attempts to wrest control of each other's railroads. At one time, Vanderbilt attempted to gain control of the Erie by purchasing its stock, but Drew and his cohorts issued so much watered stock that Vanderbilt gave up.

MANUFACTURING

Technological advances in transportation were only part of the industrial revolution in the nineteenth century. In Illinois in 1836, John Deere developed a steel plow. In the decades that followed, factory-made John Deere plows turned soil all across the midwestern prairie. In combination with Cyrus McCormick's reaper and other new developments in agricultural machinery, the steel plow helped to more than double farm production between 1840 and 1860. From the Civil War, when 80 percent of the population still lived on farms, the shift of people from farm to city never ceased as machinery continually replaced manual labor.

In the 1840s, Charles Goodyear developed practical methods for the manufacture of rubber, and Elias Howe developed a practical sewing machine. In the 1850s, Gail Borden developed evaporated milk. During the same decade, oil began flowing from wells in Pennsylvania. There are many other examples of inventions and developments during the last century: the telegraph and the telephone, the electric light, the electric generator, and the automobile.

These inventions not only brought about remarkable changes in manufacturing but in certain cases greatly facilitated the settling of the West. The railroad and the telegraph are notable examples in this respect. Another invention, less well known perhaps but one that also helped considerably in settling the western United States, was the Colt revolver. Samuel Colt invented the revolver in 1836, and it found its first widespread use with the Texas Rangers starting in 1840.

Prior to that time the Rangers and all others used single-shot weapons. This proved to be a disadvantage when fighting Indians who could shoot several arrows in the time it took to reload a single-shot gun. Time after time, therefore, a badly outnumbered band of Indians would force the Rangers into a complete and hasty retreat. Primarily to assure their successful getaway, the Rangers insisted on having the fastest horses available. If they could not outfight the Indians, the Rangers wanted to be sure they could outrun them.

When the Rangers began using the Colt six-shooter in 1840, however, they quickly demonstrated their superior firepower. Until the Indians got their own revolvers and rifles, it became their turn to make hasty retreats from most skirmishes with the Rangers.

The Colt revolver spread throughout the West. The horse enabled people to conquer the vast open spaces, while the gun provided food and offered protection. As was observed, "God made some men large and some small, but Colonel Colt made them all equal."[1]

The gun and the horse, along with barbed wire, were vital to the development of the West. Farming, ranching, mining, and other industries all benefited

[1]Walter Prescott Webb, *The Great Plains* (New York, Grosset & Dunlap: 1931), p. 494.

from the security of the gun, the mobility of the horse, and the protection of barbed wire fences. With the expansion of the West as a market and as a producer of goods and services, along with all of the developments in transportation, agriculture, and manufacturing, the stage was set for tremendous business expansion following the Civil War. Prior to the war most companies were relatively small. During the latter part of the nineteenth century and into the twentieth century, men such as Andrew Carnegie, George Westinghouse, John D. Rockefeller, and J. P. Morgan headed companies of unprecedented size and power.

EMPIRE BUILDING

One could choose from among a dozen examples to illustrate the rapid growth of a company or industry following the Civil War. Andrew Carnegie and the steel industry are as good as any. The demand for iron and steel often exceeded the supply in the years following the Civil War. Fortunately, the Bessemer process, developed earlier in England, and the open-hearth process of steel making not only helped to increase production but yielded better quality as well. Production increased from 1,000,000 tons of iron in 1860 to over 10,000,000 tons of iron and steel by 1900.

Carnegie entered the steel industry full time in 1865 after having invested in several iron foundries. He installed the Bessemer process in his plant in the early 1870s and added the open-hearth process in the late 1880s. Constantly adding new mills and improving the production process, Carnegie relentlessly pursued lower costs, higher production, and better quality. He also bought up smaller steel companies and in 1893 formed the Carnegie Steel Company.

But the best was yet to come for Carnegie. Along with Charles Schwab and Henry Clay Frick, he continued to expand his steel empire. Through all these years the demand for steel was never satisfied. Steel went into railroad tracks, U.S. Navy ships, buildings, and bridges at ever-increasing rates. Ten million tons of production in 1900 reached 30 million by 1910 and 50 million by 1920.

Already retired by 1901, in that year Carnegie entered into a deal with J. P. Morgan and his associates whereby Carnegie sold his interest in the Carnegie Steel Company for $492 million. This sum reputedly made Carnegie the richest person in the world at that time. With his retirement nest egg, Carnegie entered a new career—building and donating libraries to cities all over the country.

J. P. Morgan and his partners had brought together several companies to combine with the Carnegie Steel Company. They named this huge combination the United States Steel Corporation. It was the first billion-dollar corporation, and it dominated the steel industry for many years. A similar story could be told about John D. Rockefeller and the oil industry, or about James B. Duke and the tobacco industry, or about others. But of more interest is the reduction in competition that these new and very large companies brought about through their domination of industries.

THE MONOPOLISTS

Hardly a major industry of 1900 could be mentioned that was not dominated by a giant company. The U.S. Steel Corporation in steel production, International

Harvester in farm equipment, the American Tobacco Company in tobacco, the American Sugar Refining Company in sugar, and the Standard Oil Company of New Jersey in oil are some of the best-known examples.

These huge enterprises typically developed through the combination of a number of smaller companies, much as described previously in the formation of United States Steel. J. P. Morgan, the famous investment banker, had his hand in several of these formations. Morgan and other promoters like him typically would form a *holding company*. The purpose of a holding company is to invest in the stock ownership of other companies. As an example, ten individuals might each invest $1 million to form a holding company. With a total investment of $10 million, the holding company could then buy or trade for stock in other companies—often to the extent of actually controlling the other companies.

Morgan and his associates would usually trade the stock of their holding company for the stock of companies that would enter the developing combination. The promoters, such as Morgan, retained majority control of the holding company and, as a result, usually had control also of the companies that were acquired through trade.

Even though Congress had passed the Sherman Anti-Trust Act in 1888, action against the monopolies by the government was generally ineffective. The courts were quite lenient at the time in ruling on whether or not monopolies actually existed. Finally, however, after the administration of President William H. Taft pressed a case against Standard Oil, the Supreme Court in 1911 ordered that company "busted" into twenty-nine entities. Even this action did not effectively limit Standard Oil's power, though, since its major stockholders were still able to act cooperatively and to function almost as a single unit.

The reign of the monopolies was largely temporary, however. There was still so much opportunity for competitors because of the growing market and technological advances that few of the dominating companies were able to retain their positions. Gulf Oil and Texaco wrested large chunks of the market away from Standard Oil, for example, and the same fate befell U.S. Steel and many of the others. Never since have companies been able to dominate markets so completely. Additional legislation, such as the Clayton Anti-Trust Act of 1914, has helped assure continuing competition in business.

THE FABULOUS TWENTIES

Following the recession after World War I, the American economy prospered. A number of major new industries contributed to the recovery leading to a period of prosperity. The most important of these was the automobile industry. Starting around 1900, automobile production had grown steadily through the teen years of the century. In the 1920s, automobiles boomed. Motor vehicle registration climbed from fewer than ten million in 1920 to almost thirty million by 1930. Henry Ford was turning out almost two million cars annually by the mid-twenties.

America on wheels enjoyed a whole new way of life. People began traveling across the continent by car, going to work by car, and courting by car. Cars became a status symbol, as did many other products. "Keeping up with the Joneses" entered the vocabulary. Keeping up meant buying radios, washing machines, vacuum cleaners, and bathtubs. It also meant going to the movies, playing golf, and perhaps even taking flying lessons. It was an era of new ideas, new products, and new technology.

It was also an era of wild speculation in buying and selling shares of stock in companies. A *share of stock* is an ownership interest in a company, of course, but people in the twenties were interested in speculation—not long-term ownership. People wanted to buy a share of stock for ten dollars today and sell it for twenty dollars tomorrow. And for awhile, many people did make a lot of money.

Everyone from the corner groceryman to Wall Street hotshots was in the stock market. No one, it seemed, was immune to the hot tip. Buying on as little as 10 percent down, and paying out in cash only 10 percent of the price of the stock, was common. For example, a person could buy $10,000 worth of stock for $1,000 in cash, with the balance to be paid later. As often happened, however, the stock was sold after it increased in value but before the balance became due. Stock worth $10,000 might increase to $12,000 and be sold. If it had been purchased on 10 percent margin for $1,000, the purchaser would realize a $2,000 profit on a $1,000 cash investment. With this sort of potential, many people regularly dreamed of becoming millionaires overnight.

Then, after some previous sharp drops in stock prices, Black Friday hit—October 29, 1929. The stock market collapsed. Prices fell and fell and continued to fall. In the weeks that followed, billions of dollars were lost. There were some recoveries or increases in stock prices in 1930, but the stock market debacle proved to be the beginning of the depression of the 1930s.

THE GREAT DEPRESSION

At times during the 1930s, unemployment reached thirteen million workers, or almost one-fourth of the work force. Banks closed, factories darkened, stores closed, and many families entered bread lines and welfare, or relief as it was called then, for the first time. Large sections of midwestern farm country suffered a population drain as drought and dust storms added to the misery and forced families by the thousands into other parts of the nation.

The federal government, under President Herbert C. Hoover and more so under President Franklin Delano Roosevelt, initiated numerous programs and legislation in the effort to turn the economy around and get it moving again. President Hoover instituted the Reconstruction Finance Corporation to loan money to banks and farmers. Under President Roosevelt, Congress passed several measures designed to aid the national economy. Among these were the Civilian Conservation Corps, which provided employment for young men to work in the national forests and in conservation projects; the Federal Emergency Relief Administration, which distributed $500 million in direct help to the states; and the National Industrial Recovery Act, which financed construction of public buildings and other public works.

In addition, Congress passed the National Labor Relations Act in 1935, which helped the organization and recognition of unions as well as guaranteeing them the right to collective bargaining—that is, the right of unions to negotiate with management over wages, hours, and working conditions. With this legislation to back it up labor successfully unionized many companies, including the important large steel and automobile companies.

For the most part, business opposed the Roosevelt administration and its program but was forced into reluctant cooperation. Despite depression problems, business continued to progress. In the airline industry, new routes were being pioneered by men such as Charles Lindbergh. Douglas Aircraft and others were developing and building bigger and better airplanes. In chemicals, the DuPont Company developed nylon, which revolutionized the hosiery industry. The depression did not completely end until defense spending started at the onset of World War II in 1939. It had been a rough decade, but business and the rest of the nation were looking ahead to better days at the end of the war.

THE MODERN ERA

After a massive dedication to the production of war materials, business and the nation turned to peace in 1945. Business accomplished the conversion to peacetime production quickly in order to meet the pent-up demand for cars, refrigerators, clothing, and all the items that had been unavailable for four long years. There were new ideas, new materials, and new methods from wartime research and development. Plastics flourished. Airplane design benefited from stronger and lighter metal alloys. With the development of Freon, mass air conditioning became possible. Television started its meteoric rise in the late forties.

Business corporations became bigger and more complex than ever. Companies began to measure their gross sales in billions of dollars. The enormity and complexity of business organizations presented a new challenge to management—one which we are still striving to meet. There was and is a need for greater skill in planning, organizing, controlling, and coordinating the new enterprise. Fortunately, there has been help. Research into areas such as organization behavior and theory, marketing, financial management, and accounting methods has expanded tremendously in the past twenty-five years, often providing specific and practical help to business management. Since its development in the early 1950s, the computer has proved a boon in solving complicated decision problems and in quickly processing vast amounts of data. The computer, along with improved communication and travel, has greatly facilitated the development of far-flung business operations. The increasing importance of the multinational corporation demonstrates this facility.

The history of business is exciting. The future will be even more exciting. There are continuing problems: inflation and recession, pollution, energy shortages, and others. Yet many opportunities remain open and available to the enterprising individual. Perhaps the reader will play a role in solving some of the problems and in capitalizing on some of the opportunities. In the remainder of the book, we want to tell you, the reader, about business—to analyze and describe business operations so you will gain a basic understanding of them. In the next chapter, we will be more specific about how business operates and the legal forms of business organization.

SUMMARY

The history of business in the United States goes back several hundred years. From 1606, when the British government chartered the London Company and the Plymouth Company to establish trade in the New World, until the present time, business has developed through several well-defined stages. Until the nineteenth century, business flourished primarily in agriculture and trade. From 1800 on, manufacturing began to play an increasingly important role.

In the 1800s in the United States, many inventions and technological advances continued the industrial revolution started in England a hundred years earlier. These developments included the steam engine for railroads, a method to manufacture rubber, and others.

After the Civil War, factories, railroads, steel mills, and oil refineries began to grow very large. Around the turn of the century and into the 1900s, many of these companies combined to form the first huge corporations that we are familiar with today.

After a period of prosperity in the 1920s, the nation plunged into the Great Depression in the 1930s. Business suffered but still progressed: in commercial aviation, in chemicals, and in other industries. Following World War II, business entered the modern era—one marked by increasing complexity but also by tools such as the computer to help business deal with its increasingly difficult world.

Business has an exciting history: it has seen ups and downs, successes and failures, and it has been witness to a steady, long-term development that justifies to the present time the economic system we use.

DISCUSSION QUESTIONS

1. The cottage system was an early form of manufacturing. Can you think of examples of the cottage system in practice today? Can the cottage system be economically justified today?

2. There were many inventions during the 1800s in the United States. Can you think of reasons why, after centuries of hardly any inventions at all, so many inventions should occur in a relatively short period of time?

3. Why was the development of better transportation so vital to business development?

4. Many large corporations formed during the late 1800s and early 1900s. Is it still possible for a large corporation to develop from a small company? Can you think of examples?

5. The Great Depression of the 1930s imposed hardships on millions of people. Yet it has been said that a country needs a depression now and then as a necessary counterpart to prosperity—to sort of keep everything in balance. Do you agree with the idea that depressions might be necessary?

6. What additional business developments do you think might occur in the next ten to twenty years?

SHORT CASES

The Marriage Was a Disaster

For many years, the New York Central and the Pennsylvania railroads were giants in their industry. They hauled millions of tons of freight and ran luxurious passenger trains such as the Twentieth Century Limited between New York and Chicago. Famous politicians, movie stars, and Mr. Average Citizen were frequent travelers on their trains.

By the mid-1950s, however, both were in trouble. Airplane travel had taken away most of the train passengers. Trucks were hauling a lion's share of the freight business. In 1957, the chairman of New York Central, Robert R. Young, proposed a merger between the two old lines. He felt that by combining equipment, facilities, and management know-how into one system, the new organization could

survive. Finally, in 1968, after much negotiation and many government hearings, the merger became a reality under the name of Penn-Central. High hopes marked the beginning, but within two years the Penn-Central was in bankruptcy.

Do you think that the failure of Penn-Central shows that railroads will eventually go completely out of business in the United States?

Do you think the government should provide enough financial support to assure that there will always be railroads?

"57 Varieties"

The H. J. Heinz Company was started in 1875 by H. J. Heinz, who was still in the throes of bankruptcy following the failure of his first business venture. But Heinz was determined to be successful, and after several more years, his new venture began to make a profit. The kitchens of the Heinz Company were making tomato ketchup, tomato soup, pickles, and a variety of other products. By the time Heinz decided on the slogan "57 Varieties," the company actually was producing far more than fifty-seven varieties of products. But Heinz liked the sound of the number 57, and it became part of the slogan.

At a time when long hours and miserable working conditions were common in most industries, Heinz introduced personnel practices in his new factory (built in 1888) that were strikingly different. There was music during lunch, free medical care, and homemaking classes for the employees. Private lockers and clean uniforms were provided. For the athletic, Heinz provided a swimming pool and a gymnasium. To top it all, employees could have as many of the "57 Varieties" as they wanted.

Why do you suppose Heinz introduced such benefits as free medical care for his employees at a time (1888) when such practices were virtually unheard of in business?

Were these practices and benefits that Heinz introduced as important to business development as the invention of the automobile or the extension of the railroads across the entire United States?

SUGGESTED READINGS

Chamberlain, John. *The Enterprising Americans: A Business History of the United States.* Enl. ed. New York: Harper & Row, 1974.

Chandler, Alfred D., Jr. *The Railroads: The Nation's First Big Business: Sources and Readings.* New York: Harcourt Brace Jovanovich, 1965.

Hicks, Herbert G.; Price, W. R.; and Powell, I. D. *Dimensions of American Business.* New York: McGraw-Hill Book Co., 1975.

Walton, Scott D. *Business in American History.* Columbus, Ohio: Grid, 1971.

THE FRAMEWORK OF AMERICAN BUSINESS

LEARNING OBJECTIVES

When you finish this chapter you should:

☐ be aware of the distinctions among sole proprietorships, partnerships, and corporations.

☐ understand what a contract is.

☐ be aware of the diversity of American business.

☐ be aware of differences in cost structure among firms.

☐ understand how supply and demand operate in a market setting.

KEY TERMS TO LEARN FROM THIS CHAPTER

agency	creditors	general partnership	quasi-public corporation
alien corporation	cumulative voting	labor intensive	sole proprietorship
articles of co-partnership	demand curve	limited partnership	special partnership
	demand schedule	normal profit	subchapter S corporation
bankruptcy	dividends	obsolescence	supply curve
capital intensive	domestic corporation	partnership	supply schedule
capital stock	entrepreneurship	preemptive right	unit cost of production
contract	equilibrium price	proxy	unlimited liability
cooperative	fixed costs	public corporation	variable costs
corporation	foreign corporation		

When Geri and Art decided to form a retail candy business, one of the first decisions they had to make concerned the legal form of their business. Since they were going to share management and ownership functions, sole proprietorship (one owner) was out. However, whether to form a partnership or corporation had to be decided.

Since the legal form a business will initially take must be decided when a business is established, this topic is examined first. Some other important legal concepts applicable to business are then briefly discussed.

Two additional distinctions are helpful in terms of understanding business. These include: (1) classification of firms by function performed, and (2) differences between *capital intensive* and *labor intensive* firms. You are then ready to take a look at how the market operates in a free enterprise system.

OWNERSHIP STRUCTURE OF AMERICAN BUSINESS

When we enter a business establishment, it is unlikely that we think about the legal form of that business. Legal form of the firm, however, is almost as important as determining its product or service.

Consider Table 3–1, for example. It indicates that sole proprietorships constituted almost 80 percent of the total businesses in America. Sole proprietorships exceed corporations by more than five to one in terms of sheer numbers. Yet total proprietorship profits are less than half that of corporations. Clearly this seems to indicate that corporations are either more profitable or larger than proprietorships (or both). It is also interesting to note that the partnership is relatively unimportant in both total numbers and profits. An examination of these individual forms will shed light on why these relationships exist.

SOLE PROPRIETORSHIP

If Geri Rogers were going into business alone, she might have considered the *sole proprietorship* form of business. Starting and managing one's own business is frequently called *entrepreneurship*.

Advantages   The most obvious advantage is that the individual owner is his/her own boss. In addition, it is quite easy to start because of the simplicity of a

Table 3-1
Ownership Structure of American Business, 1973

Ownership Type	Number (in thousands)	%	Profit (in billions)	%
Proprietorship	10,648	78	$ 47	27
Partnership	1,039	8	9	5
Corporations	1,905	14	120	68
Total	13,592	100	$176	100

Source: **Statistical Abstract**, 1976.

one-owner proprietorship. As long as one remains within the laws and customs of the community, state, and nation, an individual is free to start a business of his/her choosing and operate it as he/she sees fit. Certainly the small business where the individual is his/her own boss represents the fulfillment of a considerable portion of the American dream.

Disadvantages   However, Geri would have found considerable disadvantages with the sole proprietorship. If one can start a business, one can also fail in that business. Sole proprietorships usually fail for one or more of the following reasons:

1. Lack of sufficient financing.
2. Lack of technical skill or ability in the area chosen.
3. Lack of managerial ability.
4. Lack of knowing how to market or sell the product or service being provided.

All of the above factors, excepting the second, are discussed in this book and should prove beneficial if you eventually become an entrepreneur.

The financing or cash shortage problem is a distinct shortcoming of the sole proprietary form. This is further affected by the proprietor's *unlimited liability* if the business fails. Should failure occur, the owner's personal assets such as house and car can be claimed by the *creditors* of the business (those who are owed money) for payment of amounts owed them.

PARTNERSHIP

Geri and Art thought a partnership might be a suitable legal form for their venture. They consulted Art's friend, Lou Simpson, a lawyer on the faculty of State College.

Lou first informed them that a *partnership* is defined as "an association of two or more persons to carry on as co-owners of a business for profit." This definition comes from the Uniform Partnership Act, which has been adopted by most states for the purpose of specifying legal aspects of partnerships.

Types of Partnerships   Most partnerships are *general partnerships*. A general partnership is created for the purpose of conducting a particular kind of business. A *special partnership*, on the other hand, is created for the purpose of carrying out a single transaction such as the acquisition and resale of a particular piece of property such as a plot of land or a building.

Occasionally a partnership formed for the purpose of operating a business will be a *limited partnership*. A limited partnership must have at least one general and one limited partner.

A limited partner invests his or her own money or other property in the partnership but does not take part in running the firm, nor can his or her name appear as part of the firm name.

The limited partner is entitled to a share of the profits and a return of his or her investment if the firm is dissolved. Unlike the general partner's, the limited partner's potential liability in the event of failure of the firm is restricted to his or her investment.

Advantages   A partnership has several advantages over the sole proprietorship. Because it has more members, it will usually have access to more funds when the business is formed.

Also, the partnership should have more expertise at its command because of the greater number of owners.

Disadvantages   The partnership has several distinct disadvantages, though. (Unless it is a limited partnership). It retains the sole proprietorship's unfavorable legal feature of unlimited liability for each partner in the event that the business is unable to pay its debts. Thus a wealthier partner could wind up saddled with the business debts of the other partners.

Another dangerous aspect of the partnership is that one partner acting alone can legally bind the other partners.

Several other factors add to the partnership's unpopularity. If a partner desires to leave a partnership and wishes to sell his or her interest to an outside party, the approval of the other partners must be obtained. In the event of the death of a partner, the partnership is terminated. The partnership might be reorganized if the remaining partners can buy the deceased partner's interest from his or her heirs or if a mutually acceptable outside party can be found who could buy the interest. Possibly the partnership could be reorganized by the remaining partners, with the deceased partner's heirs retaining the interest. In any event, problems certainly arise in most partnerships if a partner desires to leave or a partner dies.

Articles of Copartnership   To some extent these problems can be lessened by carefully spelling out in the *articles of copartnership* exactly what should be done in these situations. The articles of copartnership is a written document that should underlie the formation of a partnership by carefully spelling out the relations of the partners relative to each other and to the partnership. Some of the more common factors which should be spelled out include:

1. How profits and losses are to be divided.
2. How much money and other property is to be invested by each partner.
3. Authority and responsibility of each partner.
4. Procedure for admitting new partners.
5. Procedure for terminating the partnership.
6. How partners are to be compensated.
7. Limitations, if any, on withdrawals from an individual's investment.

CORPORATION

Despite the drawbacks to the partnership, Geri and Art thought it might be appropriate for their business. Nevertheless, they decided to find out more information about the corporation from Lou Simpson.

Advantages   The *corporation* itself is viewed as an artificial person in the eyes of the law. It thus has the rights, duties, and powers of a real person. It can own property in its name and sue and be sued, for example. While the individual owners of the corporation may transfer or sell their ownership shares, the corporation itself is unaffected. Here we have one of the principal advantages of the corporate form: its relative permanence over time.

There is, perhaps, an even more important advantage of the corporate form over its two rivals, one which stems from its nature as a legal person: liability of the owners is limited to their investment in the *capital stock* of the firm. Ownership interests in a corporation are represented by the number of shares of capital stock held by each owner.

Personal assets of owners, then, are unavailable to creditors for satisfaction of the corporation's debts. This seemingly simple advantage should not be underrated. Without it, it is unlikely that large firms could arise in a free enterprise system, because large amounts of funds would probably not be invested without the limited liability benefit.

Closely related to limited liability for large corporations is an owner's ability to dispose easily of presently held capital stock or to acquire more shares of stock through organized security exchanges such as the New York Stock Exchange and the American Stock Exchange. These institutions are nothing more than huge marketplaces for the buying and selling of stocks and other corporate securities.

CHARLES L. FARROW

Some businesses succeed . . .

Disadvantages   The process of incorporation, even for the small firm, can be a relatively expensive proposition. In addition to the filing fee that must be paid to the state, costs for competent legal and financial advice can be considerable. The small firm should make sure that this form is desirable before making any hasty decisions to incorporate.

There are, however, some corporations that are treated as if they were a partnership or sole proprietorship. These corporations are called *Subchapter S* corporations after the Internal Revenue Service code section discussing them. To qualify, the corporation must have no more than ten shareholders and all must

Higher corporate taxes can make the corporate form unattractive for new and relatively small sized operations. Corporate income is taxed by the federal government at 22 percent for the first $25,000 of income and 48 percent for amounts above $25,000.[1] On the other hand, sole proprietorships and partnerships are not directly taxed. Their annual income, whether left in the firm or withdrawn by owners, becomes part of each individual owner's taxable income. It will then be taxed at the rate applicable to the particular individual.

There are, however, some corporations that are treated as if they were a partnership or sole proprietorship. These corporations are called *Subchapter S* corporations after the Internal Revenue Service code section discussing them. To qualify, the corporation must have no more than ten shareholders and all must

[1] However, the Tax Reform Act of 1976 extended temporary favorable rates through December 31, 1978. These lower corporate rates are 20 percent on the first $25,000 of income, 22 percent on the next $25,000, and 48 percent above $50,000.

Some businesses fail

STEVE BAKER

elect to be taxed as individuals. Furthermore, the shareholders themselves must be individuals or estates. Shares cannot be owned by another corporation. Subchapter S treatment is desirable if the individual rates at which the shareholders are taxed lie below the corporate rate.

State income taxes are also generally higher for corporations than for sole proprietorships and partnerships.

Because of the higher costs of incorporation and the higher tax structure, Geri and Art decided to form a partnership rather than a corporation. There are, however, several other aspects of the corporation that should be discussed.

Formation   How is the corporation formed? If the bulk of the prospective firm's business is to be done within a particular state, then *articles of incorporation* are filed with the secretary of state of that particular state. When the articles are approved they essentially become the corporate charter. Among other things, the charter will specify:

1.   Purpose and type of business the new corporation can conduct.
2.   Maximum amount and kinds of capital stock that can be issued.
3.   Voting rights and powers applicable to the capital stock.
4.   Names of the incorporators and directors of the new corporation.

Domestic and Foreign Corporations   Corporations created under the laws of a particular state are *domestic corporations* relative to that state. *Foreign corporations* are those incorporated in a different state.

A domestic corporation is subject to the laws and regulations—including tax laws—of the state in which it is incorporated. A foreign corporation is likewise subject to regulation and taxation in each state in which it does business. Foreign corporations are usually required to register to do business in other states.

Corporations originating in foreign nations are known as *alien corporations.*

Stockholders   Stockholders have the following rights:

1. The right to vote for the board of directors at the annual meeting (or by *proxy,* which is essentially an absentee ballot). The number of votes a stockholder has would be equal to the number of shares owned.

2. The right to vote at the annual meeting on certain matters such as any changes in the corporate charter, profit sharing or pension plans, and dissolution of the corporation as these issues arise.

3. The right to hold their proportionate ownership interest in the company if the decision is made by the board of directors to issue more stock (called the shareholder's *preemptive* right).

4. The right to sell, transfer, or buy more ownership shares, as the stockholder sees fit.

5. The right to receive *dividends* when and if declared by the board of directors (a dividend is a return, usually of cash, to the stockholder for the use of his money).

Chase Manhattan Bank common stock certificate.

In a small, closely held corporation where a small number of people own all the shares of stock, all of these rights and privileges would be important. However, in large nationally based corporations, the shares may be owned by hundreds of thousands of people. The owner even of hundreds of shares may have an extremely small vote and thus effectively have little ability to influence corporate decisions.

However, some states require a process known as *cumulative voting,* which tends to enable smaller shareholders to gain representation on the board of directors. In cumulative voting, the shareholder's total votes equal the number of shares owned times the number of directors to be elected. Shareholders are entitled to distribute their votes in any fashion they please. If desired, an individual can cast all his or her votes for one director.

Nevertheless, the rights which are of most importance to the average stockholder owning shares in a major corporation are numbers 4 and 5: the right to buy and sell stock and the right to receive dividends as declared by the board of directors.

Board of Directors   The board of directors of a corporation is responsible for:

1.   Appointing the top management team of the firm.

2.   Resolving major policy issues.

3.   Declaring dividends.

The board of directors is the link between the stockholders of a corporation and its top management. The board, as noted above, is elected by the stockholders and, in turn, is responsible for appointing top management officials. The latter, in the form of the president or chief operating officer, reports to the board. The board is, of course, ultimately responsible to the shareholders.

Major policy issues decided by the board would include decisions relating to expansion of the corporation by building new plants or buying existing firms (the opposite situation, selling off plants or divisions, would also require the board's approval). It would also be responsible for setting or approving broad financial policies if the firm is growing or contracting. For example, building new plants might be financed by selling additional shares of stock, borrowing the necessary funds, or getting the funds from the corporation's own earnings. Carrying out the board's policy would be the treasurer of the firm.

The board is also responsible for declaring dividends on the stock. Usually a board will try to maintain a minimum annual dividend which will be increased during good years. During extremely lean times a board may cut or even eliminate the annual dividend. Also, as noted above, the board may finance expansion by investing the corporation's earnings in a new plant and equipment instead of paying dividends. The stockholders hope to sacrifice present dividends for larger dividends in the future in this situation.

Board members are usually elected for one-year terms. They sometimes receive compensation for their services. In large corporations, board members are often prominent individuals from banks and other financial institutions, lawyers with influential connections, well-known men from public life such as college presidents, and leading corporate executives from related industries. A refreshing new trend in board memberships includes individuals having important constituencies outside the traditional establishment. For example, Leon Sullivan, a black minister and advocate of minority entrepreneurship, became a member of the General Motors board in 1971. A trend is also developing toward the selection of more women as directors of corporations.

Separation of Ownership and Management   This leads us to another issue: the separation of ownership and management in the large corporation. The great bulk of the stockholders of major firms do not work for the corporation. As a result, they are often unaware of important events affecting them. Top management, while they often own shares in the corporation, are separated from the vast majority of owners. Management actions may not always be in the best interests of the stockholders.

An admittedly extreme example of this problem involved the Texas Gulf Sulphur Corporation. A large strike of bauxite, the mineral from which aluminum is produced, was found on corporate property in the wilds of northern Quebec in October 1962. No announcement of the find was made until April 1963, a six-month period of time. The announcement would have caused the stock price to rise because of the great value of the mineral deposit. Thus information that obviously would have affected buy and sell decisions as well as the immediate value of the stock was withheld from the owners. Furthermore, there was a lot of acquisition of ownership shares by the corporation itself during this six-month period. While this case, fortunately, is admittedly extreme, it does illustrate the problem of separation of ownership and management.

While the three forms of business discussed are by far the principal types, there are two other organizations in the nonprofit sector of the American economy that should be briefly mentioned. Proprietorship, partnership, and corporation are compared in Table 3–2.

OTHER ENTERPRISE FORMS

Public Corporation   The *public corporation* is chartered by either the federal government or a state government to achieve a goal deemed to be in the public interest. The Tennessee Valley Authority (TVA) is a good example. It was created by the U.S. Congress in 1933. Its principal goals included providing low-cost electric power. While originally viewed by its opponents as a socialistic experiment that would fail, it is generally conceded today that the TVA successfully accomplished its goals.

At the state and local government level, *public corporations* include city governments, county governments, and school districts. These governmental units are established for the purpose of administering public affairs under authority granted them by the state.

The *quasi-public corporation* owned jointly by the federal government and private industry has recently become prominent. The Communications Satellite Corporation (COMSAT) is owned jointly by the federal government and American Telephone and Telegraph.

Cooperative   A private nonprofit organization is the *cooperative*. Cooperatives are chartered under state law for the purpose of enhancing the economic welfare of their members. Agricultural cooperatives are the most important example of this form. While operated like a business, profits are distributed to the

Table 3-2
Advantages and Disadvantages of Legal Forms
of Business

Type	Advantages	Disadvantages
Sole proprietorship	1. Easy to form 2. Can make all the decisions without interference by others as long as operating within the law	1. Subject to limited expertise, managerial skill, and marketing ability of the proprietor 2. Often lacks sufficient financing 3. Unlimited liability
Partnership	1. Access to more funds than the sole proprietorship because there are more owners 2. More potential expertise available than with the sole proprietorship	1. Unlimited liability 2. One partner acting alone can bind other partners 3. Potential difficulty of selling a partnership interest if a partner desires to leave the business 4. Termination of partnership if a partner dies
Corporation	1. Limited liability of owners 2. Easier to raise large amounts of capital 3. Unlimited life of the firm 4. Relative ease of selling one's ownership interests	1. Higher taxes 2. Higher costs of formation

members at the end of the year in proportion to their purchases. Members also receive interest on their ownership shares.

One of the obvious benefits of the agricultural cooperative is the lower cost of goods to its members as a result of its buying power. The cooperative also provides marketing economies to its members when they sell their produce, often resulting in higher prices received for their products.

SOME IMPORTANT LEGAL CONCEPTS

Important legal differences underlie the different ownership forms of business. In this section a few important legal concepts affecting business are introduced. However, it should be very strongly stressed that complex legal questions and problems should always be referred to a lawyer.

CONTRACTS

The basic legal concept underlying virtually all business transactions is the *contract*. The word *contract* probably brings forth an image of a long legal document replete with fine print, and this is certainly the case in many complex and important situations. However, a contract is often present though it may be unwritten and even when the parties involved are unaware of its existence. Without the idea of a contract, it would be extremely difficult for people to deal with each other in a business relationship because one party would not have a valid claim against the other party in the event of the presumed nonperformance of part of the deal.

The components of a contract include an *offer* by one party to do something for the other. There must be an *acceptance* by the second party, which is an agreement to accept the first party's offer. Each party must give *consideration,* which is something of legal value that is given to or performed for the other party. In addition, both parties must be *competent,* meaning in many states that they are at least eighteen years of age and don't fall into categories such as mental incompetency, intoxication, or status as an alien. Finally, the contract must have a *lawful purpose.*

As you can see, as simple an act as buying goods at the grocery store embodies the basic elements of a contract: the seller offers the buyer the goods; the buyer accepts by saying "give me a half dozen of those" or simply taking the goods to the check-out register; consideration is provided by both parties when the buyer pays for the goods or signs a charge slip. Simple transactions are entered into by those under twenty-one (eighteen in some states), but anything as complex as buying a car requires a competent adult's presence in the form of cosigning the contract.

It is interesting to note the word *contract* as used in the world of crime has a close but perverted relationship to its ordinary business meaning. It contains all of the elements of its traditional usage except lawful purpose of the agreement.

AGENCY

Agency arises in situations where one party (the agent) is empowered to act for a second party (the principal) in transactions with a third party. Agency is an extremely common form of arrangement. It often arises where the agent is a party who has specialized expertise.

A common example arises when a firm or individual hires a law firm. One of the newest agency relationships occurs when an athlete hires a representative (usually a lawyer) to deal with a team for the athlete's services.

The agent has a duty to be loyal to his or her principal and not to further his or her own or a third party's benefit at the expense of the principal. The agent must follow the principal's instructions.

The principal must grant the agent sole authority for dealing with particular third parties. Also, the agent must be compensated for the services provided and must be reimbursed for any expenses incurred in the principal's behalf.

It should be clear that an agent is not an employee of the principal. While the agent is given a charge by the principal, he or she is free to carry it out in the manner believed to be most appropriate. Legally speaking, an employer has more control over the actions of an employee than over an agent. An employee while on company duty may create a traffic accident as a result of his or her own negligence or carelessness. Nevertheless, the employer may well be held responsible. If an agent were responsible for an auto accident while carrying out work for the principal, the latter could not be held responsible.

BANKRUPTCY

Bankruptcy occurs when a firm or individual is unable to meet their monetary obligations. It may be either voluntary (initiated by the debtor) or involuntary (initiated by the creditors).

If the court deems that the debtor is bankrupt, the case is transferred to bankruptcy court, where a referee is appointed for the purpose of liquidating (selling off) the debtor's assets so that the claims of creditors can be met to whatever extent possible.

First claim on the assets goes to the federal government for tax claims. Next claim is for wages and commissions owed to employees that were earned within the three months prior to the bankruptcy proceedings. Costs of administering the bankruptcy proceedings also take precedence over the general claims of creditors. Often little is left for the members of this last group.

Star running back Ricky Bell with his agent Mike Trope (with necktie) at the NFL draft. Bell signed a contract with the Tampa Bay Buccaneers for five years at a reported $1.2 million.

After the proceedings, if the debtor is an individual, he or she is free to make a "fresh start," even if the creditors have not been fully paid. Of course, if it should be known that the individual has been bankrupt, it may become difficult for the individual to buy goods on credit.

FUNCTIONAL CLASSIFICATION OF BUSINESS

The yellow pages of a phone book in a medium-sized American city start with abdominal supports and end with zippers. In between lies a wide range of both ordinary and exotic goods and services. On the more unusual side are lapidaries (rock and gem specialists), waterbed dealers, and portable toilet suppliers.

The product of American business and industry is indeed rich. A primary form of classification is by general type of function performed in the complex chain of activities that supplies us with the goods and services that we consume:

1. Agriculture, fisheries, mining, and other extractive industries.
2. Manufacturing and construction.
3. Transportation, communications, and public utilities.
4. Wholesaling and retailing.
5. Finance, insurance, and real estate.
6. Service.

A breakdown showing the importance of each of these functions is shown in Table 3–3.

These broad functional categories can be viewed, in a very general fashion, as showing what firms do in terms of satisfying wants and needs of consumers. Farm-

Table 3-3
Functional Breakdown of the American Economy, 1973

Function Performed	Number of Firms (in thousands)	%	Net Profit (in billions)	%
Agriculture, forestry, and fisheries	3,586	26	$11.4	6
Mining	86	0.1	6.3	3
Construction	1,099	8	7.7	4
Manufacturing	449	3	65.0	34
Transportation, communications, and public utilities	434	3	10.3	5
Wholesale and retail trade	2,945	22	47.2	24
Finance, insurance, and real estate	1,576	12	17.2	9
Services	3,367	25	26.6	14
Total	13,542	100	191.7	100

Source: **Statistical Abstract,** 1976

ing, manufacturing, construction, mining, and extractive firms change the shape and texture of the basic materials with which they work (form utility). Transportation, communications, and public utilities provide services of place utility as well as intangible services. Wholesaling and retailing firms perform services of possession, time, and place utility. A more extensive explanation of possession, place, and time utilities is given in Chapter 9. Wholesalers and retailers are middlemen between manufacturers and consumers. Their function is to transfer the goods from producer to consumer. In doing this, the objective is to have the goods on hand at a time and place which is convenient for consumers. These activities are part of our complex marketing system and will be discussed in Chapters 9 and 10. Finance, insurance, and real estate firms provide specialized services, some of which will be discussed in Chapter 12. Service firms provide a wide variety of personal, professional, and convenience services. Their activities are as varied as drilling our teeth, preparing tax returns, and preparing meals that are "finger lickin' good."

CAPITAL INTENSIVE AND LABOR INTENSIVE FIRMS

The next form of classification concerns the means by which the firm produces its output. In terms of turning out goods and services, there are three productive factors to be considered: materials, labor, and capital.[2] Capital includes land, buildings, machinery, and equipment.

All firms use some blend of these productive factors (as well as management) to manufacture their product or service. It is a process of converting inputs into output. Input for a steel manufacturer consists of iron ore. Conversion occurs as the iron ore is refined by the use of labor and capital into various types of steel.

Similarly, for an income tax preparation firm, the input is each individual client's records of income and expenses for the year. The conversion process involves the preparation of the tax return and requires the labor of the preparer and possibly the use of a computer. Output would be the completed tax return.

Of the productive factors mentioned above, materials are an input, while labor and capital are used for conversion. The relationship between labor and capital costs as they apply to conversion is important.

Capital covers all of the various costs of buildings, machinery, and equipment that are utilized in manufacturing the firm's products. The higher total capital costs are in a firm's cost of production, the more *capital intensive* the firm. Similarly, the higher a firm's labor costs, relatively speaking, the more *labor intensive* it is. Heavily automated industries such as steel making and automobile manufacturing are examples of capital intensive industries. An extreme example of a labor intensive industry would be diamond cutting. The cutter must be extremely skilled though he works with relatively simple tools, mallet and chisel.

---

[2]From the economic standpoint, land, labor, capital, and management are the productive factors which transform materials into economically valuable end products. However, from the business viewpoint, materials are a valid productive factor. Materials, labor, and capital correspond to the breakdown of costs shown in a firm's periodic statement of income, to be discussed in Chapter 14.

There is one extremely important distinction between capital and labor intensive firms. Since capital intensive firms have heavy machinery and equipment costs, they have less flexibility than labor intensive firms should a downturn in business activity occur. Labor intensive firms can ride out a downturn more easily than capital intensive firms because they can cut loose or eliminate a greater proportion of costs by releasing excess labor. Rehiring would then occur when the economy revives.

Capital intensive firms, however, become more trapped during a downturn. Plant and equipment simply become idle. But just because they become idle does

The Trojan nuclear power plant on the Columbia River is representative of the investment in plant and equipment that must be made in the capital intensive electric power industry.

EPA-DOCUMERICA. GENE DANIELS

not necessarily mean that their costs decline considerably. Property taxes are still levied on plant and equipment. A certain amount of maintenance work must be done whether or not equipment is used. Moreover, insurance must be maintained to protect the firm against fire and other potential disasters. Finally, as equipment grows older it suffers a cost which arises whether or not the equipment is used. This cost is called *obsolescence.* It arises because improved methods of production are continually being developed. As a result, older machinery loses its value because improved methods of production are cheaper. The diesel locomotive, for example, caused the steam locomotive to become obsolete because the diesel is cheaper to run.

However, capital intensive firms gain the advantage over labor intensive firms as production expands during good times. As production is increased, equipment is used more intensively. That is, more production is turned out with

Watch repair is an example of a labor intensive industry.

CHARLES L. FARROW

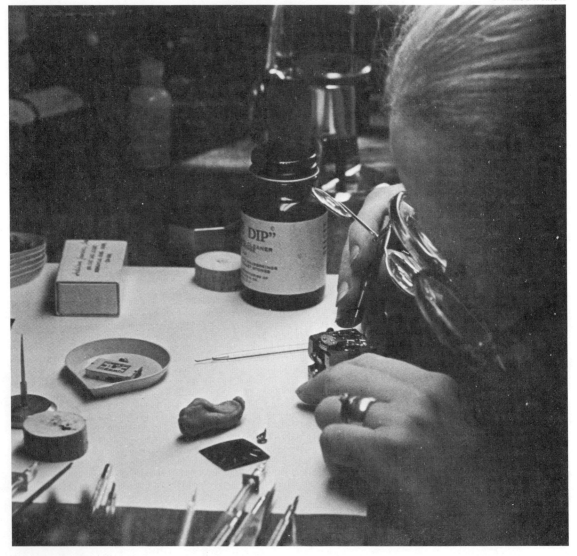

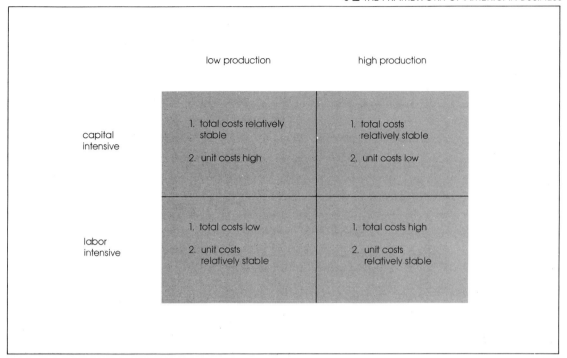

	low production	high production
capital intensive	1. total costs relatively stable 2. unit costs high	1. total costs relatively stable 2. unit costs low
labor intensive	1. total costs low 2. unit costs relatively stable	1. total costs high 2. unit costs relatively stable

Figure 3-1 Production costs of the capital intensive and labor intensive firms.

the given equipment than occurs during slack times. Since a large part of capital costs come from obsolescence, taxes, maintenance, and insurance, these costs do not change excessively as production increases. The result is a lowered *unit cost of production* during periods of relatively high output. Unit costs are determined by dividing total cost of production by total units of product manufactured. On the other hand, labor intensive firms must add more labor during good times in order to increase productivity.

Generally speaking, then, the more labor intensive a firm is, the more its total costs will change proportionately with production during a given time period such as a month or year. Costs of capital intensive firms are less susceptible to total cost changes as production varies during a given time period.

The concepts we are discussing here are frequently referred to as fixed costs and variable costs, terms which are useful in planning and analyzing business performance. To summarize, *fixed costs* remain relatively stable within wide swings of production; *variable costs* change proportionately with production. Capital intensive industries have a relatively heavy proportion of fixed costs, and labor intensive firms ordinarily would be relatively high in variable costs. The relationships discussed in this section are shown in Figure 3–1.

THE PRICE SYSTEM

As mentioned in Chapter 1, Adam Smith's great work, *The Wealth of Nations*, showed how the market system brings about the determination of prices for the goods and services produced in a free enterprise economy. The beauty of the system is that the overall benefits for society at large are maximized with each person acting in his or her own self-interest. This assumes that neither buyers nor sellers have any undue control over the supply or demand of any of the economy's goods or services.

This can be seen through a simple hypothetical example and some of the tools of the economist: a set of demand and supply curves.

AN ILLUSTRATION

Let's assume that a very exciting game called Chessers is invented. The game requires a simple cardboard board and pieces. Assume that there are no patent or copyright laws. Further, manufacturing of the game is extremely simple, allowing individuals to get into or out of manufacture of the game easily.

The Demand Curve   Now for any period of time, such as a year, there must be various quantities of the game that could be sold at different prices. Since individuals who might be willing to buy the game have only a limited number of dollars at their disposal, it would follow that they would want to spend their money as wisely as possible. Therefore, it follows that the lower the price of Chessers, the more games could be sold during a given time period.

Assume that for the year 1978 we are able to estimate the number of games that can be sold at various prices. We call this a *demand schedule* and it is shown in Table 3–4.

In Figure 3–2 the demand schedule is shown in graphic form and called a *demand curve*.

Each point on the curve (a straight line in our example) represents an intersection on the graph for the number of sets that can be sold at the various prices. For example, lines have been drawn showing the intersection for 14,000 sets at $1.60 and 13,000 sets at $1.70. Also, all individual points have been connected to form a line since there are undoubtedly many other numbers of sets that can be sold at prices other than those indicated in the demand schedule, but they would surely follow very closely to the line that we have drawn.

Table 3-4
Demand Schedule for Chessers, 1978

Price	Sales (units)
$2.00	10,000
1.90	11,000
1.80	12,000
1.70	13,000
1.60	14,000
1.50	15,000
1.40	16,000
1.30	17,000
1.20	18,000
1.10	19,000
1.00	20,000

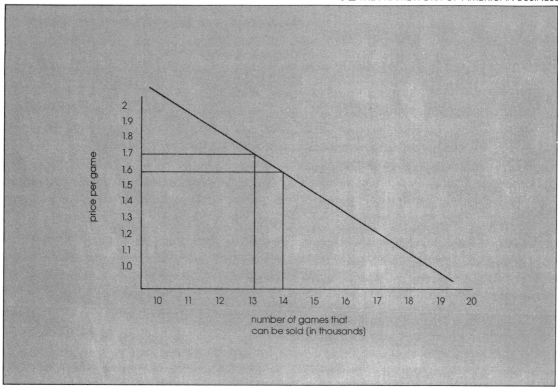

Figure 3-2 Demand curve for chessers, 1978.

The demand curve is described as downward sloping because at higher prices smaller quantities are sold. This is virtually universal for all goods and services.[3]

The Supply Curve Similar to the demand schedule is the *supply schedule*. The higher the price received by suppliers (manufacturers) during the period, the more games they would be willing to produce. The supply schedule is shown in Table 3–5.

As with the demand schedule, the supply schedule can be shown graphically as a *supply curve*. In Figure 3–3 the supply curve is shown in conjunction with the demand curve. Since the horizontal axis (baseline) refers to both the quantity that can be sold and the number of units that would be produced at various prices, we have simply labeled it as "Quantity." Otherwise, the diagram is the same as Figure 3–2, in which only the demand curve appears.

The demand and supply curves intersect at a price of $1.50 and 15,000 units. The price at the intersection is called the *equilibrium price*. It is only at this price that the market is cleared: the number of units produced equals the number of units sold.

At any other price, there will be a tendency to move to the equilibrium price. For example, at a price of $1.60 only 14,000 units would be demanded but 16,000 units would be produced. Suppliers would be left with excess inventory stocks that they did not want, which would tend to force the price down. Simi-

[3]Occasionally a prestige item might not sell if the price is too low. People might think a chinchilla coat at $1,500 looks "too cheap." At $5,000 the same coat's quality might appear to be much better.

The factors of supply and demand are key elements in the determination of prices at this concessions stand at a major sports stadium.

larly, if the price were $1.40, 16,000 units would be demanded but only 14,000 units produced. The supply shortage would tend to drive the price up and bring forth more production. Despite the simplicity of our example, the importance of price in making production decisions can be seen.

Changing Demand Curves   Sometimes factors can cause the entire demand curve to change. For example, let us assume that for the first time in history an

Table 3-5
Supply Schedule of Chessers, 1978

Price	Units Forthcoming
$1.00	10,000
1.10	11,000
1.20	12,000
1.30	13,000
1.40	14,000
1.50	15,000
1.60	16,000
1.70	17,000
1.80	18,000
1.90	19,000
2.00	20,000

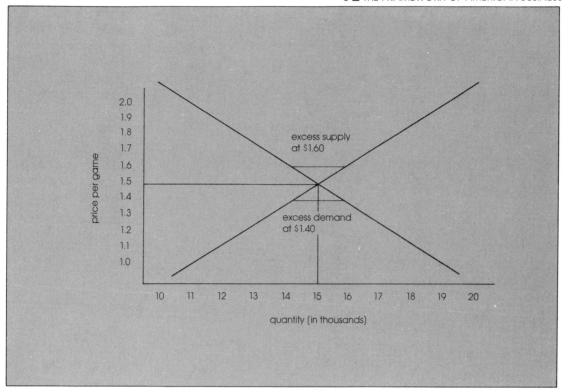

Figure 3-3   Demand and supply curves for chessers, 1978.

American were to win the Chesser championship of the world. The result might be an increased interest in Chessers by Americans. If so, the entire demand curve would move or shift to the right, as shown in Figure 3–4. Advertising is another factor which is capable of shifting the demand curve to the right if it is effective.

Notice first that the equilibrium price and quantity of goods increases from $1.50 and 15,000 units to $1.60 and 16,000 units as the entire demand curve shifts to the right. Also note that at any given price a greater quantity will now be demanded than previously. Similarly, for any given quantity, consumers are willing to pay a greater amount than before. One of the tasks of an effective marketing management is to understand market conditions and shifts and to respond with an appropriate pricing policy.

Profits   The dollar amounts (prices) on the vertical axis refer to the amount paid by consumers and received by suppliers. Total dollars involved are arrived at by multiplying the unit price times the particular quantity for the given point on the demand curve ($1.50 times 15,000 units equals $22,500 at the original equilibrium point, for example). The curves say nothing about profits of suppliers. It is again a simplification, of course, but for reasons to be stated shortly, it is presumed that the price received just covers all of the supplier's costs of production with just enough left over to allow each supplier to receive a normal profit on the investment. *Normal profit* can be defined in several ways, but we can think of it as being just large enough to keep the supplier in the present industry or line of business.

If profits are higher than normal, they will be reduced to a normal level as a result of new firms coming into the market attempting to get their share of the

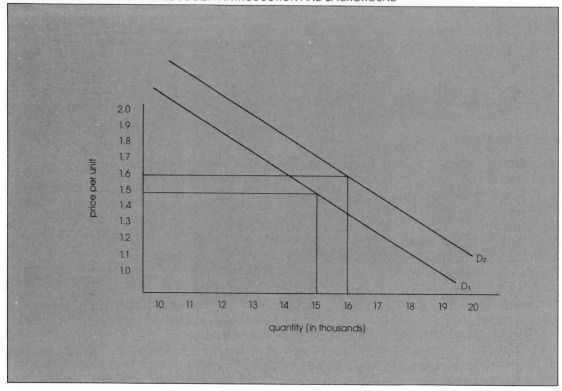

Figure 3-4   Change in demand for chessers.

higher profit. The result of more suppliers coming into the market is to move the supply curve to the right, increasing the quantities forthcoming at all prices. The rightward shift of the supply curve resulting from new firms coming into the industry in search of higher profits is to lower the equilibrium price to $1.50, eliminating the excess profits (see Figure 3–5).

Similarly, if profits are below normal, the opposite process will occur: an exodus out of the industry will move the supply curve to the left, reduce supplies forthcoming at all prices, raise the equilibrium price, and bring profits back to normal for the industry (using S_2 as the original curve and S_1 as the curve after departure of firms demonstrates this effect).

The situation that we have developed here is called *perfect competition*. One of its key assumption is that no firm or individual on either the demand or supply side is large enough to have any appreciable influence on the market. No one firm or individual has enough power to set price. All are "price takers" rather than "price makers." It is the result of interaction of all participants. The "invisible hand" in the form of the market itself is thus instrumental in setting prices, allowing only normal profits to be made by suppliers, and generally maximizing consumer satisfaction in the economic realm. The market system in a free enterprise economy thus brings about the satisfaction of consumer needs.

Imperfect Competition   However, competition in most industries is not perfect because sellers (and sometimes buyers) have some degree of control or influence over the market. Large capital investment often results in a relatively

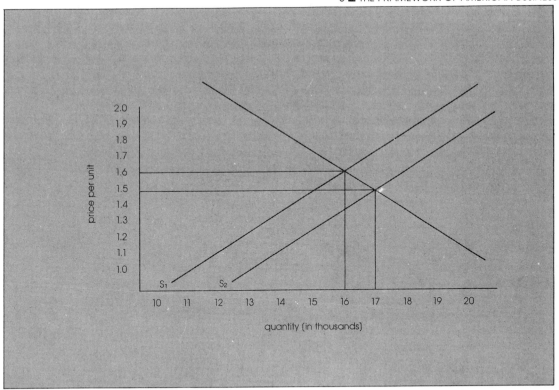

Figure 3-5   Change in supply of chessers.

few firms in an industry. Entrance by new firms is often extremely difficult. For example, the last major attempt to expand the number of firms in the automobile industry was made by Kaiser-Frazer in the late 1940s.[1] Of course, competition has been intensified by the various European and Japanese manufacturers who have entered the American market, a subject which we will examine in more detail in Chapter 11, "Multinational Business."

Going along with limited entrance and a few firms in many industries is the ability of large firms to set prices at an amount above what would be the equilibrium price. In turn, output is below equilibrium output and earnings are in excess of normal profits.

To this extent, our previous analysis must be modified. Nevertheless, despite its simplification, our example does help to explain how some parts of our economy work and, perhaps, how other parts should work. Furthermore, one trend against the concentration of economic resources and continued growth of large companies has been a resurgence of interest in small business. It presents the chance to be one's own boss and can provide the rewards and satisfactions of doing a good job of providing necessary services. There are many areas in our society where economic wants could be far better satisfied. One interesting example of this arose a few years ago when several graduates of the Harvard Business School banded together and opened an automobile repair service (a garage!).

[1] A new car, the Bricklin, was being manufactured in Nova Scotia recently, but the company went bankrupt.

The great bulk of American businesses are sole proprietorships. However, the problem of unlimited liability of owners makes it difficult to raise funds if the firm is to undergo major growth. Consequently, sole proprietorships are usually quite small in size. The partnership also has the problem of unlimited liability. In addition, it is somewhat inflexible if a partner dies or desires to sell his or her interest.

SUMMARY

Only the corporation has limited liability, enabling the firm to grow in size as opportunities arise. Before incorporating, however, a firm should carefully weigh the extra legal costs of incorporating and the higher taxes.

A contract is the basic legal concept signifying agreement between buyer and seller that underlies business transactions. Other important legal concepts of great importance to business are the law of agency and bankruptcy law.

Businesses can be classified in terms of function performed and structure of costs. Capital intensive firms have heavy fixed cost structures, while labor intensive firms lean more to higher variable costs.

In a capitalistic or free enterprise society, prices are determined by the law of supply and demand. While concentration of economic power prevents the system from working perfectly, supply and demand interaction are still the basic determinants of price in the American economy.

DISCUSSION QUESTIONS

1. Why is the partnership the least popular of the three legal forms of business?

2. Why are almost all large businesses, except those specifically prohibited by law, incorporated?

3. What is the function of a board of directors of a corporation? Is it their job to represent either top management or the stockholders?

4. Why do you think the quasi-public form of corporation, for example COMSAT and AMTRAK (the passenger train operation), has become relatively important?

5. It is often said that labor and capital are "opposing forces." Explain what you think this means.

6. It might appear that obsolescence is a benefit to a firm rather than a cost since it means that better productive equipment is coming on the market. Explain.

7. A half gallon of milk costs 90 cents and a full gallon costs $1.75. We expect to get a price break, as with the milk, for buying larger quantities of goods. Is this inconsistent with the idea of an upward sloping supply curve?

8. A firm lowered its price for a product and increased the quantity that it sold. Do you think there has been a movement of its demand curve?

SHORT CASES

Mike's Problem

Mike Hagen desires to go into business for himself. He has two opportunities. A gasoline station selling a major brand of gasoline has just come on the market. Mike knows that the location is good and the station has been profitable. The equipment in it is in top shape.

His other opportunity involves opening a new, high-quality restaurant serving French food. It would be the only restaurant in his town serving French food. It is his opinion that there would be a big demand for this type of food, though most of his friends disagree with him.

Mike wants you to tell him whether he should set up a sole proprietorship or incorporate in both of these opportunities.

Jerry and Sue's Problem

Jerry and Sue Smith manufacture widgets. A piece of equipment has worn out and some

59

3 ■ THE FRAMEWORK OF AMERICAN BUSINESS

form of replacement must be made. A highly automated machine can be acquired, which will result in a low cost provided that production is high. The other alternative is a machine which costs a great deal less but requires much more labor per unit of output. This second machine is not as efficient at higher levels of output, but cost per unit will be less at lower levels of output. What are some of the factors that should be considered before making the acquisition decision?

SUGGESTED READINGS

Anderson, Ronald A., and Kumpf, Walter A. *Business Law: Principles and Cases.* 6th ed. Cincinnati: South-Western Publishing Co., 1975.

Heilbroner, Robert L., and Thurow, Lester. *Understanding Microeconomics.* 3d ed. Englewood Cliffs, N.J.: Prentice-Hall, 1975.

*

MANAGEMENT OF THE ORGANIZATION

☐ A business must provide competent management for all of its functions and parts such as production operations, marketing, finance, and accounting. The purpose of Part Two is to introduce you to the basic concepts of management as well as the importance of organizational structure to a successful business operation. In addition, Part Two explains the important managerial areas of human assets, labor relations, and production operations.

☐ Chapter 4 defines organization and management and describes the managerial jobs of planning, controlling, and organizing. It also explains how business organizations function as open systems and how they sometimes grow from very small to very large organizations.

☐ While a business produces a product or service, the problems and methods of managing the people who are responsible for turning out the product or service must be carefully considered. Thus, human assets management is the topic of Chapter 5.

☐ Often, the employees of an organization are represented by a labor union in their dealings with company management. This situation, in turn, requires special knowledge and skill on the part of company management. Chapter 6 discusses these special demands on company management as well as the nature of the relationship between a company and a union.

☐ Chapter 7 explains how operations or the conversion of inputs to outputs is the core process of a business. It also discusses the relationships between operations and other functional areas such as marketing, finance, and purchasing.

*

MANAGEMENT AND ORGANIZATION

LEARNING OBJECTIVES

When you finish this chapter you should:
- [ ] have a basic understanding of organization and management.
- [ ] be familiar with what it takes to become a manager.
- [ ] understand why an organization is an open system.
- [ ] know the management functions of planning, organizing, and controlling and why they are important.
- [ ] be familiar with the stages of growth through which many organizations progress.
- [ ] understand the importance of synergy and philosophy to an organization.

KEY TERMS TO LEARN FROM THIS CHAPTER

centralization	management	operating manage-	single-use plan
chain of command	management by ex-	ment	span of control
control	ception	organic organization	staff personnel
conversion process	management phi-	organization	standing plan
decentralization	losophy	organizing	strategic plan
division of labor	matrix organization	planning	synergy
dynamic equilibrium	merger	planning horizon	top management
dynamic growth	middle management	policy	traditional craft
forecasting	multinational company	production	unity of command
line personnel	open system	rational administration	

In the first three chapters, we learned the reasons why business enterprise is necessary to the effective functioning of our society as well as some basic ideas on how business works. In addition to a description of our economic system, we developed an understanding of the various forms of business enterprise. We did not, however, look inside a business to find out about its management and internal organization. That is the purpose of this chapter, and our attention will be directed first toward business organization.

Businesses vary in size—from a newsstand run by one person, for example, to a corporation such as General Motors—and size and an associated degree of complexity will affect the type of organization structure utilized by a business. Our initial concern will be with the large and relatively complex business organization because this will enable us to learn some principles of organization that have broad application. Later in the chapter, we will examine how an organization changes with size, and we will investigate the effects of the type of business on structure.

THE COMPLEX BUSINESS ORGANIZATION

Over the past one hundred years, many businesses have grown very large and complex. There are a variety of reasons for this. Some businesses require substantial organization by the nature of their operations. A steel mill, for example, or a mass producer of automobiles requires substantial investment, size, and complexity in order to successfully compete. Can you imagine 100 or even 1,000 people trying to run the Ford Motor Company?

Advanced technology plays an important role in the developing need for complex organization. Today's products—the automobile, computer, television, aircraft—force complexity upon manufacturing organizations. At the same time, sophisticated communications networks and data processing methods facilitate far-flung enterprises and the employment of thousands of people.

In many markets, massive demand for a variety of products and services encourages the formation of large-scale businesses. There are companies that are international in scope—not only selling in countries throughout the world but building manufacturing plants and research centers in those countries. These are *multinational* countries. They are global in outlook and are willing to consider investment, production, or marketing opportunities anywhere.

IS THERE A LIMIT TO SIZE AND COMPLEXITY?

Occasionally someone will voice a fear that businesses are so huge that efficiency and effectiveness surely must suffer. As customers, no doubt all of us feel frustration at times over a mixed-up bill or other error that seems to take forever to straighten out. Large organizations do make mistakes, but they have no monopoly on errors. Small organizations make mistakes, too. By and large, and in spite of difficulties in trying to correspond with a computer, big business appears to be more responsive and efficient than in the past. This opinion is not meant to whitewash business for responsibilities beyond those of simple efficiency, but strictly in terms of operational matters—production, marketing, accounting, finance—business has no absolute, scientifically established limitations on size.

There are certain legal limits if a business seeks growth in directions that foster monopoly or restraint of trade. But there is ample opportunity for growth within the law. Does this mean that small business eventually will cease to exist? Hardly. Small business frequently has the ability to move more quickly in developing a product or reaching a specific market segment than does large business. Familiarity with local conditions often gives the small business person a built-in advantage.

Certain dealer or franchise operations combine aspects of big business and small business. The national or international organization—an automobile or food-service chain, for example—may be quite large, but the dealers or local franchise holders operate predominantly as small business persons. In a franchise operation, usually a large company arranges with an individual to operate an outlet in a local area. The individual usually buys or leases the location, the building, and the equipment and also pays a fee for the right to use the company's name—McDonald's, for example. The local owner agrees to abide by the franchise rules and, in exchange, benefits from advice and help from the parent company. The local owner probably buys most of the necessary supplies from the parent organization, but outside of the franchise relationship, the owner operates much as any other small business person. But before going further with our discussion, we need formal definitions of *organization* and *management*.

A FORMAL DEFINITION OF ORGANIZATION

Any organization has a number of component parts which must work together to achieve desired results. In other words, an organization is a system with component parts or subsystems which must be interrelated and integrated before the system (organization) can effectively operate. Important subsystems in an organization include people, management, technology, structure, and physical facilities (Figure 4–1). All businesses require at least these five subsystems, though if we were to cite specific kinds of businesses, other subsystems also might be important.

Are the subsystems all equally important? They are in the sense that business success requires all of them. From another view, however, management appears to possess an overriding value since it bears responsibility for coordinating and molding the other elements into a cohesive system. What is suggested is that a business can survive for a time with poor personnel, ineffective management, obsolete technology, faulty structure, or inadequate physical facilities, but if the business wants more than mere survival, management is the key.

Continuing the positive tack, the route to success lies more in the hands of management than anywhere else. Management can attract good people, adapt or generate up-to-date technology, design appropriate organizational structure, and buy or build adequate physical facilities. It seems far less likely that any of the other subsystems would build or attract good management.

These concepts are incorporated in the formal definition: *an organization is a*

Figure 4-1 The organizational system.

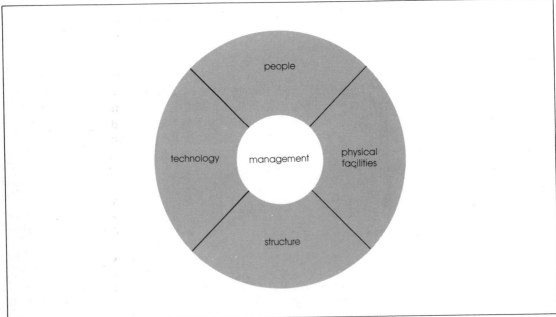

system —containing people, management, technology, structure, and physical facilities as required subsystems—in which management interrelates and integrates all the system elements into a cohesive whole in order to achieve organizational objectives.

A FORMAL DEFINITION OF MANAGEMENT

In leading up to our definition of an organization, we emphasized the key role of management in bringing together all the organizational subsystems and guiding them to successful goal achievement. In order to do this, management constantly must make decisions in many areas: setting priorities for action, dealing with people, handling operating problems, and working with people and organizations in the external environment. All of these decisions usually fall into three broad categories of management activity: planning, organizing, and controlling.

Being able to make decisions effectively requires that a manager possess knowledge about important areas of business and available tools. The important or functional areas include finance, people management, operations management, marketing, and accounting. Available tools include the computer, information systems, management science, and behavioral science. We could not expect any one manager to be expert in everything, but the total management of a business organization should include expertise in all the functional and tool areas (Figure 4–2).

The formal definition then is: *management is that component of an organization which guides the organization through decisions based on knowledge and experience toward achievement of established objectives.*

THE MAKING OF A MANAGER

What does it take to become a good manager? Is management now so scientific that book learning alone will do the job? Does experience count? These are important questions that anyone who aspires to a management career must ask.

Modern management is a combination of scientifically developed knowledge and artistic application of that knowledge. Harold Koontz describes this relationship:

Managing is an art, but so are engineering, medicine, accounting, and baseball. For art is the application of knowledge to reality with the view to accomplishing some concrete results. . . . As can be readily recognized, the best art arises where the artist possesses a store of organized and applicable knowledge and understands how to apply it to reality.

Thus engineers have long understood that the best designers are those who are well grounded in the underlying sciences and who have an ability to conceptualize a problem in the light of goals sought and the further ability to *design* a solution to the problem to accomplish goals at the lowest system cost.

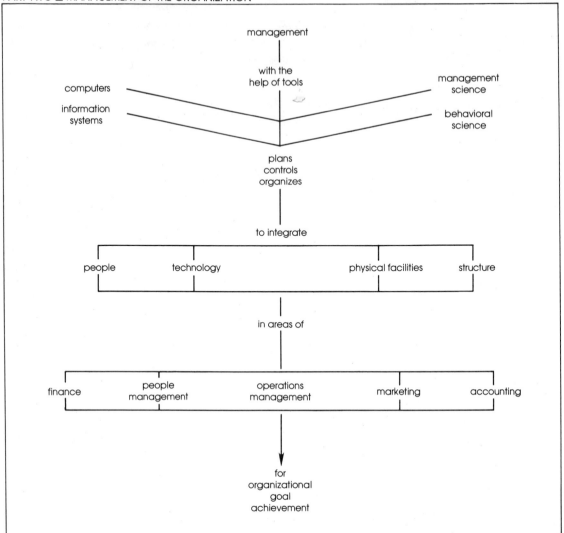

Figure 4-2   The management job.

The same can be said of the task of managing. As an art, there is every reason to believe that it will succeed best if the practitioner has a store of applicable and organized knowledge to serve him. This knowledge, when organized, is science. When it is organized in such a way as to serve practice best, it becomes a truly operational science.[1]

Most management aspirants acquire their store of applicable and organized knowledge through formal education, although self-instruction and tutoring are alternative routes. But the possession of theoretical knowledge clearly is not enough in most cases to assure success in a managerial slot. To develop the requisite art or skill requires experience.

[1]Harold Koontz, "A Model for Analyzing the Universality and Transferability of Management," *Academy of Management Journal* 12, no. 4 (December 1969): 420.

THE SCHOOL OF HARD KNOCKS

Just as theoretical knowledge alone usually is not sufficient for managerial success, so experience alone frequently proves ineffective—at least in complex organizations. There are exceptions, of course. We all know or hear of individuals who pulled themselves up by their bootstraps and became the owners of successful businesses or achieved high executive positions in an ongoing organization.

Aside from the rare exceptions, however, experience can be a deceptive commodity. Twenty or thirty years of experience sounds impressive but should not be taken at face value. It is possible that experience can be rich and varied, affording many opportunities for learning and developing skills. Experience can also be the mere repetition of the same behavior and application of knowledge over and over. One year of experience repeated twenty times is still basically one year of experience and not twenty.

The requisite experience for managerial success should be rich and varied, and many organizations strive to provide these kinds of experiences for their new people who possess managerial potential and ambition. Under the umbrella of training, companies use many methods. For example, new employees (trainees) may rotate from one job to another; they may stay in one job but be given challenging assignments immediately; they may serve as "assistants to" and receive coaching from their immediate superiors; or they may participate in formal training sessions that utilize role playing and case studies.

Whatever the method, the astute trainee may soon discover that what business really looks for is the ability to find and identify problems and opportunities and the ability to solve problems. Formal education has a fine track record in developing problem-solving skills, but it is not set up to refine potential skills in problem and opportunity discovery. The latter come about principally through on-the-job experience. The following case illustrates the importance of the difference between finding and solving.

THAR'S GOLD ON THEM SIDEWALKS

Jack and Bill were buddies in school, and during one summer vacation they managed to find jobs with the same short-order restaurant in a resort town. They figured it an ideal set up—working from two in the afternoon until ten at night, they still had time to swing after work and could sleep late in the morning.

One afternoon when they reported for work, their boss was out front picking up glasses, dishes, and assorted silverware. It seems customers liked to take their orders outside to eat and drink while they observed the scenery. Anyway, the bossman was grumbling and complaining, and he asked his hired help what could be done.

Jack immediately offered a solution by suggesting that he and Bill simply enforce a house rule about eating inside by watching carefully and stopping anyone about to walk outside with an order. Bill, however, perceived an opportunity and suggested that as long as customers like to eat outside, why not set up tables and chairs on the sidewalk and take orders as well as serve outside.

Well, Mr. Bossman liked the idea, got permission from the city fathers, and made a mint by moving half his operation out on the sidewalk. Jack had a solution for an obvious problem, but Bill found an opportunity.

THE BUSINESS ORGANIZATION AS AN OPEN SYSTEM

Before moving to further study of what management does, we should examine one characteristic of a business organization which affects all of its activities—that it is an *open system.* It was mentioned earlier that organizations are systems, with component parts that must mesh together for effective operation. A business organization does not exist in isolation, however. It cannot ignore its environment as it strives to make its system work. It affects and is affected by many aspects of the external environment.

One area of interaction with the environment involves the organizational input-output system. Any organization takes in certain inputs such as raw material, money, people, management, and technology. These inputs make possible and carry on the *production* or *conversion* process which results in the organizational output—goods and/or services. A number of the inputs also become important organizational components. These include people, management, and technology. Figure 4–3 illustrates the input-output system.

Factors in the environment which interact with any business include customers, stockholders, governments, suppliers, and competitors. There is not one activity in a business operation which in some manner will not relate to an external factor. Hence any successful business will pay close attention to what goes on outside the organization, including the impacts of its own actions on others.

In Figure 4–4, important functional areas and other activity areas have been added to the basic organizational system as illustrated in Figure 4–1. The arrows

Figure 4-3   The organizational input-output system.

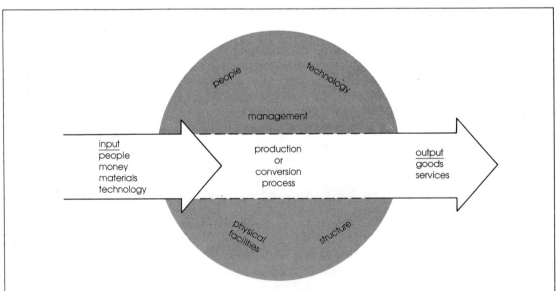

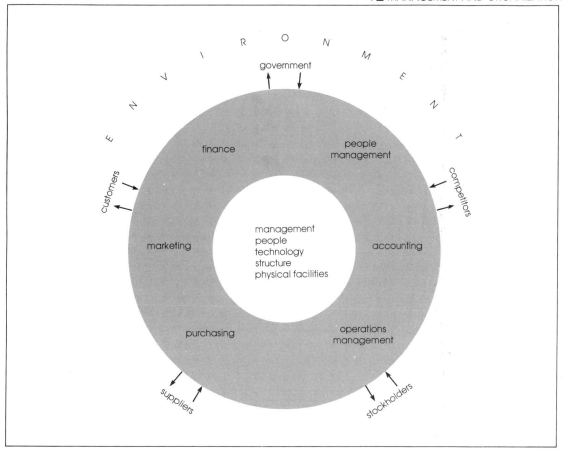

Figure 4-4   The organization as an open system.

in Figure 4–4 indicate the interaction between a business organization and its customers, for example, or between the organization and the government. Particular component parts of the organization will do most of the interaction with particular parts of the environment. Marketing, for example, will interact to the greatest extent with customers. Marketing will attempt to influence customers through its promotional efforts such as direct selling and advertising, and will be influenced in turn by customers through their tastes, complaints, and praise. Similarly, purchasing will do most of the interaction with suppliers. All functional areas will probably have considerable interaction with the government because of its regulations and requirements.

MAINTAINING STABILITY

Changes from within and from outside constantly threaten the stability of any system. If left alone, certain changes could eventually cause the system to die. In a closed system, one that does not actively interact with its environment, there is no possibility for the system itself to correct threatening changes. A clock, for example, can do nothing by itself to replace a broken mainspring—it must wait for some outside party to do the job.

Open systems, on the other hand, have a capacity for self-repair or for making the adjustments necessary to adapt to environmental changes. The human body, for example, is a biological open system. When the external temperature turns hot or cold, the body quickly reacts to maintain a constant internal temperature. When injury occurs, the body immediately initiates a repair process. Eventually, of course, even the body loses its ability for self-repair and ceases to live.

A social system such as a business, however, can exist indefinitely, provided it maintains its capacity for successful interaction with environmental forces. A *dynamic equilibrium* or stability is the result of this interaction. It is dynamic because every time an adjustment is made, there is a new equilibrium position in some respect. The old saw which says you have to move backward or forward but you can't stand still roughly approximates this concept.

The Importance of Information Vital to a successful relationship with the environment is adequate and accurate information flow—feedback—from the environment. It is apparent that a business must keep informed about what is going on in government, what is happening to consumer tastes and habits, and what competitors are doing. There are many ways to obtain information, ranging from simply reading newspapers to using sophisticated survey techniques. Occasionally companies even resort to industrial spying.

It is important to obtain two basic kinds of information: (1) that which pertains to changes initiated by forces in the environment, and (2) that which pertains to changes in the environment caused by actions of the organization itself. With respect to the former, new laws or changes in weather patterns represent external changes which the business can only react to. In the second case, a company may initiate a substantial public relations campaign and will want information on its external impact. We can represent these information needs with a feedback model (Figure 4–5).

In a broad sense, maintaining system equilibrium represents the managerial

Figure 4-5 Information needs of a business.

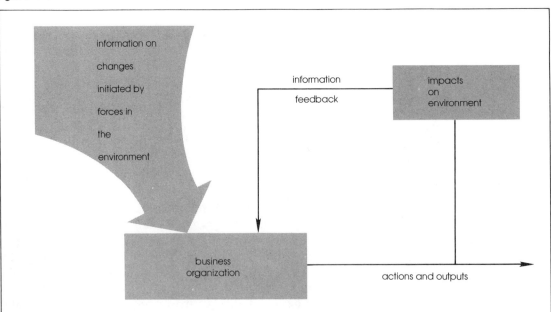

job. Of course, there are specific activities involved—planning, organizing, controlling—and these are topics we want to investigate next.

THE MANAGEMENT JOB

Management functions at three general levels of responsibility in most companies: *top management, middle management,* and *operating management.* At the top level, there are the president, vice-presidents, and top staff officers. Such jobs as sales manager, purchasing agent, advertising manager, and production supervisor fill the middle level, while the operating level encompasses foremen, branch managers, section chiefs, and others.

Managers at all levels must plan, control, and organize, though the amount and nature of each activity will vary from level to level. Long-range planning is an important responsibility of top executives. Theirs is a broad and overall view, and they must establish plans and policies in several areas: organizational structure for the total business, the types of control systems to use, overall coordination of all subsystems, principal areas of emphasis for future operations, and interaction with environmental forces. The latter area is particularly important because adjustments to environmental changes may affect one or more of the other areas of responsibility. Top executives accomplish their missions under the general guidance of a board of directors, though the guidance varies from little or none to close control.

Middle-level managers often hold responsibility for some functional area such as sales or production, though they may have charge of a geographic area or plant that includes all functions. The range of jobs held by middle managers is quite large, encompassing relatively minor entry-level jobs usually filled by persons just out of school to plant managers or chief accountants. Middle managers carry out the plans of top management, and must establish their own intermediate-range plans. They may also be viewed as intermediaries between top management and operating management, coordinating resource inputs and their conversion to outputs. The work at middle levels is more routine than at top levels and is oriented more to internal affairs than to the external environment.

Managers at the operating level translate the intermediate-range plans of the middle level to short-range plans for getting the work done. Planning often is on a day-to-day basis, sometimes hour-to-hour, and there is much routine activity. Specialized technical knowledge and human relations skill challenge the operating manager more than the top executive, since the foreman or section chief works closely with his people all day long and may spend a good portion of his time ironing out the human and technical problems that invariably arise. Figure 4–6 illustrates managerial levels in a business organization.

PLANNING

In discussing the levels of management, *planning* was mentioned several times. Certainly this activity is prominent in the managerial job, and anyone who rightfully carries the title of manager invariably will discover how important planning is to long-term success. To define planning is quite easy: it is the *determination of*

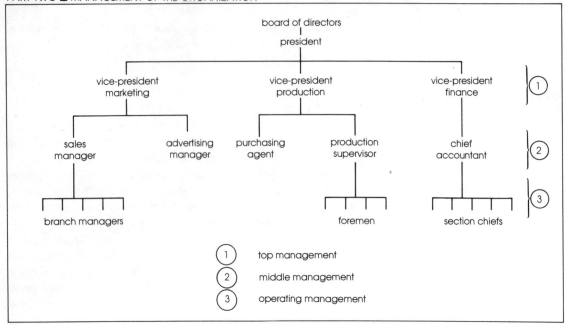

Figure 4-6 Managerial levels.

goals and the specification of ways and means to achieve those goals. To plan successfully is a bit harder.

When we think of managers engaged in planning, some of us may envision feet propped up on a desk and eyes glued to some distant horizon while the mind conjures up dramatic new ideas. This may be part of planning, all right, but there is lots more to it. In fact, research studies indicate that the complete planning process is sufficiently difficult that planning often is put off while routine work gets done.

It is not hard to find busywork, and this is exactly what many managers apparently do when they should be planning. If you suspect that such procrastination reduces managerial effectiveness, you are entirely correct. One study showed that the more efficient managers spent 61 percent more time on planning work duties than did less efficient managers.[2]

Why Planning Is So Important   We stated the importance of planning but offered no specific reasons for this importance. George Steiner offers the following:

> Effective planning prevents ad hoc decisions, random decisions, decisions that unnecessarily and expensively narrow choices for tomorrow. Effective planning gives an organization a structural framework of objectives and strategies, a basis for all decision making. Lower-level managers know what top management wants and can make decisions accordingly. But there are also ancillary benefits. An effective planning organization, for example, provides a powerful channel of communications for the people in an or-

[2]Donald Ervin Williams, "An Analysis of Selected Work Duties and Performance of the More Effective Versus the Less Effective Manager," *Academy of Management Journal* 12, no. 4 (December 1969): 516–17.

ganization to deal with problems of importance to themselves as well as to their organization.

It is difficult to exaggerate the importance of effective comprehensive planning to an organization. It has, for many companies, provided that margin needed for outstanding growth and profitability.[3]

Hence planning aids in coordinating all units of an organization and introduces a measure of certainty and predictability. This is important to organizational members, for they prefer the security of knowing where they are supposed to be going and what they are supposed to be doing, as opposed to working in a limbo of ambiguity and uncertainty. Before getting into the planning process, let us first examine some characteristics and types of plans and planning.

Variations on Plans   Planning, of course, takes place prior to any action, though we may modify plans once action is underway. We may plan a picnic, for example, but then change our plans when it starts raining—even though we are already at the park. As alternatives, we could return home, look for a shelter house, or possibly eat our picnic lunch in the car and then go to a movie. In other words, plans should be flexible—capable of modification when conditions change.

A plan for a picnic is a short-term plan, encompassing a few hours and therefore having a short *planning horizon*. In a business organization, top-level executives work to a long planning horizon—often five to ten years or more. Operating managers work with short planning horizons, anywhere from a day to several weeks or months.

Typically having a long-range planning horizon, *strategic plans* often determine organizational success. These plans establish goals and set forth those actions deemed most likely to achieve the goals. Naturally there is a certain amount of risk involved since the future is always uncertain, but a business needs this kind of general guide. On the basis of strategic plans, managers make many other short-term plans.

People often confuse policies with a strategic plan. But a *policy* derives from a strategic plan and has no particular time horizon. A policy will change only when the strategic plan changes. For example, a business may have a strategic plan with a goal of improving its community relations. A derived policy, then, will be the encouragement of organizational members to participate in various community activities.

There are two additional and rather standard types of plans—*single-use plans* and *standing plans*. As the name suggests, the single-use plan develops for one time and one purpose only. It may involve the building of a special piece of equipment or making arrangements for a visiting dignitary. When we as individuals move from one location and house to another, we often develop a single-use plan—that is, we contract with a moving company, set a date, establish a schedule for packing, and perhaps arrange for temporary accommodations at a motel.

A standing plan covers repetitive activities which are likely to take place under similar circumstances. A business may have a standing plan for the purchase of raw materials when orders increase or for repairs when equipment breaks down. Standing plans permit the implementation of an important

[3]George A. Steiner, "The Critical Role of Top Management in Long-Range Planning," *Arizona Review* 14, no. 4 (April 1966): 5–13.

concept—*management by exception.* Given certain circumstances, actions can be taken, such as ordering more raw material or fixing equipment, without having to gain the approval of higher management. In this way, management at various levels does not have to bother with relatively routine matters. Only in the exceptional cases would managerial attention be required—such as the un-availability of certain raw materials. Having gained some knowledge of the importance of planning and types of plans, let us go on to the steps in planning.

The Planning Process   The planning process includes several well-defined steps:

- Setting a goal.
- Generating alternative courses of action.
- Evaluating the courses of action.
- Selecting a course of action or a plan.
- Implementing the plan.
- Following-up or monitoring planning activities.

These steps are explained in detail below.

Setting a goal is the important first step in planning. This may entail nothing more than the solution of a simple problem: one is tired, so getting to bed and sleeping becomes the goal. On the other hand, if starting and establishing a business is the goal, this major objective spawns many other subgoals. That is, there will be many problems to solve on the way to having a successful business. Most organizations have multiple goals as well. Making a profit is a traditional business goal, but in recent years business has voluntarily taken on or been forced to accept some form of social responsibility as a second goal. In addition, a company may list among its goals a satisfied and prosperous work force, continuous growth, or leadership in its field.

In setting goals, a business should be careful that goals are stated clearly and communicated to organizational members, that there is some way to measure progress toward goal achievement, and that people perceive some benefit in working toward goal achievement. It is not enough to state that less pollution is a goal. We must state precisely what kind of pollution, how results will be measured, and how pollution reduction will benefit the organization and its members.

Goal succession is an interesting phenomenon that may be observed from time to time. Many government agencies and some organizations are set up with a specific mission to accomplish. What happens when they achieve their goal? Do they fade away like old soldiers? Rarely. Instead, they usually find some new goal that will continue to justify existence. A case in point was the National Foundation for Infantile Paralysis. When polio was conquered, the foundation searched for other goals, finally settling on childhood diseases in general. Naturally the executives wished to extend their positions of power and prestige and to continue their commitment to organizational growth in the field of health as well.

The second major step in the planning process is the *generation of alternative courses of action.* Having established goals, an organization must search for all the ways by which its goals may be achieved. It is highly unlikely that an organization will be able to discover all possible alternatives, since its knowledge and capability is usually limited in this respect. If you have a goal of making a million dollars, you will probably never consider all the ways of doing this since there are no doubt at least a million alternatives. Even such a simple act as going out for dinner offers many possibilities.

Companies generate alternatives in various ways. Several individuals may sit around and brainstorm. Past experience of both individuals and the organization may suggest alternatives. Outside help may be brought in. Books and trade journals offer many ideas. Usually most companies will seek ideas from any available source.

Having gathered some alternatives, the next major step is *evaluation.* If there are clearly defined, specific criteria, the job of evaluation may be relatively easy. Cost is always a factor, of course, and the relationship between costs and benefits takes on great importance in most evaluation processes. In addition, criteria may involve ecological considerations, ethics, and company philosophy. Applying all of the relevant criteria, the organization *chooses* or selects one or more alternatives as the best means to goal achievement.

The final steps are *implementation* and *follow-up.* All of the planning goes for nothing if implementation is not well done. Management must carefully draw up a budget and allocate resources—people, material, equipment, and money—and then *monitor* or follow-up all activities so the plan stays on course. If conditions change, the company must make appropriate modifications in the plan. It is rare, perhaps, when a plan can be executed in precise accord with its original version.

Forecasting   Being able to say something about future events is important to any kind of planning. Perhaps the forecasts we most commonly encounter in our planning pertain to weather. Most of us check these forecasts daily and modify our plans accordingly. Similarly, business needs constant forecasting to plan effectively.

Of course, the further into the future one ventures, the more uncertain forecasts become. Nonetheless, if an organization is to do long-range planning, it also must do long-range forecasting. In certain areas, a company can make reasonably sound long-range forecasts. Projection of energy needs, for example, are reasonably dependable ten to twenty years ahead. As a result, a company knows that new sources of fuel must be developed to meet large increases in the demand for energy.

In the intermediate and short ranges, planning must be more frequent and more reliable. In the fashion industry, seasonal forecasts of changing fashions are vital to success. Nations as well as businesses need short-range forecasts of agricultural production. It is apparent that the types of forecasts required are limited only by the number of products, services, and organizations needing them.

How are forecasts made? We know that in weather prediction, there is a lot of scientific input. Some also predict weather on the basis of aching corns or the feel of the air. So it is with most forecasting, ranging from a simple hunch to highly sophisticated mathematical methods.

CONTROLLING

Planning and controlling go hand in hand. There may be a beautiful set of plans, but unless there is some system to assure that *actual results conform to planned results,* a firm could wind up just spinning its wheels. This is where control comes in, and it is management's responsibility to set up a control system for the total organization as well as for its component parts.

A good plan will set up certain standards which allow measurement of future actions and results. If there is conformity with the standards, nothing need be done. But if there is some deviation, management must take steps to get results back into line with planned standards.

For example, given a projected upswing in the economy, a business may plan to increase its total sales by 20 percent over a twelve-month period. The company expects the increase to be gradual, so there should be a 5 percent boost in sales every three months. If at the end of the first three months, there is only a 1 percent increase, sales have fallen below standard, and the company will have to take corrective action. On the other hand, if the economic improvement did not occur, perhaps the plan should be modified so a 1 percent increase becomes standard.

It is common to represent control systems in the form of loops, more specifically a closed loop and an open loop (Figures 4–7 and 4–8). Note that in the closed loop, information is gathered on some ongoing activity—sales, for instance. The information is then compared to some planned standard—a 5 percent increase in sales at the end of every three months—and if there is an intolerable deviation, a correction is made or the standard is changed. Hence a closed-loop system is entirely involved with one activity.

In the open-loop system, on the other hand, one activity is compared with another. In Figure 4–8, activity A could be national economic conditions, while activity B could be a projected level of future sales. As it receives information about the state of the economy, a company will initiate certain actions with respect to sales—perhaps increasing or decreasing inventories—and/or change its plans (and standards), increasing or decreasing projected sales levels.

Most closed-loop systems concern internal activities of an organization, while most open-loop control systems seek to adjust internal operations to some environmental change. Of course, many variations are possible, and businesses

Figure 4-7   Closed loop control.

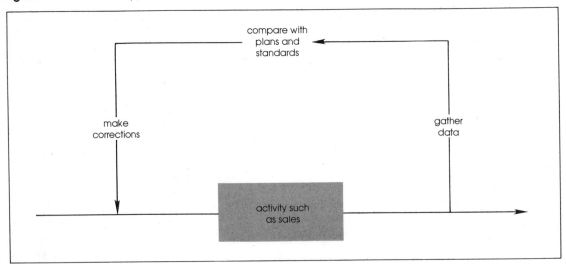

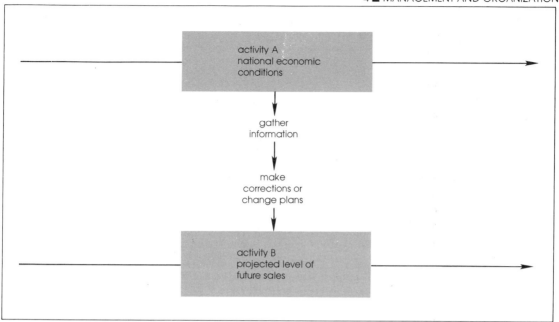

Figure 4-8 Open loop control.

with sophisticated control setups will have many combinations, including loops within loops. But no matter how complex a system may get, we usually depend on two basic types of control to make the system work. These are direct and indirect control.

Direct Control Walking a dog on a leash is an example of direct control. The dog must go where the master goes, stop when the master stops, and start when the master is ready to start. Thus direct control involves an ability to specifically guide or check some process or activity. Inspection is another example. If you run an ice cream store and inspect every ice cream cone made by your clerks, you are directly controlling that operation. Of course, direct control is expensive and time consuming. As the owner of an ice cream store, it would be more economical and efficient if your clerks could function on their own and not require your constant attention. This is where indirect control can be helpful.

Indirect Control It is often possible to select and train people so they perform their work without needing constant checking. This is the essence of indirect control. In the ice cream store example, if the manager can select and train the clerks so that they will use the proper amount and kind of ice cream in making cones, there will be no need to constantly check on them.

The desirability of indirect control explains much of the basis for the many varied training and developmental programs which businesses carry on. The more reliable people the business has performing job duties, the less need there is for inspection and close supervision. Business and other organizations spend a great deal of money trying to find ways to make indirect control more effective.

The trend in organizations in recent years has been to charge a single individual or office with responsibility for the control system for an entire organization. The intent of this arrangement is to help assure an integrated and coordinated system, and it does not in any way relieve individuals and units of their responsibility for control. Setting up the system would be in part an organizational problem, and this leads us into the next major area of management activity—organizing.

ORGANIZING

Management bears the responsibility for organizing all the component parts of a business so as to facilitate communication and coordination. The number of ways to do this is unlimited, but there are also some rather standard overall approaches that will be described. A business typically will have personnel ranging from chairman of the board of directors to errand boys, and operations ranging from sales to floor maintenance. The problem, then, is to get all of these people and operations into a harmonious relationship so the company can achieve its goals.

First, it is recognized that some people are better at doing certain jobs than others, so organizations apply the principle of *division of labor*. There are specialists in sales, in production, in purchasing, and so on. Second, there must be individuals throughout the organization who direct and coordinate the work of others. So the organization is divided into levels, and people are assigned to be vice-presidents, superintendents, supervisors, foremen, and section chiefs. The result is a *chain of command* and is an application of the *scalar process*. And within the chain of command, companies try to make sure that for the most part, people report to only one boss—an application of the principle of *unity of command*. At this point, the organization structure might look something like Figure 4–9.

Another thing to watch for is that any one boss does not have too many direct subordinates—that is, the boss's *span of control* should not be too large. For example, if you were supervising the construction of a large building and had

Figure 4-9 Basic organizational structure.

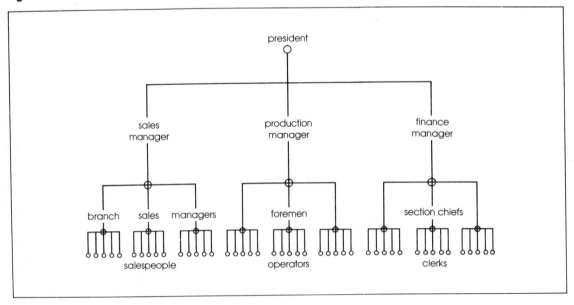

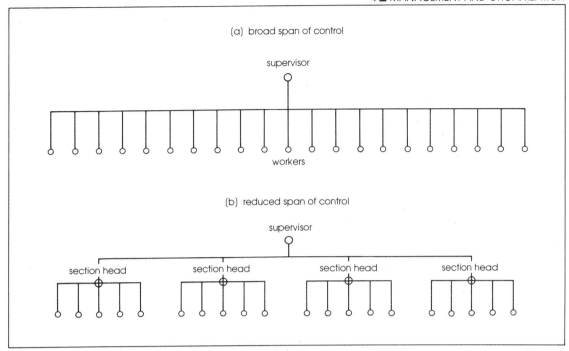

Figure 4-10 Changing span of control: (a) broad span of control; (b) reduced span of control.

several hundred people reporting directly to you, it would not be possible for you to do much coordination with any one individual. You probably would appoint sub-bosses or foremen and reduce your span of control to the point where you could effectively supervise each of your subordinates.

There is no hard-and-fast rule about how many subordinates one boss should have. Span of control depends on many factors such as the type of work, the abilities of the boss, the abilities of the subordinates, and the organizational level involved. There is a rule of thumb which states that the span of control should be no more than eight at the highest executive levels, while it should be no more than thirty at the operative level. This is at best only a rough guide, however. Figure 4–10A illustrates a broad span of control, while Figure 4–10B shows how to reduce the span by interjecting another supervisory level.

Becoming More Sophisticated   The structure we have just described may be satisfactory for simple operations, but it will hardly suffice for most business organizations in today's complex world. Specializing on the basis of division of work—that is, sales, purchasing, production—may not be adequate to cope with the multiple demands on an organization. It may become necessary to specialize also on the basis of products, customers, geographic areas, and/or manufacturing processes.

A very large company such as General Motors, for example, may well specialize or departmentalize on all of the bases that were mentioned. The company might first break out some broad product divisions—cars and trucks, for instance. Each product division could have several functional areas such as production, purchasing, sales, and finance. Sales might be divided by geographic territory, while production may be conveniently separated into component parts

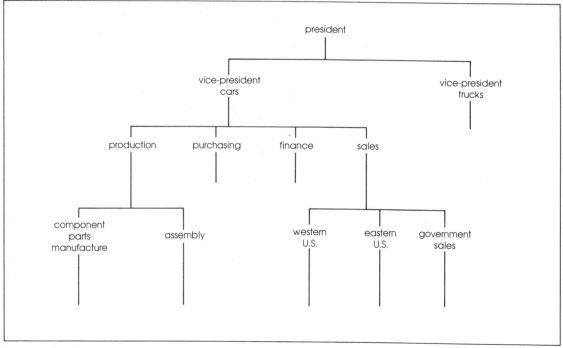

Figure 4-11 Specializing organization activities in several different ways.

manufacture and final assembly. Finally, both the car and truck divisions may want to have special offices for government sales. Figure 4–11 illustrates this type of organization structure.

It becomes necessary to differentiate the organization in the above manner because one person in a functional area of a large company would be overwhelmed by multiple responsibilities. Take sales as an example. Can you imagine one individual in General Motors trying to handle the sales of both cars and trucks all over the country as well as selling to the government and other institutional buyers? As was suggested, the company needs geographic and product sales managers as well as persons assigned to special customers. But even the structure just described is not enough. Inevitably, each of the managers in a business organization will find highly specialized help necessary from time to time, and this is the topic of the next section.

The Role of Staff Personnel   The people discussed so far in organizations are *line* personnel; that is, they bear responsibility for carrying out the business of the company—producing, selling, and financing. An organization could be departmentalized on a line basis—by products, geographic areas, customers, or whatever—to an extreme degree and still run into difficulties. Let us illustrate this by looking at the production area.

Let us stay with the manufacture of automobiles for the moment and consider the production managers and foremen in an auto assembly plan. There is a great deal involved in putting together a car—quality control, scheduling, maintenance of equipment, and control of parts inventories. It would be a terrific burden for each line manager to be expert in and responsible for each of the foregoing areas in addition to having the normal supervisory tasks involving workers and a particular segment of the production process.

In short, line managers need expert, specialized help in areas such as quality control and production scheduling. And the experts who provide this help and advice are *staff* personnel. We have been talking of only one major business function, operations or production, but business requires staff assistance in all line functions. Personnel management, accounting, and the legal department are other examples of staff activity.

The result of the above is an organization structure—*line and staff*—which is quite typical, though with many variations, of most businesses today. The staff function itself may be divided into three basic types. The first is that which has been discussed—functional staff. Its purpose is to give expert help and advice to the line. The second is more of a service function and may be illustrated by the maintenance and upkeep of physical facilities. A personal assistant to a line manager represents a third type. The assistant may work on special assignments and act in the capacity of an internal consultant. Figure 4–12 shows a line and staff organization structure.

Variations on Structure   We indicated that there are many variations on and departures from the line and staff structure. One important way to vary a struc-

Figure 4-12   Part of a line and staff organization.

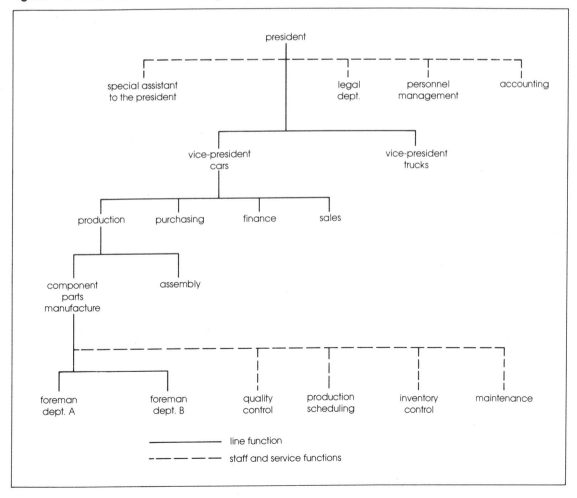

ture involves the amount of *decentralization* of decision making in conjunction with the number of managerial levels. If a company wants lower-level managers to make most of their own decisions, it will decentralize. This approach is often facilitated through use of a relatively flat structure with large spans of control. The idea, in part, is that a manager with a large number of subordinates will be forced to allow them to make most of their own decisions since the boss will have neither the time nor the ability for close supervision.

On the other hand, a desire to *centralize* decision making often will result in a rather tall structure with many levels and short spans of control. In this way, it is possible for each boss to closely supervise his or her subordinates and make most decisions for them. What an individual business does with respect to decentralization depends in part upon its philosophy of decision making and in part upon circumstances.

A retail chain, for example, may want to decentralize decision making to store managers because they know local conditions and, as a result, are simply in a much better position than top management to make local decisions. An army, on the other hand, may want highly centralized decision making because the general is the only one who can possibly know all the circumstances which could affect the actions of even the smallest unit.

There are numerous departures from the line and staff structure. These days most of them incorporate more freedom and informality than would be found in traditional designs. Perhaps the aerospace industry is most notable in this respect for its use of the project team concept. For many developmental projects in spacecraft technology and hardware, the industry assembled persons with various skills and types of knowledge into a working team (see Fig. 4–13). There was no line or staff as such; communication channels flowed in all directions, and authority was distributed more on the basis of knowledge and contribution than through the use of a formal structure.

Figure 4-13 Project team.

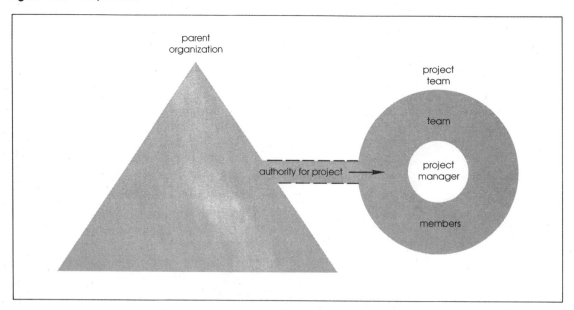

Today other industries and organizations use and are experimenting with various types of free-form structure. Even within the line and staff organization, staff teams may draw members with diverse skills from throughout the company to work on temporary or relatively permanent problems. These arrangements sometimes evolve into a kind of *matrix organization* in which persons from a particular functional area, such as production, are also members of some special task group or program.

The term *organic* is used to describe the organization structure which facilitates innovation, informality, interaction among members, and a fluid transfer of authority and control dependent upon circumstances. The organic form, of course, contrasts with the more rigid and formal traditional or mechanistic structure. Line and staff tends to be traditional, though the organic approach can be incorporated through devices such as the multidisciplinary staff team that was described above.

No One Best Structure   Having gained some familiarity with various kinds of organization structure, you may now feel that there is no best structure for all types of business. This is true. Each case depends on existing and predicted conditions and requirements. In a broad sense, a business that needs to be innovative and highly flexible will probably do best with some form of the organic approach, while a business incorporating a great deal of routine, steady activity may do well with a more traditional form. These issues, of course, are largely apart from the question of whether a business should be a single proprietorship, partnership, or corporation.

We have now studied several aspects of the management and organization of a business enterprise. There are many interesting facets in the life of a business organization, of course, and perhaps one of the most fascinating is growth. What growth phases does a business go through? What are the characteristics of each growth phase? These are the questions of concern in the next section.

GROWTH OF A BUSINESS ENTERPRISE

It is important to discuss growth for two reasons: (1) business growth is a constant phenomenon, and (2) the style of management and the type of organization structure usually change as a company moves through various growth phases. It may appear that the large corporation dominates the business world, but there are still many small businesses which thrive and which start up all the time. Not too many years ago, a young man just two years out of college borrowed $25,000 to start a leasing company. Today that organization is a billion-dollar corporation.[4]

Business growth occurs in different ways. We read, for example, of *mergers* and instances in which one company buys another. These certainly are legitimate growth patterns, but our interest will center on the company which exploits a particular product base. This means that a company could start from scratch and

[4]"Don't Take No for an Answer Says Builder of Billion Dollar Corporation," *The MBA Executive* 1, no. 3 (March 1972).

develop a product or products so that sales, assets, and employment continually increase. It is assumed that where there is more than one product, they are similar to the extent that they arise from the same technological and resource base. In other words, a company manufacturing and selling a line of hand and power tools would fall within the model, but a company which is making tools and then also starts making soap or doing commercial printing would not.[5]

It is also assumed that environmental conditions, including such factors as demand and the surrounding culture, are not limiting to growth. Most small businesses today fall within the scope of the first growth phase—*traditional craft*. In this stage, ownership typically resides in one or a few individuals, often within the same family. The boss usually makes most or all of the important decisions as well as many of the minor ones. And what traditionally has proven successful frequently provides the basis for decisions on future actions. Owners seek to establish a good living for themselves rather than pursue constant growth and expansion into new product opportunities. In sum, we have a business where things are done pretty much as they always have been, where everyone knows everyone else, and where there is little interest in becoming a large corporation.

Dynamic Growth   Occasionally one of these small companies will begin to grow and will continue to do so in rapid and exciting fashion. What are the factors that cause this dramatic change? There are at least two: (1) an innovation such as an invention, a new product, or a new service, and (2) a new kind of leader—a daring entrepreneur and promoter, an individual who can inspire others to great faith and hard work. This new person could be a member of the family who takes over the reins, someone who buys the company, or an innovative outsider who comes in to run the business.

Dynamic growth is the second growth phase and is an exciting time for everyone connected with the business. There are great expectations for future reward as employees and owners realize a full identification with their confident and optimistic leader. The nature of the organization is similar in many respects to that of traditional craft during the dynamic growth phase. It is informal, with few formal policies and procedures.

The leader or boss runs the show, though he or she may have several trusted personal assistants. Sometimes the business has a product or service of a highly technical nature. In these cases, the boss may be forced to delegate substantial authority in operations management to his or her technical specialists. If success and growth continue, the company begins a gradual shift into the third phase of growth—*rational administration*.

Formal policies and procedures, professional management, and formal staff characterize rational administration—the growth stage claiming most large, complex organizations. No longer does one individual dominate. Instead, in decision-making matters, staff personnel prepare well-documented reports, committees deliberate at length, and the final decision may be announced by the chief executive but is rarely the result of his or her work alone. The line and staff structure that was described earlier predominates under rational administration. Figure 4–14 illustrates the grow cycle.

[5]The material on the growth model is adapted from Alan C. Filley and Robert J. House, *Managerial Process and Organizational Behavior* (Glenview, Ill.: Scott, Foresman, and Co., 1969), chapter 18.

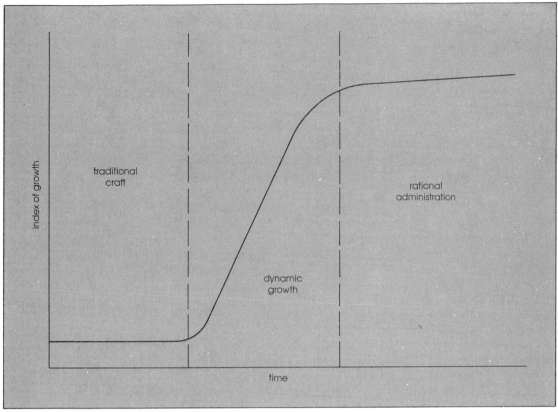

Figure 4-14 The growth cycle.

A Fourth Stage?   Is rational administration the end of the road? It would be foolhardy to claim that rational administration is the last stage of organizational evolution as the result of growth. It is likely that growth continues and that, currently at least, some form of organic structure appears. This means that a business again becomes more informal, that management action is more spontaneous, that teamwork becomes increasingly important, and that interpersonal relations achieve greater emphasis.

It may appear that the organic style is quite similar to management during the dynamic growth phase. There are surface similarities, but in the organic structure, one person does not dominate decision making, staff work continues to be important, and the emphasis is on teamwork. The same kinds of work must be done as under rational administration, but the organic approach adopts a different and perhaps more effective and innovative style toward getting the work done.

Knowledge of the growth cycle enables management to predict future changes, to prepare for them, and to enhance the learning experience involved in progressing through the various growth phases. Hence management is less likely to be surprised as events unfold throughout the life cycle of a business, and as a result, the business is less likely to be hurt because management is unprepared. We have studied some important aspects of management and organization in this chapter. We want to finish by describing the phenomenon that occurs when management and organization are effectively meshed in working partnership.

SYNERGY

In this chapter, we discussed the separate activities which make up the managerial job as well as the components which enter into organizational structure. By themselves, the various activities—planning, organizing, and controlling—and the structural components—line, staff, scalar chain, departmentation, decentralization, and span of control—can have only limited, if any, effect on organizational purpose. But working in concert as a result of human effort, all of the activities and components comprise a system which results in what is called *synergy*.

When a business has synergy, it means that the business is operating as an integrated system. All of the people who are doing the planning, organizing, and controlling and who are fulfilling line and staff roles are acting in a cooperative and harmonious manner. The result is greater than if planning is done independently of organizing and controlling, or if line and staff people go their own ways and never consult with one another. It is the same idea that applies when two or more people work on any project. They will do better work more quickly if they work together rather than each one doing something without regard for what the others are doing. Teamwork is the key, and it is essential to maximizing success.

MANAGEMENT PHILOSOPHY

The philosophy developed by top management provides the overall guide to a company's activities and has a major effect on the development of company goals. That is, a business will act in accordance with its philosophy—to be conservative, to be daring, to be socially responsible, to maximize employee welfare, and so on. A philosophy encompasses all aspects of a company's behavior and usually changes very slowly.

Management philosophy is beneficial in that it helps people to know how to act and how to integrate all system components for maximum effectiveness. But it involves danger also. For example, over time a business with a conservative philosophy will attract and tend to keep individuals who are conservative. Hence the organization membership may become quite homogeneous, with everyone holding more or less the same attitudes, values, and approaches to problems.

A condition of this nature tends to stifle innovation and to smother awareness of certain problems and opportunities. There is a need for heterogeneity also, for people who perceive things differently and who may hold somewhat different attitudes and values. So we see that up to a point, likemindedness is valuable in making a philosophy work and in helping to assure a smoothly running business. But we should also see that too much of the same can hurt a business by causing it to overlook opportunities and problems that might be obvious to someone with a different perspective.

Incidentally, gaining a different viewpoint explains much of the reason for bringing in outside consultants. A management philosophy is extremely important to a business for the guidance it offers in bringing all the system components together in orderly fashion. But if it is too rigidly enforced, a philosophy may bring about tunnel vision and a serious undercutting of organizational synergy.

In this chapter we studied the relatively large and complex business organization in order to develop concepts that apply to many kinds and sizes of companies. We said an organization is a system in which management plays a key role in coordinating all subsystems toward achievement of objectives. Our main emphasis was on the nature of the managerial job. **SUMMARY**

A good manager usually develops through a combination of formal education and experience. He or she faces a variety of challenges which demand decisions. He or she must keep in mind that the business organization is an open system—that it affects and is affected by the external environment. Hence managers at all levels must maintain this awareness as they develop strategic and operating plans.

Planning, along with organizing, and controlling is one of three important managerial activities. Planning reduces uncertainty and enables everyone in a company to have a better idea of where they are going and what they are supposed to be doing to get there. Control helps assure that actual results conform to planned results, and management must structure control systems that will keep an organization on track.

Management also must make decisions on how best to organize a business. The most common structure is line and staff, a design intended to motivate action while incorporating the advice and service of experts in various fields. There are many ways to structure a business organization, however, and one of the newer approaches stresses greater informality and teamwork with an aim of stimulating innovation and achievement. Designs in the latter category include project, matrix, and organic organization structures.

A growing business organization passes through at least three phases of growth in which the style of management and the organization structure change. The stages are traditional craft, dynamic growth, and rational administration. There may be a fourth stage, which would be of the organic or more informal variety emphasizing teamwork.

And finally, there is a synergistic effect that results from combining all the organizational system components, including management, into a cohesive whole. The result should be far more than could be achieved by any one set of components alone. We also recognized that management philosophy will determine the nature of the synergistic effect—a conservative philosophy, for example, will result in the type of component interaction which will produce conservative company actions. It should be apparent that a business needs excellent management and an appropriate organization structure in order to succeed.

DISCUSSION QUESTIONS

1. As a customer, do you have any preference about dealing with a large company or a small company? If so, what are the reasons for your preference?

2. What does it mean to operate a business as a system? What would happen to a business if it forgot it was a system?

3. Does a person need to go to college to become a good manager in a business organization? What advantages, if any, would a college education provide?

4. If a business successfully adapts to its environment, could the business exist forever? Are there any absolute guarantees for business survival?

5. Do you think a manager's job is harder at the top of the organization, in the middle, or near the bottom? What are the reasons for your answer?

6. What is the relationship between planning and controlling? Why is this relationship so important to a business organization?

7. Do you think a large department store should be organized in the same way as a bank? What are your reasons?

8. Which of the three phases of growth that were discussed in the chapter do you think would be most interesting when working for a business? Why?

9. Would it be easy or difficult for an organization to change its philosophy? What are some occasions when a business perhaps should change philosophy?

SHORT CASES

When It Rains, It Pours[6]

From 1972 to 1976, the National Semiconductor Corporation of Santa Clara, California, increased its earnings from $2 million to $19 million. The price of its stock went from $9 to $55. In 1976, investors felt that 1977 might see another large increase in profits.

Then it began to rain. The company's consumer products division—watches and hand calculators—expected a loss in 1977 of $8 million or more, according to investment analysts. The company was late in getting into production on new component parts for computers. There were delayed deliveries and shortages of materials and parts.

Then it began to pour. A strike stopped production of vital watch parts. There were reported to be organizational and control problems in some manufacturing plants. A retailer said that the company's consumer products—actually of high quality—were regarded as "low-end junk" by other retailers and consumers.

National Semiconductor responded. It put a new person in charge of consumer products. It brought manufacturing of consumer products under the direction and control of the consumer products chief. The company began

to follow market trends more closely. To gain more variety and better quality in some instances, more components were being bought on the outside. At the time of this report, it is too early to know the results of the efforts at National Semiconductor.

Do you believe National Semiconductor's problems were the result of poor management? In what ways?

How could it come about that high-quality products would become known as "low-end junk?"

Will the changes that National Semiconductor made help to solve its problems?

The New President

The Blue Grass Lawn Mower Company had been a family business for many years. Its president, old Ben LaCrosse, was seventy-eight years old but still active in the business. LaCrosse was conservative and so were his employees, most of whom had been with the company for many years.

LaCrosse had no sons and just one daughter. But he had a grandson, George Anders, who was five years out of college and working in the business as vice-president for sales. Anders was bright, energetic, and as daring as his grandfather was cautious. The two were friendly, but they differed on many aspects of running the business. For example, young Anders wanted to go to national distribution with some new product ideas. LaCrosse wanted to stay regional with lawn mowers.

At 5:30 p.m. one Friday afternoon, La Crosse was still hard at work in his office. Suddenly he collapsed over his desk. The doctor said it was a heart attack. He had died instantly. With the consent of his mother, who was now the major stockholder, Anders assumed the presidency immediately.

Will it be possible for young George Anders to quickly put some of his ideas into practice now that he is the president of the Blue Grass Lawn Mower Company?

Do you think someone else should have been named president while Anders gained more experience and maturity?

Will Anders' mother actually be running the company?

---

[6]Adapted from "Dog Days at National Semiconductor," *Business Week*, February 28, 1977, pp. 70–72.

SUGGESTED READINGS

Dessler, Gary, *Organization and Management: A Contingency Approach.* Ref. ed. Englewood Cliffs, N.J.: Prentice-Hall, 1976.

Lundgren, Earl F. *Organizational Management: Systems and Process.* San Francisco: Canfield Press, 1974.

Robbins, Stephen P. *The Administrative Process: Integrating Theory and Practice.* Englewood Cliffs, N.J.: Prentice-Hall, 1976.

Trewatha, Robert L., and Newport, M. Gene. *Management: Functions and Behavior.* Dallas: Business Publications, 1976.

HUMAN ASSETS MANAGEMENT

LEARNING OBJECTIVES

When you finish this chapter you should:
- [ ] be familiar with the various activities associated with human assets management.
- [ ] understand the importance of company planning for future employment in terms of numbers of persons and their skills and potentials.
- [ ] be aware of the general legal requirements with respect to recruiting, hiring, and paying employees, and employee safety and health.
- [ ] be familiar with the many different kinds of personnel changes that can affect employees.
- [ ] understand the potential value of human asset accounting.

KEY TERMS TO LEARN FROM THIS CHAPTER

achievement test	graphic rating scale	leave of absence	replacement chart
application form	human assets accounting	management development	selection
apprenticeship			sensitivity training
aptitude test	human assets management	on-the-job training	simulation
classroom training		orientation	supplemental unemployment benefits
coaching	incentive plan	personnel administration	
cost-of-living factor	intelligence test		test (employment)
discharge	interview	personnel management	training
effectiveness	job analysis		transfer
efficiency	job description	personality test	unemployment compensation
employee relations	job rotation	preliminary interview	
escalator clause	job specification	promotion	vestibule training
evaluation	labor relations	quit	workers' compensation
exit interview	layoff	recruiting	

Back around 1810, when Napoleon Bonaparte, the emperor of France, was recruiting fresh troops for his armies, he used a rather direct method. Spurning recruitment posters and enlistment bonuses, Napoleon chose instead to send recruiting officers traveling around France searching for likely prospects. When one was discovered, the young lad was invited to join the army. There was no physical examination or long forms to fill out. There was no attempt to match the prospect's skills and aptitudes with a particular branch of the army. The prospect was simply invited to be an infantry soldier in Napoleon's army. If the recruit proved to be reluctant, the recruiting officer seemed always to find a way to persuade the young man to join up.

Recruiting practices have changed since Napoleon's time, but their purpose remains the same. It is to find qualified applicants to fill open positions in an organization. Recruiting is part of *human assets management.* Other parts include training, pay, and employee health and safety. Human assets management is the topic of this chapter, which will provide an understanding of what human assets management means, what activities are associated with it, and why it is one of the necessary functions in running a business.

THE NATURE OF HUMAN ASSETS MANAGEMENT

An organization is nothing without people. Only people can make an organization work through planning, organizing, producing, and marketing. And yet, it does little good to fill an organization with people who just happen to come along. Napoleon did not want just anybody in his army. He wanted strong young men. And so it is with any organization. It needs people who have certain skills, abilities, and knowledge. And that defines the basic job of those in charge of human assets management. They must acquire, train, pay, and provide for the health and safety of organization members.

Organizations often use more formal titles to identify their human assets management function. These titles include *personnel management, personnel administration, employee relations,* and *labor relations.* The relationship between an organization and a labor union is often a part of the human assets management function, but we will delay discussion of this important topic until Chapter 6.

Selecting and hiring people, training them, paying them fairly and regularly, and helping to assure their health and safety are continuing and vital activities. Employees resign, die, get fired, receive promotions, and transfer from one job to another. To keep an organization successfully operating throughout all of these personnel changes requires careful planning, and the first topic in our discussion will be employment planning.

EMPLOYMENT PLANNING

Business organizations introduce new products and services, drop old products and services, and grow and contract because of economic cycles and market success or failure. Hence there is a continuing need to adjust the size of the organization's labor force as well as the mix of skills (see Figure 5–1).

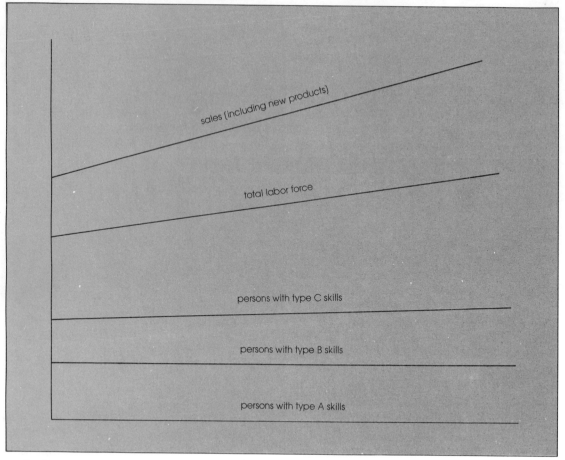

Figure 5-1 Relationship between sales of new products and the labor force.

In order to maintain *efficiency* and *effectiveness*, the organization should do its best to forecast future changes and their effects on personnel requirements. For example, new product development may cause an organization to anticipate a need for more people and different skills than the organization currently possesses. On this basis, the personnel officer will prepare to recruit the needed additional people who have the required new skills.

THE PERSONNEL INVENTORY

Basic to any planning for future personnel requirements is an inventory of current personnel, their skills, and potential. Using past experience on terminations, promotions, and other actions, an analysis of the inventory will indicate those jobs most likely to need replacements or changes in the number of job-holders in the event of expansion or contraction. Particularly for managerial personnel, a *replacement chart* is helpful in determining which subordinates might be promoted in the event of a vacancy. Figure 5–2 illustrates this type of chart.

Note in Figure 5–2 that each individual who might be promoted to a superior position has a code by his or her name showing an evaluation of present performance and an estimate of his or her readiness to be promoted to the higher position. In the event that there is no one qualified and ready to move up when a vacancy occurs, the organization will have to go outside to seek a replacement. With aids such as inventories and replacement charts, a manager is better able to keep his or her particular unit fully and adequately staffed.

JOB ANALYSIS

Employment planning may suggest a need for additional persons to be hired, but before the personnel department can do any actual recruiting and hiring, it must have detailed descriptions of the jobs to be filled and specifications for the people to fill them. This knowledge comes from a continuing and systematic process called job analysis.

Figure 5-2 Manpower replacement chart.

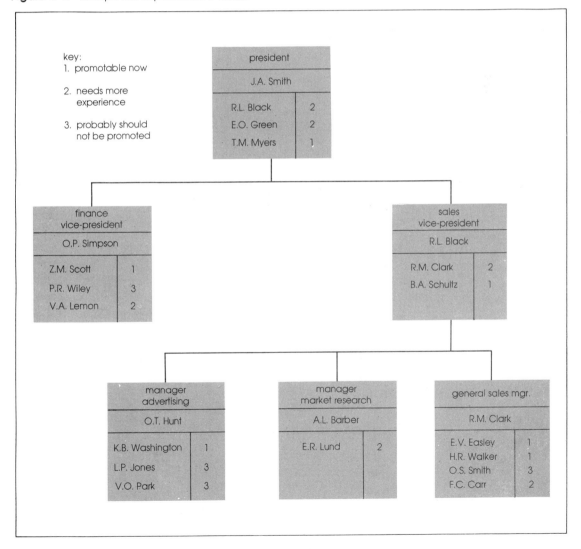

CHARLES L. FARROW

Hiring, training, paying, and providing for the health and safety of employees are the principal functions of human assets management.

Job analysis involves an overall study of a job to determine its exact content in terms of duties, operations, working conditions, and worker requirements such as skills, knowledge, and physical and mental demands. We do this initially in setting up a business and then review the job analysis periodically because jobs change over time, and it is important for recruiting and hiring purposes to keep job requirements up to date.

JOB DESCRIPTION AND JOB SPECIFICATION

As a result of job analysis, an organization prepares two documents: a *job description* and a *job specification*. The job description identifies the nature of the work to be performed, providing a summary of the job and a listing of the specific duties, as shown in Figure 5–3. The job specification is a statement of the minimum acceptable human qualities which are required to perform a job properly. The job "spec" usually includes a summary of the duties and responsibilities of a job

job title: shipping department manager
salary_____ date of job-analysis_____

summary of job: supervises the preparation
    of cartons for shipping.
    maintains records of all shipments.
    works under general supervision of production superintendent.

specific duties:
    1. estimates future needs and requisitions necessary shipping materials.

    2. maintains control of all shipping materials in inventory.

    3. checks all shipping documents for accuracy.

    4. makes weekly reports to production superintendent on shipments.

    5. accepts returned shipments and sends notification of returns to inventory control.

    6. makes sure shipments leave on schedule.

Figure 5-3   Job description.

Safety goggles are one of the many ways this machinist
protects himself while on the job.

CHARLES L. FARROW

job title: shipping department manager

summary of job: supervises the preparation of cartons and boxes for shipping.
   maintains records of all shipments,
   works under general supervision of production superintendent.

job requirements:
      education: graduation from high school necessary. two years of college desirable.

      knowledge: familiarity with shipping procedures, documentation, and packing techniques.

      experience: work in some phase of shipping helpful but not absolutely essential.

      skill: needs supervisory skill in working with people and ability to plan, organize,
              and control shipping operations.

Figure 5-4 Job specification.

but emphasizes requirements such as education, knowledge, physical condition, experience, and skill (see Figure 5–4). Used together, these two documents provide an excellent beginning basis for the recruitment, selection, and placement of people.

RECRUITING

Before a business organization can select or hire people, it must have a supply from which to choose. The function of *recruiting* is to assure sufficient job applicants so the organization has a choice in its selection of employees. The reader has probably observed a number of recruiting methods, such as newspaper ads, army and navy recruiting posters, and billboard advertisements. The methods employed range from a simple "Dishwasher Wanted" sign in the window of a restaurant to sophisticated and expensive private employment agencies.

Newspaper advertising is the most common method. Other recruiting techniques include the use of public and private employment agencies, educational institutions, present employee recommendations, labor unions, and professional meetings and conventions. Companies sometimes send a recruiting van to various cities to seek applications for employment. When a private employment agency is used, the company doing the hiring usually has to pay a fee to the agency for each person actually hired.

EFFECTS OF ECONOMIC CONDITIONS

The intensity of the recruiting effort depends to a large degree on the relative scarcity or abundance of potential employees. If unemployment is high, a business may have to do little more than interview people who walk into the personnel office looking for work. When unemployment is low, however, the supply of people looking for jobs is limited, and then an organization must engage in intensive recruiting in order to provide an adequate work force. In the latter situation, companies may attempt to lure people to work by offering high wage rates, liberal fringe benefits, pleasant working conditions, or some combination of these plus other special inducements.

SPECIAL CONSIDERATIONS IN RECRUITING

Starting in 1957, the United States Congress passed a series of eight civil rights acts that were designed to prevent discrimination in voting, the payment of wages to males and females, hiring, and the renting and selling of real estate. The most comprehensive act was the *Civil Rights Act of 1964* (amended in 1972). Among the important provisions was the prohibition of discrimination in the hiring of people on the basis of race, color, national origin, sex, or religion. Any business which employs fifteen or more persons must observe this law except in cases where a particular sex or religion is an obvious requirement. For example, a particular religious denomination has the right to employ ministers or priests of the same denomination. An all-girl baseball league may be granted the right to employ only female ballplayers.

The Civil Rights Act established the Equal Employment Opportunity Commission to enforce the law. When the commission receives a valid charge of discrimination, it may go through a U.S. District Court or take action itself to stop the discrimination. In addition, the Civil Rights Act requires many organizations, such as universities, to develop affirmative action programs in their recruiting and hiring. If, for example, a university's affirmative action program does not meet federal standards, the commission may withhold federal funds that the university depends upon for financial support.

Under an affirmative action program and generally under the law, an employer must do more than just depend upon people who walk in looking for a job or who may have heard there are job openings. The employer must make a diligent and extensive effort through advertising, the use of employment agencies, and other means. These requirements are especially enforced if an employer has a lopsided number of a certain class of people. A partial list of the conditions of employment where discrimination is illegal include hiring, layoff, discharge, pay, vacation time, insurance coverage, pension benefits, and recreational activities.

Voluntary Efforts   Since before passage of the Civil Rights Act, many business organizations have voluntarily allocated a portion of their recruiting effort to seeking out persons with handicaps, with no marketable skills, or with no working experience. These people have been hired in a deliberate attempt to aid in a program of employing and training individuals who in many cases had never developed work skills and habits and were thus victims of chronic unemployment. These people learn a work skill and often receive additional training in the simple responsibilities of reporting to work every day, being on time, and keeping themselves healthy and capable of maintaining regular employment.

For example, the National Alliance of Business has been instrumental in encouraging businesses all over the country to be active in this program. In some instances, a company will experience only limited success in hiring, training, and employing chronically unemployed persons, but with greater experience and learning, the proportion of successes should increase until success is the expected result and failure the rare exception. Unfortunately, these programs do vary in intensity with changes in economic conditions. Under adverse conditions, it is difficult to have a strong program to employ disadvantaged persons when heavy layoffs might be occurring.

With respect to handicapped persons, employers have long noticed that these workers have very low absenteeism and turnover rates and often work at the same rates as or at better rates than workers without handicaps. It is important to place handicapped workers at jobs where their skills can be fully utilized. When so placed, they usually become excellent, reliable workers.

RECRUITING FROM WITHIN THE ORGANIZATION

A final, important recruiting opportunity exists in sources within an organization. Through transfers and promotions, the company's own personnel have a chance for better jobs and more interesting work. By utilizing these internal sources, a company may improve employee morale and face less risk, since it already knows a great deal about the people being considered for selection and placement in a new job.

SELECTION

Selection of personnel is a critical component of organizational success. An organization needs talent, especially in such key jobs as those involving supervisory responsibility, important staff work, and the accomplishment of the executive mission. As a result, great amounts of time and effort go into the selection process. An organization has a responsibility to select its members on a fair and equitable basis. If you are looking for a job, you should be able to expect that all applicants for that job will go through the same selection process and be judged solely on the criteria set up for that job.

STEPS IN SELECTION

Tools of the selection process include *application forms, interviews, tests,* and *physical examinations.* Organizations usually arrange these tools into some sequence that suits particular needs. For example, a company might first conduct a preliminary interview, then have the application form completed, have the tests administered, hold another interview, and give a physical exam (Figure 5–5). During this process, appropriate persons in the company receive the results of reference checks and confer about the applicant.

In some systems, failure at any point in the selection procedure means that the applicant will be rejected. In other systems, all steps are completed, a total score calculated, and the applicant is accepted or rejected in relation to a previously set acceptance level or score. Many companies favor the latter method, since a high score or rating on one step may offset a low rating on another step, and this averaging out seems fairest for the applicants. If one step is critical to the job, however, failure at this point always means rejection. This step will usually be the first one in the selection process. For example, airline companies al-

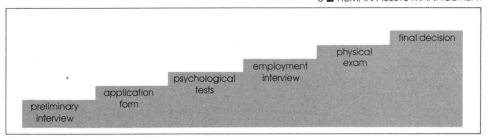

Figure 5-5 Steps in the selection procedure.

ways reject applicants for the job of pilot if a physical examination reveals very poor eyesight. And since good eyesight is so critical, an airline logically might want an eye test as the first step in selection.

The Preliminary Interview The *preliminary interview* aims to determine quickly if there are obvious reasons why a person should not be considered for employment. If we are hiring fashion models, appearance is an important factor which can be quickly judged during a preliminary interview. If an applicant for a flying job comes in wearing thick glasses, we might quickly suggest he or she think of some other line of work.

The Application Form Completion of an application form provides much of the relevant information that a company needs to make a decision about an applicant, and the completed document becomes part of the personnel record of an individual if he or she is hired. Thus the form requests the person's name, address, Social Security number, education, work experience, and other pertinent background information and data. The applicant may also list references on this form. In some cases today, companies do not request personal references under the philosophy that no one will list a reference who is unfavorable. Employment managers often investigate work and school references, however. If an applicant is employed elsewhere, the employment manager must obtain his or her permission to ask for a reference from the present employer.

Testing Since World War II, *employment tests* have been widely used as a step in the selection process. Tests measure a sample of the applicant's total behavior and thus provide some indication of future success or failure on a job. Tests should be used in conjunction with the whole selection process and not be relied upon as the sole determinant of whether an applicant is accepted or rejected.

Some persons might score low on a particular qualifying test but succeed on the job in question if given an opportunity. Other persons might fail at a job even though they may have scored high on a selection test for that job. Tests are not perfect predictors because their results are based on probabilities involving groups of people and cannot be applied with precision to an individual case. Tests also attempt to provide information on factors such as determination and drive, but these are difficult factors to measure.

Types of Tests A company may use a variety of tests, and the reader may have taken one or more of such tests during his or her work or school experience. *Aptitude tests* are commonly used and are quite reliable. These tests measure a person's potential ability for a given job or for an area of work application. For example, there are aptitude tests for particular factory or office jobs and tests for mechanical comprehension and finger dexterity.

Achievement tests measure knowledge or skill that an applicant already has. These tests may range from a simple typing demonstration to written tests covering an entire trade or craft. *Intelligence tests* provide a measure of mental alertness and awareness, and companies often favor them because some provide a relatively quick appraisal of a person's ability to cope with varying levels of job difficulty. An intelligence test may take as little as ten minutes to administer and score.

Personality Tests   Psychologists have devised a variety of *personality tests* in an attempt to measure emotional adjustment and the numerous dimensions of individual personality such as how aggressive a person is, how outgoing, and how dependent upon others. These tests have been criticized on two principal counts. First, personality dimensions are difficult to measure at best, and the difficulty is compounded by the knowledge that at least some of the tests can be analyzed sufficiently by a perceptive applicant so that the results can be roughly tailored to a personality pattern that the individual wants the test to indicate. For example, on a personality test for a sales job, the applicant may be able to answer the questions in such a way that the test results indicate an aggressive, outgoing person when in fact the applicant is shy and retiring.

The second criticism charges that personality tests pry unnecessarily into the private lives of applicants. Some tests seek information on the person's relationship with parents, sexual habits, or other intimate aspects of the life of the applicant that we might usually consider to be strictly private. While organizations normally consider these tests as confidential records, there have been instances in which unauthorized persons have gained access to them.

When filling executive positions, firms sometimes employ industrial psychologists to appraise the personality characteristics of applicants. Projective techniques may be used in which the applicant is asked to interpret ambiguous pictures or inkblots. Many industrial psychologists look primarily for potential problems in the applicant, such as alcoholism, emotional instability, and the use of drugs.

Testing and Discrimination   Psychological testing has been criticized in general because it may discriminate against people of some cultural backgrounds. On some intelligence tests, for example, it may not be surprising that the person with an excellent background in mathematics, literature, and grammar may do better than the person with a poor background in such areas who may have attended overcrowded, understaffed schools or come from a family that tended to de-emphasize education. The latter person may have high intelligence, but the tests administered do not reflect this.

Test experts are trying to develop tests that take cultural differences into consideration; however, some companies have discontinued, temporarily at least, many of their testing programs because of possible cultural discrimination. Rather than discontinuing the use of tests completely, however, perhaps an organization should use them with greater care and also emphasize changing job requirements to meet the abilities of culturally disadvantaged persons.

Under the law, tests are not discriminatory if they are not designed or used to distinguish among people of different races, colors, sex, religions, or national origins. On the other hand, the employer must be prepared to prove that the tests used measure only a person's present or potential ability to do a job.

The Second Interview   While the personnel department of an organization normally handles most of the steps in the selection procedure, the head of the department where the applicant would work if hired generally also interviews the applicant and makes the final decision on whether to hire or reject. In this way, the department head or supervisor is working with people he or she has helped to select rather than simply taking those new employees assigned by the personnel department. Thus the department head shares responsibility with the personnel people for the hiring of job applicants and should feel a corresponding interest in helping the new employee to succeed.

While recruiting is positive in that it encourages people to contact the company for possible work, selection has a negative aspect since applicants are being rejected as well as selected. However, some organizations try to place the applicant in another job if that individual cannot qualify for the job originally applied for. The aspiring pilot who flunks the eye test may be encouraged to go into administrative work. Placement of people into alternative jobs occurs predominantly during periods of low unemployment when applicants are relatively scarce.

ORIENTATION

After selection, a company's responsibility to the new employee just begins. Of course, the employee also bears a responsibility for contributing to the organization in exchange for wages and other benefits. But our concern here is how the organization can help employees to maximize their contributions and make them with satisfaction and pride.

A good point for the company to start is with a comprehensive *orientation* for the new employee. Such a program includes a general review by personnel department staff members of general policies on pay and fringe benefits—including medical and insurance benefits—and how the new employee's department fits into the overall organization. In many cases, a new employee will be given a copy of the company's policy and procedure manual.

The immediate supervisor has the major responsibility for a successful orientation, however. The supervisor must explain the job to the new person, introduce that individual to workers, and cover many other items such as coffee breaks, lunch periods, locations of cafeterias, restrooms, and so on. Sometimes a coworker is assigned to continuously help the new employee until that person feels comfortable and at home.

Starting on a new job is always hard. Not only are the job and the surroundings strange, but the new employee usually receives a certain amount of teasing from the veterans. Helping the new person through the difficult first few weeks prevents excessive discouragement and assures the new person that he or she has started work with an organization that has concern for employees. A study at Texas Instruments showed that new employees who went through a friendly, thorough orientation procedure were more productive, required less training, and had less absenteeism and tardiness than did new employees who received no orientation.[1]

THE CANDY EMPORIUM HIRES ITS FIRST EMPLOYEE

To illustrate some of the personnel activities that we have been discussing, let us see how Geri Rogers and Art Lindstrom, owners of The Candy Emporium, go about hiring their first employee. After being in operation for awhile, Geri and Art find their business has increased until they are working twelve to fourteen hours per day. Seeing every indication that business will continue to increase, they plan to hire someone as soon as possible.

After some analysis, they decide that the new employee will work primarily in production but will have to wait on customers when the store gets busy. In a very informal way, they jot down on paper the essentials of a job description and a job specification. The job description states that the principal duty of the new employee will be to run the enrober, the machine that coats candy centers. Other duties will include packing finished candy in boxes, helping to stock the candy cases, and occasional clerking.

Since the job requires a variety of duties and a knowledge of arithmetic in working with customers and customer orders, Geri and Art decide the new employee should be a high school graduate. Some experience in kitchen work and retail clerking would be desirable but not essential. By these decisions, Geri and Art have made a basic job specification.

Finally, they decide that a newspaper ad would be the best way to offer notice of the open job. They place a want ad in the local newspaper to run for a week, and then they wait for results. Their selection procedure will be quite simple, consisting of an interview and the completion of an application form. They had obtained the application forms from the Retail Confectioners International, a trade association they had joined earlier.

Geri and Art had found out about the trade association from one of their suppliers. The supplier pointed out that the trade association could offer many advantages, such as having application forms available that were tailored to the candy industry, providing notices of candy conventions all over the country, and issuing newsletters and other items of valuable information about candy making and selling. So far, Geri and Art are happy with the results of their membership.

During the week the want ad was running, Geri and Art interviewed ten applicants for their job. They finally decided to hire a twenty-two-year-old woman, a high school graduate, who had retail clerking experience. She had no commercial kitchen experience but loved to cook at home. She also expressed great interest in learning how to make candy.

Geri and Art both helped introduce their new employee to The Candy Emporium. They tried to make her feel at home and spent many hours teaching her

[1]Earl R. Gomersall and M. Scott Myers, "Break-through in On-the-Job Training," *Harvard Business Review* 44, no. 4 (July-August 1966): 62–72.

the kitchen duties, how to pack candy, and the details of clerking. Within a week, their new employee had made good progress, and Geri and Art were satisfied with their first attempt at employment planning, recruiting, and hiring.

TRAINING

Beyond initial orientation, every new employee needs *training*—either for the initial job or, later on, for a possible future job. For both managers and operative personnel, learning the skills and knowledge necessary for successful accomplishment of a job is important. Prior to starting a training program, members of the personnel staff must study the job to be performed in order to determine two types of information: (1) the knowledge and skills required to perform a given task, and (2) the type and content of training programs that will best develop the required knowledge and skills. Once these determinations are made, there are several forms of training that may be used.

ON-THE-JOB TRAINING

The most common form of training, *on-the-job* training, casts the supervisor or a senior employee into the role of an instructor who works directly with the new employee. The instructor in this case will tell the trainee how to do the job, then show the trainee, and finally have the trainee do the job under the watchful eye and guidance of the instructor. The fact that training occurs under normal working conditions has both an advantage and potential disadvantages.

The advantage is that the new employee learns while at the same time picking up the tempo of normal production. The trainee does not have to make an abrupt change to new and strange surroundings upon the completion of training. The potential disadvantages are: (1) the instructor may tend to emphasize production and become impatient with the trainee, and (2) the activity, noise, and other possible factors in normal production may distract the trainee and interfere with effective learning.

VESTIBULE TRAINING

Sometimes it is advantageous to learn a job on equipment which is identical to that used in actual production but which is away from the production area. Such an arrangement basically defines *vestibule* training. Instructors and trainees can concentrate totally on the learning to be done, and there is no problem with disrupting the flow of work in an actual production department. In addition, it is easier to assess the progress of the trainee under vestibule conditions. One study showed that vestibule training was the most successful of several training methods used as later measured in on-the-job performance.[2]

[2]William H. Holley, Jr., "Evaluation of Programs to Facilitate Effective Performance of the Disadvantaged Worker," *Training and Development Journal* 27, no. 2 (February 1973): 18–21.

CLASSROOM TRAINING

Low cost is perhaps the primary advantage of *classroom* training. A company is able to place many trainees into one classroom with only one instructor. While the "hands on" approach of on-the-job and vestibule training is invaluable, classroom training can be effective for certain kinds of learning. The theory of electricity or metal cutting, for example, or the principles of light construction are essential knowledge components for the budding electrician, machinist, and carpenter. If the lecture and textbook approach can be effectively augmented with films, slides, and other audiovisual materials, the classroom can be valuable.

APPRENTICESHIP TRAINING

Some jobs require highly developed skills, thorough knowledge, and considerable experience. For these jobs—such as electrician, tool and die maker, and engraver—*apprenticeship* training is the answer. It lasts several years. Trainees receive training both on and off the job. They receive careful and close instruction and guidance. Examinations are often given as part of the training, and for certain jobs such as electrician, there is often a state or local requirement for a final examination before an individual can practice the newly acquired trade as a full-fledged craftsman.

SIMULATION

For some jobs, learning in or on a piece of equipment that exactly and realistically imitates the real equipment is very effective. Pilots learn to fly in part by operating simulated airplane cockpits. The astronauts practiced for many hours in simulated space vehicles before actually going on the job—manning a space vehicle in flight.

There are other forms of job training, but these illustrate the types commonly used in business and industry. Training time varies greatly. To learn a simple assembly task may take only an hour. To learn to be an engraver takes four to five years. However, increased pay usually accompanies the job that requires the longest training.

MANAGEMENT DEVELOPMENT

All organizations appear to be interested in developing managerial personnel, from first-line supervisors on up. There are two important reasons for this interest and concern: (1) to help assure competency in the job currently held by the person, and (2) to help individuals realize their full potential and prepare for possible promotion to a higher-level position. Thus *management development* is important to an organization. It helps assure a continuing supply of people who can not only perform effectively now but are also prepared for greater responsibilities and authority.

To increase knowledge and skill, companies use a variety of training methods. These include *job rotation, on-the-job coaching,* being a *special assistant* to an executive, course work at universities, attendance at special seminars, and special assignments. There has been an emphasis in recent years on self-development on the job. The company encourages the supervisor or manager to make more decisions on his or her own, to take on more responsibility, and to be more independent. This pattern of encouragement also means that more mistakes will likely be made, and the organization must be prepared to tolerate these mistakes as young and aspiring managers try out their wings.

Changing Attitudes and Behavior   Another aspect of management development is the encouragement of change in attitudes and behavior so that interaction among fellow workers will be more productive and satisfying. One of the principal methods used to accomplish this has been *sensitivity training.* In its pure form trainees gather at some location away from the hustle and bustle of work. They meet in small groups of twelve to fifteen and spend one to two weeks in training.

In the training sessions, participants become very honest in their appraisals of one another. What happens, really, is that the participants provide mirrors for one another so that each person learns the others' view of himself or herself. These revelations can be shocking, of course, and there is usually a trained psychologist who acts as guide and counselor if necessary. As a result of sensitivity training, participants grow close to one another and develop substantial mutual liking. Another result is the learning of new attitudes and ways to behave which are not based solely on a desire to protect oneself from others. People learn to trust one another and to confront differences honestly and openly.

Unfortunately, unless all members of a department or a company attend sensitivity training, there is a tendency for its good effects to disappear. If only one person out of a department attends, the individual returns to a group which is the same as before. Unless that one person has had an opportunity to develop strength and confidence in his or her new attitudes and behavior, that employee is liable to revert to old patterns of behavior upon returning to the old group. For this reason, many companies using sensitivity training insist that all members of a department must attend if any are to attend.

PAY

In exchange for their contributions to an organization, people expect to receive something in return. The "something" is usually money, although in times past room and board sometimes served as pay—particularly for domestic help and farm labor. Pay rates vary, of course, but there is a minimum rate of pay established by the Fair Labor Standards Act of 1938 and subsequent amendments to the act. In addition to paying a minimum level of pay, the law requires most companies to pay time and one-half for hours worked beyond forty in any week.

Once past the minimum, many factors affect the level of pay. The supply of and demand for labor is an important determinant. In good times, when labor is relatively scarce, pay rates tend to rise. In poor economic times, many people are looking for jobs, and pay levels tend to remain static or drop. At times, however, inflation and high levels of unemployment occur simultaneously. Then we see the strange phenomenon of increasing wages and low demand for labor.

This phenomenon may be partially explained by the cost of living. In a period of inflation, there is tremendous pressure to increase wages even though there is high unemployment. Those who are working want pay increases to keep up with higher and higher costs of living. Many unions have a *cost-of-living factor* built into their contracts. When the cost-of-living price index goes up, the wage rate also automatically goes up to match the price increases. In labor contracts, this provision is called an *escalator clause*.

BARGAINING FOR WAGES

Where there is a union, the company bargains with it every one to three years to set appropriate wage levels for the union members. When the parties cannot agree, there may be a strike. Then it becomes a test of strength to see who can hold out the longest against the heavy economic pressures of a strike. If the strike involves an industry that is very important to the nation, such as transportation or energy, the government may seek to force a settlement. Unions, however, do not always want higher wages at any cost. There have been cases where a union has accepted a wage cut in order to help an ailing business get back on its feet.

INDIVIDUAL VARIATIONS IN PAY

An organization has many different rates of pay based on position and type of work. The president in most companies receives the highest pay, and it may be as high as $300,000 to $400,000 per year. In order to help assure a fair distribution

Figure 5-6 Sales incentive system with a guaranteed minimum.

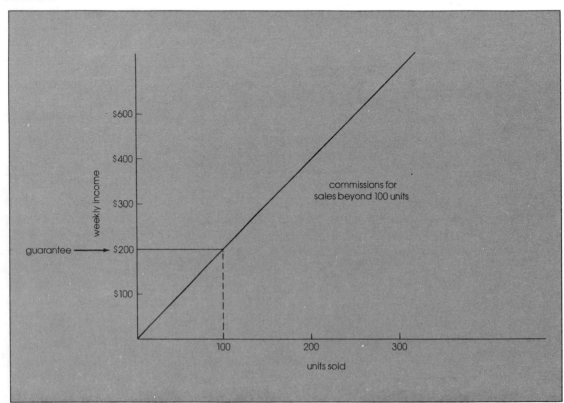

of wages or pay structure, most business organizations use a process called *job evaluation*. Persons trained in the method evaluate jobs on the basis of required skills, knowledge, mental and physical effort, responsibility, and working conditions.

For example, there might be two jobs which are equal in all factors except working conditions. One job might be done inside under very pleasant conditions, while the other is on the outside under all kinds of weather conditions. Because of the less desirable working conditions, the outside job probably would be assigned a somewhat higher rate of pay. Similarly, night work usually pays more than day work.

Incentive Plans   In addition to differences in pay based on organizational level and the nature of the job, differences also come about through the operation of *incentive plans*. Simply stated, the more one produces, the more one is paid. Salespeople who work on a commission basis are on an incentive plan. The more items or services a salesperson sells, the greater the pay. Figure 5–6 illustrates a type of incentive commission with a guaranteed minimum.

PERSONNEL CHANGES

Having selected, hired, trained, and paid a person, a company cannot assume that person will always remain in the same job. Many personnel changes occur: *transfers, promotions, discharges, quits, leaves of absence*, and *layoffs*.

TRANSFERS

A *transfer* is a change of job assignment that does not carry increased responsibility or pay. In other words, a transfer is not a promotion. It may mean moving to a different kind of job or to a different geographic location. Sometimes transfers occur because the employee wants to move. At other times, transfers are at the convenience of the company.

Many companies have made a practice of transferring young managers from job to job around the country in order to give them a variety of experience. A person may spend three years in California, two years in New York, four years in Montana, and perform several different jobs during that same span of time.

PROMOTIONS

A *promotion* is a change that does involve increased authority, responsibility, and pay. Most people hope and expect to be promoted, and it is a great incentive to hard work. There are some workers, however, who prefer the security of familiar work and surroundings and who do not wish to be promoted. When asked to step into a higher-level job, such as supervisor or foreman, these workers will turn it down.

Evaluations for Promotion   Companies commonly use *evaluations* as a basis for promotion. The evaluations primarily try to measure performance on a job, but personal factors such as cooperation are often part of the total evaluation. There are a wide variety of evaluation methods, none of which is entirely satisfactory. A common one is the *graphic rating scale*. The scale lists several factors pertaining to performance of a job and perhaps the personal characteristics of the person. The evaluator, usually the person's boss, then checks or circles a point on each circle to indicate an appraisal of the employee. Figure 5–7 shows a form of graphic rating scale.

Another basis for promotion is seniority—that is, the person with the longest time on a job is the one promoted. Railroads, for example, typically use a seniority system for promotion through train crew ranks.

DISCHARGES AND QUITS

A discharge, or being fired, is usually unpleasant but sometimes necessary. Many managers do not like to fire an employee, even though the employee is clearly incompetent. It is far more difficult to fire a competent employee, which is occasionally necessary when a company must reduce operations. In fact, discharging an employee presents such a problem that a number of companies such as Exxon and Mutual of New York have hired consultants to help solve the problem.[3]

The consultants do not always do the actual firing but often advise a company on how to handle the firing. In addition, the consultant will usually work with the person who was fired to help him or her find a new job. A consultant will advise a company that a firing should be brief and to the point. It should be

[3]"How Consultants Make Firing Easier," *Business Week*, July 20, 1974, pp. 67–68.

"I think Personnel took my request for a move further south too literally when they transferred me to the Amazon."

employee's name_____   department_____
supervisor_____   date_____

check the square ☐ that most appropriately describes the employee in the current job.

	unsatisfactory	fair	satisfactory	very satisfactory	outstanding
1. knowledge of work: clear understanding of all phases of job	☐	☐	☐	☐	☐
2. quality of work: dimensional accuracy and appearance	☐	☐	☐	☐	☐
3. initiative: willingness and ability to start and work without close direction	☐	☐	☐	☐	☐
4. cooperation: willingness and ability to work with supervisor and coworkers	☐	☐	☐	☐	☐
5. overall effectiveness: quantity and quality of work and personal qualities such as initiative, cooperation, and leadership	☐	☐	☐	☐	☐

Figure 5-7   Graphic rating scale.

stated in a matter-of-fact manner and should be done in a conference room or the employee's office so the firer can leave and avoid the embarrassment of dragging out an uncomfortable task. In addition, the person who was fired would most likely want to be alone after hearing the news. Consultants are used predominantly in those cases in which executives must be fired. This does not mean it is easier to fire lower-level employees. It simply means that companies can afford consultants only for a limited number of their employees. General advice on how to fire someone, of course, may be used throughout the organization.

Quits or leaving a job voluntarily are more common than firings and stem from a variety of reasons: moving to a better job, moving to a different location, and going back to school are just a few.

Frequently when a person quits, the personnel department will request an opportunity for a talk with the individual who is leaving. Termed an *exit interview*, the intent of the talk is to determine what the individual leaving can relate about experiences and attitudes while with the company. It is felt that when someone is leaving, there is no longer much reason not to be completely honest in comments about the company. In this way, the organization may discover facts about itself that can lead to improvements in policies and practices. While many people do tend to be more frank and open in an exit interview, there are others who do not want to burn any bridges behind them. These latter people may not be honest, therefore, in criticisms of the company. On the whole, exit interviews have not proven to be consistently helpful.

LAYOFFS AND LEAVES OF ABSENCE

In times of economic slowdown for a company, industry, or the nation, layoffs do occur. A layoff is a temporary termination of employment with an expectation of recall. Layoffs last anywhere from a few days to a few months. In most cases, employees who are laid off can receive *unemployment compensation.* This is money paid out by the government but derived from a special tax on employers. Unemployment compensation can be paid for as long as six months. In addition, many workers, particularly in the automobile industry, receive *supplemental unemployment benefits* (SUB) when laid off.

SUB plans are privately arranged between the employer and employees, usually as the result of collective bargaining. The combination of state unemployment compensation and SUB income can result in payments that reach as high as 90 percent of regular wages. Before actually having to lay off employees, many employers will resort first to short work weeks of three or four days in order to stretch the work. If business keeps falling, however, layoffs become inevitable.

One company that has successfully avoided the layoff problem is IBM.[4] The company claims it has never had to lay off a worker for economic reasons in over thirty-five years of operation. IBM has experienced almost constant growth during its history, of course, but an important contributing reason for zero layoffs is its retraining program. If one part of the organization is decreasing in size and eliminating workers, they are not laid off but are retrained for different jobs. One person went from secretary to sales representative, while another moved from warehouse work to field service. Both received substantial training for their new positions.

A leave of absence ordinarily is at the request of the employee and may come about because of military service, a desire to return to school, or many other reasons. If granted, the individual on leave usually does not receive any pay during the period of the leave.

MORE PERSONNEL ACTIVITY AT THE CANDY EMPORIUM

Under the management of Geri Rogers and Art Lindstrom, The Candy Emporium had continued to grow. Geri and Art had decided to hire another employee. Since they had already been through the hiring process once, things moved quickly this time. It had become apparent that a full-time clerk was needed, so they drew up a job description and job specification for this kind of job.

About halfway through the interviewing, their first employee, Ann, asked to

[4]"How IBM Avoids Layoffs Through Training," *Business Week,* November 10, 1975, pp. 110–112.

talk with them. Ann had been working primarily in production as planned, but she surprised Geri and Art by asking if she could fill the job of clerk while the new person would learn production. It turned out that Ann had really enjoyed the small amount of clerking she did and felt she had a real aptitude for it. After some discussion, Geri and Art agreed.

It was not hard to switch gears. Geri and Art continued interviewing using the job description and specification that applied to Ann's job in production. Within a week, they hired Tom for the production job, and Ann transferred to retail.

EMPLOYEE HEALTH AND SAFETY

Job-related accidents and illnesses are serious problems for most businesses. The costs are large and include not only direct medical expenses but lost production, the time to investigate causes of accidents, and personnel replacement costs. Hence there are not only moral and ethical reasons to provide safe and healthy working conditions but cost reasons as well.

Despite these reasons, many companies have been guilty of not providing the working conditions that will minimize accidents and sickness. Because of this, the federal government in 1970 passed the *Occupational Safety and Health Act* (OSHA). The act sets forth standards for safety and health, requires on-site inspections, and stipulates various penalties for violations.

Companies should make sure that workers have adequate lighting; that the noise level will not be injurious to hearing and, if possible, will not be disturbing; that atmospheric conditions are healthy; and that physical facilities in general are as attractive, clean, and neat as possible. All possible safety precautions should be taken with respect to equipment, worker education, accident investigation, and elimination of hazards.

Larger companies usually maintain one or more nurses on duty and, in some cases, employ a doctor on a regular basis. In addition, supervisors and security personnel frequently receive training in first aid. If a worker is injured on the job, all states now have laws, called *workers' compensation laws,* that provide for payment to a worker of a percentage of the individual's normal wages while away from work as a result of injuries. There are also provisions for at least partial payment of medical and hospitalization expenses. Many companies carry additional insurance, or at least make it available to employees, to cover disability periods and medical expenses more fully than the minimums specified by law.

Companies should also recognize that people who are emotionally upset, younger persons, and inexperienced workers tend to have relatively high accident rates. It is important, therefore, to be especially careful with new employees and those who are known to have some difficult personal problems.

SERVICES AND BENEFITS

A feeling of security is very important to most employees, and one of the greatest benefits that can be provided an employee is a guarantee of retirement income. In conjunction with Social Security provisions for retirement, many companies also have private retirement income programs. Some companies completely finance these plans, and in other cases, the employees contribute to the retirement fund along with the employer. The amount of retirement income usually depends on length of service and income received while employed. Up to a point, the longer a person works for a given organization and the higher the wages or salaries earned, the more that person will receive in retirement income.

One of the current problems of retirement plans involves *mobility* and *vesting*. Vesting refers to the claim an employee has to company-contributed money in the retirement plan at any given time. For example, a company may say that an employee with less than ten years' service has no claim to any money the company has contributed for that employee to the retirement fund, but after ten years each has a 50 percent claim, and after twenty years the employee has full rights to all money the company has contributed. This means that a person who moves around quite a bit may never build any funds in a private plan and may never receive retirement income from private sources.

For this reason, much thought has been given to improved vesting and to portable pension plans, where a person would simply transfer accrued personal pension funds from one company to another or have the funds in a large pool in which many companies would participate. Recent federal legislation has taken steps to improve the handling of retirement funds from the standpoint of employee rights to money contributed by companies. Of course, any money that an employee has contributed out of his or her own pay always belongs to the employee.

PRERETIREMENT COUNSELING

A valuable adjunct to company-assisted financial planning for retirement is preretirement counseling. Research evidence indicates that relatively few companies provide such counseling for their employees. Yet there is also evidence that preretirement counseling is valuable in helping to assure adequate financial planning, deciding where to live in retirement, setting up retirement activities, and generally helping to achieve a satisfying life in retirement.

OTHER SERVICES AND BENEFITS

There are many other services and benefits that a company may provide. Typical of these are credit unions, various insurance programs, recreational programs, assistance in finding housing, personal counseling, food services, and the financing of social functions. While it has never been proved that any of these benefits or services contribute to greater production, they do enhance the image of an organization as a good place to work.

HUMAN ASSETS ACCOUNTING

Some companies are quite interested these days in placing a value on people or groups of people. This new idea does not envision placing these people values on a published financial statement. Rather, the intent is to use *human assets accounting* as an aid to managerial decision making.

Companies always place a value on assets such as equipment and furniture. The value might be the purchase cost, the cost of replacement, or the contribution a piece of production equipment might make over several future years. People can be valued in the same way. What does it cost to hire and train an individual? What would it cost to replace someone? What is the value of an individual's contribution over the next twenty years?

Human assets accounting can be helpful in personnel actions such as transfers of personnel, rewarding of individual employees, and in placing a human assets value on the total organization. In transfers, human assets accounting makes possible the computation of loss of value to one part of an organization and the gain to another. Reward practices would probably be more equitable if individual rewards were geared to individual value. And the total human value of an organization could be determined in dollars by adding up all the dollar values placed on individuals. Human assets accounting has a brief history, but it will likely develop further in the future.

SUMMARY

We have seen that the need for people involves an organization in many activities—recruiting, selecting, placement, paying wages and salaries, training, safety and health programs, and providing employee services and benefits. These can all be grouped under the heading of personnel management or personnel administration. This is a vital function in all businesses, and the personnel manager or industrial relations director is often at the vice-presidential level.

In a small business, one person may handle all of the activities involved in the personnel function. In a large company, you will find much specialization, and a person can make an entire career in areas such as wage and salary administration or training. In the large company, however, it is usual for personnel workers to gain experience in several of these different areas since those who gain promotions to higher levels in personnel management should have knowledge of all the activities they direct. Thus, there are many opportunities in the personnel area of business management, and it is a challenging and fascinating component of the total business system.

DISCUSSION QUESTIONS

1. Would a family-owned business with fifty employees need a personnel inventory to keep track of anticipated openings and possible replacements? Why or why not?

2. Do you think that job descriptions, which spell out the duties of a job, are viewed by employees as restricting their freedom at work? Would employees rather not have job descriptions?

3. Companies sometimes recruit widely—at college campuses, for example—even though the companies will hire very few or no new employees. Why do firms do this? Do you think this action is fair to the person who interviews with such a company for a job?

4. Why do companies train people who have been to college? Should not these individuals already have enough education and training to hold a job successfully?

5. Incentive pay plans allow workers to earn wages according to how much they produce. If this seems to be a fair system to you, why should not all wage and salary plans be on an incentive basis?

6. Working hard for a promotion seems almost to be an American tradition. Can you think of any circumstances in which an individual might not want a promotion?

7. Human assets accounting seeks to place values on human beings. Do you believe this is a proper way to view people? Why or why not?

SHORT CASES

Work on a Steel Island[5]

The Mobil Oil Company employs another company, Zapata Off-Shore Company, to drill for oil in the Gulf of Mexico. One of Zapata's offshore rigs is the Concord, which works as much as 100 miles from the Texas coast. Some seventy people are always at work on the Concord, which is twenty-three stories high and as long and wide as a football field. Work goes on twenty-four hours a day, seven days a week.

The crew has comfortable quarters, including a lounge, but the noise of the machinery and the motion of the sea are constant. Each person works a twelve-hour shift and has seven days in a row on the rig and then seven days ashore. For recreation, workers have reading, movies, TV, fishing for sharks, and conversation. The work is dirty and sometimes dangerous, but the pay is good.

Would you enjoy working on an offshore oil rig like the Concord? Why or why not?

What particular personnel problems might be encountered in staffing and operating offshore oil rigs? How would these problems compare with those in staffing and operating a large insurance company office?

The Decompression Tank[6]

The Xerox Corporation has a division called Xerox Consultants, Inc. Called XCI, it is an internal consulting group staffed by Xerox executives who are nearing retirement age. However, executive officers as young as fifty-three have been assigned to XCI. XCI functions as a decompression tank because it allows executives to break away gradually from their regular demanding duties with the parent company by doing internal consulting with Xerox as well as a gradually increasing amount of external consulting for other companies.

However, some of the executives assigned to XCI have left after only a few months or a year or two to take regular managerial positions with other companies. Salaries of officers assigned to XCI are gradually reduced as their internal consulting obligations decrease. Only the chairman and the president of Xerox are exempt from going to XCI no later than age sixty. The president of Xerox recommends the executives who will go into XCI.

Do you think that assignment to the XCI division of Xerox Corporation is the same as being fired?

Should people be forced to retire at age sixty or earlier? What are the benefits and costs of early retirement?

Will other companies pattern their retirement systems for executives after the Xerox system?

SUGGESTED READINGS

Chruden, Herbert J., and Sherman, Arthur W., Jr. *Personnel Management.* 5th ed. Cincinnati: South-Western Publishing Co., 1976.

French, Wendell L. *The Personnel Management Process: Human Resources Administration.* 3rd ed. Boston: Houghton Mifflin, 1974.

---

[5]"Offshore Drilling Is a World Apart," *Fortune,* no. 6 (December 1976): 74–81.
[6]"A Decompression Tank for Xerox Executives," *Business Week,* May 16, 1977, p. 64.

LABOR UNIONS

LEARNING OBJECTIVES

When you finish this chapter you should:
- [ ] have a basic understanding of unions and the labor movement.
- [ ] be familiar with the basic types of unions and how unions are organized.
- [ ] have an awareness of how the labor movement struggled for survival and recognition.
- [ ] be familiar with the major laws governing the relationship between companies and unions.
- [ ] understand the labor-management bargaining process and the development of a contract.
- [ ] be familiar with the basic terms of a contract that is the result of bargaining.
- [ ] understand the role of unions in the economic system, including the benefits of the labor movement.

KEY TERMS TO LEARN FROM THIS CHAPTER

agency shop	craft union	labor union	secondary boycott
arbitration	fringe benefits	lockout	seniority
bargaining	grievance	management rights	strike
(collective)	grievance pro-	mediation	union security
boycott	cedure	picket	union shop
closed shop	industrial union	preferential shop	wages
contract	injunction	primary boycott	yellow-dog contract

If you were to go out on the street and ask ten different people to tell you what a *labor union* is, you would probably get ten different answers. Some answers would reflect a highly favorable view of unions, while others may embody deep distrust and hatred. Some answers would be couched in highly colorful language, while others would be drab and impersonal. Any discussion of unions frequently arouses emotional reaction. It is important, therefore, to have a clear understanding of the relationship between unions and business.

A union is a private organization of workers who have joined together to advance their common interests. In its method of operation, a union most resembles a private lodge or church group. With respect to its relationship with a business organization, a union typically strives to improve wages and working conditions, to help insure employment security for members, and to institute a system of justice to help assure equitable treatment of all workers.

Beyond its immediate relationship with a specific business organization, unions also seek to influence the political process through support of political candidates and lobbying efforts to influence legislation. Union members pay dues, hold meetings, elect their own officers, and vote on whether to accept employment terms offered by their employer. Unions vary in size and in the characteristics of the members. The local union is at the base of the total union organization structure. A local union may deal with one or more employers, but it usually operates within a limited geographic area. Most negotiations over contracts occur at the level of the local union.

TYPES OF UNIONS

There are two basic varieties of unions: *craft* unions and *industrial* unions.

CRAFT UNIONS

Craft unions organize all workers of a particular skill into one local union in a given geographic area. The building craft unions are perhaps the best known. These include plumbers, electricians, bricklayers, carpenters, and so on. A craft union of electrical workers, for example, may negotiate with several employers who employ members of that particular union. Instead of the workers themselves doing the negotiating, perhaps through an elected representative, the craft unions typically hire a full-time business agent. The agent not only does the negotiating for the craft union but represents the union in all its relationships with employers.

To gain membership in a craft union, a person must first go through an extensive apprenticeship program to learn a particular skill. Since craft unions often join in the administration of apprenticeship programs with employers, the unions typically control entry into the training programs as well as into the union. Because of this form of monopoly power over the supply of skilled labor, craft unions are usually very effective in bargaining with employers over wages and working conditions. When the electricians, for example, walk off a construction site to strike for higher wages, all other building craft unions stay away from the construction site as well. In this way new construction is completely stopped and the employing contractor stands to lose considerable amounts of money every day.

In recent years, however, increasing numbers of construction workers have been willing to work on a nonunion basis because of the limited demand for new construction and, therefore, a limited demand for construction workers. The power of a craft union, as with any union, varies with economic conditions. When times are prosperous and there is a high demand for labor, unions enjoy peak power. In a period of recession when there is low demand for labor, the power of the union is tempered considerably.

INDUSTRIAL UNIONS

The second major type of local union is the industrial union. The principal difference between an industrial union and a craft union is that while the craft union organizes one particular type of skilled labor, such as the electricians, the industrial union organizes all levels of skilled labor within a given plant. It is a wall-to-wall union within a plant and may include such diverse types of employees as assemblers, drill press operators, lift truck operators, and janitors. A local union of the United Auto Workers is an example of an industrial union.

Industrial unions bargain over wages, working conditions, and other matters just as craft unions do. Since industrial unions have little or no influence over hiring, however, they tend to have much more complex and comprehensive labor-management agreements than do craft unions. Through its contract, the industrial union attempts to gain for itself the same sort of protection that a craft

union does through controlling its membership and entry into the craft. Industrial union contracts specify in great detail provisions for seniority, methods of layoff, and even the amount of work that may be expected from certain kinds of employees.

Unless they are quite large, industrial unions do not hire a professional business agent. Instead, they conduct their affairs through their own elected officers. The elected officer most responsible for the day-to-day conduct of union affairs is the shop steward. In each department of a manufacturing plant, there is very likely to be a shop steward. In many respects the union steward is the counterpart of the foreman. The steward is the local leader, and one of his principal duties is to see that the company adheres to the union contract. The shop steward also holds a regular job as an employee of the company.

If an individual worker feels the contract has been violated in some way that affects him or her, the worker will go to the steward. The steward then has the responsibility to present the *grievance* to the foreman and ask that the foreman take action to correct the grievance. If the foreman cannot or will not take action, then the grievance goes to a higher level—perhaps to the foreman's supervisor. If the supervisor cannot settle the disagreement, it goes on up in the organization, eventually perhaps reaching top management. If, finally, no settlement can be reached, the company and the union usually agree to call in an outside third party, usually an arbitrator, to make a settlement.

Figure 6-1   A sample grievance procedure.

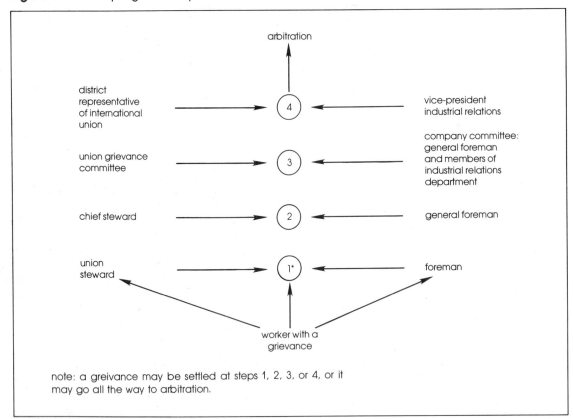

note: a greivance may be settled at steps 1, 2, 3, or 4, or it may go all the way to arbitration.

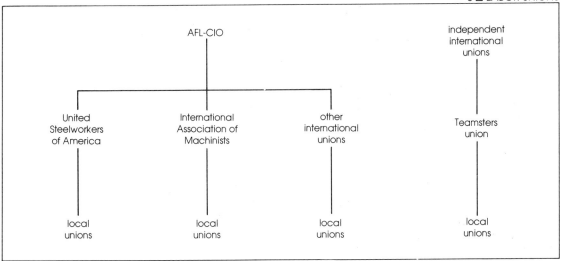

Figure 6-2 Local unions, international unions, and an independent union.

The process we have just described is a *grievance procedure.* Over 90 percent of contracts between industrial unions and companies have provisions for a grievance procedure. Figure 6–1 illustrates the basic steps in a grievance procedure.

NATIONAL UNIONS

When one or more local unions form themselves into a larger union, the larger union is a national union. The big national unions are frequently in the news, and the reader will probably recognize several of them. They include the United Auto Workers (UAW), the United Steelworkers of America (USA), the International Association of Machinists (IAM), and the United Mine Workers (UMW).

National unions can exercise fairly close control over their locals. The national unions constantly try to organize more workers and more unions. They help the local unions with their bargaining activities and attempt to influence legislation on both state and federal levels. Many of the national unions are affiliated with the American Federation of Labor and the Congress of Industrial Organizations (AFL-CIO). Major exceptions to membership in the AFL-CIO include the United Mine Workers, the United Auto Workers, and the Teamsters Union. These powerful, independent national unions do not share the AFL-CIO umbrella either because they feel no need for it or because they differ philosophically from the AFL-CIO.

The AFL-CIO functions predominantly on the national and international level. The president of the AFL-CIO interacts frequently with members of Congress as well as with the president of the United States. It is a powerful political organization and frequently has a major impact on the outcome of national elections. Being a loosely organized federation, the AFL-CIO exercises little or no control over international and local unions, but it presents a powerful voice for all of its members on the national scene. Figure 6–2 shows some of the relationships between local unions, national unions, and parent organizations such as the AFL-CIO.

UNIONS: THE DESPERATE STRUGGLE TO GROW

The development of the labor movement in the United States is marked by great struggle and moments of high achievement. American workers began to organize themselves into formal labor unions in the early part of the nineteenth century. Shoemakers, for example, organized one of the first unions in 1820. Little progress was apparent, however, until after the Civil War. Then, with fast growth in railroads, steel mills, and factories, many more unions formed. By 1880, there were about forty unions in the country with a membership approaching 300,000.

Among these unions were the Brotherhood of the Footboard (which subsequently changed its name to the Brotherhood of Locomotive Engineers), the Sons of Vulcan (Ironworkers), and the Knights of Saint Crispin (a new label for the old shoemakers' union). Then in 1869, the Knights of Labor was formed. It was an umbrella organization, similar to the present AFL-CIO in that respect. The Knights welcomed all comers—highly skilled craftsmen, unskilled labor, literally anyone who staked a claim to labor.

The Knights grew to over 700,000 in membership after supporting and winning some strikes, most notably against the Missouri Pacific Railroad. It was also involved in violence in connection with some strikes. And as the violence continued, a large segment of the public began to turn against unions, particularly the Knights of Labor. Three events finally spelled the end for the Knights: (1) the loss of a strike against several southwestern railroads, (2) a failure to support a general strike for the eight-hour day, and (3) a bombing in Haymarket Square, Chicago, where the Knights had called a meeting. The bombing killed several people, and the Knights were unfairly blamed for the incident. Thus, the year 1886, when these events occurred, spelled doom for the Knights of Labor.

The failure of the Knights gave fresh opportunity to another labor organization, the National Federation of Organized Trades and Labor Unions, started in 1881 under the leadership of Samuel Gompers. In 1886, Gompers recruited the craft assemblies—the highly skilled craft workers—from the faltering Knights and renamed his National Federation the American Federation of Labor (AFL). In that year the AFL had twenty-five affiliated craft unions and a membership of roughly 300,000. By 1905, however, the AFL had close to two million members and has survived every challenge to the present day.

THE FACTORY WORKER: NO PLACE TO GO

With the demise of the Knights and the rise of the AFL and its restricted membership (highly skilled craft workers only), the unskilled and semiskilled factory workers were left without a home. For a brief time before World War I, the Industrial Workers of the World (IWW or the "Wobblies" as they were called) offered some hope to the factory worker. But the IWW was organized by radicals, some of whom preached and practiced violence. Their strikes against equally violence-prone employers were nothing short of small wars. The violence, the radical philosophy of the IWW, and the steadfast opposition of the AFL turned many workers away from the "Wobblies." By World War I, the IWW had faded away as an organization.

During the depression of the 1930s, a powerful labor leader came into his own—John L. Lewis, president of the United Mine Workers (UMW). The UMW was a member of the AFL and was the only industrial union in that organization. Lewis had been successful in organizing all the independent mines, but he had had no success in organizing the captive mines—those owned by steel mills. And he rightly figured that the only way to do that was to organize the steel mills first.

However, the AFL was opposed to organizing an entire company, factory, or mill because that would mean including all the semiskilled and unskilled workers in the union. As a result of this dispute and other problems, Lewis was expelled from the AFL. Along with several other union leaders, he then organized the Congress of Industrial Organizations (CIO). The CIO was dedicated to industrial unionism and organizing entire plants and companies and every worker in them.

The CIO was successful. Its two greatest victories, perhaps, were the organization of the steelworkers and the auto workers. Out of these efforts came two of today's most powerful unions—the United Steelworkers of America and the United Auto Workers. For many years, the AFL and the CIO went their separate ways. Finally, in 1955 these two great international unions united to form the present-day AFL-CIO.

While the history of labor was unfolding, there were court cases and laws passed by the United States Congress which affected how unions and companies could behave with respect to one another. In a sense, these laws and court decisions governed the play of the game.

THE RULES OF THE GAME

In the early 1800s, unions attempting to organize often ran smack into possible legal action for criminal activity. It was the conspiracy doctrine, under which unions could be charged with the illegal act of conspiracy if they attempted to organize and exert economic pressure on an employer. Then in a court case in 1842, *Commonwealth* v. *Hunt,* earlier interpretations of the conspiracy doctrine with respect to unions were reversed. Being set free from the possible charge of conspiracy was a major victory for unions.

Early federal legislation included the Arbitration Act of 1888 and the Erdman Act of 1898. These laws were directed toward settlement of disputes in the railroad industry through encouragement of voluntary actions by the two parties. Since the government had a degree of regulatory power over the railroads, the laws had some power behind them. The Sherman Anti-Trust Act of 1888 sought to prevent monopoly control by business organizations, but business also used it against unions.

In 1903, for example, the hatters' union boycotted and encouraged others to boycott the products of a Danbury, Connecticut, hat company. In a *boycott,* the union members and others are encouraged not to buy the products of a particular company. The hat company sued for triple damages in the amount of $240,000 under the Sherman Anti-Trust Act. The Supreme Court ruled in favor of the company, and the union had to pay the full amount of the damages. Later on, the Clayton Act (1914) exempted unions from many provisions of the Sherman Act.

MODERN LEGISLATION

Prior to the 1930s, labor unions and companies stood toe to toe and slugged it out. There were very few laws to govern the relationship between a union and a company. Workers in a company who wished to organize a union frequently encountered violence and returned violence. In the Homestead Steel strike of 1892, workers fought and defeated armed Pinkerton men employed by the company but then were in turn defeated by government troops. Many other incidents of violence involving workers and troops or police occurred in the following years. There were company spies, boycotts, blackmail, and *yellow-dog contracts*—whereby any newly hired worker would sign a pledge promising never to join a union. And it was very easy for a company to get a court order or an *injunction* that would force a union to stop organizing activities or even to stop a strike.

The beginning of fairness in the union-company relationship came in 1932 with passage of the Norris-LaGuardia Act, which severely restricted the use of injunctions by business in labor disputes. Under this act the yellow-dog contract was not forbidden but was made unenforceable by the courts. The big change came in 1935, however, with passage of the National Labor Relations Act or Wagner Act. This act was so far reaching in its benefits for the labor movement that it has been called the Magna Carta of labor.

THE WAGNER ACT

The Wagner Act was the first nationwide labor law to set out a reasonably comprehensive set of rules for organizing a union and for carrying on bargaining

Figure 6-3 Federal laws affecting management and labor.

1888	Arbitration Act	encouraged settlement of disputes in railroad industry
1890	Sherman Antitrust Act	used by business to stop boycotts, picketing, and other union activity
1898	Erdman Act	encouraged settlement of disputes in railroad industry
1914	Clayton Act	restricted use of Sherman Act against unions
1932	Norris-La Guardia Act	made the yellow-dog contract unenforceable and restricted use of injunctions
1935	Wagner Act	Guaranteed workers the right to organize and bargain over wages, hours, and working conditions. Set up NLRB
1947	Taft-Hartley Act	balanced power by restricting certain union actions
1959	Landrum-Griffin Act	protects rights of union members

between a company and the union. It guaranteed workers the right to organize and to bargain collectively, and it prohibited employers from interfering with or discriminating against workers who support the formation of a labor union. The act also set up a procedure whereby workers could hold an election to determine if they wanted a union, and it set up the National Labor Relations Board to administer the law. From 1935 to 1947, labor union membership grew from fewer than five million workers to over fifteen million.

THE TAFT-HARTLEY ACT

By 1947 many people, most notably employers, felt that the Wagner Act was too one-sided in favor of labor. The law prohibited several unfair practices on the part of employers—for example, an employer could not refuse to bargain with a union—but none on the part of labor. As a result of this and a rash of strikes in 1946 and 1947, the Labor Management Relations Act or Taft-Hartley Act of 1947 was passed. This act prohibited several unfair labor practices on the part of unions. Among other items, this law did not allow unions to refuse to bargain collectively or to force an employer to discriminate against the nonunion employee. The Taft-Hartley Act also set up rules for the fair administration of unions by union people and required secret ballots in all cases in which workers were voting on whether or not to have a union. Unions generally disliked the Taft-Hartley Act, and many union leaders referred to it as a "slave-labor" act.

THE LANDRUM-GRIFFIN ACT

The 1950s were marked by a great deal of publicity about alleged skulduggery in the labor movement. Finally, the U.S. Senate established the McClellan Committee. Under the leadership of Senator McClellan, the committee investigated many local and national unions as well as several national union leaders. Their findings pointed out the lack of democracy in many local unions and revealed a substantial amount of local racketeering going on. In addition, the committee discovered union funds being used for the personal benefit of some union leaders, the continuing use of violence, and unsavory connections between some union leaders and known gangsters.

The upshot of the investigation and its attendant publicity was passage of the Landrum-Griffin Act in 1959. This law required the reelection by secret ballot of local union officers at least once every three years and of national officers at least once every five years. There were provisions in the act to protect individual union members against union discrimination, and the act also required all unions to file periodic reports on their constitutions and particularly on their financial transactions.

These laws as we have briefly described them set up the rules for organized collective bargaining and the internal administration of unions. Interpretation of these laws by the National Labor Relations Board and the courts has resulted in a complex body of knowledge that now requires expert advice by specialized labor lawyers. Nonetheless, these are the rules, as many managers and labor leaders have learned to their chagrin after violating some provisions of the laws. Figure 6–3 shows the sequence of congressional approval of these labor laws as well as their primary purposes.

THE BARGAINING PROCESS

For the purpose of illustrating the process of organizing and bargaining, let us assume that an imaginary union, the Amalgamated Union of Flat Iron Workers, wants to organize the workers in the Jones Flat Iron Company. First of all, union representatives approach the workers during their lunch hour, on their breaks, or at their homes. They ask the workers if they would like to have a union and seek to get the workers to sign authorization cards. When 30 percent or more of the employees of the Jones Flat Iron Company sign authorization cards, the union is then in a position to request the National Labor Relations Board (NLRB) to hold a hearing. The purpose of a hearing is to determine if a representation election should be held. In our case, the NLRB ruled yes and so an election was held within sixty days, as required by law. Using a secret ballot, a majority of the employees of the Jones Flat Iron Company voted to have the Amalgamated Union of Flat Iron Workers represent them. The NLRB certified the results of the election, and the Jones Flat Iron Company now deals with a union.

The union is authorized to bargain for wages, hours, and other terms and conditions of employment for the employees it now represents.

The first phase in the *bargaining* process is preparation on the parts of both the union and the employer. The union will study the wage structure of the company, its seniority and layoff provisions, job descriptions, and other matters pertaining to the potential contract. One of the things the union will do is to compare the information they get from the Jones Flat Iron Company with conditions of employment at other similar companies. In the bargaining they will attempt to make conditions at Jones equal to, or better than, conditions at other companies. At a meeting of the union the members then will appoint a committee to draw up a list of demands to be presented to the company.

The company also needs to prepare. If the company does not have exact information on its cost structure, it should get it. The company should determine in advance in what areas it wishes to hold fast and in what areas it may wish to yield. The company will also want to do some comparative studies of other companies and their conditions of employment.

THE FACE-TO-FACE MEETING

Finally, the two parties meet face to face. There will be a bargaining team to represent the company and a bargaining team to represent the union. In smaller companies, the bargaining team may be composed of the president and several other executive officers. The union typically will send its president and its other elected officers to bargain.

Since the union is a political organization with elected officers, these officers usually desire to put on a show for its members. If the president, for example, presents the union demands, there may be a considerable display of dramatics so that the other officers will report back to the membership that he is really trying and doing a good job. Depending upon the personality of the company representatives, they, too, may engage in a certain amount of overacting. Eventually, however, if a settlement is to be reached, both sides will have to take a reasoned approach in the give and take of the bargaining.

There are two basic strategic approaches that unions use in bargaining. One is the piecemeal approach, and the other is the total approach. In the piecemeal approach, unions try to get one small item settled at a time, gradually working toward a complete settlement and signed contract. In the total approach, nothing is ever regarded as being settled until the two parties finally reach a total agreement on everything. The union may well prefer the piecemeal approach since it feels it may be able to get certain items nailed down early while carrying on a vigorous attack on following items. The company on the other hand often wants to see the whole package before finally making any agreement.

When Negotiations Break Down   What happens when collective bargaining breaks down and the two parties just cannot come to any agreement? There are several options. The company and the union may decide to take a break for a few days and then resume negotiations. They may ask a third party to come in to help them out. The federal government through its Federal Mediation and Conciliation Service offers this kind of assistance. When requested, the mediation service will send a person who acts as an independent, impartial, third party in an effort to bring the union and the company together. The mediator talks to each side alone, talks to both sides when they are together, and simply tries in one way or another to get the company and the union finally to agree.

In some cases *arbitration* may be the answer. Typically neither the union nor the company generally favors arbitration. Arbitration differs from *mediation* in that a ruling of the arbitrator must be accepted by both parties. Usually neither party is willing to take this risk when negotiations over contract terms are at stake.

The last alternative we will mention, the most dramatic of all, is the *strike*. The strike is the ultimate economic weapon of the union. Its intent is to close down a plant and cause the employer to suffer daily losses. Ordinarily a vote on a strike will have been taken by the union early in the negotiations. This vote lets the company know that the union is prepared to strike if necessary.

A strike can be costly to a union as well. It members lose wages, the company may hire other workers to replace the strikers, or the company may even go out of business. For the individual worker, the strike means at least a loss of some income and at most some possibility that his or her job will disappear. In addition, when a person has never been on a strike, it is so contrary to long-established work habits that many workers find it extremely difficult to stay home or stay away from work on the day a strike is to take place. More than one called strike has been ruined for the union because some workers at least were unable to stay away and reported to work as usual.

Mediation can still go on during a strike with some third party still attempting to get the company and the union together. In the vast majority of cases, ultimately some agreement is reached as one party or the other or both make certain concessions. There have been cases, however, when the union has been completely defeated, with the company replacing all the union workers with other people. There have been other cases when a company has been completely defeated and forced out of business. A strike itself is relatively rare, however, given the total number of negotiations that go on in the country every year, and the final defeat of one party or the other is even more rare.

A strike is the ultimate economic weapon of a union.

The vast majority of collective bargaining negotiations are peaceably settled without a strike or without the need for mediation or arbitration. The strikes that hit the newspaper and command attention usually involve one of the national unions or some badly needed service such as airplane travel or even police protection. The collective bargaining process does work and works successfully most of the time.

THE CONTRACT

What is the nature of the *contract* that comes out of the collective bargaining negotiations? It is usually in the form of a little booklet and covers such items as grievances and the *grievance procedure, arbitration, union security, management rights, wages, seniority,* and various *fringe benefits.* We have discussed several of these but have not touched upon union security or management rights.

UNION SECURITY

A union seeks to secure its position with respect to the company by one of several forms of recognition. The strongest form of legal recognition for an industrial union is the *union shop.* Under the union shop arrangement a person does not have to be a union member in order to get a job, but must join the union within a certain period after being hired. The net result is that all employees in the bargaining unit are dues-paying union members. The union shop is a considerable source of strength, therefore, to the representative union.

Some states, however, have right-to-work laws which prohibit the union shop. To get around these laws to some extent, certain states allow a union to bargain for an *agency shop.* In this arrangement, members of a bargaining unit are not forced to join the union, but must pay the same initiation fees and dues as the regular members. The rationale for this arrangement is that the dues and the initiation fee are service charges paid to the union for representing all the workers in the bargaining relationship.

Craft unions enjoy the strongest form of recognition of all—the *closed shop.* Strictly speaking, the closed shop means a person must be a union member before he or she can be hired. The Taft-Hartley Act outlawed the closed shop, but it still exists with a slight variation as the *preferential shop.* Technically, an employer has the right to hire a nonunion person in one of the craft occupations, but after only a seven-day probationary period, the worker must join the union. In actual practice such a short probationary period is unrealistic, and most employers prefer to go to the union hiring hall for union members when hiring new workers. Hence there is in fact a closed-shop form of recognition.

These are the principal forms of the union recognition which enable unions to build and maintain membership as a source of strength for the bargaining relationship. Companies also seek to preserve and maintain certain conditions and prerogatives with respect to their relationships with unions.

WHAT ARE MANAGEMENT RIGHTS?

Managers of companies which are nonunion enjoy or think they enjoy great freedom in running their companies as compared to managers who operate in unionized companies. When a company is first organized, there is no doubt great fear on the part of management that it will lose many of its so-called rights of management. This fear initiates the attempt to perpetuate whatever management rights are perceived. But there is also a constant struggle to preserve freedom of operation in companies that have been organized for a long time.

Most unions, however, are not seeking and do not want to take over the operation of any company. They are, by and large, seeking to protect the rights of the individual employees who happen to be members of the union. Managers increasingly perceive this and are able to distinguish demands for protective devices for employees apart from limits to the freedom of operation required to run a business organization successfully. Nonetheless, management typically does seek agreement that will allow flexibility in certain areas of operation. These include: "1. discretion to organize, integrate, and coordinate operations; 2. discretion to deploy the work force and maintain discipline; and 3. discretion to deal with the outside world or environment including (within an organization) other units of the organization."[1]

In other words management wants the flexibility to provide the proper inputs to the production operations of an organization and to see that production is carried on in as efficient a manner as possible. Further, management wants the right to use workers where they can most effectively be used, and it also wants the right to discipline workers when they commit acts which violate certain policies of the company. Finally, management wants the right to market its products or services in a manner which it deems to be most effective. Certainly there are few unions, if any, in the United States who would want to take over the marketing, production, finance, accounting, and other functions found in a typical business enterprise. While management seeks to preserve its rights, therefore, it does so more to establish a position than to counter any real threats raised by unions.

Management Rights under the Law   In addition to the rights built into the labor contract, management has certain rights under labor law. While the Wagner Act of 1935 prohibits certain unfair practices on the part of business, management still retains the right to lock out employees in a labor dispute. While rarely used, it is the counterpart to the union threat of strike. If a company decides to have a *lockout,* it closes its doors and refuses to let employees enter the plant to work. As with the strike, a lockout is costly for both the company and the union. The company expects, of course, that a lockout will be more costly to the union and will force the union to come to terms.

Another right a business has under labor law is to continue to employ workers even though a strike is going on. People who accept such employment are generally nonunion workers and must cross *picket lines* that the union has in front of the plant during the strike. Unions label these employees "scab labor"—a derogatory term that illustrates the union feelings toward these nonunion workers who are helping the company during the strike. The union, of course, has the right to picket or to have its members walk in front of the plant entrances while a strike is in progress. People working during a strike must pass through a picket line and sometimes endure the taunts, threats, and occasionally even violence that occurs at the plant gate.

It is understandable that emotions run high in a strike, but threats and violence certainly cannot be tolerated. If there is trouble, the company has the right to call on the local police to insure peaceful picketing and the right of its nonunion employees to come to work. It should be emphasized again that in the vast majority of cases, picketing is peaceful and orderly, and the strike runs its course to an ultimate peaceful settlement.

Management also has the right to seek an injunction for certain causes that will prevent the union from taking certain actions. Most common among the reasons for seeking an injunction through the courts would be if the union were carrying on a *secondary boycott* against the company. A secondary boycott means that the union would be preventing third parties from engaging in business with the company the union is striking. For example, suppose a union is striking against a large retail outlet and has pickets in front of the store entrances. If the

---

[1]Edwin F. Beal, Edward D. Wickersham, and Philip Kienast, *The Practice of Collective Bargaining* 4th ed. (Homewood, Ill.: Richard D. Irwin, 1972), p. 318.

union actually prevented customers from entering the stores, this would be a secondary boycott and would be illegal. Under the law the department store could go to court and get an injunction that would prevent the union from doing this.

BENEFITS OF THE LABOR MOVEMENT

Many people have the impression that the labor unions create a constant hassle between the union and the company, frequently involving the general public as well. Occasionally this is true. There have been railroad strikes, strikes of sanitation workers, teachers, truck drivers, and others which have seriously inconvenienced the general public. Oftentimes in these cases the government will step in to help or will force a settlement before serious injury is done to the consuming public. These cases, however, are the exception.

Not only are most labor-management relations peaceable, but the labor movement has brought benefits not only to workers but to companies and to the public at large as well. The benefits to workers are fairly obvious: increased wages, better and safer working conditions, and more security. Benefits to the business community include: a more structured situation which provides clear and effective channels of communication between management and the union, and the establishment of policies and procedures which assure fairness and equity in most cases to both management and labor. Finally, the actions of both parties in a mature relationship bring about respect to each party for the other.

Benefits to the public include the assurance that negotiations between labor and management will be conducted under law in a fair and peaceful manner. Since some twenty-five million of us are union members, we benefit directly, of course, from the labor movement. For those of us who are nonunion members, we find that our wages and working conditions and provisions for employment security often increase as a result of the activities of unions in other organizations. The general public has the assurance under law that neither party will be able to take extreme unfair advantage of the other, nor will the parties be allowed to engage in the sort of violence that was much more typical many years ago.

THE EXPANDED ROLE OF UNIONS

Today we observe unions fulfilling a larger role than they have in the past. Unions actively cooperate with management on safety practices and the assurance of healthy and safe working conditions. We find cooperation also between management and labor in the effort to employ minority and handicapped workers. There are other areas of cooperation.

Unions today find a better reception in organizations such as universities, hospitals, insurance companies, and local, state, and federal governments. In other words, growing white-collar and professional groups increasingly look upon unionism as a way to maintain or improve their position with respect to management. Hence there is a new look to the labor movement. No longer is it composed exclusively of people who do manual labor. Its *role has expanded* and will continue to do so.

This does not mean the labor movement goes without challenges. Minority membership in unions has not been completely fulfilled. Labor's own house is not completely in order. There are still jurisdictional battles between unions over which unions will represent certain groups of workers. Some individuals think that unions have lost some of their former political clout. Inflation and recession always pose serious problems for unions as they attempt to keep their workers' wages abreast of increased costs of living as well as confront the difficulties posed by widespread unemployment. As an institution, however, unions have survived for many, many years and will no doubt continue to do so.

SUMMARY

A major force in the environment of many business organizations is a labor union. Unions often arouse emotions to a point of bitter attack or passionate defense. Every business manager, however, is well advised to have a clear, rational understanding of the structure and workings of the labor movement.

The basic structural unit of unions is the local. A local is the bargaining unit for one plant or a limited geographic area. Local unions belong to and pay dues to international unions. The larger unions support their locals with help at bargaining time and with research and money when necessary. There are two basic types of local unions: industrial and craft. Industrial unions organize many different kinds of workers in one plant, while craft union membership consists of one particular skill such as electricians.

Several federal and many state laws regulate the relationship between a union and a company. These laws specify unfair practices on the part of both management and labor as well as regulate much of the internal affairs of unions.

Bargaining over wages, hours, and other terms and conditions of employment occurs periodically—in most cases once every three years. In between bargaining times, labor and management live under the rules of the contract drawn up and agreed upon at the previous bargaining session. When the two parties cannot agree to a contract, one of several different events may occur. A mediator may be called upon to help the parties reach agreement. Where an important public interest is at stake, such as in transportation, the government may step in and use heavy persuasion to bring about a settlement. Sometimes the union will go on strike, refusing to work until the company comes to terms. In rare cases, the company will use a lockout, refusing to let union members come to work until the union comes to terms.

Since bargaining is a power confrontation between two parties, each one seeks to protect its security and perceived rights. The union would like management to agree that all employees in the bargaining unit must be union members. This arrangement is a union shop. Management wants to protect its right to set marketing and production policies—generally to be free to run the company in areas outside of employer-employee relations.

Many companies have found that unions bring benefits as well as some additional problems. A union sets up a structured, systematic way to go about adjusting wages and many other matters. A union often helps bring about stability and a state of orderliness and peace that companies had never enjoyed in their nonunion days. The relationship between a company and a union is no more and no less than what the two parties want to make it.

DISCUSSION QUESTIONS

1. What are the principal differences between an industrial union and a craft union? Which type of union offers its members the greatest employment security?

2. From the viewpoint of an employing company, what are the advantages, if any, of a grievance procedure?

3. What is the relationship between the AFL-CIO and one of its local unions? Is this relationship the same as that which exists between General Motors headquarters and a local Chevrolet dealer?

4. Why are laws necessary to govern the relationship between management and labor? Which party do you believe benefits the most from labor law?

5. Collective bargaining may appear to be time consuming and inefficient. Do you think it would be better to have an outside person such as an arbitrator specify the terms of the contract between management and labor?

6. Unions sometimes seem to be willing and even eager to go out on strike. By and large, do you believe workers want to strike, or would they prefer to continue working?

7. What is the purpose of the contract or agreement between management and labor?

8. What are some benefits that labor unions have brought to their members and to business organizations? Do these benefits offset the problems sometimes caused by union demands?

SHORT CASES

Leadership in the United Auto Workers[2]

Walter Reuther became active in the labor movement in the 1930s, and in 1946 he was elected president of the UAW. Until Reuther was killed in 1970 in a plane crash, he was the driving force and inspirational leader of the UAW. After Reuther was killed, Leonard Woodcock, a member of Reuther's old team, became president of the union. When Woodcock retired in 1977, it appeared that another member of the old team, Douglas Fraser, would become president.

But the union leaders are worried. What will happen when Fraser, if he is elected, leaves the presidency after two terms (six years)? All of the members of Reuther's team will be too old to take on the active role of president. The younger members of the UAW seem disinterested in taking an active role in union affairs. Attendance at union meetings is at an all-time low. The young members don't seem to have the dreams and passions of the older leaders. Fraser says, "I see guys in the labor movement who lose their ability to become angry, and I don't like it. A person who doesn't get angry with injustice should retire." The main concern of many UAW members seems to be poor working conditions in the auto plants.

Why should people in the labor movement have an ability to become angry as Douglas Fraser suggests?

Despite the apparent apathy in the UAW, do you believe the UAW will have effective leadership after Fraser retires?

Why do you think labor union members are apparently uninterested in taking an active role in union affairs?

[2]Adapted from "UAW's New Chief: An Ear to the Young," *Business Week*, May 16, 1977, pp. 135–40.

The Determined Strikers

Contract negotiations between the union and management at Perfection Packing Company had dragged on for months. Increased pay was the main issue. The old contract had been extended once, but the union members were becoming increasingly impatient for action. A vote by the members to strike if necessary had been passed before negotiations even started. Now the union leadership decided a strike was the only course of action left open to them. They informed the membership, and a strike was called.

Almost immediately, the company began hiring nonunion workers to keep the plant open and operating. These workers had to pass the picket lines of the union members and endure their jibes and catcalls about being "scab" workers. The strike went on. After two months, the company had almost a full work force of nonunion workers. After three months, some of the union members began to look for and take jobs with other companies. The union leaders were very worried about the outcome of the strike.

Did the union make a mistake in calling a strike against Perfection Packing Company?

What is your opinion of the company hiring "scab" workers while the strike is in progress?

Some of the union members have taken jobs with other companies. Are they disloyal to the union?

SUGGESTED READINGS

Beal, Edwin F., Wickersham, Edward D., and Kienast, Philip. *The Practice of Collective Bargaining,* 4th ed. Homewood, Ill.: Richard D. Irwin, 1972.

Brody, David, ed. *The American Labor Movement.* New York: Harper & Row, 1971.

Dulles, Foster R. *Labor in America: A History.* 3d ed. New York: Thomas Y. Crowell Co., 1966.

OPERATIONS MANAGEMENT

LEARNING OBJECTIVES

When you finish this chapter you should:

☐ understand the basic concept of operations management – converting inputs to outputs.

☐ understand how operations management is the core process of a business but is highly dependent upon other functions such as marketing, finance, and purchasing.

☐ be familiar with process design.

☐ know how operations control assures that the right inputs are converted into the right outputs at the right time.

☐ know why there is a continuing need for study of the conversion process through operations analysis.

☐ understand the meaning of quality and how the desired level of quality is maintained.

☐ be aware of the importance of inventory control in minimizing cost and meeting demand.

KEY TERMS TO LEARN FROM THIS CHAPTER

capacity analysis	Gantt chart	operations analysis	process analysis
carrying cost	inputs	operations manage-	process design
control of	inspection	ment	quality
operations	inventory	opportunity cost	quality control
conversion process	learning curve	outputs	safety stock
critical path	network technique	PERT	scheduling

When Nancy Clark was nearing the end of her first year in college, she knew she was lucky to have a job in an ice cream parlor already set for the summer. Still, she wondered if she could not add to her summer income in some way. Talking it over with a hometown friend, they hit upon the idea of house sitting. While people were away on summer vacations, Nancy and her friend, Lorraine, would live in the vacationers' home. In this way, there would not be a house sitting empty for days or weeks—an invitation to vandalism and burglary.

Advertising in their hometown newspaper, they soon lined up their first job for the first two weeks in July. Later on, through more advertising and by word of mouth, they were able to fill almost the whole summer with house sitting. And they could also keep their other jobs.

In house sitting, Nancy and Lorraine were providing a service to their customers by *converting* the insecurity of an empty house to the relative security of an occupied house. And the word *converting* or *conversion* strikes the essence of operations management. It is the conversion of certain kinds of *inputs* into *outputs*—goods and services—that people want or need.

In the case of Nancy and Lorraine, the inputs they provide are basically themselves and their occupancy of a house. Their service or output is a house that is safer from burglary and vandalism than it would be if unoccupied.

THE CORE PROCESS

All organizations have an operations function—that is, all organizations convert the factors of production (which were discussed in Chapter 1) into products and services. The factors of production are land, labor, capital, and management. The factors of production are often called inputs to an operations function, while products and services are called outputs. The factors of production or inputs usually include facilities and equipment, manpower, money, and management.

Important inputs to a hospital, for example, include doctors, nurses, medicine, the hospital building and facilities, and sick or injured people. All of these inputs are used in the conversion process which transforms sick or injured people into well people. A bank converts inputs of money, management, and facilities into outputs of loans, security, and earnings on savings. A school uses teachers, buildings, blackboards, and books to yield a very important output—increased knowledge and skill.

Hence the conversion process of operations is the core process of any organization. In business, automobile manufacturers convert steel and other materials into finished cars. A bakery converts flour and other ingredients into bread and pastry. The Candy Emporium converts chocolate and other ingredients into delicious candies. Operations is very important but is very dependent upon other functional areas in a business—such as personnel management, finance, marketing, accounting, and purchasing—in order to be both efficient and effective.

Marketing, for example, has a major influence on what the outputs should be as well as on aspects of the output such as design, packaging, and quality. Finance helps to assure the supply of funds needed to acquire inputs and oversee the equitable distribution of funds to areas within the organization, including operations management. Purchasing carries the major responsibility for buying appropriate inputs at the lowest possible price. Unless the conversion process receives the right kind and amount of support from all other areas of the organization, there is little chance for long-term success.

Our purpose in this chapter will be to gain an understanding of *operations management* through a breakdown of its component functions, the study of these, and then a reassembly of the parts into a complete whole. The parts we will study are process design, control of operations, quality maintenance, and control of inventories. We will also see how operations management, along with the other business functions, fits into the total business organization.

OPERATIONS MANAGEMENT IN THE CANDY EMPORIUM

Let us return to The Candy Emporium in order to further clarify the exact nature of operations management. We know that Geri Rogers and Art

The conversion process by which this oil refinery turns crude oil into petroleum products is heavily automated.

CHARLES L. FARROW

Lindstrom run The Candy Emporium and manufacture a variety of candies. They employ a full-time production employee and a full-time sales clerk. They all pitch in when necessary, however, to get candy packed or to clean up the store. Art generally oversees the production operation and decides how much of each kind of candy to produce.

Inputs include materials such as chocolate, caramel, coconut, and nuts; candy boxes; wrapping paper; and other miscellaneous materials and supplies necessary to the conversion process. Direct inputs also include the labor of the production worker and the diagrams which show how the candy is to be packed in boxes.

Somewhat more indirectly, inputs also include money to buy materials as well as pay the wages of the employees. In addition, there is the contribution by Art, Geri, and their part-time bookkeeper in keeping records straight and in billing customers for credit sales. Geri also provides marketing information that helps in deciding how much of each kind of candy to produce, and styling and design information for special products such as Valentine boxes and Easter baskets.

Their outputs are candies sold individually and in boxes and candy catering services for weddings and parties. If the conversion process is efficient and effective, their output can be sold at a profit, and an important step toward overall success will have been made.

Every organization will be different in terms of the exact nature of its inputs, the exact nature of the conversion process, and the exact nature of the output. Every organization has an operations or conversion process, however, that can

Figure 7-1 A conversion process for the Candy Emporium.

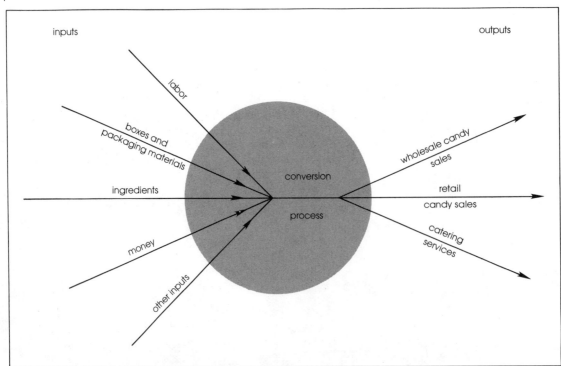

be specifically determined through study and analyzed. Figure 7–1 illustrates the conversion process for The Candy Emporium.

PLANNING THE PROCESS DESIGN

Every conversion process has some design that determines how inputs will be transformed into outputs. The design may just evolve as an organization grows, or the *process design* may be carefully planned in advance. In order to maximize efficiency and effectiveness, we fully recommend that planning be done in advance.

Two basic questions must be answered with respect to process design: (1) What is the best flow of inputs through the organization in order to reach the output stage, and (2) What kind of work must be done and how will it be done in order to complete the conversion process? Finding the answer to the first question is called *process analysis;* finding the answer to the second question is called *operations analysis.*

In The Candy Emporium, there will be both raw materials which must be processed into finished candy and purchased candy which is ready to sell as is. There must be storage space for both raw materials and finished candy. In the flow between raw materials and finished candy, the owners—Geri and Art— will have figured out where and how to do the manufacturing operations such as forming candy centers and enrobing the centers. Then all of the finished candy, both purchased and manufactured, will need to be distributed to the packing area, the storage area, and the retail display cases. Geri and Art will also have designed certain ways to pack their boxes and display the candy for retail.

Finally, packed boxes of candy will flow to storage and to the retail display cases, and Geri and Art will probably also want a packaging area to prepare candy for mailing. All of these aspects of the conversion process must be analyzed and then put back together for a complete process design. Figure 7–2 shows a possible process design for The Candy Emporium.

When we move from these simple examples to large-scale manufacturing or service operations, process design becomes much more complex. As an illustration, process design for an automobile assembly plant can only maximize efficiency with the aid of a computer. Process design for a large hospital entails setting up areas for departments such as obstetrics, surgery, intensive care, and so on. Nurses and doctors become highly specialized in order to know what work to do and how to go about doing it. Once a business has set up a process design, its next challenge is to control it.

CONTROL OF OPERATIONS

The purpose of control is to insure that the right inputs are converted into the right outputs at the right time. Thus, *scheduling* is an important element of the *control of operations.* In The Candy Emporium, Geri and Art must make sure that they and their employees are making and packing sufficient quantities of the different kinds of candy to meet customer demand. There must also be sufficient quantities of raw materials and supplies available to make whatever candies Geri and Art have currently scheduled.

Keeping operations running smoothly—that is, avoiding frantic peaks of activity followed by periods when there is nothing to do—is an important subgoal of operations control. Business attempts to smooth operations in several ways. One of these is through the use of *inventories*. During slack sales periods, inventories are stockpiled while production continues on at a smooth rate. During busy sales periods, then, these stockpiles are depleted in order to meet demand while production continues at about the same rate as always. In this way, inventories are used as a buffer in order to keep conversion going along at about the same level even though sales go through periods of highs and lows. Many businesses are highly seasonal, and inventory planning becomes an important activity for smoothing operations.

ADJUSTING THE LABOR FORCE

When inventory adjustments are not enough to smooth production completely, the business organization must be prepared to take over actions. These include the use of overtime, additional hiring, reduced work weeks, or laying off workers. When inventories are simply not adequate to meet peak demand periods, there will be a need to work overtime, to work double shifts, or to hire additional workers. In many department stores at Christmastime, for example, permanent employees often work longer hours, and the stores usually hire temporary employees to handle the Christmas rush. When companies are subject to the summer doldrums, vacations and shorter hours usually help to meet decreased demand for output.

We find, then, that operations control seeks to achieve two objectives: (1)

Figure 7-2 Process design — the Candy Emporium.

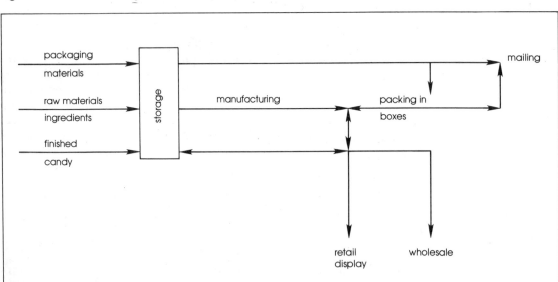

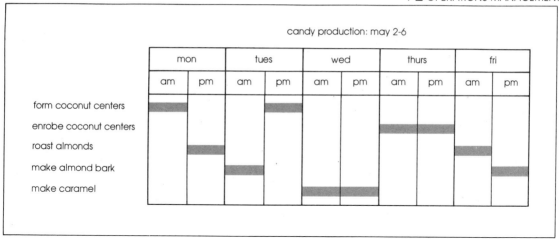

Figure 7-3 A Gantt-type bar chart for candy production.

having the right inputs in the right place at the right time in order to produce or market the right output, and (2) smoothing out the conversion process and keeping it functioning at about the same level throughout the year.

MECHANICAL AIDS FOR CONTROL

Managers have invented various devices to aid in the control of operations. A number of different kinds of charts, for example, have been used to display schedules and the assignment of inputs. A chart that The Candy Emporium might use to schedule production for one person for a week is illustrated in Figure 7–3.

   This type of chart is a bar chart and was first put to use by Henry Gantt, an industrial engineer, during World War I. It has been widely used since then, and as can be seen in Figure 7–3, the *Gantt chart* clearly shows what has to be done during a given period of time. Note that a chart of this type helps to assure that materials will be ready when needed. In the above figure, the forming of coconut centers is finished early in the week so they are ready to be enrobed on Thursday.

PERT Another aid to production planning and scheduling is the *network technique.* The best known is *PERT* (Program Evaluation and Review Technique). PERT was developed by Lockheed Aircraft to help in the development of the Polaris missile for the Navy. PERT is particularly useful for relatively complex projects in which several activities have to occur at the same time and when there is a deadline or target date for all activities as well as the whole project to be finished. A network technique such as PERT forces careful planning and facilitates control over several activities at once.

   To illustrate PERT, let us suppose that Geri Rogers and Art Lindstrom of The Candy Emporium want to remodel their store and have allocated four weeks for the project. They want to paint, lower the ceiling, add some wall dividers, and do some electrical work for spotlights. A simple PERT network for this project might appear as in Figure 7–4.

   The circles represent the beginning and end of activities, while the lines show the various activities. In this simplified version of PERT, the numbers by

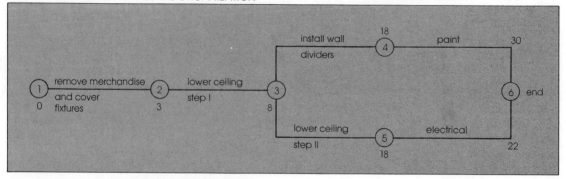

Figure 7-4   A PERT network for remodelling.

the circles show the beginning and ending times for an activity in days. For example, activity 1–2 takes three days, while activity 2–3 takes five days (eight days less three days). Since activity 4–6 (painting) takes twelve days while 5–6 (electrical) only takes four days, the electrical could be delayed until only four days before the end of the project.

It also means that the electrical activity has eight days of free or slack time since painting and electrical occur at the same time and painting takes twelve days while electrical takes only four. Slack time is important in many projects because it is possible that labor and equipment could be taken from the activity with slack time (electrical) and used in another activity (painting) if the latter were being delayed. Of course, in this example, it is unlikely that an electrician will paint, but many times the transfer of resources is practical. And the additional help can put a delayed activity back on time.

In more sophisticated networks, each circle will show the earliest and latest times for the completion of the previous activity and the beginning of the next. Look at circle 5 in Figure 7–4. The earliest possible starting time for the electrical activity is eighteen days into the project, while the latest possible starting time is twenty-six days if the project is to be done on time. Knowing all the earliest and latest starting times is convenient in computing slack times.

There are two final observations on PERT networks. Some activities must be done before others can start. Geri and Art must remove all their candy and other merchandise before any remodeling can even start. Hence this removal and storage is the first activity. Other activities can occur at the same time, such as painting and electrical. The longest path through the network is known as the *critical path*. It identifies the minimum amount of time it will take to complete a project. In the illustration, the critical path is 1–2–3–4–6, and the time involved on that path is thirty days.

Gantt charts, PERT networks, and other mechanical aids do help tremendously when used properly. They increase efficiency, which is a continuing effort, as the next section suggests.

OPERATIONS ANALYSIS

Establishing a satisfactory process design and control system does not mean that a business can ignore operations management. There is a continuing need for study and analysis of the conversion process. Among the questions a business should periodically ask itself about operations are the following: Are there alternative ways to produce our product or provide our service that would be more efficient or more effective? Are we using the least expensive labor, equipment, and material inputs that will still meet our quality and performance standards? Do we have enough capacity or do we need more capacity to introduce a new product or a new service? Do we have enough capacity to handle increasing amounts of business in the future?

A business needs to continually analyze its ongoing operations in order to minimize cost while still maintaining efficiency and effectiveness. When a company plans to manufacture a new product or offer a new service, there is a particular need for operations analysis in order to maximize efficiency and determine future costs. Of special importance in this respect is a phenomenon called the *learning curve*.

THE LEARNING CURVE

With any new product or service, some amount of research and development work must be done. The purpose of the R&D (research and development), in part, is to help assure the best possible product or service design. The R&D is necessary to determine that a new design, possibly involving the use of new materials as well, will work out satisfactorily. For example, when a major defense contractor takes on the development of a new weapons system, there may well be millions of dollars involved in R&D. Even a toy manufacturer may spend large sums of money researching the design and development of a new toy.

There will also have to be development of a process design and control system for a new product or service. Once these design and development requirements have been met, presumably the new product or service is ready for introduction to the market. There is, however, still one beneficial aspect involved in the introduction of a product or service that should be considered. The benefit is provided by the learning curve.

Initial cost estimates for producing a new product, based on test runs or paper figures, may be unnecessarily high. As we learn to do something, we generally become more proficient at it. For example, when we first learn to drive a car our movement tends to be uncoordinated and perhaps somewhat clumsy. With practice and experience, however, we become more skillful and more efficient in making all the motions necessary to handling an automobile successfully. The same phenomenon occurs in a business when it first starts to manufacture a new product. Workers may tend to be relatively clumsy when they first attempt to assemble a product or even to make component parts for a product. Equipment and facilities are perhaps not designed as well as they could be. With experience, however, the workers become more skilled, equipment may be modified, and facilities redesigned. The result is greater efficiency and lower costs. Hence in many cases, as cumulative units of output increase, the conversion time per unit of product decreases.

As an example, assume you want to begin making and selling wooden toys. Your only equipment is an old jigsaw. At first, your production is very slow. You make mistakes, the old saw has the wrong type of blade, and you make one complete toy at a time. Then you buy the right kind of saw blades. You become more skilled and accurate in your work. You begin making several component parts at one time and then assembling several complete toys when all the parts are ready. After a month, you find your production rate has increased dramatically. In short, you have benefited from the learning curve.

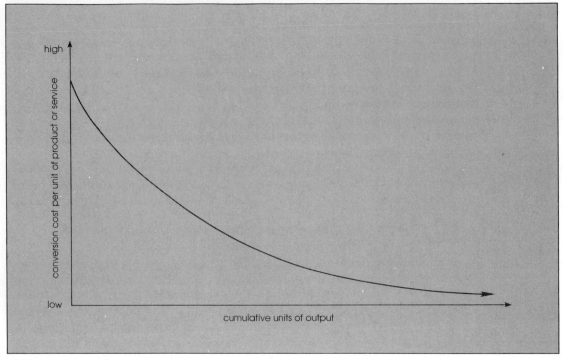

Figure 7-5 The learning curve.

A business, therefore, should consider the learning curve and its possible beneficial effects on costs when introducing a new product. As the volume of sales increases and costs decrease, the business owner or manager may find considerable satisfaction in an expanding profit margin. Figure 7–5 illustrates the concept of the learning curve.

CAPACITY ANALYSIS

There is one more important consideration before finally deciding to go ahead with a new product or any anticipated large expansion of business. Does the business have the productive or service capacity to handle the new product? Will there be a need to rent or build more space, buy more equipment, or whatever else it will take to increase production? Perhaps the investment in facilities and/or equipment would not be justified by the return from sales in profit expected from the introduction of a new good or service.

Hence *capacity analysis* must consider the required investment and the estimated earnings and costs associated with the new product. Capacity analysis is important not only from the standpoint of the specific investment involved but also from the standpoint of what is called *opportunity cost*. That is, money invested to increase capacity by adding space or buying equipment to produce something new is not available for other opportunities. Perhaps the money could be better used to expand the market for present products or to replace present equipment which is worn out.

Analysis of alternative investment opportunities is important to any business enterprise, and methods of doing such analysis will be discussed in Chapter 13, "Financial Management."

MAINTAINING QUALITY

All businesses are interested in the level of *quality* of their products or services. This interest does not necessarily mean the highest level of quality possible, but rather a level of quality that matches the goals of the organization. For example, a company that manufactures component parts for space vehicles ordinarily must maintain a very high level of quality. The chance of failure may have to be less than one in a million. We would not send a person into space if there were only a fifty-fifty chance of successfully completing the mission. On the other hand, there are occasions when companies are satisfied with a lower level of quality in order to market the product or service at a very low price. For example, a contractor can build a house of very high quality that will have to sell at a high price. A contractor could also build a house of lower quality in order to sell it at a much lower price. We have probably all had the experience of buying a very inexpensive product and not expecting much quality to be built into it. The old saw that you get what you pay for is generally true.

Hence quality control means only the assurance of quality at the targeted level. The quality-level decision should be made early in the planning for a new product or service. In this way, the business can also help assure that the appropriate amounts of time, money, and effort will be allocated to maintaining quality. The quality-level decision is important since it affects other decisions that will subsequently be made.

It affects the quality of materials that are purchased, the kind of employees that are hired, and the kind of equipment that is used to build the product or provide the service. One way, therefore, to help assure high quality is to buy the

"I think we made a mistake somewhere in our capacity analysis."

best materials, hire the best and most skilled labor available, and use the best equipment available. Conversely, for low quality output inexpensive materials, labor, and equipment can and probably should be used. Beyond these initial considerations the method most commonly used to assure a given level of quality is inspection. Let us take a look at The Candy Emporium for an example of how Geri Rogers and Art Lindstrom control quality.

QUALITY CONTROL IN CANDY

Before they opened the door for business at The Candy Emporium, Geri and Art decided to make and sell only high-quality candy. Perhaps the most important step toward this goal is to buy only the best raw materials. They have been doing this—buying the best chocolate available, buying the best ingredients for making centers, and in general always looking for the best inputs. While this costs more, Geri and Art have found that their customers are happy to pay more for a product of known high quality.

They also keep their equipment clean and in good operating condition. They spend time with their employees, training them in the appearance and taste of good candy. They ask their employees to inspect every piece of candy that is made and to throw out those that do not meet the standards of high quality. Geri and Art also randomly inspect the candy made in their kitchen and also carefully check every incoming shipment of raw material to insure it is of good quality. As a result of these activities, The Candy Emporium sells only high-quality candy, but in order to do this, the quality control program must be constant—it must be accomplished every hour of every day.

COST OF QUALITY CONTROL

There are, of course, costs associated with *quality control.* The more one inspects, for example, the higher is the cost of *inspection* and the lower is the cost of poor quality in terms of bad products and dissatisfied customers who may not return. On the other hand, with less inspection there is a lower cost of inspection but a higher cost resulting from poor-quality output. Figure 7–6 graphically illustrates this relationship between inspection costs and the costs of good or bad quality.

Note that we can add together the two individual cost curves—inspection cost and cost of poor quality—to form a curve that shows total cost of inspection. Then we drop a line straight down from the bottom of the total cost curve and through the intersection of the two individual cost curves. Where this vertical line hits the bottom of the figure is the optimal amount of inspection. This amount is optimal because it trades off one cost—inspection—against the other cost—cost of poor quality—and minimizes total cost.

Of course, any business firm may decide to inspect less or more depending upon the quality level desired in the good or service. Hence if you buy a Rolls Royce and get bad quality, you have a right to complain. On the other hand if you buy a 25¢ hamburger in a run-down restaurant, you can expect and, no doubt, will receive low-quality service and product.

There are many consumer complaints about poor quality, and certainly many of these complaints are justified. There does seem to be a place for products of lesser quality, however. Every time someone buys a good or service, there is not a need for the best quality possible. Many times, people are willing to settle for less.

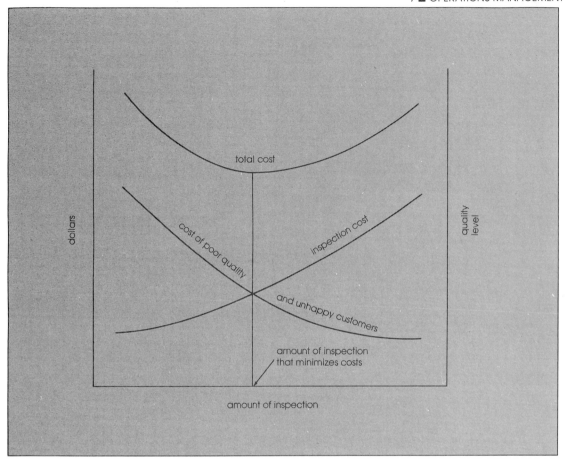

Figure 7-6 The costs of inspection.

If you need a hammer to nail together a doghouse, you probably do not want the finest hammer available. The difference in price between a hammer that will do the job and the best hammer is several dollars. Trouble arises when the lower-quality product is not even adequate to its purpose. If you break your hammer the first time it hits a nail, you feel cheated.

Hence from the standpoint of the individual consumer as well as society, there appears to be some minimum level of quality that ought to be built into every good and service. An expectation that a product will work and that a service provides what it is supposed to does not seem unreasonable. Where this is not true, it would seem that the individual and society, acting on good faith, are being cheated in their purchases of goods and services.

RESPONDING TO CHANGES IN DEMAND

One way that The Candy Emporium could meet demand would be to wait for orders, and then Geri, Art, and their employees could frantically race about producing the required candy to meet the orders. Another way would be for

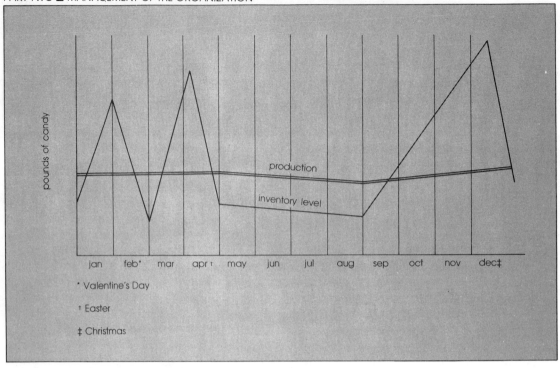

Figure 7-7   Adjusting inventories to smooth production.

them to produce larger amounts of candy than are currently needed to meet demand and put the excess in *inventory* to meet future demand. In this way, Geri and Art can keep their production operation running at a fairly smooth rate and also avoid excessively frantic activity when demand is high. This idea of building up inventory during low demand periods and reducing inventory during peak demand periods, all the while keeping production at an even keel, is illustrated in Figure 7–7.

If Geri and Art decide to maintain inventories, an immediate question arises: How much inventory should they maintain? This question breaks down into two other questions: (1) How much of any one type of candy should be produced at one time? and (2) When should a given kind of candy be produced? In order to answer these questions, Geri and Art must consider certain associated costs. One of these is the cost associated with setting up to produce a particular kind of candy. Different equipment and materials may be required. The packaging may be different. Space may have to be cleared. All of this requires time and, therefore, money. Every time the switch is made to a different kind of candy, there will be some of these *setup costs*.

They must also consider the *carrying cost* of the inventory of candy that is built up. Carrying costs could include such items as breakage, insurance, the use of storage space, and an interest charge on the money tied up in inventory. There would be an interest charge because of the opportunity cost involved with the inventory. That is, if the money were not tied up in inventory, Geri and Art could use that money for some other purpose, which they hope would produce income. If nothing else, they could put the money in a bank and draw interest. We graphically illustrate these two costs in Figure 7–8.

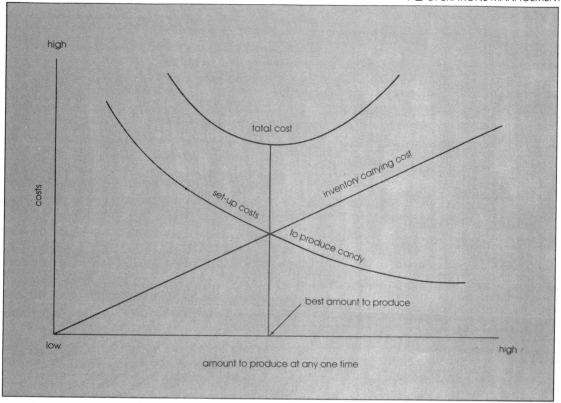

Figure 7-8   The cost of inventory.

Note that as setup costs decrease, the carrying costs increase. This occurs because Geri and Art would be producing less frequently and would have to carry a larger inventory in stock. Conversely then, as setup costs increase, carrying costs decrease. Again, we can obtain a total cost curve by adding these two individual costs. Then, by dropping a line straight down from the bottom of the total cost curve, we determine the economic order quantity or the least-cost amount of candy that Geri and Art should produce at any one time. By producing this amount of candy at each setup, Geri and Art will minimize their overall inventory cost.

THE PRODUCTION PATTERN

Suppose Geri and Art have found that for peanut clusters, 1,000 units is the proper amount to produce on a once-a-month basis. Assume also that it takes ten days to produce the 1,000 pieces and that they are sold at the rate of 1,000 per month. The total pattern of production, sales, and restocking is shown in Figure 7–9.

In Figure 7–9 the diagonal lines sloping down to the right show the steady demand for peanut clusters that would reduce inventory from 1,000 units to 0 in one month. Ten days prior to the end of the month, however, Geri and Art set up to produce 1,000 more peanut clusters. It takes ten days to produce the candy, so just as the last peanut cluster is sold on the last day of the month, 1,000 more peanut clusters are put into inventory to take care of the next month. If demand and production time remain unchanged, this cycle could repeat itself

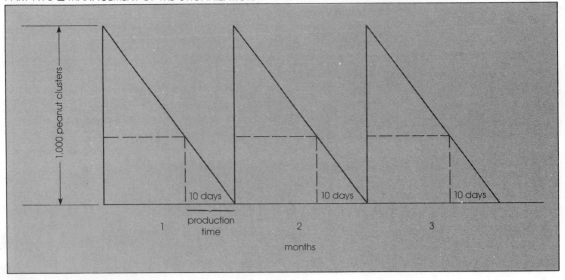

Figure 7-9 Inventory patterns for peanut clusters.

many times over. The illustration is one of perfectly constant demand, however, and in reality demand will vary, as may production time. More sophisticated inventory models take these variations into account and provide for such factors as *safety stock* in case demand would exceed expectations.

Inventory control is very important since even in a small business thousands of dollars may be tied up in inventory. The opportunity cost involved could be very high. Business managers, therefore, tend to be very careful about the size of their inventories and pay a great deal of attention to demand predictions and cost changes.

SUMMARY

Operations management or the conversion of inputs to outputs is the core activity of any business organization. Other functions of a business—such as personnel, finance, and marketing—aid in making operations management efficient and effective. It is also important to recognize that operations management is often crucial to the success of other types of organizations such as hospitals, volunteer charitable organizations, and governments.

An important aspect of operations is the process design that determines how inputs will be transformed into outputs. A good process design identifies the best flow of inputs through the organization in order to reach the output stage, the kind of work that must be done, and how the work is done to complete the conversion process.

Effective control of operations assures that the right inputs are converted into the right outputs at the right time. Control also strives to keep the amount of work in operations relatively constant through inventory adjustments even though sales may vary widely throughout the year.

The operations function requires constant study and analysis to remain effective. In special situations, such as the introduction of a new product, this analysis becomes particularly critical. Questions concerning the adequacy of the process design, control system, and operations capacity must be satisfactorily answered before a new product can be seriously considered.

Finally, operations management bears responsibility for quality and inventory control. The business organization must determine the appropriate level of quality and level of inventories in order to meet market demand and minimize costs.

DISCUSSION QUESTIONS

1. We have said that every organization has a conversion process that converts inputs to outputs. How would you describe the conversion process in a legal firm? A laundry? A resort hotel? A commercial airline?

2. Why is it important to determine the best flow of inputs through an organization? Would there be a natural flow in many cases so that no actual study would have to be done?

3. If you owned a fishing resort in Canada, would it be possible to smooth the operations function of this business?

4. Assume you own a small chemical plant and you have just discovered and introduced on the market a new kind of lawn fertilizer. Demand for your new product grows at a rapid rate. Very quickly, demand exceeds your productive capacity by a wide margin, and you have to turn down many orders. Is this a serious problem that should have been avoided?

5. We suggested that some businesses may deliberately try to produce a low-quality good or service. Is it not more logical for any business to produce a good or service that has as high a quality level as possible?

6. Jim Smith started a retail sports supply store and decided to advertise a policy of never being out of stock on any item he carried. Is this a wise policy for Smith? Is it a practical policy?

SHORT CASES

Building a Railroad[1]

Out of the remains of the Penn Central Transportation Company and five other bankrupt railroads, a new railroad was formed in 1976—the Consolidated Rail Corporation (Conrail). Confronted with bad track, broken locomotives, and rusty rolling stock, Conrail—which hauls freight only—embarked on a major rehabilitation program.

Conrail is a seventeen-thousand-mile system that serves sixteen states in the Midwest and East. In nine months in 1976, Conrail installed almost five million new ties, laid 727 miles of new welded rail, and smoothed out the rough spots on over eight thousand miles of existing track. It also rehabilitated hundreds of locomotives and almost twelve thousand freight cars.

Bankrolled by the United States Congress through the U.S. Railway Association, Conrail has done well. Even though it lost money in 1976, it is running ahead of projections. A principal problem seems to be that it is difficult for Conrail to run a large proportion of long hauls—the kind of rail service on which profits are made. Instead, it gets involved in a lot of switching and short-haul jobs. As the chairman of Conrail has observed, its basic problem is that it is mostly a gigantic switch yard.

Is it fair for the government to provide financial support for Conrail when Conrail is in competition with other forms of transportation such as trucking?

What can Conrail do to gain a greater share of the long-haul business?

[1]Adapted from "Conrail's First Year: A Good Track Record," *Business Week*, April 11, 1977, pp. 96–99.

A Fifty-Year Inventory[2]

The Weyerhaeuser Company of Tacoma, Washington, "has the largest timber inventory, in volume and value, of any company on earth." It is the largest lumber producer in the United States. It owns nearly six million acres of timberland in the U.S. and is the largest private landowner in the state of Washington.

Weyerhaeuser plans to cut down almost all of the old trees on its land by the end of the century. Some of these trees are more than two hundred years old and were full grown before white people ever got to the Pacific Northwest. The company will replant with high-yield trees that will be ready for harvest in fifty years. All of the Weyerhaeuser timberland is replanted with tree crops in perpetuity. Within a year after trees are cleared from land, new seedlings are planted—to be harvested fifty years later. Weyerhaeuser likes to think of itself as an agricultural firm.

[2]Adapted from "Weyerhaeuser Gets Set for the 21st Century," *Fortune* 95, no. 4 (April 1977): 75–88.

Since the Weyerhaeuser Company owns so much timberland, should it have the complete right to make whatever decisions it chooses with respect to the trees on its land?

What kinds of special problems do you see in growing a crop that will not be ready for harvest for fifty years?

Would you like to be in this kind of lumber business?

SUGGESTED READINGS

Laufer, Arthur C. *Operations Management.* Cincinnati: South-Western Publishing Co., 1975.

Timms, Howard L. *Introduction to Operations Management.* Homewood, Ill.: Richard D. Irwin, 1967.

Vollmann, Thomas E. *Operations Management: A Systems Model-Building Approach.* Reading, Mass.: Addison-Wesley Publishing Co., 1973.

PART THREE

MARKETING MANAGEMENT AND INSTITUTIONS

☐ Marketing decisions are some of the most important you have to make in managing a business. Management must decide to what group of consumers its goods or services and marketing efforts will be directed. A thorough knowledge of the consumer characteristics as well as an understanding of consumer buying habits and motivations are needed to build a successful marketing program. Then critical decisions must be made regarding what specific products — brands and grades — will be offered, what prices will be charged, how the products will reach consumers, and what promotional programs will be utilized to communicate with consumers.

☐ Chapters 8–10 deal with these issues. In Chapter 8 a foundation is laid for analyzing markets (collection of consumers). In addition, major decisions of product management are covered. Chapter 9 discusses pricing, distribution, and promotion decisions. The major marketing institutions available to aid management in its distribution operations are analyzed in Chapter 10. Finally, Chapter 11, "Multinational Business," extends the concepts developed in Chapters 8–10 to world markets.

☐ Students will find that marketing involves not only some of the important decisions which have to be made in both business and nonbusiness organizations but also some of the most challenging decisions.

*

MARKETING MANAGEMENT:
CONSUMERS
AND PRODUCTS

LEARNING OBJECTIVES

When you finish this chapter you should:

☐ understand the function of marketing in business and nonbusiness organizations.

☐ know what it means for an organization to embrace the marketing concept.

☐ be aware of the elements of the marketing mix.

☐ know what basic questions need to be answered about a potential market before developing an effective marketing strategy.

☐ understand how an organization attempts to match its products (services) to consumer needs.

KEY TERMS TO LEARN FROM THIS CHAPTER

brand	industrial consumer	market segmentation	product manager
cognitive dissonance	marketing	motivation research	shopping goods
consumer behavior	marketing concept	product life cycle	specialty goods
convenience goods	marketing mix	product line	ultimate consumer

Most of us have some vague notion of what marketing is about. After all, someone in each of our households spends time "marketing" in the supermarket at least weekly. We encounter daily radio, television, newspaper, or billboard commercials. We may have a relative or a friend who makes his living "selling" or as a "marketing rep" for a company. We may even occasionally answer the doorbell or telephone and be greeted with the remark, "I'm taking a marketing survey. . . ." Each of these situations portrays a small part of marketing, but neither one alone nor all together give a comprehensive picture of the marketing function. The functions of securing, developing, and maintaining customers in the modern firm is the responsibility of marketing.

WHAT IS MARKETING?

Consistent with the systems approach to management as discussed in Chapter 4, marketing may be defined as *a total system of interacting business activities designed to plan, price, promote, and distribute want-satisfying goods and services to current and potential consumers.* Marketing management under this definition is concerned with the total marketing system—how it works, what functions are performed, what institutions are embraced, how these institutions relate to each other, the limitations imposed on the system by the external environment and the firm's resources, and the implications of a firm's decisions on society as a whole. Marketing is a comprehensive system—not just selling, buying, or distribution. Each is a part, interrelated and interdependent.

An example may serve to illustrate the systems approach in marketing management. Suppose that a manufacturing company is considering a major advertising campaign for the next three months. Management has to consider what effect the campaign will have on inventories at the manufacturing, wholesale, and retail levels; production scheduling; field sales staff; cash flow; funds available for new production planning and development; sales of the advertised product; sales of other products in the company's product line; and return on investment. In addition, consideration must be given to probable reactions of competitors as well as any possible conflicts with government regulations of advertising.

THE MARKETING CONCEPT

Closely interwoven in the system's approach to marketing is the marketing concept. As the American economy passed from a primitive, self-sufficient stage to the industrial revolution of the nineteenth century, production specialization and division of labor provided American business with the know-how and technology to mass produce goods and services. With the post-industrial revolution era of twentieth-century America, the major emphasis of business management was turned to the consumer rather than the factory. This new phase of management signaled the emergence of the marketing concept.

Prompted by the built-up, unsatisfied consumer demand following World War II and pioneered by a few prominent companies in the early 1950s, the marketing concept emphasizes a consumer orientation for all business activity. In addition, this new philosophy of business stresses the importance of an integrated effort for all aspects of business management, along with the goal of a profitable sales volume. Under the marketing concept, top management recognizes that the total firm is a marketing organization in business to serve the consumer with profitable sales. Complete embrace of the marketing concept suggests that general management is responsible for administrative aspects of marketing; research and development is responsible for basic research and product design aspects of marketing; the controller, for the financial part of marketing; advertising, for the communication side of marketing; manufacturing, for the production part of marketing; and finally, marketing is concerned with consumer aspects of marketing. The total network represents an integrated effort with the consumer as the focal point.

In order to implement the marketing concept, a change in the organizational structure of management is often necessary. Marketing is given the same authority in management as other functional areas. Under the title of vice-president of marketing, marketing director, or marketing manager, responsibility and authority are placed for all marketing activities in the company. Sales, advertising, marketing research, product planning and development, traffic management, and other marketing services are coordinated under this top management person. Figure 8–1 presents structurally an application of the marketing concept within a company. The organization chart shows that all marketing activities are coordinated under a vice-president of marketing, who has the same line authority as other major division heads in the company and answers directly to the president.

While some businesses are attempting to implement the marketing concept in their operations, too many have failed even to recognize the marketing philosophy as a way of doing business. Still others have made only superficial

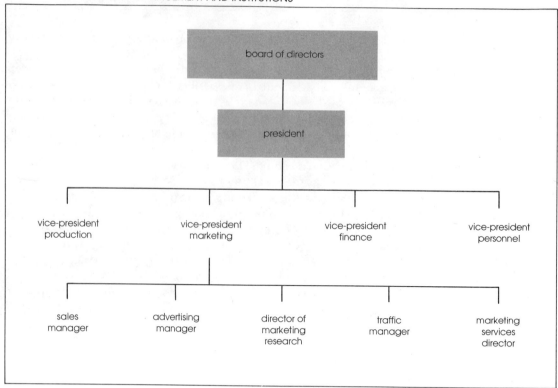

Figure 8-1 Organizational chart showing a company's application of marketing concept.

changes—for example, changed the title of the sales manager to marketing manager but kept the same person in the position with a sales orientation to business management. With increasing competition among businesses and growing consumer concern over product offerings of firms, a larger proportion of companies will be forced into embracing the marketing concept for survival.

THE MARKETING MIX

Using the marketing concept, the elements of the marketing manager's job are shown diagrammatically in Figure 8–2. As we have previously discussed, the consumer is the center of all marketing activities. Within the control of marketing management are the company's products, the price which can be charged for the products, the promotional strategies which may be used to influence consumers, and the distribution system which may be utilized to reach consumers. Jerome McCarthy[1] has coined the phrase, "the 4 Ps of marketing—product, price, promotion, and place"—as the elements of the marketing mix. In pursuing the right mix of product, price, promotion, and place, marketing management must operate within an uncertain and largely uncontrollable environment. Nevertheless, management must be aware of, analyze, and adjust to the various limitations imposed by these environmental factors. Production technology, company know-how, and skills are limiting factors on the product offerings of management. Economic, social, and cultural aspects of the environment deter-

[1]E. Jerome McCarthy, *Basic Marketing: A Managerial Approach,* 5th ed. (Homewood, Ill.: Richard D. Irwin, 1975), p. 75.

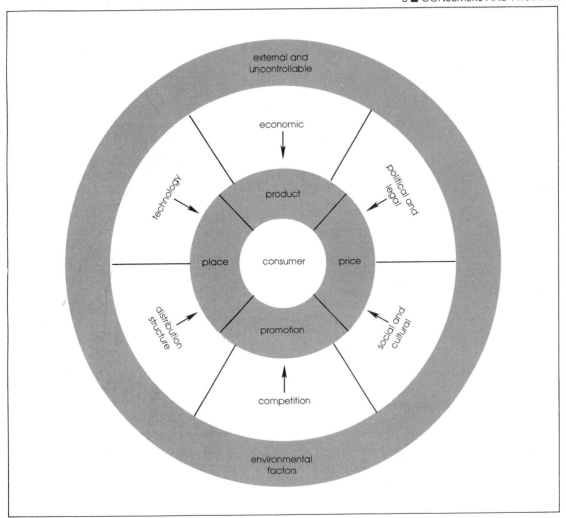

Figure 8-2 A company's marketing system.

mine product wants of consumers, control product prices, and are the bases of selecting the appropriate promotional and distribution strategies. Marketing management must be fully cognizant of the limitations and opportunities of the competitive environment in which the company operates. For example, a gasoline service station manager must be aware of the possible consequences and reactions of competitors if the price of gasoline is raised five cents per gallon on all grades. How will competitors react? Will they raise their prices or hold the line? What will be the effect on sales? On market share? How will profits change as a result of a price increase? Finally, but certainly not the least important of the environmental constraints, are those imposed by legal and political factors. Historically, government regulations such as the Robinson-Patman Act and Resale Price Maintenance Laws have tended to control the pricing activities of business. More recently, with the renewed interest in consumer rights, product safety, product obsolescence, and ecology, many new laws have been passed by Congress during the period from 1962 to 1976. In addition, some states are adding to the barrage of rules and regulations governing business activities. Further discussion of the legal and political environment is reserved for Chapter 17.

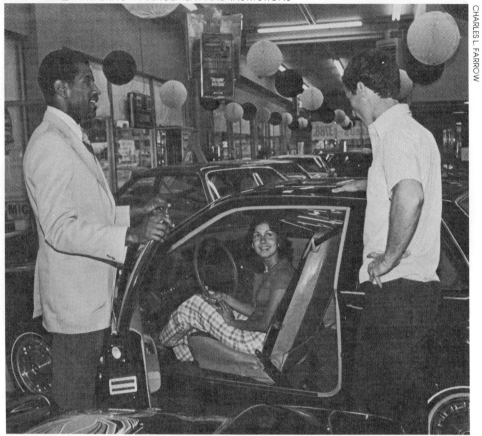

CHARLES L. FARROW

Buying an automobile is often a family matter.

DEVELOPING A MARKETING PROGRAM

An effective marketing program begins with a thorough analysis of the consumer. For marketing purposes consumers are classified broadly as either *ultimate* or *industrial* consumers, depending on the motive of the purchasers. Ultimate consumers buy for personal, family, or household use. Basically they are satisfying nonbusiness wants and constitute what is termed the "consumer" market. A mother who buys food and clothing for herself and her family or a glass candleholder as a wedding gift is an ultimate consumer. Similarly, a father who buys a new automobile for his family is an ultimate consumer.

Industrial consumers buy goods and services to use directly or indirectly in the production of other goods and services. Industrial consumers include businesses, institutions, farmers, and government bodies; they constitute the "industrial" market. An insurance company who buys accounting ledger paper is an industrial consumer because the paper is used indirectly in the "production" of a service. Similarly, when Ford Motor Company buys steel, tires, plastic, and glass for use in manufacturing automobiles, an industrial consumer purchase is being made. An Iowa farmer who purchases fertilizer for use in commercial farming is an industrial consumer. However, a home gardener who buys fertilizer for his family garden is an ultimate consumer.

The segmentation of all markets into two groups—consumer and industrial—is extremely useful from a marketing point of view. Different marketing plans, frequently referred to as strategies, are used to reach the two market segments. Even when the same product is sold to each, different strategies are employed since the two markets have diverse buying patterns, motives, uses, and intensity of need for the product. Regardless of whether the potential market to be served by a firm is consumer or industrial or both, certain key questions need to be answered in developing a marketing program. These questions will be discussed in the sections which follow.

WHO ARE MY CONSUMERS?

A clear identification of the existing and potential customers for a company's product is of prime importance in initiating a marketing program. We have already discussed the basis for distinguishing between ultimate and industrial consumers. Ultimate consumers may be men or women; young children, teenagers, or retired persons; college students; whites, blacks, Native Americans, or Spanish-Americans; truck drivers, welders, college professors, or lawyers; bachelors, young married couples without children, or middle-aged couples with children; middle-class families or blue-collar class families. In other words, ultimate consumers may be classified on the basis of sex, age, education, ethnic background, occupation, marital status, family life cycle, and social class for marketing purposes. The demand for many consumer products is influenced by these factors. With an increasing number of people attaining higher levels of education, for example, we can expect to see changes in product preferences and buyers with more discriminating taste. With an increasing number of married women working, we have already seen a great expansion of the market for prepared foods, home appliances, and services outside the home. The decline in the birthrate of the early 1970s has not only had a significant effect on the baby food business but will next have its effect on nurseries, then on grade schools, on high schools, on colleges, in marriages, on the furniture purchases for first homes, and so on. "Today's birth dearth will have to pass through a whole generation before it works its way out and before the next population wave comes through—whatever that wave is," says William H. Francis, Gerber's population analyst, whose company has experienced the initial shock of decreased sales and profits due to the birthrate decline.[2]

For many products the number of households or families is the critical variable for marketing purposes. A household is defined as one or more persons living in the same dwelling unit; a family is a group of two or more related persons living together. A manufacturer of washing machines is more interested in the total number and type of households in a market than the total number of individual consumers. A useful classification for market analysis is the stage of household in the family life cycle. The seven categories below combine several family composition factors—marital status, presence or absence of children, and ages of children—into a single classification variable:

[2]"The Lower Birthrate Crimps the Baby-Food Market," *Business Week*, July 13, 1974, p. 44.

Household Type	I	II	III	IV	V	VI	VII
Marital status	Singles	Newly married	Married	Married	Married	Married	Surviving spouse
Children		No children	All children under 10	Some children 10–19	Children 10–19 only	No children	No children

The implication, of course, is that certain types of households represent greater market potential for certain products than do other households. For example, the washing machine manufacturer might determine that household type I would tend to use laundromats; household types II and VI, the portable washer-dryer machines; and household types III, IV, and V, the regular washer and dryer machines. Similarly, a home builder could estimate and project the housing needs of a community based on the number of households in each of the seven categories. Household types I, II, VI, and VII may be excellent prospects for apartment living, while household types III, IV, and V have needs for various sizes of single-unit dwellings.

Industrial consumers may be classified on the basis of size of firm in terms of number of employees, annual sales volume in dollars, number of years the establishment has been in business, and the number of operating units within the business organization. The marketing significance of these data for industrial consumers is that a seller may choose to serve only a segment of the total market—that is, the seller may serve a small segment very well rather than serve the total market fairly well.

HOW MANY CONSUMERS DO I HAVE?

Closely related to the identification of a company's actual and potential consumers is the estimation of size of market. Management must determine whether the potential size warrants investment or expansion in fixed facilities and manpower. For some basic products such as food and clothing, total population data may be significant. Other companies, those that sell home appliances, for example, may be interested in the total number of families or households in the market. An automobile dealer may be interested not only in the total population of an area but also in the number of households of a specific type whose income is above a certain level. The United States census provides data on total population and on such characteristics of the population as age, sex, race, income, nationality, occupation, and family composition. These data may be extremely useful in attempting to gauge the size of a potential market.

WHERE ARE MY CONSUMERS LOCATED?

Compared with most societies the American population is probably the most mobile in the world. About one-fourth of Americans change their home address at least once a year. The average American changes residences about fourteen times in a lifetime, as compared with eight times for the average Englishman and five times for the average Japanese.[3] Beginning as early as the 1800s, the movement of the American population has been from the farm to the cities. By 1972, slightly less than 5 percent of the U.S. population were farm dwellers.[4] The shift from farm to city has been accompanied by a new shift to the suburbs. The 1970 census reported 75 million suburban residents, 63 million in central cities, and 63 million in nonmetropolitan areas. The shift to the suburbs has been primarily made by middle-class families and has resulted in radical changes in the traditional patterns of retailing in the cities, which has led to a disintegration of the downtown core shopping areas of many cities. It has also made the traditional political boundaries of some cities, and even states, meaningless.

To accommodate urban and marketing planners, the Census Bureau has developed an improved classification system for urban data. Data are now collected in urban areas on the basis of a Standard Metropolitan Statistical Area (SMSA). An SMSA is defined as a county or group of contiguous counties with a total population of at least 75,000 and a central city with a minimum population of 50,000 (or two closely located cities with a combined population of 50,000). The boundaries of SMSAs may cross state lines, but counties must constitute a socially and economically integrated unit with practically all employment nonagricultural. During the mid-seventies SMSAs constituted about two-thirds of the population of the United States. By 1980, the ten top tanking metropolitan areas will include:

	(in 000)
1. New York, NY–NJ	9,415
2. Chicago, IL	6,977
3. Los Angeles–Long Beach, CA	6,787
4. Philadelphia, PA–NJ	4,770
5. Detroit, MI	4,425
6. Boston, MA	3,473
7. Washington, D.C.–MD–VA	3,254
8. San Francisco–Oakland, CA	3,223
9. Nassau–Suffolk, NY	2,840
10. Dallas–Fort Worth, TX	2,680

These areas will include about 25 percent of the total United States population.

In recent years there has been a slight countertrend movement of the population to the central cities with the development of high-rise apartments and condominiums to take advantage of living closer to places of employment and cultural and recreational points of interest. This trend has been identified mostly with households without children. The central cities also include almost 60 percent of the nonwhite population of the nation. Unique marketing opportunities are available to marketers who are willing to take a special effort to analyze the

[3]Larry H. Long, "On Measuring Geographic Mobility," *Journal of the American Statistical Association*, September 1970.

[4]*Statistical Abstract of the United States*, Vol. 65, no. 331 (Washington, D.C.: U.S. Department of Commerce, Bureau of the Census, 1973).

buying behavior, attitudes, interests, and motivations of the central-city residents.

The market for industrial products in the United States is much more concentrated geographically than the market for consumer goods. The eight states comprising the Middle Atlantic and East North Central census regions account for slightly over 50 percent of the manufacturing, according to the 1967 census of manufacturing.[5] The industrial market is concentrated not only geographically but also in a limited number of firms. For example, four automobile manufacturers dominate the domestic automobile market; four automobile tire producers supply about 70 percent of the tire output; one company, International Business Machines, controls about 70 percent of the electronic data processing market. The marketing strategy used in serving the industrial market is strongly influenced by concentration geographically and by number of firms. The limited use of middlemen, and use of personal selling rather than advertising, are aspects of marketing strategy resulting from concentrated markets.

HOW MUCH PURCHASING POWER DO CONSUMERS HAVE?

Successful marketing depends not only on population but also on income! Consumers must have purchasing power to translate their wants into effective demand. Consequently, a thorough analysis of income, how it is distributed, and how it is spent is essential in formulating marketing strategy.

Economists refer to different forms of income. For example, a nation's wealth is often measured in the form of its gross national product (GNP), which is the market value of all goods and services produced in the economy during a given period. Marketing specialists are more interested in forms of income available to individuals, families, or households than the broader aggregation of GNP. As a result, one of the key forms of income used in determining purchasing power of markets is disposable personal income (DPI), which is the income available for consumption expenditures and savings. For the typical wage earner it is gross wages less income taxes, or "take-home" pay. Usually, the higher the levels of disposable personal income in a market, the higher the absolute level of expenditures for goods and services. Some sellers, particularly those selling luxury goods or first-class services, are interested in a more specialized form of income, referred to as discretionary income. Discretionary income is income over and above that required to meet fixed commitments and essential household needs. Travel agencies, manufacturers of high-priced automobiles, and swimming pool builders, for example, would be interested not just in the changes and levels of disposable personal income within markets but also in the changes and levels of discretionary income.

In addition, *money* income, *psychic* income, and *real* income are terms frequently used in economic analysis. Money income is the amount an individual receives in actual cash or checks for wages, salaries, rents, interest, and dividends. Psychic income is an intangible but highly important factor associated with climate, pleasant surroundings, independence, or enjoyment of one's job. Some persons prefer to earn less money income but rather to have the satisfaction of running their own business. Real income is what money income will buy in goods and services. For example, during 1973 the percentage increase in the

[5] These eight states are New York, Pennsylvania, and New Jersey of the Middle Atlantic region and Illinois, Indiana, Ohio, Wisconsin, and Michigan of East North Central.

Consumer Price Index[6] was about 6.2 percent. The typical wage earner's income would have to increase by more than 6.2 percent to realize an increase in real income during 1973.

During the twelve-year period from 1960 to 1972, total disposable personal income increased from $350 billion to $797 billion in the United States, an increase of 128 percent. Average (median) family income increased from $5,620 to $11,116 during the same time period. On a per capita basis, income increased from $1,937 to $3,816. Does this mean that the average family's or individual's purchasing power increased during this period? No. The Consumer Price Index about doubled from 1960 to 1972 (see Table 8–1), which means that the average family or the typical individual had about the same purchasing power in 1972 as in 1960. Inflation "consumed" most of the increase in money income.

For the same period, 1960 to 1972, discretionary purchasing power increased from $142 billion to $375 billion, as shown in Table 8–1. Even allowing for inflation, more and more discretionary spending power is available for Americans. Since average American individuals or families did not improve their economic lots during this period, this undoubtedly means that persons in the higher income brackets are enjoying greater discretionary spending. Such persons have the choice of trading in the old car for a newer model or taking that longed-for Hawaiian vacation.

How do consumers allocate their incomes among goods and services as income increases? Over a century ago a German statistician, Ernest Engle, and an American, Carrol D. Wright, collaborated in studying the spending patterns of workingmen's families in Germany and the New England area of the United States. Together they formulated what has become known as Engle's Laws of Consumption. They postulated that as family income increases:

1. A smaller percentage of expenditures goes for food.
2. Approximately the same percentage is spent for clothing.
3. The percentage spent on lodging remains invariably the same.
4. The percentage spent on sundry items (other items such as recreation, education, and medical care) will increase.

[6]The Consumer Price Index measures the change in retail prices for the goods and services generally purchased by urban wage earners.

Table 8-1

Disposable Personal Income, Median Family Income, Per Capita Disposable Personal Income, and Discretionary Income in the United States for 1950, 1960, and 1972

	1950	1960	1972
Disposable personal income (billions)	$ 207	$ 350	$ 797
Median family income	$3,319	$5,620	$11,116
Per capita disposable personal income	$1,364	$1,937	$3,816
Discretionary purchasing power (billions)	$ 88	$ 142	$ 375
Consumer Price Index	110	185	367

Source: Personal and disposable income: Survey of Current Business. Discretionary purchasing power: The Conference Board.

Are Engel's Laws still valid today? Yes and no. Based on modern-day consumption studies, Engel's Laws would have to be modified somewhat to be valid. Law 1 seems to be clearly descriptive of today's consumption patterns. Note the key word *percentage*. Even though high-income families will spend a greater absolute amount on food purchases, these purchases represent a smaller percentage of their income. Law 3 is still roughly correct in today's society. Law 2 is invalid today. Undoubtedly one of the main reasons for the lack of validity of Law 2 is today's fashion cycle in clothing expenditures—unheard of in the 1850s. Law 4 presents problems because of its broad coverage. According to consumption studies today, medical and personal care seems to remain constant as income increases, but recreation, transportation, and education behave roughly as Engel predicted.

Engel's Laws provide a background against which marketing management can forecast expenditures for product categories as income increases. Of course, a great deal of refinement beyond Engel's generalizations is needed in forecasting tools and methods before a forecast can be useful to a specific company. Consumers with wants to satisfy and money to spend must be willing to spend

Product display is an important part of supermarket operations.

CHARLES L. FARROW

before purchase takes place. In the next sections we shall examine consumer motivation and buying patterns.

WHY DO CONSUMERS BUY?

Two homemakers are doing their weekly family shopping in the same supermarket. One chooses a one-pound can of Maxwell House coffee, a giant size of Oxydol, and one fifteen-ounce package of Kellogg's Rice Krispies. Another chooses a jar of Nescafé instant coffee, a regular-sized box of Rinso, and a twelve-ounce package of Post Toasties Corn Flakes. Two men are having an after-work refresher at their favorite tavern. One chooses a Budweiser and his buddy chooses a Schlitz. Two families are shopping for a new automobile. The first family returns to the dealer from which they bought their present car and purchases a new Ford Gran Torino station wagon. The second family spends considerably more time in comparing deals among dealers and ends up buying a new Pontiac Grandville four-door sedan. Why did the consumers in each situation choose the products they did? Why the particular brands or models or sizes? Why the particular retailers? Why did they purchase at particular times?

An understanding of the reasons why consumers behave in a given way is one of the most interesting but difficult topics in marketing. Marketing specialists do not know the complete answers to the above questions. There are a number of hypotheses (educated guesses), some bits of information, and much current research attempting to explain consumer behavior. Most marketing people would agree, however, that an understanding of consumer behavior is critical in building a sound marketing program.

Explanations of why consumers buy are based on economic, sociological, and psychological theories. Economic theorists view consumers as reasoning, calculating, and comparing individuals who allocate their incomes among products so as to maximize their total satisfaction from goods and services. The limitations of this theory are obvious. The theory does not include the sociological and psychological aspects of behavior. While the economic explanation of buyer behavior may be applicable to the industrial buying sector, studies at the University of Michigan's Survey Research Center have provided doubts and contradictions about its validity for ultimate consumer buying.[7]

Many consumers buy products in order to "keep up with the Joneses." A well-known sociologist, David Riesman,[8] divides societies into three groups: tradition-directed (oriented toward the past and resistant to change); inner-directed (guided by internal personal values); and other-directed (dependent upon others for guidance). Riesman hypothesizes that today's society is other-directed—that is, people are susceptible to external social influences in their behavioral patterns. Applied to consumer behavior, Riesman's theory argues that purchases of goods and services are influenced to a large extent by the formal and informal groups to which consumers belong. We look to others—neighbors, friends, and business, professional, or fraternal associates—to guide our purchasing behavior.

Still other aspects of consumer behavior are explained by delving into the field of psychology. Some psychologists say that consumers are driven by deep-seated, hidden, and often unknown drives and tensions. Others suggest that our

[7]See, for example, George Katona, *The Powerful Consumer* (New York: McGraw-Hill Book Co., 1960).

[8]David Riesman, *The Lonely Crowd* (New Haven, Conn.: Yale University Press,1950).

behavior patterns are learned from our total set of life experiences. The concept of a person's *field* or *life space*, which is a key element in this psychological theory, may be defined as the totality of existing facts pertaining to the individual and his or her environment at the time of his or her behavior. In other words, our total environment—past and present—affects our attitudes, images, and motives and consequently, our buying behavior.

Unfortunately, there is no comprehensive theory of consumer behavior. Some of the implications of the various theories are discussed in the next section, which deals with the various stages in the buying decision process.

Marketing specialists use motivation research to attempt to uncover the "why" behind consumer behavior—that is, what it is that drives consumers to select a particular product or a specific brand. Motivation research uses various psychological techniques, such as depth interviews, picture descriptions, word-association games, and story telling, to discover images, attitudes, motives, and personality traits of consumers. Given some valid information about consumer behavior, marketing management can attempt through product design, promotion, pricing, or distribution policies to make the company's products and policies compatible with as many potential consumers as possible.

HOW DO CONSUMERS BUY?

In addition to understanding why consumers buy, manufacturers, wholesalers, and retailers must also understand how consumers buy. Two related questions are when and where do consumers buy? Basically this set of questions refers to the topic of consumer buying habits.

William J. Stanton[9] describes five steps in the consumer buying decision process. The Stanton model is shown in Figure 8–3. In this simplified portrayal of the decision process, a potential buyer may exist at any of the five steps. All five steps, as shown in Figure 8–3, are used only in certain buying situations—the first-time purchase of a product, or when buying a high-priced, infrequently purchased item. For many items, such as toothpaste, the purchase becomes a routine affair in which an aroused need is satisfied in a habitual manner by repurchasing the same brand. That is, past learning experiences lead directly to step 4. However, if some factors change (new product, service, price, or advertising message), the decision process may be reopened.

Step 1. The decision process begins when an unsatisfied need creates tension. It may be a biological need (for example, hunger); a social need (for example, a new dress for an approaching party); or a need aroused by an external stimulus such as an advertisement or having seen the product in a friend's apartment. At the time a need is aroused, conflicts may occur. For example, the wife who recognizes the need for a new dress might also have unsatisfied needs in other areas, such as for a new piece of furniture, or an approaching tuition payment for one of the children. Conflicts must be resolved before proceeding to the next step; otherwise, the decision process stops at step 1.

Step 2. Once a need is aroused, and any conflicts are resolved, the identification of both product and brand alternatives is next. The need for additional transportation may prompt a family to consider several product alternatives—an additional car, a car pool arrangement, public transportation, a motorcycle, or

---

[9]William J. Stanton, *Fundamentals of Marketing*, 4th ed. (New York: McGraw-Hill Book Co., 1975), p. 119.

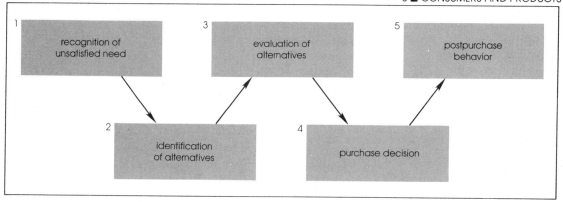

Figure 8-3 Stages in the buying decision process.

maybe even a bicycle. If one of the product alternatives is chosen—for example, an additional car—then there is the task of model and make selection. Advertisements, shopping trips, conversations with friends and associates, and ratings published in *Consumer Reports* are some of the ways to gather brand information. Sellers may assist potential buyers in the decision proces with displays, product demonstrations, or knowledgeable sales personnel.

Step 3. The time spent in the evaluation of alternatives will depend on the urgency of the need, the price range of the product, and the educational and income level of the decision maker. Some studies suggest that potential consumers with more education and income are more likely to do a thorough evaluation job. The criteria used by consumers in evaluating alternatives include past experiences, opinions of reference groups, and reliability of sources.

Step 4. When the potential buyer has completed the search for alternatives, has evaluated the alternatives, and has selected a particular product brand or model to purchase, the actual purchasing step involves when, where, price, cash or credit, color, and quantity decisions. Anything a marketer can do to simplify decision making at this stage will be meaningful to a buyer and may be influential in the repurchase. Frequently, sales promotion materials suggesting alternative uses, or "packaged" selling may be appropriate. The package tour is an example of a seller (travel agency) simplifying the buyer's decision by offering transportation, local transportation, hotels, and selected tours in one sale.

To do an effective marketing job, at this point the seller needs to understand how much time the potential buyer is willing to spend in the final purchasing process. Traditionally, consumer goods have been classified on the basis of how much effort consumers are willing to spend in the shopping process. The three classes are: convenience goods, shopping goods, and specialty goods.

Convenience Goods *Convenience goods* are those for which (1) the potential buyer is willing to spend little or no effort in comparative shopping; (2) repurchase occurs frequently; and (3) items purchased are of low unit value. For most buyers, grocery items, tobacco products, health and beauty items, and staple hardware items are convenience goods. The marketing implications of convenience goods classification are that the distribution must be extensive and intensive—that is, since a product must be accessible when the need arises, a manufacturer must have a wide variety of retailers in all areas to carry the product. The convenience good must be competitively priced, enticingly packaged, and heavily advertised.

Shopping Goods   Since *shopping goods* are purchased infrequently and have high unit value, the consumer is willing to spend considerable time in shopping, comparing prices and quality. Examples of shopping goods include homes, automobiles, diamond rings, furniture, and other durable items. The reputation of the retail outlet is important to the manufacturer since the consumer is concerned about reliability, warranty, repair services, and financial arrangements. Cooperative advertising between manufacturer and retailer is a part of the promotional strategy. Retail store location is often an important factor in the marketing mix since there are only a selected number of outlets.

The modern shopping mall tries to appeal to people as a place that offers more than just goods and services.

CHARLES L. FARROW

Specialty Goods *Specialty goods* are defined as those with unique characteristics and/or brand identification for which a significant group of buyers are habitually willing to make a special purchasing effort. Presumably, the buyer has complete knowledge about the particular product before the shopping trip begins. The buyer will accept only a particular brand or model. Apparently, the consumer will be willing to incur significant expenditures to secure his choice. For some consumers, only a London Fog topcoat or a Cadillac automobile will satisfy their needs for rainwear or automotive transportation. One outlet (exclusive distribution) in a given market may serve the needs of the potential consumers because of their willingness to seek only a given brand or model.

Step 5. Steps 1–4 take place either before or during the buying process. Step 5, even though it occurs after the sale, is equally important since how the consumer evaluates his or her purchase will influence his or her repeat sales and what is said in word-of-mouth advertising.

Consumer behavioralists say that most purchasers experience some anxieties in all but routine purchases. This state of anxiety is referred to as *cognitive dissonance.* Simply stated, most of us strive for some kind of internal harmony among our cognitions (knowledge, attitudes, values, beliefs). Any interference in these cognitions produces dissonance. Postpurchase cognitive dissonance may occur if negative information is received after the purchase or if through use of the product negative experiences are encountered. For example, the news that the contraceptive pill may produce cancer can create cognitive dissonance among users. An automobile purchaser may have cognitive dissonance upon learning that all models of the make he has recently purchased have been recalled to the dealers because of some defective parts.

A consumer attempts to reduce or minimize postpurchase cognitive dissonance by avoiding reading advertisements of the rejected products, spending more time in the prepurchase decision, or reading advertisements of the chosen product. Anything the seller can do to reinforce the purchaser through advertising or personal selling and postsale servicing will increase the likelihood of repeat purchasing. An effective postsale service program is extremely important for high-unit-value, infrequently purchased products.

MARKET SEGMENTATION

While attempting to answer the six questions involved in developing a marketing program, Geri and Art, owners of The Candy Emporium, discovered that there are at least three submarkets in the market for candy. One of these they termed the "treat yourself" buyers. This market includes those consumers who on passing by an attractively displayed candy store are enticed to buy candy to satisfy that urge for something sweet. A great deal of the purchasers in this submarket buy on impulse. They see candy, a need arises, and they immediately satisfy their need. Particularly in a college town, Geri and Art reasoned that many students will be reminded that a bag of homemade candy would go well with their late-night studying. Still others might be encouraged to go a block or so out of their way to make a purchase, if they had sampled some of the goodies from previous purchasers.

Another important segment of the candy buying market Geri and Art learned to recognize is the gift-buying customers. Gifts for birthdays, wedding anniversaries, Valentine's Day, Christmas, and other special occasions often include a box of candy with that unwritten special message, "I remembered." Geri and Art found out that much of the gift business is telephoned in for later pickup or delivery by the store. This suggested one of the marketing services a reputable store would be expected to offer.

A more distinct and less obvious segment of the candy market which Geri and Art hoped to develop is the market for special events of groups. This includes receptions, after-dinner gatherings, meetings, and other group events where a candy refresher is often appropriate and expected. This business could be serviced directly from their production facilities, and almost all of the business is on a production-to-order basis. Geri and Art knew that the marketing program for this latter segment would have to be quite different from that of the first two submarkets. In fact, the owners reasoned correctly that in order to service these three submarkets effectively, three different marketing strategies would have to be developed. Certainly the promotional program and pricing policies would vary among the three submarkets. Also, to some extent the product offering and the channels of distribution would be different for the three segments. The Candy Emporium owners decided to go after all three submarkets and to keep on the watch for other possible submarkets.

Other marketers might engage in market segmentation, as Geri and Art have done, but find that the potential market is too large, the consumers too diverse, their wants too varied, and the company's resources too limited to satisfy all of the consumers in the total market. A young entrepreneur who is considering going into the restaurant business might find that consumer needs and tastes are too varied to attempt to satisfy all of these in his or her food-service business. He or she finds some consumers who want quick, low-cost food service; others who prefer to eat out in a high-class facility; some whose eating-out preferences are for family-style restaurants; and some who would prefer to frequent standard-menu, moderately priced restaurants. According to the type of food offered, he or she would find some whose taste would be for gourmet foods, some for Italian cuisine, some for Chinese foods, others for "soul" foods, and so on. Rather than attempt to satisfy everyone, which he or she would quickly discover is impossible, the young entrepreneur would decide to satisfy the wants of a smaller, more homogeneous submarket within the total market. The process of taking the total heterogeneous market and dividing it into several homogeneous submarkets is called *market segmentation*.

Some firms, like The Candy Emporium, will choose to service all the submarkets with modified marketing programs involving product, promotion, price, and distribution. Others, like the young entrepreneur contemplating the restaurant business, will limit themselves to one or a few segments within the broad heterogeneous market.

The lack of homogeneity within a market may be due to buying habits, motives for buying, product use, life cycle of family, income, and other factors related to buyers. If markets can be properly segmented, marketing management can adjust its marketing strategies for each segment. In some instances a firm may sell the same product to different markets through use of different promotional appeals. Motherhood Maternity Shops, Inc., the country's largest chain of maternity specialty shops, now does 30 percent of its business among nonpregnant women. ("You don't have to be pregnant to shop at Motherhood" urges a sign in the shops' windows.) Frequently, however, market segmentation is accompanied by product differentiation—by developing a different product for each market segment or a selected few of the most promising segments. General Motors, for example, offers different automobile makes and models for each market segment, while Volkswagen concentrates on the economy-minded segment of the automobile market. The two approaches to market segmentation are termed *differentiated* and *concentrated* marketing, respectively.

MATCHING PRODUCTS AND CONSUMERS

Having laid the foundation for developing a sound marketing program with a thorough market analysis, marketing management must now turn its attention to matching its products or product plans to consumer needs or wants. In this process management may decide to serve only a limited segment of the market or may attempt to serve all the segments of the market with a number of different product offerings. Most of today's markets are far too sophisticated and varied to attempt to offer only one product for the entire market, as Henry Ford did successfully for a while with the Model T. Instead, some form of market segmentation is followed either by design or by default. Careful planning, designing, implementing, and control of the product-customer matching process is necessary for a continuous successful operation. Details of product management are discussed in the next section.

PRODUCT MANAGEMENT

What is a product? This seemingly simple question will be examined with several illustrations. A family who purchases a new RCA twenty-three-inch color television is buying more than a metal cabinet with electronic tubes, wiring, and metal knobs. They are buying a brand name, hours of entertainment, a warranty plan, and services from a dealer who delivers, installs, and repairs the set and may even provide credit to the purchaser. A wealthy individual who buys an original painting is buying more than a mixture of watercolors on canvas in a wooden frame; he is buying prestige, distinctive decoration, and the enjoyment of friends' admiration. A father, in purchasing an insurance policy, is buying more than a lottery with the insurance company; he is seeking security for his family, contentment, peace of mind, and perhaps some collateral against which he can borrow money at some future time.

In each of these examples the purchaser is buying want satisfaction. The product can possess physical or chemical ingredients, or it can be a service. In some cases it may be a symbol. In a marketing sense, then, a product is a combination of physical, chemical, service, and symbolic attributes designed to produce consumer want satisfaction.

THE PRODUCT LIFE CYCLE

Products, like humans, are born, grow, mature, and die. In other words, products pass through a series of stages from birth to death as depicted in Figure 8–4. The period from birth to death, or the length of the four stages—product introduction, growth, maturation, and decline—will vary from product to product. For example, the entire product cycle for the hula hoop may take six months; for a fashionable clothing item, one year; while Coca-Cola's product life cycle may be hundreds of years. The marketing strategy employed by management depends on the stage of its product in product life cycle.

In the introductory stage, for example, a firm usually incurs heavy promotional expenditures, and, if the product is truly new, it prices the product so that only those potential consumers with the most intense demand are satisfied. This pricing policy is often referred to as skimming-the-market pricing. Even with this pricing strategy, total costs usually exceed total revenue since the market at this point is composed only of the early adopters of a product. As the product enters the growth stage, prompted by widespread promotional exposure, sales begin to increase more rapidly than costs; thus a profit is enjoyed. Competitors, however, are attracted to the profitable market. To offset competition, the new

Figure 8-4 Product life cycle as related to sales volume and profit margin.

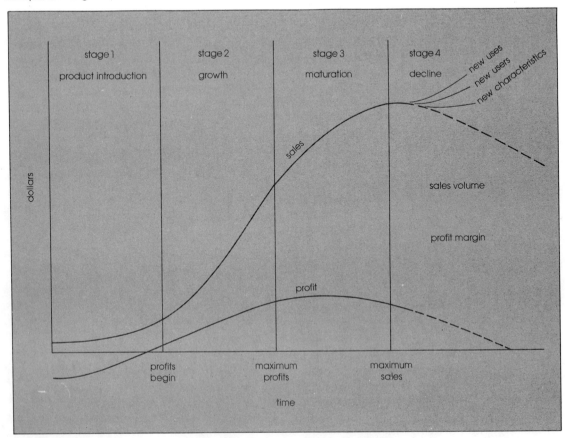

product marketer lowers price, emphasizes brand advertising, and concentrates on developing an effective distribution system.

Theoretically, the end of the growth period and the beginning of the maturation stage is reached when sales change from increases at an increasing rate to increases at a decreasing rate. Further, it is during this stage that profits begin to decline. In addition to profit decline, the maturation stage is characterized by market saturation and severe product competition. While the consumer becomes increasingly selective in his product choice at this stage, the market becomes glutted with products which offer only slight differences. In an attempt to penetrate the market, many price deals are offered by the competitive firms. To offset further profit decline and possibly even sales decrease, a company's product planning efforts should be devoted to innovation. Product innovation may occur by promoting new uses for the existing product such as Arm & Hammer's new emphasis on using baking soda as a household cleanser; by discovering new users, such as Gerber's marketing some of its baby food for adult consumers; and by providing new characteristics of products, such as the soft beverage producers increasing their container sizes from six ounces to ten, sixteen, and thirty-two ounces for family consumption, and offering a low-sugar drink for the diet-conscious segment of the market. Appropriately planned innovation may spark new growth trends, as shown in stage 4 of the product life cycle in Figure 8–4.

The major advantage of the product life cycle concept is that it provides insight about developments at the various stages of the product life. Knowledge that product profits follow a predictable pattern through the various stages and that promotional emphasis must shift from product information in the introduction stage to brand promotion in the latter stages allows the marketing manager to improve his or her future planning.

DEVELOPMENT OF NEW PRODUCTS

A marketing-oriented top management provides both the attitude within a company and an organizational setup for generating ideas and developing new products. Prior to the introductory stage in the product life cycle, considerable company resources are spent in generating new product ideas, screening these ideas, performing economic analyses of potential profitability of product ideas, converting ideas into pilot models, product testing, and marketing testing. Minnesota Mining and Manufacturing Company, the producer of the successful Scotch brand name, estimates that at any one time it is developing twenty-five to forty new products. "Maybe one-tenth of 1 percent go on to the market stage," says Chairman Harry Heltzer, "but with that much experimentation going on, it's an odds-on chance that some of them will become commercially successful."[10]

For a billion-dollar corporation such as 3M, most of its new product ideas come out of its research laboratories. Excellent product ideas may also come from salespeople or servicepeople, employees, consumers, middlemen, government agencies, competitive producers, trade associations, private research organizations, and private inventors. The particular source of ideas is not nearly as important as management's system for stimulating, acknowledging, and reviewing new ideas, and rewarding their inventors. At 3M the researcher who prefers

[10]"How Ideas Are Made into Products at 3M," *Business Week*, September 15, 1973, p. 224.

CHARLES L. FARROW

The career of the Edsel is a classic case of product failure.

to get lost in a laboratory can spend his career there and be well rewarded for his work, but the ambitious inventor is free to move on. Managers are always promoted from within, and promotions are frequent. It is just as common for inventors as it is for marketing and production men to ride with their products to become product managers, then heads of departments, and to keep going from there. "The guy who creates a product has a right to be involved in all aspects of it," says D. W. Mahew, vice-president for marketing at 3M.

THE PRODUCT MANAGER

A widely used form of organization for product planning and development is the product manager structure. Generally, however, a product manager's responsibility is not limited just to new products. This executive—sometimes called a brand manager or a merchandise manager—is ordinarily an administrator in the marketing department, reporting to the marketing manager.

The scope of a product manager's responsibilities varies widely among different companies, which is probably as it should be since businesses differ in their product and market requirements. In some companies the product manager's job is to plan and execute sales and promotional activities for the company's product(s). In others, such as Kimberly-Clark, Pillsbury, and Colgate-Palmolive, the product manager has much broader responsibilities. In such companies the product manager has responsibility for planning the complete marketing program for his or her brand or product group. Thus, he or she may be concerned with new product development, modification of existing products, setting marketing goals, and planning strategies for meeting these goals. Strategies include preparing budgets, pricing, developing advertising and sales promotional plans, and working with sales managers and salespeople to do a more effective selling job. However, the product manager generally has no line authority over the field sales and advertising personnel. This lack of authority over key persons critical to the success of his or her plans represents the biggest single weakness of the product manager system of management.

The Association of National Advertisers, in a recent study, found that the following percentages of participating companies used product managers: 85 percent of consumer packaged goods, 34 percent of other consumer product firms, and 55 percent of industrial product firms.[11]

PRODUCT LINE POLICY

Most successful companies do not sell a single product but offer a multiple product line. In many cases these products are related to each other in production (common raw material sources), marketing (the sales force can call on the same customers and offer a wider product line), or management (utilize common management skills). Products in a multiple product line may be substitutes—that is, one product may be purchased by the consumer instead of another in product line. For example, a tire company may sell several grades of automobile tires. Alternatively, products may be complements—that is, one product may contribute to the sale of another product in the same product line, such as IBM computers and IBM cards. Or products may be independent of other products in a multiple product line—that is, the sale of one has little or no relationship to the sale of others. Swift and Company's product line includes a dog food (Pard brand name), a plant food (Vigoro brand name), and a shortening (Swiftning brand name). Even though these three products are derived from a common raw materials source, they are relatively independent in sale.

An interesting question is why companies offer seemingly substitute products in their product line. At one time Proctor & Gamble's detergent line included Oxydol, Tide, Cheer, Dash, Dreft, and Ivory Snow. Ford Motor Company markets Lincoln, Mercury, Thunderbird, Ford, Maverick, Mustang, and Pinto as well as various models within each make. It appears that the firms are selling competing products. As discussed previously, both firms are confronted with broad, heterogeneous markets. By following a strategy of differentiated market segmentation they are able to satisfy different segments within the broad market and distinctively identify their products from those of competitors.

BRANDING

Many business firms use a name, term, symbol, or design (or a combination of these) to identify their products and distinguish them from those of competitors. This procedure, known as branding, facilitates marketing since the consumer can usually expect consistency in quality and performance of products. From the standpoint of manufacturers, branding facilitates promotion and enables them to control a "small market" through product differentiation. It also helps them to

[11]Victor P. Buell, "The Changing Role of the Product Manager in Consumer Goods Companies," *Journal of Marketing* 39, no. 3, July 1975, p. 3.

segment their markets through different price lines, quality levels, and different consumer motives in purchase.

Products closely related in use often utilize a family brand name such as Heinz, Campbell, or General Electric to cover an entire product line. Individual brand names are used by some sellers to differentiate product appeals to different segments within the market. Some companies employ separate brand names for groups of products—for example, Kenmore, Craftsman, and Homart are brand names for Sears-Roebuck. Still other manufacturers sell unbranded products and allow middlemen to place their brand names on the products. Firestone, Goodyear, and Goodrich tire companies may sell unbranded tires to Sears-Roebuck, Montgomery Ward, and Standard Oil and permit them to sell the tires under the Sears, Ward, or Atlas brand names.

Because a well-established brand name is a valuable asset, companies spend large sums of money in the quality control and promotion of their brands. Sometimes they are so successful that an entire product class becomes known by its leading brand name—such as aspirin, nylon, linoleum, adhesive tape—rather than by its more common descriptive name. When this happens, the brand name may be ruled generic and the original owner loses his exclusive claim to it. Legal brand names, such as Frigidaire, Kleenex, Kotex, Scotch tape, Coke, Band-Aid, and Jeep are often used by consumers as descriptive names. To prevent their brand names from being ruled as descriptive and available for general use, most of their owners take deliberate steps to inform the public of the exclusive ownership of the name. The Coca-Cola Company uses the ® symbol for registration immediately after the name Coca-Cola and Coke to indicate exclusive ownership. The company also will send letters to printed media who use the name Coke with a lower-case first letter, informing them that the name is owned by Coca-Cola.

PACKAGING

The packaging of a product serves both the production and marketing functions. It protects the product after production and before consumption as well as assists in promotion. An attractive package with informative labeling may catch the eye of the potential consumer in a supermarket and lead directly to purchase. As a part of the product differentiation strategy, a distinctive package also distinguishes a product from those of competitors. With the trend toward self-service retailing, packaging has become an extremely important aspect of the product mix in marketing.

SUMMARY

Marketing in the modern firm has the responsibility of securing, developing, and maintaining customers. Although marketing may be viewed from several perspectives, the systems view sees marketing as a total system of interacting business activities designed to plan, promote, price, and distribute want-satisfying goods and services to current and potential consumers.

The marketing concept implies that the system revolves around the consumer, who is the focal point of all business activities. Additionally, the marketing concept suggests that the total business is a marketing organization with efforts devoted to profitably satisfying consumer wants. Although certain organizational structures are recommended for implementing the marketing concept, the key to successful implementation is a positive commitment on the part of top management.

Marketing management uses four basic tools in satisfying consumer wants—product, price, promotion, and place—referred to as the four Ps of marketing. In striving for an optimum mix of the four Ps, management must recognize the opportunities and limitations posed by the economic, social, cultural, technological, political, and legal environment in which the company operates.

In developing a marketing program, management seeks answers to six key questions:

1. Who are my consumers?
2. How many do I have?
3. Where are they located?
4. How much purchasing power do they possess?
5. Why do they buy?
6. How do they buy?

After information is gathered on these questions, management's strategy might be to satisfy homogeneous segments or submarkets, rather than the total heterogeneous market. The policy of selecting submarkets or segments within the total market is known as market segmentation. Market segmentation may be approached by differentiated marketing (product for each segment) or concentrated marketing (product for one or a promising few segments). Consumer markets may be segmented on the basis of product use, buying habits of consumers, and motives for buying as well as demographic, economic, social, and psychological variables. Some useful variables for industrial market segmentation are geographic location of the market, type of business, size of firms, and buying patterns for different products.

It is important for a business to define its product(s) in terms of consumer want satisfaction. In a marketing sense, a product is a combination of physical, chemical, service, or symbolic attributes designed to produce consumer want satisfaction. Products, like humans, follow a life cycle. The various stages in the product life cycle are introduction, growth, maturation, and decline. Sales and profit curves behave differently during the various stages as management adjusts its strategy to meet changing environmental conditions. Effective product management includes developing new products, branding, packaging, and maintaining the right combination of products in the product line.

DISCUSSION QUESTIONS

1. What is meant by a systems approach to marketing?

2. Discuss the elements of the marketing concept and why it is important for businesses operating in today's environment.

3. Marketing and production depend on each other. Discuss how and why.

4. What are the four Ps of the marketing mix? Delineate the four Ps in each of the following businesses: a bank, a supermarket, a dairy, and IBM.

5. In each of the following situations, indicate whether the buyer is an ultimate or industrial consumer:
a. A student buys a copy of *Contemporary Business: Challenges and Opportunities* from a college bookstore.

b.   A homeowner purchases a power saw to use in repairing and remodeling his house.

c.   A farmer buys fertilizer for his farm.

d.   A hardware wholesaler purchases office typewriters for his company.

6.   Distinguish between disposable personal income and discretionary income.

7.   Select a company (your employer, or a company to which you are related or in which you have general interest). Evaluate your company in terms of its application or lack of application of the marketing concept.

8.   For your company selected in problem 7, analyze the company in terms of the six questions recommended in this chapter for developing a marketing program.

9.   Lever Brothers has recently introduced a new brand of toothpaste, Aim. Is this an example of market segmentation? Discuss.

10.   Have you ever experienced cognitive dissonance about a purchase? Cite some recent examples.

11.   Define *product* in a marketing sense. How would a marketing person's definition of *product* differ from a production specialist's definition?

12.   What would you consider to be the characteristics of a good brand name?

13.   Under what circumstances would you recommend the use of a family branding policy?

SHORT CASE

Add Another Product Line?

After several months of successful operation, management of The Candy Emporium is con-templating adding a line of children's toys and games to its retail operations. Geri points out that the candy displays use only about one-third of the space in the retail store and that the owners can enjoy about a 30 to 40 percent markup on all toys and games. The toys can be purchased through a broker in Kansas City. Art is not convinced that the product line should be added. He points out to Geri that the new products will add to inventory costs and do not really complement the marketing of high-quality candy. Art is more interested in finding and developing some other submarkets for the candy business than in adding toys and games.

You have been asked your opinion. What recommendation would you make? Does the new product line complement any of the current submarkets now serviced by The Candy Emporium discussed in the chapter?

SUGGESTED READINGS

Boone, Louis E., and Kurtz, David L. *Contemporary Marketing.* 2d ed. Hinsdale, Ill.: Dryden Press, 1977.

Buell, Victor P. "The Changing Role of the Product Manager in Consumer Goods Companies." *Journal of Marketing* 39, no. 3 (July 1975): 3–11.

Buzzell, Robert D. "Marketing in 1970s: What's Ahead for Marketing Managers?" *Journal of Marketing* 34, no. 1 (January 1970): 3–6.

Kotler, Philip. "Behavioral Models for Analyzing Buyers." *Journal of Marketing* 29, no. 4 (October 1965): 37–45.

Schwartz, David, J. *Marketing Today.* 2d ed. New York: Harcourt Brace Jovanovich, 1977.

MARKETING MANAGEMENT:
PLACE, PRICE,
AND PROMOTION

LEARNING OBJECTIVES

When you finish this chapter you should:

☐   have a knowledge of the basic operations of the distribution and pricing systems within a business organization.

☐   be familiar with different elements of a promotional program.

☐   understand the interrelationship among the four Ps – product, place, price, and promotion – in developing a sound marketing strategy.

KEY TERMS TO BE LEARNED FROM THIS CHAPTER

advertising	functional middlemen	oligopoly	quantity discount
cash discount	geographical pricing	personal selling	sales promotion
channel of distribution	merchant middlemen	promotion	trade discount
demand elasticity	monopolistic	promotional discount	uniform delivered
discount pricing	competition	psychological pricing	pricing
F.O.B. pricing	monopoly	pure competition	zone pricing

Essential as well designed and attractively packaged products are to management, the marketing task is not complete until products have been appropriately priced, adequately promoted, and effectively distributed to meet the demands of the target markets. This chapter will deal with these remaining three Ps of the marketing mix—place, price, and promotion.

DISTRIBUTION SYSTEM

The magnitude and complexity of a company's distribution decisions depend on whether the business is a manufacturing, a wholesaling, or a retailing operation; whether the company serves a local, regional, national, or multinational market; whether the firm is marketing one product or a multiple product line; and whether the company is a multiple-unit or single-unit operation. No business, however, is exempt from distribution decisions. Even a local gasoline service station has a critical distribution decision with regard to the best available location in terms of traffic patterns so as to maximize its sales potential. A bank which is offering financial services in a market is confronted with decisions regarding not only the most favorable location but also the number of outlets in a market to reach effectively its objectives. Manufacturers of consumer or industrial products must not only make plant and warehouse location decisions but also must be concerned with the most effective system for moving products from production to the consumers. Distribution management thus involves the channel of distribution decisions, the number and location of market outlet decisions, the selection of the best modes for the physical movement of products, and the supervision, motivation, and control of the distribution outlets.

CHANNELS OF DISTRIBUTION

The route or course taken by a product in terms of the middlemen who take title or assist in the transfer of title in the distribution process is known as a *channel of distribution* or marketing channel. A channel of distribution includes the producer and consumer as well as the middlemen in the distribution process. For example, in the automobile industry the channel of distribution generally followed is: manufacturer → retailer → consumer. For grocery items, the typical channel of distribution is manufacturer → wholesaler → retailer → consumer. Many industrial products follow a more direct channel of distribution from manufacturer or producer → industrial consumer. Figure 9–1 shows the major channels of distribution used in both the industrial and the consumer markets.

Middlemen involved in a channel of distribution are generally of two types: *merchant middlemen* and *functional* or *agent middlemen*. Merchant middlemen, such as wholesalers, retailers, and industrial distributors, are differentiated from functional middlemen in that they take title to the products they handle. Functional middlemen, such as selling agents, manufacturing agents, and brokers, do not take title but assist in the distribution process by performing a specialized function, generally selling and sometimes other promotional activities. Frequently, functional middlemen are used in lieu of a company's own sales force.

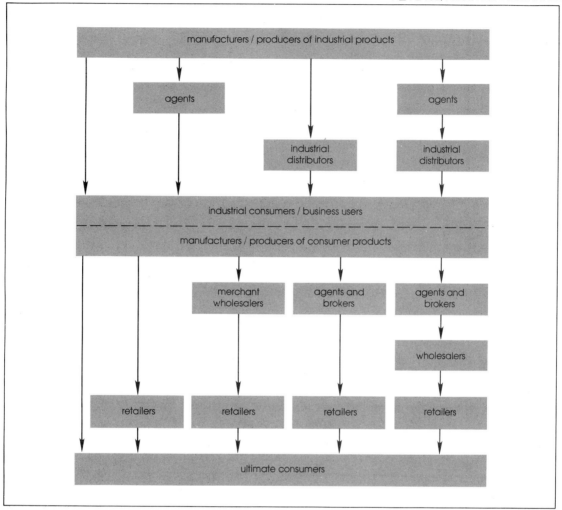

Figure 9-1 Major channels of distribution in the marketing system.

IMPORTANCE OF MIDDLEMEN

Why middlemen? Think for a moment of the difficult and probably impossible task you would have in assembling all the goods and services you have consumed today. If you arose early enough to have a hearty breakfast, you may have had orange juice from oranges grown in Florida; eggs from a poultry farm in North Carolina; bacon grown and processed in Iowa; toast from wheat grown in Kansas and processed in Kansas City, Missouri; with butter from a Wisconsin dairy; and coffee from Brazil. After breakfast you read a newspaper delivered to your doorstep and published in your hometown. As you started to drive to work or school in your automobile manufactured in Detroit, you discovered you were low in fuel and purchased gasoline made from crude oil found in and refined in Texas. Now you are reading a textbook which was published in Minnesota. It simply would not be physically possible or economically feasible to deal *directly* with all the producers or manufacturers of products we consume in our daily routine. Business firms operating as middlemen are needed to assemble and concentrate products made by producers. Others are needed to equalize and distribute these products to ultimate and industrial consumers. The important jobs of assembling, concentrating, equalizing, and distributing goods and services are performed by brokers, agents, industrial distributors, wholesalers, and retailers acting as middlemen in the distribution process.

CHANNEL STRATEGY

The marketing manager is confronted with the task of selecting the marketing channels which will best serve the customer requirements of his or her market. Among the available channels of distribution, the decision maker must determine which routes will take the products to places of demand (place utilities) and provide the needed services to satisfy consumer wants (possession utility). Management must seek solutions to the following questions in formulating a channel strategy:

1. Shall we use a direct or indirect channel of distribution?
2. If indirect, what type(s) of middlemen shall we use?
3. How many components of each type shall we use to achieve market coverage?
4. Should we use more than one channel of distribution (multiple channels)?
5. What special assistance or control activities will be necessary to maintain an effective channel system?
6. How shall we move the products physically to the consumers?

Direct or Indirect Distribution   It is generally economically feasible for a steel company to sell directly to an automobile manufacturer or for IBM to sell a

The fork lift is an indispensable tool at the distribution centers of major retail chains.

CHARLES L. FARROW

computer system directly to an insurance company or for an aircraft manufacturer to deal directly with the federal government. While a direct channel of distribution is widely used in the industrial sector, it is much less significant in consumer markets. Manufacturers' salespersons selling door-to-door and farmers' roadside stands, for example, are declining in importance in the American economy. Generally, because of the widely dispersed nature of the consumer market, the practice of ultimate consumers buying only what will be immediately consumed, and consumers' desires for variety and convenience in shopping, most consumer products are sold through indirect channels of distribution. If there is a traditional channel for consumer goods, it is: producer → wholesaler → retailer → consumer. Many consumer services, however, are sold directly from producer to consumer for obvious reasons.

On the other hand, many industrial markets are concentrated in limited geographical areas and in relatively few firms within an industry. In addition, industrial consumers purchase in relatively large quantities (raw materials or semimanufactured products) or products of high unit value. There is frequently the need to maintain considerable control over the sale and after-sale servicing of an industrial good—for example, a computerized system or an automated packaging process. These factors support a direct channel between the producer and the industrial consumer. Industrial distributors and manufacturer's agents (commonly referred to as manufacturer's "reps") are used in the distribution of standardized industrial goods.

Types of Middlemen   The marketing job which needs to be done dictates the type of middlemen used in the channel of distribution. Merchant middlemen, such as merchant wholesalers, retailers, industrial distributors, mill supply houses, and jobbers, generally perform a full range of marketing functions, including storage, transportation, bulk breaking or dividing, financing, risk bearing, buying, and selling. Functional or agent middlemen typically perform fewer services for their clients and principals. Generally, functional middlemen act as a substitute for a manufacturer's own sales force or serve as an addition to the sales force, enabling the manufacturer to sell beyond the limits of its own sales staff. Accordingly, functional middlemen specialize in performing the selling function, and they sometimes provide other promotional assistance for the manufacturer. Readers interested in a more detailed description of individual types of functional middlemen should consult some of the excellent textbooks in introductory marketing.

Number of Middlemen Needed   Depending on the characteristics of consumers and their buying patterns, management determines whether only one (exclusive distribution), several (selective distribution), or many (extensive distribution) outlets are needed in the market. In other words, the degree of market coverage needed to meet consumer demand determines the number of each type of middlemen used in the marketing channel. Consumers, for example, may be willing to spend considerable time and effort in shopping for a 35mm camera but would expect to be able to purchase film on a convenience basis. Selective distribution would be suggested for cameras, while extensive distribution is needed for film. A furnace manufacturer may need only one outlet in an area to meet the demand, depending on the size of the market.

Multiple Channels of Distribution   A manufacturer may use multiple channels of distribution either to reach different markets or to sell in the same market. A manufacturer of hydraulic brake fluid may sell direct to an original equipment manufacturer (commonly referred to as an O.E.M. market); sell the unbranded product direct to major oil companies for their service stations; and sell through automobile jobbers, who will in turn sell to automobile dealers, garages, and some service stations. The hydraulic brake fluid manufacturer is servicing both the industrial and the consumer markets. A producer selling in widely varying geographical markets or markets of different population densities will often use multiple channels. A domestic producer selling in international markets cannot use the same channel as he uses in his home country. Similarly, a food manufacturer may sell directly to large grocery chains, but to reach independent food stores in the same market he may use wholesalers. In more sparsely populated areas, the same food manufacturer may use manufacturer's agents (commonly referred to as food brokers in the trade).

A manufacturer with a widely varying product line such as Minnesota Mining and Manufacturing would clearly use different channels of distribution for product lines varying from graphics systems to health care products to tapes and allied products to electrical products to abrasives to advertising services to photographic services.

Channel Management   In order to maintain an effective channel system, it is often necessary for the manufacturer to provide direct personal supervision of middlemen. Missionary salespersons and factory representatives work directly with middlemen in implementing the promotional programs of the manufacturer, informing them about price changes and new products, and feeding back to the company recurring problems in the field. Management services such as training centers for servicemen, sales training for dealer and distributor salespeople, and advice on store location, store layout, or store modernization may be needed to maintain competitive distributors. In addition, the manufacturer may wish to stimulate sales through dealer contests and cooperative advertising plans with dealers. In order to keep abreast of the distribution system, market research should be conducted on the performance of middlemen by geographical markets, product line, and customer group. It may be enlightening for the manufacturer to discover his image among distributors—that is, how the distributors view him, his products, and his policies relative to those of other suppliers. Such research may lead to valuable information in formulating new or modifying existing marketing plans.

Physical Distribution Management   Closely allied to the decision of what channels to use and what middlemen, if any, will be involved in the distribution process is the question of how the products will be physically moved from the factory to the consumer. The objective of management is to minimize the physical distribution cost within the constraint of meeting the requirements of the market.

The transportation network available for intercity shipment of freight includes railroads, motor trucks, waterways, pipelines, and airlines. The distribution of freight among the above common carriers in 1971 is shown in Table 9–1. Railroads are still the principal mover of intercity freight but are receiving

Table 9-1
Total Intercity Ton Miles by Type of Service, 1971

Carriers	Amount (in billions of ton miles)	Percentage
Railroads	746.0	33.4
Motor trucks	445.0	19.9
Waterways	593.2	26.6
Pipelines	444.0	19.9
Airlines	3.5	0.2
	2,231.7	100.0

Source: ICC Annual Reports, 1975.

increasing competition from waterways, motor trucks, and pipelines. Railroads continue, however, to be an effective method of moving bulky freight on long hauls. Ships and barges are probably the cheapest and also the slowest method of moving freight along inland and coastal waterways. Airline costs are generally prohibitive for moving freight except for products of high unit value or when speed is important. For instance, a machine part may be needed immediately to continue production. The combining of one or more components of the transportation network, such as piggyback (loaded truck trailers carried on railroad flatcars) and fishyback (loaded truck trailers on barges or ships) service, offers promising methods of decreasing the cost of transportation. Because of the relatively high cost of transportation and the complicated rate structures of common carriers, many companies will use a traffic manager whose responsibility is to select means of transportation to satisfy the requirements of the market at the lowest possible costs.

In addition to decisions about how to transport goods, companies must determine proper location of warehouse facilities, set up efficient materials-handling systems, and organize an inventory control system. Inventory management was discussed in Chapter 7, "Operations Management."

PRICING CONCEPTS AND POLICIES

Pricing, the third element in the marketing mix, is often the most difficult to understand, as well as to manage, of the four marketing variables. Yet it is of major importance to management. A company may waste millions of dollars in research and development by pricing its product too high or may fail to realize an optimum return on its investment by pricing too low. In general, price is determined by three considerations: (1) the competitive environment of the industry in which the company operates; (2) consumer demand for the product; and (3) the firm's cost structure and pricing objectives and strategies. Each of these considerations will be discussed in relationship to price determination and policy formulation. In addition, attention will be devoted to some of the legal constraints placed upon a firm's pricing policies.

COMPETITION

Economists classify the competitive structure of markets into pure competition, monopolistic competition, oligopoly, and monopoly. In the real world there are no doubt numerous types of competitive structures representing blends of the above classes. These four models, however, provide us with a framework for analyzing the degree of pricing discretion open to management in the competitive world.

In *pure competition* numerous sellers are offering virtually identical products to many buyers. No individual seller can exert any real influence in the marketplace since the products are completely undifferentiated in the minds of consumers and each seller is supplying a relatively insignificant part of the market. A Kansas wheat farmer may be an example. Sellers operating in pure competitive market structures have no pricing discretion but must sell at the market price set by the forces of supply and demand. In some cases, particularly in agriculture, attempts have been made at gaining some degree of less than pure competition by controlling the supply of farm products through cooperatives, farm organizations, and government intervention. In addition to agriculture, fisheries and lumber mills are confronted with near pure competitive conditions.

At the other extreme from pure competition is *monopoly*. A monopoly exists when one seller, confronted with many buyers, dominates the market. The product(s) of the monopolist have no close substitutes. In other words, buyers have little choice but to select the offerings of the monopolist. While monopolies and the attempt to monopolize in this country are illegal under the Sherman Anti-Trust Act of 1890, they tend to exist in local markets. Many small towns may have only one doctor or lawyer or other professional service sellers. In such cases the seller enjoys complete discretion in setting prices so as to maximize his profits.

In many would-be monopoly industries, however, such as utilities (gas, electricity, water, and telephone), rates are regulated by government. Government bodies such as state commissions represent the interest of consumers in rate (price) determination. At the national level there is a substantial number of regulatory agencies that set or approve prices for specific industries, such as railroads, airlines, and natural gas. Chapter 17 will deal in more detail with the regulatory role of government in business.

Somewhere between pure competition and monopoly is the competitive model of *monopolistic competition*. Monopolistic competition exists when numerous small firms are selling to a market with many buyers but are able to differentiate their product(s) to some extent by changing prices or other elements in the market mix. While firms within monopolistic competition have some degree of price discretion, they must be constantly sensitive to the prices of competitors. The operations of gasoline service stations illustrate the behavior of firms in monopolistic competition. Price differences do exist among service stations, but out-of-line differentials often result in price wars. Other examples of monopolistic competition are the retail grocery and drug industries.

Some industries are characterized by "few" sellers, at least most of whom are large and serve a market of many buyers, and in which the actions of each seller definitely affect the others. The products of competing firms may be differentiated from one another in customers' eyes by some characteristics but are still considered substitutes for another. Since the degree of substitutability will vary among industries, *oligopoly* industries are sometimes classified as homogeneous-product oligopolies (high degree of substitutability in eyes of consumers) and differentiated-product oligopolies (low degree of substitutability). The steel, sulfur, and aluminum industries are frequently cited as examples of the former, while the automobile industry is mentioned as an example of the latter.

Pricing in an oligopoly industry is a major problem. Price differences do in fact exist among firms, usually to the extent of product differentiation. If a firm raises (or lowers) its prices, competitors may, depending on market conditions and their own strengths or weaknesses, raise (or lower) their prices, ignore the price change, or adjust other elements in the marketing mix, such as product features, promotion, or services, to meet the price change. An interesting phenomenon frequently referred to as *price leadership* occurs in an oligopoly industry. Not always by choice or by being the largest firm in an industry, an oligopolist may become the price leader among competitors. Usually the competitors will follow once the leader has made his price determination. General Motors and United States Steel are often recognized as the price leaders in their respective industries. In the August 22, 1974, issue of the *Wall Street Journal* it was announced that General Motors was increasing the price of its 1975 vehicles by an average of $430, or nearly 8.6 percent. The article stated:

> Since GM is the acknowledged auto industry price leader, its boost is likely to be followed by its competitors, assuring a record price boost by all Detroit auto makers this fall.

ELASTICITY OF DEMAND

In Chapter 3 we discussed how market prices are determined under pure competition using supply and demand curves. At this point you may want to review this section on the market system.

Another important concept in price determination is elasticity. *Elasticity of demand* refers to the responsiveness of quantity demanded by consumers to changes in price. If a price change elicits an even greater change in quantity purchased, the demand is elastic—that is, highly responsive to price change.[1] On the other hand, if quantity purchased changes less than a given price change, the demand is inelastic—that is, not very responsive to price change.

Perhaps the most insightful and useful view of elasticity of demand is from the vantage point of sales revenue. *Sales revenue* is defined as price times quantity $(R = P \times Q)$. From the demand schedule in Table 3–4, we obtain the data given in Table 9–2.

From $1.50 to $2.00 we observe that revenue decreases as price increases, and revenue increases as price decreases from $2.00 to $1.50. In other words, price and revenue move in the opposite direction. This occurs in the elastic portion of the demand curve. Why does revenue behave in this manner in the elastic range? Demand is elastic or responsive to price changes when a product has close substitutes. Thus, as the price for the product decreases, it will gain many of the customers who formerly purchased the substitutes, and as the price increases, it will lose many of its customers to the substitute products. Thus, at the higher price level many other games are considered by consumers to be substitutes for Chessers.

In the price range from $1.00 to $1.50, revenue increases as price increases, and revenue decreases as price decreases from $1.50 to $1.00. Within this range, price and revenue move in the same direction. This behavior is characteristic of the inelastic demand segment. Since an inelastic demand occurs when a product has no close substitutes, price decreases do not result in the gain of many customers (decreased revenue), and price increases do not result in the loss of many customers (increased revenue). By now, you should be asking, so what? What are the implications of demand elasticity to pricing on an individual firm basis?

In the real world, all other things are seldom equal, as assumed in supply and demand analysis. But demand is clearly affected by prices, and it is important for a marketing manager to have some notion of what the elasticity is for his

[1] The changes are usually measured on a percentage basis.

Table 9-2
Demand Schedule with Resulting Sales Revenue
for Chessers

Price	Quantity Demanded (units)	Sales Revenue
$2.00	10,000	$20,000
1.90	11,000	20,900
1.80	12,000	21,600
1.70	13,000	22,100
1.60	14,000	22,400
1.50	15,000	22,500
1.40	16,000	22,400
1.30	17,000	22,100
1.20	18,000	21,600
1.10	19,000	20,900
1.00	20,000	20,000

or her industry and for his or her company's products. A price decision that does not take into account price elasticity of demand can be disastrous. An example may illustrate this point. Many cities have been faced with the possibility of bankrupt mass transit systems in recent years. Confronted with declining sales revenues and rising costs, some mass transit companies attacked the problem with periodic increases in fares along with reduced service. The result was further decreases in sales revenues, followed by higher fares and again falling revenues. Undoubtedly, the consumers' reaction to higher fares and reduced service was to use substitute methods of transportation, such as driving their own automobiles, car pools, taxi service, bicycling, motorcycling, and maybe even walking. While the solution to intercity mass transit systems is indeed much more complex than a simple demand analysis indicates, one of the answers is apparently not higher consumer fares.

COST CONSIDERATIONS

Along with competition and demand, one of the key determinants of price is cost. As discussed in Chapter 3, there are several types of cost. Using the relationship fixed costs plus variable costs equal total cost, we can estimate the break-even levels for the prices presented in Table 9–2.

Assuming fixed costs of $10,000 for the production of Chessers and variable costs of $0.80 per unit, total costs can be computed for various quantities in the demand schedule. These data are presented in Table 9–3. The total break-even units can be obtained for each price level. For example, at a price of $2.00, 8,333 units must be sold in order to break even.[2] According to the demand schedule, 10,000 units can be sold, however, yielding a sales revenue of $20,000. The result at a $2.00 price level is a profit of $2,000 (sales revenue minus total costs

[2]The break-even level may be determined by the following formula where x = number of units sold:

$$\$2.00x = \$10,000 + \$0.80x$$
$$\$1.20x = \$10,000$$
$$x = 8.333$$

Table 9-3
Sales Revenue, Costs, and Profits for Chessers

Price	Quantity Sold	Sales Revenue	Profits	Total Costs	Variable Costs	Fixed Cost
2.00	10,000	$20,000	$2,000	$18,000	$ 8,000	$10,000
1.90	11,000	20,900	2,100	18,800	8,800	10,000
1.80	12,000	21,600	2,000	19,600	9,600	10,000
1.70	13,000	22,100	1,700	20,400	10,400	10,000
1.60	14,000	22,400	1,200	21,200	11,200	10,000
1.50	15,000	22,500	500	22,000	12,000	10,000
1.40	16,000	22,400	− 400	22,800	12,800	10,000
1.30	17,000	22,100	−1,500	23,600	13,600	10,000
1.20	18,000	21,600	−2,800	24,400	14,400	10,000
1.10	19,000	20,900	−4,300	25,200	15,200	10,000
1.00	20,000	20,000	−6,000	26,000	16,000	10,000

equals profit). The price level which maximizes profit is $1.90. As you can readily see from Table 9–3, a $1.90 price with sales of 11,000 units results in a profit of $2,100. This is a higher profit than can be obtained from any of the other price levels in the schedule.

The pricing concepts discussed thus far are derived from economic theory. As you have probably surmised, in the real world, price determination is not quite so clear-cut. Most firms have difficulty estimating their costs for various levels of output and find it almost impossible to estimate their demand schedule. Notwithstanding these problems, a successful marketing manager must have some knowledge or rough estimates of competition, demand, and cost for company products if the management expects to achieve the optimum price in their marketing mix.

PRICING OBJECTIVES

Let us now turn our attention to some of the pricing objectives and strategies actually used in the business world. Few firms, however, explicitly state their pricing objectives. In some cases the objectives are a part of the marketing plan formulated by product managers. The following pricing objectives are often cited by business firms:

1. Achieve target return on investment or on net sales.
2. Maintain or increase market share.
3. Meet competition.
4. Stabilize prices.
5. Maximize profits.

The first objective seems to be the one cited most often by business leaders. Profit maximization is seldom mentioned as a pricing goal of business firms. This could be due to the unfavorable connotation which profit maximization has in the mind of the public. It may be that a profit maximization goal could be sheltered under the objective of a specific target return on investment or net sales.

PRICING POLICIES AND STRATEGIES

How are prices quoted? List prices are generally quoted to potential customers. They are usually determined by a cost-plus formula.[3] Sticker prices on automobile windows are examples of automobile manufacturers' list prices.

Discount Pricing   The price that the customer pays may or may not be the same as the list price. *Price discounts* or allowances result in a deduction from the list price. The **deduction** may be in the form of cash or some other concession, such as extra **merch**andise. The underlying reason for price discounts is that the customer per**forms** some function for the seller which results in a cost savings. A

---

[3]If a product cost $10.00 to produce, for example, and the target margins to cover administrative cost, marketing costs, and profits are 15 percent, 20 percent, and 10 percent, respectively, based on selling price, the list price would be $18.18. It is determined in the following manner. Since the three margins total 45 percent of selling price, cost must represent 55 percent of selling price. Thus $.55x = \$100.00$; $x = \$10.00/.55$; $x = \$18.18$.

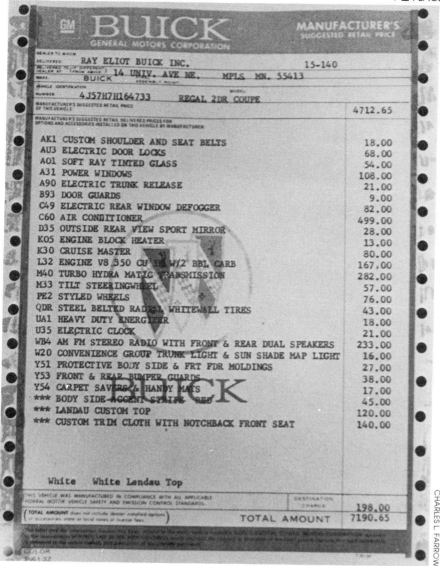

The automobile price sticker tells the potential buyer both
the list price of the car and the cost of all optional extras.

quantity discount, for example, is given customers to encourage large orders
(noncumulative quantity discount) or repeat purchases (cumulative).[4] Presumably, quantity purchases result in cost savings to the seller in bookkeeping and
billing, transportation, and sales effort. Other commonly used forms of discount
are trade, cash, seasonal, and promotional.

A *trade discount* recognizes the different functions performed by agent middlemen, wholesalers, and retailers. Trade discounts, frequently referred to as
functional discounts, are based on the different levels within the channel of distribution in which the marketing functions are performed. Generally, the closer

[4]Cumulative discounts are based on the total amount a customer purchases over a
given period, while noncumulative discounts are used to encourage large single purchases.

CHARLES L. FARROW

Price discounts are often used by merchandisers to boost
sales volume.

the middleman is to the manufacturer or producer, the higher the discount,
presumably because the closer middleman is performing functions the manufacturer would be performing without this middleman. For example, if the list
price, which is frequently the price charged the retail customer, is $45 and the
trade discount is 33⅓ percent, the wholesaler's price to the retailer is $30.

Cash discounts are offered to buyers as an inducement to pay bills promptly
or within a certain period of time after goods have been delivered. The cash
discounts take many forms, but one of the most common is 2/10, net 30—that is,
the buyer may deduct 2 percent from the total bill if the invoice is paid within ten
days after its date. If the buyer chooses not to pay the bill within ten days, he has
twenty additional days to pay the full amount before the bill becomes overdue.

Promotional discounts are offered to buyers who can assist the seller in performing promotional activities. Usually this is known as cooperative advertising
or sales promotion ventures between manufacturers and retailers. Retailers are
offered discounts from list prices for advertising the manufacturers in the retailer's market area.

Geographical Pricing Arrangements Geographical considerations are important in pricing shipments of heavy and bulky materials. Prices may be quoted
in which either the buyer (F.O.B. shipping point) or the seller (F.O.B. destina-

tion) pays the shipment cost.[5] When prices are quoted F.O.B. shipping point, the buyer pays the base price plus transportation charges from the factory or mill. The apparent limitation of F.O.B. pricing is that it limits the geographical area in which the seller can reasonably operate. The farther away a customer is from the shipping point, the less likely he is to buy from that particular seller. Thus, it is argued that F.O.B. pricing tends to create localized monopolies.

To offset the formation of local monopolies, three other types of geographical pricing arrangements are used in selected industries. One of these is *uniform delivered pricing,* in which the same price (including transportation expenses) is quoted to all buyers regardless of their location from place of origin. Such pricing is the exact opposite of F.O.B. shipping point. It is the same system as used by the mail service for first class letters; thus it is sometimes referred to as postage stamp pricing. Since the transportation costs are averaged among all customers, those customers close to place of origin are paying more than actual costs, and those at distant points are paying less than actual costs. The practice of paying more than actual costs is called *freight absorption.* Uniform delivered prices are generally legal provided they are applied to the seller's entire market.

A modification of the uniform delivered system is *zone pricing.* In zone pricing the market is divided into different geographical zones with a uniform delivered pricing system operative within each zone. The telephone company uses zone pricing for long-distance calls. Mail-order firms located in the East or the Midwest often quote higher prices "west of Rockies."

Even though it is of questionable legality, *basing-point pricing* is important from the standpoint of the industries using the system. Among the industries who are using or have used this arrangement are steel, cement, sugar, plate glass, chemicals, and lumber products. Under basing-point pricing, the final price to the customer includes the base price plus transportation charges from an industry-agreed-on basing point. The actual shipping point may have no bearing on the final price to customer.

A well-known single-basing point system was the Pittsburgh-plus, used in the steel industry. Regardless of the location of customers, prices were quoted with transportation charges from Pittsburgh. With the passage of time other steel centers, such as Chicago-Gary, Cleveland, and Birmingham, emerged. Customers located in the Chicago area, for example, objected to the payment of freight costs from Pittsburgh. Eventually, a multiple-basing-point system developed in the steel industry, and several other cities were designated as official basing points for various classes of steel products. An illustration may explain the operation of a multiple-basing-point system. Let's assume that Pittsburgh and Chicago are designated as official basing points. A customer in Kansas City, Missouri, purchases steel from a Birmingham mill. The final price to the customer is the base price of steel plus transportation charges from Chicago. The Birmingham supplier absorbs a share of the actual transportation costs.

Proponents of the basing-point system argue that the system permits competition among sellers in all markets since all customers in a given area pay the same delivered price. In essence, however, the system eliminates price competition and allows competition in other variables of the marketing mix, such as technical services, product features, advertising, and promotion. The legality of basing-point pricing is not entirely clear. Courts have not declared the system to

[5]A literal translation of F.O.B. is "free on board."

be illegal per se, but rather have tended to be concerned with the issues of collusion and conspiracy in restraint of trade.

New Product Pricing   The pricing of new products presents a unique problem for management since there is little or no direct experience in price determination. Basically two alternatives are available: skimming-the-market pricing and penetration pricing. A skimming-the-market policy chooses a relatively high entry price. The rationale of the policy is to allow the marketer of the new product to recover its research and development costs before competitors enter the market. Ballpoint pens were introduced at prices near twenty dollars but now may be purchased at prices closer to twenty cents. Penetration pricing is the opposite policy in new-product pricing. It results in pricing management believes to be lower than the long-term price. The purpose of such a policy is to discourage competition from entering the market since the existing low price is not very attractive to competition.

Psychological Pricing   Various types of *psychological pricing* are used by retail firms, in particular, to entice consumers to buy. However, there is little research basis to support the value of psychological pricing. Odd pricing is a good example of psychological pricing. For example, a price of $5.95 is supposed to give the consumer the impression that the items have been reduced from $6.00. Another common pricing technique of retail stores is to price certain items at or below cost to attract customers to the establishment. Such pricing is referred to as *loss-leader pricing.* In attracting customers to the retail establishment to purchase the reduced-price item, management's thinking is that customers will purchase other

Bargain prices, price wars, and psychological pricing are all tools of marketing.

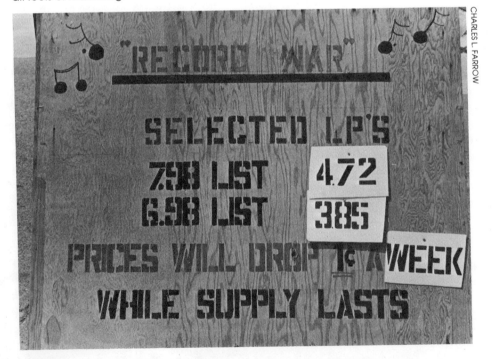

items, thus increasing overall sales. Still another pricing technique used by some retailers or manufacturers is to price above competitive market levels. *Prestige pricing* is used by firms that follow a temporary or permanent strategy of skimming the market or by firms that have acquired a unique or distinctive status in the market. Most cities have prestige clothing, jewelry, furniture, and even food stores where prices are generally above the competitive market levels.

Regulation of Pricing   Pricing strategies and policies of business firms are constrained by several statutes of law on the federal and state levels. These statutes include: (1) the Sherman Anti-Trust Act, (2) the Robinson-Patman Act, and (3) the Resale Price Maintenance Laws, commonly known as State Fair Trade Regulations. These will be discussed in Chapter 17 on government. The important point to remember is that marketing managers are not completely free to manipulate the pricing variables but must be guided by the legal and political framework of society.

PROMOTIONAL ACTIVITIES

Perhaps because of its dynamic nature and also the fact that it is observed in action daily, the promotional variable is probably the most interesting and most controversial of the marketing manager's tools. It is essential, however, to view promotion objectively. The fact that there are misleading advertising persons and disreputable salespersons does not discredit the promotional tool but suggests that users do not always apply their tools properly. The purpose of promotion is to inform, influence, and persuade potential consumers through the dissemination of product and company information. Basically, promotion activities are processes in communication. Included in promotion are advertising, personal selling, and sales promotion. The critical task confronting management is to combine the correct proportions of the three ingredients into an effective promotional strategy. In addition, marketing management must be concerned with those elements of communications, such as publicity and word of mouth, which cannot be completely controlled by management.

TOYLAND, INC.: A CASE

Let us assume that you are the marketing director for a relatively new and growing firm, Toyland, Inc. The firm manufactures a line of toys and games for preschoolers. Your competition includes such well-established companies as Playskool, Remco, Ideal Toys, Tonka Toys, and Topper Corporation, who are generally not as highly specialized as Toyland.

   Among the managerial tools that you rely on as marketing director is research, particularly that provided by Toyland's unique nursery school. The school is run by paid teachers, and the preschoolers unwittingly serve as test subjects for the company. As preschoolers probe, examine, accept, or reject a toy in the developmental stage, researchers are watching through a one-way mirror to detect anything unusual in their reaction to a toy or a game. These reactions are relayed to a management team of psychologists and marketing specialists, who decide whether children will learn anything from a specific toy, whether they will enjoy certain features, or whether the toy will help them to communicate.

While many other toymakers are trying to offset the risk of sales decline from a declining birthrate by diversification—camping equipment, recreational parks, and so on—Toyland is staying with toys and games for the preschool market segment. The company utilizes product managers for groups of toys organized by age brackets within the preschool category—that is, infant toys for infants, for one-to-two-year-olds, and for three-to-four-year-olds. The toy industry relies heavily on advertising as the form of communication to sell products. In fact, Toyland has stepped up its promotion budget from $300,000 to $3 million in the last five years.

Toyland has recently introduced a new toy, Tootmobile. As marketing director you must decide how to promote the new toy effectively along with the existing line of Toyland's products. What channels of promotion are open to you? What promotional mix is appropriate? What objectives does the company hope to achieve from its promotional expenditures?

OBJECTIVES OF PROMOTION

Toyland, Inc. like any company, should first decide what specific tasks it expects to accomplish from its promotional expenditures. The answer to this question can be as varied as companies are—their products, financial resources, market targets, stage of products in product life cycle, and other factors. Generally, however, the following can be considered the most important objectives of promotion:

1. Provide consumer information.
2. Stimulate consumer demand.
3. Differentiate the company's products.
4. Increase the value of the product.
5. Stabilize sales.

The traditional role of promotion has been to provide consumer information on the availability of products, their prices, location of products, and purchase terms. Want-ad sections of newspapers represent the consumer information role of promotion in the purest sense. Closely related to the consumer information function is the objective of stimulating consumer demand. Particularly for a new product during the product introductory stage, the role of promotion is to stimulate the demand for a good or service. In terms of demand curves of basic economics, successful promotion can shift the demand curve to the right, as shown in Figure 9–2. Existing demand for a product may be denoted by Line A in Figure 9–2. The objective may be to shift the demand schedule to Line B with successful promotional activities, thereby increasing sales at all possible price levels.

Product differentiation is often an objective of promotion. A flat demand schedule, as shown in Figure 9–3, means that the firm has no control over the price of its product. Through brand promotion the firm hopes to change the shape of its demand curve to greater inelasticity than the flat curve so as to permit some flexibility in its pricing strategy. Successful product differentiation

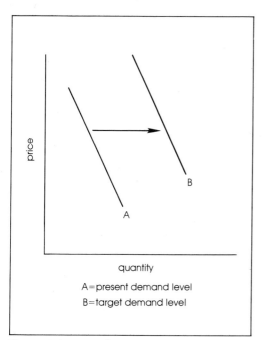

Figure 9-2 Promotional effect of stimulating demand.

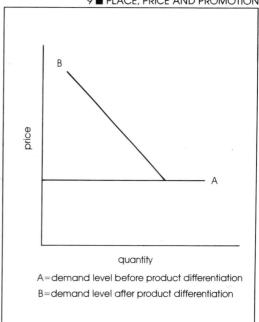

Figure 9-3 Promotional effect of product differentiation.

permits the company to operate along Line B, as shown in Figure 9–3, rather than Line A. As mentioned in a previous section on product management, brand advertising is used in the growth stage in order to differentiate the company's products from encroaching competition.

Some sellers use promotion to build up the prestige of a product or company in the minds of consumers. Status-oriented advertising may be observed in some retail store advertising as well as that of some manufacturers. Notice some of the advertisements for Lincoln and Cadillac automobiles, for example. The demand curve for a prestige product or store may be less responsive to price changes than that for a competitor without a quality image.

A company's sales are not uniform over time. Sales may fluctuate seasonally, cyclically (with changes in the business cycle), or irregularly (strikes, unfavorable publicity, and so on). Changes in sales patterns may also be caused by longer-run conditions than those mentioned above, such as changes in the birthrate, technological changes, or changes in consumer taste and preferences. Promotion aimed at building up "brand loyalty" or repeat buying may assist management in stabilizing sales or avoiding the fluctuations which may result from the previously mentioned factors. Confronted with declining birthrates, Toyland, Inc., would certainly want to avoid the declining sales pattern which could result in the toy industry. It may wish to establish itself as the company which manufactures safe, reliable, educational, entertaining, quality toys and games. How should the company allocate its budget among the various forms of promotion, given that its objectives have been established?

ADVERTISING

Toyland may wish to follow the industry practice of spending most of its promotional budget on advertising. Advertising is an impersonal form of communica-

CHARLES L. FARROW

The L'eggs pantyhose display is one of many marketing
devices found in department stores and supermarkets.

tion which involves transmitting information about a company or its products to
a mass audience by a variety of media, such as newspapers, magazines, radio,
television, billboards, and direct mail.

What should an advertisement accomplish? Regardless of the media used,
an advertisement should achieve one or more of the following steps: *awareness,
interest, desire,* and *action.* An advertisement that fails to create even an awareness
of a product or company is completely ineffectual. The task assigned to some
advertisements is to create awareness, interest, and desire for the product, but
the final action step is left to personal selling or sales promotion to accomplish in
the promotional strategy.

One of the most important decisions in developing an advertising strategy is
the selection of the media to be employed. Media decisions involve three basic
steps:

1. Determining the audience to be reached.

2. Determining the type of medium to be employed.

3. Selecting the specific media for the task.

Usually the job of identifying the target market and its size and characteristics is handled by market research. Then management must match as closely as possible the available media with target audience. The goal is to achieve adequate media coverage without advertising beyond the identifiable limits of the target market. Finally, alternative costs of the available media are compared. One method of expressing relative costs is the *cost per thousand persons (or homes) reached,* which can be calculated as:

$$\text{cost per thousand} = \frac{\text{price of space or time unit} \times 1{,}000}{\text{circulation of (or audience reached by) medium}}$$

The decision is to select those media which will provide adequate market coverage at the lowest cost per thousand of audience reached.

Toyland's target audience includes preschoolers and their parents. Even though the child may initially request a toy he or she sees in an advertisement, the purchase decision will ultimately be made by a parent. The thrust of Toyland's advertising campaign may be directed toward young parents in magazines, such as *Parent's Magazine,* and on television programs generally viewed by young families.

Essentially, there are two broad types of advertisements: product and institutional. Normally, when we think of advertising, we think of a nonpersonal message regarding a particular good or service. "Coca-Cola. . . . It's the real thing" and "When you're out of Schlitz, you're out of beer" are examples of product advertisements. Institutional advertising, by contrast, is concerned with promoting a philosophy or the goodwill of a company or industry. The American Cancer Society's advertising campaign against cigarette smoking is an example of persuasive institutional advertising. Dupont's advertisement of "Better Living through Chemistry" is attempting to build goodwill for the company through institutional advertising.

IMPORTANCE OF ADVERTISING

Unquestionably, advertising is big business in the United States. In the early seventies, total annual advertising expenditures passed the $25 billion mark. The largest volume of advertising expenditures is in newspaper advertising on a local rather than the national level. In recent years television has taken over second place—a spot held for many years by direct mail. Table 9–4 shows the total advertising bills for the country for 1973, 1975 and 1976 as well as the relative importance of the major advertising media for each year.

Is advertising effective? The answer to this question is not simple. A successful nineteenth century retailer, John Wanamaker, is reported to have said: "I know that about half of my advertising is wasted, but I don't know which half."[6] Several problems make the task of measuring advertising effectiveness particularly difficult. First, a precise outline of the objectives of advertising must be

[6] S. Watson Dunn, *Advertising: Its Role in Modern Marketing,* 2d ed. (New York: Holt, Rinehart and Winston, 1969), p. 591.

made. Is the task to create awareness, develop interest, stimulate desire, or effect sales? Second, the advertising variable must be isolated from all the other marketing variables which can contribute to the objective(s). Personal selling or number of distribution outlets, for example, may also contribute to awareness, interest, desire, or sales. A third problem in measuring the effectiveness of an advertisement is the lag between the time an ad is seen or read and a positive response is made. An advertisement seen last year may provoke a response this year. The problem is during what time period should responses be measured— during the period the ad is run, three months after, six months after, or longer?

In spite of the difficulties in measuring advertising results, some techniques are available for approximating effectiveness. Readership reports published on certain magazines and newspapers by Daniel Starch and Associates, an organization of consultants in marketing research, seek to ascertain the effectiveness of advertisements based on three measurements. The results are in the form of "noted," which means that the reader recalled seeing the advertisement; "seen-associated," which shows that the reader associated the advertisement with the advertiser; and "read most," which means that the reader read over one-half of the advertising message.

One of the major problems with measuring results of radio and television advertising is to determine who is listening to the programs. One procedure is to call a random selection of homes during the broadcasting time in order to discover if the radio or television sets are turned on and, if so, to which stations or channels they are tuned. This test is known as the coincidental method.

The Nielsen audimeter is probably one of the most controversial methods of ascertaining listenership or viewership for radio and television programs. The fate of many national television programs hangs on the evidence revealed by the

Table 9-4

Annual Advertising Expenditures for Selected Years
(in billions of dollars)

Medium	1973		1975		1976[b]	
	Amount	Percent	Amount	Percent	Amount	Percent
Total	25.1	100.0	28.2	100.0	33.4	100.0
Newspaper	7.6	30.0	8.4	29.9	10.0	30.0
Radio	1.7	7.0	2.0	7.0	2.2	6.7
Television	4.5	18.0	5.3	18.6	6.6	19.7
Magazine	1.5	6.0	1.5	5.2	1.8	5.3
Direct mail	3.7	15.0	4.2	14.8	4.7	14.1
Business publications	.8	3.0	.9	3.3	1.0	3.0
Outdoor	.3	1.0	.3	1.2	.4	1.2
Miscellaneous[a]	5.0	20.0	5.6	20.0	6.7	20.1

Source: **Advertising Age**, August 12, 1974 and December 27, 1976.

[a]Includes cost of advertising departments, transportation advertising, weekly newspaper advertising, regional farm publications, point-of-purchase advertising, material not included in direct mail expenditures, and other legitimate advertising expenditures not already covered.

[b]Preliminary estimates.

"On business trips
these days,
you've got to make
every minute,
every dollar count!

That's why
you need Hertz
more than ever."

O.J. Simpson

You can depend on Hertz. Hertz has more good
people to take care of you, so you can get
away fast into a
clean, reliable car.
More locations. More
cars. More kinds of
cars. And with Super
Saver Rates, you
save money, too.
With all this, wouldn't
you rather rent from
Hertz?

Hertz

The Superstar in rent-a-car.
HERTZ RENTS FORDS AND OTHER FINE CARS.

THE HERTZ CORPORATION

Many businesses use famous personalities to endorse their products or services. Here football star O. J. Simpson advertises Hertz rent-a-cars.

audimeter. The audimeter is a mechanical device installed in the home near the radio or television set, and it records on tape the times when the set is turned on and to what station or channel. The national sample consists of some 1,100 households. Criticisms are raised over the quantity and quality aspects of the sample. Some think the sample is too small. Further, the method does not ascertain the quality of the audience. If the set is turned on, who is listening or watching? Nielsen maintains, however, that the sample is adequate and represents a statistically accurate picture of the listening or viewing public. In addition, weekly diaries of television viewing are filled out by other samples of households and used as a basis for determining the size of the television audience for various programs. A serious limitation to using audience size as an approximation of advertising effectiveness is that the size of the audience may have little or no relationship to the attention value, believability, and comprehension of the advertisement.

In addition, the keyed-response method is used to measure advertising effectiveness. This method involves devising a procedure whereby those who are exposed to the advertisements to be tested are induced to clip the ad to purchase or to make inquiries about the advertised merchandise. The inquiries or returned ads are counted to determine the relative drawing power of the ad and/or the advertisement with the greatest number of responses. Readers of such advertisements in newspapers or magazines, for example, may be encouraged to reply by the use of coupons that are keyed to reveal the media from which the advertisements were obtained. Consumer panels or juries are used to pretest advertising copy (message) that have not been released for publication, for the purpose of selecting the one that appeals to them the most. They may be asked to rank the advertisements in terms of attractiveness, attention getting, or persuasion.

In general, all of the above methods have some real limitations in determining advertising effectiveness. More scientifically designed experiments and mathematical techniques have been developed to test the selling power of advertisements, to determine optimal allocation of advertising budgets, and to select media. These methods involve financial and personnel resources that are usually beyond the limits of the typical business.

ADVERTISING AGENCIES

While the ultimate responsibility for the advertising function rests with top marketing management, the organization of the function varies among companies. The major tasks of art, copywriting, media analysis, and advertising research are usually handled within an advertising department, headed by an advertising director or advertising manager who reports directly to top marketing executives.

Many major advertisers also use independent advertising agencies. An advertising agency is an independent company set up to render specialized services in advertising and related marketing services. If the advertising activity is given to an agency, management can expect the agency to plan and execute the entire advertising campaign. Many agencies are becoming marketing agencies, offering services such as marketing research and consultation on other aspects of the marketing mix.

PERSONAL SELLING

As a form of communication, *personel selling* attempts to match up specific products with specific customers through personal communication in order to effect sales. Personal selling has a relatively high cost per message received. With salespersons a company can reach its target market with a minimum of waste. However, this may be offset by the high cost of recruiting, developing, and maintaining a sales force. Partly for this reason, many retail firms operate on a self-service basis. A major advantage of personal selling, however, is the immediate feedback made possible with personal communication and the opportunity for the salesperson to modify the message or offer counterselling strategies if previous attempts were unsuccessful.

Relative to advertising and sales promotion, personal selling is the most important form of promotion in the marketing of industrial goods, in selling consumer goods to middlemen, and in sales of high-unit-value products to ultimate consumers. Figure 9–4 shows the relative use of advertising and personal selling between consumer and industrial products as the value of products goes from low to high.

Judging by Figure 9–4, the management of Toyland, Inc., would be expected to spend a relative high proportion of its promotional budget on advertising compared to personal selling, since toys and games are consumer goods of low unit value. Salespersons would be needed to work with the large retail accounts and wholesalers in the channel of distribution. In addition, missionary salespersons might be used to work with smaller retail outlets as well as to handle trade shows, in-store demonstrations, and to feed information back to the company regarding problems and reactions of middlemen.

Personal selling is essential to this insurance agent's sales program.

CHARLES L. FARROW

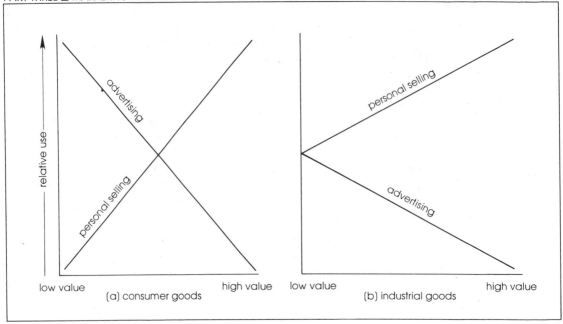

Figure 9-4 Relative use of advertising and personal selling.

MANAGEMENT OF SALES FORCE

Historically, selling and marketing were used synonymously in the business world. Frequently, the sales manager was the top marketing person in the company. Today, however, while the job of sales manager is no less important, it is recognized as being only one of the marketing managerial functions. Sales management includes selecting, training, supervising, and evaluating salespersons' performance. In addition, sales management must be concerned with delineating sales territories, determining sales quotas, and designing compensation and other incentive plans.

SALES JOBS

Most of us know persons who make their living selling. Sales jobs are numerous and varied. One of the basic differences among the wide variety of sales jobs is the degree of creativity required in the communication process. Essentially, creative selling involves transforming negative or neutral buying attitudes to positive buying decisions. Some sales jobs, such as route salesmen and order takers in retail or wholesale firms, require a minimum of creativity on the part of the seller. On the other hand, a sales engineer and a seller of intangibles such as insurance or computer installations require a high degree of selling creativity and adaptability. Perhaps the house-to-house salesperson selling vacuum cleaners or encyclopedias has one of the most difficult sales jobs since the potential customer may not have a recognized need for the product or realize how the product may satisfy his or her needs.

SALES PROMOTION

To supplement and coordinate advertising and personal selling, many marketers use sales promotion techniques such as store displays, store demonstrations, trade shows and exhibitions, and samples or premiums or trading stamps. Particularly for products purchased by consumers on a convenience or impulse basis, sales promotion at the retail level can be used effectively to supplement advertising and personal selling. Attractive displays and packaging can also be used successfully to effect sales.

Toyland, Inc., should allocate some of its promotional budget to sales promotion. Demonstrations and exhibitions at trade shows as well as store displays on the retail level can supplement the primary selling function of advertising and the efforts of salespersons.

This chapter has focused on the managerial aspects of the marketing system within the firm. Marketing management is concerned with developing a total marketing strategy using the company's products, pricing, distribution, and promotion. The objective is to achieve the correct proportions of these four elements so as to satisfy consumer needs at a profit to the company. **SUMMARY**

Management of the distribution process includes solutions for the following questions:

1. Shall we use a direct or indirect channel of distribution?
2. If indirect, what type(s) of middlemen shall we use?
3. How many components of each type shall we use to achieve market coverage?
4. Shall we use multiple channels of distribution?
5. What special assistance or control activities will be necessary to maintain an effective channel system?
6. How shall we physically move the products to the consumers?

Pricing determination is made on the basis of a company's competition, consumer demand for the company's products, and the firm's cost structure and pricing objectives and strategies. Studies suggest that most companies use a target return on investment or net sales pricing objective. In addition, other firms price to maintain or increase market share, meet competition, stabilize price levels, and maximize profits. The pricing strategies of F.O.B. pricing, discount pricing, basing-point pricing, uniform delivered pricing, penetration, and skimming the market are used in the real world. In formulating pricing strategies, management must be aware of the legal constraints imposed on the pricing variable.

Promotion is one of the most interesting and controversial of the marketing variables. It includes processes in communication—personal selling, advertising, and sales promotion. Largely uncontrollable by management, publicity and word of mouth also inform, influence, and persuade consumers about a company and its products.

Advertising is big business in the United States. Annual expenditures for the advertising function now exceed $25 billion. It is important for management to combine the correct proportions of advertising, personal selling, and sales promotion in its promotional strategy.

DISCUSSION QUESTIONS

1. What is a channel of distribution?

2. Distinguish merchant middlemen from functional middlemen.

3. Why would a manufacturer choose more than one channel for his product?

4. If generally low unit value consumer goods use indirect (middlemen) channels of distribution, how do you explain the marketing policy of Fuller Brush?

5. Differentiate among the following types of competition: pure competition, monopolistic competition, oligopoly, and monopoly.

6. Where is the break-even point for a product with a selling price of $25.00, an average variable cost of $16.00, and fixed costs of $126,000?

7. If *Fish and Stream* magazine reduces its price from $1.25 to $1.00 a copy and the number of copies sold increases from 750,000 to 1 million, what can you say about the elasticity of demand?

8. What are the three main forms of communication within promotion?

9. What is the difference between advertising and sales promotion?

10. What mix of the different promotional channels would you use for each of the following?

a. a management consulting firm

b. lawn mowers

c. car batteries

d. rental equipment service

e. life insurance

SHORT CASE

What Promotional Strategy?

Geri and Art are concerned about how many people know about their business in Warrenstown. A marketing student from State College is hired to conduct a survey among students and townsfolk. Results of the survey indicate that only 10 percent of the students and 25 percent of the town's people are aware of The Candy Emporium. Of the 10 percent of students who express an awareness, seven out of ten have eaten some of the candy, and almost all of these plan some future purchases. Of the 25 percent of the community people who express knowledge of The Candy Emporium, 80 percent have tasted their candy and 95 percent say they plan to patronize the store, if and when the opportunity arises. Geri and Art are wondering how best to spend their tight promotional budget of $2,500 for the next year. How would you recommend the $2,500 promotional budget be spent? What specific objective would you establish for their promotional strategy?

SUGGESTED READINGS

Bowersox, Donald J.; LaLonde, Bernard J.; and Smykay, Edward W., eds. *Readings in Physical Distribution Management*. London: Macmillan Co., 1969.

Hartley, Robert F. *Marketing Mistakes*. Columbus, Ohio: Grid, 1976.

Webster, Frederick E. Jr., *Marketing Communications: Modern Promotional Strategy*. New York: Ronald Press, 1971.

MARKETING INSTITUTIONS:
RETAILING, WHOLESALING, AND OTHER FACILITATING BUSINESSES

LEARNING OBJECTIVES

When you finish this chapter you should:

☐ understand the role of middlemen or intermediaries in the marketing process.

☐ be aware of the distinction between wholesaling and retailing; between wholesale merchants and agent wholesalers; between voluntary chains and corporate chains; and among various types of retailing establishments.

☐ be able to explain some of the recent trends in wholesaling and retailing institutions.

KEY TERMS TO BE LEARNED FROM THIS CHAPTER

agent wholesalers	integrated wholesaling	voluntary chains
corporate chains	retailing	wheel of retailing
department stores	universality of marketing	wholesale merchants
discount houses	functions	wholesaling
franchising		

As discussed in Chapter 9, the marketing process involves middlemen at different stages as products pass from producers to ultimate consumers. Two important groups of middlemen in the channel process are wholesalers and retailers. Their importance can be realized by noting that only 3 percent of dollar volume of all consumer goods passes directly from manufacturers to ultimate consumers. The bulk of consumer goods are sold through wholesalers and retailers. In this chapter we will examine the role played by these two marketing institutions in the marketing process.

WHOLESALING AND RETAILING COMPARED

While most of us, as ultimate consumers, come in direct contact almost daily with retail firms, we seldom have access to wholesalers. Some discount stores carry the word *wholesale* in their names when in fact they are retailers. What then is the basic difference between wholesaling and retailing?

"I say, Attila, are we pillaging on a wholesale or a retail basis these days?"

Wholesaling includes all those activities involved in selling, or negotiating sales, to customers who buy for resale or industrial use. On the other hand, *retailing* includes all those activities involved in selling, or negotiating sales, to ultimate consumers. Since a particular firm may make both wholesale and retail sales— that is, to middlemen or industrial users and to ultimate customers—the classification of a business as a wholesaler or retailer depends on who buys the majority of its products. If a majority of sales are made to ultimate consumers, even though occasional sales are made to industrial users or other middlemen, the firm is classified as a retailer. Similarly, a majority of sales to industrial or intermediate buyers by a firm would constitute a wholesaling classification.

How do the dollar sales of wholesaling and retailing compare? Since retail prices are generally higher than wholesale prices, it might seem on first thought that retail sales would exceed wholesale sales for a given time period. Table 10–1 presents a comparison of wholesale and retail sales for selected years. On the average, wholesale sales are about 146 percent of retail sales. Figure 10–1 offers a partial explanation for the difference. As can be observed, all of industrial marketing is wholesaling. In addition, sales made to middlemen who sell consumer products are also included in wholesaling. Only sales made to ultimate consumers are classified as retailing. Even though retail prices may be higher, on the average, than wholesale prices, sales made to industrial users, duplication, and export sales are sufficient to more than offset the higher retail prices.

Why is it necessary to distinguish between wholesaling and retailing? Marketing specialists are interested in studying the relative efficiency of the two institutions. To facilitate such analyses, data on "value added" in dollars are compared with costs between wholesaling and retailing institutions.[1] In addition to marketing analyses, a clear distinction is needed for certain legal and tax purposes. A retail sales tax, imposed by many states, is levied against sales to ultimate consumers and not to industrial users or middlemen. Under the Robinson-Patman Act, discussed in Chapter 9, manufacturers are permitted to offer larger discounts to wholesalers than to retailers, since they are not competing at the same level of distribution. Some laws apply to one institution but not to the other. For example, resale price maintenance laws and special chain store taxes apply to retail but not to wholesale firms. Thus for accurate accounting and analyses, correct assessment of taxes, and proper implementation of laws, a clear distinction between wholesaling and retailing is warranted.

[1]Value added is the difference between the cost of goods and their selling prices.

Table 10-1

Comparison of Wholesale and Retail Sales for Selected Years (in billions of dollars) between 1954 and 1974

Year	Retail	Wholesale	Wholesale Sales as a Percent of Retail Sales
1954	$169	$247	146%
1958	200	284	142
1962	244	358	147
1967	310	459	148
1972	448	680	152

Source: U.S. Census of Business.

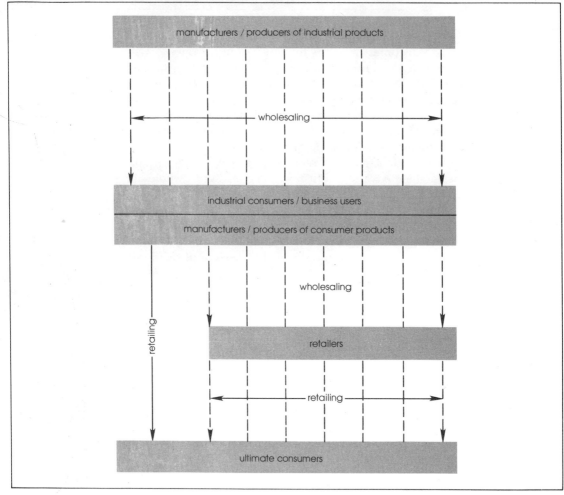

Figure 10-1 Comparison of wholesale and retail sectors of marketing system.

WHOLESALERS: TYPES AND FUNCTIONS

Middlemen who market to retailers, to other middlemen, or to industrial users are classified by the Census of Business as merchant wholesalers, manufacturers' sales branch offices, agents and brokers, petroleum bulk plants and terminals, and farm product assemblers. The number of establishments and sales for each category are given in Table 10–2.

WHOLESALE MERCHANTS

Merchant wholesalers (known as industrial distributors in the industrial sector), who take title to the goods, perform a wide variety of functions and services for the retailers or industrial purchasers. They generally provide storage, extend credit, transmit market information through their selling activities, and make deliveries. The costs of these services are estimated to be as high as 20 percent of wholesale sales. Attempts to reduce these costs have led to the appearance of limited-function and specialized-function middlemen. Cash-and-carry wholesalers eliminate financing and delivery and attempt to offer merchandise at lower prices than regular wholesalers. Drop shippers do not physically handle products but consolidate and direct shipments to their customers. Truck and rack jobbers specialize in deliveries to retailers and assist in sales promotion of the merchandise they handle. In each of these cases, the wholesalers are attempting to perform their function more efficiently by specialization.

AGENT WHOLESALERS

In addition to wholesale merchants, agents and brokers are also independent businesses. Unlike merchant wholesalers, however, agent middlemen do not take title to the goods and services in the marketing process. As discussed in Chapter 9, these independent wholesalers assume a specialized role of selling, as a substitute for or an adjunct to the manufacturers' sales force.

An example may illustrate the job performed by agent middlemen. The Gibson Manufacturing Company produces a limited line of automobile parts and accessories. Its plant is located near Detroit, and about 40 percent of its output is sold directly to one automobile manufacturer. The remaining 60 percent is sold to the replacement market through company salesmen to distributors located in the major metropolitan cities east of the Rockies. Gibson management is now considering tapping the replacement market in the major cities of the Rocky Mountain and Pacific Coast states. Since the limited available financial resources are needed to support the expanded production, the company does not have the extra capital to employ and train a sales force to cover the area. The marketing manager recommends the use of manufacturers' agents in key locations to sell the products. Even though the manufacturers agents' commission is 8 percent of sales, management believes that their knowledge of specific markets will more than compensate for this cost. In addition, manufacturers' agents have the experience, facilities, and sales force for assisting the company in product introduction.

INTEGRATED WHOLESALING

In spite of the efforts of wholesale merchants to improve their competitive position by limiting their functions and specializing in others, many large-scale man-

Table 10-2
Wholesale Trade by Type of Operation, 1972

Type of Operation	Number of Establishments (000)	Sales (billions)	Percent of Total Sales
Merchant wholesalers*	238	224	49
Manufacturers' sales branches and offices	47	175	38
Agents and brokers	26	61	13
Total	311	460	100

Source: U.S. Census of Business preliminary estimates for 1972.
*Includes petroleum bulk plants and farm product assemblers.

ufacturers and retailers choose to circumvent the wholesaler. Their activities in assuming the wholesaling functions are referred to as *integrated wholesaling.* To support their wholesaling activities, manufacturers operate sales branches and offices, and retailers maintain their own warehouses. Almost 40 percent of all products were involved in integrated wholesaling in 1972. In the industrial market alone, over 50 percent of industrial products pass through a vertically integrated wholesaling system. In the consumer product market, automobiles, meat, bakery and dairy products, and ready-to-wear items are sold in integrated wholesaling systems.

VOLUNTARY CHAINS

To compete with vertical integrated marketing systems, some wholesalers have created quasi-integrated systems of their own. Voluntary chain operations in food, drug, and dry goods industries have successfully enabled many independent retailers and wholesalers to compete with corporate chain organizations by contractually linking retailers to wholesale organizations. Super Valu in the food industry, Rexall in drugs, and Ben Franklin in variety stores are examples of successful wholesale-sponsored voluntary chains. The essence of the contract in a wholesale-sponsored chain is that the wholesaler will furnish a number of ser-

This Super Valu food store is an example of a voluntary chain.

CHARLES L. FARROW

vices to the independent retailers, who in turn will buy all or almost all of their merchandise from the wholesaler. The buying power of the combined retailers enables the wholesaler to buy at prices competitive with corporate chains. The service package of the voluntary chain organization for their retailers usually includes store location and layout advice, accounting and stock control systems, promotional aids, combined advertising, and credit. Voluntary chains will frequently offer their own private brands, thereby avoiding direct price comparison by the ultimate consumer. With successful development and continued expansion of voluntary chains in new fields, the future of the independent wholesaler seems assured.

UNIVERSALITY OF MARKETING FUNCTIONS

An important marketing lesson becomes apparent in the development of integrated marketing systems. Manufacturers may establish a distribution system of warehouses, sales branches and offices, and salespersons for providing market coverage. Or the manufacturers may attempt to push these functions on the retailers. Large retailers face the same choice. The marketing lesson involved: marketing functions must be performed by someone in the channel of distribution; they may be shifted backward to the manufacturers or forward to the retailers, but they cannot be eliminated from the channel of distribution. Whether an integrated marketing system will be more profitable than selling through independent wholesalers will depend on whether the shifted or transferred functions can be performed more efficiently than in alternative channels of distribution. Some manufacturers and retailers have discovered that the best choice is not always to circumvent the wholesaler.

RETAILERS: SCOPE AND TYPES

Retailing represents the final link in the distribution channel chain. Under the marketing concept, however, this point is not final, since marketing has not completed its task until feedback about consumer satisfaction or dissatisfaction with the product is received by the producer. Retailing, as previously defined, is concerned with all the activities involved in selling to ultimate consumers. Included under retailing are not only selling through retail stores but also mail-order and telephone-order selling, sales through automatic vending machines, house-to-house selling, and roadside selling. Actually the latter groups are relatively insignificant in their total retail sales.

SMALL-SCALE RETAILING

As with the young child who decides to sell lemonade on the street corner, it is often said that it is easier to go into retailing than virtually any other line of business. And when the child packs up his lemonade and lemonade stand in disgust as his buddies start competing businesses on opposite corners, it must be remembered that **ease of entry results in fierce competition**. This highly com-

CHARLES L. FARROW

Many small businesses, such as this unpainted-furniture store, compete successfully against large-scale operations in their product lines.

petitive environment produces a mortality rate among retailers higher than that of any other line of business.

In spite of the high entry and exit rate in and out of retailing, many small retail establishments compete successfully alongside large-scale operations in grocery, drug, and hardware businesses. In other areas, such as fashion clothing, bookstores, and sporting goods, specialty shops offer consumers a wide assortment in a limited product line, personalized services, and often convenience. It is interesting to observe that the most highly recommended restaurants in an area are still independently owned and operated establishments.

Small-scale retailers' primary competitive disadvantages are in management and buying. Often a manager of a small retail store has to be a "jack of all trades," serving in the capacity of accountant, promotion manager, buyer, and chief policy maker. It is too easy for the manager to become so engrossed in detail that little time, if any, is spent in formulating policy and planning strategy. Even though some assistance, as provided by the Small Business Administration management programs and university-sponsored programs, is available to small businesses, problems are often not recognized by management until it is too late.

In buying, small-scale operators are at a distinct disadvantage: they have to pay higher prices for goods since they buy in smaller quantities than larger-scale retailers and have little access to research and buying experts. It is for this reason that the previously discussed wholesale-sponsored voluntary chains have enjoyed success in some areas. In addition, retailers have formed their own cooperative buying groups to enable them to compete in price with the voluntary and corporate chains. Associated Grocers and Certified Grocers are examples of retailer cooperatives in the food field.

The competitive environment of retailing exemplified by many small firms operating alongside large-scale establishments reflects the spirit of a free enterprise system and offers added value for consumers. It is true that large-scale enterprises exist in retailing, and in some markets there is substantial concentration of business in relatively few firms. But even these firms compete vigorously with each other in their marketing activities, and the consumer generally benefits.

LARGE-SCALE RETAILING

Much of the color and drama of retailing are associated with large-scale operations. In many ways the growth and development of mail-order houses, department stores, discount houses, and corporate chains have added a vitality and flexibility to retailing unmatched perhaps in any other business sector. Combine with these shopping center developments, supermarket movement, and more recently the franchised system, and we can present a retailing picture unique to the American scene. In this section we will single out several major types of retailing institutions for special attention. Department stores, corporate chains, discount houses, supermarkets, and planned shopping centers will be discussed because of their major contributions to retail marketing. In addition, the rapidly expanding franchise system will be analyzed.

Department Stores   Department store development is closely associated with the growth of urban America. Today the department store is the symbol of many large urban centers, such as Macy's of New York, Marshall Field of Chicago, Neiman-Marcus of Dallas, Famous-Barr of St. Louis, and Bullock's of Los Angeles. Actually, a department store is a composition of many specialty stores in one operation. While most of the departments are operated by the department store management, some are leased to operators independent of the store itself. The lessee pays a fee to the store in return for space and use of such store services as delivery and charge accounts. Typical among leased departments are shoe, millinery, optical goods, photographic products, and special services such as repair and food services. These departments are perceived as high-risk operations which require the skills of specialized experts in management and buying.

In competing with other types of retailers, the regular department store has some characteristic strengths and weaknesses. Among the competitive strengths are its wide consumer appeal, rising from its product lines and services; the advantages of large-scale purchasing; and sufficient financial resources to undertake community projects to create a favorable public image. Department store sales represent about 10 percent of total retail sales.

Department stores' high operating costs reflect their liberal return policies, the costs of customer services, and the high overhead costs of a large, complex organization. Average gross margin as a percent of sales is estimated to be about

36 percent, with average gross operating costs of about 31 percent. Some department stores also suffer from a lack of flexibility in their operations. The failure to establish suburban branches or to compete with discount houses' prices have spelled the doom of some conventional department stores.

Corporate Chains   Unlike voluntary chains, previously discussed, corporate chains are centrally owned and managed, with all the units in the company handling the same product lines. Volume buying through a central organization and in some cases ownership of producing and processing operations enable chain store organizations to offer consumers generally lower prices than independents. In addition, through mass promotion which covers many units and standard operational procedures, corporate chains can often reduce substantially the cost of retailing.

It is thus not surprising that corporate chains, beginning with the Great Atlantic and Pacific Tea Company (A & P) in the 1850s, have enjoyed a phenomenal growth in this country. Even though chain stores represent only about 12 percent of all retail stores, they account for about one-third of all retail sales. Along with food retailing (A & P and Safeway), prominent chain store organizations are found in the variety store business (F. W. Woolworth and Kresge), the department store business (Federated Department Stores and May Department Stores), drugs (Walgreens), and the mail-order business (Sears Roebuck and Company and Montgomery Ward).

Chain stores suffer the limitations of most large-scale retailing institutions plus a few unique to chains. Earlier resentment against the corporate chain movement resulted in anti-chain-store laws in the 1930s at both the federal and state levels designed to restrict the number of operating units. The standard operational procedures of chain stores are both a disadvantage and an advantage. In some cases the standardization and inflexibility in operations have prevented individual units from adapting to local conditions. Well aware of the need for adjustment in certain markets, chain store managements have given individual store managers some freedom in merchandising and personnel policies. In addition, locally, chain stores have frequently had a poor public image growing out of absentee ownership, poor wages and long hours for local employees, and the fact that some independents are driven out of business because of chain store competition. While some of these may be misconceptions on the part of the public, chain stores have not always enjoyed a high degree of public esteem. Undoubtedly, enlightened management is working to improve the image in areas crucial to the continued growth of chain stores.

Discount Houses   The economic stage was set in the 1930s and 1940s for the development of "discounters" in the 1950s. The adoption of so-called fair-trade laws during the 1930s provided a widely recognized and legally supported system of "normal" prices among retailers. For example, it became widely accepted in the drug industry that a gross margin of 33 1/3 percent was normal and fair. In the period following World War II, there was a tremendous pent-up demand resulting from the unavailability of many consumer durables and accumulated savings during the war. With the introduction of some new products such as televisions and automatic washing machines, the stage was set for some major changes in retailing.

Most conventional retailers, however, either failed to discern the situation or ignored it. A class of retailers referred to as *discounters* seized the opportunity to offer nationally advertised products at prices lower than those suggested by manufacturers with few of the services generally associated with conventional retailers. Discount houses such as E.J. Korvette of New York and Polk Brothers of Chicago began to develop in most of the major cities throughout the country. Their operating methods enabled them to cut expenses, reduce their operating margins, and offer the consumers big price reductions. As a result, some small-scale retailers were forced to discontinue the discounted products or to adopt more efficient methods. Many large-scale retailers, such as department stores, responded by starting discount operations of their own through warehouse sales.

In the 1960s the line of demarcation between discount houses and conventional retailers became blurred. Many discount houses began offering more of the traditional retailing services, moving to suburban shopping centers, adding product lines, and upgrading their image to that of a "promotional" department store. Regular retailers such as Kresge (K-Mart), Woolworth (Woolco), J.C. Penney (Treasure Island), Federated Stores (Gold Circle), May Department Stores (Venture Stores), and Dayton-Hudson (Target and Lechmere) began to operate discount department stores themselves. Unlike the promotional department stores that reduce prices on selected merchandise, these so-called mass merchandisers offer storewide discounting.

Supermarkets   Supermarkets were started by independents to enable them to compete successfully with chain stores. The idea of retailing merchandise on a self-service basis void of credit or delivery services was quickly grasped by the corporate chains. The feature of reduced service along with volume buying power by large-scale organizations enabled supermarkets to sell at low prices.

Supermarkets are by far the dominant method of retailing in the food industry. In addition, self-service operations are common among variety stores, promotional department stores, and mass merchandisers. Among conventional supermarkets the trend is toward a wide product offering. Most of the grocery supermarkets have added nonfood lines, while many of the dry-goods supermarket operations are expanding into grocery products.

A competitor of the conventional supermarket is the convenience food store. Interestingly, many of these "superettes" have higher prices, limited product lines, and less assortment within a line, but they offer the consumer conveniences in the form of long shopping hours and many locations. Superettes such as Stop and Go and 7-Eleven, which enable the consumer to make pickups or fill-in purchases, experienced exceptional growth during the early 1970s.

Planned Shopping Centers   The success of planned shopping centers demonstrates again the adaptability of retailing institutions to population shifts, changes in consumer shopping habits and preferences, and consumers' desire for convenience. With the growth of suburbia in the 1950s, many retailing institutions responded either by moving out of downtown areas or by opening branch stores in suburban areas. The coordinated efforts of a number of different stores toward providing consumers with one-stop shopping, free parking, and a variety of merchandise lines and services resulted in the development of planned shopping centers. A shopping center developer suggests that the modern shopping center attempts to integrate all retail and commercial functions of modern life that people want in entertainment, recreation, health, shopping, education, and eating.[2]

Successful centers are generally organized around one or more major department stores, with smaller shops which complement each other in merchandise line and services. Most centers offer consumers the opportunity to shop in the evenings and on weekends in an informal and often climate-controlled atmosphere. Family shopping has become a custom in shopping centers.

From the viewpoint of retailers, planned shopping centers attract traffic. Some regional centers consisting of more than a hundred stores, including one or more major department stores, may draw customers from a trading area with a radius of as much as twenty to thirty minutes' driving time. With aggressive promotion from the center as a whole, individual stores benefit. Unless downtown areas are able to solve problems of parking, traffic congestion, and general environmental deterioration, planned shopping centers will continue to enjoy an increasing proportion of all retail sales.

Franchising Systems   Although franchising is not new, franchising systems enjoyed spectacular growth during the 1960s. Associations of independent retailers sponsored by wholesalers or retailers in the grocery field have already been discussed—a type of franchising. In addition, franchised auto rentals (Hertz and Avis), dance studios (Fred Astaire and Arthur Murray), and restaurant-motel systems (Howard Johnson's and Holiday Inn) are firmly established as retailing service units. During the 1960s, however, the franchising boom occurred mostly in the fast-food business. The likes of McDonald's, Kentucky Fried Chicken, Big Boy, and Sambo's became household names.

The big shakeout of the franchising operations occurred in the late 1960s and early 1970s. A combination of bad business conditions, incompetent management, overexpansion, and some just plain shady operators played havoc with small business people and forced some firms (A to Z Rentals and Minnie Pearl Chicken among them) into bankruptcy.

Conceptually, a franchise is a contractual arrangement between a franchiser (manufacturer or wholesaler) and a series of independent franchisees (wholesalers or retailers). The franchiser grants the franchisee the right to sell certain goods and services in generally defined markets. Additionally, the franchiser provides the franchisee with equipment and managerial services. In return, the franchisee agrees to market the goods and services in a manner established by the supplier. There are two general types of franchising systems: (1) wholesaler-or-retailer-sponsored franchised systems and (2) manufacturer-sponsored systems.

In both systems, since the independent retailers are recognized as a group, the competitive advantages of cooperative promotion, group buying power, and management assistance are realized. Franchising also allows many persons to operate their own businesses. Capital acquisition is generally easier for the small business person to secure since his or her investment is backed by the reputation of an established firm.

[2]"Shopping Centers Grow into Shopping Cities," *Business Week,* September 4, 1971, p. 34.

In the early 1970s the growth areas of franchising changed. Recreation, entertainment, travel, and business services displaced fast-food services as the fastest-growing areas of the franchising business. Between 1969 and 1971, for example, sales of recreation, travel, and entertainment franchises soared 106 percent, and the number of new units rose 26 percent, according to the Commerce Department. Business and tax services also notched a 26 percent gain in new outlets and a 25 percent rise in sales for the same period.

A roundabout trend appears in manufacturer-sponsored franchising. Some of the large franchise companies are owning and operating an increasing proportion of their own outlets. Pizza Hut, for example, now owns about 70 percent of its units as compared to an earlier mix of 291 franchised outlets and 5 company stores in 1968. Similar patterns exist for McDonald's and Ponderosa System. On balance, the future of franchising looks bright as expansion occurs in new fields.

NONSTORE RETAILING

Represented in nonstore retailing are some of the oldest as well as some of the most modern types of retailing. The Yankee peddler of the eighteenth century who mounted his horse with his merchandise and rode off to the distant countrysides to sell his wares was engaging in one of the oldest forms of retailing. Today, door-to-door or in-home retailing includes such companies as Avon, Fuller Brush, Stanley Home Products, World Book Encyclopedia, and Electrolux.

In addition to in-home retailing, automatic vending, roadside or streetside stands, mail and telephone ordering through catalogs represent other forms of nonstore retailing. Particularly in the case of retailing through computerized telephone ordering, we have one of the newest forms of nonstore selling.

In each of these forms of nonstore retailing, convenience is the key motive in consumer purchases. Plus in some cases, consumers are seeking specialty products and personalized services in utilizing nonstore purchasing services.

Some critical limitations are inherent in each of the nonstore retailing methods. In in-home retailing, prices are generally higher than for comparable products bought from stores. Combine with this the objection of many citizens to door-to-door solicitation, and we can understand the relative insignificance of in-home retail sales. Some marketing experts estimate that in-home sales are less than 1 percent of all retail sales.[3]

Mail-order firms, such as Sears, Montgomery Ward, Spiegel's, and J.C. Penney, must overcome the reluctance of consumers to purchase merchandise without physical inspection. Telephone ordering usually has the same disadvantage. To offset this disadvantage, most firms using mail and telephone selling will offer liberal return and guarantee policies.

Automatic vending is generally restricted to products of low unit value and high rate of turnover. Even though vending machines are available which are sensitive to large denominations of money, consumers are reluctant to make purchases in machines involving high dollar values. As a marketing process, it appears that the disadvantages associated with most of the nonstore retailing methods will continue to restrict their importance in the total retailing picture.

[3]See, for example: James M. Carman and Kenneth P. Uhl, *Phillips and Duncan's Marketing: Principles and Methods,* 7th ed. (Homewood, Ill.: Richard D. Irwin, 1973), p. 188.

WHEEL OF RETAILING

A marketing scholar, M.P. McNair, has attempted to explain the patterns of change in retailing as the *wheel of retailing*. The explanation suggests that new types of retailers, by reducing or eliminating services, gain a competitive advantage in the marketplace by offering lower prices to consumers than established retailers. Once established, the new types add more services, and their prices gradually rise. Then other new retailing types enter the market with lower-priced offers to gain a stronghold. So the wheel turns!

Many changes in retailing institutions seem to follow the above hypothesis—introduction and growth of department stores, chain stores, supermarkets, and discount houses. On the other hand, planned shopping centers, vending machines, and convenience superettes appear to be exceptions to the wheel of retailing hypothesis. In the latter cases, introductory and growth appeals are based mostly on convenience. On balance, however, the wheel of retailing offers at least a partial explanation of the dynamics among retailing institutions.

SUMMARY

The institutions involved in the marketing process were discussed in this chapter. Three principal components of wholesaling were examined: wholesale merchants, agent wholesalers, and integrated wholesaling. Wholesale merchants take title to goods they handle. Agent wholesalers may take possession, but they do not take title to the goods. In integrated wholesaling, manufacturers and retailers perform the wholesaling function through manufacturers' sales branches and offices and through retailers' warehouses. Even though independent wholesalers such as wholesale merchants and agent middlemen are by-passed in the channel of distribution, their functions cannot be eliminated. They may be transferred backward or forward in the channel process. This demonstrates the universality of marketing functions.

Retailers comprise the last link in the channel of distribution chain. Ease of entry in retailing produces a competitive environment where small-scale firms operate alongside large-scale companies. Many small-scale operations provide consumers with a wide assortment of a limited product line, personalized services, and convenience. Their competitive disadvantage is in management and buying power.

Large-scale retailers have provided most of the color and drama associated with retailing. From the department store to chain stores to supermarkets to discount houses to planned shopping centers, retailing institutions have responded and adapted to changes in population, consumer income, and consumer buying patterns. Franchising represents one of the fastest growing types of retailing in recent years. It again demonstrates the flexibility and adaptability of retailing in responding to consumers' desires for convenience, services, and diversity of products.

DISCUSSION QUESTIONS

1. Distinguish clearly between wholesaling and retailing.

2. Why is it necessary to have a clear distinction between wholesaling and retailing?

3. In what ways are independent wholesalers attempting to maintain their competitive position against integrated wholesaling systems?

4. If a large department store decides to bypass the wholesaler and buy directly from the manufacturer, what marketing functions are eliminated? Discuss.

5. Identify an agent wholesaler in your area. Arrange a personal interview with the manager and find out how the four Ps of marketing management are combined in this business.

6. What are some reasons for the high mortality rate among retail firms?

7. Is the task of marketing management completed with the retail sale? Discuss.

8. What are some of the recent changes taking place in retailing in your hometown? What are the bases for these changes? To what extent will the changes contribute to greater consumer satisfaction?

9. What are the underlying reasons for shopping center development and growth?

10. What is the "wheel of retailing"? Does the concept explain the recent development of catalog discount stores? Discuss.

SHORT CASE

Expansion and Distribution

The Tri-State Canning Company is a relatively small canning plant. The company has prospered in recent years and is in excellent financial condition, with a large surplus of uninvested capital. Up to the present time, the entire annual pack has been sold to several large food chain organizations. Sales arrangements have been made by Mr. Thomsen, the president and principal owner. The entire production has been packed under the private label of the company's customers. There is no sales organization, and the company has never used any outside marketing assistance.

In recent years, the population has been growing rapidly in the three-state area in the midst of which the company is located. Mr. Thomsen believes that there is an excellent opportunity to expand his production facilities, to bring out a line of canned products under the company's own brand, and to sell them widely throughout the region that can be reached with low transportation costs. After making an analysis, he was surprised to learn that there were actually several hundred prospective customers within this area (grocery wholesalers, chain store warehouses, and large institutions).

If the plan to expand the company is carried out, what method of distribution would you recommend? Explain your reasons in some detail. If your recommendations were followed, what major problems would Mr. Thomsen encounter in putting them into effect?

SUGGESTED READINGS

Bearchell, Charles A. *Retailing: A Professional Approach.* New York: Harcourt Brace Jovanovich, 1975.

Lipson, Harry A., and Darling, John R. *Marketing Fundamentals: Text and Cases.* New York: John Wiley, 1974.

MULTINATIONAL BUSINESS

LEARNING OBJECTIVES

When you finish this chapter you should:
- ☐ grasp the underlying motivations for trade among nations.
- ☐ be familiar with the major barriers to international trade.
- ☐ know the difference between the balance of trade and balance of payments.
- ☐ understand the growing role of multinational corporations and their impact on world trade.
- ☐ be aware of alternative ways for marketing in other countries.

KEY TERMS TO BE LEARNED FROM THIS CHAPTER

balance of payments
balance of trade
embargoes
joint ventures
licensing

multinational
   corporation
principle of abso-
   lute advantage

principle of compara-
   tive advantage
quotas
tariffs

wholly owned
   subsidiaries

In the United States we grow wheat and sell it to the Russians. We manufacture farm and construction machinery and sell it throughout the world. In turn, we import transistor radios and small cars from Japan, wine from France, clocks and watches from Switzerland, oil from Saudi Arabia, coffee from Brazil, and cocoa beans from Ghana.

Why do nations trade among themselves? Why doesn't each nation become self-sufficient and avoid the agonizing problems of the balance of payments?[1] Trade takes place among nations for exactly the same reasons that individuals trade with each other. After all, nations are simply broader geographical and political units than counties, states, or regions. If it pays individuals to have exchange between counties, states, or regions, international trade simply represents an extension of boundaries one step further to a country.

In this chapter we will discuss first the economic basis of trade between individuals, with special attention to individuals in different countries. Recognizing that trade between nations does, in fact, give rise to unique problems, we will examine next some of the barriers to international trade and how they may be resolved. The international balance sheet will be analyzed next, with attention to the balance of trade and balance of payments problems confronting the United States. Finally, the challenges and opportunities for businesses in multinational markets will be discussed as we deal with the following questions: Is multinational marketing merely an extension of domestic marketing? How does a company go about organizing for foreign marketing opportunities? What are some of the strategies employed by multinational firms? What are some of the current problems confronting multinational corporations?

WHY NATIONS TRADE

The main reasons for trade between individuals as well as nations are based on two economic principles: (1) the principle of absolute advantage and (2) the principle of comparative advantage. These principles are the underlying reasons for the development of international trade, often in the midst of discouraging obstacles.

PRINCIPLE OF ABSOLUTE ADVANTAGE

Sue and Barb have been friends since childhood. Their diverse talents have led them in different directions professionally. Sue is an accomplished seamstress; she has developed her skill into a successful business. Barb, on the other hand, can't sew a stitch, but after completing an accounting program at the local university, she obtained her CPA. She is particularly adept at financial and tax management for small businesses. Sue hates book work, so consequently she needs the assistance of an outside consultant. It can be argued that Sue has an absolute advantage over Barb in dress design and dress making, while Barb has an absolute advantage over Sue in accounting. They both can be better off economically if they specialize in their respective professions, trade for the other's services, and continue to be friends.

[1]Balance of payments measures the flow of money in and out of a country during a given accounting period. See the section on International Balance Sheet for a more detailed discussion.

Between nations, the diversity in natural resources, climatic conditions, production skills, and cultural patterns often gives rise to absolute advantages for certain goods and services. In a broad sense it can be said that the northern portion of the North American continent has an absolute advantage in wheat production, while the southern portion has an absolute advantage in growing bananas. Specifically, the United States has an absolute advantage in growing wheat over Costa Rica. On the other hand, Costa Rica has an absolute advantage in producing bananas over the United States. The two countries do in fact trade the respective products of their absolute advantages. Compared with the United States, South Africa has an absolute advantage in the production of diamonds (natural resources), Brzil in coffee production (climatic and production conditions), and France in fine wines (cultural background and production skills). At the same time, the U.S. has an absolute advantage in the production of many capital intensive products, such as manufactured farm, construction, and data processing equipment. Although nations are capable of producing the same products, trade will occur in instances in which certain countries are able to produce goods more cheaply.

PRINCIPLE OF COMPARATIVE ADVANTAGE

Ken practices law in a small southwestern town. He is reputed to be the best lawyer in town. Among his other talents he is also an excellent typist. In fact, few typists can match his speed and efficiency. In other words, Ken has an absolute advantage over most people in his town in both practicing law and typing. But as long as there are some people who can do an adequate job of typing, it would pay Ken to specialize in his legal practice and hire someone else to do his typing. In

"You see, we're interested in expanding our operations to the spirit world and we're having some problems . . ."

economic terms, as long as there are comparative differences between Ken's legal expertise and typing skills with someone else's, both persons should specialize in that area in which they have comparative advantages, and trade for the services of the other.

Let us illustrate this principle further with a simplified example between nations. Table 11–1 shows the amount of labor used to produce food and cloth in country A and country B, respectively.

We shall assume that the other resources needed are the same for the two products in both countries. It can be readily seen that country A has an absolute advantage in both products, since less labor is required when compared with country B. However, in country A one unit of food costs one-half unit of cloth, since for every unit of food produced, country A has to give up one-half unit of cloth. Using similar reasoning, we can say that one unit of cloth costs two units of food. For country B, one unit of food costs three-fourths of a unit of cloth and one unit of cloth costs four-thirds or one and one-third units of food. The analysis can be summarized as follows:

Country A

1 unit of food = ½ unit of cloth

1 unit of cloth = 2 units of food

Country B

1 unit of food = ¾ units of cloth

1 unit of cloth = ⁴⁄₃ or 1⅓ units of food

Comparatively, food costs less in country A and cloth costs less in country B, even though country A has an absolute advantage in both the production of food and cloth. So long as there are differences in the relative efficiencies of producing the two products in the two countries, we can be sure that even the "poor" country has a comparative advantage in the production of some commodity.

In the above example, country A should concentrate on the production of food, and country B, on the production of cloth. If the two countries would then trade with each other for the product of which each country has a comparative advantage, the economic lot of both countries could be improved. Of course, you should recognize immediately that this example is framed in a narrow economic vacuum. Barriers usually develop among nations which place limits on free trade. In many economies of the world the trend has been to place barriers, usually in the form of tariffs, which serve to equalize the cost differences on products coming from countries that are able to produce them at less cost. Let's examine some of these barriers to free trade among nations.

Table 11-1

Labor Resources Needed to Produce Food and Cloth in Countries A and B

Product	Country	
	A	B
1 unit of food	1 day's labor	3 days' labor
1 unit of cloth	2 days' labor	4 days' labor

TRADE BARRIERS

Barriers to international specialization and trade can be grouped into three broad categories: economic, political, and cultural.

ECONOMIC BARRIERS

Even though the principle of comparative advantage is one of the fundamental reasons for specialization and trade, it may exist only at certain levels of production. As production is expanded for a given commodity, production costs may become higher at the expanded levels, causing a nation to be an exporter and importer of the same commodity. At the lower cost production levels the country may enjoy a comparative advantage with some countries and be an exporter of a commodity. But at the higher cost levels, the country may lose its comparative advantage with other countries and become an importer of the same commodity, if additional quantities are needed to meet domestic consumption. In the United States, petroleum is an example of a product which exhibits these characteristics.

POLITICAL BARRIERS

All countries, for various reasons, interpose political restrictions which limit the free movement of trade between their borders. Some barriers may apply to exports, such as the prohibition of military equipment and strategic raw materials from the United States to countries behind the iron curtain. For the most part, however, restrictions are placed on imports in the form of quotas, embargoes, and tariffs. *Quotas* are restrictions on the number of physical units or value of a product coming into a country. An *embargo* is the prohibition against the movement of a commodity into and out of a country during a stated time period. *Tariffs* are taxes levied on goods being imported into a country. A tariff may be a revenue tariff or a protective tariff. Revenue tariffs are levied on imports to generate revenue for the government of the country receiving the products. Usually such tariffs are relatively low so as not to discourage imports as a source of government revenue. Protective tariffs, on the other hand, are used primarily to discourage imports in order to protect domestic industry. High tariffs on Swiss watches limit the degree to which the Swiss can specialize in watchmaking and tend to protect the watchmaking industry in the United States. For similar reasons import quotas are placed on sugar imports to protect sugar beet growers in the U.S.

The industry-protection argument needs further elaboration. The argument holds that if foreign products are kept out of a country, the domestic industry does not have to compete with, in many cases, the lower-cost products from the foreign country. This allows the domestic industry to enjoy a larger market, sell at higher prices, and be protected from foreign competition. Clearly this argument, which is used by certain business groups, tends to be in the interest of certain industries rather than in the long-run interest of a country.

Frequently, the industry-protection argument is used for new and growing industries within a country. The argument is advanced that new, developing industries need a chance to become well established before being subjected to foreign competition. While this argument does have some merit under a general

Coca-Cola is marketed the world over as these Coke trademarks in (left to right) Japanese, Hebrew, Amharic (the official language of Ethiopia), English, and Arabic indicate.

goal of national self-sufficiency, it is filled with contradictions and inconsistencies. On one hand, infant industries seldom grow up. Once protection is given, it is politically difficult to remove. Further, each new industry requires a different time period to reach maturity, which contributes to the administrative difficulties in implementing an industry-protection program. Perhaps more importantly, if another country does in fact have a comparative advantage in the production of a product which needs protection in a domestic economy, shouldn't the domestic country continue to import the product at least until the exporting country loses its comparative advantage? If this is done, the long-run interest of both countries would be served. Exceptions to the latter argument would be necessitated for products involved in the national security of a country.

CULTURAL BARRIERS

In addition to economic and political limitations to international specialization and trade, differences in cultures may restrict the free movement of products among nations. Cultural differences suggest that, in many cases, the mere extension of successful domestic market products to foreign markets may not work without modifications in the product or marketing strategy. While the soft drink bottlers Coca-Cola and Pepsi Cola market abroad exactly the same product with the same promotional themes that they do in the United States, other companies are not quite so fortunate. Another U.S. company spent several million dollars in an unsuccessful effort to capture the British cake mix market with the American-style fancy frosting and cake mixes. The company discovered, however, that Britons consume their cake at teatime, and that they prefer a dry, spongy cake suitable to be picked up with the left hand while the right hand manages a cup of tea.[2]

The unfortunate experience of discovering consumer preferences that do not favor a product is not confined to U.S. products in foreign markets. Corn Products Company, a European firm, attempted to popularize Knorr dry soups in the United States. Dry soups apparently dominate the European market. Taste tests conducted in the United States indicated a strong taste preference for the soups. However, these taste tests did not include the preparation time for the dry soups. Dry soups require fifteen to twenty minutes of cooking time, while liquid soups are ready to serve as soon as heated. This difference in preparation time for "busy" Americans was sufficient to spell doom for the product in the American market.[3]

Even more fundamental differences in cultural patterns restrict the movement of products altogether, or radical changes are needed in the domestic-

[2] Warren J. Keegan, "Multinational Product Planning: Strategic Alternatives," *Journal of Marketing* 33, January 1969, p. 58.
[3] Ibid., p. 59.

The grain being loaded into these barges may be destined for shipment to the Soviet Union, which is one of the United States' biggest customers for grain.

CHARLES L. FARROW

marketed products. A well-known paper company discovered that most countries around the world, especially in Asia and Africa, will not purchase disposable products. It runs counter to their culture, along with their economic level, to use a tissue, towel, or sanitary napkin only once and toss it away. In some cases successfully marketed domestic products can be changed to meet needs and uses in multinational markets. This will be discussed in more detail in a later section.

THE UNITED STATES IN WORLD TRADE

In terms of material goods, the United States is the dominant economic force in the world. With only about 7 percent of the world's population (200 million out of 3 billion), the United States produces and consumes about one-third of the world's output. In the early 1970s exports were about 7 percent of the gross national product (GNP) of the United States. For other nations as much as 30 to 40 percent of their national incomes are derived from exports.

Even though international trade represents only about 7 percent of GNP of the United States, in absolute dollars exports totaled $42 billion and imports were $40 billion in 1970. By 1974 exports had soared to $97 billion, with imports slightly above $100 billion. Much of this increase in dollar value was due to the extraordinary rise in world petroleum prices resulting from the world oil crisis of the early 1970s. Table 11–2 summarizes the trade picture for the United States during this period. Historically, this country has generally enjoyed a trade surplus—that is, exports exceed imports. For three of the first five years of the 1970s, a trade deficit (imports exceed exports) is shown in Table 11–2. Undoubtedly, the rising oil prices, increasing competition from foreign manufacturers in product markets such as automobiles and machine tools, and continued dependence on other nations entirely for some products—bananas, coffee, spices, tea, raw silk, nickel, tin, natural rubber, and diamonds—are contributing to this trend.

INTERNATIONAL BALANCE SHEET

Like businesses, nations must summarize their trading transactions at the end of an accounting period to show their net balance of trade and net balance of pay-

Table 11-2

Exports and Imports, United States, 1974–1977
(in millions of dollars)

Year	Exports	Imports	Balance of trade
1974	$ 97,908	$100,908	− $ 2,344
1975	107,130	96,115	11,104
1976	114,807	120,677	− 5,870
1977*	49,849	59,595	− 9,746

Source: U.S. Bureau of Economic Analysis, Survey of Current Business, March 1975, March 1976, March 1977, and June 1977.
*First 5 months of 1977 only.

ments. *Balance of trade* represents the difference between exports and imports for a given accounting period, usually on a quarterly or annual basis. *Balance of payments* measures the flow of money in and out of a country during a given accounting period. The two measures are arrived at in the following manner:

balance of trade = exports − imports

trade surplus = exports > imports
trade deficit = imports > exports

balance of payments = balance of trade − "balancing transactions"

payments surplus = exports + net capital inflows > imports
payments deficit = exports + net capital inflows < imports

Table 11–3 shows a simplified international balance sheet for a given year. With exports of $100 billion and imports of $96 billion, a net trade surplus of $4 billion is incurred. However, with gifts and grants to foreign individuals or governments of $4 billion, and net capital movement from the United States to other countries of $3 billion, a balance of payments deficit of $3.5 is incurred (with $.5 billion of errors and omissions debited against the United States). This means that the outflow of gold or dollars from the United States of $3.5 billion will take place in order to pay our net international debts.

Table 11-3

Simplified U.S. International Balance of Payments
(in billions of dollars)*

U.S. exports		+ $100
Goods and services	+ $70	
Income on U.S. investments abroad	+ $20	
Travel and transportation	+ $ 8	
Miscellaneous	+ $ 2	
U.S. imports		− $ 96
Goods and services	− $68	
Income on foreign investments in U.S.	− $10	
Travel and transportation	− $12	
Defense expenditures	− $ 5	
Miscellaneous	− $ 1	
Net		+ $ 4
Balancing transactions		
Net unilateral transfers (gifts and grants)		− $ 4
Net capital movements (U.S. investments)	− $ 5	
(foreign investments)	+ $ 2	− $ 3
Net outflow of gold from the U.S.		+ $ 3.5
Errors and omissions		− $ .5
		$ 0.0

*+indicates credits; −indicates debits.

BALANCE-OF-PAYMENTS DIFFICULTIES

Most governments try to maintain fixed exchange rates between their own currencies and those of other countries. Even if not absolutely fixed, the exchange rate is ordinarily allowed to fluctuate only within a narrow range of values. The following exchange rates existed for the United States dollars as of June 21, 1977:

Country	Currency	Rate for 100 Units
Australia	Australian dollar	111.75
Canada	Dollar	96.00
France	Franc	20.80
India	Rupee	12.00
Mexico	Peso	4.80
United Kingdom	Pound	172.75
West Germany	Deutsche mark	43.50

In other terms, the Canadian dollar was worth 96 cents in United States currency, while the British pound was valued at $1.73 as of the indicated date.

Fixed rates facilitate trade because they eliminate the uncertainty arising out of a fluctuating rate. If the rate fluctuates, either the exporter is uncertain as to the revenue he will earn from his sale or else the importer is uncertain as to what his purchase will cost him in terms of domestic currency. The maintenance of a fixed rate requires each government to keep a foreign exchange reserve, typically maintained in gold or in a major currency such as the United States dollar or the British pound sterling. This reserve is drawn upon whenever the nation experiences a deficit in its balance of payments.

A persistent deficit in a nation's balance of payments is economically undesirable. Sustained outflow of gold or currency causes the nation's reserve to run low. In a crisis, this situation may force the government to devalue the nation's currency—that is, to give it a new and lower value in the foreign exchange markets. For the United States, for example, it would take more of the nation's dollars to pay for its imports, or it would receive less for its exports. This condition is generally held to be inflationary on the domestic economy. Economists consider the ideal situation to be a long-term stable performance in the net balance of payments without wide swings in either direction.

POSSIBLE SOLUTIONS TO BALANCE-OF-PAYMENTS DEFICIT

Is the problem of a persistent deficit in a nation's balance of payments solved by imposing higher tariffs, import quotas, or embargoes in order to reduce imports? Generally no! Such techniques will lead to retaliatory actions on the part of affected nations, thereby reducing the demand for exports and inducing perhaps an even greater deficit.

Undoubtedly, the ideal solution is a healthy domestic economy. An economy in which advances in technology are giving rise to increases in productivity—that is, lowering costs of producing goods and services—improves its ability to compete successfully in a world market. Further, effective government policies, as discussed in Chapter 17, to control inflation as well as deflation (recessions and depressions) contribute to the stability of a nation's currency and to the willing-ness of other nations to do business in that nation. This includes the purchase of products, which increases exports, and the attraction of foreign investment. Both of these, as we have seen in Table 11–3, represent credits in a country's international balance sheet.

Specifically, in the case of the United States, defense expenditures in other countries have been a substantial part of our international debits. During the early 1970s these expenditures were between $4 and $5 billion annually. As other nations assume a larger share than at present of our mutual defense, we can expect to show improvements in our balance of payments.

FROM INTERNATIONAL TRADE TO MULTINATIONAL BUSINESS

The term *international trade* suggests that nations trade among themselves. Most trading among nations actually takes place in the buying and selling activities of business firms. The term *multinational business* refers to a growing number of firms whose home bases are in one country but whose operations extend to many countries of the world. A multinational business does not consider its interna-

As this Kentucky Fried Chicken shop in Tokyo, Japan indicates, many U.S. fast food companies have international operations.

KENTUCKY FRIED CHICKEN

tional operations merely an adjunct to its domestic operations. American companies whose international operations are a significant part of their total operations include International Business Machines, Coca-Cola, Exxon, Gillette, Dow Chemical, International Telephone & Telegraph, and Xerox. A list of multinational foreign companies includes Royal Dutch/Shell Group, British Petroleum, Nestlé, Volkswagenwerk, Toyota Motor, and Bayer Chemical. The above companies are incorporated to do business in many nations, even though they may consider their home base the United States, as in the case of the first group, or the Netherlands, Great Britain, Switzerland, West Germany, or Japan, as in the case of the latter group. See Table 11–4 for a listing of the twenty-five largest multinational corporations.

Table 11-4
Twenty-Five Top Multinational Corporations
(Ranked by Sales)

Rank	Company	Headquarters	Sales (in billions of dollars)
1	Exxon	New York	48.6
2	General Motors	Detroit	47.2
3	Royal Dutch/Shell Group	London/The Hague	36.0
4	Ford Motor	Dearborn, Michigan	29.0
5	Texaco	New York	26.5
6	Mobil	New York	26.0
7	National Iranian Oil	Tehran	19.6
8	Standard Oil of California	San Francisco	19.4
9	British Petroleum	London	19.1
10	Gulf Oil	Pittsburgh	16.4
11	International Business Machines	Armonk, New York	16.3
12	Unilever	London/Rotterdam	15.7
13	General Electric	Fairfield, Connecticut	15.7
14	Chrysler	Highland Park, Michigan	15.5
15	International Telephone & Telegraph	New York	11.8
16	Standard Oil of Indiana	Chicago	11.5
17	Philips' Gloeilampenfabrieken	Eindhoven (Netherlands)	11.5
18	ENI	Rome	10.0
19	Francaise des Petroles	Paris	10.0
20	Renault	Paris	10.0
21	Hoechst	Frankfurt	9.3
22	Shell Oil	Houston	9.2
23	BASF	Ludwigshafen on Rhine	9.2
24	Petroleos de Venezuela	Caracas	9.1
25	Daimler-Benz	Stuttgart	9.0

Rankings reflect 1976 sales figures. This table is adapted from "The Fifty Largest Industrial Companies in the World," **Fortune** 96 (August 1977): 240. Reprinted from the 1977 Directory by special permission; © 1977 Time Inc.

A multinational philosophy and organization offers several advantages. It enables management to deal more directly with the specific needs of diverse markets, a logical extension of the marketing concept discussed in Chapter 8. The interchange of products and personnel among nations may contribute to product technology and refinement and to the development of specialized managerial skills for business. More broadly, the transfer of technology and production to developing countries gives them increased income to spend on products in which other nations may have a comparative advantage.

A serious limitation to multinational operations is the rising tide of nationalism. Governments all over the world are attempting to obtain for themselves a bigger share of the profits, jobs, markets, and technical and managerial skills that multinational companies create or control. To achieve this, governments are using the multinationals to promote a variety of their own objectives.[4] For example:

- Mexico is pushing auto makers such as Ford Motor Company and Volkswagenwerk to export more from their Mexican plants, requiring them eventually to sell as much abroad as in the local market.

- Columbia plans to put branches of foreign banks under majority Colombian control, thus shrinking the supply of local credit for subsidiaries of foreign companies and forcing them to bring in more capital from abroad.

- Saudi Arabia is asking oil companies to set up joint venture refineries and petrochemical plants in return for long-term supplies of crude oil.

- France has insisted that Motorola, Inc.'s semiconductor division set up a research and development department to qualify for investment incentives.

- Canada requires foreign companies to show that they will bring "significant benefits," ranging from jobs and increased productivity to manpower training and development of depressed areas, to get approval for corporate takeovers.

The day of the big multinational firm dominating governments appears to be declining. According to C. Fred Bergsten, a senior fellow at Brookings Institution and former economic adviser to Secretary of State Henry Kissinger, "We are seeing increasing effectiveness on the part of governments in harnessing the (multinational) firms."[5] A major concern of some economic and political leaders is that the proliferation of government performance requirements and incentives for multinational companies could trigger retaliatory measures by other countries similar to trade wars. In order to reduce such frictions, an international agency similar to the General Agreement on Tariffs and Trade[6] might

---

[4]"Multinationals Find the Going Rougher," *Business Week,* July 14, 1975, p. 64.
[5]Ibid., p. 64.
[6]The General Agreement on Tariffs and Trade, commonly known as GATT, was established in 1947 at Geneva, Switzerland. The United States, along with seventy-one other governments, is associated with GATT. Member governments agree to a set of rules by which their mutual international trade will be conducted. It provides a means of reducing tariffs and other government-imposed barriers to international trade through negotiation.

be needed to work out basic agreements on the whole range of investment problems, including antitrust, taxes, transfer pricing, and corporate disclosure.

ALTERNATIVE MULTINATIONAL SYSTEMS

Businesses desiring to market their products in other countries have several alternative methods of doing business open to them. These methods differ in terms of investment, organization, costs, and the degree of risk management is willing to assume.

The simplest way of reaching foreign marketing is by *exporting* products from the firm's home country. This can be done indirectly through export-import middlemen, or directly by selling to distributors and/or commercial firms in the foreign country. For relatively small firms or those without experience in multinational operations, selling through export-import middlemen is often recommended. These specialized middlemen handle all the problems of shipping, customs, duties, and insurance. For these services, the middlemen are compensated by a percentage commission or discount from purchase price. Even with direct selling to distributors in another country, it may be difficult to achieve close identity of interest between a distributor or agent in one country and a firm in another.

Another basic system of operating in multinational markets involves the *licensing* of local firms and *joint ventures.* A licensing agreement permits a company in another country to manufacture and sell a firm's product, in return for royalty fees. This approach involves little risk if results are unsatisfactory. The disadvantage to licensing arrangements, if things turn out well, is that long-term licensing agreements may block a change to more profitable operations such as a subsidiary.

In a joint venture, a home-based company joins with a local firm in another country to form a new, jointly owned manufacturing and/or marketing subsidiary. This method can offer the advantages of local knowledge and contacts and possibly the pooling of resources and technical skills. Possible conflicts may arise in joint-venture arrangements over control of operations, selection of personnel, and government requirements. Some governments insist on "buy-back" clauses in joint-venture and licensing agreements with multinational companies.

Wholly owned subsidiaries represent a much greater commitment in multinational operations. When a United States–based company opens up a subsidiary in France, for example, the company provides capital, technology, and personnel for the unit's operation and assumes full risk for its success or failure. The costs of providing all of this can be justified only if the expanding company projects a sales volume sufficient to warrant such an investment. Many multinationals may operate subsidiaries in countries that have a large sales volume, such as Western Europe, Canada, and Japan, and continue to sell through agents or distributors in countries with small sales potential. Subsidiaries may be established in manufacturing and/or marketing operations. A manufacturing subsidiary represents, perhaps, the strongest commitment in multinational operations.

Which system a company chooses—exporting, licensing, joint ventures, or subsidiary—for the multinational operation depends on a number of factors. Such factors as market potential, capital availability, management experience, technical skills required, and stability of the host's national government are critical. It is thus impossible to generalize on the "best" system for multinational operations.

MULTINATIONAL MARKETING STRATEGIES

In an earlier section, we described some of the product and marketing changes necessitated in multinational operations by differences in cultural patterns among countries. In addition, varying physical and economic conditions give rise to different consumer needs and product uses among national markets. The recognition of sometimes dramatic differences in consumer needs and conditions of product use from country to country suggest several strategies in approaching multinational markets.[7]

The simplest strategy is to sell the same product with the same promotional and advertising themes and appeals in foreign markets that the company uses in its home market. This strategy of extending both the product and marketing is based on the awareness that the product satisfies the same basic needs and is used roughly under the same conditions in foreign markets as in the home market. Pepsi Cola and Coca-Cola use this approach in their multinational operations. Both are sold all over the world with approximately the same advertising themes. The obvious advantage of this strategy is the savings in research and development and marketing costs. However, not too many companies can simply extend both their product and their marketing as the soft drink industry has done.

When a product fills a different consumer need under roughly the same use conditions, the only adjustment required is in marketing communications. In the United States, bicycles, motorscooters, and outboard motor equipment are sold largely as recreational vehicles. In many European markets the bicycles and motorscooters provide basic transportation, and outboard motors may be sold in fishing or transportation industries in other countries. Another example is provided by the sale of lawn and garden equipment to the household market in the United States, but the same products are being used as agricultural implements in developing countries. In Ghana, where the average size of a farm is five acres, American-type lawn and garden equipment fits that scale of operation. In such cases no adaptation is needed in the product, but marketing communication must be adjusted to appeal to the different consumer needs. This strategy of extending the product and adapting marketing represents a savings in production costs but added costs in marketing.

A third approach is to extend without change the basic communications but to adapt the product to local use conditions. In other words, the product meets some basic consumer needs, but environment dictates varying conditions under which the product is used. Different weather dictates changes in octane ratings for gasoline; fertilizers are altered to meet different soil conditions; and soaps and detergents are adjusted to local water conditions. This strategy of adapting the product and extending marketing is in general more costly than the previous two since some changes in production are incurred.

---

[7]Most of the material in this section is obtained from the article by Warren J. Keegan, "Multinational Product Planning: Strategic Alternatives," *Journal of Marketing* 33, January 1969, pp. 58–62.

In some cases both the product and communications have to be adapted to local market conditions in multinational marketing. When this stops short of complete product innovation, a strategy in which both product and marketing are adapted is used. The greeting card industry is cited as an example in which both product and communication changes are made. Americans seem to prefer greeting cards with sentimental messages for special occasions. Europeans, on the other hand, prefer greeting cards which provide space for senders to write their own messages. European greeting cards are cellophane wrapped, necessitating a product alteration by American greeting card manufacturers selling in the European market. American manufacturers selling there must make adjustments in both their product and their marketing communications in response to this set of environmental differences.

To develop a completely new product with new marketing strategies is the most costly of the multinational marketing approaches, but it may be the only alternative if both need and use conditions are incongruous with those in the home market. An estimated 600 million persons around the world still scrub their clothes by hand. These people have been served by multinational soap and detergent companies for years, but it took an "inventing backward" approach by a leading washing machine manufacturer to develop a relatively inexpensive (under $10.00), all-plastic, hand-powered washer that has the tumbling action of a modern automatic machine. In another example of a "product invention" strategy, National Cash Register invented backward to develop a cash register to serve the needs of many small merchants who operate in outdoor marts in other countries.

Before any of the above strategies are pursued, a multinational firm must begin with a thorough product-market analysis of the local markets, followed by an assessment of the company's resources. Such questions as the following should be answered: What are the basic needs of the market segments? Are the needs basically the same as in the domestic market? How is the product used? Does it require power sources available in local markets? (For example, many

Many foreign products compete with comparable American-made products in the U.S. market.

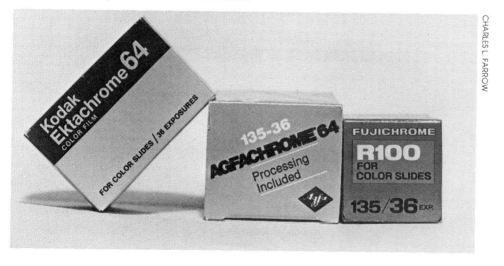

U.S.-manufactured appliances require 220 volts, but only 120 voltage may be available in prospective foreign markets.) Will the product appeal to a narrow market segment or a broad mass market? Does the firm have access to needed resources to meet the needs of the market? In other words, can the product be profitably marketed over the long run under the proposed strategy?

SUMMARY

Multinational companies, probably the most successful secular international organizations in history, are moving into the most critical stage of their evolution. Based on the principles of absolute and comparative advantage among nations, multinational operations have had a dramatic impact on the economies of many countries as well as on the profit ledgers of their companies. Recently, however, the firms are running up against a growing tide of nationalism. The most dramatic confrontation involves the world's major oil companies and the Middle East kingdoms.

Will the multinationals survive? Undoubtedly they will, but many will have to adjust to the changing political tide in their host countries. In the future, the companies will provide technology, managerial skills, and marketing networks to the nationally controlled economies for a share of the market.

Tougher times ahead for the multinationals will call for prudent planning on the part of management, preceded by a thorough analysis of the local markets. It is anticipated that multinational operations will continue in the future. For many companies, it is a matter of retaining access to raw materials in an increasingly resource-short world. For others, it is a matter of remaining in those areas where sales growth is taking place. Foreign sales for some American-based companies are already more profitable than domestic sales. Multinationals can be expected to meet these critical adjustments in this stage of their development.

DISCUSSION QUESTIONS

1. Referring to the example in the text of Sue and Barb (p. 225), how would the conclusion change if Sue were both an accomplished seamstress and an excellent accountant, and if Barb were a competent accountant?

2. What is the difference between a protective tariff and a revenue tariff? Would you say a tariff on U.S. imports would fall in the protective or revenue category?

3. Can a nation have a trade surplus and yet experience a balance of payments deficit during the same time period? Explain.

4. In the first half of 1977, the United States was incurring a trade deficit. What circumstances do you think were giving rise to this unusual occurrence in the United States international trade picture?

5. How would foreign investments in United States industries affect our balance of payments?

6. From a profitability and risk viewpoint, compare the alternative organizational structures for operating in multinational markets.

7. Explain how the strategy of market segmentation can be applied to multinational marketing.

SHORT CASE

The Battle of the Beers

European brewers are stepping up their assault on the U.S. beer market. France's Kronenbourg hopes to copy the success of the Netherlands' Heineken and West Germany's Lowenbrau in weaning Americans from their domestic brands. Kronenbourg is part of a group of beers which lays claim to 60 percent of its home market. But the three-hundred-year-old brewer's grip on the French market is slipping in the face of competition from the Dutch, the Danes, and the West Germans. Part of Kronenbourg's response is to cross the Atlantic.

Kronenbourg is not the only European beer receiving heavy promotional attention in the U.S. Denmark's Tuborg, already being brewed in the U.S., has just kicked off a $7 million campaign that the company hopes will boost its U.S. sale to one million barrels this year.

As a foreign import desiring to break into the U.S. beer-drinking market, what organizational method of becoming established would you recommend for the French brewer? What preliminary marketing investigations would be necessary before entering the market?

SUGGESTED READINGS

Fayerweather, John. *International Marketing.* Englewood Cliffs, N.J.: Prentice-Hall, 1970.

Keegan, Warren J. "Multinational Product Planning: Strategic Alternatives." *Journal of Marketing* 33 (January 1933): 58–62.

Thomas, Michael J., ed. *International Marketing Management.* Boston: Houghton Mifflin, 1969.

*

PART FOUR

FINANCIAL INSTITUTIONS AND MANAGEMENT

☐ Previous sections of this book have shown that a business needs a product and the people who constitute an organization. To be successful, a firm must also have adequate funding. In a technologically advanced capitalistic society such as the United States, the finance function is supported by an extremely complex web of organizations and institutions.

☐ Chapter 12 presents an introduction to this web of financial organizations and institutions which will provide a framework for understanding this difficult but fascinating area. The topics discussed in Chapter 12 include money, the Federal Reserve System, the nation's private banking institutions, the role of insurance in business, and the stock and commodities markets.

☐ Chapter 13 examines the problem of how a business firm raises funds or capital at the lowest costs and invests them to bring about the greatest return. This chapter includes an analysis of a very important problem which is often overlooked: How does a new business go about the difficult task of raising its initial capital?

*

FINANCIAL INSTITUTIONS

LEARNING OBJECTIVES

When you finish this chapter you should:
- [ ] understand the properties and functions of money.
- [ ] understand the structure and functions of the Federal Reserve System.
- [ ] be aware of the various types of banks and related institutions and their services.
- [ ] be aware of the basic elements of insurance.
- [ ] understand how securities markets work.

KEY TERMS TO LEARN FROM THIS CHAPTER

annuity
best-efforts
    arrangement
capital markets
closed-end investment
    companies
coinsurance
commercial banks
commercial finance
    companies
consumer finance com-
    panies
consumer installment
    loans

credit union
demand deposits
electronic funds transfer
endowment policy
factor
Federal Home Loan
    Bank
Federal Reserve System
insurance premium
investment bank
limit order
line of credit
margin

market order
money markets
mutual funds
no-fault insurance
odd lot
open-end investment
    companies
ordinary life insurance
over-the-counter
    market
real estate loan
round lot

sales finance companies
savings and loan asso-
    ciations
savings banks
securities dealers and
    brokers
security loans
selling short
term insurance
term loans
trust company
vesting

Financial management (Chapter 13) is concerned with raising funds at the lowest cost and investing funds to maximize returns. The major financial institutions that support and underlie the financial management function of business will be discussed in this chapter.

The institutions mentioned here are important in terms of controlling the money supply and providing credit to business enterprises for both short periods of up to a year (called the *money market*) and for long periods (called *capital markets*).

Money and the American banking system are discussed first. Since insurance companies are important suppliers of funds to American business and provide as well an important financial service, their role is then examined. Another part of our financial structure that will be analyzed is the market for buying and selling securities and the institutions that are involved with investing and dealing with stocks, bonds, and commodities.

MONEY

Simple economies in very ancient times did not need money. The tasks to be done were relatively few and related to the most basic needs: providing food and shelter for and raising the family within the tribal group. Small families or groups were completely self-sufficient. Where work differed, among groups such as hunters and simple toolmakers, for example, a barter system was used in which products were directly exchanged.

The barter system obviously breaks down where even a low degree of specialization and division of labor performing a variety of different jobs and tasks arises. A common commodity generally acceptable to all parties has to be used as a medium of exchange in the buying and selling of goods and services. At first articles such as animal furs and oxen teeth served as money.

PROPERTIES OF MONEY

To serve satisfactorily as a medium of exchange, a commodity would need the following properties:

1. Easily storable.
2. Transportable.
3. Divisible.
4. Durable.
5. Difficult to counterfeit.

Cheese might be a valuable commodity, but it could not be stored without an elementary refrigeration system. Extremely heavy items, such as hundred-pound stones, could not easily serve as money where mobility is required. Divisibility refers to the property of breaking down or dividing. A two-thousand-pound ox cannot be broken down into ten-pound segments. A commodity which is valuable but subject to spoilage or evaporation restricts the owner's ability to

Stacks of newly minted money at the Federal Reserve Bank in Minneapolis, Minnesota ready to go into circulation.

hold it over periods of time. Finally, if money can be easily counterfeited, it cannot remain valuable.

Early commodities such as furs and teeth serving as money were eventually replaced by valuable metals such as gold and silver.

FUNCTIONS OF MONEY

In addition to serving as a *medium of exchange* in transactions for goods or services, money has several other functions.

Money also serves as a *standard of value*. In this function it is a common denominator for valuing goods and services. One example of this function is the balance sheet of a firm in which all assets, liabilities, and owners' equities are valued in terms of dollars.

Finally, money is a *store of value*. It can be held indefinitely until the owner is ready to dispense with it. Safety becomes an important consideration in this function. Money stored in a bank account is usually safer than money stored in a mattress.

The appropriate properties of money relative to the functions it performs have led to the use of paper currency as well as coins. Even these, however, have the drawback of bulkiness in very large transactions and present security problems as well. Consequently, money evolved into a new form of *demand deposits,* which is the more formal term for checking accounts.

Let's next examine the American banking system, which is responsible for storing and regulating the supply of paper currency and demand deposits of the country.

THE BANKING SYSTEM OF THE UNITED STATES

UNITED STATES TREASURY DEPARTMENT

Functions   Among the principal functions of the United States Treasury Department is that of providing part of the nation's currency supply—roughly 13 percent—as well as managing the national debt of the federal government. The Treasury Department is also the custodian of gold mined in this country and shipped to us from abroad. In addition, the Treasury Department collects taxes for the United States government through its subsidiary agency, the Internal Revenue Service.

Monetary Panics   The private banking system that was in effect prior to the creation of the Federal Reserve System was unable to prevent a series of financial panics from wracking the country due to an inability to regulate properly the monetary supply. The worst panics were in 1873, 1884, 1893, and 1907. Panics occurred as banks were unable to pay legal tender currency on demand. The Treasury alone appeared unable to control the situation.

THE FEDERAL RESERVE SYSTEM

The Federal Reserve Act of 1913 resulted in the creation of the Federal Reserve System, which is, in effect, the central banking system of the nation. Federal Reserve Banks have also been called the "bank for bankers," for reasons which you will shortly see.

Organization   The board of governors of the Federal Reserve System is its most important policy-making group. Its seven members are appointed by the president of the United States for fourteen-year terms, with confirmation by the Senate. A continuity of membership in the board of governors is always maintained because membership terms expire consecutively rather than all at the same time.

The United States is divided into twelve Federal Reserve districts with a Federal Reserve Bank located in each district. Several of the largest districts in terms of area covered also have Federal Reserve branch banks located in major cities. A map of the Federal Reserve districts is shown in Figure 12–1.

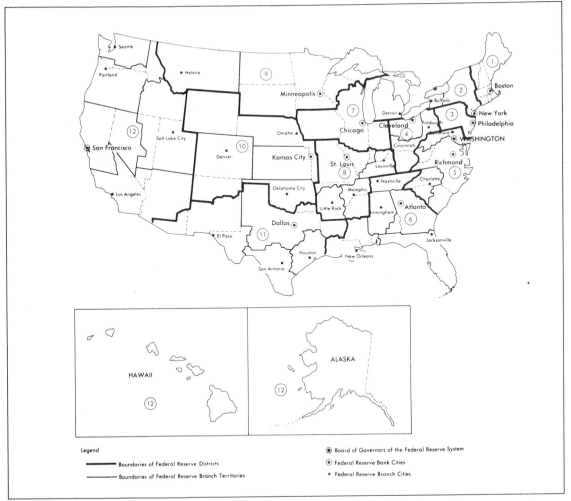

Figure 12-1 The Federal Reserve districts of the United States. (Courtesy Board of Governors, Federal Reserve System)

Each Federal Reserve Bank has a board of directors consisting of three members from the banking community, three from the business community, and three representing the general public (the latter three are appointed by the board of governors). The banker and business community members are selected to represent small, medium, and large banks or businesses. The board of directors of each bank thus represents a fairly broad segment of interests.

All nationally chartered commercial banks (to be discussed shortly) must belong to the Federal Reserve System. In addition, state chartered commercial banks may also belong to the system. In general, the larger state chartered commercial banks have joined the system but not the smaller ones.

Ownership of each of the twelve Federal Reserve Banks is by the commercial banks of the respective districts that are members of the system. Each member bank subscribes for capital stock in an amount equal to 6 percent of its own owners' equity. So far only 3 percent of this investment has been demanded. Dividends equal to 6 percent of the capital stock holdings are received by members.

It can be seen that the Federal Reserve System is a unique blend of public and private institutions. Ownership is by the member banks, which are, in turn, privately owned, but the board of governors of the system is selected by the president and approved by the Senate. An overview of the organization of the system and its functions is shown in Figure 12–2.

Monetary Creation and the Federal Reserve System

Before we specifically discuss the functions of the Federal Reserve System, it is important to understand how the monetary system of the country can expand and contract relative to business demands through the fractional reserve system.

Commercial banks are the only banks which are empowered to issue demand deposits (checking accounts) to business and other depositors. When a business or individual, company X, for example, deposits $100 in the Springfield State Bank, the bank need keep only a fractional portion of the deposit as a "reserve." It can issue additional credit—thus in effect creating money—up to a specified maximum amount.

For example, assume that there is a 25 percent reserve requirement. This means that the Springfield State Bank must keep $25 of the above demand de-

Figure 12-2 Organization of the Federal Reserve System.

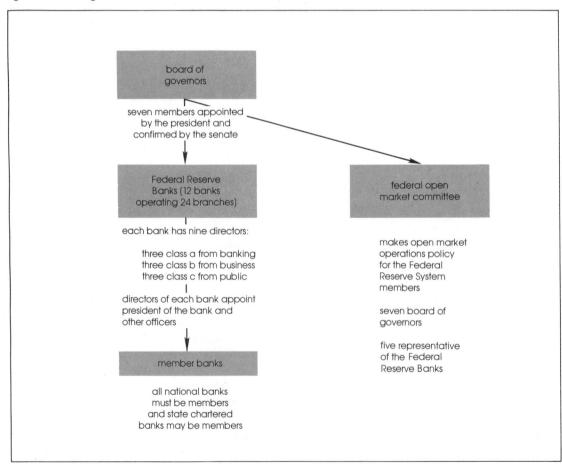

posit either in its own vaults or in the form of a deposit with the Federal Reserve Bank of its district.

Notice that in the event that the money is kept on deposit with its Federal Reserve Bank, the latter is acting as a banker's bank. This relationship is shown in Figure 12–3.

What happens to the other $75 of company X's deposit? The Springfield State Bank can lend this amount in the form of another demand deposit, in effect creating money.

Moreover, notice that the process can continue. If a check for the $75 deposit is sent by the borrower to another party to pay a bill and it is deposited in a checking account at another commercial bank, then that bank could lend out up to 75 percent of the $75 deposit, thus creating another $56.25 of potential additional lending power.

As you can see, still further money-creating transactions can occur. The maximum money-creating potential of the original transaction of $100 by company X is $400, as shown in Table 12–1, assuming the 25 percent reserve requirement. How much will actually be lent depends on the needs of business for money.

Credit Controlling Functions of the Federal Reserve Systems   Several of the most important functions of the Federal Reserve System relate to regulation of the reserves of commercial banks. Hence they deal with the problem of regulation of the money supply, an extremely important economic factor. If not enough money and credit are available in the nation, economic activity may be listless, with high unemployment and relatively low output of goods and

Figure 12-3   Following a deposit from a bank to the Federal Reserve.

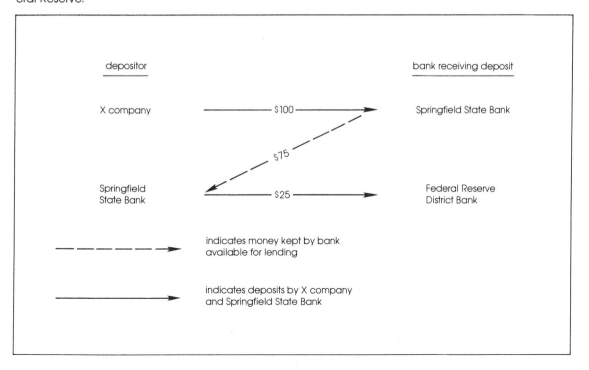

Table 12-1

Money-Creating Potential of a Fractional Reserve System

Transaction	Amount Deposited in Checking Account	25% Reserve Requirement	Excess Reserves Available for Lending
1	$100	$ 25	$ 75
2	75	18.75	56.25
3	56.25	14.06	42.19
4	42.19	10.55	31.64
5	31.64	7.91	23.73
6	23.73	5.93	17.80
7	17.80	4.45	13.35
8	13.35	3.34	10.01
9	10.01	2.50	7.50
10	7.50	1.88	5.62
11	5.62	1.41	4.21
12	4.21	1.05	3.16
13	3.16	.79	2.37
14	2.37	.59	1.78
15	1.78	.45	1.33
16	1.33	.33	1.00
	$400	$100	$300

services—conditions of recession or depression. On the other hand, if too much money is available in the economy, the result can be inflation. Clearly, controlling the money supply is an extremely important activity of the Federal Reserve System.

One means of controlling the money supply lies with the board of governors, who are empowered to *set the specific fractional reserve requirement*. The board was given this power by the Banking Act of 1935. In 1977 this rate was 17½ percent for banks having $400 million or more of demand deposits.

This power has been infrequently used by the board of governors. Should reserve requirements be lowered, increasing the credit-producing potential of the commercial banking system at a time when there is little demand for additional credit, then the net result would simply be additional excess reserves. Similarly, if the economy is expanding too fast and inflation is the threat, an increase in reserve requirements to eliminate excess credit-producing potential could well fall short of the mark if all the slack in the commercial banking system is not eliminated.

A second way in which the board of governors can affect the level of reserves (which in turn affects the amount of credit available to banks for lending purposes) is by *changing the discount rate*. In order to understand this, let's examine discounting operations of the Federal Reserve System.

Commercial banks can increase the balance of their accounts with the Federal Reserve System by taking notes receivable in their possession resulting from loans to business and selling them to the Federal Reserve System. When this occurs, their available reserves—hence their lending power—increases. The Federal Reserve Bank in buying the note will "discount" it. This simply means that they will pay less than the maturity value of the note. This is shown in Table 12–2.

Now it should become clear that increasing the discount rate will discourage commercial banks from discounting notes with the Federal Reserve System because their proceeds are reduced. Decreasing the discount rate will have the opposite effect. Therefore, available reserves can be influenced by means of the board of governors' ability to change the discount rate.

The third tool available to the board of governors for influencing reserves is by means of *open market operations*. If a Federal Reserve Bank buys a United States government security from a member bank, it will pay the commercial bank with a check drawn upon itself. When the check is deposited in the member bank's account with the Federal Reserve System, it increases the member bank's reserves and credit-granting potential. Similarly, selling United States government securities to member banks results in reducing the commercial bank's account with the Federal Reserve System, in turn reducing its credit-granting potential.

Open market operations are directed by the system's Federal Open Market Committee, which consists of the board of governors and five representatives of the Federal Reserve Banks.

Future Problems of Controlling the Money Supply   It may become more difficult for the board of governors to control the money supply in the future. One new factor that began to take hold in the country during 1975 was *electronic funds transfer* (EFT) or credit card banking.

By means of a magnetically encoded plastic card, similar to an ordinary credit card, entered into a computer terminal located in a supermarket or shopping center, the individual can deposit or withdraw cash or transfer money between savings and checking accounts. Hence banking transactions can occur without entering a bank or writing a check.

If shoppers pay for their goods at stores equipped with computer terminals by transferring amounts from their savings or checking accounts, the dollar volume of transactions is increased without using traditional "money"—checks or currency.

As a result, the Federal Reserve's ability to control the economy by regulating the supply of traditional money may be severely restricted. The long-run effects of this are hard to assess. It has been predicted that by 1983, electronic

Table 12-2
Discounting a Note at a Federal Reserve Bank

Principal amount of a 60 day 6% note	$1,000
Interest on above	10
Maturity value of note	1,010
Discounted at 8% by commercial bank at a Federal Reserve Bank after holding note for 30 days ($1,010 × 30/360 × .08)	6.73
Proceeds credited to commercial bank's account	$1,003.27

banking will eliminate 14 percent or roughly $7 billion worth of the checks that might otherwise have been used.[1]

THE BANKING SYSTEM

COMMERCIAL BANKS

Commercial banks, as mentioned above, are the only type of bank that can accept demand deposits. In addition, they accept time deposits (savings accounts) and make loans to businesses and individuals. Typically, loans by commercial banks have been largely to businesses and are generally not long-term (beyond ten years) in duration.

Types of Loans   A *line of credit* is an open amount that can be borrowed by a business up to a specified maximum. When funds are needed, the company contacts the bank, which simply credits the funds to the firm's account. The company is required to pay off the loan, usually on an annual basis, prior to renewal. The bank often requires the maintenance of a minimum average balance by the borrower.

Term loans are granted for periods of one to ten years (occasionally longer). The borrower signs a promissory note requiring payment at a particular date or dates in the future at a stated rate of interest. Term loans usually require installment payments each year until the loan is repaid.

Consumer installment loans to individuals began to grow during the depression of the 1930s and are today in excess of $65 billion. This category includes automobile loans and the very rapidly growing area of credit cards. Visa and Master Charge cards come under this last category.

Security loans are made for the purchase of securities by individuals and security brokers or dealers. These loans are secured by the stocks and bonds purchased.

Real estate loans to individuals by commercial banks for the purchase or construction of homes have grown to over $70 billion.

Other Services   Commercial banks also provide a full slate of other financial services, such as maintaining trust departments, whose function is estate and trust management, payroll services such as preparing paychecks, safety deposit box services, and advisory services which concern local business and economic trends and conditions.

Chartering   Commercial banks can be chartered (granted the right to operate) by either the federal or state government. As mentioned previously, national banks—those that are federally chartered—must become affiliated with the Federal Reserve System. State chartered banks may also join the Federal Reserve System.

Insurance and Examination   All banks belonging to the Federal Reserve System as well as many nonmember commercial banks have their depositors' savings

[1]"Bank Lords Take Over the Country," *Business Week,* August 4, 1975, p. 44.

CHARLES L. FARROW

As banks have attracted more and more customers, their financial services and facilities have grown correspondingly.

accounts protected by the Federal Deposit Insurance Corporation (FDIC). Depositors are fully insured against loss up to a maximum of $40,000 per account.

Our banking system is regulated by three federal and fifty state governing agencies. As a result, there is a great deal of overlap and competition among the regulating agencies. In view of the fact that three large bank failures occurred in the early 1970s, including the very large Franklin National Bank of New York, we can expect more centralization of regulation by federal agencies and possibly greater control over bank investments.

SAVINGS BANKS

Savings banks accept time deposits but not demand deposits. These banks make extensive investments in real estate mortgages for apartment buildings and commercial real estate developments. Generally, their loans are on a long-term basis. They also have large holdings of United States government securities and corporate bonds among their assets.

Chartering, Ownership, and Protection Savings banks are chartered solely by the state in which they are located. Stock company types of savings banks are owned by their stockholders, who receive dividends on their shareholdings like any other stockholders. Mutual savings banks are owned by their depositors. Profits are distributed to them on the basis of the size of their accounts. Most of the mutual savings banks are located in the northeastern section of the nation.

Approximately two-thirds of all savings banks have their depositors' accounts insured through the FDIC.

SAVINGS AND LOAN ASSOCIATIONS

Savings and loan associations are the primary lenders to home buyers. These institutions grew tremendously after World War II when there was a strong pent-up demand for home ownership.

Until a few years ago, savings accounts held in savings and loan institutions paid an interest rate that was approximately one percent higher than corresponding accounts at commercial banks. The latter have since become more competitive in seeking savings deposits. At the present time, regular savings accounts at savings and loan associations carry a maximum interest of 5.25 percent, and savings certificates have a maximum interest of 7.75 percent. Savings certificates require the holder to keep his money invested over stipulated periods of time. Penalties are imposed for early withdrawal.

The Federal Home Loan Bank   Savings and loan associations may be chartered by the state or can receive a federal charter from the Federal Home Loan Bank Board.

The *Federal Home Loan Bank* (FHLB) for savings and loan associations corresponds rather closely to the Federal Reserve System relative to commercial banks. The twelve regional banks of the FHLB system are owned by the member

savings and loan associations. State chartered savings and loans may join the system. FHLB banks have provided liquidity to their members in the form of seasonal or long-term loans (up to ten years). Savings accounts of depositors are protected through the Federal Savings and Loan Insurance Corporation. Depositors are fully insured up to $40,000 per account.

TRUST COMPANIES

Trust companies take legal possession of personal assets and manage them in accordance with the wishes stipulated by the creator of the trust. The trust company not only manages the assets turned over to it but also distributes interest and principal in accordance with the trust agreement. Tax minimization often underlies the creation of a trust.

Trust companies, like commercial banks, may also act as estate executors in carrying out the wills of deceased persons, a closely related function.

CREDIT UNIONS

While *credit unions* are not banking establishments in the sense that the previously discussed institutions are, the savings and lending function that they perform justifies their mention here. Credit unions are owned by their members. They are organized by specific groups, such as the employees of a particular company, organization, or institution. They are usually managed by their members, often on a voluntary basis. Credit unions provide a place of savings and are an important source of consumer credit for their members.

OTHER LENDING INSTITUTIONS

Although they do not provide the savings source that banks and other related institutions provide, other institutions are also important providers of credit.

CONSUMER FINANCE COMPANIES

Consumer finance companies make installment loans directly to consumers for the purchase of durables such as automobiles, television sets, and washing machines as well as for personal loans. They are often criticized for their high rates of interest, but it is important to note that they are acting as retailers of credit. Frequently, their source of funding comes from commercial banks, and they often serve clientele that may be unable to secure bank credit.

SALES FINANCE COMPANIES

Sales finance companies acquire installment sales contracts from the retailer, thus unburdening the seller from the problem of providing credit. These companies are particularly active in financing automobiles, major consumer appliances, and farm equipment. Sales finance companies also provide inventory financing for this same category of dealers and retailers.

COMMERCIAL FINANCE COMPANIES

Commercial finance companies provide loans to businesses that are quite marginal in terms of their credit standing. Because of the extreme risk involved, their interest rates are usually quite high. Most of the loans provided by commercial finance companies are secured by the assets of the borrower.

FACTORS

Factors buy accounts receivable from business firms at a discount to cover their costs of collection, administration, and risk as well as for the profit. Factoring is an old, established custom in the textile industry. The factor usually assumes the risk and responsibility for collecting the account after it has been sold to him.

INSURANCE AND RISK MANAGEMENT

Insurance deals with the problem of minimizing the result of unfortunate events. While death cannot be avoided, its timing—when it occurs—is uncertain. Events such as loss from fire and flood damage are not certain to happen for any particular business. However, their occurrence can be so devastating in loss of property and disruption of business that most firms are wise to provide protection by means of insurance.

HOW INSURANCE WORKS

Insurance protection works through the principle of the law of large numbers. Let us say that a fire insurance company examines its past records and estimates that for every thousand buildings insured, twenty, or 2 percent, will suffer fire damage. Of course which twenty buildings it will be is completely indeterminate, though the estimate in total is usually quite accurate unless unforeseen circumstances arise.

While some of the approximately twenty buildings may be totally destroyed, others may have only small amounts of damage. Damage, let us say, will average $15,000 per building suffering from fire during the year. In addition, it is estimated that expenses of the insurance company will total $50,000, and a profit of $25,000 is desired.

In spreading the risk among all insured businesses, each firm will pay the insurance company an annual *premium* for fire insurance protection of $375, as shown in Table 12–3.

Of course this example is highly simplified. Factors such as the size and value of insured buildings must be considered. Potential risk must also be taken into account. A brand new steel and glass building with an up-to-date sprinkler system will probably have less chance of a major fire than a rickety old wooden warehouse. Location of property relative to the hazard of fire is another important consideration.

The complex job of prediction of the various unknown factors is done by persons who are called actuaries. They must be highly trained in mathematics and statistics.

Table 12-3
Computation of a Hypothetical Fire Insurance Premium

Total Expected losses (20 × $15,000)	$300,000
Expenses	50,000
Desired profit	25,000
Total costs and profit	375,000
Divide by number of units insured	÷ 1,000
Premium per company	= $375

COINSURANCE CLAUSES

One factor that may have occurred to you about casualty risks such as fire insurance is that a complete loss is so rare that it does not pay the firm to insure against a 100 percent loss. Since the insurance company also knows this, they have instituted a system known as *coinsurance* or the coinsurance clause.

Coinsurance clauses require that insurance must be maintained at the instituted rate if smaller losses are to be paid in full.

For example, a building with a value of $50,000 would require insurance coverage of $40,000 if an 80 percent coinsurance clause were in effect ($40,000 /$50,000 = 80%) if smaller losses are to be fully covered. If insurance of $30,000 were carried and a fire loss of $20,000 occurred, the insurance company would pay only $15,000. This would be due to the fact that only 75 percent of the minimum required insurance is carried ($30,000 carried divided by the required coverage of $40,000). In turn, the payment of $15,000 is also 75 percent of the loss of $20,000.

Let's next quickly examine the various types of policies and protection offered by life and casualty insurance.

LIFE INSURANCE

Life insurance can provide protection both against dying too early and living too long.

Term Insurance   Unlike other types of insurance policies, term insurance provides protection but without any savings element present at the end of the contract. The premium thus covers pure insurance cost plus coverage of expenses and profits for the insurance company. As the name implies, term insurance coverage is written for a specific number of years, though provision for automatic renewal or conversion to another type of policy may be provided in the contract.

Group insurance provided for employees of businesses or organizations also provides life and health benefits. Rates on these contracts are usually changed each year due to rising medical costs as well as the amount of payments made for the group during the preceding year.

Ordinary Life   This type of policy is also called straight life and whole life insurance. It is probably the most prevalent form of insurance used in the United States. The insured pays the same premium each year—called the *level* *premium*—during his or her lifetime.[2] However, the policyholder may borrow against the policy or even turn it in, receiving the *cash surrender value.* The latter represents the savings portion of the premium payments (as opposed to the pure insurance portion) including interest.

Endowment Policies   These policies pay the entire amount of the contract either at the end of the contractual period or upon the death of the insured, should that occur first. The intent of the insured is often to provide both insurance coverage or accumulation of a stipulated amount at the end of the contract period if the insured survives. This type of policy might be used by a father or mother who wants to save enough money for a daughter or son to go to college, for example.

FIRE, PROPERTY, CASUALTY, AND HEALTH INSURANCE

A very wide variety of insurance protection is available. Types and amounts of insurance coverage should be tailored to the needs and potential hazards of the individual firm. Listed below are some of the many forms of protection:[3]

[2]However, premium payments may be increased so that they occur over a specified number of years rather than the individual's lifetime.

[3]List derived from Donald P. Jacobs, Loring C. Farwell, and Edwin Neave, *Financial Institutions* (Homewood, Ill.: Richard D. Irwin, 1972), p. 279.

Businesses need insurance to protect them against unexpected problems like fire.

CHARLES L. FARROW

1. Fire, lightning, and smoke damage.
2. Wind, hail, water, and earthquake damage.
3. Ocean marine transportation and inland marine transportation.
4. Medical costs and loss of income resulting from accident or illness.
5. Property damage, medical costs, and legal liability for drivers of automobiles and owners of aircraft.
6. Workmen's compensation claims arising from work-connected illness and death.
7. Theft, burglary, robbery, and forgery losses.
8. Employee infidelity, covering embezzlement (stealing) of funds and property.
9. Title insurance, protecting a buyer's claim to title (in effect, sole legal ownership) of real property (land and buildings).
10. Unexpected credit losses on accounts receivable.
11. Miscellaneous loss coverage including rain, crop, glass breakage, boiler explosion, and even nuclear explosion.
12. Public liability insurance, covering faulty products of manufacturers and negligence.

Insurers in fire, property, and casualty have been hit hard by double-digit inflation in the early and middle 1970s. The year 1975 was financially disastrous for them. The courts have been quite liberal in terms of extending liability of insured companies in cases in which the product has not been the primary cause of an accident. These include the case of a child who died after drinking furniture polish and a boy whose T-shirt caught fire when he climbed a power pole and brushed a wire.[4]

Insurers have begun to regain control by raising their premiums and being more selective in their acceptance of risks they are willing to insure.

No-Fault Automobile Insurance   A revolution has begun in the automobile insurance industry. Prior to no-fault insurance, automobile accidents often resulted in lengthy investigations to determine who was at fault. Liability was then assumed by the insurance company of the faulty driver in terms of paying the "innocent" parties as well as providing basic coverage for the faulty driver. Many state laws now require that insurance companies be made liable to their own policyholders without the problem of determining who is at fault. The right of victims to sue the other driver's insurance companies for excessive damages has been limited. While no-fault automobile insurance appears to be effective, in many states it does not go far enough. In these states, no-fault covers only the first $1,000 of medical claims, a relatively small amount given today's skyrocketing medical costs. Those with injuries above the $1,000 limit are free to sue for exorbitant amounts, as was the case under the old system. Whether this glaring loophole will be covered by states individually raising their no-fault limits or whether federal legislation will need to be passed remains to be seen.

[4]*Business Week,* September 6, 1976, p. 46.

INSURANCE COMPANIES AND CAPITAL MARKETS

An important point to remember is that insurance companies, particularly life insurance companies, possess very large amounts of cash from their premium income. As a result, they are potent forces in the supplying of funds to the capital markets. Life insurance companies are particularly important because of the delayed payments to their policyholders.

Life Insurance Companies   Life insurance companies have investments in various securities totaling nearly $300 billion. The largest segment of investment is in corporate bonds ($100 billion). One reason for this is the use of *direct placements,* where corporate bonds are sold directly by the issuer to an individual life insurance company or group of companies. Another important area of life insurance investments, totaling $90 billion, is in the form of mortgages on business, residential, and farm properties.

Capital stock investments ($30 billion) are relatively small because prior to 1951, life insurance companies having offices in New York State (a very important segment of the industry) were allowed by state law to invest in neither common nor preferred stock.

Fire, Property, and Casualty Insurance Companies   Insurance companies outside of life insurance have about $50 billion in investments. They are particularly heavy in United States government bonds and state and municipal bonds.

PENSIONS

A pension is an annuity paid to an individual after retirement for the remainder of this person's life. An *annuity* is a fixed amount per time period, usually a month for pension plans. Insurance policies often allow for this form of payment of proceeds to the insured or survivors.

Pension plans are quite common among companies as part of their fringe benefits. Often both the company and the individual employee contribute amounts to the pension fund, which is administered by a trustee, often a life insurance company. Qualified pension plans allow the employer to deduct his pension contributions for tax purposes. The employee, however, is not taxed until the money is received during retirement, when the recipient is presumably in a lower tax bracket than during his or her working life. Qualified plans essentially require a fair treatment of all employees as determined by the Internal Revenue Service. Groups such as unions and teachers' organizations are also important groups providing pension plans for their members.

The nation's Social Security system is a public pension fund controlled by the federal government. At the present time it is in deep trouble because the fund's assets have declined despite steady increases in Social Security rates, while the number of covered individuals is increasing.

Pension funds, like insurance companies, have become an important supplier of funds to the capital markets, particularly since World War II. Total investments by private pension plans is currently in excess of $120 billion.

A massive pension law was passed by Congress in 1974. The law is called the Employee Retirement Income Security Act and is frequently referred to as

ERISA. Its main intent is to make sure that covered employees actually get their pension benefits when they retire. One of the principal parts of the act is a tightening of vesting standards. *Vesting* refers to the time an employee's rights to his or her pension benefits become legally binding upon the employer in terms of honoring the commitment.

SECURITIES MARKETS

In Chapter 3 it was mentioned that the corporate form of business organization had an extremely important advantage over partnerships and sole proprietorship: limited liability. Limited liability means that one's personal assets are not legally available to creditors for satisfying debts of the firm. This important safety device has made it possible to raise extremely large amounts of capital. Virtually every major business in the United States is incorporated.

Limited liability thus makes it easier to raise large amounts of money from owners (stockholders) who are in no way involved with running the firm save for their right to vote at the corporation's annual meeting.

It should thus become clear that an institution would develop to provide a very important need: the bringing together of potential buyers and sellers of securities—both stocks and bonds—of large corporations. These institutions are called *stock exchanges*.

STOCK EXCHANGES

In essence then, a stock exchange is nothing more than a marketplace for the bringing together of buyers and sellers of corporate securities. Securities exchanges are a marketplace for securities that have already been issued rather than for new sales of stocks and bonds by the issuing company.

The two major stock exchanges in the country are the New York Stock Exchange (NYSE), and the American Stock Exchange (AMEX). Both are located in New York City. Together they handle approximately 90 percent of the securities transactions of the country measured in dollar value of transactions. The NYSE alone handles about 75 percent of the entire business of securities that have already been issued.

The New York Stock Exchange   Only *listed securities* can be traded on the two major exchanges. For the NYSE this means that stocks and bonds must be registered for trading with the Securities Exchange Commission (SEC) of the United States government and admitted to trading by the NYSE's board of governors. To qualify for listing by the NYSE, a company must meet the following standards:

1. Annual earnings must be at least $2.5 million before taxes.
2. A minimum of one million shares must be publicly held.
3. At least two thousand shareholders must own one hundred or more shares of stock.

The floor of the New York Stock Exchange on a busy day.

CHASE MANHATTAN BANK
PHOTO BY ARTHUR LAVINE

4. Outstanding common stock must have a market value of at least $16 million.

5. Net tangible assets of the company must be at least $16 million.

To comply with SEC requirements for trading securities on a national stock exchange, a firm must send an annual report to its stockholders. The annual report must contain financial statements audited by a certified public accountant. Approximately two thousand stocks and twelve hundred bonds are listed for trading on the NYSE.

The American Stock Exchange   Approximately one thousand stocks are on the AMEX. For common stock to trade on the AMEX, a company must meet the following requirements:

1. Net tangible assets must be at least $3 million.

2. Annual before-tax earnings must be at least $500,000 and after-tax earnings at least $300,000.

3. Outstanding common stock must total 300,000 shares having a market value of at least $2 million.

Stocks that are listed for trading on the AMEX cannot also be listed for trading on the NYSE. Similarly, stocks listed for trading on the NYSE cannot be traded on the AMEX. However, securities listed for trading on either of the two major exchanges can also be listed on the regional exchanges.

Regional Stock Exchanges In addition to the two major exchanges, there are thirteen regional stock exchanges located in major cities throughout the country.

These are particularly important for trading in the securities of smaller regional or local corporations whose securities are not traded frequently enough to establish going market prices. Through the use of the computer, these regional exchanges are hooked together, and potential buying and selling prices for securities can be disseminated throughout the regional exchanges. The regional stock exchanges are listed in Table 12–4.

Over-the-Counter Market Stocks not listed for trading on any of the national or regional stock exchanges are traded in the *over-the-counter market.* This market is not a particular place as are the other exchanges. Instead it is simply the hundreds of offices of security dealers where transactions in unlisted securities occur very frequently. Stocks of many financial institutions including insurance companies are traded in the over-the-counter market. In addition, government bonds and municipal bonds issued by cities and states are sold in this market. Many securities listed on one of the exchanges are also frequently traded in the over-the-counter market.

SECURITIES DEALERS AND BROKERS

The actual buying and selling of shares on the major exchanges are carried out through securities dealers and brokers.

These firms carry out two slightly different functions. As *dealers* they buy and sell securities for themselves with the intent of making a profit or gain on trading. As *brokers* they are agents of their customers, carrying out the latter's

Table 12-4
Regional Stock Exchanges

Exchange	Remarks
Boston	Regulated by the Securities and Exchange Commission.
Cincinnati	Regulated by the Securities and Exchange Commission.
Detroit	Regulated by the Securities and Exchange Commission.
Honolulu	Not regulated by the Securities and Exchange Commission.
Midwest	Trading floor in Chicago with offices in Cleveland and St. Louis. One of the three largest regional exchanges. Regulated by the Securities and Exchange Commission.
Pacific Coast	Trading floors in both Los Angeles and San Francisco. One of the three largest regional exchanges. Regulated by the Securities and Exchange Commission.
Philadelphia–Baltimore–Washington	One of the three largest regional exchanges. Regulated by the Securities and Exchange Commission.
Richmond	Not regulated by the Securities and Exchange Commission.
Salt Lake City	Specializes in mining and all shares that are under $1 per share. Regulated by the Securities and Exchange Commission.
Spokane	Specializes in mining and all shares that are under $1 per share. Regulated by the Securities and Exchange Commission.

buying and selling orders. For example, a broker-dealer may be ordered to buy 100 shares of General Motors common stock at a price not to exceed $50 per share. The broker-dealer earns a commission on transactions of this type based on the dollar value of the transaction or on a per share commission based on the selling price per share.

TRADING SECURITIES ON THE MAJOR EXCHANGES

The actual buying and selling of stocks and bonds on the floor of either major exchange is done by individuals representing the major brokerage firms who have "seats" on the exchange. There are only a limited number of seats, and their cost has gone as high as $625,000 in 1929. More recently the price of a seat has tumbled from $515,000 in 1969 to $35,500 in 1977.[5] Brokerage firms not

[5]It is interesting to note the market price of a taxi medallion (license) in New York City cost $48,000 in 1977. Thus it is cheaper to buy a seat on the New York Stock Exchange than to license a taxi in New York City.

For many brokers and financial analysts the Quotron machine, which electronically presents a visual display of market figures and information, has replaced the traditional stock ticker tape machine.

CHARLES L. FARROW

having a seat would carry out their business by means of a correspondent firm having a seat.

When an individual wishes to buy or sell a particular security, he or she contacts a broker, who relays the order to a representative on the floor of the exchange. Records are kept there for each individual security of bid prices by potential buyers and asking prices of potential sellers. Sales occur when the highest bid price meets the lowest asking price.

Prices can change extremely rapidly. Securities dealers throughout the country are constantly updated on prices through electronic communications with the stock exchange's ticker tape record of round lot (usually 100 shares) transactions.

After purchasing a security, individuals must make a downpayment—called the *margin*—equal to 50 percent of the purchase price. The power to fix minimum margin requirements was given to the board of governors of the Federal Reserve System by Congress in the Securities and Exchange Act of 1934. Very low margin requirements was one of the underlying factors which caused the great stock market crash of 1929.

Selling Short   If an investor expects the market to go up, that individual buys today with the expectation that the market will rise. A rising market is called a *bull market.* A declining market, on the other hand, is called a *bear market.*

Should an individual anticipate a declining market, he or she might well "sell short." *Selling short* is selling shares today that you do not own. The shares are essentially borrowed from a lender. The stock must be acquired later for return to the lender. If the market does indeed decline, the seller will make a profit because the shares will have been bought for replacement to the lender at a lower price than they were sold for.

Stock that is sold short is either borrowed from other customers of the broker, from stock temporarily left with the broker, or by the broker from other brokers. The lender benefits because the funds received from the sale are turned over to the lender as collateral until the shares are returned by the short seller. The lender thus has an interest-free loan over the period of time that the stock is lent. The borrower of the stock can get these funds at any time by returning the borrowed shares. Similarly, the lender of the stock can call for the return of the shares at any time.

Stock Market Particulars   If an investor asks a securities broker to buy or sell a stock at the current market price, then a *market order* is placed. If, however, the investor asks for a stock to be bought or sold at a particular price, then a *limit order* is placed.

Stock trading is done in 100-share blocks. These are called *round lots.* Many investors cannot afford round lots of stock. Orders placed for fewer than 100 shares are called *odd lots.* Purchases or sales of lots are grouped until a round lot or lots can be formed. When this occurs, the appropriate number of shares are distributed to each odd-lot purchaser.

Commissions   Securities dealers receive a commission for their role in the buying and selling of stocks and bonds. Table 12–5 shows the minimum commission rate schedule for the New York Stock Exchange for odd-lot transactions as of February 1, 1977. Costs consist of a commission plus a fixed amount for each

Table 12-5
Minimum Commission Rate Schedule

Cost of Shares	Percentage Charge	Fixed Charge
0–$100	7.5%	0
$100–$800	2.4%	$ 7.50
$800–$2,500	1.5%	$15
$2,500–$5,000	1.1%	$26
$5,000–$20,000	1.1%	$28

transaction. There is a maximum commission of $65 on any round lot of 100 shares.

Before October 10, 1975, odd-lot transactions carried a commission rate of an additional 12½ cents per share.

INVESTMENT COMPANIES

Instead of buying and selling shares directly, an individual may desire to buy the shares of an *investment company*. The Investment Company Act of 1940 defines these institutions as having over 40 percent of their assets in securities other than those of the United States government and subsidiaries of other firms. The investment company presumably provides expertise and diversification in ownership of securities that the individual does not have. There are two principal types of investment companies.

Closed-End Investment Companies   The securities of these companies are traded in the market like any other corporate issues. The value of these securities may be above or below the value of the securities in its investment portfolio. These companies rarely issue new securities of their own, which is why they are called closed-end companies. Buyers of closed-end company shares pay a brokerage fee similar to that for any other securities transaction.

Open-End Companies   These companies are usually called *mutual funds*. Mutual funds frequently offer new shares for sale and will buy back their shares whenever investors desire. The value of a share in a mutual fund, for both selling and refunding purposes, is based on the market value of all its security holdings divided by the number of its own shares outstanding. Mutual fund shares, unlike the shares of closed-end companies, are not sold through securities dealers on a regular brokerage fee arrangement. Instead, a *loading charge* based on the net market value of the mutual fund's investment portfolio is added to the price to compensate the seller. These charges are roughly 7 to 9 percent of the net value per share of the mutual fund's common stock.

Reading the Financial Pages of Your Newspaper   Knowing current prices of securities is extremely important to investors. Virtually every daily newspaper throughout the country has a stock market page informing investors of the latest prices and other important information. How to read the stock market page is shown in Figures 12–4 and 12–5.

Computer printout on the Spectra 70 stock transfer system.
An example of the data processing equipment used by
the banking and financial industry.

CHASE MANHATTAN BANK
PHOTO BY ARTHUR LAVINE

INVESTMENT BANKS

One more important institution relative to security issuance remains to be discussed. The *investment banker* is an intermediary between the issuer of new securities and the ultimate initial buyer.

They *underwrite* new security issuances by buying them from the issuer and
selling them to institutions such as insurance companies and security dealers.[6]
They make their profit on the difference between their buying and selling prices.
If the security issue is particularly large, a group of investment bankers might
join together and divide the purchase among themselves in agreed amounts.
Such a group is called a *syndicate*.

Often investment bankers will minimize their risk by taking an issue on a
best-efforts arrangement. Here they will simply sell the issue for the best price that
they can obtain. In these arrangements, investment bankers are paid a commission on their sales.

[6]Commercial banks also perform this function for municipal, state, and federal government bonds. They are precluded by law, however, from underwriting corporate stocks
and bonds.

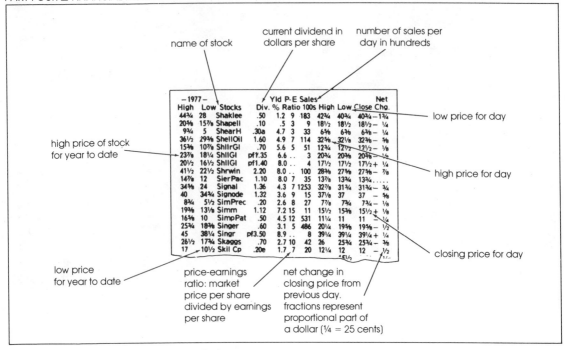

Figure 12-4 Reading the stock market page.

Figure 12-5 Reading the bond market page.

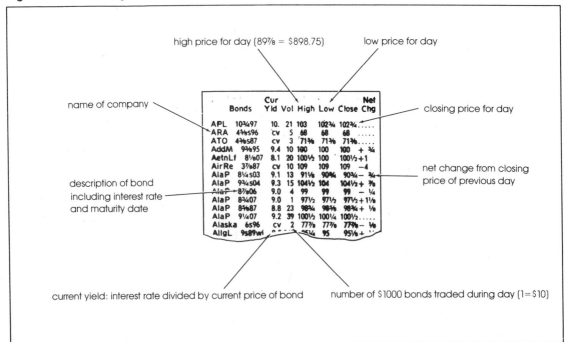

Investment bankers must be extremely knowledgeable about stock market conditions. As a result, they are extremely influential people. They often sit on boards of directors of major corporations.

COMMODITIES MARKETS

Organized markets also exist for the trading of agricultural commodities and livestock. Commodities and the exchanges at which they are traded are shown in Table 12–6.

The price board at the Minneapolis Grain Exchange.

Table 12-6

Commodities and Exchanges: Where They Are Traded

Commodity	Exchanges trading
Cattle (live)	Chicago Mercantile
Corn	Chicago Board of Trade, MidAmerica Commodity
Cotton #2	New York Cotton
Gold	Commodity Exchange, Chicago Mercantile, Chicago Board of Trade, MidAmerica Commodity, New York Mercantile
Hogs (live)	Chicago Mercantile, MidAmerica Commodity
Pork bellies (frozen)	Chicago Mercantile
Silver	Commodity Exchange, Chicago Board of Trade, MidAmerica Commodity
Soybeans	Chicago Board of Trade, MidAmerica Commodity
Sugar #11	New York Coffee & Sugar
Wheat	Chicago Board of Trade, Kansas City, MidAmerica Commodity, Minneapolis

Source: **Business Week**, September 20, 1976, p. 130.

These markets all work in roughly the same way. You either buy a contract whereby you agree to accept delivery of a fixed amount of the commodity at a specified future date or you sell a contract agreeing to make delivery of the commodity at a specified future date. Traders, however, rarely if ever actually take delivery of a commodity. They are speculative middlemen between farmer or rancher and an ultimate buyer such as General Mills or Swift & Company.

Margin requirements are small in commoditites, but losses can be extremely large. According to *Business Week,*

> You would put up $1,000 in cash, for example, to buy a 5,000-oz. silver contract that is worth roughly $21,000. If the value of that silver falls to $20,000, you will be asked to put up another $1,000—and still another $1,000 if the price falls to $19,000. You either keep meeting these margin calls or say goodbye to some of the cash you have already put up.[7]

Traders in commodities are urged to study the markets very carefully because small margins and large fluctuations can mean enormous gains—or losses.

[7]"Commodities," *Business Week*, September 20, 1976, p. 130.

SUMMARY

Financial institutions underlie the financial management function of the firm.

The Federal Reserve System is basically responsible for controlling the nation's money supply. It does this by means of three possible tools: changing the reserve requirement, changing the discount rate, and open market operations. However, its ability to control the money supply may well be challenged as electronic funds transfer systems grow in importance.

Among the nation's banks, commercial banks are the most important to business because they are the only type of bank that can accept demand deposits.

Insurance works through the law of large numbers. In addition to life insurance, protection is offered for a very wide range of risks in the fire, property, casualty, and health areas.

Corporate securities—both stocks and bonds—are traded through a system of national and regional stock exchanges. The most important exchanges are the New York Stock Exchange and the American Stock Exchange. Important exchanges also exist for the trading of commodities and livestock.

DISCUSSION QUESTIONS

1. Why does an increase in business activity tend to "expand" the money supply?

2. How does the Federal Reserve System regulate the money supply?

3. What advantages and disadvantages do you see in terms of credit card banking (electronic funds transfer) replacing more traditional forms of money such as checks and currency?

4. Why is it necessary for insurance companies to include coinsurance clauses in casualty insurance policies?

5. Why does life insurance provide protection for both dying too early and living too long?

6. What is the no-fault principle and why do you think that many lawyers have fought against it?

7. What is the over-the-counter market?

8. Do traders in commodities markets actually perform a useful economic function?

9. If ten shares of XYZ stock are acquired at a cost of $81 per share, what is the commission that would be paid the broker?

SHORT CASES

Investing Someone Else's Money

T. K. Linn is a married man in his late twenties. He has a good job and three children ranging in age from three to eight years old. He has saved $20,000 and asks you for some preliminary advice on how to invest it. What considerations would govern a potential investment program for T. K., and how might his money be invested?

Steady and Up-Down Companies

You are thinking of buying several shares of either Steady Company common stock or Up-Down Company common stock. Both securities are registered for trading on a national securities exchange. Each company has had 10,000 shares of common stock issued and in the hands of the public. Steady Company's stock is presently selling for $80 per share, while Up-Down's sells for $67.

Dividends and earnings for each company during the last four years have been:

	1975	1976	1977	1978
Steady Company				
Total earnings	$100,000	$120,000	$150,000	$160,000
Dividends per share	$5	$6	$7.50	$8
Up-Down Company				
Total earnings	$160,000	$ 80,000	$210,000	$140,000
Dividends per share	$3	$0	$10	$2

What factors might account for the different trends in earnings and dividends for the two companies? Which stock would you prefer as an investment with the given information? It should be noted that dividing total earnings by the number of shares outstanding gives earnings per share, which is useful for comparative purposes.

SUGGESTED READINGS

Cohen, Jerome B.; Zinbarg, Edward D.; and Zecker, Arthur. *Investment Analysis and Portfolio Management.* Homewood, Ill.: Richard D. Irwin, 1977.

Denenberg, Herbert S.; Eilers, Robert D.; Melone, Joseph J.; and Zelten, Robert A. *Risk and Insurance.* 2d ed. Englewood Cliffs, N.J.: Prentice-Hall, 1974.

Goldsmith, Raymond W. *Financial Institutions.* New York: Random House, 1968.

Jacobs, Donald P.; Farwell, Loring C.; and Neave, Edwin. *Financial Institutions.* Homewood, Ill.: Richard D. Irwin, 1972.

FINANCIAL MANAGEMENT

LEARNING OBJECTIVES

When you finish this chapter you should:

☐ understand the problem of raising funds by new ventures.

☐ be aware of the principal sources of funds.

☐ be aware of the principal uses of funds.

☐ understand the problems of raising long-term funds at the lowest cost and investing them at the highest return.

KEY TERMS TO LEARN FROM THIS CHAPTER

accounts and notes
    receivable and
    payable
assets
budget
callable bonds
capital budgeting
capital gain
cash discount
commercial paper
common stock
convertible bonds and
    stocks
copyrights, trademarks,
    and patents

coupon and registered
    bonds
creditors
cumulative bonds
current assets and lia-
    bilities
debenture bonds
default
depreciation
discounting
equities
fixed assets
funds
going public
indenture

inventories
invested funds
invoice
lease
lessee
lessor
leverage
long-lived assets
long-term debt
maker
mortgage bonds
open account
par value and no par
    value
participating

payee
portfolio management
preferred stock
principal
private placement
retained earnings
risk
secondary liability
short-term debt
sinking fund
time deposits
Treasury bills
trustee
venture capital com-
    panies

You may be aware of cases in which a newly started business that looked like a "can't miss" proposition went under shortly after opening. One of the main reasons this often occurs is that the firm is underfinanced: the owners did not invest enough money to carry the firm through its initial start-up period, and they were unable to get additional funds during the crisis. All this despite the fact that the defunct firm's future earnings prospects may have looked good even at the time the firm went under.

The problem of underfinancing, however, is not restricted to newly started companies. Old, established companies (including such well-known giants as Penn Central Railroad, Lockheed Aircraft, and Chrysler) may for numerous reasons find themselves in a situation in which a cash shortage threatens to topple the company.

While appropriate financial management is only one of the ingredients constituting a successful business, it might easily be viewed as the life blood of the firm.

Before discussing the finance function in greater detail, its relation to later chapters should be made clear. Institutions providing important financial services, such as banks and insurance companies, have already been discussed in Chapter 12. Accounting, discussed in Chapter 14, is concerned with financial statements which help us to evaluate the financial condition of a business. Understanding accounting reports is thus essential for those involved with the financial function.

WHAT IS THE FINANCE FUNCTION?

The finance function centers upon how a business acquires the assets needed for its operations. Let's look at this process in more detail.

ASSETS

Assets are resources of value owned or controlled by the firm. They are necessary for producing the goods or services offered by a business which hopes to make profits. Assets include capital (land, buildings, machinery, and equipment). They include a number of other necessary elements as well. Assets include stocks of goods or inventories bought for resale by wholesalers and retailers as well as raw materials that are converted into new products by manufacturers. Furthermore, when goods are sold, new assets are created either in the form of money received from customers or claims against them arising from the sale. These are a few of the many elements composing a business's assets.

SOURCES OF ASSETS

But if a firm is to own or control assets, the money must come from various sources. These sources can be classified in several ways.

Equities *Equities* refer to money coming from owners. Owners are, of course, risk takers. The return on their investment is the profit that the firm earns from its operations. Equity funds can be subdivided into two types.

Invested Funds   This type consists of money or other personal assets of the owners that are invested in the business either when it is founded or when additional funds are later needed for expansion.

Retained Earnings   These arise from profits that have been earned by the firm from successful operations. A decision is made by the board of directors of a corporation, the partners, or a sole proprietor to keep the funds at work in the business rather than returning them to owners as dividends or return on investment.

Debt   Debt refers to those sources of assets provided by creditors. Money owed to *creditors* becomes due to them at very specific dates. Debt is classified according to when amounts become due.

Short-term Debt   Short-term debt is payable within a year of the particular date at hand.

Long-term Debt   Long-term debt becomes due beyond a year from the particular date at hand.

   As of July 1, 1977, an obligation that becomes due on January 2, 1978, would be short-term debt. If that same debt were in existence on December 1, 1976, it would be classified as long-term debt as of that date.

THE FINANCE FUNCTION

Finance is involved with both the raising of funds from owners and creditors of a business and appropriate investment of these funds in assets. In a nutshell, then, the finance function attempts (1) to raise funds at the lowest cost to the business and (2) to invest these funds in a manner that will maximize the earnings on these assets to the firm and its owners. *Funds* is a rather general term referring to the various assets in which a firm invests as well as the means by which assets have been financed.

"When I asked Mom and Dad for a loan, I didn't expect them to charge me interest."

The balance of this chapter will examine in more detail the sources of funds to the firm and the general categories of assets in which they may be invested. Some of the basic concepts underlying the financial problem of maximizing the return on investment and minimizing the cost of funds will then be discussed.

However, the starting point is a special but important problem: how a new firm goes about the ticklish problem of raising funds.

RAISING FUNDS BY NEW VENTURES

After Geri Rogers and Art Lindstrom decided that they wanted to go into the retail candy business together, they made a list of the various assets that they would need in order to open a store. In order to make various kinds of candy in a medium-sized retail operation with hopes of expanding into wholesale and specialty orders, they needed the following manufacturing equipment:

· A stove.

· A refrigerator.

· An oven.

· A freezer.

· An enrober (chocolate coating machine).

These were all going to be located in the back of the store in the production room. In the front of the store in the retail area three display counters, a cash register, and a scale were needed. They also needed display shelves for their toys, but Art decided to build and finish them himself in his carpentry shop, leaving only the wood to be purchased.

Geri and Art had several friends who were in various retail businesses. From them, they got the names of several wholesalers of the types of equipment they needed. In addition, they learned of a wholesale outlet in Kansas City that had used equipment. They decided that if the used equipment were in good shape and the savings over new equipment were substantial, they would go the cheaper route.

After checking with the wholesalers in their region and the Kansas City used-equipment dealer, they made a tentative selection of their equipment. All of it was from Kansas City except the enrober and the cash register. The used-equipment dealer required immediate cash payment, while the regional wholesalers required payment thirty days after delivery. Geri and Art made a $150 down payment on their equipment in Kansas City. The dealer agreed to hold it for sixty days until they got the balance of their cash. The enrober and cash register could be ordered at any time from the wholesaler with delivery guaranteed in fifteen days.

Over and above buying their equipment, Geri and Art knew they would have other cash requirements. Geri found a beautiful 90 × 40-foot store on Seventh Street just off Main Street, the principal downtown shopping area in Warrenstown. She preferred this location to the newer shopping center just out of town because downtown was still thriving in Warrenstown. More importantly,

State College bordered on downtown. Geri felt that the students would be a very important part of their clientele. She felt that the rental of $350 a month was quite reasonable given the excellent location of the shop, its size, and its very good condition. No painting was required and only a minimum amount of cleaning up was necessary. The owner wanted three months rent in advance. After the first three months, rent was to be paid on the first of each month. Geri and Art decided to sign the lease immediately and pay the three months rent rather than take a chance on losing the excellent location. The store was leased for a one-year period.

Other cash needs of Geri and Art had to do with operating the store. Two full-time employees were needed. Geri required a second person to help her in the production room, and a full-time salesperson would be needed in the retail section.

The operation also required candy ingredients. Several different varieties of fine chocolate were necessary for Geri's chocolates. Nuts, cherries, and raisins were needed for the centers. Not too much credit was available from suppliers because bills had to be paid thirty days after delivery.

CASH BUDGET

After talking with an accountant friend, Geri and Art drew up a budget of the total cash requirements needed to launch The Candy Emporium. Although they felt that a candy store would eventually catch hold in the town, they were also aware that the first few months after opening might be quite slow. Consequently, the total amount of start-up capital was to include six months of labor and ingredient costs as well as a generous "safety fund" to guard against unforeseen contingencies. A plan applicable to a future period of time expressed in dollars is called a *budget*. Geri and Art's cash budget for launching The Candy Emporium is shown in Table 13–1.

Now that they knew their start-up needs, Geri and Art did not hesitate to ask their accountant friend for advice on how to raise the money (the accountant also foresaw that The Candy Emporium might well become his client). Four possible sources of start-up money were eventually pinpointed:

1. Geri and Art themselves and other members of their families.
2. Venture capital syndicates providing ownership money.
3. Commercial banks for a loan.
4. The Small Business Administration of the United States government for a loan.

PERSONAL SOURCES OF MONEY

Unfortunately, neither Geri nor Art nor any of their relatives had a large bundle of excess cash that could be tapped to cover their entire needs.

However, they were surprised to find that they had access to more cash from personal sources than they had anticipated. Geri's mother owned her own home and agreed to take a second mortgage (loan) for part of her equity (ownership interest) in the house. This source produced $2,000. Art had an insurance policy on his own life against which he was able to make a loan at a rate far below what

Table 13-1
Candy Emporium Six-Month Cash Budget,
January–June 1978

Cash payments	
Balance due Kansas City equipment dealer	$ 5,850
Acquisition of cash register and enrober	3,500
Three months of rent	1,050
Six months of salaries	12,000
Chocolate	7,500
Other ingredients	2,500
Stock of toys	3,500
Taxes and licenses	2,100
Safety fund	3,000
Total required cash needs	$41,000
Cash receipts	
Estimated sales for first six months of operations	$ 6,000
Total budgeted cash needs	35,000
Invested by Geri and Art	10,000
Additional investment needed	$25,000

the banks were charging. The insurance loan generated $2,500. From their own personal savings accounts Geri took $3,000 and Art, $2,500. This gave them a total of $10,000 for their initial start-up needs.

It was also in accordance with their desire to have a partnership in which their individual investments were equal (they had already agreed to share profits and losses equally). They now had to shop around for the additional $25,000 of start-up money.

VENTURE CAPITAL COMPANIES

Geri and Art did not want to incorporate immediately because of high state taxes. They did not want to pay immediately the costs of incorporating as a Subchapter S corporation either, though they held this option open once The Candy Emporium got on its feet.

While they had a great deal of faith in their venture, their first desire was to avoid borrowing debt capital because if The Candy Emporium were unsuccessful, their own personal assets would be liable for satisfying the firm's debts. They were thus first interested in raising $25,000 of ownership funds.

Geri and Art found out from their accountant that a special type of firm called a *venture capital company* exists for the purpose of investing equity money in new businesses.

Their role has traditionally been one of nursing young companies along until they are ready to *go public*. Going public refers to the process of switching from the status of a corporation whose stock is closely held (not traded frequently) by a relatively few people to one in which the stock is registered for trading on a local or even national stock exchange. The venture capital company has an excellent chance of making a large gain on the holding of its stock in the fledgling company when the stock becomes publicly traded.

Geri and Art decided that they would not pursue the venture capital possibility, at least at the present time. Their product (candy) was not so unique as to offer a particularly strong probability of their operation becoming a relatively important national or even regional company. Furthermore, since 1969 venture capital companies have generally steered clear of completely new businesses. They have concentrated more on young but relatively well established companies that show great promise of reaching the stage of going public.

At this point, Geri and Art decided that they would pay a visit to their friendly banker.

COMMERCIAL BANKS

Before going to the bank, Geri and Art were told by their accountant friend that the bank would want to know how fast any potential loan would be repaid. At this point Geri and Art did some very careful calculating. They figured that sales should grow from approximately $50,000 in their first year to about $75,000 by the third year of operations and stabilize at that point. They figured that the profits from sales would enable them to repay their loan over a five-year period.

Geri and Art then made an appointment with Joe Tearney, the loan officer at the Warrenstown State Bank. This bank was a commercial bank, one whose functions include lending money to businesses (see Chapter 12 for further discussion of commercial banks).

Mr. Tearney was impressed by the fact that they had drawn up a cash budget of their initial needs as well as a projection showing how they expected to repay the bank. Mr. Tearney was also personally impressed by Geri and Art. Although Joe Tearney fought to give them a five-year loan, he was overruled by the bank's loan committee.

There were several reasons why Geri and Art did not get their loan. In the first place, banks feel that new businesses are extremely risky, and they hesitate to make unsecured loans to them. Second, banks do not care to make loans ($25,000) that are larger than the owners' equity investment ($10,000). Finally, banks generally prefer to make loans for periods considerably shorter than five years unless the business is a very successful venture, which, of course, The Candy Emporium wasn't.

However, Joe Tearney had an excellent piece of advice for Geri and Art. He suggested that they talk to the Small Business Administration (SBA) in their Kansas City field office.

THE SMALL BUSINESS ADMINISTRATION

The SBA is a permanent, independent agency created by Congress in 1953. Its purpose is best expressed in the Small Business Act itself:

> It is the declared policy of the Congress that the Government should aid, counsel, assist, and protect, insofar as is possible, the interests of small business concerns in order to preserve free competitive enterprise . . . to maintain and strengthen the overall economy of the nation.

While the SBA offers many services, it was obviously the area of financial assistance that interested Geri and Art most. They found out that although the SBA does make some direct loans, these are reserved for extremely marginal cases.

The financial assistance program that was most applicable to them was the SBA's loan guarantee plan. For firms that qualify as small businesses which are unable to get a loan on reasonable terms elsewhere, SBA can guarantee up to 90 percent of a maximum $350,000 bank loan.

While the SBA's purpose is to foster small business, its intent is not to back failures. The agency, in fact, has a surprisingly good record in terms of borrowers repaying loans in the loan guarantee program.

Geri and Art filled out the appropriate papers for a guaranteed loan. Shortly thereafter, their application was approved. Armed with their SBA guarantee, they again saw Joe Tearney at the Warrenstown State Bank. The loan committee was now quite willing to make the five-year loan to Geri and Art. As a result of the SBA's 90 percent loan guarantee, the bank stood to lose at most $2,500 of the $25,000 loan.

Although the cash budget (Table 13–1) shows $25,000 required, it was not all needed immediately. Consequently, the bank agreed to allow Geri and Art to withdraw the money as it became needed, with interest charged on just the amount borrowed. Repayment was still to be made over a five-year period. Individual repayments were geared to the amount of the loan outstanding.

It took Geri and Art approximately one month from the time of filing their papers with the SBA to the receipt of their loan from the bank. Shortly thereafter, The Candy Emporium was successfully launched.

FINANCING ASSETS IN ESTABLISHED FIRMS

If an established firm desires to grow in size, its management, like that of The Candy Emporium, must decide how the assets should be financed. Should debt or equity or a mixture of the two be used? How much earnings that have been retained in the business should be used? Questions like these are extremely important in terms of financial management. Even if a firm remains the same size, as liabilities become due, questions relative to replacing the matured liabilities must be answered.

In this section, sources or means of financing will be surveyed briefly.

SHORT-TERM DEBTS

As mentioned before, debts are classified in terms of when they become due. Debts maturing within a year are called short-term debts or current liabilities. It is an important source of financing for virtually all businesses.

Accounts Payable   Most goods that are bought for resale as well as basic raw materials used by manufacturers are bought on *open account*. In other words, cash is not immediately due when the goods or materials are received by the buyer. Terms of sale usually depend on the custom of the particular industry.

Furthermore, the buyer is often entitled to a small saving called a *cash discount* for paying a bill promptly when it becomes due. For example, if the terms of sale are "2/10, net 30" on a $1,000 purchase, the buyer can either remit $980 to the seller ($1,000 less 2 percent thereof) within ten days after receiving the seller's bill (called an invoice), or the entire $1,000 can be paid thirty days after receipt of the invoice.

Notice a very important fact here. When goods are bought on credit, the seller is actually financing the buyer until payment is made.

Notes Payable   A note is a written promise to pay a specific amount of money on a particular date. Both the payer or *maker* and receiver (called the *payee*) are clearly specified. In addition, the note must be dated and signed by the maker. Notes often include an element of interest. Notes are frequently used if a buyer is temporarily unable to pay a seller when a bill comes due.

If a seller desires, the note can be *discounted* at their bank. When a note is discounted, the bank will pay the seller the amount due them less an interest factor. The bank will notify the maker that payment should be made to the bank. The seller then has a *secondary liability* to the bank. If the maker does not pay the note when it comes due, the seller is required to pay it.

Other Current Liabilities

Salaries and Wages   In most businesses, salaries and wages are paid to employees after the money has actually been earned. For example, when salaries and wages are paid every two weeks, a particular payroll will be for the preceding two weeks. As a result, salaries and wages are an important form of short-term financing for business.

Amounts Due the Government   Federal and state income tax withholdings from employees are remitted by the company to the appropriate government agency either monthly or quarterly.

The same applies to the employer's own income taxes if the firm is incorporated. Essentially the same thing happens if the firm is either a sole proprietorship or a partnership. In these situations it is done in the form of quarterly estimated tax payments by proprietors and partners.

Other taxes on both employers and employees that are remitted periodically by the firm to appropriate government agencies include Social Security taxes and unemployment taxes.

LONG-TERM DEBTS

When discussing long-term debts and equity sources of funds, we enter the fabled and complex world of "high finance." A few of the more important aspects are covered here.

Bonds   A *bond* is a written certificate or document in which the corporation promises to pay a stated amount of interest per year as well as to repay the amount borrowed at a specific future date. Only corporations can issue bonds.

The essentials of a bond issue are actually quite simple. The corporation borrows money from lenders. In return for the use of this money, the corporation pays a stated amount of interest. At a designated date in the future, the

A sample corporate bond.

"face" amount of the bond, called the *principal*, must be repaid to the holders of the bonds. The principal amount of each bond is usually $1,000. Each bond contract is called an *issue*. A corporation may have many issues of bonds outstanding at any given time. Each individual issue is governed by the provisions in the contract, called an *indenture*.

Trustee   The most important point about bonds is that they are debt. Unlike other forms of long-term debt, a bond issue must have a trustee.

The trustee is usually a bank. While the trustee may perform certain "housekeeping" tasks relative to the bond issue, such as keeping records of who the owners are, its principal function lies in protecting the bondholders in the event of *default* (nonpayment of either interest or principal when they become due).

Depending on the terms of the indenture and the seriousness of the default, trustees may take steps such as suing the corporation for payment of principal and unpaid interest or filing a bankruptcy petition with the federal district court for reorganizing the corporation. In less serious cases, as when the corporation has adequate cash to meet its obligations, the trustee might take equity proceedings asking for a writ (order) to the corporation ordering the corporation to fulfill its obligations.

Debenture and Mortgage Bonds   Debenture bonds are backed only by the general credit standing of the corporation. Mortgage bonds have specific assets pledged for satisfaction of bondholder claims in the event of default of interest or principal. Pledged property is called *collateral.*

Registered and Coupon Bonds   Registered bonds provide more safety than coupon bonds because records are kept relative to who the owners are. Coupon bonds, on the other hand, are payable to the bearer and are transferred to a new owner by simply giving the owner the bond. The bond itself contains coupons which are clipped and presented to a commercial bank for payment when interest is due. The coupon is then sent to the corporation or its agent for reimbursement.

Since the mid-1960s registered bonds have become far more prevalent due to the protection that registration provides. A hybrid bond which contains coupons for the interest but is registered as to principal is still somewhat popular.

Other Features   If the corporation has the right to buy back the bonds before the stipulated maturity date, the bonds are *callable*. Should it be required that a set amount of money must be put aside each year to provide for retirement, the bonds have a *sinking fund* provision. If bondholders have the right to convert each bond into a designated number of shares of common stock, the bonds are *convertible*.

Setting Interest Rates on Bonds   You are probably wondering how interest rates are set on bond issues. The issuing corporation should take the following factors into account:

1. The general level of interest rates prevailing in the bond market at the time of issue.

2. The general credit standing of the corporation.

3. The length of life of the bond issue (generally the longer the life of the issue, the higher the rate).

4. The various provisions of the bond indenture mentioned above, particularly whether the bonds are debenture or mortgage.

Bond Trading Board.

CHASE MANHATTAN BANK
PHOTO BY RAYMOND JASCHKUS

Investment banking firms (Chapter 12) can provide the issuing corporation with expert advice on setting the appropriate interest rate for bonds as well as on many other aspects of the indenture.

Long-Term Notes   Long-term notes are often used in *private placements* rather than being sold through stock exchanges. For example, an automobile manufacturer borrowing directly from a large bank or insurance company might use a long-term note. Long-term note issues usually do not require a trustee. However, the provisions of the contract embodying factors such as collateral and call provisions can be as complex as bond indentures.

Long-term notes can also be used by unincorporated businesses. The loan secured by The Candy Emporium from the Warrenstown State Bank was a note of this type.

EQUITY FUNDS

Equity funds, as mentioned previously, consist of two basic types: (1) investments of money or other assets of owners into the business and (2) profits earned by the firm which are kept in the firm rather than returned to owners. Division of partnership profits was mentioned in Chapter 3, so our attention here shall be devoted to the corporation.

Capital Stock   All corporations must have at least one type of capital stock. The basic type is called *common stock*. If other types of capital stock are present, these are called preferred stock. The following basic characteristics apply to both common and preferred stock.

Stock sometimes has a *par value*. Par value is simply a figure appearing on the face of each stock certificate. It does not represent the value of the stock. However, because of the confusion that can be created, most newly issued common stock today does not carry a par value and is known as *no-par-value stock*.

A stock's value is based on economic factors relative to the firm and the industry it is in and can only be determined in the marketplace. The idea of a "par value" arose as a result of attempting to convince potential buyers that it was the "true value" of the stock.

Common Stock   Common stock is the ultimate risk security from the standpoint of the investor. Common stock provides its owners with the least protection of all corporate securities. One can easily lose an entire investment if the corporation fails. On the other hand, the rewards to the common stockholder can be enormous if the corporation is very successful. A very modest investment in IBM at its inception would make one a millionaire today. The problem, of course, is to be able to identify the IBMs and the Xeroxes, which is where the risk comes in.

In return for their investment, stockholders hope to get (1) dividends and (2) capital gains. *Dividends* are a return of money coming from the corporation's profits to the stockholders for the investment of their funds. Since stockholders are owners of the firm rather than creditors, no legal problems arise if the board of directors of the corporation does not declare a dividend. In fact, some companies such as Litton Industries have seldom, if ever, paid a dividend. *Capital gain* refers to the rise in market value of common stock holdings in a given corporation. A drop in this value would be a *capital loss*. Capital gains arise because the firm's future operating prospects look good.

Preferred Stock   While preferred stock is an ownership type of security, it has less risk than common shares in the same corporation. Preferred stockholders are entitled to their dividends ahead of common stockholders. Preferred stockholders can receive a dividend when none is declared on common stock. However, common stockholders cannot get a dividend without the preferred shareholders getting their dividend. Also, should the corporation dissolve—go out of business—preferred shareholders would be entitled to the return of their investment ahead of common stockholders.

Preferred stock, unlike common stock, usually has a par value because the annual dividend is based on the par value. For example, 5 percent preferred stock with a par value of $100 would be entitled to an annual dividend of $5 per year. However, since it is an ownership type of security, if the board of directors does not approve a preferred dividend for a particular year, preferred stockholders—unlike bondholders—have no legal recourse against the corporation.

As a result, most issues of preferred stock have a *cumulative* provision. This means that any preferred dividends of previous years that were not paid must be made good before common stockholders can receive a dividend.

Occasionally, preferred stock issues are *participating*. If so, they may receive some amount of dividends above their stated annual amount.

Preferred shares are occasionally *convertible* into a designated number of common shares. In these cases, the owner has the right to convert them into the stated number of common shares if he or she desires.

Preferred stock usually does not have voting rights. The particular rights and privileges of an issue of preferred stock must be stated in writing in the terms of the issue.

Retained Earnings   Earnings of a corporation that are not paid back to owners as dividends remain within the firm to be used for investment in assets. Funds coming from this source are an important source of financing in corporations as well as in sole proprietorships and partnerships. The term *retained earnings* is used only in the corporate form, however. In sole proprietorships and partnerships, earnings left in the business are added directly to the investment of the owner or owners in accordance with the agreement of how profits are to be divided.

In corporations, retention of earnings by the enterprise often goes hand in hand with a rise in the market value of the common stock. This is the capital gains factor mentioned previously.

A summary of the principal sources of financing is shown in Table 13–2.

USES OF FUNDS

Just as the debt portion of the firm's sources of funds is divided into short-term and long-term portions, investment in assets is similarly divided. Current assets include cash and other items which either "turn over" or are used up within a year. When goods are sold on open account, an *account receivable* is created. When the account receivable is collected, it turns over. When materials are used in the manufacture of goods, on the other hand, they become used up.

Assets having a life or period of use ordinarily extending beyond a year are called *long-lived assets* or investments.

CURRENT ASSETS

Cash, marketable securities, accounts and notes receivable, and inventories make up the principal current assets of retailing and manufacturing concerns. Service enterprises would not hold stocks of inventories. Each of these categories will be briefly discussed.

Cash Cash is, in a sense, the ultimate current asset. When goods are sold, an account receivable is created unless payment occurs immediately. You might think that the objective of a firm is to have as much cash as possible. This, however, is not true. Business is continuous or cyclical in nature. When cash comes in, a portion must be used to pay for goods and services, salaries of employees, and other necessities. Obviously a firm desires to have more cash come in than goes out. If the business is fortunate enough to be generating a sizable surplus of cash from operations, a good financial manager will want to put the excess cash to work, at least temporarily, to increase the return or earnings on the firm's assets. Idle cash earns nothing.

Cash has three basic forms. Coin and currency is the type with which we are all familiar. Coin and currency form only a small part, however, of most firms' cash holdings. The reason, of course, is that coin and currency are not overly

Table 13-2
Principal Sources of Financing

Type and Examples	Main Characteristics
Short-term debt	Liabilities coming due within a year
Accounts payable	Arises from buying in the regular course of business from various suppliers.
Notes payable	Written promise to pay a specific sum at a specific date.
Salaries and wages payable	Amounts due employees.
Amounts due government	Various taxes and withholding from employer and employee.
Long-term debt	Liabilities maturing beyond a year
Bonds	Usually sold through investment banker or other financial intermediary and traded in the securities market.
Long-term notes	Directly negotiated by borrower and lender.
Equity funds (corporate)	Ownership funds
Common stock	Ultimate bearer of risk.
Preferred stock	Less risky but smaller return than common stock.
Retained earnings	Earnings kept within firm rather than being paid to common stockholders as dividends.

safe in terms of security. Nevertheless, firms, particularly retail establishments, must keep some amount of cash in this form for transactions requiring currency. Adequate safeguards should be employed to minimize the possibility of theft.

The bulk of a firm's cash holdings are ordinarily in the form of checking account deposits with a bank. Payment for virtually all transactions between businesses is made by check for safety and convenience. Checking accounts do not receive interest.

The last major form of cash holdings is *time deposits* or, as they are more commonly called, savings accounts. Checks may not be written against time deposits, which do bear interest.

Marketable Securities and Temporary Investments   Temporary amounts of excess cash are often invested in stocks and bonds of major corporations. The return, in the form of dividends or capital gains, is expected to be higher than interest on time deposits. These investments are classified as current assets because the securities can easily be sold at any time through a national or regional stock exchange. Investments of this type do not include acquisitions of common stock in other companies that are made for purposes of owning or controlling those enterprises. This more permanent type of investment will be discussed shortly.

Temporary investments can also be made in various types of short-term notes issued by departments and agencies of the federal government. For example, *Treasury bills* have a ninety-one-day maturity and are issued by the United States Treasury Department. They are interest-bearing notes which combine security, because they are obligations of the United States government, with liquidity, because they can be sold on the market any time prior to their maturity if the company desires.

Another popular form of temporary investment is *commercial paper*. Commercial paper consists of four to six month unsecured promissory notes of the strongest major private corporations of the United States. They usually carry a high rate of interest (for short-term securities) and are likewise highly marketable if the firm desires to sell them prior to maturity.

Accounts and Notes Receivable   When firm A buys goods on credit from firm B, the transaction results in an account payable from A's standpoint and an account receivable from B's view. Consequently, what was said relative to accounts and notes payable likewise applies here. One other factor should be mentioned, though.

When a firm sells goods on account, there is a danger, however slight, that the buyer may not be able to pay his or her bill. Large firms maintain credit departments for the purpose of evaluating the credit worthiness of potential customers. Dun and Bradstreet is a nationally known organization whose service consists of preparing credit reports for evaluating the credit standing of businesses throughout the country.

Inventories   Inventories consist of (1) goods bought or produced for sale to customers and (2) raw materials that are used as part of the manufacturing process. Steel, for example, would be an important element of an automobile maker's inventories. Inventories are an extremely important asset of almost all manufacturing and retailing firms.

Inventories are needed if sales are to be made. Retailers must have goods on hand for customers to see and buy. Even manufacturers of standardized goods with which buyers are familiar must keep some amount of inventories on hand to ensure rapid deliveries.

On the one hand, then, inventories must be kept on hand to ensure sales and prompt deliveries. At the same time, however, an enterprise does not want to keep more inventory items on hand than are really necessary because funds are tied up that could be used elsewhere. In addition, there are risks of spoilage and obsolescence. Obsolescence occurs when goods or equipment become out-moded. Relative to machinery and equipment, it was mentioned in Chapter 3 that the diesel locomotive made the steam locomotive obsolete in railroading because diesel is cheaper to operate. Another type of obsolescence—style obso-lescence—exists for certain types of inventories. If hemlines go down, a cloth-ing store would not want to get caught with an excess of above-the-knee dresses.

The problem of inventory management is one of balancing the conflicting needs of minimizing the inventory investment without reducing sales resulting from shortages of goods.

LONG-TERM INVESTMENTS IN OTHER ENTERPRISES

The great merger movement of the 1960s was discussed in Chapter 2. When an enterprise acquires common stock of another company for purposes of owner-ship and control, the acquisition is considered to be a long-term investment. Long-term investments and marketable securities acquisitions differ in terms of the firm's underlying intent or purpose.

Large retail chains have to have a substantial inventory of goods on hand at all times to meet fluctuations in customer demand.

CHARLES L. FARROW

LONG-LIVED ASSETS

Virtually all businesses, no matter how small, will have some assets which fall into this category. The Candy Emporium's enrober, refrigerator, oven, and freezer would be examples. For major manufacturing enterprises, long-lived assets are generally the most important use of funds in dollar terms. As a rule of thumb, the more capital intensive (Chapter 3) a firm, the larger will be its investment in long-lived assets. Another commonly used name for long-lived assets is *fixed assets*.

Land, Buildings, Machinery, and Equipment   The human factor aside, the heart of most industrial enterprises consists of their factories and the productive equipment inside. Keeping plant and manufacturing facilities up to date is a very important part of the financial management problem because of the size of the investment and the long period of time that the investment is tied up.

Land, unlike the other components of long-term investments, does not become used up over time. Machinery and equipment, and even buildings, decrease in value for two basic reasons. Even when properly maintained, machinery and equipment tend to deteriorate through wear and tear from use. The second reason is obsolescence of the cost variety. It is often cheaper to scrap or otherwise dispose of presently owned equipment, even though it may still be serviceable, for newer and more efficient equipment. The technical name for this process of wearing out is *depreciation*.

Leasing of Productive Facilities   Extremely complex financing arrangements often underlie acquisition of major equipment and facilities. When acquisition is needed, an appropriate long-term means of financing must be arranged if the firm does not have excess cash (as is often the case).

A method of financing which has become extremely popular during the last thirty years is *leasing*. A lease is a contractual arrangement whereby the user or *lessee* pays periodic rents to the owner or *lessor* for use of an asset for a specified period of time. Leasing is a particularly important means of financing major assets such as railroad cars, oil tankers, and airplanes.

Intangibles   Intangibles include patents, copyrights, and trademarks. All have in common the conferring of an exclusive right or privilege to the owner for a specified number of years.

The owner gains the exclusive right by registering his patent, copyright, or trademark with a United States government agency. In addition, all three may either be purchased or developed by the enterprise itself.

Patents   *Patents* are issued by the United States Patent Office. They guarantee the owner the sole right to produce and sell for a period of seventeen years the product that has been invented or developed.

A patent does not automatically assure success. A very small percentage of all the items ever patented have been carried through to commercial success. Many potential items have little or no appeal to the potential consumer. In addition, many inventors do not have the money or know-how required to promote and sell successfully their patented items.

Patented Mar. 1, 1938

2,109,678

UNITED STATES PATENT OFFICE

2,109,678

CONTACT SWITCH FOR BALL ROLLING GAMES

Nels A. Nelson, Chicago, Ill., assignor to Raymond T. Maloney, Chicago, Ill.

Application January 12, 1937, Serial No. 120,256

5 Claims. (Cl. 200—52)

The invention relates to a contact switch for use in ball rolling games, or the like.

These games usually embody a table cover which a ball is freely rollable to contact suitable targets disposed thereon, said targets in the present instance being in the form of a special means adapted to be bumped or contacted by the ball to cause momentary closing of a circuit with a suitable source of energy, said circuit including an electromagnetic relay to operate a score register, dispenser, or like game auxiliary.

More particularly, the invention relates to the target structure which in the present instance is in the form of a resilient circuit closer, to disposed on the game table as to be contacted by a freely rolling ball or other playing piece, momentarily to close the associated circuit.

The main object of the invention is to provide a novel form of obstacle or target for use with ball rolling games.

Another object is to provide such obstacle in the form of a normally open resilient switch or circuit closer, which when bumped or contacted by a free rolling ball momentarily closes to establish an electric circuit.

Still another object is to provide such a contact switch in the form of a pendant coil spring carried above a game board, and including a leg or ferrule, or the like, disposed in the board; both the spring and ferrule constituting electrical conductors disposed in a circuit.

Other important objects will become apparent to those skilled in this art as the disclosure is more fully made.

Briefly, these objects may be attained in a ball rolling amusement game having a table cover which a ball or balls may be propelled, or otherwise rolled with the object of causing the ball to bump or contact the switch structure of this invention. Said switch comprises a conductor standard mounted in the table and carries a coil spring having a leg pendantly disposed in a conductor ring located in the table slightly offset from the standard. The standard and ring are wired in a circuit with a source of energy and a relay coil in such a manner that when a ball rolling on the table bumps the coil spring from any angular direction whatsoever, the leg of the spring will be caused momentarily to contact the conductor ring in the board to establish the circuit for operating the relay coil and any desired game auxiliary device.

In the sheet of drawings:

Figure 1 is a front elevational view of the bumper obstacle mounted on a game board, and.

Figure 2 is a side sectional view thereof, taken along the line 2—2 of Figure 1, looking in the direction of the arrows, a wiring diagram being also shown in illustrative form.

The game board or table is shown at 10, the same being either disposed horizontally or slightly tilted from the horizontal in a manner well known in this art. A support or standard 11 is mounted in an upright position on the board, the same having a reduced threaded shank 12 passed through the board, or table 10, as shown, there being provided a metallic clip 13 and nut 14, below the table to secure the standard to the table, in an obvious manner.

The upper end of the standard also is reduced to form a threaded shank 15, the shoulder thus provided, carrying a horizontal washer 16. The shank above the washer 16 carries a cup-shaped cap 17 and between the cap and washer is the end of a coil spring 18, which at its lower end terminates in a pendant spring leg 19. The spring assembly is made secure by a lock washer 20 and nut 21, as shown.

Below the leg 19 and offset from the standard 11, the table 10 is formed with an aperture in which is securely seated a conductor ferrule 22 into which the leg 19 is suspended and normally out of contact therewith. Said ferrule at its lower end is formed with an inturned annular flange 23 and an integral depending extension 24.

The clip 13 and extension 24 are disposed, for example, in an electrical circuit 25 for an electromagnetic relay coil 26, and with a source of energy, such as the battery 27.

In use, when a ball rolling on the table 10 bumps or hits the spring 18 to rebound therefrom, the impact moves the spring sufficiently to cause the leg 19 thereof to contact the flange 23 of the ferrule, momentarily to close the circuit 25 and cause energization of the coil 26 for any desired purpose. It can be seen since the leg 19 is normally disposed at the center of the annular ferrule 22, that no matter from what angular direction a ball strikes the spring it will be operative to close the circuit in the manner described.

In a ball rolling game any desired number of such spring switch obstacles or targets may be placed on the board in any suitable spaced relationship and consequently, as in pin ball games generally, a single ball may successively bump and close a number of the switch devices.

It is the intention to cover all changes and modifications of the example of the invention

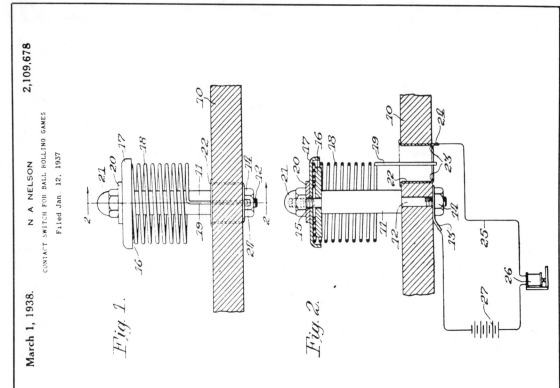

March 1, 1938.

N A NELSON

2,109,678

CONTACT SWITCH FOR BALL ROLLING GAMES

Filed Jan. 12, 1937

Fig. 1.

Fig. 2.

Trademarks *Trademarks* are symbols, words, or designs used by business enterprises as a means of identifying their products. The legalizing of a symbol, term, or name is called a trademark. The general area of branding was discussed in Chapter 8.

Copyrights *Copyrights* cover written, drawn, illustrated, or designed materials. They protect the owner against infringement by unauthorized users. Copyrights are registered with the Library of Congress. They are granted for a twenty-eight-year period and are renewable for one additional twenty-eight-year period.

A particular problem arising from copyright protection today is presented by the ability of individuals to photocopy easily and cheaply large segments of copyrighted material without paying the owner.

A summary of the principal uses of funds is shown in Table 13–3.

PROBLEMS OF THE FINANCE FUNCTION

Now that you have had a short survey of the principal asset categories of business and the means of financing them, let's take a brief look at some of the principal problems of the financial manager.

Table 13-3
Principal Uses of Funds in Business Enterprises

Type and Examples	Main Characteristics
Current assets	Become cash or turn over within a year
Cash	The ultimate current asset.
Marketable securities and temporary investments	Temporary investments to keep money "working" or earning a return.
Accounts receivable	Arise from selling goods to customers.
Notes receivable	Written promise to receive a specific sum at a specific date.
Inventories	Goods purchased for resale or for use in manufacturing.
Long-term investments in other enterprises	Common stock acquisitions of other companies for purposes of control
Long-lives assets	Useful life extends beyond a year
Land	Does not depreciate.
Buildings	Depreciate slowly over time.
Machinery and equipment	Depreciate and can be subject to rapid cost obsolescence.
Leases	Contractual right to use property for specified period without ownership.
Intangibles	Confer valuable rights upon owners
Patents	Sole right to produce and sell for seventeen years a product that has been invented or developed.
Trademarks	Symbols, words, or design for identifying a product.
Copyrights	Covers written, drawn, illustrated, or designed materials for twenty-eight years.

RAISING LONG-TERM FUNDS AT THE LOWEST COST

Relatively permanent financing comes from long-term debt and the various equity sources discussed previously. As a firm grows, the financial manager's task is one of issuing debt and equity in a "mix" or proportion that will minimize the cost of long-term funds to the firm.

As mentioned previously, bonds carry less risk to their owners than stock. However, the opposite is true from the corporation's standpoint. Since bond interest is a legal liability, it must be paid to avoid grave problems for the firm. Consequently, though bond interest is cheaper than debt, the use of too much debt by the enterprise will raise the total cost of long-term funds because of increased risk. Indeed, one of the great problems of United States industry has been an excessive use of debt, causing a huge increase in risk to the entire economy. Thus John C. Whitehead, a senior partner of Goldman, Sachs & Co., calculates that "the debt-equity ratios of industrial companies have gone from 25% to 40% in just 10 years . . . cyclical swings can bring the whole structure down."[1] In any event, it is the individual financial manager's job to seek the best mix of bonds and stock for his firm given the conditions that are expected to prevail in the economy.

The use of too much *leverage* (proportion of bonds to stocks maintained by a firm) is particularly dangerous if the firm's annual earnings are subject to a great deal of fluctuation. Assume that two firms are exactly the same except for their proportion of bonds to stock. Their respective structures of bonds and stock are:

Firm A			Firm B		
5% bonds	$ 200,000	20%	5% bonds	$ 800,000	80%
Common stock	800,000	80%	Common stock	200,000	20%
	$1,000,000			$1,000,000	

In two consecutive years the earnings are $100,000 and $30,000 before any distributions to long-term funds providers. For simplicity we will ignore taxes. The return on common stock will be expressed as a percentage, with the dollar amount of stock issued divided into earnings after coverage of bond interest. The results are shown in Table 13–4.

The extremely high degree of leverage for firm B causes a very high return on common stock in good years but a very poor return in relatively lean years in comparison with a less levered structure like that of firm A. As a result of this we might expect the price of firm B's stock to drop and the cost of additional debt issued to rise significantly because of the use of too much debt relative to the fluctuation of their earnings.

Consequently, a high degree of leverage should only be used by firms that are not subject to high degrees of change in their earnings. The classic example of firms falling into this category has been public utilities such as power and telephone companies because of stable demand for their services. However, recently many firms in this segment of the market have become over-levered due to large increases of debt issued. The result has been to raise significantly the cost of additional potential debt to this industry, which is ultimately passed on to the consumer in the form of higher prices.

[1] "The Crushing Burden of Corporate Debt," *Business Week*, October 12, 1974, p. 54.

Table 13-4
Return on Common Stock with Different Leverage
for Two Years

Firm A	Year 1		Year 2	
Earnings before bond interest	$100,000		$ 30,000	
Bond interest[a]	10,000		10,000	
Earnings after bond interest	90,000		20,000	
Return on common stock	$\dfrac{90,000}{\$800,000}$ = 11-1/4%		$\dfrac{20,000}{\$800,000}$ = 2%	
Firm B	**Year 1**		**Year 2**	
Earnings before bond interest	$100,000		$ 30,000	
Bond interest[b]	40,000		40,000	
Earnings after bond interest	60,000		– 10,000	
Return on common stock	$\dfrac{60,000}{\$200,000}$ = 30%		$\dfrac{-10,000}{\$200,000}$ = –5%	

[a]$200,000 × 5% = $10,000
[b]$800,000 × 5% = $40,000

CAPITAL BUDGETING

Capital budgeting refers to the process of investing in long-lived assets such as land, buildings, and machinery and equipment.

Since the firm's own funds coming from long-term sources cost money (in the form of interest and dividends), the financial manager wants to invest the funds in a manner that will maximize their earnings or profits over future years.

The process of capital budgeting requires the use of cash budgets for each project or investment. These cash budgets will show when cash inflows and outflows occur for each investment project. In addition, because periods of time in excess of a year are involved, the effect of interest on the inflows and outflows must be considered.

BALANCING SHORT-TERM AND LONG-TERM SOURCES AND USES OF FUNDS

At the beginning of this chapter, it was mentioned that financial management could be viewed as the life blood of a business. The comparison is quite meaningful. Blood circulates throughout the human body. Assets, liabilities, and owners' equities go through a process that is quite similar to circulation. As accounts payable are paid, they are replaced by new accounts payable. Cash is eventually used for the payment of purchases or salaries, for example, or the acquisition of assets.

Even the longer-lived elements have this same pattern, though it occurs over an extended period. As plant and equipment become worn out, they are eventually replaced. Bonds payable, when they are paid, are often replaced with other bond issues.

The financial task is one of keeping harmony or balance between the various short-term and long-term sources and uses of funds. For example, if current liabilities exceed current assets, the firm might be in danger of being unable to pay its bills. If additional cash is temporarily needed to pay bills, a short-term loan is far more appropriate than a long-term note. Similarly, long-lived assets should not be financed through short-term sources of credit. The financial manager is aided in this task by analysis of the firm's financial statements (Chapter 14).

PORTFOLIO MANAGEMENT

Portfolio management is concerned with maximizing the return from investment in the stocks and bonds of other corporations. Return should be maximized consistent with the amount of risk the firm is willing to undertake. *Risk* refers to the amount of danger present in an investment. For example, stock in a Canadian uranium mining company would be considerably riskier, in terms of losing one's investment, than stock in General Motors. Generally, it is expected that the riskier an investment, the greater the potential earnings. One would not consciously make a riskier investment except for the possibility of a greater return.

Portfolio management is a major function in financial firms such as banks and insurance companies, where the investment in securities of other companies may be very considerable.

SUMMARY

The financial function is concerned with acquiring funds at the cheapest cost and attempting to invest them to gain the greatest return.

Sources of funds include short-term liabilities such as accounts and notes payable, salaries and wages payable, and amounts due government agencies.

Long-term sources include both debt and equity. In the debt category are bonds and long-term notes. Only corporations can issue bonds. Bond issues, unlike long-term notes, must have a trustee, one of whose functions is protection of the bondholders. Since both bonds and long-term notes are debt, interest payments as well as repayment of principal must be made on time in order to avoid very serious consequences for the business.

Equity consists of invested funds, represented by common stock and sometimes preferred stock in corporations, and earnings retained in the firm rather than returned to stockholders as dividends. Common stock is the ultimate risk investment for the investor. If a corporation has preferred stock, dividends on preferred stock must be met before anything can be paid to common stockholders. However, since both common and preferred shareholders are equity investors, dividends can be ignored without creating the legal problems that arise if interest is not paid on debt.

Uses of funds are for both current and long-lived assets. Current assets include cash, marketable securities, accounts and notes receivable, and inventories. Long-lived assets include land, buildings and equipment, and intangibles such as patents, trademarks, and copyrights. Leasing, a form of using long-lived assets without actually owning them, has become popular since approximately 1950. Investment in the common stock of other firms for purposes of control would be a long-term type of investment.

Among the specific problems with which financial managers must concern themselves is maintaining an appropriate balance among long-term and short-term sources and uses of funds. Minimizing the cost of long-term funds is accomplished by attempting to get the right "mix" or proportion of long-term debt and equity funds. Capital budgeting is a process of cash budgeting which attempts to determine which long-term investments are best for the firm. Portfolio management concerns maximizing investment in bonds and stock of other companies consistent with the amount of risk the firm wishes to undertake. Portfolio management is particularly important for financial firms such as banks and insurance companies, which have very large amounts of money to invest.

DISCUSSION QUESTIONS

1. When businesses apply for a loan, why do you think that banks are favorably impressed by the presentation of a cash budget?

2. Why are salaries and wages due employees and amounts owed the government viewed as means of financing assets?

3. What is obsolescence, and how does it arise?

4. What is depreciation and how is obsolescence related to it?

5. If bonds are a generally cheaper source of financing than stock, why don't firms use larger amounts of this type of financing?

6. As a potential owner of securities, if you wanted to minimize your risk, would you tend to prefer bonds or stocks?

SHORT CASES

The Problem of Leverage

Business A and business B both have total assets of $1,100,000, of which $100,000 is financed from short-term debt sources. The balance is to be financed from a combination of 6 percent bonds and capital stock. The objective of the owners is to maximize the return on common stock.

Prospective earnings for the next four years for both firms are:

	A	B
Year 1	$80,000	$70,000
Year 2	40,000	50,000
Year 3	30,000	50,000
Year 4	100,000	80,000

Assume that you can issue either $600,000 in bonds and $400,000 in stock or $400,000 in bonds and $600,000 in stock.

Based on these figures, which company should have the greatest amount of leverage?

Keith and Norton

Keith and Norton are planning to open a garage. Both are experienced mechanics. They estimate that their business will generate cash receipts from repairs of $1,000 in the first month of operations, $3,000 per month during the next three months, and $6,000 per month thereafter.

They need equipment costing $10,000, which will be due in sixty days. Monthly salaries for two mechanics is a total of $2,000. An office person is needed who will cost $500 per month. Rent and other expenses are expected to be $750 per month. You may ignore taxes.

Keith and Norton have decided to set up a partnership. Each has $1,000 to invest.

What possible sources of financing might they consider? Assuming that the money has to be borrowed, how much do you think they should borrow and for how long? (Hint: you will want to set up a cash budget based on the above figures.)

SUGGESTED READINGS

Johnson, Robert W. *Financial Management.* 4th ed. Boston: Allyn and Bacon, 1971.

Nemmers, Erwin E. and Grunewald, Alan. *Basic Managerial Finance,* 2d ed. St. Paul, MN: West Publishing Co., 1975.

PART FIVE

MANAGEMENT TOOLS AND TECHNIQUES

☐ As the skilled craftsman must understand how and be able to use properly the available tools in his trade, the manager has a similar responsibility in running a business. The effective use of the appropriate tools is necessary if managers are to be successful in earning a profit or in meeting other objectives in their businesses. This section will examine the basic tools available for successfully managing a business organization.

☐ Chapter 14 discusses the role of accounting in providing data to measure the financial health of the business and in assisting managers in planning and controlling the operations of the organization. In Chapter 15 the information needs of a firm are further explored in terms of how research and computers can assist in providing timely and relevant information for decision making. Finally, Chapter 16 deals with another important tool which can aid managers to better understand people related to the business, primarily employees and customers. This tool is called the behavioral sciences and draws heavily upon the disciplines of psychology, sociology, and anthropology.

ACCOUNTING

LEARNING OBJECTIVES

When you finish this chapter you should:
- [ ] understand the accounting process.
- [ ] be able to read financial statements.
- [ ] understand the significance of financial statement ratios.
- [ ] understand why accounting is important to the management planning and control processes.

KEY TERMS TO LEARN FROM THIS CHAPTER

account	current ratio	journals	profit ratio
accounting	double entry system of	liquidity	quick assets ratio
balance	accounting	manufacturing	return on investment
balance sheet	expenses	overhead	revenues
break-even point	financial statement	net income	standard costs
budgeting	ratios	net income before fed-	transaction
capital turnover	income statement	eral income taxes	variance
cost of goods sold	inventory turnover	net income from	
cost-volume-profit		operations	
analysis			

It should be clear at this point that the main elements of a business consist of a product(s) or service(s) which is produced, marketed, and financed. However, a whole host of underlying staff functions are necessary to support the primary operations.

Certainly management and owners will want to know how well the business is doing and where it stands. Thus information must be provided in order to enable these groups to assess the situation. It is the task of the accounting function to provide this information to the appropriate parties.

Accounting can be defined as that part of the information system within an enterprise which is responsible for recording, processing, and preparing financial statements from the basic data arising from the transactions of that enterprise. Preparation and analysis of financial statement ratios and various techniques and information stemming from the accounting system for management planning and control purposes are part of the accounting task.

We shall start by examining the accounting process in more detail. We will then be ready for a more detailed discussion of financial statements. We then move to tools of financial statement ratio analysis and next, to the use of several accounting oriented tools for management planning and control. Finally, we discuss the problem of accounting under inflationary conditions.

THE ACCOUNTING PROCESS

The activities of a firm consist of a mass of transactions. A *transaction* is a specific act, occurrence, or deal affecting the enterprise's assets, liabilities, or owners' equities. For example, goods are bought or sold for cash or credit. A bond issue is sold to raise funds. Machinery and equipment wear out as a result of usage. The federal government is sent money owed to it for taxes. Employees are paid their monthly salaries. The board of directors of a corporation votes to pay stockholders a dividend. These are some examples of the numerous transactions affecting a business. Notice that transactions often occur between the firm and outside enterprises or parties. However, the term is used here broadly enough to include events happening within the firm itself (wearing out of machinery and equipment).

RECORDING

The accountant is responsible for entering or recording transactions in the firm's accounting records or "books." If a delivery truck is bought for cash, that fact must be duly recorded.

Transactions are recorded in chronological sequence in books called *journals*. Firms use some degree of specialization relative to journals. For example, almost all firms have separate journals devoted to transactions resulting in cash receipts and cash payments. The recording process results in entering the transaction in the firm's records and nothing more.

PROCESSING

After the transaction is entered in the journals, it must be processed or classified. The amount of cash spent for the truck must be deducted from the total of the firm's cash. If other delivery trucks are owned, the cost of the new truck must be added to their total. Processing results in organizing the raw data from transactions into like or similar groups with the appropriate increases or decreases being made.

CHARLES L. FARROW

This gun-like device is an optical scanner which reads the Uniform Product Code and/or the price on the label of a retail item. Scanners are just one of the many machines that may be used in the accounting process.

By reading the brand name and type of item on merchandise labelled with the Uniform Product Code, symbolized by the vertical lines and numbers on this package, a retailer can obtain current information on inventory and sales that is essential to the accounting process.

CHARLES L. FARROW

TRANSLATING INTO OUTPUT

The acquisition of the truck would be one of many transactions occurring during any specific time period. The last step in the accounting process is to arrange the information in the accounting system into a meaningful form to enable users to evaluate operations and assess where the firm is going in the future. This output is in the form of financial statements, which will be discussed shortly. The accounting process and the accountant's role are shown in Figure 14–1.

OTHER ASPECTS OF THE ACCOUNTING FUNCTION

Money Is the Standard of Value   If financial statements are to be meaningful, all elements applicable to an enterprise must be measured in terms of a common denominator. The common factor or standard of value in accounting systems is money. A firm's delivery trucks as they appear in financial statements will be measured in terms of dollars. Total horsepower or cubic feet of space may be useful measurements, but they do not allow combination of delivery trucks with other assets of the firm. Assets can be added together only if they are measured in terms of a common factor such as the dollar.

The Account   After a transaction is recorded in the books, the processing step requires that all elements of an enterprise be brought up to date. If a delivery

Figure 14-1   The accounting process.

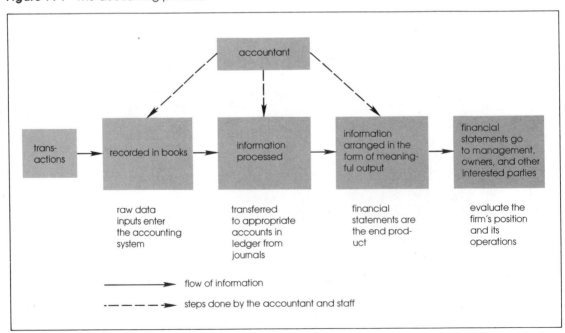

truck is bought, its cost must be added to the balance applicable to previously acquired delivery trucks. If cash is paid, it must come out of the cash balance. The type of record in which operations of this type are done is called the account. An *account* is that part of an accounting system in which transactions affecting all similar elements are processed. The result of these operations will show the *balance* of each account. The balance is simply "how much" is in each account, measured, of course, in dollars.

FINANCIAL STATEMENTS

The output of an accounting system is in the form of financial statements, which are useful for analyzing the operating performance of the enterprise and evaluating how the firm stands. Two statements that aid in accomplishing these tasks are the balance sheet and the income statement. These two statements have traditionally been provided to corporate stockholders in annual reports of publicly owned corporations. This information is also extremely important for managers and outside parties such as lenders.

BALANCE SHEET

The *balance sheet* or statement of financial position shows the wealth of an enterprise at a given date. It shows the firm's assets and how those assets were acquired in terms of debt and equity sources of financing. You are already familiar with the principal categories of assets, liabilities, and owners' equities from Chapter 13. Before examining some simple balance sheets, let's see what determines the order of the accounts on the statement.

Assets and liabilities are listed on the balance sheet in their approximate order of *liquidity*. An asset's liquidity is determined by how rapidly it turns over and becomes cash. For liabilities, it refers to how rapidly the obligation becomes due. In other words, current assets and current liabilities are more liquid than long-lived assets and long-term sources of funds.

After Geri and Art secured their loan from the Warrenstown State Bank, the balance sheet for the Candy Emporium would appear as shown in Table 14–1. The balance sheet shows a $25,000 liability to the Warrenstown State Bank, though conceivably less was borrowed under their line of credit type of arrangement. Geri and Art's personal investments are shown in the owners' equity section of the statement.

The amounts spent for the down payment with the Kansas City wholesaler and the prepaid rent are both valuable rights. They are thus classified as assets in Table 14–1. The money for them was split equally by Geri and Art. It is thus added to their respective investments. The word *capital* is traditionally used to describe owners' equity investments in sole proprietorships and partnerships.

After acquiring the various assets for cash, the balance sheet would appear as shown in Table 14–2. The total cost of the long-lived assets comes from Table 13–1. As a result of acquiring the assets, The Candy Emporium no longer has the $150 claim on the Kansas City wholesaler. They also paid another $9200 in cash, which is subtracted from the firm's cash. In accounting, assets and liabilities are divided into two types: current and long-term.

Table 14-1
The Candy Emporium Balance Sheet, January 2, 1978

Assets		Liabilities		
Cash	$35,000	Notes payable due to		
Down payment to Kansas City wholesaler	150	Warrenstown State Bank		$25,000
Prepaid rent	1,050	**Owners' Equities**		
		Geri Rogers, capital	$5,600	
		Art Lindstrom, capital	5,600	11,200
	$36,200			**$36,200**

Each balance shows the wealth of the firm in terms of the composition of the assets at a given date as well as how those assets have been financed (liabilities and owners' equities).

Balance Sheet Equality   Notice that as its name implies, the left and right portions of the statement are equal. The reason for this is that all assets must be financed from some source. Even if a business is successful, and operations result in a growth of cash which is not returned to the owners, the balancing characteristic is maintained. The source of financing which would increase in this situation would be the owners' capital accounts in The Candy Emporium.

Double Entry System of Accounting   The mechanism that brings about equality between assets and the total of liabilities and owners' equities is called the *double entry system of accounting.* It is not necessary to learn this system in order to understand how to use the output (financial statements) of the accounting process.

Table 14-2
The Candy Emporium Balance Sheet, January 5, 1978

Assets		Liabilities and owners' equities		
Current assets:		Current liabilities:		
Cash	$25,800	Notes payable (due to Warrenstown		
Prepaid rent	1,050	State Bank in a year)		$ 5,000
Total	26,850	Long-term debt:		
Long-lived assets:		Notes payable (due to Warrenstown		
Machinery and		State Bank beyond a year)		20,000
equipment	9,350	Total liabilities		25,000
	$36,200	Owners' equities		
		Geri Rogers, capital	$5,600	
		Art Lindstrom, capital	5,600	
		Total owners' equities		11,200
				$36,200

Balance Sheet Equation   Balance sheet equality gives rise to what is called the balance sheet equation:

assets = liabilities + owners' equities

The equation may be rearranged by subtracting liabilities from both sides of the equation to show the owners' investment in the enterprise's assets:

assets − liabilities = owners' equities

We shall return to the balance sheet and its uses after we examine the income statement.

INCOME STATEMENT

Whereas the balance sheet shows financial position at a given date, the *income statement* shows the results of operations for some given period of time. Thus in talking about income, we concern ourselves with how successful the firm is in carrying out its designated functions and tasks.

Revenues   The first main section is the revenue section. *Revenues* are the product of the firm's operations, be it sales of product by a manufacturing or retailing firm or performance of professional services by a medical clinic, legal firm, or similar enterprise. As a result of either sales of product or service, the firm receives either cash or cash claims (accounts or notes receivable) from its customers. In arriving at net revenues, factors such as sales returns and discounts for prompt payment would be deducted from the amount of gross revenues.

Expenses   *Expenses* are assets or resources of the enterprise that have been used up during the period in the course of operations.

Cost of Goods Sold   *Cost of goods sold,* or cost of sales, is a category found in manufacturing and retailing firms but not service firms. This section of the income statement attempts to measure those costs applicable to goods that have been sold during the period. For retailing firms, this would consist of the costs paid by the firm to its suppliers for goods it has sold to customers during the period. In the manufacturing firm, three types of costs are applicable to manufactured goods: raw materials, labor, and everything else. The latter is a catchall for a whole host or variety of costs and is called *manufacturing overhead*.

When deducting cost of goods sold expense from net revenues, the result is called *gross profit* or gross margin on sales. The relationships among net revenues, cost of goods sold, and gross profit are usually watched quite closely by operating management.

Operating Expenses   After arriving at gross margin, the remaining operating expenses are deducted. These are usually broken down on a functional basis into selling expenses and general and administrative expenses. Depreciation expense represents an estimate of the cost of long-lived assets used up during the period. The result of deducting these expenses from gross profit leads to *net income from operations* or net operating income. It thus represents net revenues minus all normal operating expenses.

Notice again that many expenses are assets that have been used up in the process of helping to produce revenues. This is obviously true for cost of goods sold: inventories that are sold become cost of sales. It is also true for assets that

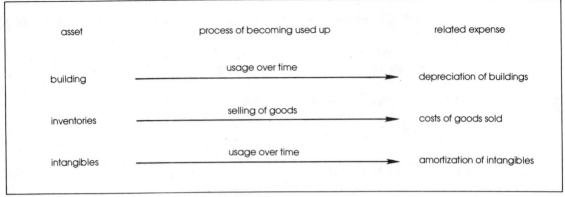

Figure 14-2 Conversion of assets to expenses. The words "depreciation" and "amortization" are commonly used accounting terms which mean using up or wearing out the particular asset.

become used up or depreciate. Expired portions of these assets provide beneficial services that are useful and necessary in terms of producing revenues. These relationships are shown in Figure 14–2.

Miscellaneous Expenses and Revenues Miscellaneous types of expenses and revenues are next listed. They include interest cost of bonds payable and notes payable as expenses and interest earned from investments as revenues. Dividend payments of corporations would not appear in the income statement because they are not defined as expenses. Instead, they would be direct reductions of the firm's retained earnings.

Net Income before Federal Income Taxes After adding or deducting the net effect of other revenues and expenses to net operating income, we arrive at *net income before federal income taxes.* Because of their overall importance and significance, federal income taxes are shown separately and deducted as the last expense in the income statement. Since sole proprietorships and partnerships do not pay federal income taxes, this category does not appear on their income statements.

Net Income The *net income* represents the increases in assets over liabilities during the period as a result of operations. Dividend payments would of course

Table 14-3
The Candy Emporium Income Statement,
Year Ending December 31, 1978

Sales		$55,000
Cost of goods sold		12,000
Gross profit on sales		43,000
Operating expenses:		
Salaries and wages	$25,000	
Depreciation	1,000	26,000
Net operating income		17,000
Other expenses:		
Interest on Warrenstown State Bank notes		2,500
Net income		**$14,500**

decrease the amount of assets staying within the firm during the period as a result of successful operations. The income statement for the first year of operations for The Candy Emporium is shown in Table 14–3.

FINANCIAL STATEMENT RATIOS

The income statement and the balance sheet are useful tools for analyzing the firm's operations and financial condition. For example, a comparison of net income for a five-year period might reveal a trend—a decline in income, let's say. An analysis of cost patterns might reveal that certain expenses were increasing as a percentage of revenues (as well as in absolute terms, assuming that revenues were increasing). Still further investigation might then reveal whether the more than proportionate rise in expenses was due to cost increases or waste. The former might be largely uncontrollable because it is due to a factor occurring outside the firm: rising prices in the marketplace (however, better purchasing policies and practices can sometimes lead to better control over costs). The latter factor, waste, would, however, be controllable. That is, management would be able to take steps to hold the cost in line during forthcoming periods.

Thus, the use of financial statements can be an important starting point in the process of evaluating results and holding costs in line. To further facilitate the process of control, various figures from the financial statements are combined in useful ways.

These figures are known as *financial statement ratios*. We can watch or monitor the course of operations and financial condition by periodically deriving these ratios and comparing them with those of previous dates or time periods.

"Well Noah, did you meet your budget on the cost of constructing your ark?"

PART FIVE ■ MANAGEMENT TOOLS AND TECHNIQUES

RETURN ON INVESTMENT

The kingpin ratio is called *return on investment.* Net income is divided by average total assets for the period (this ratio is usually computed annually) or total assets on hand at the beginning of the period. Hence return on investment shows the relationship between the two statements: the firm's assets generate income.

Return on investment gives us a view of the forest. It is usually broken down into two component ratios in order to get us closer to the trees: profit ratio and capital turnover.

Profit Ratio *Profit ratio* (net income ÷ sales) involves income statement factors only. It shows the amount of income per dollar of sales. It is thus a test or measure of efficiency because the larger the income per dollar of sales, the smaller expenses must be.

Capital Turnover *Capital turnover* (net sales ÷ average assets) indicates the ability of the firm's assets to generate revenues.

The two component ratios, when multiplied, equal return on investment because net sales cancel. Using the figures from Tables 14–2 and 14–3, we get the following results:

$$\text{profit ratio} \times \text{capital turnover} = \text{return on investment}$$

$$\frac{\text{net income}}{\text{net sales}} \times \frac{\text{net sales}}{\text{total assets}} = \frac{\text{net income}}{\text{total assets}}$$

$$\frac{\$14,500}{\$55,000} \times \frac{\$55,000}{\$36,200} = 40.1\%$$

or   or

$$26.4\% \times 151.9\% = 40.1\%$$

Profit ratio and capital turnover focus on different facets of operations and can reveal trends that return on investment alone might tend to hide. For example, in the next year, a lower profit ratio might be offset by increasing capital turnover.

$$\text{profit ratio} \times \text{capital turnover} = \text{return on investment}$$

$$\frac{\$16,040}{\$66,000} \times \frac{\$66,000}{\$40,000} = 40.1\%$$

or   or

$$24.3\% \times 165\% = 40.1\%$$

Increasing investment here might be going into high-turnover, low-profit sales. Hence using both ratios gives more potentially useful information than just the single overall ratio.

TURNOVER RATIOS

Another important type of ratio reveals *turnover* or the rapidity of collection of accounts receivable or sale of merchandise inventory. The measure involves the relationship between a balance sheet item and its related income statement account. *Inventory turnover* is determined by:

cost of goods sold
─────────────────
average inventory

For The Candy Emporium for 1978, the calculation would be:

$$\frac{\$12,000}{\$2,105} = 5.7$$

This tells us that the average item of inventory "turns over" 5.7 times a year, or that it is carried in stock for slightly more than two months (12 months ÷ 5.7 = 2.1 months).[1]

The answer is relative in the sense that a comparison with previous periods may reveal trend changes. For example, a declining turnover might indicate that obsolete goods are present in the inventory. Maximizing the turnover should not necessarily be the firm's objective either, because it might indicate that the firm is understocked: not carrying enough inventory relative to its sales.

Similarly, dividing net charge sales by average receivables would indicate how rapidly receivables are turned into cash. A decline in the rate might indicate that sales have been made to marginal customers or that the firm's collection process is not functioning smoothly.

CURRENT RATIO

Another group of ratios that provide helpful information are those that show the relationship between current assets and current liabilities. The *current ratio* simply shows the amount of dollars of current assets per dollar of current liabilities. For The Candy Emporium on January 5, 1978, the current ratio would be:

$$\frac{\$26,850}{\$5,000} = \$5.37$$

The firm thus has $5.37 of current assets for each dollar of current liabilities.

Quick Assets Ratio   Again, the importance of the ratio would be in the trend indicated by the change in the ratio over time. The *quick assets ratio* simply cuts off the current assets at the level of the receivables and computes the number of dollars of these assets per dollar of current liabilities.

Many other ratios are used, but this sampling gives the principal ones and shows how they can be used to monitor the firm's financial condition and its operations.

PLANNING
AND CONTROL

You have seen how information stemming from the financial statements is useful to management for controlling operations and financial condition. The control

───────────────

[1]We assume the average inventory for the year is $2,105. Average inventory is computed by adding the beginning and ending inventories and dividing by 2.

process consists of evaluating and comparing actual operations with planned operations as well as monitoring trends indicated by the financial and operating ratios.

Control, then, is closely linked to planning, because analyzing and correcting poor trends (as well as emphasizing factors underlying good performance) affects future operations.

In this section examination will be made of some planning tools and techniques stemming from the firm's accounting system as well as some additional control tools.

BUDGETING

Budgeting is an important tool for both planning and control. The process of *budgeting* consists of setting goals for a particular time period for operating factors such as sales, production, and the various elements of production costs. Budgets are also used to anticipate changes in balance sheet elements such as cash. The budget should then be followed up by comparing actual results with budget.

Sales budgets should be a motivational tool because they give employees goals or targets to shoot for. The motivational aspects of budgeting can probably be maximized when individuals being evaluated by budgets participate in the setting of budgetary goals. Budgets are usually unsuccessful where top management imposes them upon the individuals who are responsible for carrying them out. Furthermore, budgets lose their effectiveness when appropriate feedback to the participants—comparison of actual performance with budget—is not provided. Hence informing individuals of their actual progress relative to plans that were previously set becomes tremendously important.

Budgeting and Coordination   Since budgeting is really planning, it helps to coordinate operations. For example, if sales of a manufacturing firm are expected to be very high in the last quarter of the year, management may have to step up production in the previous quarters of the year if the firm is to avoid losing sales because of inventories running out. Similarly, having to produce inventories well before sales occur could lead to a drain on the firm's cash. Budgeting enables the firm to anticipate this problem several months prior to its occurrence; thus it could make appropriate plans in advance to make sure that cash can be borrowed during the rough period. Thus budgeting helps the firm to look at its future and helps it to anticipate problems before they arise.

Budgeting and Feedback   Another way that budgeting is helpful to the firm stems from the feedback process mentioned previously. When actual results and budget are materially out of line, the situation should be investigated in order to determine the underlying causes. If the causes can be found and corrected, future profits should be favorably affected.

Bringing Budgets Up to Date   However, care should be exercised to make certain that the original budget is brought up to date in terms of intervening circumstances that were not foreseen earlier. For example, assume the following budgetary estimates and actual facts:

	Budget	Actual
Industry sales for period	1,000,000 units	800,000 units
Our firm's sales	200,000 units	180,000 units
Our firm's share of its market	20%	22.2%

A comparison of actual and budgeted sales for the period shows that we are below budget by 20,000 units or 10 percent of our budgetary estimate. However, total sales of our industry are below expectation, which is a factor beyond the control of our sales staff. Hence a better benchmark for comparison can be constructed by taking our budgeted share of the market times industry sales (800,000 × 20% = 160,000). Thus we can see that our sales force actually did quite well once we take into account the poor performance of our industry.

Thus the budget is an extremely valuable tool for management from the standpoint of both planning and control. Closely related to the budgetary process is another useful technique called cost-volume-profit analysis (C-V-P).

COST-VOLUME-PROFIT ANALYSIS

This form of analysis stems from an important condition existing in virtually all business, as mentioned in Chapter 3: most costs behave or change in a relatively predictable manner. For example, the amount of steel and other materials going into an automobile will be uniform for each individual model and make. Consequently, the amount and cost of steel and other materials going into production will vary according to the number of automobiles produced during any given time period. Costs of this type are said to be variable—that is, they vary pretty regularly with the number of units produced.

The opposite type of cost behavior prevails for cost factors such as annual rent for factory buildings. When a firm is renting a factory, the lease will ordinarily specify the exact amount of rent to be paid per year. Since rent costs are unaffected by the level of production for any given time period, rent is called a fixed cost.

For many businesses, we can predict with a high degree of certainty how most costs will behave. Thus cost behavior is a very powerful tool to employ in the budgetary or planning process.

Since variable costs change with sales and fixed costs remain the same during a given time period such as a year, the amount of income for any given level of sales can be estimated. For example, assume that variable costs are forty cents per dollar and fixed costs are $1,000,000 dollars per year. Given different potential amounts of sales, income can be predicted:

assumed level of sales	−	variable costs	−	fixed costs	=	income
$1,000,000	−	$ 400,000	−	$1,000,000	=	$−400,000
2,000,000	−	800,000	−	1,000,000	=	200,000
3,000,000	−	1,200,000	−	1,000,000	=	800,000
4,000,000	−	1,600,000	−	1,000,000	=	1,400,000
5,000,000	−	2,000,000	−	1,000,000	=	2,000,000

As part of the budgetary process, a business may have a desired or target level of income. This desired level of income may represent an absolute or percentage increase over the previous year's income, or it may be geared to the assets employed by the firm, thus being a target return on investment.

Given our target rate of income, we can determine the level of sales needed to arrive at the desired income. For example, taking the cost relationships just mentioned and a desired profit of $1,250,000, we can find the necessary sales by solving the following simple formula (let x = the necessary sales):

$$x - .4x \text{ (variable costs)} - \$1,000,000 \text{ (fixed costs)}$$
$$= \$1,250,000$$

Solving for x, the necessary sales to achieve the target profit would be $3,750,000.

Cost-volume-profit (C-V-P) relationships are often shown graphically in the form of a break-even chart (Figure 14–3). Notice that the total sales line crosses the total cost line at the zero profit point, which is called the *break-even point*. To the left of the break-even point the firm operates at a loss, and to the right, at a profit. The total cost line starts above the zero point because fixed costs will arise even if the firm does not have any sales.

It is not simply in solving for unknowns or viewing profits at different levels that C-V-P analysis is an important management tool. Because C-V-P stresses cost relationships and behavior, it helps us to focus on factors that can be changed in the short run that might influence profits. In our little example,

Figure 14-3 Break-even chart.

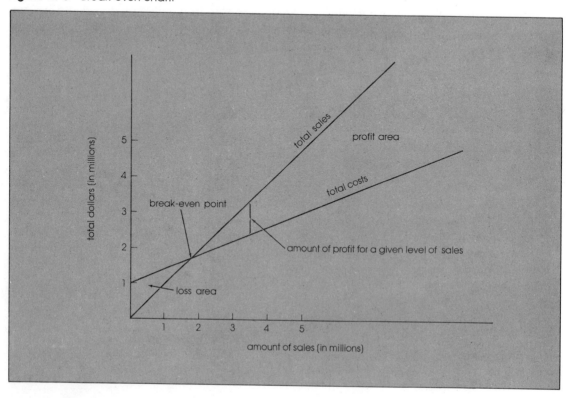

management might feel that it cannot achieve the necessary level of sales. Some of the possibilities open to management would be:

1. Raise the selling price of the product and hope for a relatively small decline in volume of sales.
2. Lower the selling price of the product and hope for a relatively large increase in volume of sales.
3. Examine fixed costs to see if any can be reduced.
4. Examine variable costs to see if any can be reduced.
5. Examine the cost structure to see if any appropriate changes can be made (buying a labor-saving machine would reduce variable costs and increase fixed costs).

The great importance, then, of C-V-P analysis to budgeting is that it helps management to focus on those factors which can be changed or altered in the short run which can affect profits. The effect on profits of these proposed changes would be assessed, and a plan of action decided upon.

STANDARD COSTS

Another accounting-oriented tool used by management in planning and control is standard costs. *Standard costs* are what costs should be under a favorable state of operating conditions. Let's say that you own a firm that makes golf clubs. One of the labor operations necessary to complete the product is buffing and polishing. After extensive engineering and time studies, you decide that a man can buff and polish a club every twenty minutes if he works relatively rapidly. Twenty minutes is not the absolute minimum, but it should more likely be a high pace that a man can maintain if he works in a reasonably efficient manner. If the labor standard is twenty minutes per club for buffing and polishing, then actual performance in terms of elapsed time can be checked against standard performance—time it should have taken—by multiplying the actual clubs buffed and polished times the standard allowed time of twenty minutes per club. For example:

Worker	Clubs completed — week of Jan. 10	Elapsed Time	Standard Time Allowed	Variance
Smith	50	954	1,000 minutes	Saved 46 minutes
Jones	30	674	600 minutes	Lost 74 minutes

The *variance* in the last column gives us the saved or lost time relative to the standard time allowed. We could put these in dollar terms by multiplying by the hourly rate.

The variance alone is not enough, though. If the variance is large enough to warrant investigation, you would want to attempt to determine the underlying cause. You might, in fact, find that a worker's unfavorable variance is caused by factors outside the individual's control—but not outside of management's control—such as faulty materials in the product or faulty workmanship in a preceding department, both of which led to problems for the buffer.

Thus by instituting standards and carefully checking performance and attempting to ascertain why costs get out of line, management can keep a lid on its costs. It should also be clear that standards are helpful in the budgeting process because they can help tell us what costs should be for standardized operations for specific levels of production.

These are a few of the accounting-oriented tools that help management plan and control operations. They illustrate how a good accounting system can help management. But remember, it is not just the figures themselves; they are only information. The important factor is still how people interact, specifically here, how they use the information to carry out the goals of the firm. Figures themselves, no matter how accurate or relevant, are still sterile.

ACCOUNTING AND INFLATION

Earlier in this chapter the point was made that money is the standard of value used in financial statements. At the present time assets are shown in balance sheets at either the actual cost paid for them or some basic offshoot of this figure (cost minus depreciation for fixed assets, for example).

But the effects of inflation can distort financial ratios and other analyses of financial statements when acquired cost figures are used. What if a building acquired fifteen years ago at a cost of $2,000,000 could be replaced today at no less than $3,000,000, as an example. Its depreciation costs and remaining balance sheet value are obviously understated.

Accounting is attempting to come to grips with this problem. In a very short time the authors expect that firms whose stock is traded publicly on regional or national stock exchanges will be required to present their annual financial statements in terms of the current cost of assets they own and use. In addition, expenses will be stated in terms of the current cost—not the past cost—of assets and resources used up.

Introduction of current costs and values will require a period of adjustment until people get used to them. The process of financial statement analysis, however, will be exactly the same as illustrated here except for the substitution of current cost and value figures in place of acquired costs.

While there are some drawbacks present, the authors believe that the use of contemporary valuations in place of outdated figures will benefit financial statement analysis and evaluation.

The accounting function deals with the recording and processing of a business's **SUMMARY** transactional data and the preparation of financial statements for use by management and owners.

The two principal financial statements are the balance sheet and the income statement. The balance sheet shows the wealth of a firm as of a given date. Wealth consists of the assets owned by the firm and the various sources— liabilities and owners' equities—from which they were financed. The assets must equal the total of the liabilities and owners' equities. The income statement shows the earnings of a firm for a particular period of time such as a year.

Financial statements can be used for further analysis by means of various ratios which give additional information relative to the firm's standing and performance. The key ratio is return on investment, which can be further broken down into the capital turnover and profit ratios. Other important ratios include inventory turnover and the current ratio.

There are many other important planning and control tools based on accounting techniques and data. These include budgeting, cost-volume-profit analysis, and standard costs. Budgeting is particularly important as a motivational and coordinating tool. Cost-volume-profit analysis is a planning tool that is helpful in terms of analyzing profits and alternatives in the short run. Standard costs is a control tool that aids management in terms of pinpointing deviations between actual costs and what costs should be.

Financial statements do not take into account presently existing costs. Instead, they are stated in terms of the costs actually incurred in the past by the firm. This is a particularly serious problem in an age of inflation. However, major changes should shortly be made which will help to solve this problem.

DISCUSSION QUESTIONS

1. A firm decides that it needs a new punch press. The firm's purchasing agent contacts a manufacturer to get a price quotation on the desired type of punch press. Has a transaction occurred?

2. Why does net income become part of the owners' equities at the end of the year?

3. Why is return on investment often considered the most important financial statement ratio?

4. "Budgeting is just a numbers game that organizations make their employees go through at the beginning of the year." Discuss.

5. Are cost-volume-profit analyses useful as part of the budgetary process?

6. Why are standard costs useful as part of the control process? Do standard costs have any relation to the budgetary process?

7. In a period of inflation why would it be important to use current costs in financial statements?

8. Zavitka Company's variable costs are 25 percent of sales. Fixed costs are estimated to be $5,000,000. What amount of sales will the firm need to break even? What amount of sales would it need to get a profit of $10,000,000?

SHORT CASE

Mohr Pump

Mohr Company is a small manufacturer of diesel fuel pumps. Bill Mohr, the company president (and owner), has made it very clear that formalized planning and control systems are more trouble than they are worth.

Manufacturing operations are carried out by a work force of fifty employees. Most manufacturing operations are highly repetitive.

The pumps are sold by a sales force of five persons, each of whom has a separate territory.

"We're just too small a company to be able to use these new accounting tools that they're teaching in school today. They're meant to be used by General Motors, not a small company like us."

Write a reply to Mohr stating whether his company should introduce accounting techniques to improve planning and control.

Oddy Company

Oddy Company's balance sheet on January 1, 1977, was:

Assets

Cash	$10,000
Accounts receivable	20,000
Inventories	25,000
Machinery and equipment	45,000
	$100,000

Liabilities

Accounts payable	$30,000
Long-term notes payable	45,000
Total liabilities	$75,000
Owner's equity	
Bill Oddy, capital	$25,000
Total liabilities and owner's equity	**$100,000**

The company's income statement for the year ending December 31, 1977, was:

Revenues	$80,000
Cost of goods sold	50,000
Gross profit on sales	30,000
Operating expenses	12,000
Net operating income	18,000
Interest expense on notes payable	3,000
Net income	$15,000

Inventories on December 31, 1977, were $19,000. Bill Oddy withdrew $3,000 of cash from the business during the year, reducing both the company's cash and his capital account. Aside from this withdrawal and the income earned during the year, no other transactions affected owner's equity. Compute as many financial statement ratios as you can. If the company's total assets were $110,000 on December 31, 1977, what were its total liabilities on that same date?

SUGGESTED READINGS

Carey, John L., and Skousen, K. Fred. *Getting Acquainted with Accounting.* 2d ed. Boston: Houghton Mifflin, 1977.

Metcalf, Richard W., and Titard, Pierre L. *Introduction to Accounting.* Philadelphia: W. B. Saunders Co., 1975.

MANAGEMENT INFORMATION, RESEARCH, AND COMPUTERS

LEARNING OBJECTIVES

When you finish this chapter you should:

☐ understand and appreciate the value of information in decision making.

☐ understand the research function in business management and how it is carried out.

☐ be able to discuss how the computer contributes to the building of an effective management information system.

KEY TERMS TO LEARN FROM THIS CHAPTER

arithmetic unit	flow chart	market potential	output
BASIC	FORTRAN	memory bank	PL/1
binary numbers	hardware	MICR (magnetic ink	population
COBOL	hypothesis	character recog-	research
computer language	input	nition	scientific method
computer program	magnetic tape	microcomputers	software
computers	management informa-	minicomputers	system analysts
control unit	tion system	nanosecond	time sharing

If there is one critical factor which pervades management at all levels, that factor is decision making. Indeed, decision making is so important that many schools of business have extensively revamped their courses and even their entire programs to more strongly emphasize this all-pervasive element.

Since decision making involves making an intelligent choice among possible alternatives, the decision maker needs appropriate information. An example of a need for information of an immediate relevance is the famous DEW line (Distant Early Warning System) of radar stations located in northern Canada and Alaska. This system is intended to give immediate information of attack on the United States by intercontinental ballistic missiles coming through the polar regions. Information of the attack would be received only a few minutes before the attack itself. However, this would give sufficient lead time to mount a retaliatory attack prior to potential destruction of our own missiles.

In business management, if the Detroit automobile manufacturers had known that an Arab oil embargo was going to signal the end of relatively cheap energy for consumers, the transition from the gas-guzzling monsters to the smaller economy cars may have been made sooner. In this situation information is of tremendous value in determining the long-term production policy of management. Both of the above examples suggest that at the heart of effective decision making in business, or any other organization, is the need for relevant and timely information.

Certainly, this book can be viewed as being built around two pillars: (1) providing appropriate information and (2) critical areas of decision making. Some chapters (e.g., 10, 12, and 17) provide important background or institutional information in specific areas that managers need to know in order to understand the environment in which business operates. The previous chapter on accounting can be interpreted as an elementary discussion of an "information system" since it deals with how basic financial and operating data are received (internal and external transactions), enter the system (accounting entries), are stored or held in the system in various accounts, and finally emerge in a useful form (financial statements) for decision makers. On the decision-making side, other chapters (e.g., 5, 7, 8, 9, and 13) are structured around the various types of decisions that arise in conjunction with the finance, human resources, marketing, and operations areas of business. This chapter will focus on: (1) the basic elements of a management information system, (2) the research function in business, and (3) the role of computers in the information process.

ELEMENTS OF A MANAGEMENT INFORMATION SYSTEM

The basic elements of a management information system are shown in flowchart form in Figure 15–1. Figure 15–1 indicates that information should be directed toward achieving certain goals or objectives. Managers or decision makers are responsible for stating the goal(s) or objective(s) and are primarily concerned with obtaining good output—that is, information which can be used to make sound decisions. In contrast, other specialists, such as accountants, system analysts, and marketing researchers, are concerned with all the elements of the

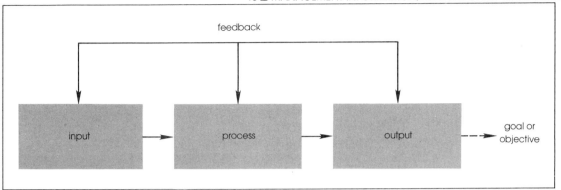

Figure 15-1   Elements of a management information system.

system outlined in Figure 15–1. Since the end result is to provide useful output, these specialists should be thoroughly knowledgeable about what constitutes good output—that is, what information is needed to make short-term as well as long-term decisions. In what form is the information needed? When is the information needed in order for a manager to be able to make timely decisions?

In addition to the output of the system, specialists must know what input (data) is needed to provide the required information. Data are facts, values, attitudes, opinions, or situations, usually quantified, which will be transformed into usable output. The transformation of data into information is illustrated as the process in Figure 15–1. This shows what methods of preparation, techniques of analysis, and treatment designs the data will undergo in order to make it into usable and understandable information. Often, the computer, which is discussed in a later section of this chapter, is used in the data processing stage.

At this point the distinction between data processing and *research* may be made. Research involves the entire process of translating relevant data into useful information, while data processing is concerned primarily with the data transformation stage in Figure 15–1. The function of research in most organizations involves the collection, organization, analyses, and interpretation of various data in order to provide information which will improve the quality of decision making.

RESEARCH IN BUSINESS

Research in business, as with any other organization, involves the application of a systematic procedure to problem solving. This systematic procedure, called the scientific method, is borrowed from science because of the method's value in yielding objective conclusions, and it is widely used in both the natural and social sciences. Problems in research are recognized not just as "wrongs" which need correction but also as opportunities which may be seized for economic or social gain. For example, a retail department store may need to conduct research to determine why sales are declining in their current downtown location. At the same time, research may be needed to determine the market potential of several possible suburban locations.

What are the important steps in the research process implied by the scientific method?

1. A clear and precise definition of the problem is made first. Terms are defined so that both the researcher and management understand what each is talking about. The scope and limits of the proposed investigation are clearly spelled out. The problem to be studied is stated in terms which can be measured. For example, what is meant by market potential? Market potential may be estimated on the basis of population, sales dollars, units sold, or other factors showing the capacity of the market to absorb a particular product. Does management need one or all of these measures to make decisions? In defining the problem, specific objectives to be achieved or *hypotheses* to be tested are outlined. These objectives and hypotheses determine what data are needed as inputs in the information system.

2. With a clear and precise definition of the problem, the researcher can formulate a research plan. Can the problem be solved with the use of already-collected data (secondary data) such as company records or government statistics, or does the problem dictate the collection of data specifically for the purpose of this study (primary data)? Oftentimes both data sources are used. If primary data are needed, should the data be collected from an experiment, a survey, observation, or a "simulated" process?

   A test designed to determine whether music or no music has a noticeable effect on productivity in a production plant is an example of an experiment. Conditions are controlled so that music is "piped" into the working area every other day, and no music is played on alternate days for a four-week period. A series of telephone calls made to randomly selected households in a *population* to determine their television viewing habits is a survey. Traffic counts to estimate the traffic flow at a particular intersection in order to determine the potential for a service station are utilizing observation as a source of data. The computer may be used to generate hypothetical data to test the usefulness of a proposed accounting system. In this case simulated data are used in the research plan. Regardless of whether secondary or primary data sources are used, the researcher should be assured that the data actually measure what is intended to be measured (validity of data) and that the data are representative of the population (reliability of data). In order to produce good output, data must be both valid and reliable.

3. Following data collection is the data preparation and analysis stage in the research process. If the investigation has been clearly defined and carefully planned, the method of data preparation and analysis has already been suggested. Techniques may range from simple frequency tabulations, cross tabulations, and percentages to basic statistical tools such as averages and measures of deviation to very sophisticated statistical and mathematical methods. In selecting the particular method of analysis, the researcher must keep foremost in mind the required information to be derived from data as well as the sophistication of the user. Certainly, the computer has enhanced the role of research with the capacity to handle masses of data and complex mathematical and statistical analyses.

4. The research process climaxes (not ends) with the drawing of conclusions from the data analyses. What information can be derived from the

data summaries? Does the evidence support or refute the previously outlined hypothesis? What answers are provided for the specific objectives detailed in step 1? Which alternative solution appears most workable in light of the evidence? If the research has been scientifically conducted and "with a little bit of luck," the researcher is now in position to provide management with some useful information.

5. A continuing stage of the research process is feedback. Throughout the research process and even after conclusions and/or recommendations are made to management, the information system must be fortified with feedback. Is the information satisfying the needs of management? Based on the additional requirements of the managers, what changes are warranted in the inputs or processing procedures? At the same time, managers should be aware of any new developments in processing capacity. In other words, an effective information flow can be achieved only with continuous feedback among the elements in the management information system.

THE COMPUTER REVOLUTION

Who can forget HAL, the jealous and ultimately treacherous computer in Stanley Kubrick's science fiction movie *2001: A Space Odyssey*? Here was a computer that not only could think but also had, beneath its monotonous voice output, human emotions. Although the impact of the computer has been somewhat less dramatic than the above science fiction example, computers have revolutionized the information process and affected the daily lives of most twentieth-century Americans. In school, computers handle your course registration, figure your grade point averages, and cumulate your credits toward graduation. In the economic market, computers figure our pay, issue many of our bills, record our payments, and check our income tax returns. In business, computers keep records of inventory, issue sales reports, handle payroll accounting, and forecast

"What's going on around here?" "Only the programmer knows for sure."

trends in the economy. Computers are also used to educate school children, to make travel reservations, to control air traffic, to monitor cardiac care patients in hospitals, and even to obtain dates for the "lonely hearts."

The widespread influence of the computer has both a quantitative and a qualitative basis. Undoubtedly, the check can be termed the life blood of our commercial system. While it is relatively simple to process an individual check manually, the sheer volume of checks processed daily would clog the banking system were it not for the computer. As an executive at the Bank of America, the nation's largest bank, puts it,

> Had we not started to use computers years ago, we soon would have had to hire every adult in California to help with our bookkeeping.[1]

Similarly, the credit card development is underpinned by the ability of the computer to process quickly a huge volume of transactions. Thus one important influence of the computer lies in its ability to rapidly sort masses of data which would be difficult, if not impossible, to do manually.

[1]Peter T. White, "Behold the Computer Revolution," *National Geographic* 138 (November 1970): 597.

These horizontal lines on a railroad boxcar are part of the system used in computer-controlled classification yards which automatically sorts freight cars.

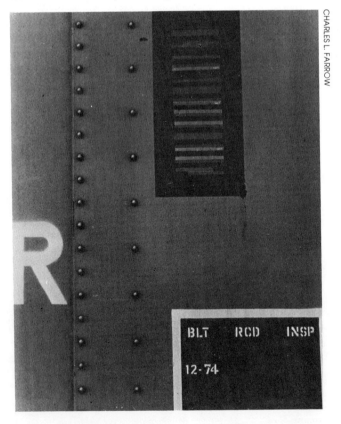

CHARLES L. FARROW

While the ability to process a mass of data quickly and economically has enormous importance, there is a qualitative as well as a quantitative aspect to the computer's operation. It has the ability to do complex calculations that would virtually be impossible by hand. Aerospace activities require so many involved calculations that space flights would be inconceivable without the computer. Indeed, the famous Apollo 13 flight of 1970, in which an oxygen tank explosion far out in space made the service module useless, was literally saved by the computer's ability to rapidly formulate new plans from a mass of data. This enabled a safe reentry by the wounded command module. In research, computers can perform complex and intricate mathematical and statistical analyses of data, providing the researcher with data summaries which may be translated into usable information—for example, a sales forecast based on years of company records and industry statistics.

A word of caution concerning computers is necessary before a brief overview of their technical operations is made. Computers are electronic machines that accept and manipulate data mathematically to solve problems and produce information. However, in spite of the science fiction story related at the beginning of this section, computers cannot think, and their output is only as good—or bad—as the data fed into the machine. The final judgment in making a decision utilizing computer-processed output is and must remain the responsibility of humans. Managers make decisions in business, not computers.

BASIC OPERATIONS OF COMPUTERS

Computer technology has improved at a virtually unbelievable rate. The present generation of computers uses extremely tiny microelectronic or integrated circuits, as contrasted to vacuum tubes, transistors, and diodes in the earlier series. This compression of circuit sizes has increased operating speed fantastically. In fact, computers can process data so rapidly that scientists have had to employ a little-used time measure called the *nanosecond,* which is defined as one-billionth of a second.

A computer system includes both computer hardware and software. Computer *hardware* consists of the machines, while computer *software* is made up of the various programs, or sets of instructions, which tell the computer what to do. A computer system will perform the following five basic operations:

1. Receive data input.
2. Store data until ready for calculation, classification, or retrieval.
3. Direct the sequence of operations through coded instructions and commands.
4. Perform various logical, mathematical, or statistical operations.
5. Print out the results, or output.

These operations relate to the elements of the computer system diagrammed in Figure 15–2.

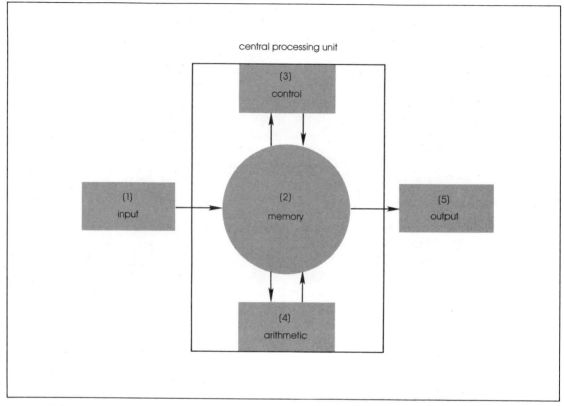

Figure 15-2   Elements of a computer system.

INPUT: RECEIVING DATA INTO THE COMPUTER

Data may be received or "read" into the computer in various forms. The most familiar computerized data input medium is the punched card, shown in Figure 15–3. Since punched cards are easily torn, bent, or mutilated (most persons today are familiar with the warning, "DO NOT FOLD, SPINDLE, OR MUTI-LATE") and they take up a great deal of space relative to data included, other input media are frequently used. Magnetic tape is the most popular data input media today in high-speed, large-volume operations because of its rapid transference into the computer.

In banking, machine-readable magnetic letters are used in check processing. The MICR (magnetic ink character recognition) method of processing checks involves the printing in magnetic ink of the depositor's bank and account number. When the payee (the check recipient) deposits the check in his or her bank, the dollar amount is encoded in the lower right corner. The check then has all the necessary data for processing by MICR reader-sorter machines, which are able to read the characters.

THE CENTRAL PROCESSING UNIT: "HEART AND BRAIN" OF THE COMPUTER

As shown in Figure 15–2, the central processing unit (CPU) consists of the memory bank, the control unit, and the arithmetic unit. These three units are responsible for storing the basic data input (memory), directing or instructing the computer as to what to do (control), and for the mathematical, statistical, and logical operations that have to be performed upon the data (arithmetic). While the operations of the CPU are extremely technical and complex, several ways to communicate with computers are discussed in a later section.

OUTPUT: RESULTS OF THE COMPUTER

The usual form of computer output is typewritten information stemming from the system's high-speed printers, frequently called *computer printouts.* In addition, output may be recorded on magnetic tapes or punched cards or paper tape, especially if the data are to be reused.

Output in the form of voice communication is used to a limited extent. In such cases, all the necessary words for replay are prerecorded on a photographic or magnetic film drum. Inquiries to the machine result in a reply message in a coded form which is then transmitted to an audio-response mechanism, which selects the words in the drum in proper sequence for a reply to the inquirer.

Visual displays similar to a television screen picture may be a form of some computer output. High-speed microfilm cameras film the output for permanent reference. Both visual displays and voice response dramatically reduce the time of the input-output cycle.

COMMUNICATING WITH THE COMPUTER

When solving a problem, the computer can do nothing without a detailed set of instructions. It can follow a set of logical instructions, but it does not reason. A set of logical instructions telling the computer what to do, how to do it, and in what order to perform each operation is called a *computer program.*

Figure 15-3 Data input card.

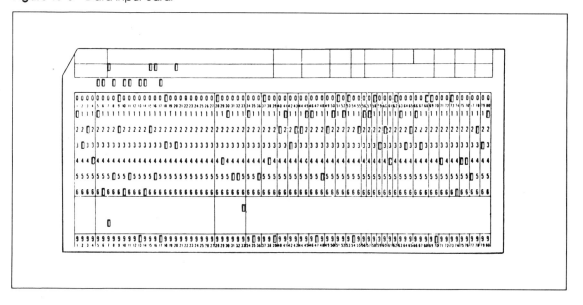

Fortunately for future generations of computer specialists, the programming of computers is being simplified tremendously by the introduction and use of automatic programs. These are commonly referred to as *canned* programs. They enable the specialist to give the computer one instruction, and the computer makes use of stored programs to do an entire series of operations.

FLOWCHARTING

For problem solutions where automatic programs are not available, the programmer outlines the logical steps needed to arrive at a proper solution. When this is done in a diagrammatical outline of the logical sequence of steps, it is called *flowcharting*. A flowchart is demonstrated using the following simple example:

> Assume that a company accumulates in the computer a record of all items received in inventory along with the cost of each item, date of receipt, and name of supplier. There are currently 600 different items in inventory. Accounting wants to know the number of items in inventory with a per unit cost equal to or greater than $10.00.

Let us assume that the arithmetic unit of the computer can add, subtract, and answer several logical questions.

Figure 15–4 shows the logical flow of steps for instructing the computer to determine the number of items whose per unit cost is equal to or greater than $10.00. There are 600 items stored in the memory of the computer where i refers to any of the 600 items. At the start of the sequence a 0 is placed in the counter, C, and the first item is reviewed. The question asked in the second box, "Is the unit cost of this item equal to or greater than 10?" If yes, 1 replaces 0 in the counter. If no, go to the next box. Both boxes 2 and 3 then feed into box 4. In box 4 the number of the inventory item advances by one. The review process continues until all 600 items are reviewed. In box 5 the number of items with a cost equal to or greater than 10, C, is stored and the computer is directed to print this number and stop.

COMPUTER LANGUAGES

At this point a very obvious question arises: How is the arithmetic logic unit directed to perform the logical operations shown in Figure 15–4? Programs must be written in such a way that the various directions can be "understood" by the machine. Computer languages have been developed for this purpose. Among the most well known are COBOL (Common Business Oriented Language), FORTRAN (FORmula TRANslator), BASIC (Beginner's All-purpose Symbolic Instruction Code), and PL/1 (Programming Language 1).

COBOL is particularly applicable to business data processing problems. It avoids the use of symbols and algebraic notations and uses English words and sentences instead.

FORTRAN is a language which is particularly useful where the computer is used for scientific research purposes; it uses mathematical and statistical computations as part of the processing operations. FORTRAN can also be used for business research purposes.

BASIC is a computer language for beginners. Developed at Dartmouth Col-

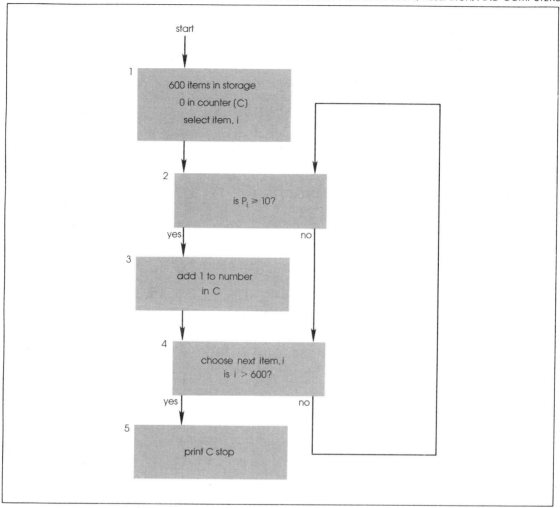

Figure 15-4 A flowchart.

lege, BASIC is an easy language to learn for individuals having little or no computer background.

PL/1 is a more recent computer language designed for both scientific and business problems. Although developed by International Business Machines (IBM) for their own computer, PL/1 can be adapted for use on other computer systems as well.

SPECIAL COUNTING SYSTEM

The numerical system used by computers during processing is not the same as the decimal numbering system used in everyday life. Rather, the computer uses a binary, or two-digit, system. Binary systems use only the digits zero (0) and one (1). Since computer switches have only two positions, on or off, the binary numerical system is readily adaptable: a one is indicated when a circuit is on, and a zero when the circuit is off.

While decimal numbers are built on a base of 10—that is, as you move a digit one space to the left and add a zero, it increases ten times as much—binary

Table 15-1
Comparison of Decimal Numeral System with
Binary Numeral System

Decimal Numeral	Corresponding Binary Numeral
0	0000
1	0001
2	0010
3	0011
4	0100
5	0101
6	0110
7	0111
8	1000
9	1001

numbers use a base of 2. As you can see from Table 15–1, with the binary numbers, every time a number is moved one space to the left, and a zero is added, it increases by twice as much. The number 347 in decimal numeration is written as 0011/0100/0111 in binary code.

COMPUTERS FOR SMALL BUSINESS

For most businesses the acquisition, or even rental, of a computer system can involve expenditures of hundreds of thousands of dollars—a considerable investment for a small business. Several recent developments in computer technology offer an opportunity for small firms to avail themselves of computerized operations. These developments include time sharing, minicomputers, and microcomputers.

Computer terminals can be established by having a direct connection with a central processing unit for instant input and data retrieval. The term *on-line computer* refers to an arrangement in which peripheral equipment is hooked directly into a main unit. *Time sharing* is the simultaneous use of an on-line computer by many users, some with many terminals in a single location, and all with a different program or set of programs. In time-sharing systems, all users communicate with a main computer via remote terminals. These terminals may not only be dispersed geographically but may be used by different companies or organizations. Thus many businesses that are too small to warrant their own systems may band together on a time-sharing basis. Time sharing is not inexpensive, but it may reduce considerably the investment in computer facilities, since the users pay only for time they actually use the computer as opposed to purchase or rental cost, where they pay whether or not the system is used.

In addition, smaller computers—referred to as *minicomputers* and *microcomputers*—now available offer another potential for the limited user. Most minicomputers are functionally capable of accomplishing almost anything a larger system costing ten to thirty times more is capable of accomplishing. However, a key difference between minicomputers and large conventional computers is capacity. Capacity is the ability to get data in, perform logic processes, use storage capabilities if needed, and create output data. Minicomputers simply cannot handle the input, do not have the storage space, and cannot produce output as rapidly as conventional computers. Most minis, for example, are not designed to handle 200 input video screens, 400 million characters of storage, or 10 output printers. But they may function quite well with 10 to 20 input video screens, 40 million characters of storage, and 2 output printers. Another important difference between minis and conventional computers is relative efficiency in handling certain types of data processing functions. Large, general-purpose

The IBM 5100 portable computer with a printer and auxiliary tape unit. The user enters this computer with statements in either the APL or BASIC programming languages.

computers are more efficient in functions which are highly repetitive, input/ output dependent; at managing large networks; at managing large data bases; at providing packaged application software; and at providing vendor support in areas of equipment maintenance and technical assistance. Buying a minicomputer is somewhat like buying a compact car. The buyer must accept the fact that he cannot go 125 miles per hour if he has the urge, nor ride six persons comfortably. But he can go 50 miles per hour, seat four people, and have a reliable means of transportation. If that's all that is needed, extra capacity is a luxury.

While minicomputers are about the size of cash registers, microcomputers are still smaller in size and lower in cost than minicomputers. The microcomputer uses microprocesses similar to those in pocket calculators; however, more memory and access to other equipment are added. Compared with minicomputers, microcomputers have less extensive instruction set, not as fully developed software, and operate three to ten times slower than minicomputers. On the other hand, the limited user may purchase a prepackaged, ready-to-work microcomputer for slightly over a hundred dollars. And just as with the pocket calculators, the price will probably decline over the next several years. However, microcomputers can range in cost up to several thousand dollars, depending on the degree of sophistication needed in the machines.

An example of a microcomputer capability is demonstrated in the following example:

> Midwest Meters, Inc., is marketing a point-of-sale computing, printing meter for liquefied petroleum trucks. The device measures the gallons sold, computes the cost including tax and prints this all on a statement for the customer. In addition this information is also recorded on cassette tape that the truck operator can leave at the office at the end of the day. These tapes can be processed on another microcomputer for a summary.[2]

COMPUTERS AND SOCIETAL ISSUES

As mentioned earlier, the computer has been an instrument of revolutionary change in our daily lives. It has made it possible for man to go to the moon and has taken over many of the routine, boring tasks in our economy. Yet some people view the computer as a threat and see many problems arising for society as a result of computer development and expansion.

Among these is the potential invasion of privacy because of the buildup of huge data banks of information on individuals. The Internal Revenue Service is one potential holder of such information. Information concerning bond interest, interest on bank deposits, dividends, and professional fees can easily be consolidated in a data bank. Other examples of agencies who seek to build up data banks of information on individuals include the national crime (e.g., the FBI) and credit agencies.

Several uncomfortable but significant questions must be answered by society. Who should have access to these data on private citizens? If incorrect data

[2]CIRAS (Center for Industrial Research and Service—Extension Service to Iowa Industry), *News for Iowa Industry* 11, no. 3 (November to December 1976).

are in an individual's file, how does the individual discover this and how can it be corrected? Visions of George Orwell's political satire *1984,* in which a society is under the control of an all-knowing, all-seeing Big Brother, take on frightening realities. Former Massachusetts governor Francis W. Sargent has perhaps placed the problem in focus with the following statement:

> The Federal Government in its incredible anxiety to computerize the lives of everyone, has made some very serious invasions into people's privacy. There has been all too much snooping. We should not get rid of computers, but we should give more thought to what goes into them.[3]

A somewhat related problem of more immediate importance to business is the whole area of industrial security and prevention of sabotage.[4] Who gains access to the computer information and the potential damage that might easily be done to a system by an individual must be carefully considered. These are some of the issues American citizens should attempt to answer as computers continue to play an expanding role in our lives.

[3]As quoted in *Time,* January 13, 1975, p. 18.
[4]For further coverage, see Brandt Allen, "Danger Ahead! Safeguard your Computer," *Harvard Business Review* 46 (November–December 1968): 97–101.

SUMMARY

At the heart of effective decision making in business, or any other organization, is the need for relevant and timely information. A management information system provides managers with the needed information on a continuous basis to make sound decisions.

In addition to accounting, which provides management with information on the financial health of the firm, research involves the collection, organization, analysis and interpretation of various data which hopefully will improve the quality of decision making. Research data in business may be collected from secondary or primary sources. Secondary data are already collected and compiled data, such as company records, government statistics, or published industry or trade data. Primary data, collected specifically for the purpose at hand, may come from surveys, experiments, observation, or simulated situations. Regardless of the source, secondary or primary, research data should be both valid and reliable.

Computers have revolutionized the information process by enabling organizations to process larger quantities of data at a higher level of complexity than could be done manually. Computers are electronic machines that accept, store, and manipulate data logically, mathematically, or statistically to solve problems and produce information. Their output is only as good—or bad—as the data fed into the machines. The final judgment in making a decision using computer-produced output is and must remain the responsibility of managers.

DISCUSSION QUESTIONS

1. What are the basic elements of a management information system (MIS)?

2. If you were given the responsibility for building an MIS for a company, what persons in the company would you consult with first? Why?

3. What do marketing research and accounting have in common?

4. What are the implications of the scientific method in conducting research?

5. What are the major sources of data available to a researcher in business?

6. How do computers aid in the building of an effective management information system?

7. What are some of the risks which confront society with continued developments and application of computer technology in our personal and business affairs?

SHORT CASES

Americana Beauty School

Americana Beauty School, one of several beauty schools in a medium-sized city in the East, desires to know how well trained their graduates are. What do the managers of beauty shops think of their graduates as compared with those of the other beauty schools? In which skills are their graduates strong and in which are they weak? What specific areas of training should be emphasized to meet the demands of the consumers? In general, how can Americana improve its training to continue as the leading beauty school in the area? A research project is planned which will involve personal interviews of about two hundred beauty shop managers in the area.

What information would you seek to obtain in the survey? Would you refer to this study as collecting secondary or primary data? Explain.

Newton Manufacturing Company

This small midwestern company with annual sales of approximately $3 million produces a limited line of industrial products—valves, gauges, compressors, and other industrial items. The company has prospered in recent years to a point at which additional plant facilities are needed. Management has isolated several alternative sites located in states with favorable labor laws. Before a final decision is made, however, management needs additional information. Which site will enable the company to meet its national market requirements with minimum transportation costs? Which location can assure the company of a continuous pool of labor with the necessary skills? How do the communities rank in other important factors such as educational system, shopping and recreational facilities, and social attitudes?

As a member of the management information team, where would you attempt to locate data on these questions? How could the use of a computerized system aid the team in providing management with the appropriate information?

SUGGESTED READINGS

Clover, Vernon, and Balsley, Howard. *Business Research Methods.* Columbus, Ohio: Grid, 1974.

Emory, C. Williams. *Business Research Methods.* Homewood, Ill.: Richard D. Irwin, 1976.

Sharpe, William F., and Jacob, Nancy L. *BASIC: An Introduction to Computer Programming Using the BASIC Language.* Rev. ed. New York: Free Press, 1971.

BEHAVIORAL SCIENCE

LEARNING OBJECTIVES

When you finish this chapter you should:

☐ know what behavioral science is and how it helps management.

☐ have gained a basic understanding of individual personality and how the individual relates to the organization.

☐ be familiar with the attractions of groups to individuals and how groups function.

☐ be aware of some of the problems in and methods for achieving motivation of workers.

☐ know the challenges and concepts of good leadership

KEY TERMS TO LEARN FROM THIS CHAPTER

aggression	empirical research	people-oriented	self-fulfillment need
anthropology	esteem need	leaders	social need
behavioral science	group cohesion	physiological need	sociology
compensation	group standard	prescriptive research	Theory X
contingency view	job enrichment	primary need	Theory Y
defense mechanism	leadership	psychology	trait theory
task-oriented leaders	motivation	secondary need	withdrawal
descriptive research	path-goal model	security need	

After a day particularly beset with personnel problems, the president of a large wholesale grocery company remarked to a colleague, "What a great business this would be if we didn't have to have people for employees." The president's remark reflected his great frustration at the end of a difficult day, but it does represent one extreme of a great range of viewpoints on employees. At the other extreme, we find employees viewed as the most important and vital component of a business organization. The truth certainly lies somewhere in between.

People—along with equipment, facilities, and money—are necessary to the effective functioning of a business enterprise. If we further accept that there are actions which management can take to provide opportunities for people to improve and make greater contributions to the organization, then we have taken the first step toward understanding that a business organization can develop a healthy, cooperative relationship between its management and its employees. To gain this understanding we need to reach into the business tool box once more and use a tool called *behavioral science.*

WHAT IS BEHAVIORAL SCIENCE?

For many years social scientists in *psychology, sociology,* and *anthropology* have been studying the behavioral and cultural patterns of people. Out of this study has developed a considerable body of theoretical knowledge. Using this knowledge base, behavioral scientists seek to develop additional knowledge and understanding in specific areas such as the interactions among organizations, individuals, and groups. We have directed much attention, for example, to individual and group behavior within business organizations.

Hence we find applicability for each of the disciplines of psychology, sociology, and anthropology. Psychology teaches us about the behavior of individuals. It is a complex study because each person is unique and does not allow complete prediction of future behavior. Psychology helps us to learn about attitudes, motivation, and leadership.

Sociology concentrates on the characteristics and behavior of groups and organizations. A lone individual has limited influence on a large organization, but a group or groups may have considerable power over the development of organizational policies and practices. Sociologists, therefore, are greatly interested in the interactions between groups and between a group and a larger organization.

Anthropology offers insights into the effects of differing cultures on the behavior of individuals, groups, and organizations. Cultural differences include not only the differences among nations but also the differences among geographic areas within one nation. In the United States, for example, there are still considerable cultural differences between the city and farming areas. Since the operations of many organizations straddle two or more cultures, a knowledge of anthropology is valuable to the practicing manager.

As a business tool then, behavioral science offers knowledge about the characteristics and behavior of individuals, groups, and organizations. In addition, the business manager can be aware of the effects of varying cultures on the functioning of his organization. Figure 16–1 shows the relationship between behavioral science and business management.

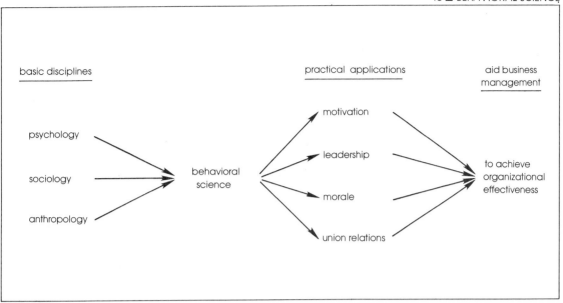

Figure 16-1 Behavioral science and business management.

HOW BEHAVIORAL SCIENCE HELPS MANAGEMENT

We have stated that behavioral science is helpful to the business manager, but we have not specified how knowledge of behavioral science translates into guides for action for the manager. First of all, behavioral science research is largely empirical in nature. That is, behavioral scientists study many specific situations and then attempt to generalize their findings to many other situations that have not been specifically studied. For example, a researcher may attempt to discover why leadership is effective or ineffective by studying ten different organizations. As a result of his or her findings, the researcher may suggest that in order for individual leadership to be successful, one kind of leadership is necessary in one situation, while another kind of leadership is necessary in a different situation.

The researcher will probably be very cautious in saying that his or her findings will have application in all organizations, however. The researcher knows that organizations differ greatly, and what works in one, or even ten organizations, may not work in another organization. Up to the current time, therefore, most behavioral science research results have been *descriptive* in nature. The researcher merely describes what happens within the specific situation of the research project and does not claim the results will always hold true. Increasingly today, however, behavioral science researchers are *prescriptive* about their results—that is, they are often willing to prescribe certain actions just as a doctor prescribes medicine. There have been so many studies in certain areas, such as leadership, that the researcher is not afraid to recommend specific courses of action in comparable situations.

The second major contribution, then, that behavioral science makes is that *empirical research* results suggest to management certain actions to be taken in specified situations. In order to use the behavioral science tool most effectively, the business manager needs a working knowledge of behavioral science research and results. Serious consequences often follow the misapplication or nonapplication of behavioral science knowledge. For example, assume a supervisor consistently reprimands subordinates for mistakes but never praises them for good work. In behaving this way, the supervisor creates a negative and unpleasant atmosphere. The subordinates, in turn, become discouraged, lose their motivation to work, and most likely will constantly look for other jobs. Perhaps through ignorance of behavioral science, the supervisor has failed to realize that people need encouragement and praise for good work in order to help them develop into productive, satisfied members of the organization. For this reason, large organizations often have a professional psychologist or sociologist on their staff to help management with organizational behavior problems, while small business managers frequently attend short courses or seek professional advice from universities or government agencies, such as the Small Business Administration.

In the remainder of the chapter, we will be even more specific about the nature of behavioral science knowledge and how it can help the business manager.

THE INDIVIDUAL AND THE ORGANIZATION

Knowledge of the general characteristics and behavior patterns of individuals is important to the success of any business manager. People are similar in many ways, and individual behavior is predictable to a limited extent. For example, most people like music, but individual taste in music varies widely. Mr. Jones may really dig hard rock, while Ms. Smith absolutely loves classical music. We can agree, therefore, with the basic idea of having piped-in music to create a more pleasant working atmosphere, but we should also recognize that we are not going to satisfy the musical tastes of each of our employees. People are similar, but they are also different in many respects. In fact, each individual is a unique entity. No two persons on this earth are completely identical.

People differ not only in their musical tastes but also in many other ways: likes and dislikes for food; preferences in sports, hobbies, and jobs; intelligence; and physical characteristics. One of the most observable differences among people is the way in which they behave. We usually talk about these differences in terms of a person's personality, and we observe that there are great differences in personality.

WHAT IS PERSONALITY?

Even given that individuals are unique, there are still some comments we can make about personality that will apply to most people most of the time. We define *personality* as the tendency of an individual to maintain attitudes and style of behavior under different conditions. For example, Mary may be a very patient person who seemingly never gets upset, while Henry is very nervous and is bothered by the slightest interruption in his daily routine. Yet under certain circumstances, Mary may lose her cool and blow up, while Henry may behave very coolly and calmly in an emergency.

Individuals, then, are never completely predictable. Consequently, the business manager faces a constant challenge which makes that job either more interesting or more frustrating, depending upon your viewpoint. The manager does have some basic knowledge of people available, however, and one part of this knowledge concerns the common drive among all persons to satisfy certain needs.

PERSONAL SATISFACTION OF NEEDS

We all try to satisfy certain *primary* needs in order to survive. We drink water, eat, breathe, and reproduce the species in order to assure our continued existence. All individuals seek to satisfy these needs. In certain societies, such as the United States, these needs are relatively easy to satisfy. In other parts of the world, the satisfaction of these needs may constitute the prime preoccupation of people over a whole lifetime.

When people satisfy their primary needs, they move on to secondary needs. In this category of *secondary* needs, we find friendship, love, status, power, and prestige. We readily observe the power and the strength of these needs in the world around us. Secondary needs provide a basis for the plots of virtually every novel, movie, and stage play. Figure 16–2 illustrates the process of need satisfaction.

To illustrate Figure 16–2, assume that an imaginary Harry Smith is a student who has an intense need for friends and social interaction. Let us also assume that Harry is just starting at a school and knows none of the other students. To gain friends, Harry becomes active in sports and on the school newspaper. He soon becomes acquainted with many other students and forms several good friendships. With at least partial satisfaction of his need for social fulfillment, Harry experiences a reduction of the tension originally created by his need. On the other hand, Harry might have failed to win any friends. His need for friendship would not have been satisfied. What would happen to Harry then?

When Needs Are Not Satisfied   People differ in the strength of their needs for friendship, power, and prestige. These differences result from inherited traits as well as from a lifetime of conditioning at home, in school, and at work.

Figure 16-2   Process of need satisfaction.

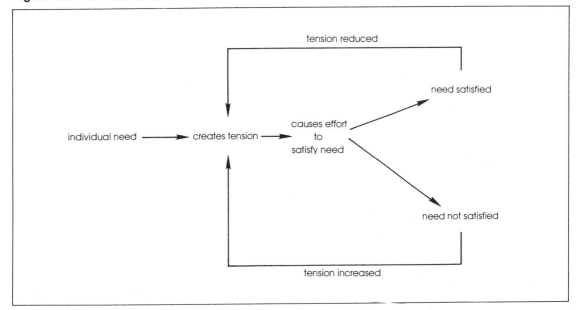

One person, for example, may have a relatively low need for social interaction and be quite content to be alone much of the time. Another person may have high need for social interaction and may seek to be with friends or family almost constantly. On the other hand, the former person may have a high need for prestige, while the latter has a very low need for prestige. What happens then if an imaginary Harry Smith, who has a high social need, is not able to develop friendships or social interaction, in general, with other people?

When needs are not satisfied, frustration results. As long as Harry is frustrated in his search for social fulfillment, he will experience stress or tension. The greater Harry's frustration, the greater will be his tension. Ultimately, Harry will have to relieve his tension either by being successful in seeking social relationships, or by taking some other course of action, as described below.

People do not always satisfy all of their needs or achieve all of their goals. Frustration is a common phenomenon in everyday life, as with Harry. If the frustration lasts long enough or becomes great enough, some action will be taken to reduce the frustration and relieve tension. One way of handling nonsatisfaction of a need is to *withdraw*—even to the point of apathy. In our illustration, Harry could stop seeking friends, withdraw into his own isolated little world, and tell himself over and over that friends are not important and are unreliable anyway.

On the other hand, Harry might become quite *aggressive* in an effort to relieve his frustration and tension. After a day of failure in the world of social affairs, Harry may come home and kick over a chair, break a dish, or kick his dog. Since he cannot make friends anyway, he may become aggressive generally toward other people. Another possible outlet for Harry is *compensation*. Since Harry cannot make friends, he may strive to achieve excellence in some other area. These areas could include almost anything: sports, a hobby, or expert knowledge in some field. By becoming an expert in something, Harry will achieve, at least in his own mind, the respect and admiration of others. In this way he will perceive increased prestige for himself and will compensate for his failure to operate successfully in the social world.

There are other ways in which Harry and all of us can relieve our frustration over failure to satisfy some need or achieve some goal. These actions we take are commonly known as *defense mechanisms*. They defend our ego against the stress, strain, and shock of failure, thereby preserving our self-respect and ability to function effectively. Hence up to a point, defense mechanisms can be healthy. They keep us going and perhaps prevent an obsession with failure. There is always a limit to these psychological deceptions, of course. A moderate use of defense mechanisms is fine. Their abuse, however, suggests that something may be seriously wrong. Then we begin to worry about neuroses or psychoses. At that point, the need for professional help is usually apparent. Figure 16–3 illustrates how defense mechanisms relieve frustration.

THE NEED HIERARCHY

Information on personality and need satisfaction is probably interesting, but of what value is it to the business organization? A famous psychologist, Abraham Maslow,[1] suggested a way to structure needs which can be helpful to the business

[1]Abraham H. Maslow, *Motivation and Personality* (New York: Harper & Row, 1954), pp. 35–58.

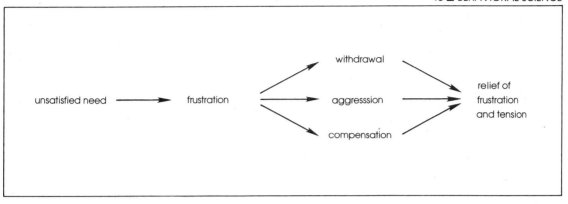

Figure 16-3 The process of relieving frustrations through defense mechanisms.

manager. Maslow pointed out that we do not try to satisfy all of our needs at the same time. We regulate our behavior and tend to attempt satisfaction of our needs one at a time and to approach them in a certain order. The first need we attempt to satisfy is the *physiological* or primary need for food, water, and the other components of life necessary to survival. Once the physiological needs are quite well satisfied, Maslow suggests we will turn to a need for *security*. We want the assurance that everything possible has been done by ourselves, the companies we work for, and our government to protect us against disasters such as a serious illness or accident. This assurance comes in the form of insurance, Social Security, good safety practices, and so on.

Once we feel quite secure, our next step up in the hierarchy brings us to the need for companionship. The *social* need is a secondary need, and we want to satisfy this need in all facets of our life—on the job as well as off the job. When we are socially satisfied, we move on to a need for *esteem* or *respect*. We want self-respect as well as the respect of others for our abilities, skills, and accomplishments. To gain this respect, we may be motivated to work very hard to learn a particular occupational skill or to achieve certain goals. When we have earned respect, we finally turn to the topmost need in the Maslow hierarchy— *self-fulfillment*. This is a need to use all of our potential to the maximum. Whatever skills, abilities, or capacities that we have, we want to use them to the maximum that is possible. We look for situations in which self-fulfillment is possible. If we cannot find it on the job, we seek self-fulfillment off the job. Figure 16–4 illustrates the Maslow hierarchy.

Business Management and the Need Hierarchy   Knowledge of the Maslow hierarchy can help the business manager to be a more effective leader. The manager can help his or her employees achieve satisfaction as well as create opportunities for motivation by making possible the satisfaction of needs up the steps of the need hierarchy. The employees' paychecks, the manager hopes, will take care of their physiological needs, and the manager will not have to worry about that. Through company insurance, health, and safety programs, the employees' need for security may well be satisfied. If the social need is being frustrated, the manager can facilitate social interaction by allowing people to work more closely together or by encouraging the employees to form bowling teams, or any other activity that tends to bring the employees into social contact.

In many jobs, the manager can also aid employees in satisfying the need for

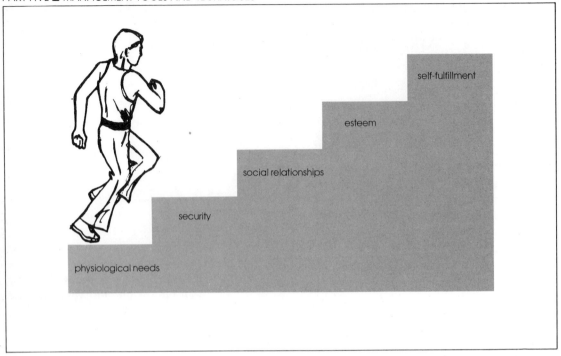

Figure 16-4 Maslow's hierarchy of needs.

esteem. Encouraging employees to perfect existing skills or to develop new skills are ways to generate respect and esteem. Giving employees the opportunity to achieve on the job and then recognizing that achievement is another way to generate esteem. If individuals satisfy their need for esteem, they then move on to the need for self-fulfillment. This need may be difficult to satisfy in certain kinds of jobs in business. For example, routine assembly line work may not challenge a person to use very much potential ability and skill, and there may be very little the supervisor or manager can do to create challenge. In some cases, however, it is possible to redesign a job so that it is more challenging and does use far more of the potential ability of an employee. This kind of redesign is called *job enrichment*. The Volvo and Saab automobile companies in Sweden have redesigned the task of assembling their automobiles to be far more challenging and interesting than work on the typical American automobile assembly line. Such changes, however, are beyond the capacity of the individual manager to bring about. They require the full commitment of the organization from the president's office on down. Nonetheless, where possible, the individual manager should make every effort to build the possibility of self-fulfillment into the jobs of subordinates.

Although there are constraints on what one manager can do, we can see that Maslow's hierarchy does offer some guidelines to the individual manager in working with employees. It is possible to structure satisfaction of their needs as well as provide motivational opportunities for them. Of course, the individual manager cannot be as effective in this as can the total organization. If the total organization makes the commitment to structure opportunities for the achievement of esteem and self-fulfillment, there is much greater likelihood of success.

Our section on the individual personality has been illustrative of how management can use the behavioral sciences as a tool to facilitate effective operation. There is, of course, far more to the psychology of the individual, and we recommend full study of this area to the practicing or aspiring business manager. Individual behavior comprises only a portion of total human behavior in any organization, however. Equally important is the behavior of people in groups, and this is the subject of our next section.

THE GROUP AND THE ORGANIZATION

We know that people have a need for social interaction, so it is not surprising that people readily form groups under all circumstances and conditions, including work. These latter groups are usually task groups that form as a result of several people working in close proximity on a job. However, these task groups may also be friendship groups for many of their members. There is a saying in psychology that the more people interact, the more friendly they become. At their own great peril, some business organizations have chosen to ignore employee groups that exist within the boundaries of their business. We say "at great peril" because groups can become quite powerful and influential with respect to the organization's ability to make a profit.

THE POWER OF A GROUP

Why does a group wield power? The obvious answer is that two people have more influence than one, that five people have more influence than two, or that ten people have more influence than five. But this easy explanation does not really explain group power, since in order to have power the group must really act as one rather than as a mere assembly of separate individuals.

In other words, the group must act with unity in order to assert power and influence. The real question, then, is how a group acquires the unity necessary to be influential. The answer lies partially in the reasons individuals join groups in the first place. There are several, and some of these reasons parallel the Maslow hierarchy.

Why People Join Groups   People join groups to satisfy needs. Group membership helps to satisfy the needs for security, social interaction, esteem, and in certain cases, self-fulfillment. To illustrate, let us say our Mr. Harry Smith has just landed a new job with a large department store. He is going to be the assistant buyer for men's clothing. The personnel department and his boss will tell Harry about the formal policies and procedures of the company, and Harry will probably follow these to the letter in order to maintain good standing and secure his job.

Harry observes, however, that there are one or more informal groups of the other assistant buyers. He also observes that the other assistant buyers seem to observe some of the policies very closely and more or less ignore others. Soon

Harry develops a strong desire to belong to one of these informal groups so he will feel more secure and comfortable in knowing what he should or should not do on the job. Harry does manage to gain membership in one of the assistant buyer informal groups and finds that learning the ropes does give him a much greater feeling of security about doing the right thing and being able to keep his job.

Group membership also satisfies much of Harry's need for social interaction on the job. The company considers the members of the group which he has joined to be the best of its assistant buyers, enabling him to gain a feeling of prestige and esteem through his membership. Finally, the knowledge and experience of his fellow assistant buyers in the group may help Harry to realize fully his potential on the job and enable him to enjoy a partial or full measure of self-fulfillment.

There are other reasons for group membership, but these are some of the most important. Figure 16–5 illustrates the parallelism between these reasons for group membership and Maslow's need hierarchy.

THE SOURCE OF GROUP COHESION

The development of *group cohesion* depends on how attractive the group is in stimulating people to join and to stay as members. The attractiveness of the group depends on the potential the group offers to satisfy needs for security,

Figure 16-5 Maslow's hierarchy and reasons for group membership.

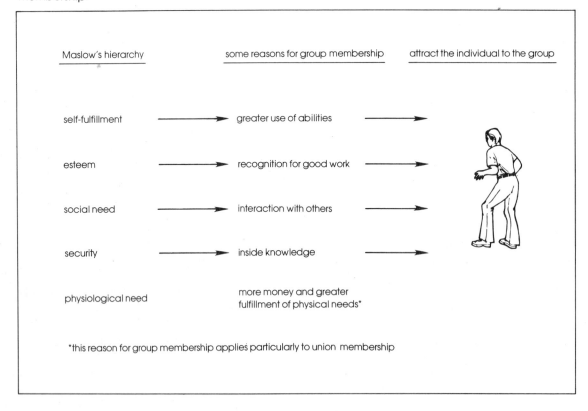

Maslow's hierarchy	some reasons for group membership	attract the individual to the group
self-fulfillment	→ greater use of abilities	→
esteem	→ recognition for good work	→
social need	→ interaction with others	→
security	→ inside knowledge	→
physiological need	more money and greater fulfillment of physical needs*	

*this reason for group membership applies particularly to union membership

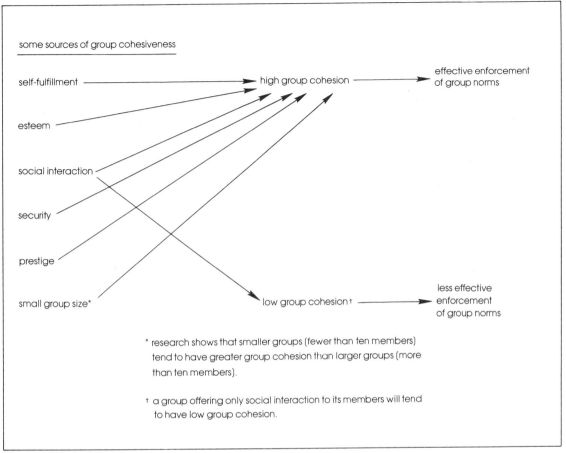

some sources of group cohesiveness

Figure 16-6 Group cohesiveness and group norms.

social interaction, esteem, and self-fulfillment. If the group that Harry joined appeared to have a high potential for satisfying these needs, the group will be very attractive to Harry, and he will very much want to remain a member.

In order to join and remain a member in good standing, however, Harry will discover that he must conform to the *group standards* for performance and behavior. Every group develops certain standards of conduct or norms. A norm is an "ought." It tells members how they ought to act. A group of high school students may enforce certain standards of dress, while a work group in a company may enforce certain standards of performance—either high or low. If a group member does not conform to these standards, the group will ultimately expel the member.

Hence there is a connection between group cohesiveness and the enforcement of group standards of conduct. The greater the cohesiveness or attractiveness of the group to individuals, the greater will be the power of the group to enforce its standards of conduct. If you really do not care whether or not you belong to a group, you are not likely to be very careful in observing the group standards. Conversely, if membership in a certain group is highly valued, you will probably be very careful to observe whatever standards of conduct the group enforces. Figure 16–6 illustrates some sources of group cohesiveness and the relationship between cohesiveness and the enforcement of group norms.

KNOWLEDGE OF GROUPS AS AN AID TO GOOD MANAGEMENT

Once again we find a valuable tool in the behavioral sciences—knowledge of group dynamics. How can this knowledge help the business manager? For one thing, the manager can realize that groups are inevitable and will always exist within the business organization. It is foolhardy to try to ignore groups and group power as some managers still do. One consequence of recognizing groups is realizing that leadership must be exercised through groups as well as through individuals.

To illustrate, suppose a supervisor, Mr. Emery, asks one of his subordinates, Jones, to work extra hard to get a special project out on time. Jones agrees but deliberately fails to complete the work by the deadline. Emery is unhappy and lets Jones know this. The latter, however, is relatively unconcerned. Why?

Jones belongs to a tightly knit, highly cohesive work group. The group has certain standards about how hard members should work and respond to requests for special favors. The group believes that if Emery needs some special help, he should approach the group, explain the problem, and ask for help. The group does not like the supervisor to approach only one member, as this action is seen as an attempt to split the group.

Hence when Emery asked Jones for special help, Jones would not outright refuse to obey Emery but neither would Jones violate his group's norms. He worked on the special project, but he worked no harder than usual. Emery, of course, should have attempted to exercise his leadership through the group and not just through one individual, Jones. If Emery is unusually perceptive, he would also note that a highly cohesive work group is not overly fearful of resisting a supervisor or even the total organization. By comparison, a lone individual or a group with very low cohesion would not resist or would be very hesitant about resisting a supervisor's request.

If a manager supervises one or more highly cohesive groups, that person should attempt to work with the groups as well as with the individuals and try to find out what some of the group norms are. This is not a suggestion that the manager attempt to manipulate the groups, but rather to work with the groups and try to make it possible for the groups to have norms that will contribute to the effective functioning of the department and the whole organization.

Can a Manager Help a Group to Change Norms?   A first step for the manager in helping a group to change its norms is for the manager to be absolutely fair and equitable in dealing with all the individuals in groups under his or her supervision. Fair managerial actions will develop confidence among the subordinates that they work for a good boss and a good company. Second, the manager should be supportive of the group and ask for their participation in some of the decisions that must be made. In this way, the group will gain a feeling of responsibility for what goes on in their department, and they should tend, for example, to develop high standards of performance. A manager who constantly fights the groups of his or her department, or even attempts to destroy them, will only arouse resentment and will very likely strengthen the very groups he or she is trying to eliminate. This course of action can only lead to increasing trouble for the manager and for the company.

So far, we have presented only a few of the reasons why a knowledge of the behavioral sciences can be a valuable tool for business management. In the last sections on motivation and leadership, we will further illustrate the value of behavioral knowledge.

MOTIVATION OF WORKERS

The question most likely to be asked by a troubled manager is, "What can I do to motivate my people?" Increasingly, research results in behavioral science suggest certain specific steps that a manager can take to increase the *motivation* of workers. While we cannot detail a specific program for increasing motivation, we can point out some of the behavioral science concepts which provide a base for the more specific step-by-step procedures. Maslow's hierarchy is one of these concepts.

A manager, hopefully in cooperation with the organization, can strive to assure that the physiological, security, social, esteem, and self-fulfillment needs of workers are being met. Research has indicated that satisfaction of the first three of these needs will tend to remove feelings of job dissatisfaction on the part of workers. Research also indicates that being able to satisfy the needs for esteem and self-fulfillment provides a strong motivational base for the individual.

A nationally known consultant and scholar, Frederick Herzberg, has found that a way to satisfy the esteem and self-fulfillment needs is to structure certain motivators into the job.[2] In his model there are five motivators:

1. A perceived opportunity for achievement.
2. Recognition.
3. Work itself.
4. Responsibility.
5. Opportunity for advancement.

In other words if a person has interesting work, is given responsibility, has an opportunity to achieve something worthwhile on the job, is given recognition for work done, and has an opportunity for promotion, then this person will be motivated. Implicit in the concept is that the work, the possible achievement, and the responsibility are of a nature to command the respect of the individual and of others. Further, the motivators must challenge the worker in terms of abilities and capacities in order for the worker to gain a feeling of self-fulfillment. Hence we see a relationship between the work of Maslow and that of Herzberg. Maslow points out the importance of the esteem and self-fulfillment needs, while Herzberg suggests the specific job factors or motivators that can make possible the satisfaction of these higher-order needs. Herzberg also suggests some specific steps that an organization can take to build the motivators into jobs.

[2]Frederick Herzberg, "One More Time: How Do You Motivate Employees?" *Harvard Business Review* 46 (January–February 1968): 53–62.

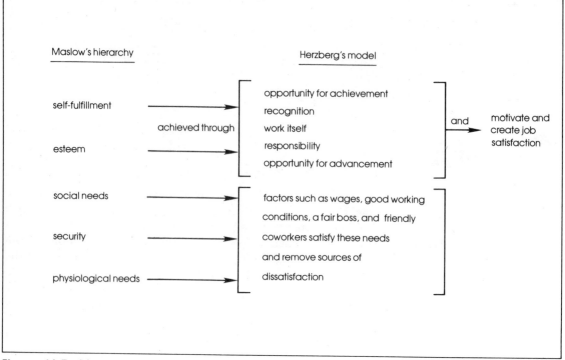

Figure 16-7 Maslow's hierarchy and Herzberg's motivators.

Figure 16–7 shows the relationship between the models of Maslow and Herzberg.

In Figure 16–7, Maslow's higher-order needs of esteem and self-fulfillment refer to job-related factors such as work itself and achievement in Herzberg's model. Since it is often difficult for unskilled and semiskilled workers to find an opportunity for achievement or other motivators on the job, we see that it is also comparatively rare for these workers to fulfill their needs for esteem or self-fulfillment. On the other hand, it is easier to fulfill the lower-order needs such as the social and security needs since almost any job can have adequate wages and working conditions, a fair boss, and satisfactory coworkers.

A POSITIVE VIEW OF PEOPLE

In the early 1960s another outstanding student of management, Douglas McGregor, pointed out that managers usually view their employees in one of two different ways.[3] He said that some employers look upon their workers as being lazy, disliking responsibility, resisting change, and generally being only interested in themselves and having no interest in the organization. While this description may be true of a very few people, it does not seem to represent an accurate portrayal of the majority of society. Hence McGregor suggested another viewpoint which he felt was a much truer description of workers and which was also supported by his own research. This view held that people do

[3]Douglas M. McGregor, "The Human Side of Enterprise," in Donald E. Porter and P. B. Applewhite, eds., *Studies in Organizational Behavior and Management* (Scranton, Pa.: International, 1964), pp. 452–63.

want responsibility, they do want to contribute to the organization, and they do want to work hard. The problem is, said McGregor, that organizations often do not allow their people to behave in this manner. Organizations put their people on assembly lines or in other very routine jobs, never ask for their opinions, and treat their employees like so many machines or robots. In this kind of organizational atmosphere, it is not surprising that employees begin to behave as the first view, which he labeled *Theory X,* would suggest. On the other hand, if an organization creates opportunities for its employees to achieve, to have interesting work, and to assume responsibility, then they will be as the second view, or what McGregor calls *Theory Y,* suggests.

If we accept McGregor's Theory Y, then it is possible also to see how Maslow's and Herzberg's models will work and will increase motivation. That is, if people do want responsibility, do want to work hard, and do want to contribute to an organization, they will respond to the motivators, such as responsibility, in Herzberg's model. In doing so, they will be seeking to satisfy their higher-order needs for esteem and self-fulfillment. Hence we can see how all three concepts tie together and provide insight into the type of structure needed to provide motivational opportunity for people to respond to. At the same time, we must recognize that not all persons will respond in the manner these theories suggest. Some percentage of the population is alienated from work. These are people who are conditioned early in life, usually by their parents, to not value work and the reward of work. As adults they tend not to respond to motivational opportunities. It does seem, however, that the vast majority of people still respond to job factors such as Herzberg's motivators.

The Pursuit of Individual Goals   A final aspect of motivation can be constructed on the foundation already built by Maslow, Herzberg, and McGregor. Sometimes called the *path-goal model,* this concept suggests making a distinct connection between individual performance and individual goal achievement. The

"I'm a true Theory X type myself. How 'bout you?"

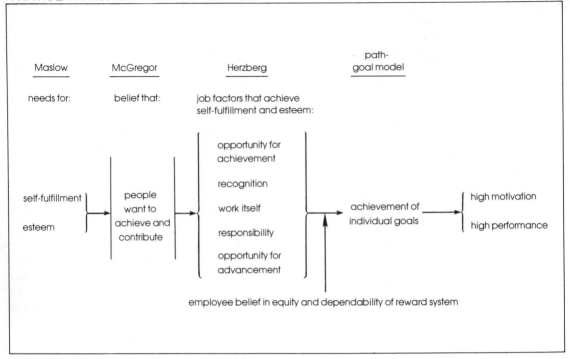

Figure 16-8 A motivational model.

worker must perceive high performance as a path to a goal that he or she values highly. Hence there are really two parts to the path-goal model. The manager must know or find out what the worker wants. Is it more money, a promotion, more responsibility, or more autonomy on the job? When individual goals are known, the manager then must see to it that high performance leads to the achievement of goal(s). In other words, if a person wants more money, that person must perceive that good performance will lead to an increase in wages or salary. If the worker does perceive this and does believe it, then that individual will be motivated to perform at a high level.

To these concepts of the path-goal model, the need hierarchy of Maslow, the motivators of Herzberg, and the positive viewpoint of McGregor, we add finally the elements of credibility and equity. With the proper job structure and the workers believing in the equity and dependability of the reward system, there is a high probability that the organization will not only have an excellent relationship with its workers but will also enjoy their consistent high performance.

LEADERSHIP

Our final illustration of the use of behavioral science as a business tool is in the topic of *leadership*. It was very common a number of years ago to say that a leader had to be strong, tall, courageous, honest, intelligent, hard working, sober, and so on. Each expert on leadership had a favorite list of traits which presumably identified the chosen few who could be leaders. While we have not today completely thrown out the *trait theory,* we do subscribe to the idea that almost anyone, with training, can be a satisfactory leader in a given situation. Some research also still suggests that certain traits such as intelligence, a desire for achievement, and awareness are characteristics common to successful leaders.

We pay much more attention today, however, to the situational or *contingency view* of leadership. As a starting point of this concept, we divide leadership into two basic styles: *task-oriented* and *people-oriented.* That is, some leaders pay most of their attention to the job at hand and how to get it done. These are task-oriented leaders. Other leaders pay most of their attention to the people working to get a certain job done. These are people-oriented leaders.

Current thinking has it that most people have a natural style of leadership that tends to be either task-oriented or people-oriented. Therefore, if we can identify work which requires a task-oriented type of leadership, a task-oriented person should be relatively successful in that leadership role. Similarly, if we can identify work which calls for a people-oriented approach, then a people-oriented person should be relatively successful in that leadership role. There are specific methods designed to identify both the nature of the work and the orientations of people—that is, either task-oriented or people-oriented. This is how the word *contingency* gets involved. The type of leader needed is contingent upon the nature of the work. If a business can successfully match its various jobs with the appropriate type of leadership, it should have reasonably effective leadership throughout.

For example, the boss of a construction gang probably should be fairly task-oriented, while the manager of a research and development unit might want to be mostly people-oriented. Ideally, we would like to have leaders who can be either task-oriented or people-oriented, as the situation demands. But these people are relatively rare, and so we do the next best thing—get the best match possible between the demands of the job and the type of person needed to fulfill a leadership role for that work.

THE DEMANDS OF LEADERSHIP

We have described the types of leaders needed for different jobs. All leaders, however, face the challenge posed by our discussion on motivation. No matter what the orientation, it is up to the leader to structure motivational opportunities for the workers. It is up to the leader and the organization to make it possible for the workers to satisfy their needs on the job, to take advantage of available motivators, and to respond time and again to fair rewards offered for high performance. It is easy to say these things, but very difficult to accomplish them on the job. The manager, the boss, the supervisor, the leader must have knowledge of the behavioral sciences and must temper this with experience. There is no easy road to good leadership, and there are very few so-called natural-born leaders. It takes study and hard work. The behavioral science portion of the business tool box will be invaluable in this task.

We have now covered three important management tools and techniques: (1) accounting, (2) research and information systems, and (3) behavioral science. These tools are invaluable to the practicing business person. The last major section of the book will deal primarily with the challenges and responsibilities facing business now and in the future.

Behavioral science is a body of knowledge and a tool that business management can and should use for more effective and efficient operations. It has its knowledge base in the disciplines of psychology, sociology, and anthropology. Knowledge of behavioral science becomes a guide for action as management works with individuals and groups within the organizational context.

SUMMARY

Each person is unique but tends to behave rather consistently under varying circumstances. We call this observable behavior personality. While personality is completely individual, all persons do seek to satisfy certain common needs. These needs cause individuals to work for physiological satisfaction, the assurance of security, social fulfillment, self-esteem, and self-fulfillment. When needs are not satisfied, people become frustrated and compensate by kicking their dogs, working in a garden, or by one of many other ways of relieving frustration. Business management can motivate employees by helping them to satisfy needs on the job.

People also form into groups on the job as well as off the job. Since groups may exert considerable power within an organization, it is important that management understand the nature of groups as well as individuals. If management is fair and supports work groups, these groups will tend to cooperate with the organization in terms of high morale and productivity.

Business has long regarded motivation of employees as a difficult and important problem. By giving employees deserved recognition and opportunities for achievement and responsibility, management builds a foundation for high productivity. By further creating the opportunity for achievement of individual goals, management can complete its motivational structure. Then it is up to the organizational leadership to maintain motivation at a high level.

Research studies suggest that natural leaders are rare but that most people can be effective leaders if their leadership styles are matched with appropriate assignments. The situational approach makes it possible for companies to have good leadership in all positions. All managers and leaders should constantly study behavioral science to improve their overall effectiveness.

DISCUSSION QUESTIONS

1. Behavioral science knowledge comes from psychology, sociology, and anthropology. Which of these three disciplines do you feel is most important in understanding organizations? Or are they all equally important?

2. Although each individual's personality is unique, we know that some people have similar personalities. As an employer, would you want a wide divergence of personalities among your employees or would you want them all to be somewhat similar?

3. Do you think that one individual will make greater use of defense mechanisms at some time than at others? If your answer is yes, what would account for the differences in depending upon defense mechanisms?

4. Do most workers in the United States fulfill their needs for esteem and self-fulfillment on or off the job? Would your answer be the same with respect to workers in England? Japan? Brazil?

5. Is there too much emphasis on groups these days as compared to individual initiative and action? Do you feel that group action or individual action was most responsible for developing the United States?

6. Is there a loss of individuality when members of a group conform to group standards?

7. As an employee of an organization, what do you believe would be the best way for your supervisor to motivate high performance on your part?

8. Do you think you are primarily a task-oriented or people-oriented type of person? Should this make any difference with respect to your choice of a career?

SHORT CASES

An Rx for Success[4]

Employees of the Donnelly Mirrors Company in Holland, Michigan, work on salaries and do not have to punch a time clock when they report to and leave from work. Through membership on their work teams and an elected committee, the employees participate in settling grievances, establishing pay policies, and handling other matters such as fringe benefits and exceptions from the company promotion policy. The work teams get involved in decision making on production, pricing, marketing, and other matters.

The Donnelly Company has 70 percent of the United States market in auto mirrors and produces many other glass products. During the ten years from 1965 to 1975, sales increased from $3 million to more than $18 million, while the number of employees rose from fewer than 200 to more than 500. The company not only maintained prices on most of their products during that period but actually reduced the prices on some items. By and large, the employees feel comfortable with their participation in company decision making. Some of the managers, however, find it threatening.

Why should some of the managers of Donnelly Mirrors Company feel threatened by employee participation in decision making?

Do you think it is a good idea for employees to participate in decisions on production and marketing? As an employee, would you like to participate in these decisions?

Since Donnelly has been so successful, why have not all companies adopted a similar system for running their businesses?

---

[4]Adapted from "Participative Management at Work," *Harvard Business Review* 55 no. 1, (January–February 1977): 117–27.

The Personal Problem

George Smith worked for the QRS Company. Smith did semiskilled work on an assembly line and had been a good worker and employee with QRS for three years. Smith's supervisor, Henry Garr, was a no-nonsense type who believed in getting the work done. Smith had always gotten along well with Garr since Smith did his work well and did not participate in the horseplay which sometimes went on.

Over the past several months, Smith's wife had begun drinking quite heavily. Smith often had to prepare the evening meal for himself and the two children—ages eight and ten—because his wife was sleeping off a daytime drinking bout. Smith worried, of course, and his worry began to show in his work with QRS. One day Garr asked him what the big problem was—why his work was slipping in both quality and quantity. Smith told Garr there was a bad problem at home which he, Smith, was very worried about.

Garr responded, "Look, Smith, I don't care about your personal life. That's your problem. But when you're here working in my department I want 100 percent. Leave your personal problems at home."

Do you agree with the attitude about personal problems expressed by the supervisor, Henry Garr?

Should Smith discuss his problem with someone else in the company—perhaps someone in the personnel department or even Garr's boss?

SUGGESTED READINGS

Chung, Kee Hoon. *Motivational Theories and Practices.* Columbus, Ohio: Grid, 1977.

Hellriegel, Don, and Slocum, John W. *Organization Behavior: Contingency Views.* St. Paul, Minn.: West Publishing Co., 1976.

Ivancevich, John M.; Szilagyi, Andrew D., Jr.; and Wallace, Marc J., Jr. *Organizational Behavior and Performance.* Santa Monica, Calif.: Goodyear Publishing Co., 1977.

*

PART SIX

RESPONSIBILITIES AND OPPORTUNITIES

☐ Our system of business management described in the preceding chapters has generated for Americans new records in consumption. In the early years of the 1970s our annual consumption levels reached a trillion dollars' worth of goods and services. Our demands will undoubtedly be even greater in the future. After all, there will be more of us, our average income will be higher, and it seems likely that in any foreseeable future we will demand more, not less, for ourselves and our families.

☐ In assessing the nature of future demands, however, business is confronted with new uncertainties. People are embracing new values and seeking greater self-expression; social and moral values are changing; many potential or long-dormant conflicts between social groups and classes — including those between women and men — have become overt; the government is intervening in the economy in new ways; and new concerns about the environment will also have an impact on the economy in ways that cannot be foreseen.

☐ As businesses respond to the new pressures of future demands, they will be held accountable to their investors, employees, and consumers. Some are saying that in addition to these groups, businesses must be held responsible for their impact on the environment, on social problems, and on the quality of life in general. In the next three chapters we will examine the relations between government and business (Chapter 17) and the responsibilities and challenges confronting business toward people (Chapter 18) and for the environment (Chapter 19). Chapter 20 will include discussions of future challenges for business in growth, development, and new technologies. Chapter 21 will discuss the resultant career patterns, especially for young people, which exist and are likely to exist in the future.

*

GOVERNMENT AND BUSINESS

LEARNING OBJECTIVES

When you finish this chapter you should:

☐ understand the role of government in carrying out the functions of equity, regulation, protection, promotion, and stability.

☐ be aware of some of the regulatory commissions and laws involved with the above functions.

KEY TERMS TO LEARN FROM THIS CHAPTER

applied research	pure research
business cycle	revenue sharing
inflation	tax shelters
investment credit	trust
negative income tax	value-added tax
progressive taxes	

To what extent is a large business involved with the federal bureaucracy? Are business's complaints about the paperwork jungle essentially a matter of unwarranted bellyaching? Standard Oil of Indiana, a major oil refiner and distributor, attempted to answer this question. They estimated that in 1975 it took the equivalent of 527 full-time employees to prepare the reports required by the federal government. The annual cost in salaries and related administrative expenses added up to $21 million. The output was in the form of 24,000 pages of reports for the year. In turn, these reports were backed up by 225,000 page of computer printouts. It is an understatement to say that these figures are staggering. Perhaps no small part of President Jimmy Carter's successful presidential campaign was his promise to reform the federal bureaucracy.

While the issue of the size and complexity of the federal government is extremely important, perhaps a good starting point is to ask what various functions are performed by Washington.

The purpose of this chapter is to provide a framework covering the role and function of government, with a few selected examples, as it appears to be evolving. The emphasis will mainly, though not exclusively, stress the relationship between business and government.

Two important limitations should be borne in mind relative to this approach. First, it is intended to describe what is, rather than discuss what we might think the relationship should be. Second, the discussion is limited to the federal government. The role and scope of state and local governments and their relation to the federal government goes beyond the bounds of this book. Indeed, the last area is of vital significance today in view of the staggering financial and societal problems of many major metropolitan areas. Like New York, many other large cities may need federal aid to avoid bond defaults.

It is probably true that most of our present societal problems cannot be solved without some collaborative effort between business, government, and the American people. How this can be done consistent with the goals of minimizing costs, maximizing benefits, and maximizing our personal freedoms is one of the paramount issues of our time. As mentioned previously, this chapter simply attempts to provide a framework for viewing government activities as they are now provided, without attempting to analyze in depth these important issues.

GOVERNMENT FRAMEWORK

The federal government is a direct producer of various goods and services as well as being an important consumer. It also greatly affects business through its concern for the common welfare by means of legislation, regulatory agencies, and policy. These areas are of concern in this chapter. The general approach in this text has been to discuss the interface between business and government in the relevant chapters. For example, the role of the Small Business Administration in backing new business in Chapter 3, safety legislation in Chapter 5, and the Federal Reserve System and Securities and Exchange Commission in Chapter 12 are a few areas of government activity affecting business mentioned earlier in this book.

To provide a workable framework, government activity can be divided into five categories:

The National Capitol, Washington, D.C.

1. Equity.
2. Regulation.
3. Protection.
4. Promotion.
5. Stability.

An overview of the approach used here is shown in Figure 17–1.

There is, to be sure, some degree of overlap in this classification scheme. Nevertheless, it is useful for analyzing the role of government.

Each of these functions, with a few illustrations, will be discussed. The focus will be mainly on the executive branch of government (the presidency and the various departments, such as Commerce, Labor, and the Treasury) as well as important legislation passed by Congress. In these illustrations, the relation between government and business should be quite clear.

EQUITY

The equity function involves the government in its role of being an intermediary that attempts to provide services, benefits, or opportunities for disadvantaged segments of our economy, including groups who are not as well off economically as others in our population. Disadvantaged groups include the elderly and those who are physically handicapped.

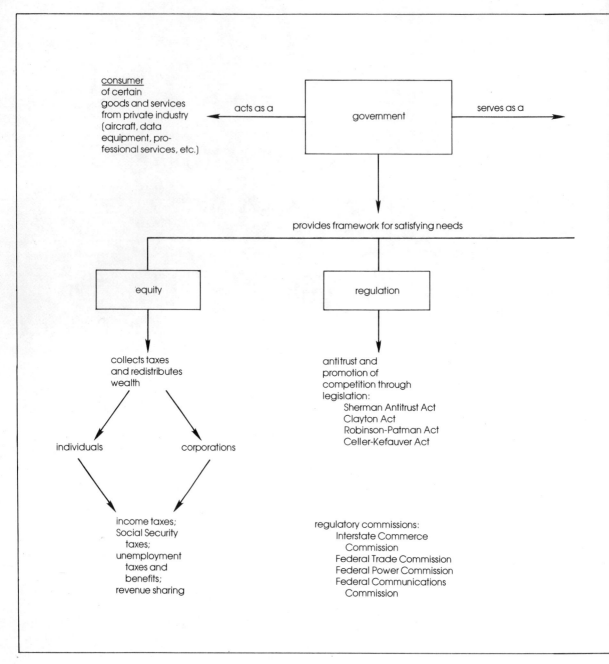

Figure 17-1 The role of government in American society.

direct producer
of certain goods
and services
(highways, national
defense, health care,
postal service

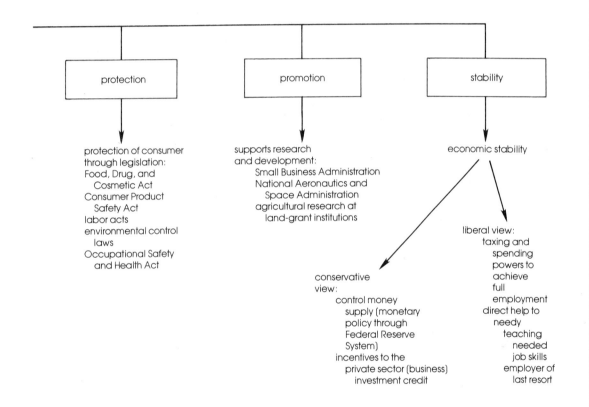

protection

promotion

stability

protection of consumer
through legislation:
Food, Drug, and
  Cosmetic Act
Consumer Product
  Safety Act
labor acts
environmental control
  laws
Occupational Safety
  and Health Act

supports research
and development:
  Small Business Administration
  National Aeronautics and
    Space Administration
  agricultural research at
    land-grant institutions

economic stability

conservative
view:
  control money
    supply (monetary
    policy through
    Federal Reserve
    System)
  incentives to the
    private sector (business)
      investment credit

liberal view:
  taxing and
    spending
    powers to
    achieve
    full
    employment
  direct help to
    needy
    teaching
    needed
    job skills
  employer of
    last resort

Some important areas where equity is attempted include the whole gamut of health, education, and welfare services and also the imposition of income taxes.

TAXATION

The Constitution of the United States in Article 1, Section 8, gives the federal government the right to raise and collect taxes.

Although there was no tax on income until 1913, today individual and corporate income taxes make up slightly more than 50 percent of the total tax revenues collected by the federal government. Sources of federal tax revenues are shown in Table 17–1.

Tax revenues obviously underpin the financing of the federal government. However, the amount of the load that various individuals and segments of the population must bear represents an instrument of equity in the hands of the federal government.

Income Tax Rates   At the corporate level, the income tax rate is 20 percent of the first $25,000 of income and 22 percent of the next $25,000 of income and 48 percent on earnings above $50,000. Sole proprietorships and partnerships are not taxed as such. However, income from these firms must be included in the total income of their owners when they compute their personal income taxes.

Table 17-1
Sources of federal tax revenue.

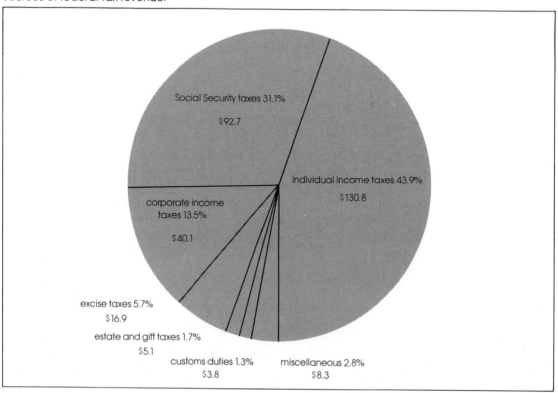

The basic structure of the individual income tax in the United States is *progressive*. In theory, this means that the higher the individual's total income, the higher the percentage of total taxes that must be paid.

While the basic structure of our income tax system is progressive, a huge layer of tax benefits for various individuals and groups casts some doubt upon the question of what groups really bear the largest share of the income tax. At their best, tax rules promote the concept of equity in a just and simple manner. For example, extra deductions from taxable income are allowed for people sixty-five years of age and over and also for the blind.

Tax benefits that aid the wealthy are often called *tax shelters*. Some tax shelters are nothing more than legal loopholes enabling the wealthy to avoid paying their proportionate share of income taxes. For individuals, the first $50 of corporate dividends received on city, state, and local governments is not taxed. (Nontaxability, however, enables municipal bonds to be sold at a lower rate.) Much more flagrant, perhaps, were tax-exempt "foundations" that were supposedly set up as charitable organizations but which were, in reality, complex fronts that enabled some wealthy people to avoid taxes. Fortunately, this loophole was largely closed by a recent tax reform act, but much more still remains to be done. On the other hand, only medical costs above the first 3 percent of income (save for health insurance) are allowed as a deduction from income. Similarly, day care costs of working mothers were also largely not allowed as tax deductions in computing taxable income.[1] Both of these aspects of the tax law work against people in the lower income brackets.

In recent years much talk has been directed to overhauling our entire tax structure, both to simplifying the tax code and applying equity to work more favorably for those in lower economic brackets. While nothing has happened on a grand scale yet, several new ideas merit our attention.

Negative Income Tax   The negative income tax extends the equity idea of taxation to its logical conclusion. An amount of income would be designated as the poverty level. Earnings above this amount for each individual or family would be taxed as it is presently done. Those below this level would receive income payments based on factors such as how far below the poverty level they are and the number of people in the family.

Negative income tax is intended to be relatively easy to administer and largely to replace our complex and costly system of social welfare programs.

The negative income tax could be set up so that individuals would always be better off as they earned more. In the hypothetical example shown in Table 17–2, subsidies begin below the $10,000 level of income. In this example, $7,500 was designated as the poverty level, the minimum income a family of a particular size must have to maintain an absolute minimum standard of living. In this example, personal incentive might well be reduced for individuals capable of earning up to $5,000 before receipt of poverty benefits.

Higher poverty levels can be set for a higher number of family members.

Value-Added Tax (VAT)   As its name implies, this tax would be imposed upon the excess of value added to a product as measured by selling price over amounts

[1]However, the Tax Reform Act of 1976 allows a tax credit or reduction equal to 20% of the employment-related expenses up to $2,000, which would reduce taxes up to $400 for an eligible child. The maximum credit allowed is $800.

paid to suppliers of raw materials plus other costs of production. VAT is an idea which has received a great deal of attention recently since it has been introduced in the Common Market countries of Europe.

Because all firms keep the basic records necessary to compute VAT, it would presumably be easy to compute and administer. Ecological interest could be promoted by lowering or eliminating the VAT rate on recycled products. From the balance of payment standpoint, exports could bear a low tax, while imports could have higher rates.

On the other hand, it has been contended that VAT is regressive—hitting the lower income groups proportionately higher than those in the upper economic strata.

VAT will probably continue to be examined carefully in this country, though its likelihood of adoption in the near future is not particularly great.

Federal Revenue Sharing   The *revenue sharing* idea is based on the premise that local government units can spend money in their regions more efficiently than the federal government. In addition, local administration will be cheaper than Washington's supervising the process. Congress enacted revenue sharing in 1972.

Basically, the federal government returns to the states a portion of taxes collected during the preceding year. Distribution of the taxes among the various state and local governments is set by a complex formula including equity aspects such as population, income, and local taxes imposed in the various municipalities at the state and local level.

Revenue sharing allocations to the states for 1975 is shown in Table 17–3.

Regulatory Taxes   An excise tax is one that is levied upon various goods and commodities that are either considered harmful or nonessential.

In the former category are excise taxes upon liquor and tobacco. Excise taxes upon luxury items have been levied upon furs, jewelry, and even certain types of cosmetics. Often major consumer goods such as automobiles, tires, and major home appliances bear this type of tax.

Table 17-2
Hypothetical Negative Income Tax Example

Net Income before Income Taxes or Poverty Benefits	Income Taxes	Poverty Benefits	Net Income after Income Taxes or Poverty Benefits
$12,000	$1,000	—	$11,000
11,000	500	—	10,500
10,000	0	0	10,000
9,000	—	$ 500	9,500
8,000	—	1,000	9,000
7,000	—	1,500	8,500
6,000	—	2,000	8,000
5,000	—	2,500	7,500
4,000	—	3,500	7,500

Table 17-3
Federal Revenue Sharing, 1975

State	Dollars Received (in millions)	Percent of Total	State	Dollars Received (in millions)	Percent of Total
Alabama	$103.4	1.7	Nebraska	42.4	.7
Alaska	8.2	.1	Nevada	13.5	.2
Arizona	62.8	1	New Hampshire	20	.3
Arkansas	64.4	1	New Jersey	193.1	3.2
California	651	10.6	New Mexico	38.8	.6
Colorado	65.3	1.1	New York	687.7	11.2
Connecticut	78.8	1.3	North Carolina	157.8	2.6
Delaware	18.5	.3	North Dakota	22.2	.4
District of Columbia	26.9	.4	Ohio	245.4	4
Florida	188.6	3.1	Oklahoma	69.3	1.1
Georgia	130.1	2.1	Oregon	61.4	1
Hawaii	26.8	.4	Pennsylvania	325.7	5.3
Idaho	24.1	.4	Rhode Island	27.3	.5
Illinois	273.5	4.5	South Carolina	84.9	1.4
Indiana	128.5	2.1	South Dakota	26.1	.4
Iowa	86.1	1.4	Tennessee	120.6	2
Kansas	57.5	.9	Texas	293.2	4.8
Kentucky	99.6	1.6	Utah	36.2	.6
Louisiana	139.7	2.3	Vermont	17.3	.3
Maine	38.2	.6	Virginia	121.6	2
Maryland	119.8	2	Washington	87.3	1.4
Massachusetts	194.7	3.2	West Virginia	60.9	1
Michigan	262.1	4.3	Wisconsin	154.8	2.5
Minnesota	122.4	2	Wyoming	10.8	.2
Mississippi	98.6	1.6	Total distributed		
Missouri	116.6	1.9	by Department		
Montana	24.9	.4	of Treasury	$6,129.4	100.0

Source: Statistical Abstract, 1976.

Excise taxes are basically added on to the cost of the goods bearing them and so are essentially passed on to the buyers of the goods. As a result, these taxes can be used as a rationing device. Thus it is proposed that the excise tax be increased upon gasoline. However, whether gasoline is currently a "luxury" item is certainly open to question. If it is not, and gasoline consumption remains largely unaffected, increased taxes will not only fail as a rationing method but those who are least able to pay may well be hurt the most.

REGULATION

Regulation by the federal government refers to its power to control various aspects of business operations in the private sector.

Regulation occurs for two reasons. Efficient operations in some industries require that the size or scale of plant be so large that only a monopoly (or near monopoly) can perform the task economically. As a result, a certain degree of regulation is necessary to protect the public from the power that could be exerted if monopolies were enabled to run unchecked. Examples of industries falling into this category include electric power, radio and television networks and stations, railroads, and airlines. These industries are often called "natural monopolies."

Second, even where natural monopolies are not the rule, pressures to grow in size could easily create monopolies.

Government regulation against monopoly and other forms of protection has taken the form of (1) the passage of laws and (2) the creation of administrative agencies or bureaus to administer the laws. These agencies operate under various departments (Commerce, for example) in the executive branch of government.

While the two phases of regulation (laws and administrative agencies) are virtually inseparable, we shall briefly examine each in turn.

REGULATORY LAWS

By the late 1800s, a significant amount of concentration and control of major industries often resided in a relatively few hands. Industries in which a large degree of monopoly was present included petroleum, sugar, and lead.

The instrument through which economic control often was exercised was known as a *trust*. The owners of majority shares of stock in competing firms transferred their shares to a trust. They would receive, in exchange, trust certificates entitling them to share in the profits of the trust, which in turn, controlled the previously competing corporations. As a result, trust profits were larger than the combined separate corporate profits would have been as a result of the growth of monopoly power and the reduction of competition.

As a result of this practice, laws intending to curb trusts were called *antitrust laws,* a name which has continued down to this day even though the trust arrangement itself has long since been illegal.

Sherman Anti-Trust Act (1890)   The act states that conspiracies and combinations in the trust form (or any other form) as well as conspiracies having as their desired end, the "restraint of trade or commerce among the several states, or with foreign nations, is hereby declared to be illegal." Violators of this act are subject to a fine of $5,000 or one year in prison or both.

While the act was useful in breaking up the Standard Oil Trust and the Tobacco Trust, it was somewhat vague and ambiguous when applied to specific interpretations.

Clayton Act (1914)   This act was intended to clarify and strengthen the Sherman Act. Its principal provisions include the following:

1. Price discrimination or differentiation which intends to "lessen competition or to tend to create a monopoly" is prohibited. Different prices could exist if they were lessened to meet competition or where quantity or quality differentials between buyers are present (further clarification on price discrimination occurred in the Robinson-Patman Act of 1936).

2. "Tying contracts" were specifically prohibited. When corporations had a patented item, these contracts had forced buyers to acquire other products in the manufacturer's line if they desired the patented item.

3. Corporations were prohibited from acquiring significant amounts of the capital stock of competing companies "where the intent was to lessen competition or to create a monopoly." This section of the act was strengthened by the Celler-Kefauver Act of 1950.

4. Interlocking directorates were prohibited. These arose when a person served on the board of directors of competing corporations.

Robinson-Patman Act (1936)   As a result of the growth of large retail chains, a common practice was the demanding of price concessions from wholesalers. Whereas the Clayton Act prevented price discrimination on the part of the seller, the same basic idea was extended to buyer-oriented price discrimination intending to lessen competition in interstate commerce. Where different costs arise due to actual differences in manufacturing, delivering, or selling, different prices are allowed. This act is enforced by the Federal Trade Commission.

Celler-Kefauver Act (1950)   This act strengthened the Clayton Act by preventing the purchase of the assets of a competing firm as well as the capital stock thereof where the intent is to lessen competition. As a result, all types of mergers were prohibited where the intention has been to lessen competition.

REGULATORY COMMISSIONS

As previously mentioned, regulatory commissions have been created to enforce the law. Much has been written about the influence upon them by the very industries that they are presumed to be regulating. Often members of these commissions having important decision-making powers either come from the industries they are supposed to be regulating or take lucrative jobs in these industries after leaving government service (and sometimes both).

Obviously a reason why individuals often come from the regulated industries is because they possess knowledge about an industry. Alternatively, a reason for taking jobs with regulated firms after concluding federal service arises because of the connections made in government circles and the presumed influence acquired by working in Washington.

If this facet of administrative and regulatory agencies could somehow be changed, decision making and enforcement of the law would become more effective. Only a few of the hundreds of governmental agencies are discussed here.

Interstate Commerce Commission (ICC) (1889)   The ICC was created by the Interstate Commerce Act for the purpose of regulating railroad rates. The problem arose because for many years the railroads had ripped off farmers through excessively high freight rates.

Today the power of the commission has been extended into most areas of interstate transportation and commerce, including bus, truck, and certain types of pipelines.

Federal Trade Commission (FTC) (1914)   This commission was created to enforce the Clayton Act and to prohibit unfair methods of competition in interstate commerce. Over the years it has worked against false and deceptive advertising and also misleading packaging practices.

Federal Power Commission (FPC) (1920)   The FPC was created by the Federal Water Power Act of 1920. In addition to controlling water power resources, the commission regulates interstate electric and natural gas utility rates (power companies operating strictly within a state have their rates controlled by state public utility commissions).

Federal Communications Commission (FCC) (1939)   The Communications Act of 1939 resulted in the creation of the FCC. The commission controls the licensing (and renewal thereof) of radio and television stations.

   This very brief sampling of the many agencies at the federal level gives an idea of the extensive involvement of the federal government in regulating business in the private sector of the economy. Whether there is too much government control and interference, or perhaps, how it should be reshaped are interesting questions. Certainly politicians desiring to play on citizens' fears of "big government" have not hesitated to use the federal bureaucracy as a very convenient whipping boy. These questions are simply impossible to be addressed in detail here. Perhaps the more responsive business itself is to societal problems and dangers, the smaller the bureaucracy will be.

PROTECTION

Much of the legislation designed to regulate business activity has been formulated to protect consumers and the general public. In recent years, due to a vigorous and vocal movement on the part of consumers to protect their interest in the marketplace, government has responded with many new laws and agencies, and has increased the authority of some existing agencies to patrol the public's interest. The protective role of government has been extended to the following areas: (1) food, drugs, and cosmetics; (2) product safety; (3) labeling; and (4) environmental control. Much of the detailed discussion of these topics is reserved for Chapters 18 and 19, with implications and possibilities for business as it plans for the future. The following applicable laws and agencies illustrate how government attempts to protect the interest of the public.

FOOD, DRUG, AND COSMETIC ACT

Although the Food and Drug Administration (FDA), now a part of the Department of Health, Education, and Welfare, was established in 1906, the authority was increased with the enactment of the Food, Drug, and Cosmetic Act in 1938 and the Food Additives Act in 1958. Powers of the FDA include insistence on sanitary methods of manufacture, purity of content, and accurate labeling of all food and drugs. Packages must show accurate weights, ingredients in proportion from greatest to smallest, and whether dyes or preservatives are used. Drugs must be labeled as to use and, if the drug is habit-forming, a statement indicating this must be included on the label. Heavy penalties are provided for violators of the law, with maximums of $10,000 in fines and imprisonment of three years for deliberate intent to defraud or mislead.

Close scrutiny of drug manufacturing has resulted in the removal of unsafe drugs from the market. In recent years the FDA has been responsible for the elimination of cyclamates from many diet-type soft drinks.

CONSUMER PRODUCT SAFETY ACT

One of the most significant consumer protection laws is the Consumer Product Safety Act of 1972. The basic goal of this law is to reduce injuries, deaths, and other economic losses associated with consumers' use of products. To accomplish this objective, Congress established an independent regulatory commission with

Federal regulations require cigarette packages to carry this warning.

Warning: The Surgeon General Has Determined That Cigarette Smoking Is Dangerous to Your Health.

two different, but complementary, areas of power: (1) the development of physical standards for product safety and (2) the dissemination of information for educating consumers on safe use of products. The latter area has received much less attention than the first, but in some respects it may offer greater potential for accomplishing the basic goal of reducing injuries and deaths.

Included among the products under the jurisdiction of the Commission are household and recreational products, flammable fabrics, and motor transport vehicles. It is estimated that some 20 million injuries and 30,000 deaths occur annually as a result of household and recreational accidents alone![2] Certainly, efforts of the Commission directed toward improving the physical standards for product safety and educating consumers in safe product use offer substantial potential in reducing economic loss to society.

LABELING ACTS

A labeling act of interest is the Automobile Information Disclosure Act of 1958, which is concerned with pricing. Under this act the manufacturer is required to show the suggested retail price of each new vehicle itemized as to base price, freight costs, and price of extra equipment.

Other labeling acts which deal with raw materials rather than price are the Wool Products Labeling Act of 1939, which requires that all wool products be labeled to show fiber weight, the percentage of nonwool filling, and the manufacturer; the Fur Products Labeling Act of 1951, which requires that the name of the animal that produced the fur as well as the manufacturer be included on the label; and the Textile Fibers Product Identification Act of 1958, which requires the use of labels that show the percentage of natural and synthetic fibers used in the manufacture of cloth and other materials. These laws are enforced by the Federal Trade Commission. In 1960 Congress passed the Hazardous Substances Labeling Act, whose jurisdiction was given to the Food and Drug Administration.

ENVIRONMENTAL CONTROL LAWS

With the public's concern about pollution, the wasteful use of limited natural resources, and urban blight, a new direction in federal protective legislation has been occurring in the 1960s and 1970s. Chapter 19 has an extensive treatment of the causes, problems, and possible social costs of pollution and environmental protection. Undoubtedly, solutions will demand the cooperative efforts of the public, business, and government.

PROMOTION

One of the often overlooked roles of government is its very active influence in promoting and stimulating scientific and technological advances. From the very beginning of this nation, the federal government has supported research and development (R&D) for and in industry. George Washington, for example,

---

[2] U.S. Department of Health, Education, and Welfare, "Accident Study, 1968" in *Product and Injury Identification*, Appendix D, Supplemental Studies, vol. I, National Commission on Product Safety, June 1970 (New York: Law-Arts Publishers, 1971).

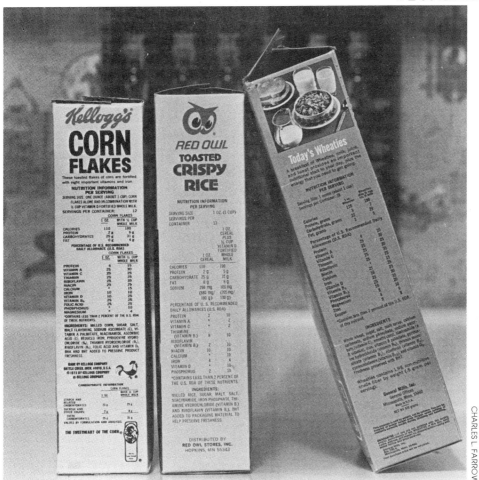

Many of the food products sold today list their nutritional content as an aid to the consumer.

wanted to create a national university centered about scientific research.[3] Through grants of land, the federal government supported the growth of railroads in our early history. With the passage of the Hatch Act of 1887, experiment stations were set up at land-grant institutions which were instrumental in stimulating the productivity revolution in agriculture. Hybrid corn, for example, is a product of agricultural research at the land-grant universities. More recently, the National Aeronautics and Space Administration (NASA) Apollo program represents billions of dollars of federal expenditures to support R&D in outer space. This has been done primarily because of the potential benefit of the space program for the military, but the possibilities of many nonmilitary applications exist in our space explorations. Communication satellites is one example of the latter.

Since the bulk of federal R&D expenditures is made through industry, the question arises: Why not spend federal funds in government departments rather than in industry? Following World War II the government abandoned the practice of spending most of its R&D in arsenals, which it owned and operated to

[3]George A. Steiner, *Business and Society*, 2d ed. (New York: Random House, 1975).

develop and produce military equipment. It was simply much more efficient and effective to look to industry rather than its own departments for research, development, and production. While it cannot be said that the aerospace industry, for example, is private like the automobile industry, the aerospace-government industrial complex follows much more closely the private industrial than the government model.

Many people argue that the government should support, to a greater extent, pure research rather than applied research. *Pure research* refers to scientific work attempting to answer basic questions but which has no immediate practical usage, though it conceivably might later. Attempts to split or smash the atom were originally seen as having no practical use, but it has led to applications in weapons and energy production. *Applied research* attempts to solve problems of immediate practical usage. Agricultural research to develop hardier strains of wheat is a good example of applied research.

While this argument no doubt has validity, it is more difficult to assign priorities to basic scientific efforts than to applied research activities. It is not easy to forecast the effects of basic scientific discoveries on the rest of science. Scientists often will disagree on the impact of basic scientific efforts on other research and ultimately society, as well as what constitutes a good balance of research funds among the scientific disciplines. It is then understandable that politicians find this a complex area in which to make decisions.

There are some signs that the federal government is giving more attention to scientific research. During the fiscal year period 1969–1975, the largest growth in terms of percent of total R&D expenditures has been in energy development and conversion, and the environment. Space R&D has decreased considerably—from 24 percent in fiscal year 1969 to an expected level of 13 percent of all federal R&D in fiscal year 1975. The relative prominence of other programs in the total R&D picture during the same period has remained fairly constant.

Breaking down federal R&D expenditures ($19.6 billion for 1975) by major categories yields the following percentages: national defense (52 percent), space (13 percent), health (10 percent), energy development and conversion (5.1 percent), science and technology—that is, basic, nonapplied research (3.9 percent), natural resources (3.8 percent), and transportation and communications (3.6 percent). It is expected that more emphasis will be placed on scientific and technological efforts, environmental, energy and natural resources research in the future. Policy decisions in the R&D area will need to be made by more technically oriented persons who also have a broad economic, political, and social outlook.

STABILITY

One of the most visible and important functions of the federal government is its role in maintaining economic stability by preventing frequent downturns in business and economic activity. A decline in business and economic activity brings in its wake a rising unemployment rate. A high rate of unemployment results in massive human misery, which can lead to social unrest and possible government instability if not overthrow.

The Apollo 11/Saturn V space vehicle carrying Apollo 11 astronauts Neil Armstrong, Michael Collins, and Edwin Aldrin lifted off on July 16, 1969 to begin the first manned lunar landing.

UNEMPLOYMENT

Unemployment today in the United States is said to be largely *structural* in nature. That is, it tends to hit some groups much harder than others. For example, in early 1977 the overall national unemployment rate was approximately 8 percent. However, among teenagers it was 19.2 percent, among blacks, 13.7 percent, and for black teenagers, 35.2 percent.

Business Cycles Declines in business and economic activity—depending upon their intensity—are called recessions or depressions. Recessions and depressions have occurred at fairly regular intervals throughout United States history. The regular recurrence of significant declines in output of goods and services followed by a rebounding of the economy to a high level of output is called the *business cycle*.

Causes   Many possible reasons have been advanced for the fluctuating pattern of business activity, including changes in sunspot activity which adversely affect agriculture which, in turn, adversely affects other areas of business activity.

Perhaps the most plausible reasons advanced are (1) declines in demand by business for investment in new plant and equipment and (2) undesired increases in inventories which cut demand for future orders. Both of these have a cumulative effect and result in tremendous declines in business and industrial activity. Adding to these declines in economic activity is a loss of confidence in business prospects. So psychological factors add further to the intensity of the downswing. When confidence returns, activity is stimulated and the economy rebounds.

INFLATION

There is a second extremely important aspect of economic stability: prevention of excessive inflation. *Inflation* can be described as a decline in the purchasing power of money or simply rising prices for goods and services.

The United States had a fairly steady inflation from the end of World War II to the early 1970s. However, since the early 1970s, the rate of inflation has

The unemployment line.

CHARLES L. FARROW

increased sharply. Consumer prices increased by approximately 48 percent between 1967 and 1974, and wholesale prices increased by a full 60 percent between those same dates.

Causes of Inflation   One of the principal causes of inflation today appears to
be a *concentration of economic power in the hands of big business and labor unions.* In
this situation large segments of the labor force can get huge wage increases when
their contracts expire. In turn, the companies and industries affected raise prices
to compensate for the rise in their labor costs. It is important, however, to remember that this is a chicken-egg type of problem. Which is cause and which is
effect is virtually impossible to say. It is clear, however, that the cycle of rising
prices and rising wages is a chronic inflationary problem affecting our society.

A relatively recent but important factor in inflation is *supply shortages.* The
outstanding example has been in petroleum, where the industrialized nations of
the West plus Japan have been unable to supply their own needs. Prices from
the oil-supplying nations have jumped sharply, contributing to the inflationary
spiral.

Growth of the government sector has also added to the inflationary spiral. It
should be remembered that the government itself is an important consumer and
also produces a vast array of diverse goods and services from swine flu shots to
construction of roads, bridges, and dams. The sheer growth of the government
sector, as well as the cost of goods and services it provides, has undoubtedly
contributed extensively to rising prices.

One of the classic causes of inflation has been *excessive demand for goods and
services.* This is a phenomenon of economics that often occurs when an economy
is operating at a full employment level. When demand for goods and services
increases, if an economy is operating at full employment, producers cannot easily increase output. The only other possibility then occurs: prices rise.

UNEMPLOYMENT AND INFLATION

In the past, unemployment has essentially been a problem of recession and depression, while inflation has mainly been a problem of good economic times. One
of the most important points about our current economic history is that unemployment and inflation have both been major problems at the same time. This
makes the problem of bringing them both under control extremely difficult, as
the Phillips curve graphically shows.

The Phillips Curve   The most important point to remember about the problems of unemployment and inflation is that remedies taken to reduce the effects
of one problem often increase the seriousness of the other one. For example,
increasing taxes, which cuts down the public's buying, can effectively check inflation. However, it could seriously affect the level of economic activity, including
increasing the level of unemployment.

The adverse relationship, or trade-off effect, between inflation and unemployment was noted by an English economist, A. W. Phillips, who showed the
results in what has become known as the Phillips Curve. The Phillips Curve for
the United States from 1960 to 1974 is shown in Figure 17–2. Notice the general
pattern of higher unemployment with low inflation rates and the opposite effect.
In 1974, a huge jump in inflation occurs *without* a reduction in unemployment.

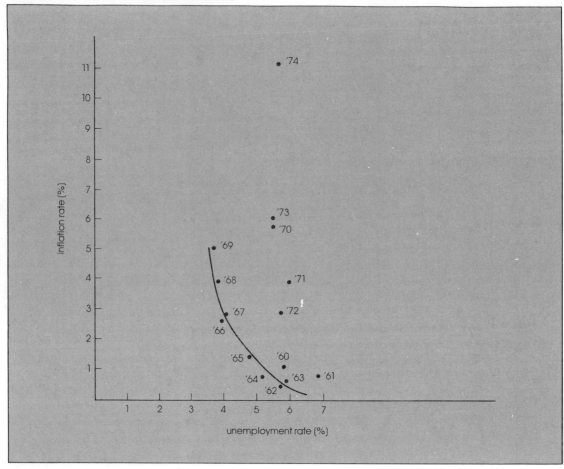

Figure 17-2 Phillips Curve for the United States, 1960–
1974. (Source: **Macroeconomics** by J. Carl Poindexter,
The Dryden Press, 1976, p. 370.)

Indeed, the years since 1970 indicate that the curve may be shifting to the right,
a potentially dangerous situation.

THE ROLE OF GOVERNMENT
IN THE ECONOMY

Given that unemployment and inflation are opposing problems, what should the
role of government be? A classic confrontation between opposing political views
has resulted. Those advocating an active role by government are called *liberals,*
while those championing a more passive governmental role are called *conservatives.* Labels are, of course, dangerous. Many people coming under the same
label may have important differences of opinion. Nevertheless, what follows is an
attempt to state the essentials of each position.

The Liberal View   Liberals have advocated a positive role by the government
in terms of its taxing and spending powers for the purpose of achieving full
employment. Thus if economic activity decreases, liberals often desire more gov-

ernment borrowing and spending to offset the decline in the private sector. Conversely, if economic activity proceeds too rapidly—affecting price increases more than output—liberals often desire an increase in taxes to check inflation.

In order to bring unemployment down to a more tolerable 3 to 4 percent level, it is estimated that the economy must grow at a rate of 6 percent a year between 1976 and 1981. Roughly 2 million more jobs a year must be created to stem unemployment and provide jobs for new entrants to the work force.

Liberals advocate very positive moves in retraining workers and teaching needed job skills to teenagers and minorities suffering from structural unemployment. Some would even go as far as making the federal government itself an employer of last resort by enlisting those who cannot otherwise get jobs in various kinds of constructive work.

The last step has occurred in the past. During the 1930s the Civilian Conservation Corps was set up by the government to utilize the unemployed in various public works projects.

The Conservative View   Conservatives are distrustful of big government. They feel that a large bureaucracy is inefficient and wasteful. Many programs eat up huge numbers of dollars and return very little in the form of benefits to those who are supposed to be helped. Furthermore, conservatives believe that big government can lead to an erosion of incentive in the private sector.

There are two important aspects of the conservative viewpoint. One positive role of the federal government should be properly controlling the money supply (how the Federal Reserve System does this was discussed in Chapter 12). To prevent excessive inflation, the monetary supply should be kept roughly constant except for allowing it to increase as population increases. Hopefully this would provide enough "liquidity" to allow the economy to operate effectively. Maintaining the fiscal integrity of the dollar is thus a paramount concern of conservatives.

The second thrust of the conservative program is to provide appropriate incentive to the private sector. This follows from their distrust of government and their belief in its inefficiency.

One example of incentives to business is in the form of the *investment credit.* For acquisition of most new machinery and equipment, business gets an income tax reduction of up to 10 percent of the cost of eligible new equipment and machinery. The desired result is to stimulate business activity in the form of new investment through the tax reduction incentive. The intended result, then, is to create more jobs in the private sector.

These opposing viewpoints—liberal versus conservative—constitute one of the most important issues facing our citizens and the businesses they own and for which they work.

SUMMARY

Government activity embraces a huge number of products, services, and activities, many of which have an important effect upon business. This chapter has attempted to develop a framework for classifying government legislation, regulatory agencies, and policy activity, particularly as it applies to business.

The equity function pertains to the government's effort to aid disadvantaged segments of the population such as the elderly and minorities. The income tax structure appears to be geared toward bringing about equity because of its progressive tax rates. However, a huge array of tax shelters for the wealthy undermines its progressive intention.

The regulatory function arises because of the need to prevent monopolies and to control those businesses which must operate as monopolies, or near monopolies, due either to technical reasons or the need to have an extremely large scale of operations in order to operate efficiently.

Another necessary facet of government operations lies in the area of protection. The rise of the consumer movement makes this a particularly important and controversial function today.

A somewhat neglected activity of government lies in the area of promotion. Government aid and grants have been instrumental in setting up America's land-grant institutions as well as aiding and developing important scientific research.

The stability function refers to the government's attempts to prevent or minimize severe economic fluctuations. At the present we have both a high rate of inflation and high unemployment.

Conservative and liberal remedies differ in terms of the role of the government in solving these problems. Liberals desire a more active role by government, whereas conservatives are more distrustful of the ability of government to overcome these problems.

DISCUSSION QUESTIONS

1. Why is our federal income tax structure, in theory at least, an instrument of equity?

2. Relative to the negative income tax, why is there a conflict between the maintenance of a minimum poverty level on the one hand and the possible losing of personal incentive on the other?

3. Do you think substantial excise taxes on gasoline will significantly lower consumption of gasoline?

4. How can price discrimination lessen competition? Is it restricted just to sellers?

5. What is the government function of protection and how does it differ from regulation?

6. Why do you think a partnership arrangement between government and industry has arisen in areas such as aerospace research?

7. What are the principal differences between the liberal and conservative views for maintaining economic stability and growth?

SHORT CASES

Kuhns Company

Some government tax policies are intended to stimulate investment through benefits to the private sector so that employment and production will be increased.

For example, take the case of the Kuhns Company. If it buys a fixed asset costing $120,000 with a five-year life, the annual depreciation is an expense which is deducted from revenues in arriving at taxable income. Most firms like to use a level or straight-line calculation of depreciation in their annual report to stockholders. This is determined by dividing the cost of the asset by the estimated years of useful life ($120,000 ÷ 5 = $24,000). If this amount were also used for tax purposes, the annual tax saving, assuming a 48% tax rate, would be $11,520 ($24,000 × .48).

Among the incentive benefits given by the government are the investment credit and accelerated depreciation. The investment credit is a flat reduction in the firm's income tax equal to a maximum of 10 percent of the cost of new fixed assets. Accelerated depreciation allows the firm to speed up its depreciation deductions for tax purposes (the firm can still use the level depreciation amounts for financial reporting purposes).

One type of accelerated depreciation for Kuhns would show the following depreciation for each of the five years:

Year	Tax Depreciation
1974	$40,000
1975	$32,000
1976	$24,000
1977	$16,000
1978	$ 8,000

For each of the five years, show the amount of the tax benefits received by the firm from the investment credit and accelerated depreciation. Is there any difference between the total allowable tax benefits stemming from accelerated depreciation versus level or straight-line depreciation? If not, why is accelerated depreciation for tax purposes considered to be so important by businessmen? Can you see any situations where the use of accelerated depreciation could actually result in smaller total taxes paid by business over an extremely long period of time? Why do you think that firms like to use straight-line depreciation for reporting to stockholders even though they use accelerated depreciation for tax purposes?

Fair Packaging and Labeling Act of 1967

The Fair Packaging and Labeling Act of 1967 includes among its provisions the following types of information on grocery products:

1. Giving pricing information per unit of weight such as cents per pound or ounce to enable the consumer to make comparisons among competing products.
2. Indicating the last date that a product should be used.
3. Giving information in units such as a bowl or glass relative to the proportion of recommended daily allowances of vitamins, minerals, and other ingredients contained by the product.

Which type of government activity (or activities) in terms of those developed in this chapter is this law attempting to accomplish? What do you think some of the arguments might be, both pro and con, relative to this law?

SUGGESTED READINGS

Alexander, Tom. "The Deceptive Allure of National Planning." *Fortune.* (March 1977): 186–189, 192, 194, 198.

"Is John Sherman's Antitrust Obsolete." *Business Week,* March 23, 1974, pp. 46–56.

Weidenbaum, Murray. "The High Cost of Government Regulation." *Business Horizons* 18 (August 1975): 43–51.

"Why the Corporate Lobbyist is Necessary." *Business Week,* March 18, 1972, pp. 62–65.

THE HUMAN CHALLENGE

LEARNING OBJECTIVES

When you finish this chapter you should:

☐ understand the consumer movement and the rise of consumerism in recent years and how it relates to business.

☐ be familiar with some of the ways businesses have attempted and may attempt to deal with consumer problems.

☐ be aware of the problems and opportunities confronting business in minority employment and how some businesses are responding to minority employment.

☐ understand selected societal issues such as urban redevelopment and black enterprise development.

KEY TERMS TO BE LEARNED FROM THIS CHAPTER

affirmative action programs
consumerism
consumer rights
reverse discrimination

Everyone does not agree on what the social responsibilities of business should be in a relatively free enterprise economy. Milton Friedman, a well-known economist, contends that the business of business is to maximize profits. His contention suggests that the notion of social responsibility for business is fundamentally at odds with the concept of shareholders' financial interest. Friedman's thesis holds that for a firm to engage in acts which cannot be clearly justified in terms of profitability is to engage in "taxation without representation." It constitutes taxation of investors by depriving them of potential earnings, taxation of consumers by making them pay more for the firm's goods and services, and taxation of employees by depriving them of the potential earnings additional profits might engender. He adds that, to the extent that investors or customers or employees want their money devoted to good works, they should be free to devote it to the good works of their choosing rather than those selected by management. This you recognize as essentially the laissez-faire credo of Adam Smith discussed in Chapter 1.

Many scholars and social critics today disagree with the point of view which assigns to business the sole goal of profit maximization. A list of well-known dissenters includes John Kenneth Galbraith, Vance Packard, the late Rachel Carson, and Ralph Nader. The position of those who call for an expanded social role for American business is summarized well by a scholar, Dr. Clark Kerr, in an essay for the President's Commission on National Goals.[1] Dr. Kerr acknowledges that our economic system has brought the average individual rich benefits in health, material goods, and leisure. But it has also created large and powerful organizations exerting an increasing amount of influence over individuals' choices, and making them more dependent on the decisions of these organizations. The economic success or failure of an individual or a private group today may depend on or may affect many others. The complexities—possible costs and potential benefits—of many projects are completely beyond the scope of private individuals to assess and undertake. Industrialization has resulted in new concepts of public responsibility and public endeavors. Certainly, many business persons today respond to the view expressed by a former chairman of the board of AT&T, Cleo F. Craig, who says:

> No one can accept responsibility in the world unless he takes it first on his own doorstep. So for us in industry, I can see only one sure course to follow. Call it common sense, call it policy, call it anything you like. To my mind, industry must aim for, and everlastingly operate for good of the community. The community can't ride one track and business another. The two are inseparable, interactive, and interdependent.[2]

It is the position of the authors of this book that business is not only accountable to its direct public—consumers, stockholders, and employees—but should also assume an expanded social role in protecting the environment, contributing to the solution of the energy shortage, assisting public bodies in urban redevelopment, and providing leadership in improving the quality of life for the general public. The remainder of this chapter will deal with businesses' respon-

[1] The American Assembly Goals for Americans, The Report of the President's Commission on National Goals, Essay No. 6 (New York: Prentice Hall, 1960).
[2] Abram T. Collier, "Social Responsibilities of the Businessman," *Management Review* 46 (July 1957): 62.

sibilities and challenges in the areas of consumers and consumerism, minority employment, and urban redevelopment.

CONSUMERS AND CONSUMERISM

In Chapters 8 and 9, the functioning of the marketing system was analyzed, basically from the viewpoint of management. We can now expand that view by noting that the social role of marketing includes the creation and delivery of a standard of living to society. Even though this system has been responsible for delivering unparalleled consumption levels, there is a growing consumer concern and dissatisfaction with the delivery system. This movement is frequently referred to as consumerism. It includes the range of programs by government, businesses, and independent groups designed to promote and protect consumers' interests from practices that infringe upon their rights as consumers.

The following hypothetical example is illustrative of the infringement upon consumer rights and need for consumer protection:

> Take the case of Clifton Berg of Tulsa, Oklahoma. His color TV conked out. No sound, very little color. Two months and $175.00 later it still wasn't working to Berg's satisfaction. For the next three months he and his wife tried to get the repair shop to make proper repairs. At first the proprietor agreed, but he never showed up. Later he refused to come to the telephone, Berg said, until Mrs. Berg disguised her voice and asked to speak to him. Then he "became abusive and hung up," according to Berg. Finally, long after the trouble began the Bergs gave up and had the set fixed at another repair shop for an additional $155.00.

Unfortunately, similar cases occur too frequently in TV repair and many other product categories. News story captions such as the following appear almost daily in the media: "Sunshine Biscuit Products Contaminated with Pesticides"; "Iowa Auto Dealer Must Tell Guarantee Limits"; "TWA Pays CAB $87,000 in Overbooking Case"; and "Brake Flaw in GM Autos." It is not surprising that such examples of abuses in the marketplace have unleashed a wave of consumer intolerance that calls for a redirection of technology and marketing practices to the satisfaction of redefined goals of society.

CONSUMER RIGHTS

Society has rejected the preeminence of the seventeenth-century doctrine of caveat emptor (let the buyer beware), and has put in its place a consumer bill of rights. In his first consumer message to Congress in 1962, President John F. Kennedy enunciated four basic consumer rights:

1. The right to safety—to be protected against the marketing of goods which are hazardous to health or life.

2. The right to be informed—to be protected against fraudulent, deceitful, or grossly misleading information, advertising, labeling, or other practices, and to be given the facts needed to make an informed choice.

3. The right to choose—to be assured, wherever possible, access to a variety of products and services at competitive prices and in those industries in which government regulations are substantial, an assurance of satisfactory quality and service at fair prices.

4. The right to be heard—to be assured that consumer interest will receive full and sympathetic consideration in the formulation of government policy and fair expeditious treatment in its administrative tribunals.

Nearly a decade later, in 1971, President Richard M. Nixon reiterated the concept of buyers' rights, thereby acknowledging the federal government's role in consumer protection. President Nixon's buyers' rights include:

1. The right to make an intelligent choice among products and services.

2. The right to accurate information on which to make a free choice.

3. The right to expect that the health and safety of the buyer is taken into account by those who seek his patronage.

4. The right to register dissatisfaction, and have a complaint heard and weighed, when a buyer's interests are badly served.

CONSUMER LEGISLATION, 1962–1976

The appendix to this chapter summarizes the significant consumer protection legislation enacted during the twelve-year period since President Kennedy promulgated his now-famous concept of consumer rights. In addition to those laws enacted by Congress, numerous federal agencies have intensified their programs of consumer protection. The Food and Drug Administration has in recent years expanded its list of banned products, which includes cyclamates, hexachlorophene, and DES. The Federal Trade Commission has embarked upon a program of corrective advertising, required care labeling of textile wearing apparel, implemented a cooling-off period for door-to-door sales, and introduced a host of other consumer protection programs.

Not to be outdone by the federal government, state and local governments have become increasingly protective of consumers' interests. Massachusetts, Minnesota, Maryland, Connecticut, Delaware, Florida, New Jersey, Oregon, and South Dakota have instituted no-fault insurance laws; Indiana has a phosphate ban; Oregon has banned the use of aerosol cans; and California has regulated the product service and repair industry. These are a few of the state laws which illustrate states' growing interest in consumer rights.

Several objections are raised by some businessmen concerning government regulation. One is that it leads to further and repressive regulation—that is, regulations seldom fade away; instead, they proliferate. The process continues with additional and ever more confining rules until innovation is choked and business operating costs are increased. A second objection to government regulation concerns lack of uniformity in application. Differences from case to case in interpretation of regulation cause government regulation to be unpredictable, inequitable, and inexplicable in application. Still another objection, directed mainly at the Federal Trade Commission, which is the principal government agency concerned with consumer protection, is that the FTC functions as both the prosecutor and judge. Since the commission is concerned with the issuance of complaints, it may be unrealistic to expect them also to rule impartially when cases are argued. Business generally sees government regulation as a mixed blessing at best. It may serve to clarify, define, and make explicit acceptable and unacceptable rules of operation within an industry. But at the same time, it may be insensitive, inept, and costly from a business point of view.

SELF-REGULATION

Self-regulation is an obvious alternative. It is repeatedly called for by business people and some government officials. What does the experience show? A few companies and associations have undertaken pro-consumer activities. The advertising industry, in conjunction with the Better Business Bureau, has established the National Advertising Review Board to review complaints against national advertisers. Plans call for the organization of state review councils to combat misleading and fraudulent advertising on state and local levels. As of this writing, about a dozen state review boards have been organized. The composition of the state councils is similar to the membership of the national board—that is, heavily weighted on the side of advertisers and advertising agencies. It is too soon to evaluate the effectiveness of the national and state advertising review boards, but if the new organizations are too protective of the advertising industry, they will obviously be self-defeating.

Too many industries do not respond unless coerced by government regulation. Until the passage of the Fair Labeling and Packaging Act (1966), the food industry did virtually nothing to eliminate package-size proliferation or higher-price large "economy" sizes. The detergent industry had to be forced into developing biodegradable detergents, and then pressured into removing phosphates and enzymes from their products. The record to date suggests that voluntary action, while desired by many, is seldom adequate.

CONSUMER ORGANIZATIONS

Two consumer organizations, Consumers' Union and Consumer Research, provide consumers with product test information through their monthly publications, *Consumer Reports* and *Consumer Bulletin,* respectively. While the two organizations do not always agree in their product evaluations, they do provide independent sources from which consumers may validate some product claims of manufacturers. *Consumer Reports,* the larger of the two publications in circulation, reaches directly about 3,000,000 families each month, and indirectly a much larger total audience through library circulation, word-of-mouth communication, and borrowed issues. Intense allegiance has been built by Consumer Union's policies of not accepting advertising, of not permitting companies to use their product rating in promotion, and of attempting to learn purchase problems of their members.

In recent years consumer organizations have become more aggressive and active in pushing for consumer legislation in areas of product safety, informational labeling, and truth-in-lending. Through the Consumer Federation of America, consumer organizations now have a common base to pool their financial and informational resources to make a greater impact in the political arena than previously.

To the extent that consumer organizations are successful in obtaining favorable consumer legislation, all consumers benefit. However, most of the members of the consumer organizations—consequently, the primary users of product test information—represent social groups that are well educated and have high incomes. Consumer Union reports the following data on the composition of its membership: 63 percent are professional or managerial; 79 percent attended college and have median age of forty years. Unfortunately, the low-income groups, who need valid product information most in their purchases, seem to use it least. As David Caplovitz points out in his book *The Poor Pay More,* low-income groups are so heavily influenced by advertising and credit sellers in their quest to "keep up with Joneses" that more of the costly models of household equipment are purchased by those least able to afford such items. Generally, brand name loyalty is high where income is low. Consumer education programs, sponsored by state extension services, adult education classes, and community service agencies offer possible ways to deal with consumer problems among the low-income groups.

CONSUMER ACTION PROGRAMS

Consumers are becoming more active in their protests against business practices deemed as unjust, wasteful, or detrimental to the environment. Such actions have ranged from individually refusing to buy a product or shop at certain stores to the organization of consumer boycotts against businesses or products.

Few consumer boycotts have had the national impact of the meat boycott during the spring of 1973. Considerable support was generated by consumers to abstain from or reduce meat purchases in order to lower the rising meat prices. One isolated study[3] of the meat boycott identified three groups of consumers: those who did not boycott (nonboycotters); those who said they participated in and supported the boycott but also reported buying or consuming meat (alleged boycotters); and those who did not buy or consume meat during the boycott period (actual boycotters). Almost half the group was identified as alleged boycotters, with the remaining half about equally divided between the non-boycotters and actual boycotters. Actual boycotters were identified as being younger, more liberal, and more educated than nonboycotters and were more likely to attribute rising meat prices to external forces such as farmers, middle-men, and government. Their action was thus perceived as bringing pressure on these external forces to lower prices.

Generalizations from an isolated study have to be made with extreme caution. In other words, the question may be raised as to what extent the sample studied represents the whole population of consumers in the United States. Even within the limits of this one study, certain clues to consumer direct action may be discerned. With approximately three-fourths of the consumers either sympathizing with or participating in an organized boycott, consumer direct action has to be counted as a future potential power in the market place.

[3]Mazis and Faricy, Consumer Response to the Meat Boycott, 1974 Combine Proceedings, Series No. 39 (American Marketing Association, 1975).

Many companies have a consumer communications office which handles all sorts of complaints and problems.

CHARLES L. FARROW

BUSINESS RESPONSE TO CONSUMERISM

Consumerism is becoming too big an issue for business to ignore. The White House Office for Consumer Affairs says the number of complaints it receives now runs about 2,500 a month. The Federal Trade Commission says that the number of written public complaints received by the agency number over 35,000 annually.[4] Public-opinion surveys still indicate a relatively negative attitude toward big business. Some companies are initiating programs aimed at appeasing complaints and improving the customer relations with their companies. Some of the programs include:

[4]Antitrust and Trade Regulation Report, February 5, 1974, pp. E-1 to E-3.

1. Appointment of top-level officers to new positions solely concerned with consumer affairs. Some of the officials, such as those at Chrysler, Pan American Airways, and RCA, are vice-presidents. Swift & Company has instituted a position of director of public responsibility.

2. Installation of toll-free telephone lines for the use of consumers who wish to bypass dealers and other intermediaries and lodge complaints directly at headquarters. Others are advising consumers through advertising to forward their complaints to headquarters in writing.

3. Revamping their corporate structures to accommodate customers. Ford Motor Company has elevated its service division to a par with its sales division. This, according to a Ford executive, will allow district service managers more time to handle repair and service problems at a local level.

4. Undertaking programs to determine consumer reaction to sales and service operations of vendors and service people. Many companies follow up service calls with a questionnaire designed to find out whether the work was performed as scheduled and how satisfied the customer was with the performance. A large publisher of reference books revamped its door-to-door sales operations because of growing complaints about selling techniques. The new policy is to have a member of the credit department double-check every order with the purchaser before it is shipped to resolve any misunderstanding by overzealous salesmen. The company goes further and calls a random sample of its customers eight weeks after an order is shipped in order to solicit reactions to the company's books—and to its salesmen. Additionally, dissatisfied customers are invited to make collect calls to the headquarters to register their complaints.

FUTURE OF CONSUMERISM

There is little question that the consumer movement has made its impact on the American economy. Consumers no longer accept docilely their inability to make rational comparisons and judgments in the marketplace. Consumerism has brought to light a wide range of product deficiencies and service flaws. In government, both the executive and legislative branches have responded with programs to protect consumer interest, symbolizing an outward expression of the government's commitment to a consumer bill of rights. Beyond laws and regulations, there are some tangible responses of business and industry through self-regulation to the increasing criticism of consumer groups. There is a growing recognition both among industry and government that we must develop a system by which technology is evaluated in the light of conflicting or competing social goals. Today industry must submit to an annual fiscal audit; tomorrow it may have to submit to a new kind of audit: a social audit. Included in a social audit may be the answers to such complex questions as these: Do your products contribute to a significant human need? What is the short-term and long-term impact of your company's policies and practices on the environment? Is the company exploiting or conserving national resources? Do you exceed minimum product safety standards where economical and feasible? Of course such social objectives are more difficult to define and measure than financial objectives. But industry and government must seek to develop methods and procedures which can ascertain the social contributions of business.

EMPLOYEES

Traditionally employees were regarded as an expendable resource in business. In recent years, with the growth of unions and increased labor specialization, businesses are recognizing employees as a scarce resource. Coerced by massive union influence, a growing number of businesses are becoming sensitized to wage and working condition demands of employees. This is exemplified by the recent Coal Pact, negotiated between the United Mine Workers and the coal mining industry. The pact encompasses such areas as comprehensive safety training, grievance procedures for employees, individual rights to refuse to work in unsafe conditions, the establishment of local safety committees, increased access for union safety representative, and increasing cost-of-living clauses.[5]

Other unions are following the lead of the United Mine Workers. While some companies view these demands as simply pressure tactics to secure higher wages, others recognize the fact that they owe their employees safe working conditions, benefit packages that ensure security in times of trouble and upon retirement, and guaranteed wage increases that are comparable to cost-of-living increases. Company obligations in many of these areas have been discussed in Chapter 5, "Human Assets Management." In addition, labor unions were treated extensively in Chapter 6.

MINORITY EMPLOYMENT

With the Civil Rights Act of 1964 (and the subsequent amendments of 1972) that prohibits discrimination in the hiring of people on the basis of race, color, national origin, sex, or religion, minority employment became a key concern of

[5]Editorial, "A Goal Pact That Increases Safety and Output," *Business Week*, December 14, 1974, p. 76.

"You know, Jones, I'll take production problems over people problems any day."

American business and nonbusiness institutions. Often to secure federal contracts or to receive federal funding, management must provide evidence of minority recruitment, employment, and promotion.

For many years, American Indians, Mexican-Americans, blacks, and women were given only the menial jobs in business, if hired at all. The argument of inadequate training and education and poor work habits was often used to justify this practice. This argument, however, can lead to circular reasoning. Does low income lead to poor education and training, or does the lack of education and training produce low income? People caught in the vicious circle need assistance from an outside source. Government is one; business is another. Particularly in a free enterprise economy, the larger the role assumed by business, the less is needed from government.

ARE NONDISCRIMINATION LAWS EFFECTIVE?

It would seem logical that an employer would seek to hire and advance those employees best qualified for the job based on the needs of the firm. Such a policy would establish criteria based on merit and seniority. As plausible as this argument may sound, Congress believed it necessary in 1964 to enact legislation specifically prohibiting discrimination against individuals on the basis of race, color, religion, sex, or national origin. Is a federal statute necessary to ensure an attitude of nondiscrimination?

The experience of the federal government may help to clarify the issue. Larry E. Short[6] analyzes the employment picture of minorities in the federal government from 1940 to 1970. Three phases of concern for equality of opportunity are identified. The first phase began with the establishment of the Civil Service Act of 1833, which resulted in the creation of a government-wide merit system. Phase two began with President Franklin Roosevelt's proclamation in the 1940s against racial discrimination in the armed forces, in the federal government, and in companies engaged in defense efforts. Explicit policies of nondiscrimination in government-related employment were instituted in order to achieve full opportunity of employment for all citizens.

By the 1960s, the federal government recognized that mere enforcement of nondiscrimination policies was insufficient to insure equality of opportunity. New policies designed to create positive programs of equal opportunity were issued by President John Kennedy, and were continued and strengthened by Presidents Lyndon Johnson and Richard Nixon. Emphasis in the federal government was changed from seeking the absence of discrimination to requiring positive action to achieve equal employment through affirmative action programs. Affirmative action programs require an analysis of areas within which the employer is deficient in the utilization of minority groups and women in comparison with the external labor area. Further, goals and timetables are set to which the employer's good-faith efforts must be directed to correct the deficiencies.

The three phases of concern are shown in Table 18–1, with the percent of black employment in federal employment compared with the percent of blacks in the total population.

[6]Larry E. Short, "Nondiscrimination Policies: Are They Effective?" *Personnel Journal* 52, no. 9 (September 1973): 786–92.

As can be seen from Table 18–1, considerable differences occurred in the employment of blacks in federal employment as compared with the employment in general population for the three phases of concern. During the merit system, which ended in 1940, the proportion of blacks in federal government employment was far below the proportion of blacks in the total population. Policies of nondiscrimination, implemented during the 1940s and 1950s, are associated with significant increases in the employment of blacks. By 1960 the proportion of blacks in federal government employment was higher than the proportion of blacks in the total population. During the affirmative action phase of the Equal Employment Opportunity Act (EEOA), the proportion of blacks increased even more relative to the proportion in the total population. In addition to the data shown in Table 18–1, with affirmative action the proportion of blacks occupying intermediate and higher-level positions in government increased substantially.[7] Short concludes that:

1. A merit system to achieve equality of opportunity is not associated with significant accomplishments in the employment of minorities.

2. Policies of nondiscrimination are associated with significant achievements in minority employment, but do not seem to result in the advancement of minority employees.

3. Affirmative action programs to promote equality of opportunity are needed to achieve results in both employment and advancement of minority employees.

What are the implications of this experience for private business? In the past, the federal government has often utilized the experiences of the private sector in developing personnel policies and practices. Personnel analysts report that federal government personnel managers relied heavily on the labor relations experience gained in the private sector in developing collective bargaining programs.[8] In developing equal employment opportunity, private employers

[7]Ibid., p. 786.
[8]William B. Vosloo, *Collective Bargaining in the United States Federal Civil Service* (Chicago: Public Personnel Association, 1966), p. 89.

Table 18-1
Percent of Black Employees in Federal Employment
Compared with Percent of Black Population
in Total Population

Phase	Year	Black Employment as a Percent of Federal Employment	Black Population as a Percent of Total Population
Merit	1940	4.2	9.8
Nondiscrimination	1950	9.3	10.0
	1960	11.7	10.6
Affirmative action	1970	15.0	11.2

Source: Adapted from Table 1, Larry E. Short, "Nondiscrimination Policies:
Are They Effective?" **Personnel Journal** 52, no. 9 (September 1973): 790.

may note that affirmative action programs may be necessary in private employment just as they were necessary in federal employment to ensure full equality of opportunity and advancement of minority persons.

RESPONSE OF PRIVATE BUSINESS

There is some evidence that business is responding. Below are the performance records of several national firms in the area of social responsibility, including minority employment:[9]

Aetna Life & Casualty, Hartford
Largest stock-owned insurance company in nation. . . . Innovative social programs planned and executed under direction of corporate officer who holds title, "vice-president corporate social responsibility." . . . Has tried to integrate social concerns into business operations. . . . Examples: Promotion of low-cost group auto insurance, disclosure of life insurance policy costs, establishment of health maintenance organization groups. . . . Not afraid of backing antimanagement proxy resolutions offered by activists. . . . Minority employment 12 percent of staff, quadrupled in ten years. . . . Blacks on the board: yes. . . . Women on the board: yes.

Levi Strauss & Company, San Francisco
Manufacturers of world-famous Levi's (jeans). . . . Social thrust that few companies can match. . . . Acknowledged leader in numerous areas—product quality, minority employment (38 percent of total, 11 percent of officials and managers), utilization of women (15 percent of officials and managers, 4 percent of sales personnel), innovative support of minority economic development. . . . Strong community relations program at all plant sites . . . Seeks to allocate at least 3 percent of after-tax profits to social responsibility efforts. . . . Encourages employees to be socially concerned and socially active. . . . Blacks on the board: yes. . . . Women on the board: yes.

Xerox Corporation, Stamford, Conn.
One of the youngest companies in America is a social pioneer. . . . Annual charitable contributions now about the $7 million level. . . . Maintains an experimental Community Involvement Program. . . . Major supporter of United Negro College Plan. . . . Also major bankroller of public television. . . . Has social service leave program enabling employees to take full-pay leaves to work on social projects of their choosing. . . . Strongly encourages social involvement of all employees at all levels . . . . Number of minority group members working for Xerox has increased by more than sixfold since 1968 . . . . Settled antitrust action by agreeing to make patents available to all newcomers. . . . Blacks on the board: yes.

The above sketches on corporate social responsibility indicate what can be done. Unfortunately, many companies can be coerced into action only with lawsuits, and then only minimally. Especially in retailing, women are going to court to obtain pay equal with men for similar positions under the 1963 Equal Pay Act. More than 5 million women and more than 6 million men are employed in the

[9]Milton Moskowitz, "Profiles in Corporate Responsibility: The Ten Worst, The Ten Best," *Business and Society Review* 13 (Spring 1974).

Census Bureau category of retail trade. Even allowing for the likelihood of greater seniority and expertise among men, a $4,000-plus differential in average annual wages between the sexes can hardly be legally justified.[10] Courts are ruling that the retailers' argument that different departments of a store constitute differing selling establishments is not a valid basis for wage differentials. A store is a single selling unit in which men and women employed on jobs requiring "substantially equal skill, effort and responsibility" must be paid the same wage, according to a district court judge in Montgomery, Alabama.[11]

REVERSE DISCRIMINATION

In order to meet the requirements of the Civil Rights Act of 1964, many businesses and nonbusiness organizations have instituted affirmative action programs designed to indicate their hiring targets for women and minority groups. These hiring plans, or attempts to implement such plans, are resulting in a new set of social goal conflicts between white males and the hiring organizations under the label *reverse discrimination*. Being challenged are the seniority rule in labor unions and the tenure system in education. Some even suggest that we are entering a new era of discrimination on the basis of race, creed, color and sex in which a large number of qualified persons will pay with their careers simply because they are white males.

When management makes a conscious decision to hire minorities and women first, is this bias in reverse? Some say yes. In Los Angeles, the local chapter of B'nai B'rith Anti-Defamation League petitioned the University of California regents to halt the practice of hiring on such "nonrelevant" grounds as race, religion, or color.[12] Others say no. Some equal rights leaders believe that their male critics are overreacting. "The white male has not had to compete with anybody and now he suddenly has to compete with blacks and women," says the affirmative action coordinator at University of California.[13] In support of their programs, HEW officials point out that reverse discrimination is also clearly prohibited under federal law. Reverse discrimination is defined as the hiring or promoting of a minority or female person who is less qualified than a competing white male candidate. In order to correct past inequities in hiring and promotion practices, it may be necessary for employers to (1) eliminate individualistic processes of hiring and promotion, (2) eliminate screening tests which are discriminatory against minorities, and (3) consciously and by design seek minority and female candidates and even give preferential treatment to them only when their qualifications are equal to those of competing white males.

More difficult problems are encountered in work force layoffs and cutbacks. Unions maintain that the seniority rule (last hired, first fired) is necessary for the smooth operation of their organizations. Tenure systems in education which offer job security to longer-termed teachers over recent hires are supported on the basis of academic freedom. How can affirmative action programs effectively deal with these widely accepted practices? Again, it may be necessary, particu-

---

[10]Editor, "Equal Pay for Women Hits Retailers," *Business Week*, January 29, 1972, p. 76.

[11]Ibid.

[12]Editor, "Faculty Backlash," *Newsweek*, December 4, 1972, p. 128.

[13]Ibid.

CHARLES L. FARROW

WE'VE GOT A DOZEN GREAT IDEAS FOR THIS BUILDING. WE NEED A DOZEN GREAT OWNERS.

Many cities are trying to rebuild their downtown areas.

larly as a stopgap measure until equal opportunity is achieved, for employers to give preference to female or minority employees only when they have same time in grade as white male employees. These are complex problems for our society, and they can be resolved only with the good sense of management and equitable laws.

URBAN REDEVELOPMENT

One of the major challenges confronting American society is the restoration of its physically decaying, economically depressed, and socially troubled urban areas. Confronted with eroding tax bases as the middle-class population and businesses flee to the suburbs, and an excessive rise in the cost of services such as police protection, fire prevention, sanitation, and education, many American cities find themselves in dire financial straits. The agonizing thought on the minds of many business and political leaders is: How many cities will be faced with the same crisis as New York City in the next decade? In this section some of the underlying causes of urban decay will be examined along with some discussion of possible means for urban redevelopment. The focus will be on the combined role of business and government in restructuring and revitalizing massive urban areas.

HISTORICAL PERSPECTIVE

American cities began their massive growth and expansion in the late nineteenth and early twentieth centuries following the industrial revolution. Methods of mass production had created the goods and services to fill the demand for a broad, emerging middle class that was moving from the farms to the city. Improvements in farm technology freed people to leave the farms and move to the cities to seek their fortunes. Developments in modes of transportation—first by rail and then by trucks—permitted wide and swift distribution of products from the farms and industrial centers to reach concentrations of urban populations. In addition, train transportation allowed individuals to travel more easily between cities and rural areas. Communication improvements such as the telephone enabled rapid communication with other urban centers in the nation as well as the world.

Within the city, modes of transportation such as the streetcar and subway trains increased the range of commuting to the central city and led to the growth of "close-in" or "bedroom" suburbs. The commuter railroad pushed the suburbs even further out. People had a chance to combine working in the city with living in a suburban or even semirural area.

Later, the automobile became the prime mode for moving millions to and from the cities as outlying areas developed into communities, in some cases linking two or more cities together. Those cities which had their principal development prior to the automobile had fairly compact downtown districts. Centralized downtown areas usually included the cities' principal department and specialty stores, financial institutions, offices, and cultural establishments such as theaters, museums, and universities. Outside of the central district were business establishments, factories, and living areas offering easy access to downtown. Cities of this type, such as Boston, New York, Chicago, and St. Louis, developed in the East and Midwest.

Cities that had their primary development after the advent of the automobile were far more spread out. While automobiles made getting around easier, they also required more room for related space such as parking lots, garages, and freeways. Cities of this type were located in the West, with Los Angeles the obvious prototype.

After World War II, the automobile brought increased growth along with tremendous problems to both types of cities. To give the automobile access to and from the cities, freeway and expressway systems were punched in, leaving old, established living areas torn out in their wake. As cities continued to grow and expand, automobile pollution became a major problem.

In addition, significant economic and sociological problems developed. The continued growth and expansion brought about a loss of community and neighborhoods and an eroding tax base in which less money was available for school, streets, parks, city maintenance, and public services. To a large extent, individuals worked in the city but returned with their money to the suburbs in the evening. As a result, business suffered in many downtown areas and moved with the population to the suburbs, leaving a decaying city occupied generally by the economically disadvantaged.

FINANCIAL CRISIS OF THE AMERICAN CITY

All of these problems of the American city have created a new problem: financial crisis for the American city. In addition to the flight of people and business to the suburbs, urban blight, and erosion of the tax base, an additional problem has occurred. There has been an excessive rise in the cost of services such as police protection, fire prevention, sanitation, medical services, and education. In the case of cities like New York, which have spent rather lavishly, the result has been a push toward the financial brink.

Solving the overall economic and financial problems of the American city will require a very careful ordering of priorities because of the conflict between economic and environmental considerations and needs. While it is obviously too late to turn the clock back on the automobile and its effects, a possible key for improving the cities may lie in better and more reliable mass transit systems. If travel preferences can be changed from private to public, the changes may be beneficial from both the environmental and economic standpoints.

THE INNER CITY GHETTO

In its early developmental period, the American city provided an arena for personal growth and upward mobility. Areas such as the West End of Boston, South Philadelphia, and the legendary Lower East Side of New York became crowded ghettos. While money may not have been plentiful for most of their inhabitants, the tempo of life was interesting, and many people were able to take advantages of the opportunities afforded them with, in some cases, dramatic improvements in their economic well-being. In short, the "American dream" worked.

Today the situation has changed. With the suburban migration of many white Americans, the predominant groups left in the inner cities are blacks, Puerto Ricans, and Mexican-Americans. Intensified by the tearing down of old but in many cases livable homes and apartments for freeways, overcrowded living conditions developed in most of our large urban centers. Heightened by discriminatory housing and employment practices and poor schools, inner city America became plagued by unemployment, crime, drug addiction, racial strife, and physical decay. In most cases societal responses to these conditions were too little, too slow, and largely ineffective.

Government housing programs to aid the disadvantaged in the inner city have largely been a failure. The nation's federal housing laws are largely a patchwork of varied programs that are not well understood, well coordinated, or well administered. While the economically disadvantaged are supposed to be the recipients of help, a considerable portion of the federal subsidies have gone for federal and local administrative expenses and tax benefits to investors. In low-rent government housing, the projects were poorly planned and often became havens of crime and drug addiction. The famous Pruitt-Igoe project in St. Louis won an architectural award from the American Institute of Architects in 1956 but was largely abandoned by 1972. Many of the buildings were empty, ruined shells which were demolished to eliminate them from the scene.

As a result, inner city residents became victims of overcrowded living conditions, experienced high unemployment rates, and were subjects of racial discrimination and prejudiced attitudes. In addition, the federal government's housing programs were largely ineffectual in relieving the living conditions. The pent-up frustrations of ghetto life finally burst in the mid-1960s, with a series of riots breaking out in major cities across the country during what has been called "the long, hot summer months." While the riots dramatically pointed out the cancerous effect of ghetto life, they did little, if anything, to solve the problems. Ironically, the riots penalized the inhabitants of the inner city much more than the absentee landlords and business owners toward whom they were apparently directed.

What are the solutions to the decaying inner cities and ghetto life in America? Unfortunately, there are no easy and neat answers to the problems. Obviously, greater economic opportunities have to be made available for inner city dwellers. Some businesses are responding by providing financial, self-help, and technical assistance to organizations within inner cities. The Young Great Society (YGS), in a rundown area of west Philadelphia, is an interesting example of needed cooperation between business and inner city inhabitants. Ghetto-run and business-aided, the YGS operates the following projects: housing rehabilitation, a medical center, a drug rehabilitation center, education and recreation programs, a day care center, and a community newspaper. Funds for the operation of the projects are provided by foundations, a government agency, local churches, along with business. In addition, business offers planning and consulting services sponsored by University of Pennsylvania's Wharton School of Business. As in the case in YGS, the key to the success of such projects is often able and dedicated leadership among ghetto residents.

In St. Louis in four of the city's largest projects, the tenants are choosing a salaried manager from the ranks of their own members. The tenant-manager then heads a staff of both salaried and volunteer workers who perform the various functions of maintenance, protection, and general upkeep. So far the self-government appears to be working quite well; crime has been reduced, the buildings and surrounding area are in better shape, and civic pride has been enhanced.

BLACK ENTERPRISES

Entrepreneurial activity has typically been the bootstrap by which urban ethnic groups have elevated themselves to the mainstream of American life. The avenue seemed to have escaped American blacks, the dominant minority group of inner city America. Typically, black businesses have been dominated by small, marginal firms, mostly in personal services and food and drinking establishments. In Milwaukee, Wisconsin, for example, out of a total of approximately 260 black-owned businesses, over three-fourths were in small-scale personal services and retail trade.[14] No businesses were represented in manufacturing, and only a few in wholesale trade.

Nationally, there are more than 322,000 minority businesses, which produce over $3.3 billion in annual sales.[15] But with 17 percent of total population, minorities control less than one percent of the nation's business assets. The rea-

[14]Eddie V. Easley, *Negro Businesses in Milwaukee's Inner Core Area* (Madison: University of Wisconsin Press, 1967).
[15]Edward Brooke, "Black Business: Problems and Prospects," *The Black Scholar* 6 (April 1975): 2–7.

CHARLES L. FARROW

This hardware store manager has to know all phases of his
business's operations.

son is simple: the fields of concentration of black enterprises—small-scale retail
trade and personal services—are growing more slowly than the economy as a
whole.

Thus the need to diversify the range and focus of black-owned business is
paramount. In addition, the scale of operation has to be increased and the efficiency improved. There is an added problem that the two basic keys to success
in business—managerial skills and capital—are restricted or absent altogether
among black would-be entrepreneurs. In spite of these factors, there are a few
success stories.

With the establishment of the Office of Minority Business Enterprise
(OMBE) in 1969, the government made its first national commitment to aid
minority business development. OMBE was designed as a catalyst to stimulate
and coordinate a joint federal-private partnership to promising minority businesses with management and technical assistance. The Small Business Administration (SBA) also has an important role in spurring minority business enterprise, as it carries out the intent of the Small Business Investment Act and the
Minority Enterprise Small Business Investment Act. Under Section 8(a) of the
Small Business Act, SBA is permitted to obtain purchase contracts from other
federal agencies and to award subcontracts to minorities to help them become
owners of self-sustaining manufacturing, construction, and other related service

enterprises. Some fifteen hundred companies were assisted in 1975, with contracts totalling $250 million. The SBA loan guarantee program seeks to ensure the availability of capital to minority entrepreneurs.

Through these programs some progress has been made. However, a large gap remains unfilled. Most of the financing of minority business is done through extension of loans. While debt financing has been pursued, equity financing has largely been ignored. Equity financing through the private sector creates an opportunity for the investor, who supplies the venture capital, to become a partner in the enterprise. This brings to the business venture not only capital but also a broad base of experience—technical and managerial—and a strong commitment to its success.

Minorities must be willing to share in joint ventures with business persons of all races and to tap the stream of risk capital flowing through the economy as a whole. Minorities must also be prepared to undertake the hard task of acquiring the technical and managerial skills required to survive and prosper in today's sophisticated business world.

A report released in January 1974 by the National Task Force on Education and Training for Minority Business Enterprise underscores the magnitude of the problem. Several basic findings are cited:

1. The alarmingly high failure rate of minority-owned businesses is attributed primarily to poor management and business skills of the owners and managers of these firms.

2. There is a chronic shortage of trained minority talent available to meet the pressing need for owners, managers, and business technicians in the growing number of new, expanding minority business firms.

3. Entrepreneurship as a career opportunity for minority youth is given inadequate attention within the total education system.

The report concludes that a comprehensive program for minority business enterprise education and training must be established if the goal of expanding business ownership is to be successful.

How can businesses from the majority community assist in the development of minority enterprises? Established businesses can offer their facilities, foremen, and workers as educational and training resources. More successful companies can render on-the-job training for the employees of minority-owned firms. The minority firms would release, with compensation, their employees for an appropriate training period with the cooperating companies. Minority youth can be encouraged to visit on-site business operations of stockbrokers, insurance companies, banks, construction companies, and other enterprises. Textbook knowledge is necessary but cannot be a substitute for practical experience and observation.

THE AMERICAN SUBURB

A final word must be added about the suburbs. The problem of the inner city may have its counterpart in the suburbs. The suburbs are largely homogeneous in terms of being made up of white, middle-class residents.

Furthermore, geographical job mobility and a system of constant corporate transferences have made the suburbs largely unstable. It is not unusual for an individual to go from, say, Denver to Minneapolis to St. Louis, back to Minneapolis, and then to Tulsa in a five-year period as personnel managers play corporate checkers with their employees. In any event, the suburbs have developed the related problems of high rates of divorce and alcoholism among adults and drug use by their youths.

CONCLUSION

Unquestionably the American city is in trouble. Appropriate federal assistance, jobs, more minority business enterprising efforts, and better schools will aid in its solution. In the long run, however, the solutions must take into account our desired priorities in the light of conflicting goals. Do we want more freeways or mass transit systems? Street improvements or parks or shopping malls? Sports arenas or civic centers? Potential solutions must attempt to examine all aspects of the problem.

Since business and its environs are interdependent, interactive, and inseparable, business's responsibility extends not only to its public (consumer, employees, and stockholders) but also to human-related problems such as urban redevelopment.

SUMMARY

There is a growing consumer concern and dissatisfaction with products, practices, and policies of some businesses. Programs directed toward the promotion and protection of consumers' interests from practices that infringe upon their rights as consumers are being sponsored by consumer groups, government, and business. This movement, including the whole range of programs, is referred to as consumerism. A possible consequence of the consumer movement is that industry may have to submit to a new kind of audit: a social audit. Included in a social audit may be answers to such complex questions as these: Do your products contribute to a significant human need? What are the short-run and long-run effects of your company's politics and practices on the environment? Do your products exceed minimum safety standards? Is your company doing everything feasible to conserve national resources?

In employee relations business should provide safe working conditions, benefit packages that ensure security in times of trouble and upon retirement, and guaranteed wage increases that are comparable to cost-of-living increases. In addition, business should provide equal employment opportunities to minority groups and women. A failure to meet the requirements of the Civil Rights Act of 1964 (and the subsequent amendments of 1972) will result in further government intervention into management operations.

Historically, the American city has provided the avenue where many people have been able to improve their economic lot in life and has provided as well a social and cultural tempo which makes life interesting for millions of Americans. Prompted by the automobile and aided by the deterioration of urban dwelling, congestion, and the loss of community, many middle-class persons have fled the city for the suburbs. Many factories and other places of employment have followed the population movement, leaving behind an eroding tax base and a rising cost of services. Some cities today are approaching the brink of financial disaster as a result.

What are the solutions for our physically decaying, economically depressed, and socially troubled urban areas? No short-run, easy solutions are apparent.

Massive programs of urban development, involving public housing correctly administered, development of minority enterprises, and a reordering of priorities offer some promise for reestablishing the American city as the hub of economic, social, and cultural activity.

DISCUSSION QUESTIONS

1. What is meant by the term *consumerism?* What factors have contributed to the interest in consumerism during the 1970s?

2. Betty Furness, a former director of the President's Office for Consumer Affairs, has suggested that consumers have a right to be fully informed by the manufacturers of the expected life of their products—for example, brand A light bulb has an expected life of 500 hours. Do you agree or disagree with the assertion? Why or why not?

3. Assume that you are thinking about the purchase of a new automobile. Where would you go to obtain reliable information on performance, cost, and design features?

4. Explain the idea of a social audit for business. What would be some of the problems in attempting to implement the idea in industry?

5. Is a firm's prime obligation to its consumers, employees, or stockholders? Support your answer with logic and rigor.

6. Some persons argue that affirmative action programs are easier to implement during rising economic conditions than in recessions. Do you agree or disagree? Explain you answer.

SHORT CASE

Trust-Us Security Service, Inc.

The Trust-Us Security Service of Las Cruces, New Mexico, operates a twenty-four-hour guard and patrol service for residential, commercial, and government customers. Their uniformed security officers are all licensed and insured. The company has been in business since 1933 and has gained a reputation for reliable and efficient service. Among their clients is the federal government, where they are charged with the responsibility of guarding the installations at nearby White Sands. Previous to the government contract, all of the 150 guards were white males between the ages of twenty-one and sixty.

In order to comply with the EEOA's affirmative action guidelines, the security service added ten black males and five females to their staff of licensed and bonded guards. Recently, the firm cut back on its staff due to a loss of some of its nongovernment contracts, which now represent about one-half of their business.

Ten of the white male guards were dismissed in the cutback, with the company claiming that it must keep its minority employees in order to comply with the government's guidelines for hiring minorities and women. The dismissed employees have threatened the company with a lawsuit unless rehired, claiming reverse discrimination and indicating that the seniority rule should be followed in the dismissals. Management is considering how to resolve this serious problem.

What recommendations would you offer management? Do you agree that this is a case of reverse discrimination? What policy should the company formulate in order to avoid this problem in the future?

SUGGESTED READINGS

Jacoby, Neil H. *Corporate Power and Social Responsibility.* New York: Macmillan Publishing Co., 1973.

Kangun, Norman; Cox, Keith K.; Higginbotham, James; and Burton, John. "Consumerism and Marketing Management." *Journal of Marketing* 39 (April 1975): 3–10.

Nader, Ralph, ed. *The Consumer and Corporate Accountability.* New York: Harcourt Brace Jovanovich, 1973.

Steiner, George A. *Business and Society.* 2d ed. New York: Random House, 1975.

APPENDIX:
CONSUMER LEGISLATION 1962–1974

Consumer Credit Protection Act of 1968

Bank Records and Foreign Transaction Act of 1970

District of Columbia Credit Protection Act of 1971

Gold and Silver Articles Consumer Protection Act of 1970

Flammable Fabrics Consumer Protection Act of 1967

Child Protection and Safety Act of 1969

National Traffic and Motor Vehicle Safety Act of 1966

National Commission on Product Safety Act of 1967

Product Safety Act of 1972

Odometer Tampering Act of 1972

Automobile Bumper Act of 1972

Radiation Control for Health and Safety Act of 1968

Natural Gas Pipeline Safety Act of 1968

Lead-Based Paint Poisoning and Prevention Act of 1970

Federal Railroad Safety and Hazardous Materials Transportation Control Act of 1970

Boat Safety Act of 1971

Federal Cigarette Labeling and Advertising Act of 1965

Public Health Cigarette Smoking Act of 1969

Fair Packaging and Labeling Act of 1966

Clean Air Act of 1963

Motor Vehicle Air Pollution Control Act of 1965

Air Quality Act of 1967

Wholesome Meat Inspection Act of 1967

Wholesome Poultry Products Act of 1968

Egg Products Inspection Act of 1970

Clinical Laboratories Improvement Act of 1967

Drug Amendments of 1962

Food Additives Transitional Provisions Amendment Acts of 1961 and 1964

Drug Abuse Control Act of 1965

Drug Amendments of 1968

Interstate Land Sales Full Disclosure Act of 1968

Consumer Education Act of 1972

Consumer Goods Pricing Act of 1975

THE ENVIRONMENTAL CHALLENGE

LEARNING OBJECTIVES

When you finish this chapter you should:
- [ ] understand the role of ecology as part of understanding the environment.
- [ ] be aware of the different types of pollution.
- [ ] understand why business activity has often created environmental problems.
- [ ] be aware of legislative attempts to combat environmental problems.
- [ ] be aware of how business might work more in harmony with our natural environment.
- [ ] be aware of our various energy sources and their environmental problems and possibilities.

KEY TERMS TO LEARN FROM THIS CHAPTER

cartel	holistic	recycling	tertiary recovery of
degradable wastes	nondegradable wastes	sanitary landfill	petroleum
ecology	persistent wastes	secondary recovery of	
		petroleum	

During the middle and late 1960s the term *spaceship earth* was used with increasing frequency. Two factors were primarily responsible for the coining of this term. Astronauts voyaging in outer space took pictures of the earth. The result changed our perspective. For the first time we saw our entire planet as a single entity, a beautiful blue marble moving around the sun.

The second factor was even more important. Again, our view of ourselves and the environment which we not only inhabit but also transform began to change profoundly. The people responsible for this reassessment go by various names: ecologists, environmentalists, conservationists, and even "eco-freaks" by those unwilling to listen to their message.

The principal objective of this chapter is to examine briefly environmental concern and the potential effects it will have upon the business and public enterprises of technologically advanced societies.

In addition to examining the issue of pollution and the environment, another problem will also be discussed: energy shortages. To a large extent, the problems tend to intertwine. For example, our energy shortage could be solved relatively quickly if we developed and utilized our vast coal reserves more intensively as a source of power. However, satisfying our energy needs through coal would be at a cost of vastly increasing the amount of pollutants pumped into the air.[1]

[1]However, research is being undertaken to attempt to eliminate or at least reduce the pollutants from coal.

"I can't afford to drop any of these."

This interaction between coal and energy illustrates a general problem prevailing in the environment and energy concerns: a trade-off effect that is present because solving one problem often has a cost of creating or intensifying other problems.

Pollution will be examined first. Of the two problems discussed, it probably has the most important long-run implications. In addition, the concepts and definitions involved are more complex than in the energy problem.

The examination of pollution is broken down into three parts. The ecological approach to the environment is presented first. Types of pollution and pollution legislation in this country are then discussed. Finally, some potential solutions to the problem are then presented.

The energy discussion centers on the main sources of energy, stressing potential long-run supply from each as well as advantages and disadvantages.

BUSINESS AND THE NATURAL ENVIRONMENT

THE ECOLOGICAL APPROACH

Ecology is a relatively new term. It refers to the interrelationships among the various life forms and the natural environment of the earth.[2] The term *life forms* is used because ecology is concerned with the connections among people, the various animal, bird, and insect species, and also lower forms such as plant life and even microorganisms. It is thus a total or all-embracing approach.

A simple example of ecology involves the relationship between the Canadian lynx and the rabbit. The former needs the latter as a food source. If the rabbit population expands, then the lynx prospers and survives in large numbers. However, if the rabbit population dwindles, the lynx is adversely affected. This type of relationship also has ramifications for the wider environment. For example, wolf packs kept the elk and moose population in the Yellowstone Park area of Montana and Wyoming in check. With the virtual extinction of the wolf from the vicinity, the elk and moose herds have increased in size, with the unfortunate side effect of consumption of an excessive amount of vegetation in the area. Ecology thus implies not only a system among living things but also the extremely important idea of the maintenance of a delicate balance in the natural world.

Systems can be extremely complex and roundabout. An important life element is the chemical nitrogen. It enters the soil from decayed plant matter and animal or human wastes as well as through bacteria and algae living in the soil. Nitrogen becomes part of the soil's humus, where it is converted into nitrate and is eventually taken up into plant roots, where it is converted into protein. Eventually the plants will be eaten by animals and humans, and nitrogen will again go back into the soil. The process is thus circular or cyclical. There is an interdependence among all living things. It is important to remember that what we refer to as "waste" is really part of this huge cyclical process:

[2]Many of the ideas expressed in this section are discussed in great detail in Barry Commoner, *The Closing Circle* (New York: Alfred A. Knopf, 1971).

In nature there is no such thing as "waste." In every natural system, what is excreted by one organism as waste is taken up by another as food. Animals release carbon dioxide as a respiratory waste; this is an essential nutrient for green plants. Plants excrete oxygen, which is used by animals. Animal organic wastes nourish the bacteria of decay. Their wastes, inorganic materials such as nitrate, phosphate and carbon dioxide, become algal nutrients.[3]

Now modern society produces a tremendous amount of waste. The problem of pollution is closely related to an elementary law of physics: physical matter is not easily created or destroyed except in extremely minute quantities.[4] If we burn a particular quantity of wood or coal, we are left with ashes and chemical residues that enter the air. Thus as matter is transformed, air, earth, or water can be adversely affected because poisonous or toxic chemical residuals directly result or a reaction occurs between a relatively harmless residual and other existing factors. For example, hydrocarbons resulting from automobile exhausts combine with nitrogen oxide in the presence of sunlight to form smog. Barry Commoner has stated the problem particularly well:

A persistent effort to answer the question "Where does it go?" can yield a surprising amount of valuable information about an ecosystem. Consider, for example, the fate of a household item which contains mercury—a substance with serious environmental effects that have just recently surfaced. A dry-cell battery containing mercury is purchased, used to the point of exhaustion and then "thrown out." But where does it really go? First it is placed in a container or rubbish. This is collected and taken to an incinerator. Here the mercury is heated; this produces mercury vapor which is emitted by the incinerator stack, and mercury *vapor* is toxic. Mercury vapor is carried by the wind, eventually brought to earth in rain or snow. Entering a mountain lake, let us say, the mercury condenses and sinks to the bottom. Here it is acted on by bacteria which convert it to methyl mercury. This is soluble and taken up by fish. Since it is not metabolized, the mercury accumulates in the organs and flesh of the fish. The fish is caught and eaten by a man and the mercury becomes deposited in his organs, where it might be harmful. And so on.[5]

Thus all matter has to go somewhere. As Commoner describes the cycle, mercury from old car batteries can eventually enter the food chain and wind up in both fish and human beings. Certainly many of the waste disposal systems of large metropolitan cities often ignore the ecological approach. Two examples should suffice.

New York City Waste Disposal   Most waste from New York City is eventually dumped into an area of the Atlantic Ocean a few miles off the coast. This area has been so badly transformed by the constant dumping of tons and tons of refuse that it is known as the "Dead Sea." As a result, these waters contain highly poisonous substances. Moreover, there is a not-too-distant threat posed to all beaches in the New York City area as a result of matter from the Dead Sea washing ashore.

[3]Commoner, pp. 39–40.
[4]Einstein's famous equation $E = mc^2$ yields the amount of energy (E) created if a mass (m) is destroyed.
[5]Commoner, p. 40.

The Case of Lake Erie   The Case of Lake Erie is even more infamous in the annals of ecology. Lake Erie is actually a huge, inland, freshwater sea. It is approximately twelve thousand years old, having been carved out—along with the other Great Lakes—by an advancing glacier, glacial melt then filling the trough and creating the lake.

Until relatively recently, the lake has maintained an ecological balance. The lake was clean and contained a high population of "quality" fish such as sturgeon and whitefish. The ecological cycle consisted of the fish eating the smaller animals and insects, which fed on algae, which in turn are supported by the inorganic matter (carbon dioxide, nitrate, and phosphate) coming from the decayed fish and animal wastes, thus closing the circle. (Algae are microscopic plants which depend upon the basic elements of hydrogen, nitrogen, phosphorus, and oxygen.)

However, since approximately the beginning of this century, the balance among the lake's elements has been disrupted. The key has been a triggering of the amount of the algae bloom. The overproduction of algae results in successive waves of algae falling to the bottom of the lake. During the process of their decay, they consume a tremendous amount of oxygen on the bottom of the lake. Where the lake is deep and circulation of the water is limited, the oxygen supply on the bottom strata of the lake has been virtually eliminated.

The result of the excess production of algae and elimination of oxygen from the lake bottom has been a disappearance of many fish species which spend part of their breeding period on the bottom of the lake. In addition, the lake waters have become black and brackish, foul smelling, and unfit for swimming. "Rougher" fish species, such as sheepshead, catfish, and carp, have replaced sturgeon, whitefish, and blue pike.

What caused the algae bloom to get out of hand, with the concomitant decay of the lake? The main problem appears to be sewage that has been dumped into the lake. As the sewage decays or becomes biologically degraded, it provides the necessary nutrients to trigger rapidly succeeding algae cycles which consume so much of the lake's oxygen.

Furthermore, modern sewage plants appear to have contributed to the algae-producing cycle. Essentially, sewage plants convert organic wastes into inorganic wastes prior to being dumped in the lake. The resulting nitrates and phosphates were then supposed to be flushed from the lake into the ocean. However, this appears not to have occurred. Instead, the nitrates and phosphates have remained in the lake and become fuel for the algae explosion.

Other major sources of nutrients for algae have come from the phosphates contained in detergents dumped into the lake and nitrates coming from the runoff from heavily fertilized farmland.

Industrial dumpage into the lake has also added to the deterioration of its quality. An extremely well known incident occurred in the summer of 1969. The Cuyahoga River, which flows through Akron and Cleveland prior to entering Lake Erie, was so heavily laden with flammable materials that it caught fire. Furthermore, the blaze was serious enough to almost destroy two bridges. Such materials entering the lake could hardly improve its quality.

In summary, it appears that dumping sewage, whether treated or untreated, into water on a large enough scale can lead to problems. For major urban concentrations, Commoner has suggested a solution which is more in accord with the natural ecological cycle. He has suggested that after removal of nondegrada-

EPA-DOCUMERICA, GENE DANIELS

West Los Angeles, California shrouded in smog.

ble elements, huge sewer pipes should transport the degradable natural wastes to rural areas where they would be returned to the soil. This approach is now being tried in the Chicago area.

The ecological viewpoint that has been stressed in this section is one which attempts to see the interrelationships among the parts of an entire system. This is sometimes called a *holistic* viewpoint because it differs from a narrow examination of the separate parts of a system. A further examination of the various types of pollution is now in order.

TYPES OF POLLUTION

Air Pollution   Chemical pollutants coming from automobiles include carbon monoxide, hydrocarbons, and nitrogen oxides. Carbon monoxide in sufficiently concentrated quantities can endanger human life. When hydrocarbons and nitrogen oxides interact in the presence of sunlight, they can produce smog. Factories, incinerators, and power plants also send sizable quantities of hydrocarbons and nitrogen oxides into the air.

The use of coal and oil for heating and generating power also led to the emission of sulfur oxides and particulates. The latter include both biologically active elements and metal particles.

How badly the air is fouled depends upon the strength or concentration of the pollutants, the quantity emitted, and atmospheric conditions such as the strength of the wind currents. In the factory town of Donora, Pennsylvania, in 1948, particular atmospheric conditions stabilized the air currents, which led to a poisoning of the air. About 20 people died, and 6,000 became ill as a result.

Water Pollution　Waste materials entering water are classified into three types. *Degradable wastes* such as raw sewage are organic in nature. In the biological sense they are living things. They are made up of complex molecular structures of the four basic chemical elements: hydrogen, carbon, oxygen, and nitrogen. Perhaps even more important than raw sewage as a source of degradable wastes are residues from chemical, food-processing, and the petroleum industries and the runoff from agricultural feedlots.

The latter have become a particular problem because they concentrate a large number of animals in a relatively small amount of space. Previously animals were more spread out in the pasture or range. The concentration of animal wastes presents a threat to both groundwater beneath the soil surface and rivers and streams from waste runoff during rainstorms. The enormity of the problem can be seen from the fact that feedlots now produce more organic wastes than the entire amount of sewage from all American municipalities.

Nondegradable wastes, as their name implies, are not broken down when they enter water. They include inorganic materials such as salts and residues from various metals. If they enter the food chain, they can be extremely dangerous. Two examples of this phenomenon occurred in Japan relatively recently: mercury poisoning resulting from eating contaminated fish (mainly tuna) and cadmium poisoning resulting from contaminated rice.

The third category of water pollutants are called *persistent wastes*. They are somewhere between the degradable and nondegradable classifications. While they are attacked by bacteria from the water which they enter, the process of chemical breakdown of persistent waste components is usually very slow. Synthetic (manmade) organic chemical products such as pesticides are the principal members of this category.

The degree of pollution of a particular body of water depends upon the quantity and type of pollutants entering it and the briskness of the water flow. Other things being equal, the faster water flows, the better its ability to cleanse or purify itself through its contact with the air.

An important distinction to be made between air and water pollution is that when the latter is restricted to inland streams and lakes, it is more controllable because it is localized. Some control can be kept over it by treating it before we drink it. Air pollution, on the other hand, is virtually impossible to control. What happens to pollutants when they are in the air is wholly dependent upon atmospheric conditions.

The Oceans　Should the oceans become polluted, however, man's very survival could be threatened. Thor Heyerdahl, the famous Norwegian anthropologist and explorer, crossed the Atlantic in a papyrus reed boat several years ago, and he noted that much of the Atlantic Ocean is already covered by a thin oily film.

A very important cause of such ocean pollution is oil spills from tankers.

The Center for the Observation of Short Lived Phenomena, in Cambridge, Massachusetts, noted that there were thirty-eight oil tanker spills of at least 25,000 gallons each during 1976.

Noel Möstert, author of a 1974 book entitled *Supership,* takes the position that the risk of spills is increased by building huge supertankers. While these ships are economical in terms of their cargo-carrying capability, the spill risk is greatly increased because of their limited maneuverability and their fragility due to their size and shape:

> The sort of accidents that have been happening to small ships will in the future be happening to the very biggest ships, the so-called VLCCs (very large crude carriers). We may confidently expect a rising rate of major big-ship disasters in the decade ahead.
>
> VLCCs were initially built without any experience or any attempt to really understand what was involved in such sizes. There have been improvements, but the fundamental structural problem of the ships is unchanged. For example, a VLCC must be able to steam through a monsoon one week, subantarctic storms off the Cape of Good Hope the next, pass through the tropics, then the Biscay or North Atlantic coast gales. These subject its great length to severe hogging and sagging, with its broad decks constantly subjected to the weight of the tremendous quantities of sea water because of the low freeboard of the loaded ship.
>
> One of the principal factors in the loss at sea of loaded older tankers has been their sudden breakup because of their worn structures. In the recent past these accidents have happened principally to smaller ships. But now the first generation of VLCCs is nearly ten years old: the world is being serviced increasingly by gigantic ships that have entered the critical and dangerous period of tanker life.[6]

Earth Pollution   In addition to air and water pollution is the category of earth pollution. The solid wastes generated in this country are staggering in magnitude. It has been estimated that each person in the United States annually discards 188 pounds of paper, 250 metal cans, 133 bottles and jars, and 388 bottle caps and crowns. Furthermore, 7 million cars and 100 million tires are junked every year.

Land Dumpage   Land dumpage takes primarily two forms: the open garbage dump and sanitary landfill. The open garbage dump is unsightly, does not utilize land space efficiently, and is a breeding ground for rats and vermin. There were 12,000 open dumps in the United States up to a few years ago. The Environmental Protection Agency's Mission 5,000 is attempting to close down 5,000 of them. The Environmental Protection Agency defines *sanitary landfill* as "an engineered method in which solid wastes are disposed of by spreading them in thin layers, compacting them to the smallest practical volume, and covering them with earth each day in a manner that minimizes environmental pollution." When a landfill is completed, the land itself can be used again for a multitude of purposes such as crop or pasture land, parks, or even golf courses.

Sanitary landfill is a vast improvement over open dumping, but it is not without problems. Proper construction must ensure that groundwater or infiltrating surface water are protected from contamination. If these waters are not protected, a substance called leachate can result. It contains dissolved solid

[6]As quoted in *Time,* January 10, 1977, p. 46.

matter and microbial waste elements. The result can be water supplies that are unfit for drinking or irrigation.

Perhaps the biggest problem with sanitary landfill is political in nature. Vigorous opposition by citizen groups has frequently resulted. People may well approve the idea as long as the landfill is not located in their community. A concerted educational effort may be needed to overcome this attitude.

Noise Pollution   A final category of pollution is noise pollution. It is caused by the constant barrage of noise of different intensities that frequently assaults our ears in a modern technological society. The danger lies in the effect of noise levels upon our hearing and also our nervous system (it is interesting to note that the noise level, measured in decibels, from rock bands has been recorded as high as the pain threshold). Noise pollution was one important reason that America abandoned the development of the supersonic transport plane in the early 1970s.

Let's next attempt to assess what the root causes might be that underlie our environmental problems in the United States.

ROOT CAUSES OF POLLUTION

Business and Social Attitudes   While many potential factors undoubtedly underlie our environmental dilemma, we will attempt to identify three important ones.

What to do with waste products is a big part of the environmental challenge.

CHARLES L. FARROW

The first condition might be stated as *business and societal attitudes toward waste and conservation.* Until very recently we have had an attitude that says our resources are unlimited and we need not worry about disposal of abandoned products because that's someone else's problem.

For example, we have long been encouraged by the automobile industry to drive new cars and get rid of the old ones. The reasons have not always been economically or technically sound. Instead, Detroit's subtle advertising techniques have attempted to instill images of conspicuous consumption and masculine virility. The result has been too many cars scrapped too early in their useful lives (automobile disposition is not Detroit's problem). If this contention is correct, it means that internal expansion of the automobile industry's productive capacity is too large in relation to the needs of the nation and the world. The result is a conflict between the short-run goal of the automobile industry (produce and sell as many cars as possible) and the long-run needs of society (conserve scarce resources and lessen solid waste disposal). Put slightly differently, too many of our resources are geared toward producing automobiles and not enough toward maintaining them properly.

Nor are Motown's environmental sins restricted to a policy encouraging early obsolescence. The industry has also attempted to push automobiles with powerful engines that encourage excessive fuel consumption.

While these attitudes are perhaps very well exemplified by the automobile, they appear throughout American business and industry. For example, since World War II, the production of nonreturnable pop bottles has increased an astounding 53,000 percent![7] The consumer, of course, does not want to be bothered with keeping bottles around the house and eventually carting them back to the supermarket. Also, production of bottles has been drastically increased, which is good for bottle manufacturers.

Free Economic Goods   Another underlying cause of our environmental condition is that our *air and water have been free economic goods* for American industry. There has been no cost to a particular business for polluting a stream or sending smoke into the atmosphere. Consequently, cost analyses of production alternatives would not take into account the pollution created. In fact, because there were no costs to pollute air and water, these resources have been intensively used. Society, of course, is eventually presented with the bill.

In a sense, we should not blame business for exploiting freely available resources. Part of the blame (perhaps encouraged by business) lies with our previously mentioned attitude that our natural resources were unlimited.

Synthetic Goods   The third factor has been extensively discussed by Barry Commoner. Since World War II, *a tremendous expansion in the use of synthetic materials has occurred.* On the one hand, the development of synthetics is a great tribute to the technological genius of American industry. On the other hand, unfortunately, synthetic materials do not easily fit into the ecological cycle when they are discarded. A good example is laundry detergents, which have captured a large segment of the market from old-fashioned soaps.

Laundry detergents are a synthetic product made from organic raw materials obtained from petroleum and other substances which are subject to chemical processes during manufacture. In contrast, soap is manufactured by a pro-

[7]Commoner, pp. 142–43.

cess creating a chemical reaction between fat, a natural product, and alkali, which is a soluble salt obtained from certain plants.

The manufacturing process of detergents produces air pollutants, while that of soap does not. Disposal differences create even worse problems.

When disposed of, soap residues are attacked by bacterial enzymes and eventually become carbon dioxide and water, creating little if any biological stress upon the ecological system of waterways. Detergent residues, until 1965, could not be broken down by bacterial enzymes when they entered water. The result was mountains of detergent foam in rivers and streams. Consequently, biodegradable detergents were introduced in 1965. The results have been depressing. Many elements of the new detergents, when degraded, have proved toxic to fish. Also, both the old and the new detergents contain relatively large quantities of phosphate, which can trigger excessive algae growth, as previously discussed.

In summary, the benefits of detergents over soap as a cleanser appear to be far outweighed by the costs to the environment. Overlooking the total ecological picture has proven to be quite costly.

Detergents are only one of many synthetic substances and materials leading to environmental hazards. Synthetic pesticides (DDT), chemical fertilizers, even synthetic fibers replacing natural fibers such as wool and cotton are just a few of the many synthetic elements abounding in our present economy that may lead to environmental dangers.[8] It should not be forgotten that plastic is a synthetic material which strongly resists biological breakdown.

Perhaps the next question to ask is how we can counteract the factors leading to a dangerous environmental situation. Legislation is one possible answer.

FEDERAL ANTIPOLLUTION LEGISLATION[9]

LEGISLATION

1948–1967 Air and water pollution laws, save for one minor exception, were virtually nonexistent until shortly after World War II. From 1948 through 1967, several laws were passed, but they were difficult to enforce and were thus generally ineffective. In the wake of great concern for the environment, Congress passed the Clean Air Act Amendments in 1970 and amended a previous water pollution act in 1972. As shall be seen, these laws became much tougher, but they may also be somewhat unrealistic.

All the way back in 1899, Congress passed an act which required a permit from the chief of the United States Engineers to discharge waste into navigable waters. The act was largely ignored until 1970, when the Engineers, under some

[8]DDT has played an important role in endangering several species of birds because its presence in their bodies has softened their eggshells and made hatching their young difficult.

[9]Much of the information in this section is derived from Allen V. Kneese and Charles L. Schultze, *Pollution, Prices, and Public Policy* (Washington, D.C.: Brookings Institution, 1974).

congressional pressure, attempted to enforce the law. However, its relation to subsequent legislation and the development of state standards tended to make it ambiguous and rendered it essentially useless.

Since World War II, a considerable amount of air and water pollution control has been enacted, as shown in Table 19–1.

The Water Pollution Control Act of 1948 was relatively timid in terms of involving the federal government. The states were left with prime responsibility for pollution control, but the federal government was given authority for secondary activities such as research, investigation, and surveys.

The 1955 Air Pollution Control Act was somewhat similar to the 1948 act in that it involved the federal government in active research. Primacy was still seen as residing with the states.

The 1956 Water Pollution Control Act Amendments got the federal government more positively involved. Federal grants for the construction of municipal waste treatment plants were authorized up to 55 percent of total construction costs. Enforcement procedures against individual polluters were also enacted.

The 1963 Clean Air Act gave the federal government enforcement powers against air polluters. The procedural system was similar to that developed in the 1956 Water Pollution Control Act Amendments.

Enforcement procedures were strengthened by the Water Quality Act of 1965, which attempted to prescribe water quality standards for streams.

Immediately after passage of the Water Quality Act, the Motor Vehicle Air Pollution Control Act was enacted. The law authorized the Department of Health, Education, and Welfare (HEW) to prescribe emission standards for automobiles as soon as practicable.

In 1967 the power of HEW was extended by the Air Quality Act. The department was empowered to oversee air quality standards developed by the individual states and to prescribe air standards if none were forthcoming.

The legislation enacted up to 1970 for both air and water control was largely a failure. The judicial process was extensive and included conferences, follow-up procedures, and finally legal action in the event of presumed violations of the

Table 19-1
Principal Pollution Control Legislation

Month of Enactment	Popular Title
July 1948	Water Pollution Control Act
July 1955	1955 Air Pollution Control Act
July 1956	Water Pollution Control Act Amendments of 1956
December 1963	Clean Air Act
October 1965	Water Quality Act of 1965
October 1965	Motor Vehicle Air Pollution Control Act
November 1967	Air Quality Act of 1967
December 1970	Clean Air Amendments of 1970
October 1972	1972 Water Pollution Act Amendments

Pollutants from automobile exhaust are one of the greatest
threats to the quality of the environment.

law. Moreover, information on discharges needed by enforcement agencies such
as HEW was extremely difficult to procure. In federal aid for water treatment
plants, incentive was really not provided for communities where it was most
needed. Furthermore, as seen with Lake Erie, waste treatment plants can stimulate excessive algae growth cycles. Finally, prescribing the quality of a stream
leads to enforcement problems in determining the effect the individual polluter
has on that stream.

1970 to the Present   As mentioned previously, the 1970 and 1972 acts became
much stiffer than their predecessors. The 1970 Clean Air Act Amendments further expanded the federal government's role in setting and enforcing air quality
standards on motor vehicle emissions. The law directed the Environmental Protection Agency to determine scientifically the threshold or essentially minimal

levels for air pollutants in terms of their human health hazard. The legislation has far-reaching implications for both automobiles and stationary sources of air pollutants.

The automobile standards set by the 1970 amendments are particularly strong. The goal was for a 90 percent reduction for 1975 cars from 1970 levels for two pollutants: hydrocarbons and carbon monoxide. In addition, a 90 percent reduction from the 1971 emission level for nitrogen oxide was set for the 1976 models. Thus significant reductions for all three pollutants were set for 1976 cars.

There are probably two strong criticisms that can be made of the 1970 amendments as they apply to the automobile. The technology necessary to bring about the desired results is quite complicated. As a result, the standards set for the 1975 models were delayed four times and postponed to the 1981 models. Once implemented, however, these standards could lock us into our present technology rather than leading us to do what may be most necessary: exploring new technologies such as steam, turbine, and electric alternatives.

Second, there is an extremely difficult problem of enforcement due to a critical factor: optimum pollution control and efficiency of automobile engines are not necessarily the same. Considerable engine tuning by owners to accomplish the latter while sacrificing the former could be largely undetectable.

The Water Pollution Control Act Amendments of 1972 set two national goals: (1) prevention of pollutants from entering navigable waters by 1985 and (2) an interim goal of water quality sufficient to protect fish and wildlife and adequate for recreational purposes by mid-1983.

The 1972 amendments call for a 1977 deadline for commercial discharge (as opposed to publicly owned treatment works) using the best practicable pollution control technology currently available. By 1983 commercial sources of discharge are required to use the best available technology for controlling pollutants.

There are some definitional problems with the terms *best practicable technology* and *best available technology*, especially concerning costs and benefits of available alternatives. Furthermore, there are economy questions in going from the best practicable technology in 1977 to the best available by 1983. There is also a question of whether industrial plants are to be treated separately or in classes or categories. Obviously laws do not always clearly specify extremely important points.

COUNTERACTING POLLUTION

Some Considerations Before prescribing remedies to counteract pollution, we should keep several factors in mind. First of all, a distinction must be kept in mind between air and water which are already polluted and additional discharge into them which further pollutes the environment. In the former case the damage has already been done, and it is usually difficult to pin down who bears responsibility for what share of the damage. On the other hand, far better control can be kept over additional discharge from stationary sources such as smokestacks or discharge pipes entering a stream.

Second, for active sources of pollution, costs of control vary between industries and even between firms in the same industry.

Third, for any individual pollution source, there may be several different methods for controlling pollution having different degrees of success and different costs.

Finally, and perhaps most importantly, the cost of eliminating pollution from an industrial process generally increases the greater the percentage of pollutants that have already been removed from that process.

The Price System Approach   Given these four factors and focusing on stationary sources of additional pollution (rather than the problem of cleaning up what has already been done), we may find it far easier and more economical to resort to the price system rather than to force industry to adopt the "best practical technology" or "best available technology." In adopting the price system, a legislative body such as Congress or a state legislature would prescribe a cost per unit that industry would be taxed for various types of pollutants sent into the air or waterways. The decision is made by the firm itself, however, considering its desired course of action. A simple example will show how this works. In Figure 19–1, curve A_1 represents the assumed additional cost per ton for removal of pollutants from an industrial smokestack. It costs $60 per ton to remove the 100th ton of pollutants from a smokestack and $70 to remove the 110th ton. P_1 represents a government tax of $90 per ton. If that were the tax, the firm would eliminate the first 120 tons of pollution from the process because that would be cheaper than paying the tax. If the tax were raised to $110 a ton, the firm would remove 130 tons of pollutants from the process. In the first case 20 tons of pollutants would come from the stack, and with the higher tax the amount would be reduced to 10 tons out of the total of 140 per period.

Figure 19-1   Taxing industrial pollution.

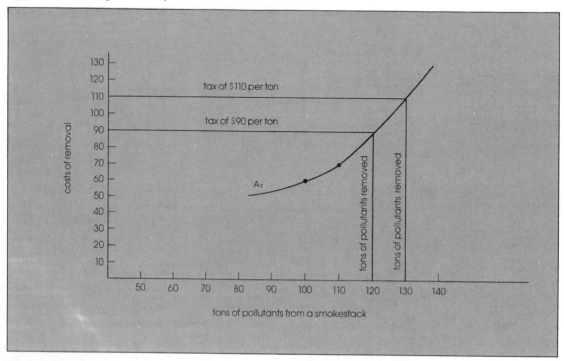

ROY DOTY © CONSUMER REPORTS

Many scientists and lay persons are worried about the toxic effects of the fluorocarbons used on propellants in aerosol sprays.

Notice that the firm makes its own decision in terms of its own welfare. The government's only problem is specifying an appropriate tax schedule. The inequities and difficulties of prescribing appropriate technology are avoided by taxing pollutants from stationary sources.

Recycling A second step would appear to lie in improving our disposition of waste products. We have already mentioned sanitary landfill, for example. A key concept here might be the idea of *recycling* waste or using it again, often in a different form. One possibility might be to use compacted solid wastes as a base for highway or roadbed (of course this could have side implications for fuel consumption and air pollution). In Japan, where space is extremely scarce, the Japanese are literally building an island of compacted solid wastes near Tokyo.

Another example of recycling would be eliminating the no-deposit, no-return bottle. A problem, however, is that making the deposit large enough to reduce throwaways significantly could also lead to counterfeiting of bottles.

Ecological Planning Another step that would be helpful is the use of total ecological planning prior to adopting or developing new products, new plants, or new processes, to be as certain as possible of the extent of potential pollution before making substantial commitments of capital. It is very likely that a government unit such as the Environmental Protection Agency would have to be involved in the decision-making process in order to have appropriate safeguards. Its exact degree of authority would, of course, have to be carefully ascertained.

The Aerosol Can A good case in point where ecological questions were not significantly raised until long after the product was introduced is the aerosol spray can, a product with which we are all familiar. It is used to dispense a multitude of household products, such as underarm deodorants, hair spray, shaving cream, oven cleaner, paint, insecticides, and air fresheners. These are but a small sample of the can's uses. The industry has put out as many as three billion cans a year, enough to put forty-five cans in each American household per year.

The utility of the aerosol can lies, of course, in the ease of dispensing the product inside. A mere press of the finger does the trick. Other methods requiring slightly greater physical effort include roll-on bottles (for underarm deodorants), rubber squeeze ball atomizers, and even plain old tubes that are manually squeezed.

The contents of an aerosol can are dispensed by means of a chemical propellant, which is released into the air along with the product. A number of potentially dangerous effects from certain propellants, mainly fluorocarbons, have only recently begun to be noticed. These include danger to many vital organs, such as the heart, liver, and lungs. Another problem is that fluorocarbons eventually rise into the stratosphere and decompose into chlorine, which in turn destroys ozone molecules. Ozone in the earth's atmosphere helps to shield us from the sun's radiation. Therefore, depletion of the earth's ozone can lead to an increase in skin cancer caused from radiation (the SST supersonic jet may be an even greater danger in the ozone depletion problem). Another danger stems from the chemical propellant entering the eyes. Finally, it has even been noted in beauty parlors that the metal in furnace combustion chambers has been corroded by aerosol propellants.

The dilemma facing us is that large capital outlays have been made by the aerosol can industry and propellant manufacturers, and changeovers would be extremely costly. Combined with this, definitive answers to the ozone depletion problem may not be forthcoming for several more years. By that time, however, it may be too late to prevent significant damage to the atmosphere. Justice thus becomes extremely difficult to dispense after large capital investments have been made.

Fortunately, action has been taken by a combined group of government agencies comprising the Environmental Protection Agency, the Food and Drug Administration, and the Consumer Products Safety Commission. These agencies issued a proposed phasing out of nonessential uses of fluorocarbon aerosol propellants by April 26, 1977.

Fluorocarbon propellants illustrate why new processes, products, and plants must be subject to extremely careful ecological scrutiny prior to the point of investment. The tragedy in the aerosol can case is that we have accepted large potential health hazards for an extremely minor labor-saving advantage that the aerosol can has over older, "obsolete" methods of dispensing.

Other Considerations   Beyond the three steps suggested here, research into environmental problems must continue. In addition, the public must be kept aware of developments in the knowledge of the environment.

One thing that appears fairly certain is that the government must be involved in the process. The danger that can be done to the environment in the name of profit is enormous. The objective is not to deprive business of its decision-making power but to strike an appropriate balance between consumer needs and investment opportunities on the one hand, and environmental considerations which affect us all—including future generations—on the other hand.

ENERGY

Along with the environment, energy is a second enormous challenge facing this country, with tremendous implications for business. As mentioned previously, the problems are closely connected, and tradeoffs are present.

The United States is the greatest energy-consuming power in the world. With approximately 6 percent of the earth's population, we consume about 35 percent of the world's total energy output. The uses of energy and power by the United States predicted for 1980 are shown in Table 19–2. Table 19–3 shows the sources from which energy and power are provided.

In the remainder of this section, energy sources will be surveyed. Included will be old established sources such as oil, coal, and natural gas; newly emerging technological sources such as nuclear power; and finally, technological sources that are on the distant horizon, such as solar energy.

PETROLEUM

At the present time the United States imports about one-third of its oil supply. Most of the imported oil comes from the politically sensitive Middle East. Despite our striving for independence from oil imports, our reliance on foreign oil could increase if present trends of use continue, even counting the effect of the Alaskan North Slope oil strike. In order to get a better understanding of the oil picture, several factors should be briefly explained. These include price controls and exploration incentive, secondary recovery and its problems, and finally, the Organization of Petroleum Exporting Countries (OPEC).

Price Controls   Crude petroleum from newly developed properties as well as all production from old properties which exceeds 1972 production levels is not subject to price control. Its price at the time of writing is around $11.50 a barrel.

Oil from existing properties (up to 1972 annual production levels) has been price controlled at $5.25 a barrel. It is presently scheduled to be decontrolled in phases, with the price becoming totally unregulated by the end of 1977.

Along with the question of price controls, there is one extremely important fact about domestic oil: it is estimated that as much as three times the oil that has been produced in this country has been left behind in the ground after the initial withdrawal. All of this oil left behind in the ground is a result of too many wells being punched into the ground with a resultant loss of pressure, which left huge amounts of oil trapped below the surface.

The oil left behind is harder to get at, but several *secondary recovery* methods have been developed, such as water and steam injections to replace the original pressure. Even today, a surprisingly large amount of our domestic production comes from these methods. (Research has even gone into *tertiary recovery* or retrieving oil still in the ground after the first two tries.)

The phasing out of price controls on "old oil" would have several effects. It would tend to raise the price of most domestic oil in line with the international price. The result would be higher prices at the gas pump. This would, to some extent, discourage consumption (hopefully by as much as 350,000 barrels per day by the end of 1977).

A second important effect of eliminating price controls would involve a reallocation of money from new exploration into improving and extending secondary and tertiary recovery methods. Most geologists agree that the chances of finding many more huge new oil deposits are relatively slim. Locations having the correct geological conditions indicating major strikes have been pretty well exhausted. The number of rigs exploring for new deposits on both land and sea was approximately three thousand by the end of 1975. This overinvestment in new oil and underinvestment in recovering oil left in the ground has resulted from the dual price structure for old and new oil.

Thus the decontrolling of old oil would tend to realign supply and demand by increasing the former and diminishing the latter through the higher price. The principal danger, though, lies in the potentially inflationary effect of the move. The high price of new oil has, of course, been a subject of worldwide importance because of the actions of OPEC, the international oil cartel.

OPEC A *cartel* is essentially an organization of producers to control price and output of its product. Many existed in the period between the two world wars. The war broke them up, and United States antitrust action as well as an increase in worldwide demand for products prevented their reappearance after World War II.

OPEC was formed in 1960 by Venezuela, Iran, and Saudi Arabia as a reaction against the attempt by the large oil companies to force prices down in the

Table 19-2
Sources of energy and power in the United States, 1980 (projected).

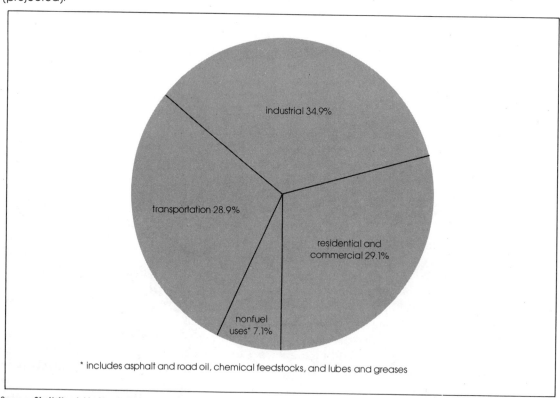

* includes asphalt and road oil, chemical feedstocks, and lubes and greases

Source: **Statistical Abstract**, 1976.

wake of a world oil glut. They were soon joined by the other nine nations making up OPEC.

The OPEC nations really sensed their power as a result of negotiations between Libya and the oil companies in 1969. As a result of the closing of the Suez Canal, Libya had become an extremely important producer, particularly because of its geographical closeness to Europe. The oil companies refused to grant a desired 5 percent increase in price to Libya. This resulted in the overthrow of King Idris and his replacement by the revolutionary Muammar Gaddafi. In the wake of a decrease in production, the oil companies knuckled under to a 20 percent price increase. As a result, the OPEC nations became acutely aware of their vast power. While prospects are generally gloomy, there are some rays of hope for future relations with OPEC.

An extremely important point to remember about cartels is that if prices are pushed too high, those outside the cartel will attempt to develop alternatives in the form of new sources of supply, synthetics, or substitutes. All of these steps are presently being pursued, to a greater or lesser extent, by the United States and Western Europe. Thus one of the dangers to OPEC lies in its very success. Most of the solutions to the problem are long-run in nature, however. They will take several years to implement.

Another danger to OPEC lies in the possibility of different policy choices

Table 19-3

Sources of energy and power in the United States, 1975 (estimated).

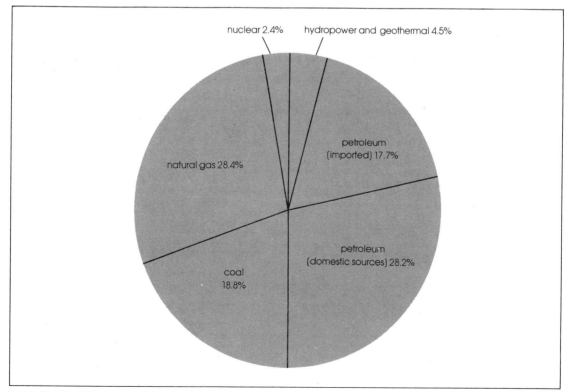

Source: **Statistical Abstract**, 1976.

Launched in 1976, the supertanker **Mobil Eagle** displaces 280,000 deadweight tons, carries 2 million barrels of oil, and is nearly as long as 4 football fields.

among the twelve member nations. Some members, such as Iran, Venezuela, and Algeria, have relatively large populations and ambitious plans for industrial development. Their desires may lie in maximizing oil revenues now with a relatively low concern for long-run considerations of market maintenance. Other members, such as Saudi Arabia, Kuwait, and the United Arab Emirates, with small population bases are more concerned with long-run maintenance of the cartel. These countries literally have more money coming into them than they can possibly use in the short run. Also, this latter group of nations has more oil in the ground than the more populous, industrially ambitious first group.

The first break in OPEC's solid front occurred in December 1976. Saudi Arabia and the United Arab Emirates agreed to raise prices by only 5 percent, while the other members opted for a 15 percent rise. The 5 percent price rise was seen as an overture to the incoming Carter administration to engineer a peace settlement in the Middle East. Despite its potential internal problems, we can expect OPEC to remain a potent force in the world of energy for years to come.

New Sources of Petroleum   Among the new sources of oil, two which have received some attention recently are tar sands and oil shale. At the present time neither is economically feasible, and oil shale, in addition, could cause environmental problems.

The tar sands of northern Alberta could provide oil but results thus far have been disappointing.

Oil can be recovered from shale rock deposits. Large deposits of shale exist in our western states, particularly Colorado. As recently as January 1974, there was great excitement about this source of oil, but costs of recovery at present oil prices have been found to be way out of reach. In addition, shale production causes tremendous waste and would despoil vast areas of the Colorado Rockies.

COAL

About coal, little need be said. About 20 percent of the world's known deposits are found in the continental United States. Our reserves are adequate for several hundred years of use. Coal, however, has several drawbacks. When burned, many varieties emit sulfur into the air, so use is presently environmentally hazardous.[10] Research, however, is attempting to clean up the pollutants.

Another environmental problem with coal is that strip mining (surface mining), where possible, is obviously economical, but in the past it has left ugly scars

[10]Coal found in the Rocky Mountains is considerably less sulfurous than coal mined in the East.

Strip mining operations on the dragline at the Navajo Mine near Fruitland, New Mexico, in the Four Corners Area.

LYNTHIA SCOTT ELLER/CPS

on the earth. At a minimum, grass could be planted to ease the ugly eyesores that have been left behind.

A last point to bear in mind about coal is that research is underway to attempt to transform it to petroleum. If this can be accomplished successfully, the energy crisis would be largely solved. However, at best this lies many years in the future.

NATURAL GAS

Natural gas has been a cheap source of energy for many years. Often found with oil, natural gas was at first "flared off"—burned as it rushed out of the well—because it was not considered economically useful. However, industries near the wells started buying gas and laying their own pipelines. Pipeline companies then grew up, extending the pipelines over large parts of the country, particularly the area west of the Mississippi.

The Federal Power Commission (FPC) has regulated the price that interstate (between states) pipeline companies can pay producers. This power was given to them by the Natural Gas Act of 1938. Intrastate pipeline companies (those lying entirely within a state) are unregulated in terms of supply price, however.

As a result of the regulation, supplies to the interstate pipeline companies have become low since approximately 1970, and many of their customers have turned to oil. In addition, price regulation has probably hindered new exploration. The new discoveries of natural gas that have been made on land have not been available to the interstates because the intrastates had been paying around four times the regulated price per thousand cubic feet. Price regulation does not apply to offshore natural gas. However, in July 1976, the FPC announced a near tripling of new natural gas prices to the interstates.

The interstate pipeline companies cannot easily import natural gas, either. Natural gas must be liquefied if it is to be shipped by tanker. The process of conversion from gas to liquid is simply too expensive to warrant its use.

Hopefully, the decision of the FPC to raise prices for new gas handled by the interstate companies will spur the exploration for natural gas and increase the supply. In addition, another positive factor is the large supply of natural gas in Mexico that will become available for sale in the United States market as soon as the connecting pipeline is built.

NUCLEAR POWER

The idea of a particle known as the *atom*, which was presumably the smallest element of the physical world, has fascinated man since the time of the ancient Greeks. The word *nuclear* refers to the nucleus or center of the atom, which is bombarded by an even smaller particle called the neutron as part of the process of splitting the atom.

The story of the evolution of atomic theory and its subsequent development for destructive and peaceful purposes covers one of the greatest intellectual achievements in the history of humans. The best-known part of the story concerns the discovery that splitting certain types of atoms can cause a chain reaction of splitting other atoms, in turn creating a tremendous source of energy. This energy was used in fashioning the atomic bomb which brought World War II in the Pacific to an abrupt end with the bombing of Hiroshima and Nagasaki.[11]

After the war we began to turn our attention to peaceful uses of the atom. By 1975 we had 56 nuclear power plants in operation, with 63 more under construction and another 100 on order. Nuclear power plants now in operation are providing slightly in excess of 5 percent of our total electricity needs. The type of uranium used as fuel in nuclear plants is in tremendous abundance in certain

[11]We were fortunate enough to develop the bomb before Nazi Germany because many of America's leading research physicists were forced to leave Germany because of their lack of "pure Aryan blood." One of the more bizarre aspects of the race between Germany and America for the atomic bomb was that one of our leading espionage agents in Europe observing Nazi progress was a former catcher for the Chicago White Sox and Boston Red Sox who was also one of the world's foremost linguists (language experts). See Louis Kaufman, Barbara Fitzgerald, and Tom Sewell, *Moe Berg, Athlete, Scholar, Spy* (Boston: Little, Brown and Co., 1975).

Final testing of the atomic reactor at Plum Brook near Sandusky, Ohio. The reactor core is contained in the round open area to the left.

PHOTRI

areas of the Rocky Mountains, so it would appear that our energy shortage could be solved by this technological miracle.

Dangers of Nuclear Energy   Yet there are dangers with nuclear energy, and they have created a deep division within the scientific community. Each side has its own array of prominent scientists. The principal dangers stemming from the use of nuclear energy are these:

1. Leakage of radiation from a plant accident could contaminate a wide area in the vicinity of the plant.
2. Individuals could steal plutonium from a nuclear power plant and build crude atomic bombs.
3. Disposal of extremely toxic atomic waste materials can be unsafe.

Notice that an atomic explosion is *not* one of the dangers of operating a nuclear energy plant. The processes of explosion and creating industrial energy are substantially different. It has been said that an accident such as the rupture of part of a plant which would enable radioactive materials to escape is a calculated but extremely small risk. The chances during a year of an individual being injured from radiation as a result of an accident have been estimated at 15,000,000 to 1 in a study of the problem under the auspices of the Nuclear Regulatory Commission. However, a near accident did occur at the Browns Ferry, Alabama, reactor plant of the Tennessee Valley Authority on March 22, 1975.[12]

Nuclear plants being built today have as one of the by-products of their energy generation, the creation of about 200 pounds per year of plutonium 239 (the number 239 refers to the substance's atomic weight). Plutonium 239 is a manmade element resulting from the transformation of uranium 238 when it absorbs a neutron during the process of splitting. Plutonium 239 is a horribly poisonous element.

Unfortunately, it can be used as the fuel to trigger an atomic bomb. The fear is that as more plants are built, control over the plutonium by-product will be more difficult to maintain. It may take as little as five pounds to build a crude—but effective—atomic bomb. With the rise of revolutionary radicalism in the world today, it is quite possible that atomic blackmail could appear as an intriguing means of bringing about a group's goals. Absolute security must be maintained at our own plants and any that we may decide to build for other nations. The problem may become more uncontrollable because both the Soviet Union and France may eventually be selling nuclear reactors to the developing nations.

Perhaps the most important of the three problems is the question of the disposal of atomic wastes such as plutonium 239, mentioned above. Nuclear wastes are extremely toxic and can remain that way for up to 250,000 years.

At the present time our atomic weapons programs have produced 81 million gallons of waste, with about 7.5 million gallons added annually. Up to now we have not found an absolutely satisfactory means of disposal. It appears that the scientists who favor going ahead feel that a satisfactory method will be devised and that we should therefore go ahead with continued development to correct our present energy crisis.

[12]See "How Browns Ferry Skirted Disaster," *Business Week*, November 17, 1975, p. 105.

The present debate has brought a halt to development of the breeder reactor, which generates its own fuel but would also add immeasurably to our waste disposal problems.

It appears that we have gone so far down the nuclear track that turning around now would be extremely difficult. This could impede the development of radically new sources of energy such as solar power.

SOLAR ENERGY

The sun is unique in the energy question because it is a limitless source of energy which is free to us, will not run down for millions of years, and is nonpolluting.

Though only a modest-sized star, the sun's statistics are staggering. It has a circumference of 2,712,000 miles containing 2.2 octillion tons of gaseous matter. Its surface temperature is 11,000 degrees Fahrenheit, but it rises to 27 million degrees in its core. The process of fusion on its surface—hydrogen molecules are transformed into helium—creates tremendous energy reaching the earth, which is 93 million miles away, in the form of sunlight.

The basic problem in harnessing the power of the sun is less a problem of technology than one of cost. One means of doing this harnessing is by means of silicon cells that convert the sunlight directly to energy. This process has actually been used in our space program, but the costs would have to be about one-fiftieth of what they presently are for this method to be commercially feasible on a large scale.

The first commercially feasible breakthrough may have been made by the Solaron Corporation of Denver, Colorado. Solaron approached George Löf, director of the Solar Energy Applications Laboratory at Colorado State University, who had designed a system for the federal government as long ago as World War II. Löf's system is used in conjunction with a conventional gas furnace/hot-air heating system:

> Solar collectors on the roof heat the air as would a series of shallow greenhouses. Fans force the heated air through a cylinder filled with rocks. The rocks store the heat. When warmth is needed, air from the rooms is circulated through the rocks and then through the conventional hot-air ducting. Over the course of a sunny day, the rocks gradually get hot enough to help warm the house after the sun goes down.[13]

The system requires a larger initial investment in the home's heating system but results in smaller monthly expenses. In spring 1977, the system was installed in a new 160-unit housing project in North Easton, Massachusetts. The results bear close watching for possible future large-scale adoption.

There are several other ways to hitch up the sun's power, but all need considerable research to make them attractive from a cost standpoint.

In summing up the energy problem, it is apparent that we are going to be in a squeeze for a number of years, probably beyond 1980, the desired date for our energy independence. Hopefully by the mid-1980s, improved technologies, new mineral sources, and a wiser use of energy will enable us to overcome this problem. How business handles these problems will indeed be a test of the responsiveness of our free enterprise system.

[13]"A Giant Step for Solar Heating," *Business Week,* October 18, 1976, p. 99.

The late afternoon sun lights up the solar heating panels on
this house.

CHARLES L. FARROW

SUMMARY

Pollution is one of the paramount problems facing the industrialized nations of
the world today. The problem has grown because of little concern for the environment, not only on the part of business but by all of society. While legislation
in the United States has become much tougher since 1970, the laws are somewhat vague and confusing. However it is brought about, much more attention
must be paid in the future to ecological relationships and environmental effects.

A second important problem facing industrialized society concerns development of energy sources as nations grow and expand. For the United States
particularly, appropriate steps must be taken because our country consumes
more than a third of the world's energy output, though only 6 percent of the
population lives here.

Too much dependence is currently being placed on foreign oil sources,
mainly in the Middle East. The picture is, of course, clouded by political problems as well as by the formidable OPEC cartel. We have ample coal supplies in
the United States for our energy needs, but coal used in its present form badly

B. H. SCHOPPER

As concern over energy supplies has grown, use of solar energy is now being seriously considered as an alternative to coal, oil and nuclear power.

damages the environment. The newer sources of energy include nuclear power and solar energy. The dangers in nuclear power are mainly the problem of safely disposing of nuclear wastes and the security problem of preventing terrorists from obtaining plutonium, which can be used to make crude atomic weapons. Solar energy is a promising source of power because it is cheap, abundant, and nonpolluting. All that remains is to make it economically feasible.

DISCUSSION QUESTIONS

1. What does the term *ecological viewpoint* mean?

2. Why is pollution of the oceans a very serious threat to people's survival?

3. What are synthetic goods and why do they create a very serious environmental problem?

4. Why has legislation to control pollutants emitted from automobiles been largely unsuccessful?

5. Why is the price system approach to counteracting pollution a promising method of controlling industrial pollution?

6. Do you think that eliminating price controls from "old oil" will help to eliminate our gasoline shortage?

7. Do you think that OPEC will be able to maintain its power over the supply and price of petroleum over the long run?

8. Why have many individuals taken a very strong stand against the further power development and expansion of nuclear power as an energy source?

SHORT CASES

Stop Pest Company

Robert Smith is the president of Stop Pest Company, a pesticide producer. The company's products are used by farmers to combat insects which damage corn, soybeans, and other crops.

The company has been experimenting with a new pesticide which has been extremely effective against insects that have caused damage to soybeans. Market analysis reveals that pesticide sales can be expected to triple or even quadruple with the new pesticide. Some additional capital investment would be needed to handle the increased production. Considerable unemployment exists in the town of Clear Springs, where Stop Pest is located. Fifty new jobs would be created by the increased production.

The only problem is that the Environmental Protection Agency's investigations have found that the new chemical used in the pesticide is suspected of causing cancer, although a final determination has not as yet been made.

What alternatives are open to Stop Pest relative to the new product? What decision would you make based on these facts if you were Smith?

Business and the Natural Environment

You are appearing at a national conference of business, industrial, and government representatives. You have been asked to prepare a position paper stating why business has tended to ignore the natural environment and what might be done about it consistent with maintaining a capitalistic system for allocating economic resources and satisfying consumer wants and needs. Prepare a short paper attempting to answer these questions.

SUGGESTED READINGS

Commoner, Barry. *The Closing Circle*. New York: Alfred A. Knopf, 1971.

"Effects of 2,4,5-T and Related Herbicides on Man and the Environment." *Hearings before the Subcommittee on Energy, Natural Resources, and the Environment of the Committee on Commerce of the United States Senate*. Washington, D.C.: U.S. Government Printing Office, 1970 (Serial No. 91-83).

Gross, Andrew G., and Ware, Warren W. "Energy Prospects to 1990." *Business Horizons* 18 (June 1975): 5–19.

"How OPEC's High Prices Strangle World Growth." *Business Week*, December 20, 1976, pp. 44–50.

Kneese, Allen V., and Schultze, Charles L. *Pollution, Prices, and Public Policy*. Washington, D.C.: Brookings Institution, 1975.

Manne, Alan S. "What Happens When Our Oil and Gas Run Out?" *Harvard Business Review* 53 (July–August 1975): 123–137.

Mostert, Noel. *Supership*. New York: Alfred A. Knopf, 1974.

"Why Atomic Power Dims Today." *Business Week*, November 17, 1975, pp. 98–106.

THE CHALLENGE OF THE FUTURE

LEARNING OBJECTIVES

When you finish this chapter you should:

☐   be familiar with the state of business ethics now and what can be done to improve business ethics in the future.

☐   be familiar with the state of the economy now and some of the suggestions for changing or modifying our economic system in the future.

☐   be familiar with the state of technology now and what can be done to improve technological development in the future.

☐   be familiar with the state of business employees now and their possibilities for the future.

☐   understand the need for organizational and individual planning in order to cope with the future.

KEY TERMS TO LEARN FROM THIS CHAPTER

business ethics
charter
productivity
technology

Throughout history, people have demonstrated a constant and lively interest in the future. And throughout history, there have been fortune-tellers, prophets, and others who have predicted events ranging from meeting and marrying a rich stranger to a cataclysmic end of the world. Thoughtful scholars in a modern "think tank" have joined palm reading and observing the groundhog on the first of February as one of the many ways to assess the future.

Anyone can make certain predictions on a short-term basis that most certainly will come true. It is quite safe, for example, to predict that the sun will rise tomorrow. It is not quite so safe to say that the sun will still rise over the earth one billion years from now. The future is full of uncertainties and the farther one moves into the future, the more uncertain it becomes.

The future usually involves change, and these days change occurs more rapidly than at any previous time in history. There are relatively few people in the world today who largely repeat the lives of their parents, working at the same farm or trade for a lifetime and then passing on the same heritage to sons and daughters. For many of us, lives are dramatically different from those experienced by our parents and grandparents.

Change today is so rapid that people often have difficulty handling it, as Alvin Toffler pointed out so well in his book *Future Shock*.[1] Toffler claims that a reason many of us have difficulty is that we often take an impersonal view of the future. We tend to look upon a predicted energy shortage, for example, as some vague, general event that may affect others but not ourselves. It is not until the prediction comes true and hits us personally that we make plans to cope with it. Twenty years ago, there were predictions of an energy shortage. These predictions were just about totally ignored by individuals until the shortages hit in the 1970s.

Toffler suggests that in order to avoid the shock of such changes and to cope with them, individuals need to assess predictions about the future in personal terms. If, for example, there are going to be periodic cutoffs of natural gas to homes five years from now, individuals should ask themselves what they can begin to do now to prepare for regular cutoffs of gas for heating and other purposes five years down the road. If the predicted event occurs in five years, the individual will not be so shocked by its impact.

In this chapter, we will look at some current problems and future challenges for business and individuals in business. We will also examine some ways in which businesses and individuals can better cope with the future by becoming better prepared now.

CURRENT PROBLEMS AND FUTURE CHALLENGES

In Chapters 18 and 19 there was discussion of some important future challenges, such as consumerism, pollution of the environment, energy, and urban redevelopment. There are other important challenges. These include business ethics, the economy, science, and people as members of business organizations. Busi-

---

[1]Alvin Toffler, *Future Shock* (New York: Random House, 1970).

ness is not only affected by events and conditions in each of these; most importantly, business is also in a position to make positive contributions to meet these future challenges.

BUSINESS ETHICS NOW

Watergate not only exposed corruption in the Nixon administration but also made the public sharply aware of the dismayingly large amount of corruption and unethical practice in public and private organizations. As a result of the Watergate investigations, 111 corporations were convicted of making illegal political contributions to candidates in 1972. Sadly, as Phillip Moore of the Project on Corporate Responsibility commented, there are probably additional thousands of illegal corporate campaign contributions that were never uncovered.[2]

But political slush funds to dispense company cash to politicians have not been the only headline grabbers. Following quickly on the heels of Watergate came disclosures of bribes, kickbacks, and payoffs by American corporations to foreign government and business officials.

> Gulf Oil admitted payments of $4 million to President Park Chung Hee of Korea and $350,000 to the political party of General Rene Barrientos, who was campaigning for the presidency of Bolivia. Ashland Oil acknowledged making payments to government officials in Gabon, Libya, and the Dominican Republic. Northrop admitted it paid $450,000 to Saudi Arabian businessman Adnan Khasshoggi to bribe two Saudi generals.[3]

These payoffs have been defended in a number of ways. Such payoffs are common in other countries; payoffs are necessary to successfully compete for foreign business; and since payoffs are confined to foreign operations, they should not be considered a domestic problem. Such reasoning has disturbing flaws, however.

Payoffs by American companies in foreign countries have apparently been taken by American companies as necessary and proper business deductions for tax purposes. This action is illegal. In addition, whatever differences in morality one may initially perceive between payoffs in foreign countries and payoffs in this country appear to disappear as foreign payoffs become more common and accepted. In other words, a company which commonly commits bribery in other countries may find it a relatively short step to offering kickbacks and payoffs in this country.

Bribery in the United States   No one is seriously suggesting that the acceptance of corrupt practices in other countries is the sole cause of corruption in the United States. But it may be a contributing factor to what is already an existing condition. In two surveys, approximately half of the business managers who responded appeared to feel that bribery and payoffs were all right as long as a good many others were also doing it.[4]

---

[2]Rick Dunham, "The Best Candidate Money Can Buy," *Wharton Account* (October 1975): 28–31.

[3]Joel Seligman, "Crime in the Suites," *MBA* (June 1976): 23–31.

[4]Ralph Nader and Mark Green, "What to Do About Corporate Corruption," *Wall Street Journal*, March 12, 1976, p. 16.

Such a collective nonethic seems to justify corruption easily in many areas. The General Accounting Office in the federal government has found, for example, that the use of entertainment, gifts, and other gratuities is common in the defense industry in order to gain and/or assure continuing business. Companies that supply 90 percent of the gypsum board used in construction were found guilty in 1975 and 1976 of a conspiracy to fix prices. During the period of the conspiracy, artificially high prices undoubtedly cost consumers millions of extra dollars.

Despite criminal prosecution and civil lawsuits, price fixing is considered widespread in some industries, partly because rewards—higher prices and bigger profits—often may seem worth the seemingly small risk of getting caught and penalized for violating the antitrust laws. In the gypsum case, Judge Hubert I. Teitelbaum gave only suspended prison sentences and imposed fines ranging from $50,000 to as little as $1,000. Still, the companies have paid out about $70 million in damages to gypsum dealers who filed private civil suits to recover the money they lost in paying illegally high prices.[5]

One could go on with other examples. The professions have collected a good share of criticism and lost prestige. Lawyers and accountants have been parties to corporate and political wrongdoing. From these and other possible examples, the picture seems clear. On an ethical level, the business community has often failed to meet the wishes and expectations of a disillusioned public. What can be done?

BUSINESS ETHICS: THE FUTURE

The public has a right to look first to business itself to improve its ethical level. There are scattered signs of hope. In 1976, Eberhard Faber, Inc.—the well-known manufacturer of pencils and similar products—turned down a lucrative investment possibility in a foreign company because the latter was making payoffs to the local government.[6] There are other similar examples.

Exxon has tightened financial controls to discourage questionable money deals and/or to discover those already made. "Today, an auditor's first task when visiting an affiliate is to make sure that Exxon policy statements are being complied with."[7]

Companies are increasingly developing codes of conduct to guide employee activity. Among the companies that have or are developing these codes of business ethics are Pitney-Bowes, Hueblein, and United Brands Company.

A few companies have instituted stiffer penalties for unethical behavior. Gulf Oil Corporation fired four top executives, including the chairman of the board, for maintaining a corporate political slush fund. Many executives in other companies, however, who admitted making illegal contributions, continue undisturbed in their executive positions.

Seminars in business ethics and signed pledges to maintain ethical behavior are among other techniques currently used. Based on the past history of at-

[5]David McClintick, "Busting a Trust," *Wall Street Journal,* October 3, 1975, p. 1.
[6]Eberhard Faber, "How I Lost Our Great Debate about Corporate Ethics," *Fortune* 94, no. 5 (November 1976): 180–88.
[7]"How Companies React to the Ethics Crisis," *Business Week,* February 9, 1976, pp. 78–79.

tempts at self-government, however, it is doubtful that other segments of society will be satisfied with the current efforts by business—well intentioned as they may be. The public and the government will be looking to some forms of external enforcement of ethical standards.

External Enforcement of Business Ethics   There are laws on the books already which specify the illegality of most of the corrupt practices that business has committed. Corporate campaign contributions, for example, have been illegal since 1948. The law against price fixing and other monopolistic practices dates back to the Sherman Anti-Trust Act of 1888. While there may be a need for specific additional legislation, this does not appear to be the whole answer.

Penalties in many cases have been notoriously light. Suspended prison sentences or no sentences at all as well as small fines have been more the rule than the exception. Many convicted executives have continued right on in their executive positions. Writing in the *Wall Street Journal,* Ralph Nader and Mark Green suggest:

> In order that punishment falls on those individuals responsible, officers convicted of willful corporate-related violations should be disqualified from serving as an officer or director in any American corporation or partnership for five years after a conviction, guilty plea, or nolo contendere plea. This is only logical. One does not reemploy an embezzler as a bank teller.
>
> Fines should be calibrated to the size of the firm and the "size" of the violation. Business crime has its own cost curve. If companies are punished with insignificant penalties, the result is predictable. Instead of absolute fines, there would be percentage fines based on gross—so the fine would fit the crime.[8]

The impact of stiff penalties should be sobering. The executive facing possible imprisonment or the corporation facing the possibility of huge fines would be less likely to knowingly commit an illegal act. Nader and Green also suggest that the federal government through its agencies should publish detailed information on which companies have violated the law and the corrective action required and taken. In addition, there could be suggestions for additional tools needed to prevent crime. These tools could include broader subpoena powers and more federal authority, for example.

Another Nader proposal is for federal *chartering* of all corporations with annual sales of $250 million or more. This proposal includes the requirement of a full-time board of directors drawn from outside the corporation. These independent directors would help prevent violations of law or disloyalty to shareholders.

Along with such preventative measures and threats of punishment, there remains the hope that more businesses will improve their self-government, will abide by their codes of conduct, and will do whatever else is required to maintain high levels of ethical behavior.

THE ECONOMY NOW

Inflation, recession, unemployment, and the energy shortage have become familiar terms to us in recent years. These are terms that do not suggest a vibrant,

[8]Nader and Green, p. 16.

healthy economy. In addition, the weather has not been kind in some years. The winter of 1976–77 blew unwanted cold and snow in vast quantities throughout the eastern United States. Losses in production and unemployment resulted. The same winter brought drought to the Far West and a loss of food supplies for the entire country. Variations in the value of the dollar have sometimes made foreign trade more difficult.

In addition, some observers suggest that *productivity* is lagging. For example, the National Commission on Productivity and Work Quality reported in 1975:

> Productivity in the United States has not fared well in recent years. Output per man-hour experienced an unusually sharp cyclical drop beginning in 1973; the rate of productivity growth during the post–World War II period as a whole has been showing signs of retardation; and apart from these unfavorable developments, the average productivity performance of the U.S. has lagged during recent decades behind most other industrial countries.[9]

Given what many persons would conclude is an unsatisfactory state of the economy, what can be said about the future?

THE ECONOMY: THE FUTURE

Economic forecasting is risky. It is even difficult to find a middle ground between the pessimistic and optimistic forecasts. Our economy assumes that high productivity is necessary for growth, yet the report on productivity quoted previously is quite gloomy. On the other hand, Douglas Greenwald, chief economist for McGraw-Hill Publications, predicts productivity increases of 2.5 percent for the economy as a whole through 1980. This is better than the 2.2 percent recorded since 1960.[10]

And with respect to employment, Peter Drucker, a well-known writer on business topics, foresees a labor shortage through 1995. Hence, rather than trying to piece together one economic forecast out of the many available, it is perhaps more significant to consider that some important people are suggesting that the capitalistic system might need changing. For example, a 1975 meeting of the National Democratic Issues Convention approved a demand for public ownership of corporations in defense, energy, and transportation. Their demands also included employee ownership and management of all corporations as well as a massive government employment program.[11]

Many economists disagree with such a radical plan. Charles Schultze, President Carter's chairman of the Council of Economic Advisers, favors keeping the present system while recognizing that it may need modification.[12] Some form of wage-price control is an example of a possible modification. Of all the topics we have discussed in this book, the economy is likely the most difficult to project into the future. Among the most important factors continuously affecting the economy is technology.

[9]"Productivity," *Fourth Annual Report of the National Commission on Productivity and Work Quality*, 1975, p. 5.
[10]"A Look at the Economy of 1985," *Business Week*, December 18, 1971, pp. 84–85.
[11]Hobart Rowen, "Tinker with Capitalism or Change the System," *Des Moines Register*, November 29, 1975, p. 5.
[12]Ibid.

TECHNOLOGY NOW

For decades the public has occupied a front-row seat to view the miracles of advancing *technology*. From automobiles and airplanes to television and trips to the moon, we have been startled and impressed. At the beginning of this century, a United States congressman suggested that the U.S. Patent Office be closed since everything already had been invented which possibly could be invented. Even today there are those who claim we have gone as far as we can with technological developments.

Most would agree, however, that technological potential is virtually unlimited. But there are problems. Money available for research has fallen off dramatically as business has become less inclined to take risks on new products.

> From its peak in 1968, total government and industry research spending has dropped more than 6 percent in real or noninflationary dollars. Going back 10 years, studies by the National Science Foundation show that real industry spending for basic research has slipped 12 percent. During the same period, the level of federal funding for basic research within industry fell 45 percent.[13]

Within business, high costs, lack of ready capital, and high failure rates for new products cause management to be very cautious about taking chances on untested products and services. There is also a failure to anticipate the future with adequate preparation. Back in 1956, Jacob E. Goldman, then director of Ford Motor Company's scientific laboratory, warned that there would need to be a major breakthrough in automotive power within the next twenty-five years in order to meet the predicted gasoline shortage. The breakthrough has not occurred.

There is the electric car, of course—expensive and perhaps not as safe as it should be. And there are other technological triumphs such as the hand calculator and the minicomputer. Both of the latter have lowered initial purchase costs tremendously. But across the board, there has been a slowdown in research and development.

Since technological improvements are important to economic growth, the decline in research and development takes on added significance. What does the future hold?

TECHNOLOGY: THE FUTURE

To help with the economy, to maintain a clean environment, and to relieve the energy shortage, continuing research is vital. There are suggestions. One is to share the risk. By working with consultants or some other intermediary, several companies may cooperate to share the cost and risk of a new development. There is a need in many companies to change the climate away from a no-risk philosophy. John R. Rockwell, head of the venture-management division of the consulting company Booz, Allen, notes:

> The whole environment of the big, publicly held corporations that dominate our economy is oriented toward the right to succeed. For some companies

[13]"The Silent Crisis in R&D," *Business Week,* March 8, 1976, pp. 90–92.

like P&G, that is almost an inalienable right. Innovation, however, is best encouraged by an environment that recognizes the right to fail. And today, nobody feels they can afford a failure. That is the thinking that must somehow be changed in the years ahead.[14]

There are also suggestions for more tax incentives for research and development as well as more federal funding where the risks are particularly high, such as in energy research. The university research potential appears to be underutilized at the present. Government and industry funding could more effectively put the university community to work. Fortunately, many persons in government and industry realize what must be done. Whether or not we meet the challenge, of course, remains to be seen.

BUSINESS EMPLOYEES NOW

From the standpoint of economics, the position of many American workers has depreciated in the last several years. Their wages and salaries have not kept up with inflation. Securing employment has been a problem for some. At the managerial level, there are complaints of overwork, stress, and problems in the supervision of subordinates. On the worker level, some observers report a feeling of alienation from work. Boredom could be a cause. The net result is often reported as indifference, lack of motivation, and/or low productivity.

[14]"The Breakdown of U.S. Innovation," *Business Week*, February 16, 1976, pp. 56–68.

"It'll travel from New York to Los Angeles at an electricity cost of $8.12, but the extension cord costs $15,000."

Under the impact of federal and state laws, business has gradually increased its percentage of minority-group employees. Women and other minority-group members are increasingly moving into the managerial ranks. There remain problems of health and safety, ineffective training, lack of information about employment opportunities, poor match-ups between aptitudes and jobs, and others. The condition of the business employee is far from perfect—worse off in some instances from previous years and better off in others. What, if anything, can be said about his or her future?

BUSINESS EMPLOYEES: THE FUTURE

A sampling of events, facts, and efforts may offer some clues as to the future condition of the business employee.

> Item: Xerox Corporation, the Mead Corporation, a United Auto Workers local union in Parma, Ohio, and others have started family counseling programs to help employees with marital, family, and personal financial problems.

> Item: A major Philadelphia insurance company, INA, and other insurance companies have instituted programs of rehabilitation for workers receiving disabling injuries on the job rather than simply paying the workers disability compensation for extended periods up to a lifetime.

> Item: A number of companies have implemented job enrichment programs to provide workers with more responsibility and more control over their individual jobs.

> Item: Dr. Herbert Benson suggests that executives try a twenty-minute period of meditation twice a day in a quiet place with few distractions.

> Item: The Bureau of Labor Statistics reports that the number of workers with at least a high school education has increased by three million. The number of non–high school graduates has declined by one million. Sixty-eight percent of all workers have at least a high school education, while 14 percent have four years or more of college.

> Item: The bureau also reports that the jobless rate for workers with some skills runs 2 to 4 percent lower than the jobless rate for workers with no skills.

A forecast cannot be assembled out of a random sampling of news items. Some observations, however, could be appropriate. There appears to be a continuation of a long-term trend for greater concern over the well-being of employees. There is great interest on the part of companies for better leadership and worker motivation as well as for family counseling and meditation. The utilization of education and training to develop job skills appears as important as ever to maximize one's chances for continuing employment.

It has not been our purpose to predict the future—only to see what current happenings might offer clues to the future. Noting such general clues and possible trends is helpful, but individuals and businesses need to make specific plans to prepare themselves for the future in terms of their own skills, abilities, and potentials.

PLANNING FOR THE FUTURE

Alvin Toffler, author of *Future Shock,* advocates viewing the future and its changes in terms of personal impact. The advice applies equally well to business and individuals. Many businesses are currently attempting to follow his suggestion. Companies such as General Electric, General Mills, Whirlpool, and the Pillsbury Company are engaged in what they call "futures research."

These companies have long-range forecasters and planners who keep track of current changes and attempt to assess conditions five to twenty-five years in the future. They are concerned with politics, economics, energy, the environment, and science and technology. Their assumptions range from worldwide political upheaval to an end to economic growth.

> American Standard . . . has factored into its plans the probability of a critical worldwide grain shortage in the late 1970s, in the wake of 5-degree wind changes that will reduce rain in the major producing areas of the world.[15]
>
> Dow Chemical has a product management team that analyzes new social and political pressures and relates them to its business. The result is what Dow calls its "ESP" (for economic, social, political) report, a formal document that attempts to evaluate risks from all of these factors.[16]

LESS FORECASTING AND MORE PLANNING

Because of the great uncertainties in the future, forecasts beyond twelve months have limited value. Companies are learning to compensate in two ways: (1) quick reaction time and (2) developing batteries of contingency plans and alternate scenarios. "If you can't forecast, all you can do is react quickly,"[17] says Gary L. Neale, president of Planmetrics, a Chicago-based company that currently is helping seventy-six corporations computerize their planning process to speed up reaction time even more. Arizona Public Service adjusts its two-year budget every month. Xerox has five different scenarios or tracks for the company through 1990.

Alternate plans are developed for many possible contingencies. What happens if the weather changes? What if there is a major breakthrough in energy technology? What if there is a major worldwide depression? For each of these contingencies, an alternate plan can be developed, a plan that relates possible future changes to an individual company.

INDIVIDUALS CAN PLAN, TOO

Individuals can plan in much the same way as business. Individuals can establish goals, learn to react quickly, stay flexible, and develop alternative plans. This kind of planning is necessary to cope with future change. Alternative plans could include switches in career tracks, working in different locations, working for

[15]"Corporate Planning: Piercing Future Fog," *Business Week,* April 28, 1975, pp. 46–54.
[16]Ibid., p. 50.
[17]Ibid., p. 47.

CHARLES L. FARROW

For some people, planning for the future means learning a
particular job or skill before entering the job market and
looking for a position.

different companies, going into business for oneself. Planning is hard work, but
very likely it will be worth the effort.

PLANNING AND THE COMPLEXITY
OF THE SYSTEM

What makes planning such hard work is not only the uncertainty of future
change but the complexity of the system. Consumerism, social change, pollution,
energy, ethics, science, and the economy are all tied together in a gigantic
worldwide system. For example, an ethical company will strive to conserve
energy, reduce pollution, and deal fairly with its customers. Political changes in
Europe could affect the economy of the United States. A solution to the energy
problem is highly dependent on scientific research and development.

Hence it is not enough to consider one component of the system only. The
components interact, and it is necessary also to consider the nature of the interactions and their possible outcomes. This complexity is why forecasting is so
difficult and why so much stress currently is placed on flexibility and fast reaction
time.

Of course, much of the planning that is of keen interest to individuals concerns future employment opportunities.

THE FUTURE JOB MARKET

As was noted earlier in the chapter, Peter Drucker has taken an optimistic outlook on the job market from the viewpoint of the person looking for a job. But

the Department of Labor in a 1977 report estimated a shortage of one million jobs for college graduates for the years 1974–1985. The report also predicts a good demand, however, for persons with vocational and/or technical training.

Hence it appears there may be competition at least for the better opportunities in business. It may be expected that areas such as accounting and operations management, which for years have experienced a high demand for qualified people, will continue to provide excellent employment opportunities. And in areas where there may be somewhat less demand, the individual who has prepared well in education and training should not have great difficulty in finding a satisfactory job. Chapter 21 provides more specific information on career opportunities.

CAN OUR PRESENT SYSTEM MEET THE CHALLENGE?

There is no question that problems and their challenges confront our society and the business community. The challenges range from meeting the energy shortage to improving the level of business ethics. In this section of the book, we have reviewed these challenges in detail and analyzed the role of business in helping to meet the challenges. It was noted that the economic system within which business operates—the capitalistic system—has been questioned as to its adequacy for future years.

Suggestions for changing the capitalistic system usually involve a major increase in government control or ownership of business enterprise and a corresponding slice out of our total package of freedoms. Government laws, controls, and regulations are necessary, but the authors do not support large takeovers of important segments of the private sector of the economy. There is certainly no guarantee that the government could do a better job of running the transportation system or the energy industry than is now being done.

There is plenty of room for improvement, of course. There appears to be a need for greater cooperation among the various forces in our society—business, government, labor, and the educational system. There needs to be less preoccupation with local, selfish interests—within business or labor, for example—and a greater concern for the well-being of the total system. To gain this commitment requires a greater awareness of the effects of the actions of one component on another as well as on the total system. Higher ethical levels of behavior in all sectors of society would help, as would superior leadership.

It would seem this kind of cooperative action and commitment is possible without the loss of basic freedoms—without the loss of the individual's right and the individual organization's right to pursue their own goals with vigor and dedication. But the pursuit must be accomplished with increased concern for the impacts of one's action on others. Our system may need modifications and adjustments from time to time, but the authors believe our basic system of capitalism is still capable of successfully meeting the current and future challenges.

SUMMARY

The future holds many changes and uncertainties that will offer a continuing challenge to business and to the total society. When dramatic changes occur, there is often a feeling of unpreparedness and shock. By preparing for the personal impact of possible future changes, individuals and business can reduce the shock effect. It is likely that current problems such as pollution, the energy shortage, the economy, and business ethics will continue to be problems and challenges in future years.

As a result of political contributions, payoffs to foreign officials for trade benefits, and other illegal events, it is apparent that business ethics currently are at a relatively low level. There are some encouraging signs that business is beginning to take the necessary steps to raise its level of ethics. In addition, there are suggestions for greater external control through stiffer penalties and enforcement.

For some years, the economy has been in varying states of ill health. Some suggestions for major changes in our capitalistic system have been made, but it is likely that the basic system, though perhaps with minor modifications, will remain to wrestle with the economic challenge.

Technology has been suffering from a lack of money. Suggestions for greater cooperation among companies in research, a greater willingness to take risks, and greater use of university research facilities may help to move research into a more productive period.

Over the past few years, members of business organizations have lost ground financially in certain cases, have suffered some physical and mental health problems in others, and in certain cases appear alienated from work. There does appear, however, to be a continuation of the long-term trend for greater concern over the well-being of employees and a mildly optimistic outlook for the employment of individuals with salable skills and knowledge.

Since forecasting is so uncertain, many companies are emphasizing planning as the best way to prepare for the future. The development of alternative plans to meet future changes is increasingly common, as is the development of an ability to react quickly to unexpected changes. Individuals could plan in much the same way as companies in order to better prepare for future change.

Despite the many problems that currently face us and that will face us in the future, the authors believe our present capitalistic system is the system best able to cope—to meet the challenges, find solutions, and successfully implement them.

DISCUSSION QUESTIONS

1. Penalties for unethical and/or illegal behavior on the part of business executives have been very limited in recent years. Do you believe stiffer penalties will make business persons more ethical and less inclined to break the law? Why cannot business police itself?

2. Productivity plays a key role in the state of our economy. It seems quite simple that if everyone worked harder, there would be no problems with economic conditions. Is this true?

3. Some persons suggest that new technological improvements are so expensive these days that only the government can afford the research and development costs. Do you believe this to be true? If so, what role do you see for private industry?

4. Why is it important for individuals to plan for the future? After all, what can one person

do about energy, inflation, the environment, and technology?

5. Do you believe our present economic and business system can cope with the future, or does it need to be changed?

SHORT CASES

Bubbles — Tiny Bubbles

In early 1977, Texas Instruments announced it was going commercial with a new bubble memory for computers. For years, magnetic disks and tapes have dominated computer-memory technology. The bubbles are also magnetic and slide around on the surface of a crystalline chip. Right now the bubble memories cost a lot more than disks and tapes, but in a few years the bubbles should be equal to or less than disks and tapes.

The bubbles can store so much data in a small space that a bubble memory can turn a small hand-held calculator into a powerful minicomputer. The bubble memory takes up only 4 to 5 percent of the space of a disk, uses less power, and operates from two to seventy-five times faster. In addition, the bubble does not lose data when power is cut off and has *no* moving parts. Texas Instruments expects the market for bubble memories to be around $500 million by 1985.

What changes do you foresee in business as a result of having a powerful minicomputer the size of a hand-held calculator?

Will other companies attempt to break into the bubble-memory market?

Why will the cost of bubble memories decrease to the point where they cost no more than disk or tape memories?

Is National Planning Necessary?

Thorton Bradshaw, president of the Atlantic Richfield Company, believes the federal government must take a leading role in planning for the energy crisis. Bradshaw suggests that the United States does not have a free enterprise system but is a mix of private and government forces. This mix operates our economic system.

According to Bradshaw, the government should assess the economic condition and prospects, set national goals and priorities, and then allow private market forces to work. He does make one exception to the interplay of private market forces. He believes the government must permanently manage the price of domestic crude oil in order to give industry the incentive to meet national production goals.

Do you agree with Thorton Bradshaw that the United States does not have a free enterprise system but rather has a mixture of private and government forces?

Do you believe it wise for the government to play an increasing role in business and economic affairs? Should the government set national goals and priorities for business?

SUGGESTED READINGS

Bradshaw, Thornton F. "My Case for National Planning." *Fortune* 95, no. 2 (February 1977): 100–104.

Toffler, Alvin. *Future Shock*. New York: Random House, 1970.

CAREERS IN BUSINESS

Throughout the text, mention has been made of the challenging opportunities available to young people in the functional areas of operations, marketing, and financial and personnel management. In addition, in the supportive areas of accounting, computer technology, research, insurance, banking, and labor unions, exciting careers exist for young men and women. Many of these areas will offer substantial increases in jobs during the next decade. This chapter, then, is an extension of Chapter 20, dealing with the future challenges. Specifically, the focus of this final chapter will be on those career alternatives which will exist between now and the mid-1980s, specifically in business management.

Many questions must be asked by young persons as they attempt to match their abilities and interests with the variety of occupational choices. What fields look promising for employment opportunities? What education and training are required to enter particular jobs? How do earnings in certain occupations compare with earnings in others requiring similar training? What types of employers provide which kinds of jobs? What are the opportunities for advancement in a particular field, and will this field lead to fulfillment of career objectives?

Answers to these important questions change as the economy grows. New products and improved methods of production as well as changes in living standards, life styles, and government policy constantly alter the types of jobs that become available. For example, the growing population, rising incomes, and increasing urbanization of society will lead to an increased payroll in the service-producing industries—government, health, education, finance, insurance, and real estate. Conversely, employment in the goods-producing industries will increase more slowly than service industries because of labor-saving technological changes in agriculture, mining, and manufacturing. Figure 21–1, prepared by the Bureau of Labor Statistics, shows these projected changes by major industries through the mid-1980s.

BROAD OCCUPATIONAL PROFILES

Occupations are often divided into two general groups: white-collar and blue-collar. White-collar jobs include the professional, managerial, clerical, and sales workers. On the other hand, blue-collar jobs include crafts workers, machine and equipment operators, and skilled and unskilled laborers. With an increasing demand for persons to perform research and development, to provide education and health services, and to process the growing amount of paperwork in all types of organizations, labor specialists see a continuation of the rapid growth in white-collar occupations through the mid-1980s.[1] Growth in the white-collar occupations will be offset by slower-than-average changes in the blue-collar jobs and a decline in farm workers because of the use of laborsaving equipment in industry and agriculture.

[1] Bureau of Labor Statistics, *Occupational Outlook Handbook, 1976–77 Edition* (Washington, D.C.: U.S. Department of Labor, 1976).

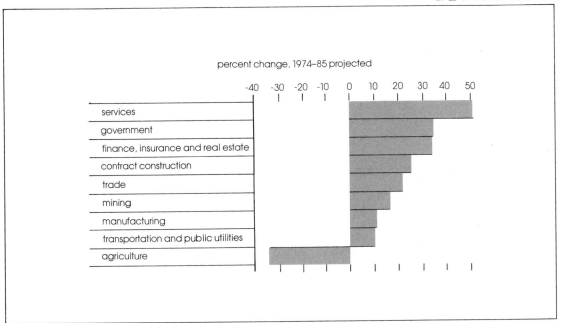

percent change, 1974–85 projected

Figure 21-1 Through the mid-1980s employment growth will vary widely by industry. (Source: Bureau of Labor Statistics)

Figure 21–2 reflects these broad occupational changes forecast for the mid-1980s. The largest growth is predicted in clerical, professional and technical, service, and managerial and administrative occupations.

Clerical workers, the largest group of workers in the mid-1970s, are expected to grow the fastest during the 1975–1985 period, increasing by about one-third. Many new clerical positions are expected to open up as industries employing large numbers of clerical workers continue to expand. The demand will be particularly strong for those persons qualified to handle jobs created by electronic data processing.

In professional and technical employment, the third largest occupational group in the mid-1970s, a 30 percent growth is expected between 1975 and 1985. This group includes such highly trained personnel as accountants, computer scientists, actuaries, and operation researchers, as well as physicians, dentists, and psychologists. These professionals will be in great demand as the nation makes greater efforts to solve our transportation, health, and energy problems, to rebuild our cities, and to protect our environment. The quest for scientific and technical knowledge is bound to grow, raising the demand for workers in scientific and technical specialties.

As in the past, requirements for salaried managers are likely to continue to increase rapidly because of the growing dependence of business and nonbusiness organizations and government agencies on management specialists. On the other hand, the number of self-employed managers is expected to continue to decline as the trend toward larger businesses continues to restrict growth of the total number of firms. However, there will still be opportunities for the small business owner-manager who offers his local market unique products and/or services.

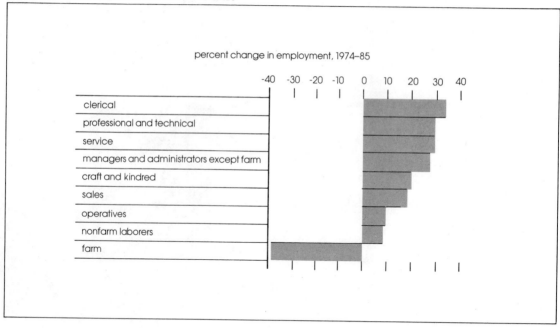

Figure 21-2 Through the mid-1980s employment growth will vary widely among occupations. (Source: Bureau of Labor Statistics)

Figure 21-3 Training needs are determined by replacement plus growth. (Source: Bureau of Labor Statistics)

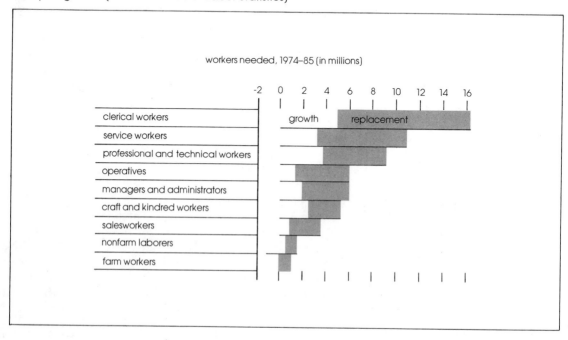

Sales workers are found primarily in retail stores, manufacturing and wholesale firms, insurance companies, and real estate agencies. Sales workers are expected to increase by about 16 percent during the forthcoming decade as the population continues to grow and business responds to the expanding population needs.

A word of caution is offered to young persons in considering only those occupations that are growing rapidly or eliminating those that are not among the fastest growing. Growth is only one indicator of future job outlook. In some occupations jobs will be available because of deaths, retirement, and other labor force separations. For example, Figure 21–3 indicates that more jobs will be available in the operators category resulting from growth and replacements combined than for craft workers, even though the rate of growth for the crafts will be considerably higher than the rate of growth for the operators occupational group.

Some specific occupational projections are shown in Table 21–1.

Table 21-1
Projections and Outlooks for Various Occupations

Occupation	Estimated Employment 1974	Average Annual Openings 1974–85	Employment Trends and Prospects
OFFICE OCCUPATIONS			
Clerical occupations			
Bookkeeping workers	1,700,000	121,000	Employment expected to increase at slower rate than average for all occupations because of increasing automation in recordkeeping. Most job openings will result from replacement needs.
Cashiers	1,111,000	97,000	Because of very high turnover and average employment growth in response to increased retail sales, thousands of job openings for cashiers expected annually. However, future growth could slow with widespread adoption of automated checkout systems.
Collection workers	63,000	4,500	Employment expected to grow faster than average for all occupations as continued expanded use of credit results in increasing numbers of delinquent accounts. Best opportunities in collection agencies and retail trade firms.
File clerks	275,000	25,000	Increased demand for recordkeeping should result in some job openings. However, employment is not expected to grow as fast as in past years due to increasing use of computers to arrange, store, and transmit information. Most job openings will be created by replacement needs.
Hotel front office clerks	54,000	4,250	Employment expected to grow about as fast as average for all occupations as new hotels and motels are built. Most openings, however, will result from replacement needs.
Office machine operators	170,000	12,800	Employment expected to grow more slowly than average for all occupations as result of more centralized and computerized recordkeeping and processing systems. Most job openings due to replacement needs.

Table 21-1 (continued)

Occupation	Estimated Employment 1974	Average Annual Openings 1974–85	Employment Trends and Prospects
Secretaries and stenographers	3,300,000	439,000	The increasing use of dictating machines will limit opportunities for office stenographers. Very good prospects for skilled shorthand reporters and secretaries.
Statistical clerks	325,000	23,000	Employment expected to grow about as fast as average for all occupations as numerical data increasingly are used to analyze and control activities in businesses and government. Increased use of computers may eliminate some routine positions.
Stock clerks	490,000	26,000	Employment expected to grow about as fast as average for all occupations as business firms continue to expand. Competition anticipated as many young people seek this work as a first job.
Typists	1,000,000	125,000	Employment expected to grow faster than average for all occupations as business expansion results in increased paperwork. Very good opportunities for typists, particularly those familiar with automatic typewriters and new kinds of word processing equipment.

Computer and related occupations

Occupation	Estimated Employment 1974	Average Annual Openings 1974–85	Employment Trends and Prospects
Computer operating personnel	500,000	27,500	Employment of keypunch operators expected to decline because of advances in other data entry techniques and equipment. Employment of console and auxiliary equipment operators should grow faster than average for all occupations in response to the expanding use of computer hardware, especially terminals.
Programmers	200,000	13,000	Employment expected to grow faster than average for all occupations as computer use expands, particularly in medical, educational, and data processing services. Best opportunities for programmers with some training in systems analysis.
Systems analysts	115,000	9,100	Employment expected to grow faster than average for all occupations in response to advances in hardware and computer programs resulting in expanded computer applications. Also, as users become more familiar with computer capabilities, they will expect greater efficiency and performance from their systems.

Banking occupations

Occupation	Estimated Employment 1974	Average Annual Openings 1974–85	Employment Trends and Prospects
Bank clerks	517,000	54,000	Excellent employment opportunities due to large replacement needs and faster than average growth as banking services expand. Best prospects for those trained in computer techniques.
Bank officers	240,000	16,000	Employment expected to grow faster than average for all occupations as increasing use of computers and expansion of banking services require more officers to provide sound management. Good opportunities for college graduates as management trainees.
Bank tellers	270,000	30,000	Good employment opportunities due to large replacement needs and faster than average employment growth as banking services expand. Many openings will arise for part-time tellers to work during peak business hours.

Table 21-1 (continued)

Occupation	Estimated Employment 1974	Average Annual Openings 1974–85	Employment Trends and Prospects
Insurance occupations			
Actuaries	10,700	700	Best opportunities for college graduates who passed at least one actuarial examination while in school and have strong mathematical and statistical backgrounds. However, competition may be keen because of large number of qualified applicants.
Claim representatives	125,000	6,600	Employment expected to grow about as fast as average for all occupations in response to expanding insurance sales claims. Limited opportunities for adjusters specializing in automobile claims in states with no-fault insurance plans; favorable prospects for other types of adjusters. Less favorable prospects for claim examiners due to increased computer processing.
Insurance agents, brokers, and under-writers	470,000	19,400	Employment expected to increase about as fast as average for all occupations as insurance sales continue to expand. Selling expected to remain competitive, but ambitious people who enjoy sales work will find favorable opportunities as agents and brokers. Good prospects for under-writers.
Administrative and related occupations			
Accountants	805,000	45,500	Very good opportunities. Because of growing complexity of business accounting requirements, college graduates, particularly those who worked part time for an accounting firm while in school, will be in greater demand than nongraduates. Employers also prefer applicants trained in computer techniques.
Advertising workers	170,000	7,100	Employment expected to increase about as fast as average for all occupations as the growing number of consumer goods and expanding competition in many product and service markets cause advertising expenditures to rise. Favorable opportunities for highly qualified applicants; keen competition for others.
Buyers	110,000	9,000	Employment expected to grow faster than average for all occupations as retailers place greater emphasis on the selection of goods they have for sale. However, keen competition anticipated as merchandising attracts large numbers of college graduates.
City managers	2,900	150	Employment expected to grow faster than average for all occupations. However, persons without at least a master's degree in public administration or related management experience likely to face keen competition.
College student personnel workers	50,000		Tightening budgets in both public and private colleges and universities will limit employment growth, resulting in competition for available positions. Over short run, most openings will result from replacement needs.
Credit managers	66,000	4,500	Employment expected to increase faster than average for all occupations due to expanded use of credit by both businesses and consumers. Best opportunities in large metropolitan areas.

Table 21-1 (continued)

Occupation	Estimated Employment 1974	Average Annual Openings 1974–85	Employment Trends and Prospects
Hotel managers and assistants	120,000	6,500	Employment expected to grow about as fast as average for all occupations as additional hotels and motels are built and chain and franchise operations spread. Best opportunities for those with degrees in hotel administration.
Industrial traffic managers	20,500		Employment expected to grow more slowly than average for all occupations. Best opportunities for college graduates with majors in traffic management or transportation.
Marketing research workers	25,000	3,000	Employment expected to grow much faster than average for all occupations as marketing activities are stimulated by demand for new products and services. Best opportunities for those with graduate training in marketing research or statistics.
Personnel and labor relations workers	320,000	23,000	Employment expected to increase faster than average for all occupations as employers implement new employee relations programs in areas of occupational safety and health, equal employment opportunity, and pensions. Although growing public employee unionism will spur demand for labor relations workers, keen competition is anticipated. Best opportunities for applicants with advanced degrees.
Public relations workers	100,000	6,500	Employment expected to increase about as fast as average for all occupations as organizations expand their public relations efforts. However, keen competition for beginning jobs as glamorous nature of the occupation attracts many applicants.
Purchasing agents	189,000	11,700	Employment expected to increase faster than average for all occupations. Strongest demand for those with graduate degrees in purchasing management. Firms manufacturing technical products will need engineering and science graduates.
Urban planners	13,000	700	Employment expected to grow faster than average for all occupations in response to need for quality housing, transportation systems, health care, and other social services. Best opportunities for graduates with advanced degrees.

PROTECTIVE AND RELATED SERVICE OCCUPATIONS

Health and regulatory inspectors (government)	110,000	7,900	Employment expected to increase faster than average for all occupations in response to public concern for improved quality and safety of consumer products. Employment of health inspectors expected to grow more rapidly than that of regulatory inspectors.
Occupational safety and health workers	25,000	1,100	Employment expected to increase faster than average for all occupations as growing concern for occupational safety and health and consumer safety continues to generate programs and jobs. Best prospects for graduates of occupational safety or health curriculums.

SALES OCCUPATIONS

Automobile parts counter workers	75,000	3,500	Employment expected to increase faster than average for all occupations as more parts will be needed to repair growing number of motor vehicles.

Table 21-1 (continued)

Occupation	Estimated Employment 1974	Average Annual Openings 1974–85	Employment Trends and Prospects
Automobile salesworkers	130,000	5,500	Employment expected to grow as demand for automobiles increases. However, employment may fluctuate from year to year because car sales are highly sensitive to economic conditions and consumer preferences.
Automobile service advisers	20,000	800	Employment expected to increase about as fast as average for all occupations as automobiles increase in number and complexity. Most openings in large dealerships located in metropolitan areas.
Manufacturers' salesworkers	380,000	9,500	Employment expected to increase more slowly than average for all occupations. Some growth will occur in response to rising demand for technical products. Good opportunities for those with sales ability. Most job openings due to replacement needs.
Real estate salesworkers and brokers	400,000	28,500	Employment expected to increase about as fast as average for all occupations in response to growing demand for housing and other properties. However, highly competitive nature of occupation will result in many beginners having to transfer to other fields of work after short period of time.
Retail trade salesworkers	2,800,000	190,000	Employment expected to grow about as fast as average for all occupations as volume of sales rises and stores continue to remain open longer. Good opportunities for full-time, part-time, and temporary employment due to growth and high replacement needs.
Route drivers	190,000	3,700	Employment expected to change little, but several thousand openings annually will result from replacement needs.
Securities salesworkers	100,000	6,100	Employment expected to grow faster than average for all occupations as funds available for investment increase. Due to competitive nature of occupation, replacement needs are relatively large. Those seeking part-time work will be limited to selling shares in mutual funds.
Wholesale trade salesworkers	770,000	30,000	Employment expected to grow about as fast as average for all occupations as wholesalers sell wider variety of products and improve services to their customers. Good opportunities for persons suited to competitive nature of selling.

OCCUPATIONS IN TRANSPORTATION ACTIVITIES

Reservation, ticket, and passenger agents	56,000	4,250	Employment expected to grow faster than average for all occupations due to anticipated increase in airline passengers. Nevertheless, applicants likely to face keen competition because of popularity of airline jobs.

SCIENTIFIC AND TECHNICAL OCCUPATIONS

Mathematics Occupations

Statisticians	24,000	1,250	Employment expected to grow faster than average for all occupations due to increasing use of statistical techniques in business and government. Favorable opportunities for those who combine training in statistics with knowledge of field of application such as engineering.

Table 21-1 (continued)

Occupation	Estimated Employment 1974	Average Annual Openings 1974–85	Employment Trends and Prospects
Health Occupations			
Health services administrators	150,000	17,400	Employment expected to grow much faster than average for all occupations as quality and quantity of patient services increase and hospital management becomes more complex. Best opportunities for those with graduate degrees.
Medical record administrators	12,000	1,100	Employment expected to grow faster than average for all occupations as increased use of health facilities will add to volume and importance of medical record systems. Very good opportunities for graduates of approved programs.
SOCIAL SCIENCE OCCUPATIONS			
Economists	71,000	4,700	Economists with master's and Ph.D. degrees may face keen competition for positions in colleges and universities but may find good opportunities in private industry and government. Bachelor's degree holders are expected to face keen competition in all areas.

Source: **Occupational Outlook Quarterly,** Spring, 1976, pp. 6–29, published by the Bureau of Labor Statistics.

SPECIFIC CAREERS IN BUSINESS MANAGEMENT

This section will involve a discussion of some of the career opportunities in the functional and supportive areas of business. It is by no means an exhaustive treatment of career possibilities but involves highlighting those careers that seem to enjoy the most attention from college recruiters.

CAREERS IN OPERATIONS MANAGEMENT

There is a variety of career tracks open in operations management. Persons starting out in operations often work in one of the specialized areas, such as production control, quality control, or process planning and design. Each of these areas usually has a manager, and in large companies, there may be one or more assistant managers. In addition to these promotion possibilities, operations people often become plant managers and vice-presidents. And as is true in other functional areas, people in operations management have as much chance as anyone else to reach the top executive levels—including the presidency.

The demand for people in operations management has been good for many years, and there seems little reason to forecast any decline in that demand. The salaries are competitive with other areas, and as the reader has probably noted, there are many different challenges in a variety of responsibilities.

While manufacturing companies have typically used the majority of persons specializing in the field of operations, other types of organizations are increas-

Most colleges and universities have placement offices
which will help students to find jobs.

ingly interested. Recognition of the critical nature of operations management in
achieving organizational success has prompted banks, hospitals, large retailers,
and many others to employ specialists in the area.

CAREERS IN PERSONNEL MANAGEMENT

Many different kinds of organizations—hospitals, government agencies, businesses, banks, and others—have a personnel management function. Most persons starting out in a personnel management career begin in one of the specific
functional areas such as employment, health and safety, or wage and salary administration. Many students may obtain early experience through internships.

An internship allows a person to spend a few hours a week working in a
personnel department. Interns often work on some special project such as
analyzing a safety program but also gain an overall view of the personnel function. Universities, colleges, businesses, and government agencies frequently use
interns for a semester, quarter, or over a summer. Although internships often
carry low salaries, they do have considerable value since an internship may be of
great help in landing that first job. Sometimes interns stay right with the organizations in which they have been working.

Success in a personnel career can lead to the position of personnel manager for an entire organization. These positions are often at the vice-presidential level and are truly top executive. A vice-presidency is not necessarily the end of the road either. A vice-president in charge of personnel is just as eligible as anyone else for an executive vice-presidency of an organization or the presidency itself.

Because of the variety of work and the constant human challenge, personnel management is highly attractive to many students. For the dedicated person, it offers a highly rewarding career channel.

CAREERS IN LABOR RELATIONS

There must be those in a company who administer the contract with a union and who do the preparation for and the actual bargaining. Similarly, there are needs in labor unions for persons to help with contract administration and to help with the preparation for bargaining as well as actual bargaining.

The most immediate and constant point of contact between a union and a company is at the supervisor–union steward level. A union steward is usually a full-time employee of the company who is elected by his fellow union members to take on the duties of the steward. It is possible to begin as a union steward and work up through the union ranks. One might become the president of a local union and then move into a national or international union. Most high union officials—presidents of international unions, for example—started their careers in the ranks.

There are other positions available, especially at the international union level. There are needs for specialists in research in areas such as economics, health and safety, and pension funding. There are lawyers, writers, and administrators in unions. While the range of positions and the quantity of positions may not be as great as in business, there are certainly opportunities for the interested person.

BUSINESS CAREERS
FOR BEHAVIORAL SCIENTISTS

All supervisors and managers must be involved with behavioral science in order to work successfully with others. But are there opportunities for specialists in behavioral science in business? Large companies, in particular, are increasingly adding behavioral science specialists to their staffs. These individuals work within the organization and concentrate on organizational development in better leadership, increased motivation, cooperation among organizational members, and improved overall organizational health and morale.

Their activities may lead them into training and development work. They may carry on research within the organization and, based on the research results, may suggest and help to implement new programs and changes. It is essential and important work but may be frustrating at times because results are often slow in developing.

Many behavioral science specialists work for consulting firms or as independent consultants. In this capacity, they do much the same work as in-house behavioral scientists, but they work on a contract for a fee. Since a consultant views the organization from outside, some companies feel that consultants gain a better overall view of an organization and its possible problems.

As a behavioral science specialist, then, there are career opportunities both within an organization and outside as a consultant. And, of course, there is movement between the two possibilities. A consultant may go to work for a company on a full-time basis, or a person from an organization may go to work for a consulting firm or set up his or her own consulting firm.

Educational requirements for behavioral scientists usually include a graduate degree. A master's degree is probably a minimum requirement, and in most cases, a doctorate is probably preferred. People with advanced degrees in psychology or in organizational behavior would have the basic educational requirements to begin a career in behavioral science. For those who qualify, it appears to offer an interesting and challenging career opportunity.

CAREERS IN MARKETING

In Chapter 8 marketing is defined as a system of interacting activities designed to plan, price, promote, and distribute goods and services to consumers in order to satisfy their needs. In other words marketing deals with the management and operation of the four Ps. Generally speaking, marketing is nothing more (or less) than almost everything that happens from the time a product or a service is conceived until it is sold, and then on to post-sale service. It is somewhat difficult to speak of careers in marketing since there are so many positions included in this broad area, from product conception to sale and to post-sale. A salesperson, an advertising executive, a sales promotion manager, a marketing researcher, a retail buyer, and a brand manager are all involved in performing marketing functions.

The American Marketing Association (AMA), the professional organization for marketing persons, published a monograph in 1976 which describes key careers in marketing in six broad areas.[2] These include careers in sales, advertising, sales promotion, retailing, brand (product) management, and marketing research. Even though marketing is more than what happens in these six areas, we will limit our discussion of careers to these six and draw heavily on the material presented in the AMA monograph.

Careers in Sales   Sales can cover many possibilities: door-to-door sales, or retail sales, or being sales representative with a firm selling either consumer or industrial products. Most likely, a young person will start out selling for a large consumer-goods company as a local representative. Tasks will typically include visits to retail stores, putting up and displaying merchandise, dusting off the stock, taking orders, and making sure the company's stock does not run low. This may not sound very glamorous or challenging, but if one is ambitious and aggressive, such work may provide an excellent background for a career in sales, or in any area of marketing.

The next step up the line may lead in one of two directions. The salesperson may become a specialist in dealing with certain types of customers, such as chain stores, drug stores, or jobbers, or special market targets such as doctors, educational institutions, or governments. Or the young salesperson may advance to other higher levels within the same or another company—to become manager of

[2]Neil Holbert, *Careers in Marketing* (Chicago: American Marketing Association, Monograph Series #4, 1976).

a region, area, division, territory, or whatever they may be called. In these later jobs, more and more management responsibility exists and may lead eventually to a national sales management or vice-president in charge of sales position. It is generally conceded that the sales ladder is an excellent route to broader responsibilities in marketing and even to top management in a company.

Jobs in sales, as pointed out earlier, are not always glamorous. They often involve travel and spending many nights away from home, filling out a lot of forms, and facing indifferent sales prospects. Successful salespersons are generally those who have an outgoing personality and a competitive spirit and can discipline themselves in work and personal habits. Sales jobs, which often start at minimum salaries, can lead to lucrative incomes and a great sense of personal achievement.

Careers in Advertising   Advertising is often seen as the glamorous field in marketing. It is associated with Madison Avenue, a fast-moving crowd, and highly creative work. A small part of advertising work may be associated with the above, but most advertising positions involve working in the many advertising agencies throughout the country, or as media representatives selling advertising space to clients (manufacturers, retailers, or service firms), or as copywriters for a retail store or mail order advertiser, or executing mass communication responsibilities for an advertiser. In this latter area, jobs in public relations for a company are included.

An advertising agency exists to create advertising—television, radio, magazine, newspaper, outdoor, or direct mail—for clients. While some agencies charge their clients on a fee basis, most of the time it is 15 percent of the total advertising bill. Perhaps the best-known job in the agency is the copywriter. A copywriter writes the words for an ad and the script for a commercial. Obviously, such persons should be skilled in use of language. Certainly, courses in creative writing and journalism as well as a knowledge of marketing are essential.

Advertising agency work also offers careers in production, traffic, and media. Production sees that the ads and commercials are made correctly and on time. Traffic involves routing the ads and commercials through all phases of the agency and client, and media arranges for buying time and space.

Finally, and not of least importance, is the account executive, who is the link between the agency and the client. Sometimes the account executive may be thought of as the sales representative of the advertising agency. Certainly, the successful account executive must know both the working of his or her agency and the client's products and needs as well. An understanding of marketing, business, management, and advertising is needed in today's business world.

So whether you work in an advertising agency or as a media representative selling time or space or as a copywriter for a retailer or as an advertising specialist for a seller of products, advertising is filled with drama, pressures, and rewards.

Careers in Sales Promotion   While most people are familiar with advertising, very few are aware of sales promotion as a marketing function. Sales promotion includes about everything beyond media advertising and personal selling used to stimulate sales. This includes premiums, trading stamps, samples, coupons, contests, sweepstakes, point-of-purchase displays, trade shows, demonstrations and a host of other activities. Most of the above activities are directed toward middlemen and their sales force within the channel of distribution.

Frequently, the work in sales promotion is carried out in a sales promotion house. These houses, especially the full-time ones, have a continuous relationship with their clients that is roughly similar to the advertising agency and their clients. Sales promotion specialists have to understand their clients' total marketing effort and attempt to blend sales promotion efforts with other aspects of the clients' marketing objectives.

Careers in sales promotion require an understanding of merchandising, marketing, and promotional function. A knowledge of the graphic arts—layout, materials, sizes and shapes, up-to-date technical possibilities—is also essential for a successful career in sales promotion.

Careers in Retailing   Retailing institutions change and adapt to consumer life styles and buying patterns; they come and go; they range in size from Sears Roebuck and Company to the corner pipe shop. But the job of retailing remains the same—that is, to match the needs of consumers with merchandise available from manufacturers and distributors.

Most sales come through direct contact with the multitude of retail clerks and salespersons. If they perform their jobs well and succeed, they get to know merchandise and their customers' needs well. They understand the important elements of consumer psychology and find great satisfaction in the day-to-day tasks of meeting the public and attempting to satisfy their product needs.

If these retail salespersons are in fact successful, they move up to assistant department managers or department managers, depending upon how the organization is structured. Here an understanding of personnel and operations management and labor relations are important along with retailing.

Another important job in retailing is that of the buyer. It often takes a great deal of product experience as well as knowledge of one's market to be able to buy thousands of units of dresses, suits, or shoes, for example, that will sell in a highly competitive retail market. The life of a buyer is frequently thought of as fast, furious, and demanding, but the successful buyer must always be able to distinguish fakery from authenticity.

Careers in retailing involve selling, supervising, buying, and merchandising. A good background in the specialties of retailing, marketing, psychology, and managements is often prerequisite to rewarding and successful careers.

Careers in Brand Management   Being a brand (or a product) manager is like running your own little (but sometimes not so small) marketing company. For the brand or product manager must be familiar with all aspects of marketing a brand but cannot be a specialty in any of these. The brand manager, simply stated, is responsible for overseeing all the activities relating to a brand, such as Tide washing powder, Crisco shortening, or Kleenex facial tissues, as well as the bottom line of the balance sheet for that brand. Sometimes this responsibility extends to a group of branded products within a company's line. In this work the brand manager must work with other managers in production, sales, R&D, advertising, transportation, and sales promotion as well as marketing research, packaging, purchasing, and legal specialists. The brand manager is neither line nor staff, is more of a generalist than specialist, has probably more responsibility than authority, and is usually one of a number of brand managers in a company.

Positions in brand or product management are often financially rewarding, challenging, and demanding. A Master of Business Administration (M.B.A.) degree is often a recommended credential for a brand manager's slot for the breadth of education it offers. A student who views brand or product management as a professional objective should pursue an undergraduate program in marketing and look forward to earning an M.B.A. later on.

Careers in Marketing Research   Marketing research offers a challenge for those who are interested in solving problems—marketing problems in this case—using different approaches and disciplines. In Chapter 15 we offered a definition of research. Marketing research is an organized, objective, and systematic approach to solving problems in marketing. It involves data gathering, data analysis, and interpretation which will help marketing managers make better-informed decisions. Understanding and skills in statistical analysis, marketing, and communications are necessary. In addition, knowledge of psychology, sociology, and mathematics is important for the researcher in many areas. Attempting to understand consumer behavior is one of the newest and most exciting aspects of marketing research.

Where can you find jobs in marketing research? You would work either with a provider of goods and services (manufacturer, retailer, media, trade association, government), a research consulting firm, or with an advertising agency.

In each of the above three settings, you may be expected to do a wide variety of research projects—test marketing, advertising research, package testing, concept testing, motivation research, and so on—and usually to do work involving a number of different approaches. It is sometimes recommended that the best place to start for a career in marketing research is with a research consulting firm for the exposure it will offer in research fundamentals and variety of research projects. With the proper experience at the entrance levels and the ability to think analytically, persons in marketing research can attain a research director's slot—often called the intelligence arm of marketing management.

CAREERS IN ACCOUNTING

Opportunities in accounting are excellent today. It is considered to be one of the best growth areas, with increasing job openings during the next decade. Accounting careers will be broken into three different sectors.

Public Accounting   Public accounting work is performed by individuals who are members of public accounting firms. These organizations are professional firms which act as agents for their clients.

Individuals joining a public accounting firm are expected to pass the Certified Public Accountants' examination. This test is prepared and administered by the American Institute of Certified Public Accountants, a national professional organization. Individuals who pass this exam and satisfy additional criteria are designated *Certified Public Accountants* (CPAs). Granting of the license and the right to practice is done by the various states. CPAs perform three major tasks.

Auditing   Auditing consists of examining the financial statements and underlying records of a firm to make sure that the accounting methods and techniques employed to record transactions and present the financial statements are acceptable to standards set forth by the public accounting profession. Outside parties such as investors and lenders can have a high degree of confidence in and can rely on the statements as a result of the CPA's opinion, assuming, of course, that it is favorable.

Income Taxes Given the increasingly complex tax regulations set forth by Congress, CPAs frequently give tax advice and compute the tax return for their clients.

Management Consulting A third area of work performed by public accountants is management consulting. Auditing and tax work familiarize the CPA with the client's accounting system and problems so that consulting in areas such as inventory ordering systems, warehouse location, new product selection, and capital acquisition analysis is a logical extension of the other services.

Private Accounting
Accountants who work for industrial, merchandising, and service firms fall into this category. Many CPAs also go into the private accounting sector after gaining experience and expertise as public accountants.

A professional examination is also offered for individuals going into private accounting. It is called the Certificate in Management Accounting examination. Those passing it are designated as *Certified Management Accountants* (CMAs). Private accounting can be broken down into several functions.

Cost Accounting In this function the accountant is responsible for determining costs of products and services. Traditionally it has been most applicable to manufacturing firms, but industries such as banks have become more conscious of computing the cost of various services, so the concept of cost accounting has extended far beyond its original bounds.

Budgeting The importance of budgeting as a management tool for planning and control purposes was previously noted in Chapter 14. Budgeting can also include the complex and interesting area of capital acquisitions analysis, where selection must be made between competing projects based on an analysis of future cash flows for the purpose of maximizing the return to the firm.

Internal Auditing Large companies employ a staff of internal auditors as well as public accountants who perform the external auditing function. Among their principal concerns are spotting incorrect applications of accounting procedures and detecting fraudulent operations, if any exist.

Tax Accounting Tax laws and regulations at both the federal and state levels are so complex that large firms usually have a staff that specializes in these laws.

Government Accounting The federal and local governments have likewise experienced a sharp increase in their demand for accountants.

In general, government accountants are responsible for keeping track of the costs appropriated for and spent by the various agencies and departments of state and local governments. The federal government has an extremely important agency performing essentially an auditing function called the General Accounting Office. This agency has been responsible for finding many irregularities in the spending of the taxpayer's money.

Another important area for accountants in the federal government (and in corresponding state agencies) is with the Internal Revenue Service of the Department of the Treasury, which is responsible for administering the collection and reporting of income taxes.

CAREERS IN FINANCE

In finance we can distinguish between financial management in business firms and careers in financial institutions.

Corporate Financial Management   A good background for careers in this area is knowledge in both accounting and finance. In general, financial management functions keep track of cash, credit granting and collections on account, investment of excess funds in stocks and bonds, and insuring the property of the enterprise as well as the lives of key executives, if desired. Accounting and finance functions often overlap.

In small firms it is quite likely that one person, no matter what the actual job title might be, will be responsible for carrying out both functions. In larger firms, the duties are usually divided. While titles vary considerably, the chief financial executive is often called the treasurer, and the principal accounting officer is known as the controller (either or both may also have vice-presidential titles).

The Financial Executives' Institute, a leading professional organization whose membership comprises upper echelon accounting and financial executives, lists the functions of each:

Treasurer (finance)	*Controller (accounting)*
1. Raising investment funds	1. Planning and control
2. Investor relations	2. Record keeping and financial reporting
3. Short-term financing	3. Evaluating and consulting
4. Banking	4. Tax administration
5. Credit granting and collection	5. Government reporting
6. Investments	6. Protection of assets
7. Insurance	7. Economic appraisal

The list is, of course, a hypothetical breakdown, but it does follow fairly closely the distinctions made here between accounting and financial management.

Financial Institutions   Financial institutions include banks, savings and loan associations, trust companies, and insurance companies. Insurance companies will be discussed separately below. Some of the principal operating positions in these firms that business administration students (usually with a finance emphasis) can strive for are briefly discussed.

Bank Tellers   Bank tellers are responsible for handling transactions with customers' deposits and withdrawals from their accounts. The person who is in charge of these operations is often called a cashier.

Loan Officers Loan officers in financial institutions are responsible for assessing the credit worthiness of loan applicants. Loan applicants can range from individuals desiring consumer installment loans for automobiles or other consumer durables or mortgage loans on a house to large businesses desiring either short-term or long-term credit.

Trust Officers Trust officers are responsible for investing and maintaining funds left with them in accordance with the wishes of the person or persons setting up the trust.

Portfolio Managers Portfolio managers are responsible for managing the investments of the financial institution itself in the securities of other firms.

The Securities Industry The securities industry embraces the issuing and trading of stocks, bonds, and other securities and also the trading of commodities. Those desiring to enter this exciting industry should have a background in finance courses, particularly those courses dealing with investments.

Customers' Representatives Persons in this position are usually referred to as *stockbrokers* or *commodities brokers* for that segment of the industry. They are responsible for carrying out the wishes of their clients in buying and selling securities or commodities. Brokers often give their customers advice on these matters.

Securities Analysts Securities analysts are individuals who do research in depth on securities and industries for brokers and dealers as well as firms that specialize in giving advice and information on particular issues of securities and industries for investment purposes. Commodities analysts perform a similar function for that area of the securities industry.

Insurance The insurance industry offers a wide range of satisfying careers for those attracted to this field.

Business administration courses with an emphasis in insurance are a helpful entry in this area. For those with a college background, several entry-level positions within insurance companies themselves are of interest.

Underwriters Underwriters are responsible for evaluating risks and selecting those risks that the company will insure. Their judgment is thus instrumental in minimizing the insurance company's claims payments so that it can realize greater profits.

Claims Examiners and Claims Adjusters Claims examiners investigate claims against the company to make sure that they are legitimate, whereas claims adjusters actually settle the claims of policyholders.

Actuaries Actuaries are responsible for statistically analyzing mortality and property and casualty loss expectations so that adequate premium rates can be set. Traditionally, many individuals who have moved to the top management slots of insurance companies have come from the ranks of the actuaries. Those desiring to enter this area should major in actuarial science, which requires a strong mathematical and statistical background, and have courses in insurance. Only a relatively small number of colleges of business in American universities have actuarial science programs.

Portfolio Managers   Since insurance companies have large investment portfolios also, portfolio management is important for these companies.

Insurance Agents and Insurance Brokers   These positions are external to the insurance companies. Agents and brokers perform a marketing function by bringing the insurance company and the individual or firm to be insured together. Insurance agents sell insurance for one or more insurance companies through independent agencies.

Insurance brokers are, to a large extent, the opposite of insurance agents. They are agents of the buyers of insurance. Their function is to acquire insurance for their clients that best meets their clients' needs in amounts of premium and coverage offered by the various companies. Insurance sales are also made by individuals who are employees of the company as opposed to independent agents.

CAREERS IN COMPUTER INFORMATION SYSTEMS

One of the fastest-growing occupations for young people is in computer operation and analysis. In most cases new skills are required which may be obtained by working directly with computers in school or on the job. As advancement occurs, a background in mathematics, statistics, computer science, and business administration is needed.

Although there are variations in titles and responsibilities, three major jobs are generally found in data processing installations.

Computer Programmer   The typical entry-level position for young men and women with at least two years of college is a programmer. This job consists of preparing computer programs based on specifications prepared by the systems analyst. The programmer needs specialized skills in writing computer instructions.

Systems Analyst   The systems analyst requires a broader background in education and understanding of organizations. This individual studies information needs and data processing requirements for managers within the organization and designs the data processing system. In addition, the systems analyst prepares the program specifications for the programmers.

Information System Analyst   As organizations develop management information systems, as discussed in Chapter 15, a key person in the analysis, design, and implementation of the formal information system is the information analyst. Basically, the information analyst is the interface between the users of the information (i.e., managers) and the technical persons, such as programmers, data base administrations, system analysts, and machine operators, who work in the system. Persons who aspire to this position need a sound knowledge of computer science as well as a broad-based understanding of organizations, management, and business administration. The responsibility often means arriving at the best mix of money, people, machines, materials, and methods for implementing the information system. A college education in business administration majoring in computer information systems with successful experience in an organization should prepare one for a career as an information system specialist.

In summary, these occupational profiles may be useful in assessing what jobs will be available in what industries. The final decision in the selection of an occupation should be based on the individual's interest and aptitude, and on his or her ability and means to acquire the necessary skills and education for a particular occupation. Getting as much education and training as one's abilities and circumstances permit should therefore be a top priority for today's youth.

SUMMARY

*

GLOSSARY

achievement test   an employment test that measures knowledge or skill that an applicant for a job already has. See also *employment test.*

account   that part of an accounting system where transactions affecting all similar elements of a firm are processed and kept up to date.

account receivable   claim created when goods are sold without immediately receiving the cash.

accounting   a system within an enterprise responsible for recording, processing, and preparing financial statements from basic data arising from enterprise transactions.

advertising   impersonal form of communication to a mass audience about a company or its products.

advertising agency   a business that plans, produces, and places advertisements in media for other businesses and may often arrange total advertising programs for their clients.

affirmative action   positive programs to achieve equal opportunities for minorities and women as required under the Equal Employment Opportunity Act.

agency   a legal arrangement whereby one party represents and performs a service for another party. The agent carries out his or her task in the best manner seen fit and is not an employee of the other party.

agency shop   a form of union recognition in which an employee does not have to belong to a union in order to work for a given company but must pay the equivalent of the initiation fee and regular dues to the union.

agent wholesaler   a wholesaler who does not take title to the goods and services in the marketing process but assumes a specialized role of selling for a client.

aggression   a reaction to frustration over not satisfying a need in which people become verbally or physically abusive toward others or toward inanimate objects.

alien corporations   corporations originating in foreign nations.

annuity   a fixed amount received (or paid) per time period. Many pension plans call for the payment of monthly annuities to retirees.

anthropology   the study of the effects of differing cultures on the behavior of individuals, groups, and organizations.

application form   a form that collects factual information about a candidate for a job; includes such items as address, past experience, and education. The candidate usually completes the application form.

applied research   research aimed at solving specific problems.

apprenticeship   the learning of new skills and knowledge over a period of years under the instruction and guidance of highly skilled craftsmen; usually includes both on-the-job and off-the-job training; may require a final examination to certify qualification to practice the newly learned skill or trade.

aptitude test   an employment test that measures a person's potential ability for a given job or for an area of work application. See also *employment test.*

arbitration   a process in which a third party

issues a binding ruling in disputes between two primary parties; often used in labor relations to settle grievances.

arithmetic unit   that part of the computer system which performs the mathematical, statistical, and logical operations.

articles of copartnership   a written document specifying the rights and responsibilities of the partners, including how profits are to be divided.

assets   resources of value owned or controlled by an enterprise.

balance   amount left in an account after increases and decreases are figured.

balance of payments   the net difference between money flowing into a country and money flowing out of that country as a result of trade and other international transactions. A favorable balance of payments means that there is a net flow of money into the country, and vice versa.

balance of trade   the net difference between the monetary value of a country's imports and exports.

balance sheet   a financial statement showing the wealth of an enterprise. Liabilities and owners' equities of the firm will equal its assets.

bankruptcy   a legal situation arising when a firm or individual is unable to pay debts due.

bargaining (collective)   the discussions between management and labor that result in a labor contract. Major issues of concern are usually wages, hours, and working conditions.

BASIC   generally thought of as a computer language for beginners.

basing-point pricing   pricing arrangement in which the final price to the customer includes the base price plus transportation charges from an industry-agreed-on basing point.

behavioral science   a body of theoretical knowledge about the behavior of individuals, groups, and organizations based on the disciplines of psychology, sociology, and anthropology.

best-efforts arrangement   arrangement in which investment banks sell a new securities issue for the best price they can get, obtaining a commission for this service.

binary system   system of counting used by computers which has only two digits, zero and one.

boycott   the situation during a labor dispute between the union and the company in which the union encourages its members and others not to buy the products of the company.

brand   a name, term, symbol, or design (or combination of these) used to identify a company's product and distinguish it from those of competitors.

break-even point   that level of output at which there is a zero level of profit.

budget   a financial plan applicable to a future period expressed in dollars.

budgeting   setting goals for a particular time period for the various operating elements of a firm and also for expected changes in cash.

business   the main instrument through which individuals practice the capitalistic or private enterprise system. See also *capitalism.*

business cycle   a period of time characterized by changing states of the economy, usually alternating periods of recession or depression, recovery, prosperity, and then again recession or depression. The decline into recession and the recovery into prosperity are often accompanied by deflation and inflation, respectively.

callable bonds   a feature of a bond issue allowing the issuing corporation to recall them prior to the maturity date. The issuer must pay a premium fee as well as the principal on the bonds if they are called prior to maturity.

capacity analysis   the process of determining if a business organization has the available labor, facilities, and/or equipment for additional production.

capital the means by which the human resource can more efficiently use land in the production of goods and services. Capital includes all types of equipment, tools, machinery, buildings, and transportation.

capital budgeting the process of selecting among long-lived assets for purposes of acquisition and usage.

capital gain the gain (or loss) from selling a bond or stock at a price higher than it was acquired for.

capital intensive firms that are highly automated. Costs of using machinery and equipment are high in these firms.

capitalism the economic system which is characterized by the right to own and use property and to earn a profit or sustain a loss, by a price system in which individual businesses are relatively free to set their own prices for products and goods, and by relatively free competition.

capital markets market for supplying of long-term debt and equity funds.

capital stock certificates of ownership in an incorporated business.

capital turnover net sales divided by average assets for the period.

carrying cost the cost of carrying inventory, which includes such items as breakage, insurance, the use of storage space, and an interest charge on the money tied up in inventory.

cartel an organization of producers to control output and price of a product. OPEC is the most important recent example of a cartel.

cash discount a deduction from list price if payment is made within a specified time period.

caveat emptor "let the buyer beware," a philosophy of business during the 1800s which advocates that consumers should be responsible for their purchases.

centralization the concentration of authority and responsibility for decision making at the top level of an organization.

chain of command the distribution of authority in an organization from the top to the bottom.

channel of distribution the route or course taken by a product through the middlemen who take title or assist in the transfer of title in the distribution process. A channel of distribution also includes the producer and the consumer.

charter the legal document issued by states which establishes the legality of corporations and gives them the right to conduct business in stated areas.

checking accounts accounts at banks allowing the account holder to write checks.

classroom training the learning of new skills and knowledge in a separate room—a classroom—through letters and the use of audiovisual materials such as films and slides.

closed-end investment companies investment companies whose shares are traded in the securities market. These companies rarely issue new securities of their own.

closed shop a form of union recognition in which a person must be a member of a certain union before gaining employment with a company in which the union is the certified bargaining agent.

coaching a form of management development in which a superior manager works closely with a subordinate to guide the latter into learning new skills and knowledge. See also *management development*.

COBOL COmmon Business Oriented Language. Short for a specialized language that is extremely close to English, used mostly in business data processing.

cognitive dissonance a mental state of anxiety or doubt which may occur after purchasing a product if negative information is received about the product or company and if unfavorable experiences are encountered.

coinsurance minimum allowable percentage of insuring in order for the insured to recover full amount of loss on smaller claims.

commercial bank a bank whose functions include lending money to business firms.

commercial finance companies companies that provide loans to businesses that are marginal in their credit standing.

commercial paper four- to six-month maturity unsecured promissory notes of the strongest major corporations of the United States.

common stock the basic risk type of equity capital that all corporations must have.

communism an economic system in which there is state ownership of virtually all the productive resources of the economy. All production and market decisions are usually made by the central government. Communism is typically associated with a totalitarian form of government.

compensation a reaction to frustration over not satisfying some need in which people attempt to become outstanding in some activity not directly related to the activity in which the need frustration occurred.

competition a component of capitalism which permits businesses to sell, advertise, promote, reduce prices, and in other ways to gain an increasing share of the total business available to a number of similar businesses.

computer an electronic system that can store, process, and manipulate large quantities of data quickly and accurately.

computer program a detailed, logical set of instructions telling the computer what to do, how to do it, and in what order to perform each operation.

consumer behavior a body of knowledge which seeks to explain the underlying reasons for consumer purchasing patterns.

consumer finance companies companies that make installment loans directly to consumers for the purchase of durables and also for personal loans.

consumer installment loans loans repayable in installments for consumer durables such as automobiles; also includes amounts borrowed through credit cards.

consumerism the movement which is concerned with promoting and protecting the interests of consumers. It includes the range of programs and actions by government, business, and independent groups.

Consumer Price Index a figure which measures the change in price of a selected group of consumer goods and services from a base period. It is a measure of inflation.

consumer rights as enunciated by President John F. Kennedy in 1962, these include: (1) the right to safety, (2) the right to be informed, (3) the right to choose, (4) the right to be heard.

contingency view a view of leadership which indicates that the style of leadership which should be used varies with conditions and circumstances. The contingency view also suggests that almost anyone can be a successful leader given the proper circumstances.

contract an agreement between two parties. One party must make an offer and the other must accept it. Each party must give consideration, which is something of legal value that is given to or performed for the other party.

contract (labor) the labor agreement between a company and a union that covers conditions of employment. It is in written form.

control action set up by a system or method to assure that actual results conform to planned results.

control of operations a production or operations process to assure that the right inputs are converted into the right outputs at the right time.

control unit that part of the computer system which directs or instructs the computer as to what to do.

convenience goods a classification of consumer products for which potential buyers are willing to spend little effort in comparative shopping; repurchasing occurs frequently; and products are generally of low unit value.

conversion the changing of organizational inputs such as raw material, money, people, and management into outputs of goods and services.

conversion process see *operations management*.

convertible bonds bonds which the owner has the right to convert or trade for a designated number of common shares of the issuing corporation.

convertible preferred stock preferred stock which can be converted into a stipulated number of common shares if the owner desires.

cooperative a private, nonprofit organization chartered under state law. It is operated like a business, but profits are distributed to the owner-members at the end of the year.

copyrights exclusive right for twenty-eight years to written, drawn, illustrated, or designed materials. A copyright may be renewed for one additional twenty-eight-year period. They are registered with the Library of Congress.

corporate chains retail stores which are centrally owned and managed with all the units within the company handling the same product line.

corporation a business form in which the owners' liability extends only to the amount of their investment.

cost of goods sold cost of inventory used during a period by merchandising firms.

cost-of-living factor a clause in a labor contract or a company policy that increases wages to match price increases as reflected in the government cost-of-living index.

cost-volume-profit analysis estimate of income at various levels of output for the period. It is used as part of the budgeting or planning process.

cottage system a system in which producers deliver raw materials to homes where families or individuals work to convert the raw materials to partially finished or finished products. These products are then picked up by the producer.

coupon bonds bonds containing coupons which are clipped and presented to a commercial bank for the interest when it becomes due. These bonds are payable to the holder and are transferred to a new owner by simply giving him or her the bond.

craft union a labor union that organizes all workers of a particular skill into one local union in a given geographic area.

creditors parties to whom debts are owed by the enterprise.

credit unions savings and lending institutions for a particular group of people such as employees of a company. Credit unions are owned by their members.

critical path the longest path through a network that identifies the minimum amount of time it will take to complete a project. See also *network technique*.

cumulative feature of many preferred stock issues. Any preferred dividends that were not paid in previous years must be paid before common stockholders can receive their dividend.

cumulative voting a method of giving more concentrated voting power to small stockholders. Each shareholder can cast a number of votes which is equal to the product of the number of shares owned times the number of directors to be elected.

current assets cash plus all assets that will become cash within a year or will be used up within a year.

current liabilities liabilities that become due for payment within a year.

current ratio current assets divided by current liabilities.

debenture bonds bonds issued only on the general credit standing of the issuing corporation.

decentralization the distribution of authority and responsibility for decision making to the lowest possible levels in the organization.

decimal system commonly used counting system which is built on a base of ten and uses ten digits.

default nonpayment of either principal or interest on a bond or note when it becomes due.

defense mechanism actions and attitudes people adopt in order to defend themselves against frustration and failure, often in seeking need satisfaction, and which may help an otherwise well-balanced person to preserve self-respect and to function effectively.

deflation a state of the economy in which wages and prices are falling.

degradable wastes waste matter which is organic in nature—that is, composed of living organisms. It can enter the food chain of bacteria, causing them to multiply, therefore creating stress upon higher living species.

demand curve a demand schedule shown in graphic form.

demand deposits checking accounts.

demand elasticity responsiveness of quantity demanded by consumers to changes in price.

demand schedule schedule of how many units of a product will be bought at various prices.

department store a retailing institution organized into a series of departments or specialty shops and which offers the customer a wide product line and a range of consumer services.

depreciation the process of wearing out over time of long-lived assets.

depression a state of the economy characterized by high unemployment, low production and sales, and a general atmosphere of pessimism.

descriptive research studies which describe what happens under particular conditions and situations, especially with respect to the behavior of individuals, groups, and organizations.

discharge the requirement that an employee leave the organization for reasons of incompetence, undesirable characteristics, or other reasons. Commonly referred to as being "fired."

discount houses retail stores which offer nationally advertised products at lower than suggested manufacturers' prices with few of the services generally given by conventional retailers.

discounting the process of taking a note receivable to the bank prior to its maturity. The bank will charge interest against the maturity value of the note based on its own holding period.

discount pricing allowing a deduction from the stated list price.

discretionary income income over and above that required to meet fixed commitments and essential household needs.

disposable personal income that part of personal income available for consumption expenditures and savings. For the typical wage earner, it is his or her "take-home" pay.

dividends a return of cash to stockholders for the use of their money.

division of labor the dividing of work into specialized segments or components, such as the dividing of organizational work into production, marketing, and finance.

domestic corporation corporations incorporated within a particular state are domestic corporations in that state.

double entry system of accounting the system of accounting that brings about equality between a firm's assets and the total of its liabilities and owners' equities.

dynamic equilibrium a position of balance maintained by an open system through its interaction with the environment. The position of balance constantly changes as the open system has new inputs and outputs. See also *open system.*

dynamic growth a stage of growth in which a business is growing very fast and is operated by one person and some personal assistants in an informal manner.

ecology the interrelationships among all living things and the natural environment of the earth. The term is used for the movement for cleaner air, water, and communities.

effectiveness the degree to which the doing of a job or task actually accomplishes the intended purpose.

efficiency the ratio between input to a task and the output. Maximum output for a given level of input means highest efficiency; often measured in terms of dollars, time, or units of output.

elastic demand when a price change elicits an even greater change in quantity purchased by consumers.

electronic funds transfer computerized or credit card banking. Computer terminals in places such as supermarkets allow one to make transactions without actually going to the bank.

embargo the prohibition against the movement of a commodity in and out of a country during a stated time period.

empirical research studies of actual behavior of individuals, groups, and organizations, in work situations, for example; as opposed to theorizing on the basis of personal experience or logic.

employee relations see *human assets management.* The term *employee relations* places more emphasis on developing and maintaining a satisfactory work role and environment for the employees.

employment test some form of examination (written or demonstration of skill, for example) which reveals information about an applicant's skills, aptitudes, intelligence, or personality concerning aptitude for a particular job opening.

endowment policies policies that pay the entire amount of the contract either at the end of the contractual period or upon the death of the insured.

entrepreneur a person who assumes the risk of organizing and managing a business in the hope of making a profit.

equilibrium price price indicated by the intersection of the supply and demand curves.

equities investment in a firm by its owners.

escalator clause a cost-of-living clause in a labor contract. See also *cost-of-living factor.*

esteem need the desire for the respect of oneself and of others for the work and activities that a person does.

ethics (business) those practices, attitudes, and behavior patterns of businesses and business people which are moral or immoral, legal or illegal, fair or unfair, good or bad. Business ethics are usually categorized as good or bad, high-level or low-level, or in some category in between.

evaluation the measurement of performance on a job; often includes measurement of personal factors such as cooperation and integrity; used primarily for promotions and pay increases.

exchange rate the units of one currency—for example, pound—needed to buy one unit of another currency—for example, dollars.

exit interview a talk with a person who is leaving an organization in an effort to determine attitudes or comments that may be helpful to an organization in improving its policies and practices.

expenses assets or resources of a firm used during the period in the course of operations.

experiment an artificially designed situation, usually with a control group, to produce data for a research project.

export movement of goods out of a country for sale in another country.

factors companies that acquire accounts receivable from business firms, relieving the latter of the financing function.

family life cycle a classification of consumers by marital status, age of family head, and number and ages of children. Generally, the family life cycle is thought to be an evolutionary process.

financial statement ratios ratios derived from financial statements which help to assess how strong a firm is and how well it is doing.

fixed assets another term for long-lived assets—those having a life or period of usefulness extending beyond a year.

fixed costs costs which remain level within wide changes in production.

F.O.B. pricing pricing arrangement where the seller quotes a base price plus shipment cost. When prices are quoted F.O.B. shipping point, the buyer pays base price plus transportation charges from factory or mill.

forecasting making predictions about events or conditions at some future date.

foreign corporations those incorporated in other states.

FORTRAN short for "FORmula TRANslator." A computer language used mostly for scientific research purposes.

franchise a business arrangement between a franchiser (manufacturer, service firm, or wholesaler) and a series of independent outlets (generally retailers or wholesalers) in which the franchiser grants the franchisee the right to sell certain goods and services in generally defined markets. In return, the franchisee agrees to market the goods and services in a manner established by the franchiser.

free enterprise see *private enterprise.*

fringe benefits those benefits which are part of the total pay package for employees but which do not represent a direct money payment. Examples include health insurance and retirement benefits.

functional middleman independent businesses who do not take title to the products they distribute in the channel of distribution.

funds both the assets in which a firm invests and the means by which assets have been financed. The term is rather general in both these uses.

Gantt chart a type of control chart in operations that shows what work has to be done on particular equipment or facilities during a given period of time.

general partnership partnership created for the purpose of conducting a particular kind of business.

geographical pricing pricing arrangements which are based on the geographical location of the buyer.

going public the process of switching a corporation from the status of one whose stock is closely held by a few people to wider ownership through listing the stock for trading on a regional or national stock exchange.

graphic rating scale a form of evaluation that lists several factors describing performance on a scale. The supervisor checks a point on the scale to indicate the evaluation. See also *evaluation.*

grievance a complaint by a worker in a unionized company that the contract has been violated in some way that affects the worker.

grievance procedure the established, formal procedure in a unionized company by which a grievance is dealt with by the company and the union. The grievance procedure is spelled out in the labor contract. See also *grievance.*

gross national product (GNP) market value of all goods and services produced in the economy during a given period.

gross profit the difference between dollar costs and dollar sales before the deduction of labor costs and other expenses.

group cohesion the attractiveness of a group to an individual which makes that person want to join the group and stay in the group.

group standard the rules, practices, and policies that a group has and which members must observe if they are to stay in the group and be in good standing with other members of the group.

hardware the electronic and mechanical components of a computer system.

heterogeneous market a market composed of consumers with diverse or dissimilar characteristics and buying patterns.

holding company a company formed for the purpose of investing in and controlling other companies.

holistic examination of all aspects of a system and their interrelationships.

homogeneous market a market composed of consumers with similar characteristics and buying patterns.

human assets accounting the placing of dollar values on the individual employees of company based on the cost of hiring and training a replacement as well as the value of the future contribution of the employee.

human assets management that part of an organization which has responsibility for providing an adequate force through specific actions such as recruiting, hiring, training, paying, and assuring a safe and healthful work environment.

hypothesis an educated guess about the relationships in a research problem.

import movement of goods into a country produced outside the country.

incentive plan a pay plan that is based on productivity. The more that is produced on a given job, the greater is the pay for that job.

income statement financial statement showing the results of operations for a firm over a given time in terms of profit or loss.

incongruous not consistent or incompatible with another position, statement, parts, or qualities.

indenture the individual provisions of a bond contract. It covers factors such as cumulative, participative, and convertible features of the individual bond issue.

industrial consumer one who buys goods and services to use directly or indirectly in the production of other goods and services.

industrial revolution a period from approximately 1700 to 1900 when great inventions and technological discoveries were made in Europe and the United States. These inventions greatly aided the development of manufacturing and transportation.

industrial union a labor union that seeks to organize all levels of skilled labor within a given plant.

inelastic demand when a price change elicits a smaller change in quantity purchased by consumers.

inflation decline in the purchasing power of money resulting in rising prices of goods and services.

injunction a court order that prohibits some action by a party from occurring. Formerly used by companies to force unions to stop organizing activities or to stop a strike.

input in a management information system, data which will be processed and translated into information for decision making.

inputs the factors of production (land, labor, capital, and management) that go into the conversion process of an organization. See also *operations management.*

inspection the process of measuring and/or testing a good or service to make sure that the desired quality level is actually being maintained in the productive process.

insurance premium amount paid by the insured for protection against a particular risk.

integrated wholesaling the combining of the wholesaling function with manufacturing and/or retailing into one business concern. Generally this occurs with large-scale manufacturers or retailers.

intelligence test an employment test that provides a measure of mental alertness and awareness. It gives an appraisal of an applicant's ability to cope with varying levels of job difficulty. See also *employment test.*

interchangeability of parts component parts which are identical so they can be exchanged for one another in a product.

interview (employment) an oral interaction between the candidate for a job and a member of the organization which has the job opening. The purpose of the interview is to provide additional information about the candidate and to give the candidate information about the company.

inventory stockpiles or supplies of raw materials, in-process goods, and finished goods that will help a business meet customer demands on time and with the right product.

inventory turnover cost of goods sold divided by average inventory for the period.

invested funds money or other resources invested by owners; part of the owners' equities of a firm.

investment bank an intermediary who performs important services for a firm issuing new securities.

investment credit a tax reduction to buyers of new machinery and equipment. Its intention is to stimulate business activity.

invoice the seller's bill sent to the buyer of goods indicating quantity and price of goods purchased as well as terms of payment.

job analysis an overall study of a job to determine its exact content of duties, operations, working conditions, and worker requirements such as skills, knowledge, and physical and mental demands.

job description identifies the nature of the work to be performed on a job and provides a summary of the job and a listing of the specific duties.

job enrichment enlarging a job to include more duties and more responsibility for planning, controlling, and organizing one's own work.

job evaluation a study of the required skills, knowledge, mental and physical effort, responsibility, and working conditions in the jobs of an organization in order to determine an equitable pay structure for all employees.

job rotation a form of management development in which individuals change jobs within a company frequently to gain skills, knowledge, and experience. See also *management development*.

job specification a statement of the minimum acceptable human qualities which are required to properly perform a job, such as education, knowledge, physical condition, experience, and skill.

joint ventures in international business, a venture in which a home-based company joins with a local firm in another country to form a new, jointly owned manufacturing and/or marketing company.

journals books used for recording the accounting transactions of a firm.

labor one of the four factors of production. It is the human resource which expends physical and mental energy in the production of goods and services.

labor intensive firms whose labor costs are relatively high.

labor relations see *human assets management*. The term *labor relations* places emphasis on

that phase of human assets management which deals with labor unions—that is, collective bargaining and contract administration specifically.

labor union a private organization of workers who have joined together to advance their common interests.

laissez-faire "let alone" or "hands off" or "let businesses compete"; an economic philosophy that advocates government's playing a limited role in economic affairs.

land one of the four factors of production. Land includes natural resources such as oil and mineral deposits, water, forests, and land.

leadership the ability of a person to cause others to take certain actions willingly and behave in certain ways that are desired by the person in leadership.

learning curve a curve that shows how the costs of producing a product, especially a new product, decrease as experience is gained over time and labor and equipment is more efficiently used.

lease a contractual arrangement in which the user has a right to solve use of a particular piece of property for a specified time although he or she does not own the property.

leave of absence a temporary absence from an organization with permission on the part of an employee. Leaves may vary in duration from a few days to a year or more.

lessee party having the right to use leased property.

lessor owner of leased property.

leverage proportion of bonds to stocks maintained by a firm in terms of how its own assets are financed. The higher the proportion of bonds, the greater the degree of leverage.

licensing in international business, the situation in which the parent firm in one country permits a local firm of another country to manufacture and sell the parent firm's products, in return for royalty fees.

limited partnership a partnership in which

one partner invests in the firm but does not take part in running it. The limited partner's liability is restricted to his or her investment in the event of failure of the firm.

limit order   when an investor asks his or her broker to buy or sell a security at a particular price.

line of credit   an open amount that can be borrowed by a business up to a specified maximum. The borrower usually must repay the loan annually before renewal.

line personnel   those persons in a business who have responsibility for carrying out the principal operations of the business—usually in production, marketing, and finance.

liquidity   how rapidly an asset becomes converted to cash or how rapidly a liability becomes due for payment.

lockout   the company's counterpart to the union's strike in a labor dispute. The company closes its doors and refuses to allow employees to enter the plant to work.

long-lived assets   assets whose life or period of use extends beyond a year.

long-term debt   debt that becomes due for payment beyond a year from the present date.

magnetic tape   one of the devices for storing, entering, and retrieving data from computer systems.

maker   the payer or writer of a note payable. It often arises if the maker needs an extension of time to pay a bill.

management   (1) the component of an organization which guides the organization through decisions based on knowledge and experience toward achievement of established objectives. See also *organization*. (2) the people who have the skill and knowledge required to guide and direct the operations of a business organization successfully.

management by exception   only exceptions from standing plans are brought to the attention of higher management for advice and/or action. See also *standing plan*.

management development   the training and education of managers to help assure competency in their current jobs and to help them realize their full potentials and prepare for a possible promotion to a higher-level position.

management information system   an organized procedure, usually supported by the computer, for processing data to provide timely and relevant information for managers to base decisions upon.

management philosophy   the attitudes and actions of management which determine the general atmosphere of an organization and the way in which an organization will operate.

management rights   rights to action that management wants in a union-company conflict. Basically, management wants the rights to control production, finance, and marketing and to employ workers in the most effective manner possible.

manufacturing overhead   productive costs of manufacturing in addition to materials and labor.

margin   down payment that must be made on the purchase of a security. It is 80 percent of purchase price today.

market   a collection of consumers with needs to satisfy, a willingness to satisfy their needs, and purchasing power to translate their needs into effective demand.

marketing   a total system of interacting business activities designed to plan, price, promote, and distribute want-satisfying goods and services to current and potential consumers.

marketing concept   a management orientation which emphasizes the satisfaction of consumer needs in all of its business activities.

marketing mix   the four Ps of marketing: product, price, promotion, and place.

marketing research   an organized, objective, and rational approach to gathering marketing data, which when processed, analyzed, and interpreted, will help the marketing manager make better-informed decisions.

market maturation stage three of the product life cycle, characterized by severe product competition among the competing firms and sales slowdown and profit decline for the individual firms; also referred to as the market saturation stage.

market order when an investor asks his or her broker to buy or sell a stock at the current market price.

market potential the total expected demand for a given product in a defined market during a stated time period. Demand may be expressed in dollars, number of units, or number of persons who will buy the product.

market saturation stage three of the product life cycle, characterized by many similar product offerings in the market with only marginal differences competing for the limited consumer demand; also referred to as the market maturation stage.

market segmentation the process of dividing up the total diverse market into one or more similar submarkets and designing a special marketing strategy for one or more of the submarkets.

mass merchandiser a retailing organization which offers all of its merchandise lines at discount prices.

mass production the manufacture of component parts in large numbers which are then assembled into a finished product. Each component part is standardized and identical.

matrix organization an organizational design which uses work or task teams that are composed of individuals with different skills and backgrounds from throughout the organization. The teams are usually permanent.

mediation a process in which a third party attempts to help two disputing parties to come to some agreement. A mediator does not make a binding ruling as in arbitration.

memory bank that part of a computer system which is responsible for the storage of the basic data.

merchant middleman independent businesses that take title to the products they distribute within the channel of distribution.

merger the coming together of two or more companies through the exchange of stock or other assets to form one organization.

MICR (Magnetic Ink Character Recognition) a standardized set of symbols used in the computer processing of bank checks.

middle management those persons in an organization who carry out the plans of top management and may often be in charge of some function such as production or sales, although they may be in charge of a geographic area or plant that includes all functions.

minicomputers smaller-sized computers which are functionally capable of accomplishing almost everything a larger system can but with a smaller capacity for storage, receiving data, and producing output.

money income amount of money an individual receives in actual cash or checks for wages, salaries, rents, interest, and dividends.

money markets market for short-term funds.

monopolistic competition a market condition characterized by many sellers competing for consumers by offering differentiated products in market place.

monopoly occurs when one company dominates a market to such an extent that there is no effective competition, enabling the monopoly company to control distribution, sales, and prices in the entire market for its goods or services.

mortgage bonds issues of bonds having claims upon specific assets of the issuing corporation in the event of default of interest or principal.

motivation an internal desire to work and to accomplish goals, often represented by the satisfaction of primary and secondary needs.

motivation research investigation into the "why" behind consumer behavior.

multinational corporation a firm whose home base is in one country but whose operations extend to other countries of the world.

mutual funds see *open-end investment companies.*

nanosecond time measurement used in connection with computer operations which means one-billionth of a second.

nationalization the taking over of the ownership and operation of a private company by the government.

negative income tax a tax structure in which families below the designated poverty level receive income payments and do not pay income taxes.

net income the difference between dollar costs and dollar sales after the deduction of labor costs and other expenses. See also *gross profit.*

net income before federal income taxes income after miscellaneous expenses and revenues but before deduction of federal income taxes.

net income from operations income after deducting operating expenses from revenues.

network technique a type of control chart for production projects that displays the work that must be done, when it must be done, and how long it will take. Networks also show where excess resources might be available for emergency use in keeping a project on schedule.

no-fault insurance insurance in which insurance companies pay the parties they insure without the problem of determining who is at fault in an accident claim. In most states this system covers only the first $1,000 of medical claims. Those with injuries above the $1,000 limit are free to sue for larger amounts, as was the case under the old system.

nondegradable wastes waste composed of inorganic or nonliving materials such as salts. Wastes of this sort do not break down or decompose when they are disposed of.

no-par-value stock stock not containing a par value figure.

normal profit the profit just large enough to keep a firm in its particular industry.

notes a written instrument indicating that a certain amount of money is due another party on a specific date. The note may carry instrument and must be signed by the maker of the note. It is a note payable from the maker's standpoint and a note receivable from the recipient's standpoint.

obsolescence decline in value of equipment because technologically improved equipment comes on the market.

odd lot less than one hundred shares of a stock.

oligopoly a market condition characterized by few sellers offering similar or differentiated products in market.

on-the-job training the learning of new skills and knowledge on the job under the guidance and instruction of a supervisor or senior employee.

open account the usual means of doing business when one firm buys from another. The money is not immediately due but the terms of payment are clearly indicated.

open-end investment companies investment companies that frequently issue new shares and stand ready to redeem their own shares from owners at any time. Regular brokerage fees are not paid for these shares. Instead, they bear a "loading charge" of 7 to 9 percent of the net market value of the fund's portfolio.

open system a system such as an organization which interacts with its environment, gathering inputs from and making outputs to the environment. Through interaction with the environment, the organization as an open system is able to survive indefinitely.

operating management those persons in an organization who carry out the intermediate-range plans of middle management. Operating management is responsible for the actual production of the company's output—goods or services.

operations analysis the determination of what kind of work must be done and how it will be done in order to complete the conversion process.

operations management the planning, controlling, and organizing of the process of converting the factors of production into outputs of goods and services in any organization.

opportunity cost the cost incurred by failing to invest in some alternative opportunity or possibility instead of the particular investment or opportunity in which money was actually invested.

ordinary life insurance provides both a protection and a savings element.

organic organization an organizational structure which facilitates innovation, informality, interaction among members, and fluid transfer of authority and control. It is in contrast to the more traditional or bureaucratic structure.

organization a system containing people, management, technology, structure, and physical facilities as required subsystems in which management interrelates and integrates all the system elements into a cohesive whole in order to achieve organizational objectives.

organizing putting together all the component parts of a business organization so as to facilitate planning, controlling, communication, and coordination for the achievement of organizational goals. See also *organization*.

orientation the introduction of a new employee to the job and company. Often includes a general review by personnel department staff of general policies on pay, fringe benefits, and how the new employee's department fits into the overall organization; also includes information from the immediate supervisor on specific job information such as coffee breaks, lunch periods, location of cafeterias, and so on.

output in a management information system, processed data or information which will be used as a basis for making decisions.

outputs the results of the conversion process in a business organization in the form of goods and services. See also *operations management*.

over-the-counter market name given to dealings in unlisted securities through the offices of securities dealers.

participating feature of some issues of preferred stock. They are entitled to share in dividends with the common stock over and above their regular dividend.

partnership an association of two or more people who form and carry on as co-owners an unincorporated business.

par value a figure appearing on the face of a stock certificate. Because of easy confusion of this figure with a "value" element, most common stock today does not contain this figure.

patents issued by the United States Patent Office. A patent guarantees the owner the sole right to produce and sell for seventeen years the product that has been invented or developed.

path-goal model a motivational model in which a person perceives high performance as a path to a goal that is highly valued by the person.

payee the recipient of money designated on a note. This party is often the seller of goods.

penetration pricing setting a low price to secure a desirable market share and discourage competitors from entering the market.

people-oriented a style of leadership in which the leader is mostly oriented toward the subordinates in terms of supporting them by being friendly and of help and counsel whenever desired or necessary.

persistent wastes wastes whose chemical breakdown is slower than that of degradable wastes. Synthetic (manmade) organic chemical products such as pesticides are in this category.

personality the tendency of an individual to maintain attitudes and style of behavior under different conditions.

personality test an employment test that attempts to measure emotional adjustment and the numerous dimensions of individual personality, such as how aggressive, how outgoing, and how dependent upon others an individual is. See also *employment test.*

personal selling form of promotion involving direct contact with perspective buyers on a face-to-face basis.

personnel administration see *human assets management.*

personnel management see *human assets management.*

physiological need the need for food, water, and the other components of life necessary to survival. See also *primary needs.*

picket in a union-company dispute the right of the union to have its members walk in front of the company to publicize the dispute and to discourage others from working for or doing business with the company.

PL/1 a more recent computer language designed for both scientific and business problems, designed by IBM.

planned product obsolescence intentionally scheduling the replacement of an existing product with a new product by a company so as to stimulate sales.

planning the determination of goals and the specification of ways and means to achieve those goals.

planning horizon the length of time encompassed by a plan. It may vary from a few seconds to many years.

policy action or attitude based on a strategic plan or a portion of a strategic plan. A policy has no time horizon and will change only when the strategic plan changes. See also *strategic plan.*

population in research, the totality of all the elements under study for a particular research project.

portfolio management process of maximizing return from investment in the stock and bonds of corporations.

preemptive right the right to maintain one's proportionate interest in ownership of stock of a corporation if a new offering is made.

preferential shop a form of union recognition; similar to a *closed shop* except that while a person does not have to be a union member to get a job, the new employee must join the union within seven days after hiring.

preferred stock has less risk than common stock. It is entitled to dividends ahead of common stock. In the event of dissolution of the corporation, preferred stockholders have a claim for the return of their investment prior to common stockholders.

preliminary interview an oral interaction in the selection process for a job which seeks to determine quickly if there are obvious reasons why a person should not be considered for employment.

prescriptive research studies which say what ought to be done under certain conditions and situations in order for certain results to occur, especially with respect to the behavior of individuals, groups, and organizations.

price system a component of capitalism in which the supply of and demand for a product or service interact and affect the level of a price for a given product or service.

primary boycott in a labor-management dispute, the situation in which the union does not allow and/or discourages its owner members from doing business with the company, as distinguished from a *secondary boycott.*

primary data data collected specifically for the purpose of a particular research project.

primary needs the basic elements needed for survival: to drink water, eat, breathe, and reproduce the species.

principal amount borrowed indicated on a note or a bond.

principle of absolute advantage a country has an absolute advantage in producing a good when it is the only country that can produce that good or when it can produce it at a lower cost than other countries.

principle of comparative advantage a country has a comparative advantage in the production of a good when it produces that good for less than the comparative cost that another country can produce the good. (See example in text.)

private enterprise the economic system in which business organizations operate. It includes the right to own property, to make a profit or loss, to set prices, and to compete with other business organizations.

private placements bond issues or long-term notes directly placed with the lender by the borrower without going through the market mechanism of the securities exchanges.

process analysis the determination of the best flow of inputs through the organization in order to reach the output stage.

process design the determination of the best flow of inputs through the organization in order to reach the output stage and the determination of what kind of work must be done and how it will be done in order to complete the conversion process.

product differentation designing products which appear different to consumers from those of competitors with the objective of attracting and holding consumers and commanding a higher price in marketplace.

product life cycle the evaluation of a product through the stages of introduction, growth, maturation, and decline.

product line the total group of products, brands, models, and grades marketed by a given company.

product management the planning, designing, implementing, and control of the product-customer matching process.

product manager a marketing executive who generally has the total responsibility for planning and implementing the complete marketing program for a brand or product group. Sometimes this executive is called a brand manager or a merchandise manager.

production see *conversion.*

productivity the efficiency of the individual worker or of the work force of a company or nation; measures the relationship between output and input. High productivity, for example, means maximum output for a given level of input.

profit the difference between dollar costs and dollar sales. See also *gross profit.*

profit and loss system a component of capitalism which gives a business organization the right to make a profit and also the possibility of taking a loss. See also *profit.*

profit ratio net income divided by sales for the period.

Program Evaluation and Review Technique (PERT) a network technique developed by Lockheed Aircraft to help in the development of the Polaris missile for the Navy. See also *network technique.*

progressive taxes an increase in the individual tax rate as one's income rises.

promotion (1) a change of job assignment in a company that brings increased authority, responsibility, and pay; (2) all forms of communication by a seller to inform, influence, and persuade potential consumers through the dissemination of product and company information.

promotional discount a deduction from list price offered to buyers (generally retailers) for assisting the seller in promoting the seller's product in the retailer's market area.

protective tariff taxes levied on imports with the primary purpose of discouraging imports in order to protect domestic industry.

Protestant ethic a belief in the eighteenth and nineteenth centuries that those who worked hard and saved their money would be successful and also earn divine favor.

proxy an absentee ballot applicable to owners of shares of a corporation.

psychic income an intangible factor associated with income of those individuals who value climate, pleasant surroundings, independence, or enjoyment of a particular occupation.

psychological pricing pricing schemes used

by sellers to entice buyers to purchase the product or patronize the seller's store.

psychology the study of the behavior of individuals with particular attention in organizational applications to attitudes, motivation, and leadership.

public corporation a corporation chartered by either the federal or a state government for the purpose of achieving a goal deemed to be in the public interest.

pure competition a market condition characterized by many sellers offering similar products in the marketplace where buyers are unable or do not bother to distinguish the offerings of the many sellers.

pure research research attempting to answer basic scientific questions rather than having any immediate practical applications.

quality the degree of reliability, attractiveness, performance, design, and manufacturing precision that is desired and that is built into a good or service.

quality control a process to assure that the degree or level of quality that is desired in a good or service is actually built into the good or service. See also *quality*.

quantity discount a deduction from the list price based on the size of the order (noncumulative discount) or the total amount purchased for a given time period (cumulative discount).

quasi-public corporation a corporation owned jointly by the federal government and private industry.

quick assets ratio total of cash, marketable securities, and accounts and notes receivable divided by current liabilities.

quit voluntarily leaving an organization for any of many reasons: moving to a different job, leaving the geographic area, going to school.

rational administration a stage of growth in which a business has reached substantial size and is characterized by professional management, formal policies and procedures, line and staff structure, and a bureaucratic atmosphere.

real estate loans loans made to individuals by commercial banks for the purchase or construction of homes. The bulk of home loans are from savings and loan associations, however.

real income purchasing power of money income.

recession a mild form of a depression. See also *depression*.

recruiting the use of advertising, employment agencies, and other methods to attract candidates for a job opening.

recycling using disposed of materials again. Used paper, for example, can be reprocessed and made into new paper.

registered bonds bond issues where records are kept by the trustee as to the owners.

reliability results of a research study are representative of the population from which the data are derived and can be repeated in another study from the same population.

replacement chart shows those jobs likely to need replacements or changes in the future due to normal turnover of personnel and also to possible expansion or contraction of the business; also includes a current inventory of skills and potentials of present employees.

research an objective, systematic, and studious investigation of a particular problem or opportunity.

retailer one who sells products to ultimate consumers for personal, family, or household consumption.

retained earnings earnings of a firm not returned to owners in the form of dividends. It is still part of the owners' investment as a result.

return on investment income before financial costs divided by average total assets for the period or assets on hand at the beginning of the period.

revenues the product of the firm's operations in terms of either sales for merchandising firms or professional fees earned for service firms.

revenue sharing the return of taxes collected by the federal government to states and municipalities for spending according to state and local needs.

revenue tariff taxes levied on imports with the primary purpose of generating revenue for the government receiving the products.

reverse discrimination an act of bias against the generally favored group or person. Some persons argue that when management makes a conscious effort to hire minorities and women, it practices bias in reverse.

risk the amount of danger present in an investment. One would accept more risk only for the possibility of getting a greater return on his or her investment.

robber barons individuals in the late 1800s who achieved great wealth at least partly through deception and dishonesty.

round lots a block of one hundred shares of a stock.

safety stock extra inventory that is maintained to meet customer demand in case that demand exceeds expectation and the normal inventory is rapidly depleted.

sales finance companies companies that acquire installment sales contracts from retailers, thus relieving them of the financing function.

sales promotion forms of communication with prospective buyers used to supplement advertising and personal selling, such as store displays, product demonstrations, and contests.

sample a portion of a population selected for study in a research project.

sanitary landfill a method of solid waste disposal which minimizes environmental pollution. The waste is compacted and spread in thin layers and covered with earth.

savings and loan associations the principal institutions making home loans to prospective home purchasers.

savings banks banks that accept time deposits but not demand deposits.

scalar process the dividing of an organization into vertical levels to separate the managerial levels and to facilitate implementation of the chain of command. See also *chain of command.*

scheduling a production process to assure that all steps in production are performed at times that will maximize efficiency.

scientific method an objective, systematic procedure used to investigate a research problem.

secondary boycott in a union-company labor dispute, the situation in which the union attempts to prevent its own members *and* third parties from doing business with the company. The fact that third parties are involved makes the boycott of a secondary nature.

secondary data from the viewpoint of research, data already collected for other purposes but that may be useful for another research project.

secondary liability potential liability of a discounter of a note if the maker does not pay on time. If that happens, the bank collects from the discounter.

secondary needs motivate people to seek friendship, love, status, power, and prestige. These needs become important after primary needs have been largely satisfied.

secondary recovery methods for procuring petroleum left in the ground due to loss in pressure from too many wells being drilled in a given area.

securities brokers as "brokers," securities firms act as agents of their customers carrying out the latter's buying and selling orders.

securities dealers as "dealers," securities firms buy and sell securities for themselves intending to make a profit or gain on trading.

security loans loans made for the purchase of securities by individuals and security brokers or dealers. The loans are secured by the stocks and bonds purchased.

security need the assurance that everything possible has been done by ourselves, the companies we work for, and our government to protect us against disasters such as a serious illness or accident.

selection the process of choosing one candidate out of the several who might be interested in a particular job opening.

self-fulfillment need the desire to use all of one's potential to the maximum, especially in work.

selling short selling securities that are not owned in anticipation of a market decline. Shares must be returned to the borrower upon demand.

seniority the length of time an employee has worked in a given job, department, or company.

sensitivity training a form of management development in which the trainees meet in groups in a nonstructured situation. Through interaction over several days, the trainees learn from one another about themselves. It helps trainees to drop disruptive defensive personality and to be more honest in personal interactions.

setup cost the cost to prepare for the production of a different good or service than has been in the production process.

share of stock an ownership interest in a company represented by a stock certificate. A stock of certificate is a piece of printed paper that proves ownership.

shopping goods a classification of consumer products for which potential purchasers are willing to spend considerable time in shopping and in comparing prices and quality.

short-term debt debt that becomes due for payment within a year.

simulation (1) a hypothetical situation used to generate data for a research project; (2) the learning of new skills and knowledge through practice in equipment which is not real but exactly duplicates real equipment.

single-use plan a plan that is used for one time and one purpose only.

sinking fund provision in some bond issues requiring that a set amount of money be put aside each year for retirement of a bond is-

sue. A trustee is designated to invest these funds.

skimming pricing setting a high initial price in order to get maximum quick return on product developmental costs.

social Darwinism a philosophy of the late 1800s and early 1900s which stated that survival and success belonged to those with the greatest strength and endurance and/or the best brains; popularly known as "survival of the fittest."

socialism an economic system in which the government owns and operates major industries such as coal mines, steel mills, railroads, and communication networks. A socialistic system is often called a welfare state. See also *welfare state*.

social need the desire for friendship, companionship, and love.

sociology study of the behavior of groups and organizations and the interactions among them.

software the programs, languages, and routines used in electronic data processing.

sole proprietorship single owner, unincorporated form of business.

span of control the number of subordinates which one supervisor can effectively control and coordinate.

special partnership created for the purpose of carrying out a single transaction such as buying and selling a particular piece of property.

specialty goods a classification of consumer products for which the potential buyers are habitually willing to make special purchasing efforts because of the unique characteristics of the products.

staff personnel those persons in an organization who provide specialized advice and assistance to line personnel. See also *line personnel*.

standard costs what costs should be for a given level of output under favorable operating conditions based upon predetermined scientific estimates for the various operations of a firm.

standing plan a plan that covers repetitive activities which are likely to take place under similar circumstances.

strategic plan plan that establishes overall goals for an organization and sets forth actions that are mostly to achieve those goals.

strike in a union-company dispute, the situation in which the union members refuse to work in an effort to force the company to come to an agreement.

Subchapter S corporations corporations treated as if they were partnerships or sole proprietorships for tax purposes.

supplemental unemployment benefits (SUB) private arrangements between an employer and employees for the payment of extra money to employees who are laid off. SUB supplement unemployment compensation.

supply curve a supply schedule shown in graphic form.

supply schedule schedule of how many units will be produced at various prices.

survey data collected from respondents in their natural environment or usual setting.

syndicate a group of investment bankers who divide a large new securities issue among themselves, in turn selling the securities to large investors.

synergy the result when an organization operates as an integrated, cooperative system. The result is better and more output through the integration and cooperation of the organizational members than if they worked as individuals without cooperating.

systems analyst one who studies and designs methods and procedures for solving business problems using the computer.

tariff taxes levied on goods being imported into a country.

task-oriented a style of leadership in which the leader is mostly oriented toward getting the job done.

technology in business, the state of theoretical and applied science is utilized by business in equipment and facilities to produce, transport, communicate, and otherwise carry on the operations of business.

term insurance type of life insurance providing protection only with no savings element.

term loans one- to ten-year loans payable in stated installments.

tertiary recovery third-try methods for procuring petroleum from existing wells after initial and secondary recovery methods have failed.

Theory X a view of people in which employers look upon their workers as being lazy, disliking responsibility, resisting change, and generally being only interested in themselves and having no interest in the organization.

Theory Y a view of people in which employers look upon their workers as desiring responsibility, wanting to contribute to the organization, and wanting to work hard.

time deposits savings accounts at banks that draw interest. Checks cannot be written against these accounts.

time sharing a method whereby a number of users may use the facilities of a single computer at one time.

top management those persons in the organization who are responsible for the planning and operation of the entire company; usually of presidential and vice-presidential rank.

trade deficit the monetary value of a country's imports exceed the monetary value of the exports.

trade discount a deduction from the list price based on position of the middleman within the channel of distribution.

trademarks symbols, words, or designs used by business enterprises to identify their products.

trade quotas restrictions placed on the number of physical units or value of a product coming into a country.

trade surplus the monetary value of a country's exports exceeds the monetary value of its imports.

traditional craft a stage of growth in which a business operates in ways which have proved satisfactory in the past. Businesses in the traditional craft stage of growth are often family operated, with all decisions made by the family or a member of the family.

training the learning of the skills and knowledge necessary to the successful accomplishment of a job and/or for promotion to a higher-level job.

trait theory a theory of leadership which suggests that only people with certain traits or characteristics such as intelligence, honesty, and courage can be good leaders; now largely discounted.

transaction a specific act, occurrence, or deal affecting an enterprise's assets, liabilities, or owners' equities.

transfer a change of job assignment in a company to one that does not carry increased responsibility or pay.

Treasury bills ninety-one-day notes issued by the United States Treasury Department.

trust an economic entity composed of a group of corporations. Owners of shares of stock transferred their shares to the trust, receiving, in exchange, trust certificates enabling them to share in the profits of the trust.

trust companies companies that take legal possession of personal assets and manage them in accordance with the wishes of the creator of the trust.

trustee usually a bank which is responsible for protecting the bond owners in case of nonpayment of either principal or interest when they become due.

ultimate consumer one who buys for personal, family, or household use.

unemployment compensation money paid by the government to unemployment workers. The money is gained from a special tax on employers and may last up to six months.

uniform delivered pricing pricing arrangement in which all buyers, regardless of their location, are quoted the same price.

union security the type of legal recognition that a union obtains from a company. The type of recognition affects the degree of control the union has over its members.

union shop a form of union recognition whereby a person does not have to be a union member to get a job but must join the union within a stated period after starting work.

unit cost of production cost of production divided by the number of units produced.

unity of command individual employees of an organization report to and are responsible to only one superior.

universality of marketing functions although marketing functions may be transferred from one firm to another firm, they cannot be eliminated from the channel of distribution.

unlimited liabilities where one's personal liabilities can be claimed for satisfying business debts.

validity in a research study, the data are measuring what is intended to be measured.

value-added tax tax on the income in value to a product performed by the manufacturer. It is measured by selling price over amounts paid to suppliers plus other costs of production.

variable costs costs which change proportionately as production changes.

variance divergence of actual cost from standard cost.

venture capital company financial firms that invest equity funds in new businesses, hoping to make a profit when the new business eventually goes public.

vestibule training the learning of new skills and knowledge away from the actual job but on equipment or facilities identical to what is actually used on the job.

vesting the claim an employee has to company-contributed money in the retirement plan at any given time.

voluntary chains a series of independently owned and controlled retail outlets which are linked together contractually with a wholesale organization to gain the advantages of quantity purchases, combined advertising, and other management services.

wages the money that employees receive in

return for their work (contribution) to the company.

watered stock shares of stock in a company which are issued beyond the value of the company. See also *share of stock*.

welfare state usually associated with socialism. The government provides free social and health care for all citizens.

wheel of retailing a retailing hypothesis which suggests that new types of retailers gain a competitive advantage in the marketplace by reducing services and offering lower prices to consumers than established retailers, but once established, these new types tend to add services and their prices gradually rise.

wholesale merchant a wholesaler who takes title to the goods and performs a variety of functions and services for retailers or industrial purchasers.

wholesaler one who sells products for resale or for use in other businesses.

wholly owned subsidiary in international business, a home-based company operates a subdivision in another country where the home-based company provides all the capital, technology, and personnel and assumes full risk for its success or failure.

withdrawal a reaction to frustration in not satisfying some need in which people remove themselves from active participation in normal activities.

workers' compensation payments to a worker while away from work as a result of injuries suffered on the job. There are also provisions for partial payment of medical and hospitalization expenses. Most companies carry insurance to cover workers' compensation.

yellow-dog contract an employment agreement whereby any newly hired worker would sign a pledge promising never to join a union; now illegal.

zone pricing pricing arrangement in which the market is divided into different geographical zones and all buyers located within the same zone pay the same price.

INDEX